The
Yorkshire County
Cricket Club Limited

Registered Number 28929R

YEARBOOK
2012

114th EDITION

Sponsors of

THE YORKSHIRE COUNTY CRICKET CLUB

Editor:

DAVID WARNER

Records and Statistics

Yorkshire First Eleven:

JOHN T POTTER

Yorkshire Second Eleven:

MICHAEL SNOOK

Production Editor:

JAMES M. GREENFIELD

Published by
THE YORKSHIRE COUNTY CRICKET CLUB LTD
HEADINGLEY CARNEGIE CRICKET GROUND
LEEDS LS6 3BU
Tel: 0871 971 1222   Fax: 0113 278 4099
Internet: http://www.yorkshireccc.com
e-mail: cricket@yorkshireccc.com

Solicitors: *Auditors:*

DLA PIPER UK LLP   KPMG Audit plc

Medical Officer: Dr NIGEL MAYERS, MBChB, MRCGP
Burley Park Medical Centre, 273 Burley Road, Leeds LS4 2EL

The opinions expressed by contributors are not necessarily those of the Board.

TELEPHONE AND FAX NUMBERS

HEADINGLEY CRICKET GROUND   **Tel: 0871 971 1222**
Fax: 0113 278 4099

NORTH MARINE ROAD, SCARBOROUGH **Tel: 01723 365625**
Fax: 01723 364287

BURNLEY ROAD, TODMORDEN   **Tel: 01706 813140**

SHIPTON ROAD, YORK   **Tel: 01904 623602**

BRADFORD & BINGLEY   **Tel: 01274 775441**

STAMFORD BRIDGE   **Tel: 01759 371545**

Produced by:

Great Northern Books
PO Box 213, Ilkley LS29 9WS
www.greatnorthernbooks.co.uk

ISBN: 978-1-905080-06-9

CONTENTS

	Page
Telephone numbers of Yorkshire grounds	2
Officers, Board and Committees	4
The President	6
Officials of the Club	10
Fixtures — 2012	11
Jonny Goes Marching On — Chris Parrott	14
Review of 2011— Graham Hardcastle	18
Yorkshire Coaching Shake-up — David Warner	22
The Queen Honours "Dickie" Bird — David Warner	23
The Second XI — Michael Snook	24
The Academy — Harold Galley	27
The Schools — Chris Hassell	30
The Farewells: David Wainwright, James Lee, Ben Sanderson and Lee Hodgson — David Warner	33
100 Years Ago — Derek Hodgson	39
50 Years Ago — Anthony Bradbury	47
Celebrity Interview: Sir Alan Haselhurst — Anthony Bradbury	58
Arthur Wood: The Late Arrival — Martin Howe	62
The Archives — David Allan	70
Riddle and a Roses Dish — Nigel Pullan	73
Yorkshire's Captain of South Africa — Anthony Bradbury	74
Final Piece of a Puzzle — Anthony Bradbury	77
F S Trueman Biography — Derek Hodgson	80
Obituaries — David Warner	81
Thumbnail Player Profiles — John T Potter	84
Highlights of 2011— John T Potter	90
LV County Championship 2011 — Scorecards, Tables, Match Pictures and Reports By Nigel Pullan, John T Potter and Simon Wilkinson	98
Clydesdale Bank 40 League 2011 — Scorecards, Tables, Match Pictures and Reports By Dave Caldwell, John T Potter and Simon Wilkinson	140
NatWest One-Day International — England v. Sri Lanka	168
Friends Provident t20 2011 — Scorecards, Tables, Match Pictures and Reports By Dave Caldwell, John T Potter and Simon Wilkinson	171
Second Eleven Squad 2011	202
Second Eleven Highlights 2011	203
Second Eleven Championship Matches 2011	204
Second Eleven Trophy Matches 2011	215
Second Eleven t20 2011	226
Second Eleven Other Matches 2011	235
Yorkshire Academy Averages in ECB County Premier League and Cup	241
Records Section	242
Annual Report and Statement of Accounts	413

Officers for 2012

4

GEOFFREY CHOSEN TO TOP YORKSHIRE LINE-UP AGAIN

By David Warner

The sequence of great Yorkshire players going on to be installed as Yorkshire County Cricket Club President was due to continue this year with Geoffrey Boycott OBE nominated to succeed Raymond Illingworth CBE, whose two-year term of office expired at the annual general meeting in March 2012.

Raymond was acknowledged by all to have performed his duties admirably, and even an unexpected heart operation during last summer did not prevent him returning to Headingley to attend various functions once he was restored to good health.

The same dedication to the Presidency will be shown by Geoffrey, who also considers it a great honour to become the figurehead of the county of his birth and the only county for which he played his cricket. In his own words,

MAGIC WAND: Geoffrey stands before the East Stand Long Room Honours Board to present Yorkshire with the bat which brought him his 100th first-class century in the Fourth Test v. Australia at Headingley on August 11, 1977

the Presidency is the icing on the cake. Just as Raymond was equally suited to hosting functions either on the international scene or at county level, so will be Geoffrey, who was a batsman without peer during his active service and one of the finest in the world at any given period.

When it comes to scoring runs, Geoffrey is among that unrivalled group of great batsmen who have served Yorkshire with pride and helped to make it the greatest cricket club in the world.

Three batsmen, as opposed to genuine all-rounders, immediately spring to mind when one considers those who have made the most significant contributions to Yorkshire and England cricket — Herbert Sutcliffe, Len Hutton and Geoffrey.

All three were mighty lions, and it is hard to imagine anyone from the modern era getting anywhere near their first-class records.

Depending on whose

HUNDRED HUNDRED CLUB: Sir Leonard Hutton and a wheelchair-bound Herbert Sutcliffe congratulate Geoffrey on completing his 100th first-class century in the Fourth Test v. Australia at Headingley in 1977 — the only three Yorkshiremen to have scored 100 first-class centuries *(Photo: Yorkshire Post)*

statistics you follow, Sutcliffe finished with either 149 first-class centuries (*Wisden*, which I prefer to recognise) or 151 (other sources), but there is no contrary opinion about Geoffrey's 151 or Hutton's 129.

Neither is there any doubt that the trio monopolised century-making for Yorkshire — Maurice Leyland's 62 centuries being well short of Sutcliffe's 112, Geoffrey's 103 and Hutton's 85.

Whenever Geoffrey chooses to look back over his remarkable career, some memories are bound to be more to the fore than others, but he will be able to recall few which gave him greater pleasure than his 191 for

HAPPY FAMILY: Geoffrey, Rachael and daughter Emma

England against Australia on his home ground of Headingley on August 11, 1977. It was during that epic innings that he became the only batsman to complete his 100th first-class century in a Test match...and how vivid, still, is the picture of him on-driving Greg Chappell to reach three figures, followed by the mass invasion of ecstatic Yorkshire fans.

Then there was Delhi on December 23, 1981, when he became the highest run-scorer in Test cricket — overtaking the 8,032 of Garry Sobers and going on to 8,114 to top the pile for a further two years.

For Yorkshire, also, there was a host of magical moments, one of them soon after I became a Yorkshire cricket correspondent in 1975. That was his unbeaten 152 against Worcestershire at New Road on May 15, when he completed the task of scoring a century off each of the then 16 other first-class counties. His 100th first-class century meant a lot to Geoffrey — and so did his 100th first-class century for Yorkshire, which he achieved against Warwickshire at Edgbaston on August 6, 1985, followed in the final home match of that season by his unbeaten 125 off Nottinghamshire at Scarborough that brought him level on Sutcliffe's 149 centuries in all matches, a figure he went on to overtake.

From beginning his career with Yorkshire in 1962 to ending it in 1986 Geoffrey totted up 48,426 first-class runs to make him the eighth heaviest scorer of all time. For Yorkshire he amassed 32,570 first-class runs...and don't forget his 8,481 runs in one-day matches, a figure not yet overtaken.

With all his broadcasting experience and time on the Yorkshire CCC Management Board, Geoffrey has kept well up to date with what is going on in the cricket world, and his vast knowledge means that he will be doing far more than just opening the drinks cabinet during his term — which includes the Club's 150th anniversary celebrations next year.

ENGLAND AT HEADINGLEY
2012-2019
EXCLUSIVE INTERNATIONAL MEMBERSHIP

2012 INTERNATIONAL FIXTURES:

SOUTH AFRICA TEST MATCH

WEST INDIES ONE DAY INTERNATIONAL

Officials of the Yorkshire County Cricket Club

President	Treasurer	Captain	Captain (Contd)
T R Barker 1863	M J Ellison 1863-1893	R Iddison 1863-1872	D L Bairstow 1984-1986
M J Ellison 1864-97	M Ellison, jun 1894-1898	J Rowbotham 1873	P Carrick 1987-1989
Lord Hawke 1898-1938	Chas Stokes 1899-1912	L Greenwood 1874	M D Moxon 1990-1995
	R T Heselton 1913-1931	J Rowbotham 1875	D Byas 1996-2001
Rt Hon Sir F S Jackson 1939-1947	A Wyndham Heselton 1932-1962	E Lockwood 1876-1877	D S Lehmann 2002
T L Taylor 1948-1960	M G Crawford 1963-1979	T Emmett 1878-1882	A McGrath 2003
Sir W A Worsley Bart 1961-1973	J D Welch 1980-1984	Hon M B (Lord) Hawke 1883-1910	C White 2004-6
	P W Townend 1984-2002	E J R H Radcliffe 1911	D Gough 2007-8
Sir K Parkinson 1974-1981		Sir A W White 1912-1918	A McGrath 2009
N W D Yardley 1981-1983	*Chairman*	D C F Burton 1919-1921	A W Gale 2010-11
	A H Connell, DL 1971-1979	Geoff Wilson 1922-1924	*Secretary*
The Viscount Mountgarret 1984-1989	M G Crawford 1980-1984	A W Lupton 1925-1927	Geo Padley 1863
		W A Worsley 1928-1929	J B Wostinholm 1864-1902
Sir Leonard Hutton 1989-1990	H R Kirk 1984-1985	A T Barber 1930	F C (Sir Fredk.) Toone 1903-1930
Sir Lawrence Byford QPM, LLD, DL 1991-1999	B Walsh, QC 1986-1991	F E Greenwood 1931-1932	J H Nash 1931-1971
	Sir Lawrence Byford CBE, QPM, LLD, DL 1991-1998	A B Sellers 1933-1947	J Lister 1972-1991
R A Smith TD, LLB, DL 1999-2004		N W D Yardley 1948-1955	D M Ryder 1991-2002
	K H Moss MBE 1998-2002	W H H Sutcliffe 1956-1957	*Company Secretary*
David Jones CBE 2004-6	GA Cope 2002	J R Burnet 1958-1959	B Bouttell 2002-5
		J V Wilson 1960-1962	Charles Hartwell 2011-12
Robert Appleyard 2006-8	R A Smith TD, LLB, DL 2002-5	D B Close 1963-1970	*Chief Executive*
Brian Close CBE 2008-10	Colin J Graves 2005-12	G Boycott 1971-1978	C D Hassell 1991-2002
		J H Hampshire 1979-1980	Colin J Graves 2002-5
Raymond Illingworth CBE 2010-12		C M Old 1981-1982	Stewart Regan 2006-10
		R Illingworth 1982-1983	

COUNTY FIXTURES — 2012

LV COUNTY CHAMPIONSHIP — Division 2

(All four-day matches)

Date		*Opponents*	*Venue*
THU 5-8	**APRIL**	**KENT**	**HEADINGLEY CARNEGIE**
THU 19-22	**APRIL**	**ESSEX**	**HEADINGLEY CARNEGIE**
Thu 26-29	Apil	Kent	Canterbury
WED 2-5	**MAY**	**LEICESTERSHIRE**	**SCARBOROUGH**
Wed 9-12	May	Gloucestershire	Bristol
WED 16-19	**MAY**	**HAMPSHIRE**	**HEADINGLEY CARNEGIE**
WED 30-2	**MAY/JUNE**	**NORTHAMPTONSHIRE** .	**HEADINGLEY CARNEGIE**
Wed 6-9	June	Glamorgan	Colwyn Bay
Wed 11-14	July	Hampshire	Southampton
Wed 18-21	July	Derbyshire	Chesterfield
Fri 27-30	July	Leicestershire	Leicester
Wed 1-4	August	Northamptonshire	Northampton
WED 15-18	**AUGUST**	**DERBYSHIRE**	**HEADINGLEY CARNEGIE**
TUE 28-31	**AUGUST**	**GLOUCESTERSHIRE**	**SCARBOROUGH**
TUE 4-7	**SEPTEMBER**	**GLAMORGAN**	**HEADINGLEY CARNEGIE**
Tue 11-14	September	Essex	Chelmsford

CB 40 LEAGUE

SUN 6	**MAY**	**KENT**	**HEADINGLEY CARNEGIE**
SUN 20	**MAY**	**DERBYSHIRE**	**HEADINGLEY CARNEGIE**
Thu 24	May	Sussex	Hove (Floodlit)
Sun 27	May	Unicorns	Scarborough (Away)
SUN 3	**JUNE**	**NORTHAMPTONSHIRE** . .	**HEADINGLEY CARNEGIE**
Sun 22	July	Derbyshire	Chesterfield
Tue 7	August	Warwickshire	Edgbaston (Floodlit)
Thu 9	August	Northamptonshire	Northampton (Floodlit)
SUN 12	**AUGUST**	**UNICORNS**	**HEADINGLEY CARNEGIE**
SUN 19	**AUGUST**	**SUSSEX**	**HEADINGLEY CARNEGIE**
Wed 22	August	Kent	Canterbury (Floodlit)
MON 27	**AUGUST**	**WARWICKSHIRE**	**SCARBOROUGH**
Sat 1	September	Semi-Finals	TBC
Sat 15	September	Final	Lord's

FRIENDS PROVIDENT TWENTY20 CUP

FRI 15	**JUNE**	**DURHAM**	**HEADINGLEY CARNEGIE**
SUN 17	**JUNE**	**LEICESTERSHIRE**	**HEADINGLEY CARNEGIE**
Mon 18	June	Derbyshire	Derby (Floodlit)
Fri 22	June	Durham	Durham ICG
SUN 24	**JUNE**	**NOTTINGHAMSHIRE**	**SCARBOROUGH**
Wed 27	June	Leicestershire	Leicester
FRI 29	**JUNE**	**LANCASHIRE**	**HEADINGLEY CARNEGIE**
Thu 5	July	Nottinghamshire	Trent Bridge (Floodlit)
Fri 6	July	Lancashire	Old Trafford
SUN 8	**JULY**	**DERBYSHIRE**	**HEADINGLEY CARNEGIE**
Tue 24-25	July	Quarter-Finals	TBC
Sat 25	August	Semi-Finals and Final	Cardiff

UNIVERSITY MATCH

FRI 13-15	**APR**	**LEEDS/BRADFORD MCCU**	**HEADINGLEY CARNEGIE**

NPOWER TEST MATCHES

(All five-day matches)

ENGLAND v. WEST INDIES

Thu May 17 . . . . Lord's   Fri May 25 . . . . Trent Bridge

Thu June 7 . . . . Edgbaston

ENGLAND v. SOUTH AFRICA

Thu July 19 . . . . The Oval   **THU AUGUST 2 . . . . HEADINGLEY CARNEGIE**

Thu August 16 . . . . Lord's

NATWEST INTERNATIONAL TWENTY20

Sun	24	June	England v West Indies	Trent Bridge
Sat	8	September	England v South Africa	Durham ICG
Mon	10	September	England v South Africa	Old Trafford (Floodlit)
Wed	12	September	England v South Africa	Edgbaston (Floodlit)

NATWEST ONE-DAY INTERNATIONALS

Sat	16	June	England v West Indies	Southampton
Tue	19	June	England v West Indies	The Oval (Day/Night)
FRI	**22**	**JUNE**	**ENGLAND V WEST INDIES**	**HEADINGLEY CARNEGIE**
Fri	29	June	England v Australia	Lord's
Sun	1	July	England v Australia	The Oval
Wed	4	July	England v Australia	Edgbaston (Day/Night)
Sat	7	July	England v Australia	Durham ICG
Tue	10	July	England v Australia	Old Trafford (Day/Night)
Fri	24	August	England v South Africa	Cardiff
Tue	28	August	England v South Africa	Southampton (Day/Night)
Fri	31	August	England v South Africa	The Oval (Day/Night)
Sun	2	September	England v South Africa	Lord's
Wed	5	September	England v South Africa	Trent Bridge (Day/Night)

SECOND ELEVEN CHAMPIONSHIP

WED	**25-27**	**APRIL**	**LEICESTERSHIRE**	**HARROGATE**
TUE	**22-24**	**MAY**	**DURHAM**	**YORK**
TUE	**26-28**	**JUNE**	**WORCESTERSHIRE**	**BARNSLEY**
Tue	3-5	July	Derbyshire	Denby CC
Tue	17-19	July	Nottinghamshire	Lady Bay Boots
Tue	24-26	July	Northamptonshire	Northamptonshire
TUE	**7-9**	**AUGUST**	**MCC UNIVERSITIES**	**YORK**
WED	**15-17**	**AUGUST**	**LANCASHIRE**	**TODMORDEN**
WED	**22-24**	**AUGUST**	**WARWICKSHIRE**	**STAMFORD BRIDGE**
Tue	3-6	September	Final	

SECOND ELEVEN TROPHY

TUE	**24**	**APRIL**	**LEICESTERSHIRE**	**HARROGATE**
MON	**21**	**MAY**	**DURHAM**	**MARSKE**
MON	**25**	**JUNE**	**WORCESTERSHIRE**	**PUDSEY CONGS**
Mon	2	July	Derbyshire	Denby CC
Mon	16	July	Nottinghamshire	Worksop College
Fri	27	July	Northamptonshire	Northamptonshire
FRI	**10**	**August**	**Unicorns A**	Abbeydale Park, Sheffield
TUE	**14**	**AUGUST**	**LANCASHIRE**	**TODMORDEN**
TUE	**21**	**AUGUST**	**WARWICKSHIRE**	**WEETWOOD**

SECOND ELEVEN TWENTY20 (TWO MATCHES IN THE SAME DAY)

TUES	**29**	**MAY**	**ENGLAND UNDER-19**	**BINGLEY**
THUR	**31**	**MAY**	**DERBYSHIRE**	**BINGLEY**
Wed	6	June	Lancashire	Ormskirk
Fri	8	June	Nottinghamshire	Lady Bay Boots
Fri	15	June	Semi-Finals and Final	TBC

SECOND ELEVEN FRiENDLIES

Wed	11-13	April	Durham	Marton CC
TUE	**1-4**	**MAY**	**LANCASHIRE**	**STAMFORD BRIDGE**
Tue	8-11	May	Kent/ Northamptonshire	Beckenham
Tue	4-7	September	Somerset	Taunton Vale

YORKSHIRE ACADEMY IN THE YORKSHIRE LEAGUE

SAT	**28**	**APRIL**	**DONCASTER**	**WEETWOOD**
Sat	5	May	Castleford	Away
Mon	7	May	Driffield	Away
SAT	**12**	**MAY**	**SCARBOROUGH**	**WEETWOOD**
Sat	19	May	Harrogate	Away
Sat	26	May	York	Away
Sun	27	May	Rotherham	Away
SAT	**2**	**JUNE**	**HULL**	**WEETWOOD**
Mon	4	June	Appleby Frodingham	Away
SAT	**9**	**JUNE**	**BARNSLEY**	**HEADINGLEY CARNEGIE**
SAT	**16**	**JUNE**	**CLEETHORPES**	**WEETWOOD**
Sat	23	June	Sheffield Collegiate	Away
Sat	30	June	Sheffield United	Away
SAT	**7**	**JULY**	**ROTHERHAM**	**WEETWOOD**
Sat	14	July	Doncaster	Away
SAT	**21**	**JULY**	**CASTLEFORD**	**WEETWOOD**
SUN	**22**	**JULY**	**DRIFFIELD**	**WEETWOOD**
Sat	28	July	Scarborough	Away
SAT	**4**	**AUGUST**	**HARROGATE**	**WEETWOOD**
SAT	**11**	**AUGUST**	**YORK**	**WEETWOOD**
Sat	18	August	Hull	Away
SUN	**19**	**AUGUST**	**APPLEBY FRODINGHAM**	**WEETWOOD**
Sat	25	August	Barnsley	Away
Mon	27	August	Cleethorpes	Away
SAT	**1**	**SEPTEMBER**	**SHEFFIELD UNITED**	**WEETWOOD**
SAT	**8**	**SEPTEMBER**	**SHEFFIELD COLLEGIATE**	**WEETWOOD**

YORKSHIRE ACADEMY IN THE YORKSHIRE LEAGUE CUP

SUN	**20**	**MAY**	**HULL**	**WEETWOOD**
Sun	8	July	Semi-Final	TBC

(Final date and venue to be confirmed)

YORKSHIRE ACADEMY IN THE YORKSHIRE LEAGUE T20

Sun	10	June	Scarborough	York
Sun	15	July	Finals	TBC

YORKSHIRE ACADEMY FRIENDLIES

Sat	14	April	Barnard Castle	Away
Mon	16	April	Durham	TBC
Mon	14	May	Derby Academy	Staverley
Thu	24	May	Leeds/Bradford UCCE	TBC
Tue	5-7	June	Durham Academy	Longhurst Hall

YORKSHIRE IN UNDER-17s' CUP

Thu	5	July	Durham	Away
Thu	12	July	Cheshire	TBC
THU	**19**	**JULY**	**LANCASHIRE**	**WEETWOOD**
THU	**9**	**AUGUST**	**DERBYSHIRE**	**WEETWOOD**
Sun	2	September	Final	

YORKSHIRE UNDER-17s' TWO-DAY NATIONAL CHAMPIONSHIP

Tue	10-11	July	Cheshire	Away
TUE	**17-18**	**JULY**	**LANCASHIRE**	**HEADINGLEY CARNEGIE**
Tue	24-25	July	Durham	Away
TUE	**7-8**	**AUGUST**	**DERBYSHIRE**	**WEETWOOD**
Tue	21-22	August	Semi-Finals	Away
Thu	30-31	August	Final	Away

(Fixtures on this page are provisional only)

13

BAIRSTOW COMES OUT TOP AFTER FRENCH LESSONS

By Chris Parrott

While 2011 might have been a disappointing year for Yorkshire, it turned out to be quite the opposite for one player in particular. From making his inaugural first-class century...to passing 1,000 Championship runs for the first time...to making one of the most impressive England debuts in the modern era...this was the year the secret got out about Jonathan Bairstow.

He came into 2011 with much to prove after impressing in 2010, and he now heads into 2012 as one of the hottest prospects in the game. To analyse properly his rapid progression last season it is important to note the particular circumstances he found himself in this time last year.

An impressive performer in all forms of the game during Andrew Gale's first year as captain, he embodied the county's development in 2010 along with a number of other emerging talents, but while many of his contemporaries went on to suffer from a bout of "second-season syndrome" Bairstow made 2011 another year to remember.

A fluent 81 in the second game of the season against Durham set the tone before two performances against Nottinghamshire in the early part of the campaign signalled the emergence of the 21-year-old into the big time. The first was at Headingley Carnegie, where he made a belligerent unbeaten 50 as Yorkshire were bowled out for 86 to lose a game they had seemed certain to win, but the second at Trent Bridge in May proved even more telling: this time he was not left high and dry by his teammates — passing three figures in first-team cricket for the first time before remarkably doubling his tally to be dismissed for 205.

If ever there can be a breakthrough knock this was it, with Bairstow's celebration upon reaching the first hundred perhaps the iconic image from Yorkshire's 2011 campaign. Bat aloft, he pointed to the sky, the affable young player admitting that it was his "moment of last season."

By this time Yorkshire were already embroiled in their unsuccessful battle to avoid the Championship drop, and with their season also deteriorating in the one-day game Bairstow was striking a rare positive note in a tough campaign. The theme would continue as the summer wore on.

Another century followed against Somerset soon afterwards, the wicket-keeper/batsman's burgeoning reputation going up another notch

CHANGE OF GLOVES: Can Jonny make it for England as a wicket-keeping all-rounder?

or two in 10 days at the start of August.

First, he passed three figures at international level for the first time — for England Lions against Sri Lanka A at Scarborough — before the one thing missing from his armoury was emphatically put to bed at the home of cricket itself.

Lord's was venue for the Clydesdale Bank 40 contest against Middlesex as the right-hander plundered 114 off 87 balls in a comprehensive Yorkshire success.

It was a brutal innings, as many of Bairstow's knocks can be, and the fact that it was his first one-day century made the achievement even more impressive.

The innings had the recognition it deserved, the normally level-headed Jonny admitting that it was the ideal time to make a big score with another Lions appearance on the cards.

It came, of course, against Sri Lanka at Worcester, but Bairstow was now firmly in line for a call to the full national set-up.

That invitation duly arrived — and before the end of the month as England announced a young squad for a one-off *Twenty20* international against Ireland in Dublin. It was a proud moment for Jonny and his family, the young Bairstow following in the footsteps of his late father, David, the former Yorkshire and England wicket-keeper/batsman, in being picked for his country.

The debut did not quite materialise. England left the Bradford-born player out of the starting eleven, but it was a clear indication that finally he was in the selectors' thoughts. It also meant that he missed Yorkshire's vital Championship game with Warwickshire at Headingley Carnegie which the Tykes lost by an innings and 58 runs to push them closer to the relegation trapdoor.

15

A proud Yorkshireman, Bairstow was "bitterly disappointed" not to be involved, his absence providing clear evidence of how vital he had become to the side. By this stage he was the leading run-scorer in every form of the game apart from *t20* for Yorkshire, and he was showing real improvement in his wicket-keeping skills.

The fact that he was publically named and then backed as N. 1 behind the stumps certainly seemed to help, with Bairstow recalling on numerous occasions the winter work he had done with England's Bruce French. He would need all of his ability for the remainder of the campaign: Yorkshire had two games in which to save themselves from Division Two, and this did not quite happen.

The draw at Warwickshire in the last-but-one game ultimately rendered victory over Somerset in Yorkshire's last match of 2011 inconsequential. The county were heading for Division Two for the first time since 2005. Most of the squad took a well-earned break at this point after the rigours of a long season. Not so Bairstow, who passed 1,000 Championship runs in the win against Somerset.

Jonny's big adventure was about to begin. Six days later he was called to the England squad again, this time for the final one-day international against India at Cardiff. In the team this time, it was his chance to shine. He took it with both hands — producing a man-of-the-match display to see England to a 3-0 series win with a stunning 41 off 21 balls. It was truly an outstanding introduction to international cricket.

Captain Alastair Cook claimed the nation had "found one", with the world Press tipping Bairstow as a "star of the future". Anyone who had watched him in Yorkshire could have told them that long before he walked to the crease in the Welsh capital.

More England success would follow on his maiden international tour to India, most notably a 53-ball century against the Hyderabad Cricket Association in October, the accolades flying in as quickly as the runs left Bairstow's bat by start of the winter.

There were two Player of the Year awards from Yorkshire among them, as well as the coveted Cricket Writers' Club Young Cricketer of 2011 prize. This last has been won by only nine players in the county's history, and winning it meant that Bairstow ended what was personally a wonderful year on yet another high.

With this comes pressure as we look ahead to the 2012 season. But, with a cool head on his young shoulders and a work ethic that is tough to match, Bairstow looks as though he is now in possession of all the attributes he needs to fulfil his huge potential.

Here's hoping.

Chris Parrott is a sports journalist who covers Yorkshire matches home and away.

A SEASON OF GLOOM DESPITE SOME SHINING LIGHTS

By Graham Hardcastle

It is difficult to say that 2011 was simply a nightmare season for Yorkshire because there were some shining lights, most notably the individual performances of young guns Jonny Bairstow, Joe Root and Gary Ballance. But, if you follow the adage that there is no *I* in *Team*, this was undoubtedly a summer to forget for the White Rose county.

Having finished third in the *LV County Championship* Division I table in 2010, coming within a whisker of winning the pennant and showing enough quality to be tipped among the runners and riders again, Yorkshire finished second bottom with three wins from 16 matches.

They beat Worcestershire twice and Somerset once, but even this last came when all was virtually settled in their final game at Headingley Carnegie in early September. Captain Andrew Gale's side also crashed out of both the *Clydesdale Bank 40* and *Friends Life t20* competitions in the group stages, only winning a combined total of 11 out of 28 fixtures.

Jacques Rudolph was missed more than anybody thought possible, while a trio of key injuries to Gale, Ajmal Shahzad and, in particular, Anthony McGrath, contributed to the Club's downfall. Mind you, Yorkshire aren't the first and certainly won't be the last team to point to injuries in summing up a disappointing campaign, whatever the sport.

Gale missed the last four matches of the season with a broken right forearm, suffered while batting against Oliver Hannon-Dalby in the Headingley nets prior to Yorkshire's clash with Sussex at Scarborough in mid-August, and Shahzad, who turned the England selectors' heads with his performances during 2009 and 2010, suffered from twin hamstring tears and an ankle problem, limiting him to only 10 four-day matches and 25 wickets.

McGrath, a seasoned run-getter with more experience than you could shake a stick at, had the first half of his season ravaged by complications following arthroscopic knee surgery which led to sciatic pain in his back. The ex-England man and county captain admitted to struggling to walk up the stairs when the pain was at its worst. He made 485 runs from 12 matches, including one century against Hampshire at the Rose Bowl.

Martyn Moxon, the county's Director of Professional Cricket, said:

Running into the future: Gary Ballance and Joe Root during their stand of 189 v. Sussex at Scarborough

"It's been a disappointing season. From a results perspective that goes without saying. It's been frustrating, though, in the fact that we've had positions of strength in pretty much every game we've played. We've let them slip for a variety of reasons, and we've then gone on to lose or draw games that we could have won. That is why we are where we are."

Four matches stick out like a sore thumb as being key to the outcome of Yorkshire's Championship season:

First came the home clash with Nottinghamshire in April when, having taken a first innings lead of 193, the hosts had reduced the reigning champions to 167-6 in their second innings. Chris Read and Steven Mullaney then shared 150 for the seventh wicket to help to set Yorkshire 145 to make to win — and they fell 59 runs short when they were bowled out for 86.

Then came the two *Roses* clashes against Lancashire, which were both thrillers and went the way of the Red Rose by a whisker: they chased down 121 in the last 15 overs at Liverpool after staunch defence in both innings from the impressive Joe Sayers went to waste as a draw slipped from Yorkshire's grasp. Then, having been reduced to 45-8 in reply to 328 in the return at Headingley Carnegie, Yorkshire were dragged back into the mix by a stunning 117 not out from Richard Pyrah. The hosts ended up chasing 284, but they were bowled out for 260.

Finally, came Warwickshire at Headingley. This was a contest the title-chasing visitors bossed for most of the time, the White Rose bowled out for 127 in their second innings during the third afternoon and evening to send shockwaves through their camp. From the outside looking in, this was the day Yorkshire's relegation was sealed.

Martyn said after this: "We went into this season with our eyes open. We knew it was going to be a challenge. With the players we had we knew everything had to slip into place if we were to be successful. We were hopeful that we would do well. But, more importantly, we wanted to give the players the opportunity to prove they were good enough."

The young trio mentioned at the top of this piece, adding Pyrah and old-head Ryan Sidebottom to that list, proved that they were good enough. They just lacked support.

Bairstow topped 1,000 Championship runs for the first time, posting a personal best of 205 against Nottinghamshire at Trent Bridge and earning England one-day and Twenty20 calls. Root had an impressive breakthrough year in the Championship, clearing the 1,000-run barrier in all first-class cricket, courtesy of 66 and 10 for England Lions against Sri Lanka A at Scarborough.

Ballance was voted the player-of-the-season by his teammates, thanks to 717 runs from 13 Championship matches, 331 from nine 40-over games and 215 from 13 Twenty20s. Pyrah also had the best summer of his career with 376 Championship runs and 29 wickets, while he led the way with 21 wickets in Twenty20, including the county's best-ever figures of 5-16. Sidebottom, re-signed from Nottinghamshire, finished as Yorkshire's leading Championship wicket-taker with 62.

Despite encouraging starts to the season against Worcestershire at New Road, players like Adil Rashid and Adam Lyth suffered a considerable dip in form, and the fact that Rudolph played only four matches proved a bigger problem than anybody had imagined. After all, you'll strike the jackpot if you replace 2,000 runs in all forms of the game at the drop of a hat.

Concentrating on one-day cricket, two thrilling *Roses* Twenty20 wins were nights to remember but so, for the wrong reasons, were two defeats against the Netherlands in the *Clydesdale Bank 40* competition. For those of us in Amstelveen, it won't easily be forgotten.

Moxon said: "We have to improve, and I think we need to bring in some extra quality and experience to help in the short-term. I think we have a long-term plan here. I think the board have accepted that, and are understanding of the situation.

"We want to try and build a successful Yorkshire team with predominantly our own players and those who have come through our system. That is an ambitious target, but one that I believe we can achieve with the current group. We are not where we want to be yet. We know that, but it was only 12 months ago that everybody was applauding the team and saying what a good young side it was.

"They haven't become bad players overnight, but what we have seen is an inability to make the most of a good situation. I'd like to think that

His best season: Richard Pyrah, batsman and bowler

we'll be better for the experiences of this season when we start again in 2012. The bottom line is that if you look at our positions in all of the three leagues we just haven't been good enough."

As for bouncing back to the top division at the first time of asking, that won't be a walk in the park, as a county like Surrey have proved. With all the resources at their disposal, it took them three seasons to earn promotion.

Martyn said: "There will be different pressures. Make no mistake. Yorkshire will have no divine right to get straight back up again. We will need to work hard and play well to win promotion. We can't take it for granted that it will just happen because we've come down from Division I. That won't be the case. We are going to have to improve."

Graham Hardcastle is a sports journalist who covers Yorkshire matches home and away

GILLESPIE RETURNS AS PART OF COACHING SHAKE-UP

By David Warner

Some familiar faces departed the Headingley Carnegie scene and some new ones were welcomed on board following the restructuring of Yorkshire's coaching staff in November.

Chairman Colin Graves made it clear at the end of last season that Martyn Moxon would continue as Director of Professional Cricket while the other coaches working below Martyn could apply for any of the four new coaching posts which would replace the previous five.

Craig White, Martyn's deputy for the past two seasons, decided to sever a continuous link with Yorkshire which went back to 1990 when he returned to his native county from Australia as a young player. He chose instead to concentrate on trying to become a first-class umpire.

Other staff members to leave Yorkshire were bowling and Academy coach Steve Oldham, who first played in 1974 and went on to become renowned for the number of top-class fast bowlers he brought on — including Darren Gough, Ryan Sidebottom and Chris Silverwood; batting coach Kevin Sharp, who played for Yorkshire between 1976 and 1990 and later rejoined the staff after being cricket-development officer in Shropshire and the first appointed coach of the Bradford-Leeds Universities' Centre of Cricketing Excellence; and John Blain, who joined Yorkshire as a pace bowler from Northamptonshire in 2004 and later became second-team assistant bowling coach.

Operations manager Ian Dews was successful in applying for the new post of Director of Cricket Development, while the three newcomers were first-team coach Jason Gillespie, the former Australian pace ace who played for Yorkshire in 2006-2007, senior second-team coach Paul Farbrace, the former Kent wicket-keeper/batsman who was the county's director of cricket last year; and Development Manager Richard Damms, who previously worked for Yorkshire Cricket Board and the age-group and Academy teams.

Both Colin Graves and Martyn Moxon stressed that the new coaching structure had been planned for some time, and was not introduced because of Yorkshire's poor showing last season when they were relegated to Division Two of the LV County Championship.

THE QUEEN SIGNALS OBE
FOR DICKIE AND CHARITY

By David Warner

Harold "Dickie" Bird, the famed former international umpire, who is an Honorary Life Member of Yorkshire County Cricket Club, received the OBE in the New Year Honours bestowed by Her Majesty Queen Elizabeth for 2012. Dickie, who received the MBE in 1986, was awarded the OBE for his services to cricket and charity.

It was in March 2004 that he set up the Dickie Bird Foundation to help disadvantaged young people under the age of 18 to participate in the sport of their choice, irrespective of their social circumstances, culture or ethnicity.

"I am very proud and delighted to have been awarded the OBE in Her Majesty's New Year Honours List," Dickie said. "I was extremely surprised when I got the MBE, and even more so when I opened the letter telling me that the Prime Minister had it in mind to put my name forward for the OBE. The Foundation has helped scores of young people to get the opportunity to better themselves at sport, and I am honoured that this has been recognised with the award of the OBE. I would like to thank all the trustees for their hard work in making it such a big success."

Born in Barnsley, where a six-foot statue has been erected near his birthplace, Dickie first played as a batsman for Yorkshire in 1956 before moving on to Leicestershire, where he was a member of the playing staff until 1964. He had a spell of coaching and playing league cricket, but then took up umpiring and it was this that made him into an international star on the sporting scene.

He umpired his first county game in 1970, and went on to umpire what was then a record of 66 Test matches and 69 one-day internationals, including three World Cup finals. His final Test appearance was at Lord's in 1996, when he walked through a guard of honour of the England and India players.

Dickie, president of Wombwell Cricket Lovers Society, has also been bestowed the Freedom of Barnsley and has received honorary doctorates at Huddersfield, Leeds and Sheffield Hallam Universities.

Yorkshire have already intimated that Dickie will be nominated by the Board as the Club's president in 2014.

NO-WIN SITUATION BRINGS
RECORD NOBODY WANTED

By Michael Snook

It was a disappointing season for Yorkshire Seconds in every competition. For the first time in their history in the Championship no win was achieved in the nine matches played; the nearest they came to victory was against Leicestershire at Hinckley, when the last man was adjudged leg-before with the scores level — the first tie recorded by Yorkshire in any Second Eleven game.

There were four defeats — to Nottinghamshire, Warwickshire, Lancashire (yet again) and Worcestershire. The other four matches — against Derbyshire, Durham, MCC Universities and Northamptonshire — were all drawn after being interrupted by rain.

Yorkshire followed on 297 runs behind Nottinghamshire's 481, and they lost eight wickets before the arrears were wiped out. Eight overs were enough for the match to be lost by nine wickets. A first-innings deficit of 102 against Warwickshire hardly enhanced Yorkshire's chance of victory, their opponents winning with 20 overs to spare.

A large percentage of Lancashire's first innings of 288 was a fifth-wicket partnership of 186. They lost seven wickets as they chased down the winning total with seven overs to go. Worcestershire declared 64 behind on first innings after bad light and rain had curtailed play on the second day. A morning was lost to the waterlogged ground, and then the second-innings bowling asked to be hit. Yorkshire set a target of 229 in 50 overs, and two were left when Worcestershire won by six wickets

Derbyshire, seemingly lacking ambition, batted on after a rain break with a last-wicket partnership of 99 to take a lead of 94 runs on first innings. Yorkshire batted well into the third evening to set them the impossible task of scoring 221 to win off the 13 overs remaining.

Durham bowled Yorkshire out for 91 soon after lunch on the first day, but it was the second afternoon before they had established a first-innings lead of 160 after three stoppages for rain. The rain returned soon after Yorkshire had started their second innings, continued overnight and, together with a saturated ground, prevented play on the third day.

Rain also interrupted play against the MCC Universities, newcomers to Yorkshire's fixture list. Sensibly, the Universities declared their first innings 180 behind, encouraging Yorkshire to set a target of 350. It was after yet another weather break that the plug was pulled on the run chase and the teams settled for a draw

Yorkshire's leading run-scorer in the Championship was Alex Lees, with 530 including five 50s. Anthony McGrath's 478 runs included two centuries, his best being 186 against the Universities. Joe Root also scored two centuries in five innings.

The leading bowler was left-arm spinner Gurman Randhawa with 22 wickets at 28.81 — half as many again as the next on the list, Oliver Hannon-Dalby, who took 14 wickets at 42.28, Randhawa bowling two more balls than Hannon-Dalby during the season.

The White Rose finished

GURMAN RANDHAWA
Leading wicket-taker

10th and bottom in the Championship group, two down from their eighth place in 2010. Marginally better results were achieved in the Trophy, where three of the group matches were won, five lost and one abandoned with no result. Victories were recorded against Warwickshire by 62 runs, Northamptonshire by 37 runs and Worcestershire by 23 runs.

The Seconds were overwhelmed by the Minor Counties' team, Unicorns A, whose victory margin of 169 runs was Yorkshire worst defeat in the Second Eleven Trophy. They lost to Nottinghamshire by four wickets, Durham by six wickets, Lancashire by seven wickets and Leicestershire by two wickets in a match reduced to 37 overs a side

Leading run-scorers in the Trophy were Callum Geldart, for the second year running, with 192 in four innings, and Gerard Brophy with 142, also in four innings. Gary Ballance was the sole centurion, with 129 against Nottinghamshire in his only Trophy innings. The leading wicket-taker with 11 was Iain Wardlaw, shading Oliver Hannon-Dalby's 10.

A Twenty20 competition for Second Elevens was introduced in 2011, with four match days, two at home and two away, each day featuring two fixtures against the same opponents, one before lunch, the other after. Derbyshire and Nottinghamshire visited Headingley Carnegie, while the Seconds visited Neston in Cheshire to play Lancashire and Riverside to play Durham. The matches against Derbyshire were lost by two and seven wickets. Nottinghamshire won the morning match by eight wickets but, just when Yorkshire had set a challenging score for the first time in the competition, rain brought about the abandonment.

A sodden ground, the legacy of heavy overnight rain, caused the morning match against Lancashire to be abandoned without a ball bowled. The afternoon match, reduced to 10 overs a side, saw Lancashire slump to 79-8, only for Yorkshire to be bowled out for 51. The matches against Durham were lost by four and eight wickets. Just two points, both from abandoned games, did not represent a satisfactory performance in this inaugural season.

Six friendly matches in formats ranging from one-day to four-day games were played, with four won and two lost. Durham were the winners by two wickets at Weetwood in the first one-day match, Yorkshire winning next day by eight wickets in the second.

Derbyshire won by one wicket deep into the last hour of a stirring three-day match at Belper, thanks to Garry Park carrying his bat for 165. A Kent-Northamptonshire XII was beaten by 174 runs in the four-day fixture at Beckenham, Lees doubling his maiden Second Eleven century with 204 in Yorkshire's first innings.

Ireland A came to Harrogate, the first match there for nine seasons, but succumbed by an innings and 75 runs before noon on the third day. Yorkshire's winning margin of 72 runs saw off MCC Young Cricketers in a three-day match at York, the last game of 2011.

Second Eleven caps were awarded to Moin Ashraf, Randhawa and Lees but, all told, it was not the best of seasons for the Seconds. There is hope that there will be improved cricket and results in 2012.

*MICHAEL SNOOK has retired after 346 scoring engagements for the Seconds and 85 more at International and First Eleven level since he was appointed in July 1996. Mike leaves with many happy memories of the games and friendships made with the players, the coaches, the umpires and the spectators on the boundaries of Yorkshire cricket.

LEES LEADS WAY IN CUP TRIUMPH SEASON

By Harold D Galley

Yorkshire Academy came good after initially struggling in the Solly Sports Yorkshire ECB Premier League. Following a 10-wicket defeat by Scarborough, they lost by eight wickets at Cleethorpes, while mid-week friendlies in May v. Durham Academy and Derby Academy saw further setbacks.

Hints of better things to come surfaced when Alex Lees scored an unbeaten 74 out of 221-4 against Harrogate. George Ross, too, gained confidence with a fine 81 not out, and James Wainman had a good match, taking 3-37 in his nine overs, but the experience of Harrogate's ex-Academy player, Vic Craven, prevailed.

ALEX LEES
Both batting awards

Two consecutive victories over Driffield in league and cup followed, Lees, Ross, Eddie Wilson and Jack Leaning showing the potential of which the coaches knew they were capable. League champions York headed the table in mid-June, and their spin attack and batsmen dominated teams.Ross, 78, and Lees, 62, steered the Academy to a total of 233 at Clifton Park, and their seam attack of John Blain, 4-37, Wainman, 4-12, and Ben Coad, 2-14, then scuttled York for 85.

The League Cup Quarter-Final saw a fine victory over Hull YPI, and league victories followed over Doncaster, Sheffield Collegiate and Cleethorpes to boost the side's confidence. By the time the Cup Semi-Final was played against York the Academy had risen to fourth in the league, and they had outstanding victories against teams above them in the table. What a transformation from the early league matches.

York's decision to bat on a bowler-friendly Weetwood was not a wise one: Alex Lilley with 7-14 decimated the leaders, and Lees, 60 not out, and Leaning, 53 not out, ran the Academy to a nine-wicket victory.

JACK LEANING   **BEN COAD**   **GEORGE ROSS**

EDWARD WILSON   **HENRY CHADWICK**   **JAMES McNICHOL**

Further league victories over Castleford and Sheffield United further boosted the rise in confidence. Lees rarely failed with the bat, and Leaning gave excellent support, while James McNichol steadily improved. Wicket-keeper Henry Chadwick finished with a batting average of 40, and Ross scored over 700 league runs. Jonathan Tattersall gained in confidence as the season progressed, taking 21 wickets with his leg-spin and scoring 395 runs. The experience of Anthony McGrath and Steven Patterson, both recovering from injury, was a shot in the arm.

September saw Scarborough visit Weetwood for the League Cup Final. Blain won the toss, and after the allotted 50 overs Scarborough had stuttered to 157-9, Coad's medium-pace claiming 3-17 in his 10 overs. The fielding was of a high standard, and seven catches were taken. Openers Lees, 90 not out, and Tattersall, 40, put on 142, and it took only 28 overs to prevent the cup from going to North Marine Road.

There were many fine performances in 2011 after a faltering start. Seamers Wainman, Coad and Lilley, off-spinner Ross and leg-spinner Tattersall had many league batsmen struggling. Lees is to be particularly congratulated on taking both the Senior and Junior League batting awards with an average of 60.33, scoring 905 runs in 19 innings, but all concerned can look back on the season with pride.

Harold Galley is Yorkshire Academy Scorer: *Photos: KAREN LEANING*

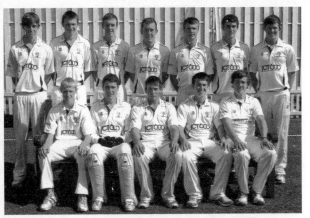

Top of the class: Yorkshire's winning line-up for the Under-17s County Championship. Back row, left to right: Ben Coad, Ryan Gibson, Graham Wiles, George Ross, Edward Wilson, Will Rhodes and Josh Shaw. Front row: Jonathan Tattersall, Henry Chadwick, Jack Leaning (captain), Jonathan Booth and Elliott Callis

All-ROUNDER ROSS UNDER-17s STAR

Yorkshire once again showed its greatness as a cricket stable and all-rounder George Ross firmly put down his marker as a young man to watch when the Under-17s won their County Championship for the first time since 2006 — beating Surrey in the final by six wickets at Grace Road, Leicester, on September 1 and 2.

Surrey won the toss, elected to bat on a flat pitch, and amassed 180-1 off the first 45 overs. As the early bowlers went unrewarded Yorkshire turned to the slow men — and they put up such a fightback that eventually Surrey were bowled out for 327. Off-spinner Ross earned his applause with 5-76 in 24 overs, and leg-spinner Jonathan Tattersall gave strong backing with 3-64 in 15.1. The second day featured a great White Rose batting performance, opener Tattersall showing the way with 46 and skipper Jack Leaning compiling 47 at No.3. Ross entered at second wicket down — and was still there at the end with 112 not out. Ed Wilson, grandson of England 1966 World Cup fullback Ray Wilson, weighed in with 76, putting on 170 for the fourth wicket with Ross.

A FIRST CLASS EFFORT BY YOUNG BARNEY GIBSON

By Chris Hassell

It was another excellent season at all age levels for the Yorkshire schools, but only the Under-15s topped their Northern group to reach the ECB County Cup finals at Oakham. The Under-14s won the Taunton Festival, as did the Under-13s. The Under-15s B team and the Under-12s were both runners-up in the Ampleforth Festival, which in future will be held at Bedford.

A total of 163 matches were played at county level. Congratulations are due especially to Ryburn Valley High School, Halifax, who won our Lord's Taverners' Trophy at Under-14 in 2010 and then represented Yorkshire in the national competition for 2011 at Under-15, beating Pocklington School, Manchester Grammar and Sedbergh to reach the semi-final, where they unfortunately lost to King's School, Grantham — a truly remarkable achievement for a comprehensive school.

Barney Gibson (Crawshaw School, Pudsey) broke a 144-year old record to become the youngest ever first-class player with his selection at the age of 15 years and 27 days for Yorkshire against Durham UCCE.

Having won the ECB County Cup as Under-13s and Under-14s, the Under-15A group hoped for a clean sweep as Under-15s, but they fell five runs short in the final following the cruel run-out of top-scorer Josh Shaw, 69, Jordan Thompson's fierce drive being deflected on to the bowler's stumps during a thrilling chase against Surrey at Oakham.

It was a tremendous experience for the boys, having won a last-ball morning semi-final against Somerset, bowling last in a 20/20 revised format. To bowl again after lunch in the revised 35-over final put them under significant physical pressure, which they handled very well. It was a strong side ably captained by Charlie Elliot (St Peter's) with seven boys in the North team for the ESCA Bunbury Festival at Monmouth — Dylan Budge (Woodhouse Grove), Callum Goldthorpe (Benton Park), Barney Gibson (Crawshaw), Ryan Gibson (Fylinghall), Mosun Hussain (City of Leeds), Alex Leyshon (Ossett) and Josh Shaw (Crofton).

Josh won the Professional Cricketers' Association Award for the most valuable player of the Festival, and Barney Gibson the Shine Trophy for the most shining performance in the field. Ryan Gibson was awarded Yorkshire's Ken Lake Trophy for the best performance at the Bunbury

Festival. Ryan, Barney and Josh were then selected for England Under-15s against England Ladies, and they were also invited to the ECB winter-development programme.

Whilst the team were undoubtedly talented they did let themselves down on occasions — but fortunately recovered, apart from one defeat against Derbyshire. Josh was the quickest bowler, and with his solid batting (272 runs) and athletic fielding was a star performer who will be one to watch. Callum Goldthorp (502 runs) and Dylan Budge (488) were a reliable opening duo, and the main run-scorers were ably supported by Mosun Hussain (397), Charlie Elliot (239) and Jack Harrison (233, Leeds Grammar School) who covered extremely well for Barney Gibson with excellent wicket-keeping which included six stumpings.

In the spin department Karl Carver (Thirsk) topped the wicket tally with 24, followed by leg-breaker Stewart Ward (Benton Park) with 16. The fielding was always of a high standard, and few catches went down, so all in all it was another fine season. The future for this group looks bright, seven boys playing a year up and Matthew Fisher (Easingwold) and James Logan (Normanton Freestone) having two more years at this level. Team manager: Andy Rowsell; coach: Richard Damms.

An outstanding season for Under-15B will be remembered for boundless enthusiasm and inner self-belief, with only one narrow defeat in a thriller against a strong Essex A. Yorkshire dominated in every other fixture, mercilessly pushing their opponents aside. The value of this squad was demonstrated with the promotion of a number of boys to the A team. Nathan Firn (Sherburn High) with his high action was a fearsome sight and won the Lord's Taverners' YTV most-improved-player award. There were many highlights including some class innings culminating in such a successful season. Captain Bradley Birkhead (Rastrick High) showed great leadership qualities, a safe pair of hands behind the stumps and was no mean performer with the bat.

The Ampleforth Festival was a resounding success which saw four victories, but a brilliant effort in chasing 328 fell just short, so the boys took the runners-up spot. Danny Wilbur (Brigshaw) battered 70 in 28 deliveries in a valiant effort with 120 required from nine overs, a fantastic effort. Josh Holling (Shelley College) won the Raymond Fox Trophy as most-improved player with Will Simpson (Sedbergh) taking the batting award and Sammy Davies (King James School, Knaresborough) the bowling award. Team manager: Bob Wincer Woodhouse Grove); coach: Peter Hepworth.

Under-14A enjoyed another successful season with just one blemish in losing to Lancashire. The weather also played its part in denying us the Northern crown when Cumbria were tottering at 46-6: being level on points, Lancashire pipped us by virtue of our head-to-head match and they went on to win the ECB County Cup with some ease at Oakham.

The boys enjoyed a wonderful week in retaining the Festival Trophy at Taunton by winning all five matches in some style and with a record points tally. The character and resilience of the team shone through in the final match of the week against Worcestershire: with Yorkshire 29-8, having been inserted on a damp pitch, in came Matthew Fisher to score 79 not out and Ben Twohig (Bruntcliffe) 48 to lift the total to 170-9. Demoralised, Worcestershire were skittled for 96. The side were capably led by Jordan Thompson (Benton Park) with good knowledge and understanding of the game and engendering a good team ethic. He also led the run-scoring chart with 652, and received the Ian Steen batting award. Top of batting and bowling averages and player-of-the-year for the Brian Willey Trophy was Matthew Fisher (Easingwold) who was under 13 — a magnificent achievement. Team manager/coach: Tony Pickersgill; assistant manager/coach: Bren Terry.

An eventful and most productive season for 14B with plenty of excellent performances, although the batting was at times fragile. There is some concern at the fielding and general fitness, which hopefully can be addressed before the new season. Captain: Tom Norman (Hymer's).

The southern tour was a particular success with four wins and one match abandoned. Toby Booth (Queen Elizabeth Grammar School, Wakefield) took the batting award with 578, although there were very good innings from George Drury (Driffield) and Matthew Fisher. Callum Bethel (Birkdale) earned the bowling award with 17 wickets, while wicket-keeper Bailey Worcester (Woodhouse Grove) claimed 23 catches and 11 stumpings. Sam Witham (Boroughbridge High) took the Michael Barker most-improved player award. Team manager/coach: Tony Pickersgill; coaches: Bren Terry and Jack Bethel.

A number of records were broken by 13A, but a disappointing performance against Nottinghamshire meant failure to retain the ECB Northern Championship for an eighth successive season. Nevertheless, the players showed tremendous spirit to come back from a debilitating loss against Leicestershire to defeat Kent and go on to win the Taunton Festival for the first time. The batting was generally good and at times outstanding. Captain Nathan Goldthorp (Benton Park) with 325 runs featured in century and double-century opening stands and with a top score of 142, while Ben Ainsley (383, Ryehills Comprehensive) and Yasser Imtiaz (342, Royds Hall) contributed well with the bat. Yasser won the most-promising-newcomer award.

Only against top-class fast bowling at Taunton and on a deteriorating wicket against Nottinghamshire did the batting fail. The bowling proved sound with spinners Danish Hussain (Tong High School, 14 wickets) and Alex Kippax (Brigshaw High, 19) doing particularly well, but the slow left-armers of James Logan (Normanton Freeston High) were quite exceptional. He claimed 23 wickets and was leading scorer with 526.

RISING STAR: A great summer for wicket-keeper/batsman Jonathan Bairstow saw him turn his maiden First Class century into a double, become the only Yorkshire player to top 1,000 Championship runs...and burst on the England one-day scene.

YORKSHIRE — 2011

APRIL LINE-UP: Front row, left to right: Richard Pyrah, Ryan Sidebottom, Anthony McGrath, Martyn Moxon (Director of Professional Cricket), Andrew Gale (Captain), Ian Dews (Director of Cricket Operations), Joe Sayers, Gerard Brophy and Adam Lyth. Middle row: Scott McAllister (1st XI Physiotherapist), Kevin Sharp (Batting Coach), Oliver Hannon-Dalby, James Lee, David Wainwright, Jonathan Bairstow, John Blain, Steven Patterson, Craig White (Assistant to the Director of Professional Cricket) and Steve Oldham (Academy Director and Bowling Coach). Back row: Tom Summers (Head of Strength and Conditioning), Gurman Randhawa, Azeem Rafiq, Gary Ballance, Joe Root, Ben Sanderson, Lee Hodgson and Moin Ashraf. *(Photo: VAUGHN RIDLEY).*

PRESIDENT IN WAITING: August 11, 1977, and Geoffrey Boycott drives Australian captain Greg Chappell under the feet of his partner, Graham Roope, for the boundary that brings up his 100th First Class century in the Fourth Test against the old enemy at Headingley. At the Annual General Meeting of 2012 Geoffrey was the Board's nomination to succeed Raymond Illingworth as President of Yorkshire County Cricket Club. *(Photo: Courtesy of PATRICK EAGAR)*

THE WAY AHEAD: Former Australian fast bowler Jason Gillespie, above, on his return to Yorkshire in 2012 as First Team Coach. BELOW: Newly appointed Senior Second Team Coach Paul Farbrace, left, and Development Manager Richard Damms, who previously worked for Yorkshire Cricket Board and the age-group and Academy teams.

DREADED FINGER: Ex-umpire Harold "Dickie" Bird introduces the Prince of Wales to his statue in Barnsley. Dickie was awarded the OBE for services to cricket and charity. *(Photo: Chris Lawton/Yorkshire Post)*

HERITAGE UNVEILED: Yorkshire's £300,000 Cricket Museum is opened on March 18, 2011, by Dr Keith Howard, chairman of the trustees of the Bingley-based Emerald Foundation who funded the fitting-out of the museum below the East Stand at Headingley Carnegie. Dr. Howard is flanked by Museum Director David Hall.

WAS THAT ME? Former Yorkshire left-arm spinner Don Wilson, extreme right, meets himself in his hey-day and is joined by ex-Test umpire Dickie Bird for the first viewing of Yorkshire's Cricket Museum.

THE YOUNGEST ONE: Wicket-keeper Barney Gibson, of Pudsey Congs, set a record that may never be broken when on April 27, 2011, he appeared at The Racecourse, Durham, for Yorkshire against Durham MCCU. At 15 years and 27 days he was the youngest ever to play in English First Class cricket — breaking a record which had stood for 144 years. He dives to pouch Luc Durandt off Oliver Hannon-Dalby for his debut victim in the 10th over of the match. *(Photo: JAMES BUTTLER)*

SILVER ON THE TABLE: If Yorkshire's first and second teams could not do it in 2011...then the Academy could...when they whipped Scarborough by nine wickets at Weetwood to clinch the Yorkshire League Cup for the fourth time in a decade. Skipper John Blain holds the giant trophy aloft and, below, the victorious squad line up. Back row, left to right: James McNichol, Henry Chadwick, Ben Coad, James Wainman, Jonathan Moxon, Will Rhodes, Edward Wilson, Jack Leaning and Jonathan Tattershall. Front row: George Ross, Steve Oldham (Yorkshire Academy Director), John Blain (captain), Alex Lees (Man of the Match), Ian Dews (Yorkshire Cricket Operations) and Harold Galley (scorer). *(Photos: KAREN LEANING)*

DOUGHTY FIGHTER WITH NEVER-SAY-DIE ATTITUDE

By David Warner

DAVID WAINWRIGHT
Only third Yorkshire player
to score century at No. 10

David Wainwright was a firm favourite with the Yorkshire fans, despite being unable to hold down a first team place. All *White Rose* followers will wish him well as he tries to rebuild his career with Derbyshire.

The left-arm spin bowler and left-hand batsman was particularly admired for his fighting qualities, and his unbeaten century batting at No. 10 against Sussex at Hove in the last match of 2008 is still recalled with great affection.

Yorkshire travelled to Hove for that game in grave danger of relegation, and their situation appeared even bleaker as they slumped to 80-6. They improved somewhat through a stand of 80 between Tim Bresnan and Adil Rashid, but two further wickets left them in big trouble again on 178-8.

It was at this stage that Wainwright joined Rashid. They defied all of Sussex's attempts to dislodge them by putting on 140 — only the second time Yorkshire had managed a century partnership for the ninth wicket at Hove.

The stand ended when Rashid was lbw to Mohammad Sami for 111, but Wainwright's innings was still far from over: he then put on an unbeaten 82 for the last wicket with Matthew Hoggard — a record for

33

THE BATSMAN: Lancashire's Luke Sutton and V V S Laxman look on as Wainwright hits out during the 2009 Roses match at Headingley Carnegie

Yorkshire's 10th wicket against Sussex. The declaration at 400-9 left Wainwright unbeaten on 104 from 169 balls with 10 fours and a six to become only the third Yorkshire player to score a century batting at No. 10. Jason Gillespie did so the previous season against Surrey at The Oval, and the only other instance was George Hirst's 115 not out off Gloucestershire's attack at Bristol in 1894.

Wainwright then turned his attentions to the ball, picking up three wickets for nine runs as Sussex were made to follow on. A century from Murray Goodwin, despite Rashid's seven wickets, enabled Sussex to draw the match when they declared on 397-9. Both sides were happy with the result, because 12 points for Yorkshire and eight for their opponents meant that they both avoided relegation at the expense of Kent.

The Pontefract-born all-rounder's never-say-die attitude was evident again at Scarborough the following season when he rapped out an unbeaten 102 against Warwickshire. Batting this time at No. 9, his innings used up 149 balls and contained 14 boundaries.

Wainwright's partnership of 144 with Gerard Brophy was only the second century stand for the Yorkshire eighth wicket against Warwickshire.

It seemed inevitable that when Yorkshire returned to Hove that year Wainwright would again make his mark: his fine all-round contribution, plus Hoggard's hat-trick,

JAMES LEE
Surprise *Roses* debut

brought Yorkshire victory by 156 runs, and again saved them from relegation. This time he enjoyed unbeaten knocks of 85 and 15 at No. 9, and followed up figures of 5-134 with 4-12 in 8.3 overs as Sussex buckled to 83 all out. Sadly for both Yorkshire and Wainwright, a combination of loss of form, injuries and strong competition from the other spinners meant that he was never able to command the regular place he so eagerly sought — and which he needed to go on improving his game.

He was loaned out to Derbyshire during last summer, but made an immediate return because of injury to Azeem Rafiq. A few weeks later Yorkshire agreed to his release so that he could join Derbyshire on a two-year contract. Wainwright, who joined Yorkshire from Loughborough University, where he played for Loughborough MCCU, scored 852 first-class runs in 28 matches for his native county at an average of 35.50. He claimed 62 wickets at 38.15 runs apiece.

In 47 List A matches he scored 150 runs, rarely getting the chance to bat early on, and captured 36 wickets at 38.38. He played 25 Twenty20 games, scoring 23 runs and helping himself to 21 wickets at 26.23.

Yorkshire also said farewell to Sheffield-born fast bowlers James Lee and Ben Sanderson, neither of whom managed to secure regular first-team places, but who turned in several excellent performances for the Second XI over the past few years.

Lee, then 18, made a surprise Championship debut in the *Roses* match at Old Trafford in 2006, but his chances were few and far between, although in 2009 he claimed seven wickets in the NatWest Pro40 League at an average of 16.57 to finish second in the averages as well as helping Yorkshire Seconds to beat Lancashire in the Trophy final.

Sanderson's debut was restricted to half a match at Riverside in 2008, when he was replaced on the third morning by Matthew Hoggard upon his release from the England squad.

He also played that summer in the *Roses* match at Headingley Carnegie, but it was another two years before his third and final first-class appearance when he ran through Loughborough MCCU with 5-50 in their only innings.

BEN SANDERSON
Deputised for Hoggard

Also in 2010, Sanderson impressed with seven wickets in the CB40 League, while last summer he enjoyed himself in the Friends Life t20 encounter at Derby with 4-21, Yorkshire's joint second-best figures of the season in the competition.

The fourth player to leave Headingley at the end of last season was Middlesbrough-born all-rounder Lee Hodgson, who Yorkshire signed from Surrey in 2009 after he had scored 63 against Nottinghamshire on his only Championship appearance for the London club the previous summer. Hodgson made 33 and 34 against Loughborough MCCU and India A at Headingley in 2010, and on his Twenty20 debut later that season he top-scored with an excellent unbeaten 39 against Nottinghamshire at Trent Bridge before picking up a couple of wickets in the next game at Derby. He was another who could not secure a regular first-team place and in the end was surplus to requirements.

DAVID JOHN WAINWRIGHT

BATTING

First Class — Yorkshire 2004-2011

M	I	NO	Runs	HS	Avge	100s	50s	Ct
29	36	11	914	104*	36.56	2	3	6

All First Class

M	I	NO	Runs	HS	Avge	100s	50s	Ct
35	43	12	1,071	104*	34.54	2	3	10

Yorkshire Domestic List A

M	I	NO	Runs	HS	Avge	100s	50s	Ct
47	20	13	150	15*	21.42	0	0	16

Yorkshire t20

M	I	NO	Runs	HS	Avge	100s	50s	Ct
26	9	6	23	6*	7.66	0	0	9

BOWLING

First Class — Yorkshire 2004-2011

Overs	Mdns	Runs	Wkts	Avge	Best	5wi
747.4	143	2,380	69	34.49	6-40	2

All First Class

Overs	Mdns	Runs	Wkts	Avge	Best	5wi
893.3	169	3,003	82	36.62	6-40	2

Yorkshire Domestic List A

Overs	Mdns	Runs	Wkts	Avge	Best	5wi
276.1	10	1,382	36	38.38	3-33	0

Yorkshire t20

Overs	Mdns	Runs	Wkts	Avge	Best	5wi
75.5	0	551	21	26.23	3-6	0

LEE JOHN HODGSON

BATTING

First Class — Yorkshire 2008-2011

M	I	NO	Runs	HS	Avge	100s	50s	Ct
3	3	0	99	34	33.00	0	0	1

All First Class

M	I	NO	Runs	HS	Avge	100s	50s	Ct
4	5	0	165	63	33.00	0	1	3

Yorkshire Domestic List A

M	I	NO	Runs	HS	Avge	100s	50s	Ct
6	2	0	9	9	4.50	0	0	1

All Domestic List A

M	I	NO	Runs	HS	Avge	100s	50s	Ct
8	2	0	9	9	4.50	0	0	4

Yorkshire t20

M	I	NO	Runs	HS	Avge	100s	50s	Ct
2	1	1	39	39*	—	0	0	1

BOWLING

First Class — Yorkshire 2008-2011

Overs	Mdns	Runs	Wkts	Avge	Best	5wi
40.5	9	158	2	79.00	1-42	0

All First Class

Overs	Mdns	Runs	Wkts	Avge	Best	5wi
49.5	10	216	2	108.00	1-42	0

Yorkshire Domestic List A

Overs	Mdns	Runs	Wkts	Avge	Best	5wi
30	1	161	4	40.25	2-44	0

All Domestic List A

Overs	Mdns	Runs	Wkts	Avge	Best	5wi
38	1	213	4	53.25	2-44	0

Yorkshire t20

Overs	Mdns	Runs	Wkts	Avge	Best	5wi
6	0	59	2	29.50	2-29	0

BEN WILLIAM SANDERSON

BATTING

First Class — Yorkshire 2008-2011

M	I	NO	Runs	HS	Avge	100s	50s	Ct
3	2	1	6	6	6.00	0	0	0

Yorkshire Domestic List A

M	I	NO	Runs	HS	Avge	100s	50s	Ct
10	2	1	14	12*	14.00	0	0	5

Yorkshire t20

M	I	NO	Runs	HS	Avge	100s	50s	Ct
4	0	0	0	—		0	0	0

BOWLING

First Class — Yorkshire 2008-2011

Overs	Mdns	Runs	Wkts	Avge	Best	5wi
55	10	190	6	31.66	5-50	1

Yorkshire Domestic List A

Overs	Mdns	Runs	Wkts	Avge	Best	5wi
42	1	247	8	30.87	2-17	0

Yorkshire t20

Overs	Mdns	Runs	Wkts	Avge	Best	5wi
12.4	0	74	6	12.33	4-21	1 x 4wi

JAMES EDWARD LEE

BATTING

First Class — Yorkshire 2006-2011

M	I	NO	Runs	HS	Avge	100s	50s	Ct
2	3	1	24	21*	12.00	0	0	1

Yorkshire Domestic List A

M	I	NO	Runs	HS	Avge	100s	50s	Ct
4	0	0	0	—	—	0	0	0

BOWLING

First Class — Yorkshire 2006-2011

Overs	Mdns	Runs	Wkts	Avge	Best	5wi
28	1	149	2	74.50	2-63	0

Yorkshire Domestic List A

Overs	Mdns	Runs	Wkts	Avge	Best	5wi
17.4	0	116	7	16.57	3-43	0

Fergie

The coach Ralph Middlebrook said Carrick had helped hundreds of young players: "He may not have been as good a bowler as Wilfred Rhodes, but for acumen I'd put him in the same bracket."

Graeme Wright, Wisden on Yorkshire

YORKSHIRE THRIVE WITH ALL-WEATHER ATTACK

By Derek Hodgson

The year 1912 will be remembered for the loss of the *Titanic*, the super liner "that even God could not sink", perhaps an omen for the shock and loss of blood and treasure that was to follow in the Great War.

Edwardian England had two and a half summers left in which to enjoy the belief that prosperity and education were still advancing. There was still time for songs and gaiety, for the music hall, for the seaside.

County cricket was at its apogee, more a national obsession than a sport, and Yorkshire followers were impatient for success. Three years had passed without a Championship — these were Kent's great years — and, to general surprise, newcomers Warwickshire had upset the natural order by winning in 1911. The Ridings demanded change.

**SIR ARCHIBALD WHITE
Fortunate to take over
such a talented band**

Everard Radcliffe had succeeded Hawke as captain in 1911 although, in fact, he had been in practical charge for most of the previous two years as the 51-year-old president and captain spent more time in the committee room. Less obvious to the casual spectator was the burgeoning strength of the team as exemplified by the emergence of three formidable all-rounders in Booth, Drake and Kilner, a young wicket-keeper in Dolphin, a superb bad-wicket batsman in Oldroyd and consistent middle-order scoring from Benny Wilson, all behind the remaining immortals: Rhodes, Hirst, Haigh and Denton.

The fortunate young man to take over this band was Archibald White, son of a baronet, from Wellington School and Cambridge University but born in Tickhill. He was no great shakes as a player, failing to make the

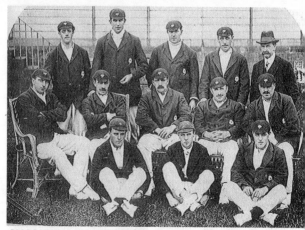

CHAMPION COUNTY 1912. Back row, left ro right: Arthur Dolpin, Major Booth, Alonzo Drake, Wilfred Rhodes and James Hoyland (scorer). Middle row: Benny Wilson, David Denton, Sir Archibald White (captain) George Hirst and Schofield Haigh. Front row: Roy Kilner, Edgar Oldroyd and Billy Bates
(Photo: Ron Deaton Archive)

Cambridge X1 and returning a career-best score of 55, but he could hit the ball and he was a disciplinarian— a much-needed quality in a team of so many talents and temperaments.

He was popular enough for the team to contribute hard-earned coin to buy a silver salver that first year, which is remembered in cricket history as the year of the Triangular Tournament when England played Australia and South Africa in a series. Rhodes thus missed six Championship matches and Haigh one. The weather was miserable, only nine of Yorkshire's 19 home matches escaping the rain. Play was washed out for four successive days at Sheffield and Huddersfield, and again at Bradford and Hull.

What this meant on uncovered pitches was that Yorkshire's attack, incredibly versatile with a man and ball for every occasion, could run riot on drying turf. Only one match was lost, and White won the Championship in his first season. Hence the salver. The defeat came at Lord's, where White chose to bat first on a day after rain. Yorkshire were 76-7 before Booth, Haigh and White managed to raise 157. Middlesex needed only 139 in the fourth innings, and duly accomplished this by four wickets, having to wait because of rain until late afternoon.

Hirst, Drake and Haigh routed Lancashire by 10 wickets at Bradford where, on a difficult surface, it was the dead-bat technique of Rhodes, 107, that made the difference. At Nottingham with 248 needed, Hirst injured and Rhodes out, Wilson, Kilner and a promising amateur, John Tasker, did the job.

Yorkshire gained some revenge for earlier reverses at Tunbridge Wells where, in mid-July, the sun did shine. Denton contributed 221 to a total of 543, only Frank Woolley, 42 and 75, sustaining resistance in an innings defeat. Yorkshire then collided with C B Fry, 186, at Southampton but Denton's 191 was thought the better innings. Hirst and Haigh were deadly after rain in a nine-wicket win.

Denton at 38 lauded it over England that summer, only Hobbs with 2,042 approaching his aggregate of 2,127 runs. Haigh on 125 was the leading wicket-taker, with Hirst and Booth also reaching three figures while Drake took 87. Haigh, then 41, wrecked the Australians at Bradford with match figures of 11-36, bowling so well the Aussies wanted to adopt him.

ARTHUR DOLPHIN: Kept wicket for 22 years
(Photo: Courtesy of www.adelphiarchive.co.uk)

The counties were unhappy at having to surrender players for six Test matches, and Kent had every reason to feel hard done by: they won 14 of their 26 matches, one more than Yorkshire who edged ahead by taking the lead more often on first innings, points for which were first awarded in 1911. The true glory in 1912 belonged to Northamptonshire, elected in 1905, who used only 12 players in finishing second, winning 10 of their 18 matches. In Kent, a schoolboy known to history as W Clarke took three hat-tricks in the first innings of a match and two in the second.

The *Titanic* was not the Empire's only loss that year. Robert Falcon Scott, gentleman and explorer, led his party in a doomed but epic attempt to be the first to the South Pole. Churchill spoke for Home Rule for Ireland; middle-class complacency was jarred by a strike of 800,000 coal-miners; China's last emperor lost his throne; a Stuttgart newspaper called for a European Union, and the Louvre was still searching for the stolen Mona Lisa.

Jamie Hood honoured

Former Yorkshire Second XI and Academy all-rounder Jamie Hood was made an honorary life member of the Yorkshire Players' Association.

Jamie, who was born in Saltburn on September 7, 1976, played several times for the Second XI between 1994 and 1997, and he appeared to have a bright future ahead of him.

His career was abruptly and tragically ended by a serious car accident in South Africa, which left him paralysed from the neck downwards. He has never lost his enthusiasm for cricket, and he keeps in close touch with Yorkshire's fortunes.

Association Secretary Geoff Cope said: "Our members were delighted to award Jamie honorary life membership, and he has now received his complimentary Yorkshire CCC membership card and an Association tie.

Jamie still has fond memories of scoring a century for Yorkshire Seconds against Worcestershire Seconds at Bradford Park Avenue in 1995, and he is proud of the record-breaking 161 he once made for Redcar against Northallerton.

Love in for players...

Jim Love was installed as President of Yorkshire Players' Association by retiring president Philip Sharpe at the Association's annual general meeting in March 2011. Jim, who played for Yorkshire between 1975 and 1989, scored 10,263 first-class runs with 13 centuries. He also scored 4,298 one-day runs for his native county, and he represented England in three one-day matches.

YORKSHIRE'S FIRST-CLASS HIGHLIGHTS OF 1912

Wins by an innings (3)

Yorkshire (330) beat Somerset (69 and 125) by an innings and 136 runs at Taunton
Yorkshire (389) beat Nottinghamshire (161 and 126) by an innings and 102 runs at Harrogate
Yorkshire (543) beat Kent (310 and188) by an innings and 45 runs at Tunbridge Wells

Wins by 10 wickets (2)

Essex (129 and 187) lost to Yorkshire (278 and 40-0) by 10 wickets at Leyton
Yorkshire (226 and 17-0) beat Lancashire (76 and 165) by 10 wickets at Bradford

Match abandoned without a ball bowled (1)

v. Surrey at Sheffield on June 3, 4 and 5. Nineteen full days were lost to the weather: 15 at home and 4 away

Totals of 400 and over (5)

543	v. Kent at Tunbridge Wells
492	v. Hampshire at Southampton
471	v. Hampshire at Sheffield
451 for 4 wkts dec)	v. Warwickshire at Birmingham
411 for 9 wkts dec)	v. Gloucestershire at Bristol

Opponents dismissed for under 100 (10)

59	Warwickshire at Hull	76	Lancashire at Bradford
68	Gloucestershire at Leeds	80	Hampshire at Sheffield
69	Somerset at Taunton	84	MCC at Scarborough
73	Somerset at Dewsbury	85	Worcestershire at Dewsbury
74	Northamptonshire at Bradford	95	Hampshire at Southampton

Century Partnerships (12)

For the 2nd wicket (4)

253	B B Wilson and D Denton	v. Warwickshire at Birmingham
197	B B Wilson and D Denton	v. Hampshire at Southampton
164	R Kilner and E Oldroyd	v. Northamptonshire at Northampton
160	E Oldroyd and D Denton	v. Kent at Tunbridge Wells

For the 3rd wicket (2)

134	D Denton and A Drake	v. Hampshire at Sheffield
118	D Denton and A Drake	v. Hampshire at Southampton

For the 4th wicket (4)

144	D Denton and G H Hirst	v. Worcestershire at Dewsbury
113	D Denton and G H Hirst	v. Hampshire at Sheffield
113	D Denton and G H Hirst	v. Kent at Tunbridge Wells
101	D Denton and G H Hirst	v Gloucestershire at Bristol

For the 5th wicket (1)

113	R Kilner and J Tasker	v. Nottinghamshire at Nottingham

For the 8th wicket (1)

120	S Haigh and Sir A W White	v. Gloucestershire at Bristol

Centuries (10)

D Denton (6)

221	v. Kent at Tunbridge Wells
200*	v. Warwickshire at Birmingham
191	v. Hampshire at Southampton
182	v. Gloucestershire at Bristol
111	v Northampton at Northampton
107	v. Hampshire at Sheffield

W Rhodes (2)

176	v. Nottinghamshire at Harrogate
107	v. Lancashire at Bradford

G H Hirst (1)

109	v. Worcestershire at Dewsbury

B B Wilson (1)

150	v. Warwickshire at Birmingham

5 wickets in an innings (33)

S Haigh (11)

9 for	25	v. Gloucestershire at Leeds, 1st innings
6 for	14	v. Australians at Bradford, 2nd innings
6 for	46	v Gloucestershire at Bristol
5 for	14	v. Somerset at Dewsbury
5 for	22	v. Australians at Bradford, 1st innings
5 for	25	v. Lancashire at Bradford
5 for	33	v. South Africans at Huddersfield
5 for	37	v. Worcestershire at Dewsbury, 1st innings
5 for	40	v. Gloucestershire at Leeds, 2nd innings
5 for	57	v. Worcestershire at Dewsbury, 2nd innings
5 for	62	v. Kent at Tunbridge Wells

M W Booth (7)

8 for	47	v. Middlesex at Leeds
8 for	52	v. Leicestershire at Sheffield
7 for	50	v. Essex at Leyton, 1st innings
6 for	31	v. Hampshire at Sheffield
6 for	52	v. MCC at Scarborough
5 for	69	v. Essex at Leyton, 2nd innings
5 for	91	v. Northamptonshire at Northampton

A Drake (7)

6 for	23	v. Middlesex at Leeds
6 for	24	v. Nottinghamshire at Harrogate
6 for	25	v. Warwickshire at Hull
6 for	33	v. Lancashire at Bradford
6 for	35	v. Essex at Huddersfield
5 for	26	v. Leicestershire at Leicester
5 for	60	v. Cambridge University at Cambridge

5 wickets in an innings *(Continued)*

G H Hirst (6)

    9 for 69 v. MCC at Lord's, 2nd innings
    6 for 30 v. Somerset at Taunton, 1st innings
    6 for 37 v. Somerset at Taunton, 2nd innings
    6 for 40 v. MCC at Scarborough
    6 for 47 v. Hampshire at Southampton
    5 for 40 v. MCC at Lord's, 1st innings

W Rhodes (2)

    6 for 102 v. South Africans at Huddersfield
    5 for 68 v. Nottinghamshire at Harrogate

10 wickets in a match (8)

S Haigh (3)

    14 for 65 (9 for 25 and 5 for 40)   v. Gloucestershire at Leeds
    11 for 36 (5 for 22 and 6 for 14)   v. Australians at Bradford
    10 for 94 (5 for 37 and 5 for 57)   v. Worcestershire at Dewsbury

G H Hirst (3)

    14 for 109 (5 for 40 and 9 for 69)   v. MCC at Lord's
    12 for 67 (6 for 30 and 6 for 37)   v. Somerset at Taunton
    10 for 138 (4 for 91 and 6 for 47)   v. Hampshire at Southampton

M W Booth (2)

    12 for 119 (7 for 50 and 5 for 69)   v. Essex at Leyton
    11 for 143 (8 for 52 and 3 for 91)   v. Leicestershire at Sheffield

Hat-tricks (2)

M W Booth (1)

    1st innings v. Essex at Leyton (P A Perrin, C P Buckenham and W Mead)

A Drake (1)

    1st innings Essex at Huddersfield (E C Coleman, G T Sutton and W Mead)

The Double (all First-Class matches) (1)

G H Hirst

    1,119 runs @ 26.08   113 wickets @ 16.91

3 catches in an innings (3)

A Dolphin (2)

    3   v. Cambridge University at Cambridge
    3   v. Leicestershire at Sheffield

H Watson (1)

    3   v. Nottinghamshire at Nottingham

3 dismissals in an innings (3)

A Dolphin (3)

    3 (2ct, 1st) v. Leicestershire at Leicester
    3 (2ct, 1st) v. Hampshire at Southampton
    3 (2ct, 1st) v. Middlesex at Leeds

5 dismissals in a match (1)

A Dolphin (1)

    5 (3ct, 2st) v. Leicestershire at Leicester

Debuts (3)
In first-class cricket: E Loxley-Firth, J H B Sullivan and J Tasker

100 YEARS AGO

YORKSHIRE AVERAGES 1912

ALL FIRST-CLASS MATCHES

Played 36   Won 14   Lost 3   Drawn 18   Abandoned 1
County Championship: Played 28   Won 13   Lost 1   Drawn 13   Abandoned 1

BATTING AND FIELDING *(Qualification 10 completed innings)*

Player	M.	I.	N.O.	Runs	H.S.	Avge	100s	50s	ct/st
D Denton	35	51	4	2088	221	44.42	6	6	8
W Rhodes	24	39	5	1030	176	30.29	2	3	20
B B Wilson	35	54	3	1453	150	28.49	1	6	3
G H Hirst	32	43	0	1119	109	26.02	1	7	25
M W Booth	34	45	7	708	75	18.63	0	4	20
E Oldroyd	17	23	1	405	70	18.40	0	2	6
S Haigh	33	42	10	577	62*	18.03	0	2	16
Sir A W White	35	43	12	557	54*	17.96	0	2	11
A Drake	35	49	2	797	65	16.95	0	4	20
R Kilner	23	39	5	570	83*	16.76	0	3	13
J Tasker	23	33	3	455	67	15.16	0	3	11
W E Bates	12	17	0	165	64	9.70	0	1	5
A Dolphin	32	35	13	185	28	8.40	0	0	33/12

Also batted

Player	M.	I.	N.O.	Runs	H.S.	Avge	100s	50s	ct/st
G W Bayes	5	6	4	42	14	21.00	0	0	1
J H B Sullivan	1	2	0	41	26	20.50	0	0	0
J T Newstead	2	2	1	12	8*	12.00	0	0	0
E Loxley-Firth	2	4	0	43	37	10.75	0	0	1
J P Wilson	2	3	0	23	17	7.66	0	0	1
H Watson	3	5	2	7	4	2.33	0	0	6

BOWLING *(Qualification 10 wickets)*

Player	Overs	Mdns	Runs	Wkts	Avge	Best	5wI	10wM
S Haigh	798.4	241	1508	125	12.06	9-25	11	3
G H Hirst	858.1	252	1911	113	16.91	9-69	6	3
A Drake	698.5	195	1629	87	18.72	6-24	7	0
M W Booth	732.5	163	1994	104	19.17	8-47	7	2
R Kilner	167.3	56	338	16	21.12	4-66	0	0
W Rhodes	340.5	65	997	45	22.15	6-102	2	0
G W Bayes	104	16	340	13	26.15	4-51	0	0

Also bowled

Player	Overs	Mdns	Runs	Wkts	Avge	Best	5wI	10wM
D Denton	2.4	1	7	1	7.00	1-1	0	0
J T Newstead	32	12	58	8	7.25	4-8	0	0
E Oldroyd	37	5	115	4	28.75	1-8	0	0
J H B Sullivan	7	0	43	0	—	—	—	—
B B Wilson	5	0	42	0	—	—	—	—
Sir A W White	1	0	7	0	—	—	—	—

SHARPE WORK HELPS TO BRING BACK TITLE

By Anthony Bradbury

The seasons of the late 1950s and early 1960s provided unexpected challenges to the then dominant teams in county cricket.

Yorkshire won wholly unexpectedly in 1959; Hampshire, who had never won the Championship, were successful in 1961, and in 1962 the challenge came from Worcestershire, a team with few resources who also had never won it. There was to be a very tight contest with Yorkshire.

Yorkshire had a formidable side in 1962 with, by the season's end, 12 players who had or would play Test cricket — one of whom was already one of the world's great bowlers; another would become one of the world's great batsmen, and two would be outstanding captains of their times.

The county came into the season having been runners-up in the 1961 Championship to Hampshire and with a determination to regain the crown that they had held in both 1959 and 1960.

They were still led by their professional captain, Vic Wilson — now in his third season at the helm — and their existing Test players

J.V. WILSON
Yorkshire

**VIC WILSON
Second Championship
in three years**
(Photo: Ron Deaton Archive)

were Brian Close, Raymond Illingworth, Doug Padgett, Ken Taylor, and Fred Trueman. Philip Sharpe, Brian Bolus, John Hampshire, Don

300 HOOKER: Ron Hooker, who was to play exactly 300 first-class games for Middlesex, lives up to his name with 50 in the first innings at Lord's in 1962 as Jimmy Binks, Philip Sharpe and Vic Wilson stay on full alert. Middlesex won by six wickets.

(Photo: Courtesy of www.adelphiarchive.co.uk)

Wilson and Jimmy Binks, all of whom had played for Yorkshire in 1961, would become England players, and two of the three new first-teamers in 1962, Geoffrey Boycott and Richard Hutton, would gain Test caps. The third newcomer, Tony Nicholson, would be chosen to go on an England tour to South Africa, and the remaining players in the regular squad — Bryan Stott, Mel Ryan, Bob Platt, and Mike Cowan — were exceptional county players. Ryan, Platt and Cowan took between them 125 Championship wickets in 1962.

As in previous years the Counties played differing numbers of games — either 28 or 32. Yorkshire played 32, and so met every other county twice. They also in their traditional way started the season with a southern tour of MCC at Lord's and Cambridge and Oxford universities. The sole touring side were Pakistan, so there was a game against them, and MCC came to Scarborough before the season closed. The first match started on April 28, and the last one finished on September 7. These 37 three-day games started on Wednesdays and Saturdays, with never any play on a Sunday — and thus with a symmetry clearly understood by players and spectators alike.

Yet financial clouds were growing even in Yorkshire, where the annual surplus was to be only £362, and this in a county with few capital assets. Quietly tucked away at the foot of the 1962 Annual Report was this statement: *"In 1963 a Knockout Cup Competition is to be inaugurated. The matches are to be played on an overs basis (65) and in order to meet any interruption by rain three days have been allocated for each round. It is hoped that this competition will be welcomed by members and the general public and will add further interest to the game."*

Though none knew it 1962 was the last year of the old regular order — and in another way, too, for amateurism was to be abolished. The last Gentleman v. Players match was held at Lord's in July 1962, and F S Trueman was captain of the Players.

Yorkshire's 16 home Championship games were played on seven grounds, including Hull, Middlesbrough and Harrogate, with only three at Headingley. Away venues included Westcliff-on-Sea, Worksop, Bournemouth and Gillingham, and with the varying conditions it would not have been a total surprise that Trueman and Illingworth took 100 wickets apiece and that none of the recognised batsmen averaged 40.

Despite their talent the opening partnership of Bolus and Taylor did not survive the season, although they went out

**PHILIP SHARPE
Genius at slip whose
catches record in 1962
may last into eternity**
*(Photo: Courtesy of
www.adelphiarchive.co.uk)*

together in the first 12 matches and in some afterwards. A young man who had scored heavily in the Second XI was given a few mid-season games: he was involved in a run-out in his first match, and again in his second, when he opened for the first time. His name was Geoffrey Boycott, and by the time of the *Roses* match at Old Trafford he was replaced by a Cambridge undergraduate playing his first match for Yorkshire. The undergraduate was Richard Hutton, and Boycott was unable to displace him for the remainder of the 1962 season.

Meantime, the opening slot had moved from Bolus and Taylor to Taylor/Boycott to Stott/Taylor to Stott/Padgett to Boycott/Padgett to Hampshire/Padgett to Taylor/Padgett and, finally, to Taylor/Hampshire. The one man who did not open but had an excellent season was Philip Sharpe, with 2,252 runs and six centuries at an average of over 40 in all of his 64 first-class innings. He was a genius as a slip fielder, the best in the country, and his 71 catches for Yorkshire beat the record of 70 set by John Tunnicliffe in 1901. A record that may now last into eternity.

CHAMPION SMILES: The title is safe, and Yorkshire line up at Harrogate. Back row, left to right: Philip Sharpe, Bryan Stott, Mel Ryan, Don Wilson, Ken Taylor and John Hampshire. Front row: Raymond Illingworth, Brian Close, Vic Wilson (captain), Freddie Trueman and Jimmy Binks. *(Photo: Ron Deaton)*

The season ebbed and flowed. Three early victories put Yorkshire in top position, but then followed three losses and three draws and Yorkshire were down to seventh. A revival of nine wins and no losses in the last 20 games started with a remarkable victory against the reigning Champions, Hampshire, at Bradford. In a low-scoring match where neither team reached 180 in any innings, Derek Shackleton took 12-145 and Hampshire were left to make 163 to win. They were 156 with only five wickets down when Illingworth and Trueman pounced, taking the last five wickets for one run, and Yorkshire ran out winners by five runs. That match and the nature of the win must have provided an additional bonus for Trueman — for the next fixture was his benefit match at Bramall Lane against Yorkshire's great Southern rivals, Surrey. The game was drawn because of a strong Surrey recovery after a big first-innings deficit. The beneficiary did not bat and took only three wickets, but his fund realised £9,331, falling just short of Sir Leonard Hutton's then Yorkshire record of £9.713. In 1962 this would be for many people more than nine times their gross annual salary.

Though Yorkshire were doing well in their matches, other teams were chasing hard. Worcestershire, Warwickshire, Surrey and Gloucestershire all had good running streaks, but ultimately Worcestershire became the team to beat: their two matches with Yorkshire were drawn, though Yorkshire were lucky to avoid defeat in one game when, needing 229 to win, they stumbled to 48-5 before recovering through defensive work from Illingworth and Vic Wilson to 103-7. If Yorkshire had lost Worcestershire would have been outright favourites for the title.

An unsatisfactory quirk in the fixtures left most counties completing their final matches on or before September 4. That included Worcestershire who defeated Nottinghamshire that day and placed themselves on top of the table with

KEN TAYLOR
Hero of Harrogate
(Photo: Ron Deaton Archive)

14 wins and some bonus points. Yorkshire, instead of playing their last Championship game, were meeting MCC as a part of the Scarborough Festival. While Worcester supporters then had no cricket to watch, Yorkshire moved across the county to Harrogate to play Glamorgan in a match that started on September 5. Whether any Yorkshire supporters remained behind in Scarborough to watch TN Pearce's XI against Pakistan starting on the same day must be doubtful. Yorkshire had to win to deny Worcestershire the Championship.

It was on an uncovered and drying pitch that Yorkshire won the toss and put Glamorgan in. Don Wilson was bowling within the hour, and promptly took 6-34. Glamorgan all out for 65, but if Yorkshire briefly felt great delight their nemesis nearly came. In the Yorkshire innings that same day 10 of their 11 batsmen scored 32 between them. Salvation came from opener Taylor, who handled the medium-pace of Ossie Wheatley and off-spin of Don Shepherd with brilliant batting and 10 fours in an innings of 67. Perhaps this was his greatest day. Next day it poured with rain, and no play was possible. On the third morning volunteers arrived before dawn. With car headlights on, they used Squeegees to rid the ground of surface water. One of the umpires who allowed play to start on time was Tom Drinkwater. Illingworth and Don Wilson got back to work: Glamorgan wickets fell steadily, and seven

PACE TRIO: Freddie Trueman, whose Yorkshire career was to continue until 1968, marked the end of an era in 1962 when he became the last captain of the Players against the Gentlemen before the abolition of amateur status. Newcomer Tony Nicholson and left-armer Mike Cowan, extreme right, are studying form
(Photos: www.adelphiarchive.co.uk and Ron Deaton Archive)

were down by lunch. Then resistance from the Welsh stiffened.

The 11,000 Yorkshire faces in the crowd showed their collective anxiety, but a final flurry of wickets left Yorkshire with a target of 66 in three hours. Surely all would be well? Out came Taylor...but he was back in the pavilion after one ball, bowled for a duck by Jeff Jones.

It was Jones's hat-trick, because he had taken two Yorkshire wickets with the last two deliveries in Yorkshire's first innings. John Hampshire, then uncapped, stood firm, and with Sharpe and Close to give him support Yorkshire were home.

The *White Rose* had 14 Championship victories — just like Worcestershire — but four more points. Vic Wilson, their captain, and Maurice Leyland, the coach, were both able to retire from their eminent positions as happy men.

YORKSHIRE'S FIRST-CLASS HIGHLIGHTS OF 1962

Win by an innings (4)

Warwickshire (108 and 171) lost to Yorkshire (386) by an innings and 107 runs at Birmingham

Essex (207 and 112) lost to Yorkshire (363-9 dec) by an innings and 44 runs at Sheffield

Derbyshire (232 and 114) lost to Yorkshire (377) by an innings and 31 runs at Hull

Somerset (105 and 128) lost to Yorkshire (246) by an innings and 13 runs at Hull

Totals of 400 and over (2)

441 for 9 wkts dec   v. Nottinghamshire at Leeds
416   v. Surrey at The Oval

Opponents dismissed for under 100 (5)

99	Sussex at Scarborough	65	Kent at Gillingham
95	Gloucestershire at Bradford	65	Glamorgan at Harrogate
70	Leicestershire at Bradford		

Century Partnerships (17)

For the 1st wicket (3)

138	J B Bolus and K Taylor	v. Cambridge University at Cambridge (2nd innings)
136	J B Bolus and K Taylor	v. Cambridge University at Cambridge (1st innings)
105	J B Bolus and K Taylo	v. Glamorgan at Cardiff

For the 2nd wicket (4)

266*	K Taylor and D E V Padgett	v. Oxford University at Oxford
124	D E V Padgett and P J Sharpe	v. Somerset at Taunton
124	J B Bolus and D E V Padgett	v. Cambridge University at Cambridge
115*	J H Hampshire and P J Sharpe	v. Lancashire at Manchester

For the 3rd wicket (3)

199	P J Sharpe and D E V Padgett	v. Surrey at Sheffield
130	P J Sharpe and W B Stott	v. Pakistan at Bradford
115	P J Sharpe and D B Close	v. Northamptonshire at Sheffield

For the 4th wicket (1)

148	D E V Padgett and W B Stott	v. Derbyshire at Hull

For the 5th wicket (2)

117	D B Close and R Illingworth	v. Warwickshire at Sheffield
113	P J Sharpe and R Illingworth	v. Gloucestershire at Bradford

For the 6th wicket (2)

120	D B Close and J V Wilson	v. Somerset at Taunton
111	R Illingworth and J V Wilson	v. Worcestershire at Leeds

For the 7th wicket (1)

130	P J Sharpe and J V Wilson	v. Warwickshire at Birmingham

For the 8th wicket (1)

116	K Taylor and J V Wilson	v. Nottinghamshire at Leeds

Centuries (22)

P J Sharpe (7)

138	v. Somerset at Taunton	
136*	v.Pakistan at Bradford	
132	v. Surrey at Sheffield	
112	v. Lancashire at Manchester	
110	v. Northamptonshire at Sheffield	
108*	v. Lancashire at Leeds	
104	v. Nottinghamshire at Worksop	

D B Close (3)

142*	v. Essex at Sheffield
140*	v. Warwickshire at Sheffield
121*	v. Somerset at Taunton

D E V Padgett (3)

125*	v. Surrey at Sheffield
115*	v. Gloucestershire at Bristol
107*	v. Oxford University at Oxford

R Illingworth (3)

127	v. Surrey at The Oval
115	v. Hampshire at Bournemouth
107	v. Warwickshire at Sheffield

K Taylor (2)

178*	v. Oxford University at Oxford
163	v. Nottinghamshire at Leeds

J V Wilson (2)

134	v. Nottinghamshire at Leeds
134	v. Warwickshire at Birmingham

J B Bolus (1)

108	v. Cambridge University at Cambridge

W B Stott (1)

145	v. Derbyshire at Hull

5 wickets in an innings (20)

R Illingworth (8)

7 for 40	v. Northamptonshire at Northampton
6 for 26	v. Essex at Sheffield
5 for 10	v. Sussex at Scarborough
5 for 31	v. Gloucestershire at Bradford
5 for 33	v. Hampshire at Bradford
5 for 52	v. Kent at Middlesbrough
5 for 63	v. Gloucestershire at Bristol
5 for 64	v. Warwickshire at Sheffield

F S Trueman (4)

8 for 84	v. Nottinghamshire at Worksop
6 for 45	v. Somerset at Hull
5 for 29	v. Lancashire at Leeds
5 for 34	v. Hampshire at Bradford

5 wickets in an innings *(Continued)*

D Wilson (4)

    6 for 24 v. Glamorgan at Harrogate

    6 for 67 v. Cambridge University at Cambridge

    6 for 70 v. Hampshire at Bournemouth

    5 for 23 v. Somerset at Hull

M Ryan (2)

    6 for 33 v. Leicestershire at Bradford

    5 for 53 v. Leicestershire at Leicester

M J Cowan (1)

    5 for 135 v. Somerset at Taunton

R K Platt (1)

    6 for 67 v. Worcestershire at Worcester

10 wickets in a match (4)

R K Platt (1)

    10 for 106 (6 for 67 and 4 for 39)   v. Worcestershire at Worcester

M Ryan (1)

    10 for 77 (4 for 44 and 6 for 33)   v. Leicestershire at Bradford

F S Trueman (1)

    10 for 142 (8 for 84 and 2 for 58)   v. Nottinghamshire at Worksop

D Wilson (1)

    10 for 72 (6 for 24 and 4 for 48)   v, Glamorgan at Harrogate

The Double (all First-Class matches) (1)

R Illingworth

    1,610 runs @ 34.25   116 wickets @ 18.92

3 catches in an innings (17)

J G Binks (8)

    5   v. Lancashire at Leeds

    4   v. Somerset at Taunton

    3   v. Cambridge University at Cambridge

    3   v. Middlesex at Middlesbrough

    3   v. Glamorgan at Cardiff

    3   v. Essex at Westcliffe on Sea

    3   v. Sussex at Scarborough

    3   v. MCC at Scarborough

P J Sharpe (8)

    4   v. Hampshire at Bradford

    4   v. Essex at Sheffield

    4   v. Worcestershire at Leeds

    3   v. Somerset at Hull

    3   v. Warwickshire at Sheffield

    3   v. Derbyshire at Hull

    3   v. Gloucestershire at Bristol

    3   v. Kent at Middlesbrough

M Ryan (1)

    3   v. Leicestershire at Bradford

3 dismissals in an innings (5)

J G Binks (5)

    6 (5ct, 1st) v. Lancashire at Leeds
    5 (2ct, 3st) v. Middlesex at Lord's
    3 (2ct, 1st) v. Oxford University at Oxford
    3 (2ct, 1st) v. Kent at Gillingham
    3 (2ct, 1st) v. MCC at Scarborough

5 catches in a match (3)

J G Binks (2)

    5 (0 + 5) v. Lancashire at Leeds
    5 (2 + 3) v. MCC at Scarborough

P J Sharpe (1)

    5 (2 + 3) v. Derbyshire at Hull

5 dismissals in a match (4)

J G Binks (4)

    6 (2ct, 4st) v. Middlesex at Lord's
    6 (5ct, 1st) v. Lancashire at Leeds
    6 (5ct, 1st) v. MCC at Scarborough
    5 (3ct, 2st) v. Cambridge University at Cambridge

Debuts (4)

In first-class cricket: G Boycott, M C Fearnley and A G Nicholson
For Yorkshire, having previously played first-class cricket: R A Hutton

Capped: M Ryan, April 18, 1962

Lyth lifts award

Yorkshire CCC Southern Group named Adam Lyth as the winner of their Neil Lloyd Award for the Young Cricketer of the Year for 2010. The 24-year-old left-hander received the honour when Southern Group visited Headingley Carnegie on September 9 for the LV County Championship match between Yorkshire and Somerset. Neil was a Wakefield-born left-hander who played for Yorkshire Seconds and England Young Cricketers, but he died in 1982 at the age of 17 from an infection caused by a rare virus. Southern Group make their award to the most promising young Yorkshire cricketer who played in the First XI and was under 23 and uncapped at the start of the previous season.

50 YEARS AGO

YORKSHIRE AVERAGES 1962

ALL FIRST-CLASS MATCHES

Played 37   Won 16   Lost 5   Drawn 16

County Championship: Played 32   Won 14   Lost 4   Drawn 14

BATTING AND FIELDING *(Qualification 10 completed innings)*

Player	M.	I.	N.O.	Runs	H.S.	Avge	100s	50s	ct/st
P J Sharpe	36	62	8	2201	138	40.75	7	7	70
D B Close	28	45	6	1438	142*	36.87	3	7	29
R Illingworth	35	55	8	1610	127	34.25	3	8	28
K Taylor	26	44	2	1372	178*	32.66	2	10	12
D E V Padgett	34	57	3	1750	125*	32.40	3	11	15
J H Hampshire	13	23	2	559	81	26.61	0	5	7
J B Bolus	21	36	1	880	108	25.14	1	4	14
W B Stott	18	32	3	685	145	23.62	1	3	11
J V Wilson	37	54	2	1226	134	23.57	2	5	29
F S Trueman	27	38	4	709	44	20.85	0	0	17
D Wilson	34	46	8	522	41	13.73	0	0	26
J G Binks	37	45	9	414	67	11.50	0	1	70/16
M Ryan	24	23	10	83	15*	6.38	0	0	13
Also played									
A G Nicholson	5	7	5	98	37*	49.00	0	0	1
G Boycott	5	9	2	150	47	21.42	0	0	4
R A Hutton	7	11	3	123	45*	15.37	0	0	2
R K Platt	11	13	6	66	17	9.42	0	0	5
M J Cowan	7	9	6	27	15*	9.00	0	0	2
P J Kippax	1	2	0	11	7	5.50	0	0	0
M C Fearnley	1	1	1	11	11*	—	0	0	0

BOWLING *(Qualification 10 wickets)*

Player	Overs	Mdns	Runs	Wkts	Avge	Best	5wI	10wM
F S Trueman	932.1	220	2171	122	17.79	8-84	4	1
R Illingworth	1047.2	412	2195	116	18.92	7-40	8	0
D Wilson	996	384	2099	97	21.63	6-24	4	1
R K Platt	398.3	124	935	40	23.37	6-67	1	1
M Ryan	767.1	189	1962	81	24.22	6-33	2	1
K Taylor	397	154	853	34	25.08	4-31	0	0
A G Nicholson	138	36	406	15	27.06	4-50	0	0
D B Close	392.5	156	885	29	30.51	3-4	0	0
M J Cowan	255.5	45	722	16	45.12	5-135	1	0
Also bowled								
W B Stott	15	6	58	4	14.50	4-34	0	0
R A Hutton	82.3	18	197	9	21.88	4-40	0	0
M C Fearnley	35.5	13	71	3	23.66	3-56	0	0
J B Bolus	69.1	23	170	7	24.28	4-40	0	0
P J Kippax	11	1	48	1	48.00	1-48	0	0
J H Hampshire	36	7	132	1	132.00	1-57	0	0
D E V Padgett	26.1	15	32	0	—	—	—	—
P J Sharpe	10	1	37	0	—	—	—	—
J G Binks	3	1	15	0	—	—	—	—
J V Wilson	1	0	6	0	—	—	—	—

Celebrity Interview: ANTHONY BRADBURY
went to the House of Commons to meet the
Yorkshire-born former Deputy Speaker,
SIR ALAN HASELHURST, and to hear about
his passion for the summer game

CRICKET DEVOTEE WHO LOOKED DOWN ON GHODS AT LORD'S

Alan Haselhurst was born in 1937 in the Yorkshire village of South Elmsall, near Hemsworth. He is now in his fifth decade as a Member of Parliament, and his distinguished service has included 13 years as Deputy Speaker of the House of Commons. Many who were born in the 1930s and who saw the renaissance of cricket as a spectator sport after the Second World War have retained their affection for that game throughout their lives. Sir Alan has been no exception, and his deep love of cricket and his affection for the county of his birth has remained steadfast. Indeed his participation in public life has given him opportunities to promote cricket and to write about it in an affectionate way.

South Elmsall has not been the birthplace of any Yorkshire First Eleven players, but the people of the village 70 years ago were as enthusiastic about the side of the late 1930s as any in Yorkshire. Alan recalls long walks with his grandfather, who lived nearby, and remembers his grandfather speaking of Hedley Verity setting his field and shaking his head at the captain, Brian Sellers, perhaps in rejection of some suggestion Sellers had made. It is Alan's earliest cricket recollection.

His father was fond of watching cricket, and Alan recalls that the first games he watched were at Doncaster and how excited he was when given the chance to sell programmes. Naturally, his hero was the great Len Hutton — and in that regard he was no different to thousands and thousands of Yorkshire schoolboys. It was an enormous excitement to be given a "Len Hutton" bat, but Alan was to find that his enjoyment came not from the playing, but from watching, reading, learning cricket history and, importantly in his latter school days, from being a scorer.

In 1946 his family moved to Birmingham, and from his preparatory school he won a foundation scholarship to King Edward VI School in the pleasant district of Edgbaston. The Warwickshire ground was but a short walk away, and another memory is of a packed stadium when the

New Zealand tourists arrived for a match in the August school holidays. Munching though a bag of sandwiches in a game where Martin Donnelly and John Reid made splendid centuries would have made for a very contented schoolboy. Opportunities to return to Yorkshire to watch county cricket did not readily arise, so his Championship-watching round included New Road, Worcester, Stourbridge, Coventry and Cheltenham.

It was at Cheltenham College that Alan had the chance to participate in an active if not playing role in important schools' cricket. He went there as a boarder in 1951, and found himself in due time as a private orderly — known in other schools as a fag — to the prefect who was also the first-team scorer.

Cheltenham was one of the finer public schools, and the lovely college ground remains as attractive a place to play and watch cricket as anywhere in England. The young Haselhurst was put in charge of the movable

SIR ALAN HASELHURST
Sporting Yorkshire colours

scoreboard. This was a cabin that had to be towed into position and which, with its antique rollers on which the numbers were positioned, provided quite a challenge to operate as soon as runs were scored.

Alan gained a reputation for such efficiency in keeping the board up to date the moment runs were scored — a task that required total concentration, often on players who would not be well known to him — that the role of official scorer for the school became his in 1954 and 1955.

The highlight of Cheltenham College cricket was the annual match at Lord's against Haileybury College. These two-day games had been played since 1893, and the full scorecards were printed in *Wisden*, together with a short report. Thus we read that in 1954, with the young scorer intently watching from the old box high in the Grandstand designed by Sir Herbert Baker, for Haileybury "Ghods, a Persian boy, unsettled Cheltenham with tantalising deliveries." The nature of the tantalising is not revealed, and what happened to Ghods? Cheltenham lost that game heavily, but when the school returned with its enthusiastic scorer in 1955 it was Haileybury who were struggling as the game ended in an exciting draw. Alan, as well as relishing use of the scorebox, sampled over those four summer days 55 years and more ago the delights of the Lord's lunchtime catering for teams and officials. It must have seemed like high heaven. *Wisden* stopped recording the full scores and report of that annual fixture in 1969, and it is now played over one day.

Schooling was nearly over for Alan, but he still has memories of the 1955 Scarborough Cricket Festival. He stayed in the Grand Hotel — when it was truly grand. The festival that year, after Yorkshire had played MCC, saw the Gentlemen v. the Players, and TN Pearce's XI v. the visiting South Africans. Both were wonderful examples of festival cricket, the Players winning their game by two wickets with five minutes to spare and the South Africans winning by four wickets with one ball to spare. Young Haselhurst was enthralled. Sadly, Len Hutton, in his last season of Championship cricket, was not well enough to play, but Brian Close, Vic Wilson, Ray Illingworth, Johnny Wardle and Fred Trueman were in the Players side, and Norman Yardley and Billy Sutcliffe were with the Gentlemen. Wardle would have enjoyed bowling Sutcliffe, and Trueman took the scalp of Yardley. How the crowd with many a schoolboy among them must have loved it.

Now more serious times claimed Alan Haselhurst. He went up to Oriel College, Oxford, and became secretary, treasurer and librarian at the Oxford Union. Later he took up employment with ICI at Welwyn Garden City. He became very active in politics, becoming national chairman of the Young Conservatives when that was far and away the largest youth organisation in the nation. Work then took him to Lancashire and selection as Parliamentary Conservative candidate for Middleton and Prestwich. Success in the 1970 General Election gave him his first taste of Westminster, but an added attraction was to travel across the Pennines to all the then Yorkshire grounds save Hull. At Headingley, Bradford Park Avenue, Bramall Lane, Middlesbrough and Harrogate he saw Championship cricket, and one-day cricket at Huddersfield. These were days when Yorkshire cricket was strong, spectator passion exciting, Brian Close a powerful captain, and Geoffrey Boycott was showing his excellence. Alan did not involve himself in cricket politics, but he enjoyed the pleasure of watching great players. He and friends, formed "Tykes on Tour" — Yorkshire supporters who with Real Ale to hand supported their team on Southern travels.

In February 1974 Alan lost his Lancashire seat, and he endured a wait of three years before a return to Parliament followed a by-election at

WAS HE OUT? A youthful Len Hutton looks on at slip as Arthur Wood breaks the furniture. Batsman unknown. *(Photo: Ron Deaton Archive)*

man, leading J M Kilburn to note that Wood could claim the record for a catch taken at the greatest distance from the wicket. Doubtless, Arthur made the claim!

Hitler brought an abrupt end to first-class cricket in England. Most of Arthur's Yorkshire colleagues speedily signed on, but he was too old to serve in the Forces — he had fought in France in the First World War. He continued his cricket with Undercliffe in the Bradford League, where many first-class cricketers were engaged when not required for military duties. He also turned out regularly in charity matches for Jack Appleyard's XI and other invitation sides. Arthur played in the Hedley Verity Memorial Match against Lancashire at Bradford in 1945, an emotional occasion for him and his Yorkshire colleagues, and also in three other matches designated as first-class. He was not picked for any of the Victory Tests against the Australian Services, when S C Griffiths was the England wicket-keeper.

Arthur was 47 when the war ended. He continued to play for Undercliffe, but he had to assume that his first-class career was over. Gibb was Yorkshire's first choice wicket-keeper in 1946, but in a mid-

MARITIME HOBBY: Perhaps surprisingly for an old Army man, Arthur chose a seafaring hobby for the "off" season — constructing models of old galleons from wood, matches, thread, clasp studs for the rigging, parchment for the sails and lashings of glue. He put together about 500 pieces, all real works of art.

season emergency Arthur was called on to substitute for Gibb in the match against the Indian tourists: he accounted for seven dismissals and conceded only a single bye, demonstrating agility behind the stumps beyond his years. He went on to keep in six matches, but after that little run of appearances, Gibb returned to the side and then shared the wicket-keeper position with triallist Kenneth Fiddling.

Yorkshire retained the Championship, rather surprisingly perhaps, given the loss of Verity, the retirement of Herbert Sutcliffe and the diminished effectiveness of a number of the pre-war stars. There was no likelihood of Wood being called upon again after 1946, and with the retirement of Wilf Barber, Maurice Leyland and Cyril Turner the great Yorkshire side of the 1930s was breaking up.

Yet there was, unexpectedly, to be one more first-class match for

Wood. In 1948 Glamorgan astonished the cricket world by winning the county championship. To that county's annoyance the usual Champion County against the Rest of England fixture was cancelled, but in its place two commemorative matches were arranged locally for the champions — one against a South of England XI at Swansea, the other against an All-England XI at Cardiff.

CHURCHMAN'S CIGARETTES

A. WOOD

It was at Cardiff that Wood, now 50 years old, was included in a strong side captained by D R Jardine, who had played only a couple of first-class matches since 1934. After Lindwall's and Miller's assaults on the England batsmen that summer the crowd would have enjoyed the reminder of the time when England's fast bowlers carried all before them. It is understood that Norman Yardley, a friend of one of the businessmen organising the matches, had a hand in the invitation. It was a draw, and proved a quiet exit from the first-class arena as Arthur scored one run in his only innings and made one stumping. He retired from club cricket in 1951 "because I'm too old."

Wood was a good enough footballer at left-back to be offered terms by Bradford Park Avenue, and he was an excellent golfer with a single-figure handicap. Outside sport his hobby was the construction of model galleons, but cricket was his profession and his passion. In 420 first-class matches he scored 8,842 runs at an average of 21.20 and accounted for 886 dismissals — 631 caught and 255 stumped. For Yorkshire his tally was 855 dismissals, 612 caught and 243 stumped. At the time this made Wood the second most successful Yorkshire wicket-keeper after the legendary David Hunter, who had 1,186 victims behind the stumps. Since Wood's time Jimmy Binks (1,044) and then David Bairstow (1,038) have exceeded his total.

Arthur Wood was a most popular cricketer, both with the crowds and with his colleagues. Spectators warmed to his effervescence. So did his teammates. They not only admired Wood's technical competence and tactical awareness, but they gave him in the words of J M Kilburn "licence to wear cap and bells in the light relief desirable to balance the intense concentration applied to business on the field." It is as one of the game's happier spirits that Arthur should be remembered to this day.

ARTHUR WOOD

FIRST-CLASS CRICKET FOR YORKSHIRE 1927 TO 1946

Right-hand batsman   Wicket-keeper

Born: Fagley, Bradford   August 25, 1898

Died: Ilkley   April 1, 1973

Debut: Yorkshire v. Derbyshire at Chesterfield   August 17, 1927

(Wood was selected to play in the previous match v. Kent at Bradford,
but it was abandoned without a ball being bowled)

Last match (last day): Yorkshire v. Surrey at The Oval   July 30, 1946

Capped: 1929

BATTING AND FIELDING

Season	M	I	NO	Runs	HS	Avge	100s	50s	ct/st
1927	1	0	—	—	—	—	—	—	0/2
1928	29	24	4	513	69	25.65	0	3	38/20
1929	35	43	8	604	63	17.25	0	2	57/13
1930	33	40	3	617	91	16.67	0	3	35/19
1931	33	30	8	516	65	23.45	0	3	48/19
1932	32	38	8	491	65	16.36	0	1	66/12
1933	36	47	8	972	85	24.92	0	5	50/22
1934	35	45	10	466	59	13.31	0	2	75/14
1935	35	51	12	1237	123*	31.71	1	7	57/22
1935/36 (Jamaica)	3	3	0	183	94	64.33	0	2	4/0
1936	35	40	3	882	97	23.83	0	4	44/21
1937	32	40	7	829	71	25.12	0	5	48/20
1938	30	34	9	554	69	19.10	0	1	31/22
1939	31	35	2	587	65	17.78	0	3	43/32
1945	2	3	0	44	25	14.66	0	0	3/0
1946	6	8	2	74	21*	12.33	0	0	13/4
Totals	**408**	**481**	**80**	**8579**	**123***	**21.39**	**1**	**41**	**612/242**

Centuries (1)

123* v. Worcestershire   at Sheffield, 1935

Sixties (25)

97 v. Somerset	at Sheffield, 1936
94 v. Jamaica	at Melbourne Park, Jamaica, 1935/36
91 v. Gloucestershire	at Bristol, 1930
85 v. Essex	at Leyton, 1933
81 v. Warwickshire	at Bradford, 1936
79 v. Hampshire	at Bournemouth, 1933
79 v. Glamorgan	at Swansea, 1936
77 v. Jamaica	at Sabina Park, Jamaica, 1935/36
74 v. Worcestershire	at Worcester, 1933
71 v. Sussex	at Eastbourne, 1937
69 v. Glamorgan	at Swansea, 1928
69 v. Nottinghamshire	at Nottingham, 1935
69 v. MCC	at Lord's, 1938
68 v. Kent	at Tonbridge, 1937
67* v. Oxford University	at Oxford, 1937
65 v. Glamorgan	at Scarborough, 1931
65 v. Surrey	at Sheffield, 1932
65 v. Lancashire	at Manchester, 1939
64* v. Gloucestershire	at Gloucester (WWG), 1935
64 v. Derbyshire	at Chesterfield, 1935

Sixties *(Continued)*

63	v. Oxford University	at Oxford, 1929
62	v. Middlesex	at Leeds, 1928
62	v. New Zealanders	at Harrogate, 1931
60	v. MCC	at Scarborough, 1930
60	v. Essex	at Westcliff-on-Sea, 1936

Century Partnerships (13)

217* for the 6th wkt	H Sutcliffe and AW	v. Worcestershire at Sheffield, 1935
180 for the 7th wkt	C Turner and AW	v. Somerset at Sheffield, 1936
154 for the 6th wkt	E Robinson and AW	v. Glamorgan at Scarborough, 1931
128 for the 8th wkt	E Robinson and AW	v. Middlesex at Leeds, 1928
126 for the 6th wkt	P Holmes and AW	v. Surrey at Sheffield, 1932
124 for the 7th wkt	A B Sellers and AW	v. Kent at Tonbridge, 1937
114 for the 7th wkt	A B Sellers and AW	v. Lancashire at Manchester, 1939
113 for the 9th wkt	H Verity and AW	v. MCC at Lord's, 1938
110 for the 5th wkt	A Mitchell and AW	v. Kent at Tonbridge, 1935
104 for the 7th wkt	F Dennis and AW	v. Gloucestershire at Bristol, 1930
104 for the 6th wkt	Turner and AW	v. Northamptonshire at Harrogate, 1935

Six dismissals in a match (6)

8 (8 ct)	v. Northamptonshire at Huddersfield, 1932
7 (7 ct)	v. Kent at Maidstone, 1934 *
7 (4 ct, 3 st)	v. Indians at Bradford, 1946
6 (5 ct, 1 st)	v. Northamptonshire at Bradford, 1934
6 (6 ct)	v. Worcestershire at Worcester, 1934 *
6 (5 ct, 1 st)	v. Derbyshire at Scarborough, 1935

* consecutive matches

Four dismissals in an innings (21)

5 (4 ct, 1 st)	v. Hampshire at Bournemouth, 1933
5 (5 ct)	v. Sussex at Hove, 1933*
5 (4 ct, 1 st)	v. Northamptonshire at Bradford, 1934
5 (4 ct, 1 st)	v. Worcestershire at Bradford, 1934
5 (2 ct,3 st)	v. Indians at Bradford, 1946
4 (3 ct, 1 st)	v. Essex at Sheffield, 1928
4 (4 ct)	v. Northamptonshire at Northampton, 1929
4 (1 ct,3 st)	v. Sussex at Hove, 1931
4 (3 ct, 1 st)	v. Indians at Harrogate, 1932+
4 (4 ct)	v. Northamptonshire at Huddersfield, 1932 (1st inns) +
4 (4 ct)	v. Northamptonshire at Huddersfield, 1932 (2nd inns) +
4 (4 ct)	v. Nottinghamshire at Nottingham, 1932+
4 (3 ct, 1 st)	v. Surrey at The Oval, 1933 *
4 (4 ct)	v. Leicestershire at Huddersfield, 1934
4 (4 ct)	v. Kent at Maidstone, 1934
4 (4 ct)	v. MCC at Scarborough, 1934
4 (3 ct, 1 st)	v. Cambridge University at Cambridge, 1935
4 (3 ct, 1 st)	v. Hampshire at Bournemouth, 1936
4 (3 ct, 1 st)	v. Hampshire at Sheffield, 1939
4 (4 ct)	v. Middlesex at Lord's, 1939
4 (3 ct, 1 st)	v. Derbyshire at Chesterfield, 1939

* consecutive innings   + consecutive matches

Wood played in four Tests — one against Australia in 1938 and three against West Indies in 1939. In five innings (once not out) he scored 80 runs at an average of 20.00. His highest score was 53 against Australia at The Oval in 1938. He caught 10 and made one stumping.

Wood played in 420 first-class matches, batted in 500 innings (with 83 not outs), made 8,842 runs at an average of 21.20 with one century and 43 fifties. He took 631 catches and made 255 stumpings. He bowled five overs (with one maiden) and took one wicket for 33.

Roy D Wilkinson

RHODES COLLECTION THE JEWEL IN THE CROWN

By David Allan

The official opening of the Yorkshire County Cricket Club Museum at Headingley Carnegie and a display of the unique collection of memorabilia once owned by the great Wilfred Rhodes were among the outstanding events in a busy and fruitful year for the Archives Committee

The £300,000 museum was formally opened on March 18 by D Keith Howard, chairman of the trustees of the Bingley-based Emerald Foundation, who funded the fitting-out of the museum below the Eas Stand. Dr. Howard and Robin Smith, a Yorkshire Management Board member and former Club President and Chairman, were introduced by Museum Director David Hall, and after the opening ceremony the offi cials and guests were able to tour the museum.

Guests included trustees of the Emerald Foundation and trustees of both the Yorkshire Cricket Foundation and Yorkshire Charitable Youth Trust, along with leading former players, honorary life members, vice-presidents and representatives of the Members' Committee and Archives' Committee. The Wilfred Rhodes display in a cabinet in the Long Room consisted of several important items from the collection of his memorabilia which had been gifted to Yorkshire by his granddaughter, Mrs Margaret Garton, the sole surviving member of his family.

Mrs Garton later paid a visit to Headingley Carnegie, and upon her return home wrote a letter expressing her gratitude for the way in which the collection had been received and much of it displayed. The Horace Fisher collection, received the previous year, was also the feature of a cabinet display in the Long Room.

The first 2011 meeting of the Archives Committee took place in February, when the chairman welcomed two new members Howard Clayton, who had replaced the retiring Peter Anderson as secretary, and Dennis Smith, a longstanding member of Yorkshire CCC. Plaques from the old Press Box in the football stand had been salvaged, and a place for them to be displayed was later allocated in the Long Room.

It was reported that new stock had been acquired of the DVDs which had been made of some of the most famous players in Yorkshire's history. There was a feeling that more information on the videos should be made available, and they were all featured in an article on the Yorkshire

FIRST VIEWING: Archives Committee member Roy D Wilkinson, second from right, who was Yorkshire's official statistician for 40 years, escorts Bryan Stott, chairman of Yorkshire Players' Association

website giving full details of price and how they could be purchased. A paper circulated by the secretary on the possible creation of an Archives database revealed that all the necessary software was available online free of charge.

He was to make further investigations with a small group of members, and further developments were reported during the year.

Gifts for the Archives included a cricket ball which had been given by Yorkshire

ON GUARD: Founding father Lord Hawke greets the guests

71

wicket-keeper Arthur Wood to a former Committee member, J C Town, in gratitude for Mr Town's help in organising Wood's benefit in 1939; the 1970 Sir Donald Bradman gold-embossed and leather-bound *Yearbook*, and a sugar bowl dating from 1902 which had been awarded to or at any rate belonged to David Denton.

Paul Dyson has researched some of the events that will reach their centenaries over the next few years, including in 2012 the centenary of Yorkshire becoming county champions for the ninth time in 23 years, a feat unequalled and greater than Surrey's eight titles; Denton's highest score of 221 v. Kent, and Hampshire losing by nine wickets to Yorkshire, despite making 441 in their first innings.

Roy Wilkinson reported in May that he had compiled a list which linked the debut of a player to his cap/badge number, and this list would be displayed in due course. The bat with which Ashley Metcalfe scored Yorkshire's highest score on debut came under discussion, and later in the year James Greenfield was able to report that Ashley had most generously agreed to donate the bat to the museum.

Members heard at the September meeting that a couple of items concerning Brian Close had been purchased on EBay and that other items connected with Frank Lowson were available. Brian Sanderson agreed to pursue these and to report on any other such items of interest.

All *Wisdens* and *Yearbooks* from the Rhodes estate had been received, along with a silver cup which was one of those presented to each member of the 1922 Championship-winning side. These items would be displayed, and plans were ongoing for winter displays. A Printers' Shield, connected to Leeds Cricket League, had also been received, as had an original water colour of Fred Trueman, loaned by Mr Ray Seal. A copy of a taped conversation with Wilfred Rhodes was to be obtained from cricket author David Frith.

Members of the Archives Committee during the year were J C David Allan, Howard Clayton, Paul E Dyson, James M Greenfield, Mick Pope, Brian Sanderson, Dennis Smith, David Warner and Roy D Wilkinson.

J C David Allan is Chairman of Yorkshire CCC Archives Committee

Wardle in line...

Johnny Wardle always wanted to live up to being in the line of left-arm spinners Peate, Peel, Rhodes and Verity. He loved to listen to the legends. He was proud to tell Pat Murphy of listening to Rhodes talk of technique at Scarborough. Most of all he desperately wanted to be thought one of them.

Derek Hodgson 1984

YORKSHIRE'S FORGOTTEN MATCHES AT AIGBURTH

By Nigel Pullan

The redevelopment of Old Trafford meant that Lancashire staged their first-class fixtures away from their traditional headquarters in 2011. The *Roses* match in May was played at Aigburth — the first time any of us had seen Yorkshire in a Championship game at Liverpool, where they had never appeared in the County Championship.

In fact, Yorkshire had already played two first-class friendly games at Aigburth. In 1958 a three-day match began on August 30, but I cannot find out why. The following year a similar match was arranged at Middlesbrough. A A Thomson says they were played for entertainment. Lancashire won at Aigburth by 243 runs as Brian Statham took 5-8 in the first innings and Roy Collins 4-5 in the second. Peter Marner made 110 for Lancashire, and Geoff Pullar 79. David Pickles took 5-42 and Don Wilson 5-51.

Yorkshire's other Aigburth fixture was in 1913 to coincide with the visit of King George V to Liverpool, and attracted a large crowd. Yorkshire lost again, mainly because of Harry Dean, who took 9- 62 and 8-29. There were wet conditions similar to last May, but when they started earlier than Dean expected he had left the ground and was not available. Let us hope King George V enjoyed the match and found a seat behind the bowler's arm.

Yorkshire also played Liverpool and District seven times between 1887 and 1894, but with no match in 1888. According to Yorkshire's records three of these are regarded as first-class and four are not. Why were they played? My assumption is that in 19th Century Lancashire, as elsewhere, travel was difficult, and there would be large local crowds at Aigburth as Liverpool was a prosperous mercantile city.

It may also be a reason that A G Steel and his brothers belonged to the Liverpool club, as did the Hornby family. In 1892 both Steel and A C MacLaren played for Liverpool and District, who could put out a strong team. They won by six wickets that year. So, last May, when we sat in the pavilion built by Cubitts in 1880 in anticipation of Liverpool CC moving to Aigburth in 1881, we were enjoying cricket on a ground with a long history and proud traditions. A final piece of historical information: I was staying in a hotel where the fifth Beatle had lived as a child.

YORKSHIREMAN CAME HOME AS SOUTH AFRICA CAPTAIN

By Anthony Bradbury

This year marks the centenary of a Yorkshire cricketer returning to his home country as the captain of another Test cricket nation.

Frank Mitchell is the only Yorkshireman to have achieved such distinction. He came to England in 1912 as captain of South Africa when they embarked on a triangular series against England and Australia.

Today he is barely remembered in Yorkshire. Yet once he was regarded as one of the foremost rising stars of Yorkshire and English cricket, highly regarded by W G Grace and by his mentor, Lord Hawke.

He played brilliantly for his school and for Cambridge University, had periods of success for Yorkshire, became a *Wisden* Cricketer of the Year, played for England in the Victorian era — and all before a

FRANK MITCHELL Played for Yorkshire, England and Springboks (*Ron Deaton Archive*)

final late and sad tour for South Africa brought his career to a close. He engaged in some journalism after First World War service, lived in South London at Blackheath, and now lies buried in a Charlton cemetery.

Frank Mitchell was born in 1872 at Market Weighton in the East Riding. His father was a successful farmer, and the farmhouse in which the young boy was brought up still stands today. He was educated at St Peter's School, York, where later an England captain, Norman Yardley, was a pupil. Mitchell was in the cricket first XI at 15 and captain at 17. In two notable matches against Yorkshire Gentlemen in 1889 and

1890 he scored two centuries, and with Lord Hawke in the opposing side of 1890 his reputation was made. Mitchell did not go to university immediately. He spent three years teaching in Hove, and played his cricket for the Brighton Club and occasionally for Sussex Club and Ground and Sussex Gentlemen. He became known for his forceful straight batting and his wicket-keeping skills.

He went up to Gonville and Caius College, Cambridge, in the autumn of 1893 to read Classical Tripos, and in 1894 on the lovely college ground he scored three centuries in seven innings including a double-hundred. He was catapulted as a freshman straight in to the university side. He played against W.G. Grace and Stanley Jackson in his opening game against Mr C I Thornton's XI, against Lord Hawke in the next match, and he was then part of the Cambridge team that defeated a strong Yorkshire side by 119 runs. His scores of 75 and 92 in that game led Yorkshire to select him in their own side before the end of May. He had gone from college to county player in six weeks. By 1895 he was leading his own team of university cricketers in a tour of North America, and while at university he played for and even briefly captained England at rugby football. His bulk and force as a front-row forward made him a formidable opponent.

He continued to play for Yorkshire during university vacations, and in his last year at Cambridge in 1896 he was captain in a notorious game against Oxford University: he had instructed his bowlers to deliver wides to avoid the risk of compulsorily requiring Oxford to follow on — as was then in certain circumstances mandatory through the Laws of Cricket. The venomous correspondence in *The Times* about such tactics perceived as unsporting made an unwelcome national name for him.

Mitchell played on as an amateur for Yorkshire, but the moments of brilliance became more fragmentary. He went again in 1898 to North America, this time with Plum Warner's side, and early in 1899 he was a member of Lord Hawke's team representing England in South Africa: he played in two games against South Africa, now recognised as official Tests, but without much success. So Mitchell is in the England records. In 1900 he returned to South Africa to participate in the Boer War as a Yorkshire Dragoon and a member of the Imperial Yeomanry.

He had a final flourish as a seasoned member of the Yorkshire side in 1901. In 45 innings he scored 1,807 runs, highest score 162 not out, but at the end of that season he had to think of full-time work. Lord Hawke secured a position for him as a secretary to Sir Abe Bailey, a South African entrepreneur who amassed a fortune from the goldmines of the Witwatersrand. Bailey was one of the backers of South African cricket, and his money financed some early South African tours. Mitchell later took up stockbroking, and became a stalwart of the Wanderers Club in Johannesburg. He played in the Currie Cup for Transvaal, and was in the South African side which toured England, without playing Tests, in

TRIANGULAR TOURISTS: The 1912 South Africans who came to play Australia as well as England. Back row, left to right: L Stricker, R O Schwarz, R Beaumont, T Campbell, G P D Hartigan and J L Cox. Centre: S J Pegler, L J Tancred, F Mitchell (captain), G A Faulkner, S J Snooke and A W Nourse. Front: H W Taylor, T A Ward and C P Carter. *(Photo: Ron Deaton Archive)*

1904. He also played a few final games for Yorkshire. In his 83 matches for the county he totalled 4,104 runs at an average of 34.20 with 10 centuries. A useful, though slightly unfulfilled, county career.

With no more first-class cricket, Mitchell bizarrely was made South Africa captain for the 1912 Triangular series in England. The series was the idea of Abe Bailey, and with no experienced South African available or suitable the call came to Mitchell. He was 39, and it was a mistake to take on the burden. He had a disastrous tour, and he dropped himself from the Test side. The public did not like the concept of the tour, and Mitchell was bankrupted over debts that had accrued from 1904.

He stayed on in England, and the First World War gave him renewed purpose: his powers of leadership earned him an immediate commission in the Territorial Army, and he finished the war after Mentions in Dispatches as a lieutenant-colonel in the West Riding Royal Field Artillery. Friendships with Lord Hawke and Pelham Warner enabled him to enjoy hospitable visits to Lord's during the 1920s, and he would have enjoyed the pleasure of his son playing cricket for Kent. He had a regular column in *The Cricketer*, and he was writing about his life when he died suddenly in 1935. In the 100 years since Frank Mitchell's last major game few other sportsmen can have had such a varied life.

THOMAS JOHN WRIGHT
— END OF A SEARCH

By Anthony Bradbury

Over 110 men have played just one first-class match for Yorkshire since 1863 as recorded in the Yorkshire *Yearbook* statistics so carefully compiled by Roy D Wilkinson over many years.

Many of those are still alive, but it is remarkable that, because of the assiduous research carried out by the late Tony Woodhouse and a band of helpers, there are very few cricketers born before the First World War whose dates of birth and death are not known.

Death certificates for players with common Christian and surnames are difficult to trace because so many with exactly the

THOMAS JOHN WRIGHT: Can anyone recognise the pavilion?

same names can be born in any calendar year and the certificates rarely record the deceased as a cricketer — save for those who are truly great.

For a long time such a problem arose for Thomas John Wright, who played one game for Yorkshire — against Cambridge University in June 1919. In *A Who's Who of Yorkshire Cricket* (1992) Tony recorded a date of birth in 1900 and education for T J Wright at St Peter's School, York, and Clare College, Cambridge. The biographical entry read: "Very little appears to be known about him. At school in 1917 to took 74 wickets at 7.00 runs each, and headed both batting and bowling averages in the following year. He also played for XVI of York against Yorkshire in 1930."

It is somewhat curious that he played for Yorkshire in the 1919

Cambridge match. He left school in 1918, and played once that summer for Yorkshire v. Yorkshire Council, batting at No. 3 behind Hirst and Holmes and scoring 19. That, of course, was not a first-class game. On the basis of his school form he played in the Freshman's match at Fenner's in early May 1919, making eight and naught. He was not picked for the next three trial games or for the Cambridge fixture against the Army in late May. The Yorkshire season had started late — with fixtures against Gloucestershire and MCC immediately before Cambridge in early June. For that southern tour Yorkshire had selected a squad of 14 under the captaincy of D C F Burton, including the professional Thomas Birtles, a batsman who played occasionally for his county from 1913 to 1924. Wright was not in that squad or named as an addition.

Birtles, who had played against MCC, was omitted at Fenner's and Wright, despite his poor form in the Cambridge trials, took his place. The *Yorkshire Post* reporter wrote: "A damaged cartilage prevented him (Wright) from doing himself justice, and through this handicap Mr Burton did not put him on to bowl, bowling being one of his qualifications for trial. This handicap was also obvious when he went into bat. However, he contributed double figures (12) before popping up a ball in front of the wicket (for a catch)."

There was no opportunity for a second innings. So another first-class career had started and finished. Yorkshire, using at times six other amateurs, won the 1919 County Championship with some ease.

Thereafter, apart from the York v. Yorkshire match in 1930, there was silence in terms of reported cricket about Mr Wright. Nothing was known of any death. Recently, interest in him revived on the *White Rose Cricketing Forum* because of the thought that if he had lived to a great age he might have become Yorkshire's longest-living cricketer.

St Peter's School had no fresh information, but Clare College had a 1929 address for Wright at The Cloisters, Windsor Castle! Was he in royal service? Various archivists at Windsor took on my inquiries. The archivist at St George's School ascertained from the Easter 1924 School Magazine that "the new master is Mr T J Wright. He will be in charge of the cricket practices next term. He has played several times for Yorkshire." Then, in the summer magazine, "Mr Wright worked hard at the nets to teach the XI the elements of batting. We are sorry his efforts were not rewarded by some success in matches." Then the archivist of St George's Chapel, Windsor, discovered that in 1927 Mr and Mrs Wright had their son, John Michael Baillie Wright, christened there.

The unusual full name of John Michael Baillie Wright was a breakthrough. Yorkshire historian Mick Pope discovered from an ancestry website that a gentleman of that name had died in York in 2004. An attendance at the Probate Registry led to the disclosure of a grant of probate for J M B Wright and the names of his two children — who were Thomas John Wright's grandchildren. An electoral-registration search produced an address for one grandchild, and she then kindly provided a death certificate for Thomas John Wright and a photograph, though she could add no more cricketing detail to the life of her grandfather whom she had never met.

Seemingly, Thomas Wright by middle-age had given up teaching and moved far away from Yorkshire to Burry Port near Llanelli, South Wales. By 1962 he was an audiologist engaged in the testing and fitting of hearing aids. That November he went to Aberystwyth on business and stayed at the Skinners' Arms Hotel. It was there that he suddenly died. The paper for his home town, *The Burry Port Star*, though reporting his death, made no mention of his cricket connections, and it has taken 48 years for our *Yearbook* to be now able to complete its brief record of another Yorkshire player.

The photograph of Thomas John Wright, reproduced with this article, shows him as a cricketer wearing a sweater with buttons down the front. Was that once fashionable cricket apparel? And if so, when? Judging by those in the background wearing hats and suits, this photograph may have been taken in the 1940s or 1950s.

Can anyone recognise the pavilion? There remains more to learn of the cricketing life of the man who in 1919 played alongside Rhodes, Holmes, Denton, Roy Kilner, Hirst, Burton, Sutcliffe, Dolphin, Blackburn and Ernest Smith in a Yorkshire team.

Yorkshire at Dewsbury

Yorkshire played there, usually during Feast week, from 1867 to 1933, and of the then first-class counties only Middlesex and Glamorgan were never visitors. In 1921 a crowd of 11,000 saw the first Saturday start to a Championship match, against Sussex. A total of 29,000 watched Warwickshire four years later. Even the *Roses* match was scheduled for Savile Town in 1886, but Lancashire never got on the field, all three days being washed out.

The Carnegie History

RICH NEW SEAM ON FST
IS EXPERTLY MINED

By Derek Hodgson

FRED TRUEMAN: THE AUTHORISED BIOGRAPHY
Chris Waters (Arum Sport, £20)

When the author first mentioned this project I was profoundly scepti-cal. "You'll find it difficult to unearth much new material on Fred," I advised. "This seam has been well mined." I could not have been more wrong. By his own diligence and by the fact that there were another 100 stories to be told about Fred, but not in his lifetime, Chris Waters has delivered an outstanding and splendid biography.

His timing was immaculate: there is a moment, when the subject's life is still in the public memory and when there are many who knew the subject intimately still alive, that a biography takes on a life and colour that is impossible either just before or just afterwards.

Fred was a mass of contradictions. The greatest English fast bowler, he worried about his place in history and could be boring and jealous about his achievements. A life-long critic of cricket's establishment and especially MCC, he was inordinately proud, I can testify, to his honorary membership. The shining example of the working-class lad made good, the son of a south Yorkshire miner, his views on modern society would have made Norman Tebbitt appear a Left-Wing loony.

Fred and I had a generous and warm relationship when, in the 1980s, we worked together on his *People* Sunday newspaper column. He pro-vided 75 per cent of the ideas, I did all the writing; we got on well and had many a laugh. Then, when he heard that I had been commissioned to write the Yorkshire CCC official history, he became a different per-son. It may have had something to do with another history he produced with Don Mosey, and he may have felt that I was trespassing.

He and Ray Lindwall remain the two best fast bowlers I ever saw, and if this should be the last Trueman book it comes as a worthy epilogue. The publishers deserve praise for an excellent production containing many previously unseen pictures. Also included is the famous photo-graph of Fred in full delivery stride against Essex in 1951, the picture that truly captures that magnificent action and what should have been the template for the statue in Skipton.

Who knows, Yorkshire might one day honour him more strikingly.

Now, for the first time, we get much more of Fred off the field, with his family contributing handsomely. This is the surge and thunder of one of the great sporting lives of the second half of the 20th Century.

EDDIE LEADBEATER

By David Warner

Eddie Leadbeater, one of only two outstanding leg-spinners in Yorkshire's history, died in a Huddersfield nursing home aged 83.

The other renowned leg-breaker, Adil Rashid, returned match figures of 11-114 in Yorkshire's first LV County Championship game of 2011 at Worcester — the best leg-spin figures ever recorded for the county, but only narrowly beating Eddie's 11-162 against Nottinghamshire at Trent Bridge in 1950.

In that same season Eddie enjoyed a 10-155 haul, including a career-best 8-83, against Worcestershire at New Road — the same ground on which Adil bamboozled the opposition.

Eddie, christened Edric, was Huddersfield-born and bred. He played in 81 matches for Yorkshire from 1949 to 1956, taking 201 wickets at 28.41 runs apiece and hitting 898 runs with a top score of 91.

Despite his undoubted skills he was never awarded his county cap, and he remains one of cricket's few players to be capped by England but not their county. He was called up by MCC for the tour of India in 1951-52, and played in two of the Test matches.

He spent two seasons with Warwickshire after leaving Yorkshire, and in 1958 he made his only first class century — 116 against

EDDIE LEADBEATER
Capped by England,
but not by Yorkshire
(Photo: Ron Deaton Archive)

81

Glamorgan at Coventry. His career was by no means over on retirement from the first-class scene: he played for Almondbury in the Huddersfield League until he was 68, taking more than 1,000 wickets for the club.

Eddie helped Almondbury to beat a very strong Paddock side in the Sykes Cup final of 1962 by claiming three wickets and scoring 105. Cricket was not the only sport in which he excelled: he was a very good footballer, and on occasions he played alongside former Yorkshire fast bowler and cricket chairman Bob Platt for Wooldale Wanderers in Division One of the Huddersfield League. Eddie had a daughter with his first wife, Betty Knott, and three sons and a daughter with his second wife, Mary, to whom he was married for 49 years up to his death.

Eddie Leadbeater   **Born: August 15, 1927**
                          Died: April 17, 2011

MARTIN SEARBY

Freelance Yorkshire cricket journalist Martin Searby, who lived in Heckmondwike, died in June aged 72.

Colleagues from around the country attended his funeral at Heckmondwike Crematorium, and mourners included many past and present first-class umpires. Martin, born in Pontefract and educated at The Haberdashers' Aske's Boys' School in London when his parents moved south, became very much a part of the Yorkshire cricket scene when he settled in Scarborough in the mid 1970s.

A gifted journalist who had done stints on national newspapers, Martin for a while covered Yorkshire county cricket for Radio Leeds, travelling to all matches home and away. He also wrote a popular column on Yorkshire cricket for the *Sheffield Star* sports edition as well as match reports at various times for several of the national newspapers, including the *Daily Telegraph* and the *Daily Mail*.

In a colourful career Martin made many close friends from the world of cricket and sports journalism, and he was particularly fond of his Yorkshire Press Box colleagues. He struck up a deep friendship with David Green, the former Lancashire and Gloucestershire batsman who went on to report cricket for the *Daily Telegraph*.

Martin was a loyal member of the Cricket Writers' Club, and his enthusiasm for the sport knew no bounds.

It was while living in Scarborough that he met his long-term partner, Hilary Woodward, who made sure that nobody who visited or was put up at the Searby household ever went away without being sumptuously fed and properly entertained. The sandwiches she packed for Martin were the envy of every Press Box in the country.

Fellah' with an umbrella...echoes of Irving Berlin as this long-lost *Yorkshire Post* cutting shows the young Bill Petherbridge sticking to his post at Old Trafford

BILL PETHERBRIDGE

Bill Petherbridge, right, Yorkshire County Cricket Club's second team scorer from 1983 to 1996, died on March 9, 2011, aged 87.

A meticulous scorer who had a lifelong interest in cricket, Bill travelled the length and breadth of the country with Yorkshire Seconds and was well respected by players and club officials alike.

A Bradford man, born and bred, Bill lived at Wibsey with his wife, Doreen, and he took up his scoring role with the county upon his retirement from the Police Force in Bradford, where he reached the rank of superintendent. Most sports appealed to Bill, and in his younger days he played football for Bradford Police. In later years he enjoyed watching Rugby Union.

His brother is Edward Petherbridge, the well-known actor whose many roles have included playing Lord Peter Wimsey in several screen adaptations of Dorothy L Sayers' novels.

The Players

Andrew William GALE

Left-hand batsman
Born: Dewsbury, November 28, 1983

First-Class cricket:
Debut: v. Somerset at Scarborough, 2004
Highest score: 151* v. Nottinghamshire
at Nottingham, 2010
Best bowling: 1-33 v. Loughborough UCCE
at Leeds, 2007

CB 40:
Highest score: 125* v. Essex at Chelmsford, 2010

FP t20:
Highest score: 91 v. Nottinghamshire
at Leeds, 2009

Philip Anthony JAQUES

Left-hand batsman, slow left-arm bowler
Born: Sydney, Australia, May 3, 1979
First-Class cricket:
Debut: New South Wales v Queensland
at Brisbane, 2000-1
Debut for Yorkshire: v. Hampshire at Leeds, 2004
Highest score: 244 for Worcestershire v. Essex
at Chelmsford, 2006
Highest score for Yorkshire: 243 v. Hampshire
at Southampton, 2004
List A:
Highest score: 105 for Yorkshire v. Sussex
at Leeds, 2004
FP t20:
Highest score: 92 v. Leicestershire at Leeds, 2004

Timothy Thomas BRESNAN

Right-hand batsman, right-arm medium-fast bowler
Born: Pontefract, February 28, 1985
First-Class cricket:
Debut: v. Northamptonshire at Northampton, 2003
Highest score: 126* for England Lions v. Indians
at Chelmsford, 2007
Highest for Yorkshire: 116 v. Surrey, at The Oval, 2007
Best bowling: 5-42 v. Worcestershire at Worcester, 2005
List A:
Highest score: 80 for England v. Australia
at Centurion Park, 2009
CB 40:
Highest score: 61 v. Leicestershire at Leeds, 2003
Best bowling: 4-25 v. Somerset at Leeds, 2005
FP t20:
Highest score: 42 v. Leicestershire at Leeds, 2004
Best bowling: 3-10 for England v. Pakistan at Cardiff, 2010
Best bowling for Yorkshire: 3-21 v. Durham
at Chester-le-Street, 2006

Ryan Jay SIDEBOTTOM

Left-hand bat, left-arm fast-medium bowler
Born: Huddersfield, January 15, 1978
First-Class cricket:
Debut: v. Leicestershire at Leicester, 1997
Highest score: 61 v. Worcestershire at Worcester, 2011
Best bowling: 7-37 v. Somerset at Leeds 2011
CB 40:
Highest score: 32 for Nottinghamshire v. Middlesex
at Nottingham, 2005
Highest score for Yorkshire: 30* v. Glamorgan
at Leeds, 2002
Best bowling: 6-40 v. Glamorgan at Cardiff, 1998
FP t20:
Highest score for Yorkshire: 16* v. Worcestershire
at Worcester, 2011
Best bowling: 3-16 England v. Pakistan at Cardiff, 2010
Best bowling for Yorkshire: 3-20 v. Durham
at Leeds, 2003

John Joseph SAYERS

Left-hand batsman, right-arm off-break bowler
Born: Leeds, November 5, 1983
First-Class cricket:
Debut: Oxford University v. Worcestershire
at Oxford, 2002
Debut for Yorkshire: v. Leicestershire at Leicester, 2004
Highest score for Yorkshire: 187 v. Kent
at Tunbridge Wells, 2007
Best bowling: 3-15 v. Durham MCCU at Durham, 2011
CB 40:
Highest score: 62 v. Gloucestershire at Leeds, 2005
Best bowling: 1-31 v. Warwickshire
at Birmingham, 2005
FP t20:
Highest score: 44 v. Northamptonshire
at Northampton, 2011

Anthony McGRATH

Right-hand batsman, right-arm medium bowler
Born: Bradford, October 6, 1975

First-Class cricket:
Debut: Yorkshire v. Glamorgan at Bradford, 1995
Highest score: 211 v. Warwickshire
at Birmingham, 2009
Best bowling: 5-39 v. Derbyshire at Derby, 2004
CB 40:
Highest score: 148 v. Somerset at Taunton, 2006
Best bowling: 4-41 v. Surrey at Leeds, 2003

FP t20:
Highest score: 73* v. Lancashire at Leeds, 2010
Best bowling: 3-17 v. Nottinghamshire
at Nottingham 2011

Gerard Louis BROPHY
Right-hand batsman, wicket-keeper
Born: Welkom, Orange Free State, South Africa,
November 26, 1975
First-class cricket:
Debut: Transvaal B v Eastern Province B
at Johannesburg, 1996-97
Debut for Yorkshire: v.Nottinghamshire
at Nottingham, 2006
Highest score: 185 for South African Academy
v. Zimbabwe President's XI at Harare, 1998-99
Highest score for Yorkshire: 177* v. Worcestershire
at Worcester, 2011
CB 40:
Highest score: 93* v. Derbyshire at Leeds, 2010
FP t20:
Highest score: 57* v. Nottinghamshire
at Nottingham, 2008

Adil Usman RASHID
Right-hand batsman, leg-break bowler
Born: Bradford, February 17, 1988
First-Class cricket:
Debut: v. Warwickshire at Scarborough, 2006
Highest score: 157* v. Lancashire at Leeds, 2009
Best bowling: 7-107 v. Hampshire
at Southampton, 2008
List A:
Highest score: 41* v. Derbyshire at Leeds, 2008
CB 40:
Highest score: 43 v. Netherlands
at Amsterdam, 2011
Best bowling: 3-28 v. Middlesex at Lord's, 2010
FP t20:
Highest score: 34 v. Worcestershire
at Worcester, 2010
Best bowling: 4-20 v. Leicestershire at Leeds, 2010

Ajmal SHAHZAD
Right-hand batsman, right-arm medium-fast bowler
Born: Huddersfield, July 27, 1985
First-Class cricket:
Debut: v. Middlesex at Scarborough, 2006
Highest score: 88 v. Sussex at Hove, 2009
Best bowling: 5-51 v. Durham
at Chester-le-Street, 2010
CB 40:
Highest score: 59 v. Kent at Leeds, 2011
Best bowling: 4-34 v. Middlesex at Lord's, 2010
FP t20:
Highest score: 20 v. Leicestershire
at Leicester, 2011
Best bowling: 3-30 v. Worcestershire
at Worcester, 2011

Adam LYTH

Left-hand batsman, right-arm medium bowler
Born: Whitby, September 25, 1987

First-Class cricket:
Debut: v. Loughborough UCCE at Leeds, 2007
Highest score: 142 v. Somerset at Taunton, 2010
Best bowling: 1-12 v. Loughborough UCCE
at Leeds, 2007

CB 40:
Highest score: 109* v. Sussex
at Scarborough, 2009
Best bowling: 0-3 v. Essex at Chelmsford, 2009

FP t20:
Highest score: 59 v. Worcestershire at Leeds, 2010

Richard Michael PYRAH

Right-hand batsman, right-arm medium bowler
Born: Dewsbury, November 1, 1982
First-Class cricket:
Debut: v. Glamorgan at Colwyn Bay, 2004
Highest score: 134* Loughborough v. MCCU
at Leeds, 2010
Best bowling: 5-58 v. Nottinghamshire at Leeds, 2011
List A:
Best bowling: 5-50 for Yorkshire Cricket Board
v. Somerset at Scarborough, 2002
CB 40:
Highest score: 69 v. Netherlands at Leeds, 2011
Best bowling: 4 for 24 v. Netherlands
at Rotterdam, 2010
FP t20:
Highest score: 33* v. Lancashire at Leeds, 2005
Best bowling: 5-16 v. Durham at Scarborough, 2011

Jonathan Mark BAIRSTOW

Right-hand batsman, wicket-keeper
Born: Bradford, September 26, 1989

First-Class Cricket:
Debut: v Somerset at Leeds, 2009
Highest score: 205 v. Nottinghamshire
at Nottingham, 2011

CB 40:
Highest score: 114 v. Middlesex at Lord's, 2011

FP t20:
Highest score: 49* v. Worcestershire at Leeds, 2010

Steven Andrew PATTERSON

Right-hand batsman, right-arm medium-fast bowler
Born: Beverley, October 3, 1983

First-Class cricket:

Debut: v. Bangladesh 'A' at Leeds, 2005
Highest score: 53 v. Sussex at Hove, 2011
Best bowling: 5-50 v. Essex at Scarborough, 2010

CB 40:

Highest score: 25* v. Worcestershire at Leeds, 2006
Best bowling: 6-32 v. Derbyshire at Leeds, 2010

FP t20:

Highest score: 3* v. Derbyshire at Leeds, 2010
Best bowling: 4-30 v. Lancashire at Leeds, 2010

Oliver James HANNON-DALBY

Left-hand batsman, right-arm fast-medium bowler
Born: Halifax, June 20, 1989

First-Class Cricket:

Debut: v Surrey at The Oval, 2008
Highest score: 11* v. Lancashire
at Manchester, 2010
Best bowling: 5-68 v. Warwickshire
at Birmingham, 2010
and Somerset at Leeds, 2010

CB 40:

Has not batted
Best bowling: 2-22 v. Worcestershire
at Worcester, 2011

FP t20:

Awaiting debut

Joe Edward ROOT

Right-hand batsman, right-arm off-spin bowler
Born: Sheffield, December 30, 1990

First-Class cricket:

Debut: v. Loughborough MCCU at Leeds, 2010
Highest score: 160 v. Sussex at Scarborough, 2011
Best bowling: 3-33 v. Warwickshire
at Birmingham, 2011

CB 40:

Highest score: 63 v Essex at Leeds, 2009
Best bowling: 1-1 v. Kent at Canterbury, 2011

FP t20:

Highest score: 46* v. Derbyshire at Leeds, 2011
Best bowling: 1-12 v.Warwickshire at Leeds, 2011

Azeem RAFIQ
Right-hand batsman, off-break bowler
Born: Karachi, Pakistan, February 27, 1991
First-Class Cricket:
Debut: v Sussex at Leeds, 2009
Highest score: 100 v Worcestershire
at Worcester, 2009
Best bowling: 4-92 v. Lancashire
at Manchester, 2010
CB 40:
Has not batted
Best bowling: 1-36 v. Sussex at Scarborough, 2009
FP t20:
Highest score: 11* v. Derbyshire at Leeds, 2009
and v. Lancashire at Manchester, 2011
Best bowling: 3-15 v. Lancashire
at Manchester, 2011

Gary Simon BALLANCE
Left-hand batsman, leg-break bowler
Born: Harare, Zimbabwe, November 22, 1989
First-Class Cricket:
Debut: v Kent at Canterbury, 2008
Highest score: 210 for Mid-West Rhinos v.
Sothern Rocks at Masvingo, Zimbabwe, 2011-12
Highest score for Yorkshire: 111 v. Warwickshire
at Birmingham, 2011
CB 40:
Highest score: 73 for Derbyshire v. Hampshire
at Southampton, 2006
Highest score: 81* v. Derbyshire
at Chesterfield, 2011
FP t20:
Highest score: 48* v. Derbyshire at Derby, 2010

Moin Aqeeb ASHRAF
Left-hand batsman, right-arm fast-medium bowler
Born: Bradford, January 5, 1992

First-Class cricket:
Debut: v. Loughborough MCCU at Leeds, 2010
Highest score: 10 v. Kent at Leeds, 2010
Best bowling: 5-32 v. Kent at Leeds, 2010
CB 40:
Has not batted
Best bowling: 1-29 v. Worcestershire at Leeds, 2011
FP t20:
Awaiting debut

YORKSHIRE'S FIRST-CLASS
HIGHLIGHTS OF 2011

Totals of 400 and over (2)

534 for 9 wkts dec	v. Nottinghamshire at Nottingham
532	v. Hampshire at Southampton

Match aggregates of 1,250 and over (2)

1,431 for 32 wickets: Sussex (398 and 333-6 dec) drew with Yorkshire (388 and 312-6) at Scarborough

1,359 for 30 wickets: Yorkshire (358 and 321) lost to Somerset (452 and 228-0) by 10 wickets at Taunton

Century Partnerships (21)

For the 1st wicket (4)

174	J A Rudolph and J J Sayers	v. Sussex at Scarborough
129*	G S Ballance and J J Sayers	v. Durham MCCU at Durham (2nd innings)
118	G S Ballance and J J Sayers	v. Durham MCCU at Durham (1st innings)
114	A Lyth and J J Sayers	v. Nottinghamshire at Nottingham

For the 2nd wicket (3)

134	J J Sayers and J E Root	v. Warwickshire at Birmingham
129	J A Rudolph and A W Gale	v. Hampshire at Southampton
100	A Lyth and A McGrath	v. Nottinghamshire at Leeds

For the 3rd wicket (1)

115	J J Sayers and G S Ballance	v. Lancashire at Liverpool

For the 4th wicket (3)

157	A McGrath and G S Ballance	v. Hampshire at Southampton
119	J E Root and J M Bairstow	v. Nottinghamshire at Nottingham
107	J E Root and J M Bairstow	v. Somerset at Taunton

For the 5th wicket (3)

189	J E Root and G S Ballance	v. Sussex at Scarborough
167	J M Bairstow and G S Ballance	v. Somerset at Taunton
120*	A W Gale and G S Ballance	v. Durham at Chester-le-Street

For the 6th wicket (2)

188	G S Ballance and A U Rashid	v. Warwickshire at Birmingham
128	J J Sayers and D J Wainwright	v. Durham MCCU at Durham

For the 8th wicket (2)

149	G L Brophy and R J Sidebottom	v. Worcestershire at Worcester
108	T T Bresnan and A Shahzad	v. Hampshire at Leeds

For the 9th wicket (2)

154	R M Pyrah and R J Sidebottom	v. Lancashire at Leeds
151	J M Bairstow and R J Sidebottom	v. Nottinghamshire at Nottingham

For the 10th wicket (1)

109	A Shahzad and R J Sidebottom	v. Worcestershire at Scarborough

Centuries (11)

J M Bairstow (2)

    205   v. Nottinghamshire at Nottingham
    136   v. Somerset at Taunton

A W Gale (2)

    145* v. Nottinghamshire at Leeds
    101* v. Durham at Chester-le-Street

G S Ballance (1)

    111   v. Warwickshire at Birmingham

G L Brophy (1)

    177* v. Worcestershire at Worcester

A McGrath (1)

    115   v. Hampshire at Southampton

R M Pyrah (1)

    117   v. Lancashire at Leeds

J E Root (1)

    160   v. Sussex at Scarborough

J A Rudolph (1)

    120   v. Sussex at Scarborough

J J Sayers (1)

    139   v. Durham MCCU at Durham

5 wickets in an innings (9)

R J Sidebottom (3)

    7 for 37 v. Somerset at Leeds
    5 for 43 v. Warwickshire at Birmingham
    5 for 53 v. Sussex at Scarborough

A U Rashid (2)

    6 for 77 v. Worcestershire at Worcester 1st innings
    5 for 37 v. Worcestershire at Worcester 2nd innings

A Shahzad (2)

    5 for 61 v. Durham MCCU at Durham
    5 for 65 v. Hampshire at Leeds

R M Pyrah (1)

    5 for 58 v. Nottinghamshire at Leeds

D J Wainwright (1)

    6 for 40 v. Durham MCCU at Durham

10 wickets in a match (2)

A U Rashid (1)

    11 for 114 (6 for 77 and 5 for 37)   v. Worcestershire at Worcester

R J Sidebottom (1)

    11 for 98 (4 for 61 and 7 for 37)   v. Somerset at Headingley

3 catches in an innings (10)

J M Bairstow (6)

5	v. Warwickshire at Birmingham
4	v. Somerset at Taunton
3	v. Lancashire at Leeds
3	v. Sussex at Scarborough
3	v. Worcestershire at Scarborough
3	v. Worcestershire at Worcester

B P Gibson (1)

4	v. Durham MCCU at Durham

A Lyth (1)

4	v. Durham at Chester-le-Street

G L Brophy (1)

3	v. Warwickshire at Leeds

J J Sayers (1)

3	v. Worcestershire at Worcester

3 dismissals in an innings (1)

G L Brophy (1)

4 (3ct, 1st) v. Warwickshire at Leeds

5 catches in a match (5)

J M Bairstow (4)

7 (5 + 2)	v. Warwickshire at Birmingham
5 (3 + 2)	v. Lancashire at Leeds
5 (3 + 2)	v. Sussex at Scarborough
5 (3 + 2)	v. Worcestershire at Scarborough

B P Gibson (1)

6 (2 + 4) v. Durham MCCU at Durham

Debuts (4)

In first-class cricket: B P Gibson, A E Lilley, G S Randhawa and I Wardlaw

---

Herst (sic)

There was, too (in 1889) a promising young player from
Tinsley, Sheffield, named Edward Wainwright, useful with
both bat and ball; also a young batsman, J T Brown, who played
11 innings, born at Driffield, while in an account of Yorkshire
v. Cheshire, Lillywhite has this note: Herst (sic) of Kirkheaton,
a left-hand bowler, represented Yorkshire for the first time in
this match.

Country Vicar 1946

LV CHAMPIONSHIP FACTFILE

Compiled by John T Potter

Versus WORCESTERSHIRE at New Road, Worcester

1. A U Rashid's 11-114 was his first 10-wicket haul in a match.
2. G L Brophy's 177* was his highest score for Yorkshire.
3. R J Sidebottom's innings of 61 was his First Class career best.
4. G L Brophy scored all the runs in Yorkshire's first-innings 10th-wicket partnership of 43. Moin Ashraf was his partner.
5. In Worcestershire's second innings D G Wright was Rashid's 250th first-class wicket.
6. Worcestershire's second-innings scorecard featured the line: V S Solanki c Bairstow b Sidebottom. The last time this dismissal entry occurred in a First Class match was in the second innings v. Leicestershire at Grace Road, Leicester, on June 7-9, 1989. This time the line was delivered by the Sons.
7. J E Root made his Championship debut.

Versus DURHAM at Headingley Carnegie

1. R M Pyrah's 3-70 in Durham's first innings was his career best.
2. Durham's first-innings opening partnership of 106 by M J Di Venuto and W R Smith was the county's highest against Yorkshire.
3. Durham's first-innings ninth-wicket partnership of 94 by L E Plunkett and C D Thorp was the county's highest against Yorkshire.
4. Yorkshire's second-innings eighth-wicket partnership by R M Pyrah and R J Sidebottom was the highest by Yorkshire against Durham.
5. The sixth-wicket partnership of 187 by D M Benkenstein and M J Richardson in Durham's second innings was the highest for Durham against Yorkshire.
6. Injury to P Mustard cost him his 100th consecutive Championship appearance.

Versus NOTTINGHAMSHIRE at Headingley Carnegie

1. R M Pyrah's 5-58 in Nottinghamshire's first innings was his career best.
2. The seventh-wicket partnership of 150 by C M W Read and S J Mullaney in Nottinghamshire's second innings was the highest for Nottinghamshire against Yorkshire.

Versus DURHAM MCCU at The Racecourse, Durham

1. This was the first match against this opposition.
2. First Class debuts for A E Lilley and G S Randhawa.
3. B P Gibson also made his first-class debut and became the younges
   player in the history of English First Class cricket at the age of 1?
   years and 27 days.
4. J J Sayers's 3-15 was a career best in Durham MCCU's first innings
5. G S Ballance and J J Sayers with first-wicket partnerships of 11?
   and 129* became only the 12th Yorkshire opening pair to stage cen
   tury stands in both innings of a First Class match. It was last don?
   in 1988, and it has been achieved only done three times since 1964

Versus NOTTINGHAMSHIRE at Trent Bridge

1. Yorkshire's first innings total of 534-9 declared was their highest i?
   Nottinghamshire.
2. J E Root's 95 in Yorkshire's first innings was his maiden First Clas?
   half-century.
3. J M Bairstow's 205 was his maiden First Class century.
4. The ninth-wicket partnership of 151 by J M Bairstow and R ?
   Sidebottom in Yorkshire's first innings was the highest for the coun
   ty against Nottinghamshire.
5. The ninth-wicket partnership of 114 by B J Phillips and A R Adam?
   in Nottinghamshire's first innings was the highest fo?
   Nottinghamshire against Yorkshire.

Versus HAMPSHIRE at Headingley Carnegie

1. T T Bresnan passed 3,000 First Class runs during his innings of 87
2. D G Cork passed 10,000 First Class runs during the match.

Versus Lancashire at AIGBURTH, Liverpool

1. This was Lancashire's first home *Roses* Championship match away
   from Old Trafford.
2. A W Gale passed 4,000 First Class runs during the match.

Versus Somerset at Taunton

1. The fifth-wicket partnership of 167 by J M Bairstow and G ?
   Ballance in Yorkshire's first innings was the highest for Yorkshir?
   against Somerset.
2. Trescothick's dismissal gave R J Sidebottom his 500th First Clas?
   wicket.
3. S P Kirby also took his 500th First Class wicket in Yorkshire'?
   second inning — R J Sidebottom.
4. This was Yorkshire's heaviest defeat by 10 wickets — 228-0.
5. M E Trescothick and A V Suppiah shared first-wicket partnership
   of 257 and 228*. It was the first time two century opening stand?
   had been achieved against Yorkshire — let alone double centuries

LV CHAMPIONSHIP FACTFILE *(Continued)*

Versus Sussex at Hove

1. The third-wicket partnership of 304 by L W P Wells and M W Goodwin in the Sussex first innings was the highest for the county against Yorkshire.
2. M W Goodwin's 274* was the highest individual score for Sussex against Yorkshire.
3. S A Patterson's 53 was his maiden First Class half-century.
4. G S Ballance's 73* was his First Class career best for Yorkshire.

Versus DURHAM at Durham ICG, Chester-le-Street

1. J M Bairstow passed 2,500 First Class career runs.
2. A Lyth passed 3,000 First Class career runs.
3. A Shahzad passed 1,000 First Class career runs.

Versus WORCESTERSHIRE at Scarborough

1. The 10th-wicket partnership of 109 by A Shahzad and R J Sidebottom in Yorkshire's first innings was the highest for this wicket in a First Class match at Scarborough. It was also the best against Worcestershire by Yorkshire.
2. Yorkshire completed a season's double over Worcestershire.

Versus LANCASHIRE at Headingley Carnegie

1. This was Yorkshire's 3,000th County Championship match.
2. The ninth-wicket partnership of 154 in Yorkshire's first innings was the highest at Headingley in all First Class matches.
3. R M Pyrah's 117 was his maiden Championship century.
4. Lancashire completed the Championship double over Yorkshire for the first time since 1989.
5. The last victory double in *Roses* Championship matches was by Yorkshire in 2001 — they went on to win the Championship that year. Lancashire were to follow suit in 2011.

Versus HAMPSHIRE at The Rose Bowl, Southampton

1. Hampshire's first-innings total of 599-3 declared was their highest against Yorkshire and the fifth highest against Yorkshire by anyone.
2. The third-wicket partnership of 523 by M A Carberry and N D McKenzie for Hampshire was the county's highest ever for any wicket — the previous best being 411. It was the highest for any wicket in a First Class match against Yorkshire.
3. M A Carberry's 300* was a career best. He became only the fifth Hampshire player to reach 300 or more.
4. N D McKenzie's 237 was a career best.

Versus SUSSEX at Scarborough

1. E C Joyce passed 1,000 First Class runs for the season.
2. The fifth-wicket partnership of 198 by M H Yardy and B C Brow in the Sussex first innings was the county's highest again Yorkshire.
3. M H Yardy scored a century in each innings for the first time in h 136th First Class match.

Versus WARWICKSHIRE at Headingley Carnegie

1. Warwickshire's total 482 was their highest in Yorkshire.
2. J E Root's 3-33 was a career best.

Versus WARWICKSHIRE at Edgbaston, Birmingham

1. J J Sayers passed 5,000 First Class runs.
2. S Chanderpaul scored his second century in consecutive innings against Yorkshire — 193 at Headingley Carnegie, followed by 11 at Edgbaston, plus 56* in the second innings.
3. The sixth-wicket partnership of 188 by G S Ballance and A Rashid in Yorkshire's second innings was Yorkshire's best again Warwickshire.
4. G S Ballance with 117 scored his maiden First Class century fc Yorkshire.

Versus SOMERSET at Headingley Carnegie

1. R J Sidebottom's 7-37 in Somerset's second innings was a caree best. He finished with match figures of 11-98, his second 10-wick et haul for Yorkshire and the third of his career.
2. J M Bairstow passed 1,000 First Class runs for Yorkshire
3. J E Root passed 1,000 First Class runs for the season.

'Schof'

The deeds of Rhodes and Hirst have tended to overshadow the right-arm bowling of Schofield Haigh. Look at his record. In 1902,05,06, 08 and 09 he headed the national bowling averages, a feat Hirst never achieved. In a career extending for 18 years he took 2,012 wickets at an average of 15.9

Roy Genders, 1952

LV Championship
Division 1 2011

Captain: A W Gale

*Captain

§ Wicket-Keeper

Figures in brackets ( ) indicate position in 2nd Innings batting order,
where different from 1st Innings.

DETAILS OF PLAYERS WHO APPEARED FOR YORKSHIRE IN 2011
(ALL FIRST-CLASS MATCHES)

Player	Date of Birth	Birthplace	First-Class debut for Yorkshire	Date Capped
W Gale	November 28, 1983	Dewsbury	July 21, 2004	Sept. 18, 2008
McGrath	October 6, 1975	Bradford	May 18, 1995	July 20, 1999
J Sidebottom	January 15, 1978	Huddersfield	July 2, 1997	July 23, 2000
T Bresnan	February 28, 1985	Pontefract	May 14, 2003	July 19, 2006
A Rudolph	May 4, 1981	Transvaal, S A	April 18, 2007	April 25, 2007
J Sayers	November 5, 1983	Leeds	August 19, 2004	June 16, 2007
L Brophy	November 26, 1975	Welkom, S A	April 19, 2006	May 31, 2008
U Rashid	February 17, 1988	Bradford	July 19, 2006	Sept. 18, 2008
Shahzad	July 27, 1985	Huddersfield	August 30, 2006	April 8, 2010
J Wainwright	March 21, 1985	Pontefract	September 10, 2004	April 8, 2010
Lyth	September 25, 1987	Whitby	May 16, 2007	Aug. 22,2010
M Pyrah	November 1, 1982	Dewsbury	August 24, 2004	Aug. 22,2010
M Bairstow	September 26, 1989	Bradford	June 11, 2009	Aug. 17, 2011
M Guy	November 17, 1978	Rotherham	May 24, 2000	—
A Patterson	October 3, 1983	Beverley	August 3, 2005	—
J Hannon-Dalby	June 20, 1989	Halifax	May 21, 2008	—
S Ballance	November 22, 1989	Harare, Zim	July 11, 2008	—
A Ashraf	January 5, 1992	Bradford	May 10, 2010	—
J Geldart	December 17, 1991	Huddersfield	May 10, 2010	—
E Root	December 30, 1990	Sheffield	May 10, 2010	—
Z Lees	April 14, 1993	Halifax	June 5, 2010	—
P Gibson	March 31, 1996	Leeds	April 27, 2011	—
S Randhawa	January 25, 1992	Huddersfield	April 27, 2011	—
E Lilley	April 17, 1992	Halifax	April 27, 2011	—
Wardlaw	June 29, 1985	Dewsbury	July 20, 2011	—

Match-By-Match Reports	NIGEL PULLAN
Scorecards	JOHN POTTER
Pictures	SIMON WILKINSON
	VAUGHN RIDLEY

LV County Championship Division 1
Worcestershire v. Yorkshire

Played at New Road, Worcester, on April 8, 9 and 10, 2011
Yorkshire won by 9 wickets at 5.32pm on the Third Day

Toss won by Worcestershire   Yorkshire 22 points; Worcestershire 4 point
Close of play: First Day, Worcestershire 286 all out; Second Day, Yorkshire 284-6 (Brophy 118
Sidebottom 50*)

First Innings	WORCESTERSHIRE		Second innings	
§ D H K Mitchell, lbw b Rashid		49	lbw b Patterson	2
J G Cameron, b Sidebottom		30	lbw b Sidebottom	1
V S Solanki, c Sayers b Rashid		15	c Bairstow b Sidebottom	1
M M Ali, c Bairstow b Patterson		18	c Lyth b Rashid	2
A N Kervezee, c Sayers b Rashid		4	c Bairstow b Patterson	5.
M G Pardoe, c Sayers b Sidebottom		26	c Lyth b Rashid	
G M Andrew, b Rashid		49	c Bairstow b Patterson	
* O B Cox, c Root b Rashid		10	not out	
D G Wright, lbw b Rashid		0	lbw b Rashid	
M S Mason, run out (Patterson)		63	lbw b Rashid	
A Richardson, not out		16	b Rashid	
Extras lb 6		6	Extras b 4, lb 2, nb 2	
Total		286	Total	13

Bonus points — Worcestershire 2, Yorkshire 3

FoW: 1-43 (Cameron), 2-91(Solanki), 3-96 (Mitchell), 4-100 (Kervezee), 5-129 (A
1st   6-191 (Pardoe), 7-197 (Andrew), 8-197 (Wright), 9-218 (Cox), 10-286 (Maso
FoW: 1-21 (Cameron), 2-49 (Mitchell), 3-53 (Solanki), 4-102 (Ali), 5-120 (Pardo
2nd   6-121 (Andrew), 7-132 (Kervezee), 8-135(Wright), 9-135 (Mason), 10-137 (Richardso

	O	M	R	W		O	M	R	V
Sidebottom	20	5	61	2	Sidebottom	11	2	36	2
Patterson	18.1	2	79	1	Patterson	14	2	43	3
Ashraf	15	4	39	0	Rashid	9.5	2	37	5
Rashid	29	9	77	6	Ashraf	4	1	15	0
Pyrah	10	4	23	0					
Root	1	0	1	0					

First Innings	YORKSHIRE	Second Innings	
A Lyth, c Cox b Wright	35	not out	29
J J Sayers, c Mitchell b Mason	15	lbw b Richardson	2
J E Root, c Solanki b Andrew	0	not out	2
* A W Gale, c Cox b Wright	27		
§ J M Bairstow, c Cameron b Mason	6		
G L Brophy, not out	177		
A U Rashid, c Andrew b Wright	4		
R M Pyrah, lbw b Ali	19		
R J Sidebottom, b Mason	61		
S A Patterson, lbw b Ali	10		
M A Ashraf, lbw b Andrew	0		
Extras b 11, lb 3	14	Extras b 4	4
Total	274	Total (1 wkt)	5

Bonus points — Yorkshire 3, Worcestershire 2   Score at 110 overs: 323-8

FoW: 1-40 (Lyth), 2-47 (Root), 3-63 (Sayers), 4-73 (Bairstow), 5-104 (Gal
1st   6-120 (Rashid), 7-155 (Pyrah), 8-304 (Sidebottom), 9-325 (Patterson), 10-368 (Ashra
FoW: 1-16 (Sayers)

	O	M	R	W		O	M	R	
Wright	28	4	79	3	Wright	4	0	15	0
Richardson	28	9	79	0	Richardson	4	0	15	0
Andrew	17	4	57	2	Mason	2.3	0	14	0
Mason	22	2	72	3	Ali	2	0	8	0
Ali	24	1	60	2					
Cameron	2	0	7	0					

Umpires: M R Benson and N J Llong   Scorers: J T Potter and N D Smith

Worcestershire v. Yorkshire
Great victory for starters

GERARD BROPHY
Career-best 177 not out

Yorkshire gained an encouraging victory in their first Championship match starting as early as April 8 over three warm, sunny days.

Mitchell and Cameron gave the hosts a good start until the introduction of Rashid — who took three wickets either side of lunch, and finished with 6-77.

Pardoe on debut and Andrew batted well, but it required a last-wicket partnership of 68 between Mason and Richardson to enable Worcestershire to reach 268 when Patterson ended the first day by running out Mason.

It was good to see Sayers back after a debilitating illness as he took three catches. Root from Sheffield and Worksop College, failed to score on his Championship debut, but he would make 21 not out second time. Yorkshire's outstanding contribution was an undefeated 177 by Brophy, playing as a batsman while Bairstow kept wicket. They had declined to 155-7 when Sidebottom joined Brophy, and the subsequent lead of 82 was due to these two who added 149 for the eighth wicket. Brophy played an excellent innings, with some accomplished straight and on-driving and, in its final stages, adventurous hitting to reach a Yorkshire career best. It would not have been possible without the durability of Sidebottom on his return to Yorkshire from Nottinghamshire, and his 61 was also a career best. Finally, Brophy put on 43 for the last wicket with Ashraf who remained tenacious but scoreless.

Worcestershire provided some resistance at first, especially from Mitchell, their new captain, and Kervezee, but wickets fell at regular intervals. When Rashid came on he began with three tentative and expensive overs, but then ran through the side, ending with 5-37 and 11-114 to record his best match analysis. The home side lost their last six wickets for 35 runs, and it was a simple task for Yorkshire to make the necessary 56 runs and for Root to get off the mark.

LV County Championship Division 1
Yorkshire v. Durham

Played at Headingley Carnegie , Leeds, on April 14, 15, 16 and 17, 2011
Durham won by 146 runs at 5.15pm on the Fourth Day

Toss won by Durham   Durham 22 points; Yorkshire 3 points
Close of play: First Day, Durham 326-9 (Plunkett 65*, Onions 6*); Second Day, Durha
Second Innings 64-3 (Muchall 6*, Benkenstein 9*); Third Day, Yorkshire 88-2 (Root 38*, Gale 3*

First Innings	DURHAM	Second innings	
M J Di Venuto, lbw b Pyrah	74	(2) c Pyrah b Sidebottom	12
W R Smith, run out (Patterson)	37	(1) lbw b Ashraf	8
G J Muchall, c Lyth b Pyrah	0	c Bairstow b Ashraf	19
B A Stokes, lbw b Ashraf	14	b Patterson	28
* D M Benkenstein, lbw b Sidebottom	0	c Lyth b Patterson	150
I D Blackwell, b Sidebottom	1	c Lyth b Pyrah	14
§ M J Richardson, c McGrath b Pyrah	67	not out	73
S G Borthwick, c Bairstow b Sidebottom	13		
L E Plunkett, not out	66		
C D Thorp, c Brophy b Rashid	41		
G Onions, c Gale b Sidebottom	6		
Extras b 2, lb 5, w 1	8	Extras lb 4, w 1, nb 2	7
Total	327	Total (6 wkts dec)	311

Bonus points — Durham 3, Yorkshire 3

FoW: 1-106 (Di Venuto), 2-106 (Muchall), 3-116 (Smith), 4-119 (Benkenstein), 5-123 (Blackwel
1st 6-134 (Stokes), 7-196 (Borthwick), 8-223 (Richardson), 9-317 (Thorp), 10-327 (Onions
FoW: 1-21 (Di Venuto), 2-25 (Smith), 3-53 (Stokes), 4-98 (Muchall), 5-124 (Blackwel
2nd 6-311 (Benkenstein)

	O	M	R	W		O	M	R	W
Sidebottom	24.2	5	72	4	Sidebottom	14	3	25	1
Patterson	20	4	61	0	Ashraf	15	3	44	2
Ashraf	15	1	58	0	Pyrah	11	1	45	1
Pyrah	19	3	70	3	Patterson	12.5	1	55	2
Rashid	19	2	59	1	Rashid	26	2	99	0
					Root	8	1	39	0

First Innings	YORKSHIRE	Second Innings	
A Lyth, c Stokes b Onions	0	c Richardson b Thorp	26
J E Root, c Richardson b Onions	45	c Richardson b Onions	38
A McGrath, lbw b Thorp	15	c Di Venuto b Blackwell	7
* A W Gale, c Blackwell b Onions	16	c Richardson b Borthwick	5
§ J M Bairstow, lbw b Onions	19	c Di Venuto b Borthwick	81
G L Brophy, not out	19	lbw b Thorp	20
A U Rashid, c Di Venuto b Blackwell	7	c Richardson b Plunkett	7
R M Pyrah, lbw b Thorp	0	lbw b Borthwick	87
R J Sidebottom, b Thorp	2	c Richardson b Plunkett	31
S A Patterson, c Richardson b Onions	1	lbw b Plunkett	0
M A Ashraf, c Stokes b Borthwick	5	not out	8
Extras b 4, lb 11, w 2, nb 22	39	Extras b 16, lb 10, w 1, nb 6	33
Total	149	Total	343

Bonus points — Durham 3

FoW: 1-0 (Lyth), 2-43 (McGrath), 3-100 (Gale), 4-108 (Bairstow), 5-115 (Root
1st 6-126 (Rashid), 7-127 (Pyrah), 8-129 (Sidebottom), 9-133 (Patterson), 10-149 (Ashra
FoW: 1-64 (Lyth), 2-81 (McGrath), 3-89 (Root), 4-95 (Gale), 5-132 (Brophy
2nd 6-158 (Rashid), 7-225 (Bairstow), 8-323 (Sidebottom), 9-323 (Patterson), 10-343 (Pyrah

	O	M	R	W		O	M	R	W
Onions	15	1	53	5	Onions	18	5	56	1
Thorp	17	5	33	3	Thorp	19	7	67	2
Plunkett	5	0	10	0	Blackwell	31	12	70	1
Stokes	2	0	10	0	Plunkett	23	5	75	3
Blackwell	18	10	12	1	Borthwick	25.4	13	49	3
Benkenstein	2	0	11	0	Benkenstein	2	2	0	0
Borthwick	1.1	0	5	1					

Umpires: R K Illingworth and S J O'Shaughnessy   Scorers: J T Potter and B Hunt

Batting frailties cost Yorkshire

The seamers had to work hard on a bright, cold morning as Di Venuto and Smith put on 106 — but then six wickets fell to Yorkshire for 28.

Benkenstein and Muchall were out for ducks, and Blackwell only a single. Di Venuto reached 74 before he was trapped by Pyrah bowling

RICHARD PYRAH: Runs off Plunkett in last-ditch fight to save the game

with energy and skill as fourth seamer. Richardson, 2nd XI young player of the year in 2010 and son of South African Test wicket-keeper Dave, made 67 after an uncertain start, and Plunkett was solid and dependable for an undefeated 66.

Lyth was out second ball to an injudicious shot, and Yorkshire struggled. Root was top scorer with a patient 45 as his county fell to a disappointing 149. Onions, returning for Durham after a long-term injury to his back, took 5-53, well supported by Thorp who claimed 3-33. Blackwell gave a fine exhibition of controlled left-arm spin, conceding only 12 runs in his 18 overs.

Durham lost three wickets on the second evening, Ashraf taking two, but they consolidated on Saturday led, as so often, by Benkenstein and well supported by Richardson. These two put on 187 for the sixth wicket, Benkenstein making 150. Richardson's 73 took him to 140 on Championship debut, and he kept wicket well as deputy for Mustard.

Durham had an unassailable lead of 489, but Yorkshire batted better in their attempt to save the match. Bairstow played very well, showing circumspection in defence and hitting 10 fours. He hit leg-spinner Borthwick for three successive boundaries, but he was caught at slip next over when a maiden century seemed inevitable.

Pyrah, who had received a shooter in the first innings, moved steadily towards a century, but he was another victim of Borthwick, who achieved a good deal of turn late in the match. Much credit should be given to Pyrah and Bairstow, but Yorkshire had lost too many wickets early in the innings, when some batting frailties were again apparent, to have a realistic chance of drawing the game.

LV County Championship Division 1
Yorkshire v. Nottinghamshire

Played at Headingley Carnegie, Leeds, on April 20, 21 and 22, 2011
Nottinghamshire won by 58 runs at 5.49pm on the Third Day

Toss won by Nottinghamshire   Nottinghamshire 19 points; Yorkshire 6 points
Close of play: First Day, Yorkshire 213-5 (Gale 47*, Rashid 39*); Second Day, Nottinghamshi
175-6 (Read 13*, Mullaney 1*)

First Innings	NOTTINGHAMSHIRE	Second Innings	
M A Wagh, b Hannon-Dalby	2	(2) b Pyrah	1
P J Franks, c McGrath b Sidebottom	1	(1) b Sidebottom	
A D Hales, c Brophy b Pyrah	85	b Pyrah	8
S R Patel, lbw b Sidebottom	0	b Sidebottom	
A C Voges, c Lyth b Pyrah	2	lbw b Pyrah	4
A D Brown, lbw b Sidebottom	11	c Bairstow b Sidebottom	1
* § C M W Read, c Bairstow b Pyrah	10	lbw b Rashid	8
S J Mullaney, c Bairstow b Pyrah	15	c Rashid b Sidebottom	8
A R Adams, b Pyrah	8	lbw b Rashid	
L J Fletcher, c Lyth b Sidebottom	4	lbw b Rashid	
C E Shreck, not out	0	not out	
Extras b 4, lb 1	5	Extras b 3, lb 4, w 1	
Total	143	Total	33

Bonus points — Yorkshire 3

FoW: 1-7 (Wagh), 2-7 (Franks), 3-7 (Patel), 4-24 (Voges), 5-43 (Brow
1st 6-56 (Read), 7-100 (Mullaney), 8-124 (Adams), 9-133 (Fletcher), 10-143 (Hale
FoW: 1-11 (Franks), 2-37 (Wagh), 3-38 (Patel), 4-143 (Hales), 5-152 (Voge
2nd 6-167 (Brown), 7-317 (Read), 8-321 (Read), 9-335 (Fletcher), 10-337 (Mullane

	O	M	R	W		O	M	R	W
Sidebottom	12	5	30	4	Sidebottom	23.1	5	67	4
Hannon-Dalby	8	0	28	1	Hannon-Dalby	20	1	77	0
Pyrah	10.4	1	58	5	Pyrah	27	8	73	3
Wainwright	3	1	14	0	Rashid	23	5	52	3
Rashid	2	0	8	0	Wainwright	21	2	61	0

First Innings	YORKSHIRE	Second Innings	
A Lyth, c Franks b Fletcher	64	lbw b Shreck	
J E Root, c Read b Shreck	0	lbw b Franks	1
A McGrath, lbw b Adams	49	lbw b Shreck	
* A W Gale, not out	145	b Fletcher	
§ J M Bairstow, b Fletcher	4	not out	5
G L Brophy, c Patel b Fletcher	4	lbw b Shreck	
A U Rashid, b Patel	40	c sub (M Robson) b Franks	
R M Pyrah, b Fletcher	0	c Read b Franks	
D J Wainwright, c and b Patel	19	c Hales b Patel	
R J Sidebottom, lbw b Patel	0	lbw b Fletcher	
O J Hannon-Dalby, c Voges b Shreck	2	c Patel b Fletcher	
Extras lb 3, w 1, nb 6	10	Extras b 1, lb 1, w 1	
Total	337	Total	8

Bonus points — Yorkshire 3, Nottinghamshire 3

FoW: 1-6 (Root), 2-106 (McGrath), 3-124 (Lyth), 4-136 (Bairstow), 5-144 (Brophy), 6-2
1st (Rashid), 7-221 (Pyrah), 8-253 (Wainwright), 9-254 (Sidebottom), 10-336 (Hannon-Dalby
FoW: 1-5 (Lyth), 2-5 (McGrath), 3-15 (Gale), 4-44 (Root), 5-51 (Brophy
2nd 6-64 (Rashid), 7-66 (Pyrah), 8-85 (Wainwright), 9-86 (Sidebottom), 10-86 (Hannon-Dalby

	O	M	R	W		O	M	R	W
Fletcher	23	2	97	4	Fletcher	8.3	2	27	3
Shreck	14.2	1	56	2	Shreck	13	3	29	3
Adams	11	1	30	1	Franks	7	1	24	3
Franks	18	1	77	1	Patel	2	0	4	1
Patel	23	7	62	2					
Mullaney	2	0	11	0					

Umpires: S A Garratt and P Willey   Scorers: J T Potter and L B Hewes

Yorkshire v. Nottinghamshire
Disaster without a cause

FIRST BLOOD: Hannon-Dalby bowls Wagh

Yorkshire played so well on the first two days — but lost when winning had seemed a formality.

Nottinghamshire were dismissed for 143 by Sidebottom, exuberant on his return to Yorkshire, and Pyrah with a career-best 5-58. Hales stood out as a batsman of quality, and was last out for 85.

Yorkshire were 213-5 by the close on Wednesday, but the innings was revived, thanks to a remarkable last-wicket stand between Gale and Hannon-Dalby: they came together at 254-9, Gale 67 not out, and they put on 82, with 78 to Gale, two to Hannon-Dalby and two extras.

Gale remained undefeated on 145 after a wonderful exhibition of hitting and running between the wickets — culminating in two successive sixes off Fletcher who nevertheless ended with a commendable 4-67.

Hales again impressed in partnership with Voges, but Nottinghamshire started the third day still 18 runs behind with only four wickets remaining.

The reasons for Yorkshire's disastrous performance were not fully apparent. In the morning Read and Mullaney took their stand to 150 without any sign of trouble, and predominantly defensive fields were set. Read offered one chance to Pyrah, who could not hold on: Read thought he had been caught, set off for the pavilion, and was run out. Gale sensibly recalled him. Rashid took three quick wickets after lunch, so Yorkshire needed only 145. Yet on a reasonable wicket against good, but not outstanding, bowling 10 out of 11 batsmen were unable to build any sort of innings as Bairstow watched in despair. The experienced McGrath and Brophy both failed to score, and some others submitted too easily. There was plenty of time in a situation that required concentration and sound defence. Only Bairstow stood firm as Shreck, Fletcher and Franks ran through Yorkshire to achieve one of the most remarkably fightbacks in Championship history.

103

LV County Championship Division 1
Nottinghamshire v. Yorkshire

Played at Trent Bridge, Nottingham, on May 4, 5, 6 and 7, 2011
Match drawn at 5pm on the Fourth Day

Toss won by Yorkshire   Nottinghamshire 10 points, Yorkshire 9 points
Close of play: First Day, 291-3 (Root 89*, Bairstow 50*); Second Day, Nottinghamshire 43-
(Wagh 2*, Edwards 29*); Third Day, Yorkshire 17-0 (Lyth 13*, Sayers 4*)

	First Innings	YORKSHIRE	Second Innings	
A Lyth, c sub (O J D Swann) b Franks		57	c Wagh b Mullaney	52
J J Sayers, c Hales b Fletcher		50	b Patel	45
J E Root, c Read b Franks		95	not out	9
* A W Gale, c Voges b Patel		32	not out	6
§ J M Bairstow, b Mullaney		205		
C L Brophy, b Fletcher		0		
A U Rashid, c Edwards b Franks		4		
R M Pyrah, c Read b Franks		9		
A Shahzad, c Phillips b Patel		18		
R J Sidebottom, not out		45		
S A Patterson	Did not bat			
Extras lb 6, w 1, nb 12		19	Extras lb 1	1
Total (9 wkts dec)		534	Total (2 wkts dec)	113

Bonus points — Yorkshire 3, Nottinghamshire 2   110-over score: 331-7

FoW: 1-114 (Lyth), 2-114 (Sayers), 3-184 (Gale), 4-303 (Root), 5-304 (Brophy)
1st   6-313 (Rashid), 7-331 (Pyrah), 8-383 (Shahzad), 9-534 (Bairstow)
FoW: 1-92 (Lyth), 2-98 (Sayers)

	O	M	R	W		O	M	R	W
Fletcher	35	8	76	2	Fletcher	9	4	13	0
Phillips	26.2	3	99	0	Phillips	11	2	40	0
Adams	9	4	20	0	Patel	10	1	23	1
Franks	30	5	135	4	Franks	9	1	23	0
Patel	39.4	7	140	2	Mullaney	12	7	13	1
Mullaney	22.5	4	58	1					

	First Innings	NOTTINGHAMSHIRE	Second Innings	
M A Wagh, b Pyrah		16	(2) not out	25
N J Edwards, c Bairstow b Pyrah		64	(1) not out	6
A D Hales, c Sidebottom b Rashid		59		
S R Patel, c Rashid b Pyrah		21		
A C Voges, lbw b Shahzad		5		
S J Mullaney, c Lyth b Rashid		49		
* § C M W Read, c Root b Rashid		30		
P J Franks, b Root		9		
B J Phillips, not out		71		
A R Adams, c Bairstow b Shahzad		54		
L J Fletcher, c Root b Shahzad		20		
Extras b 3, lb 10, w 1, nb 16		30	Extras	0
Total		428	Total (0 wkts)	31

Bonus points — Nottinghamshire 5, Yorkshire 3

FoW: 1-88 (Wagh), 2-105 (Edwards), 3-143 (Patel), [3-145 (Hales 28* retired hurt),] 4-158
1st   (Voges), 5-222 (Read), 6-264 (Hales), 7-269 (Mullaney), 8-291 (Franks), 9-405
    (Adams), 10-428 (Fletcher)

	O	M	R	W		O	M	R	W
Shahzad	23.5	4	99	3	Rashid	5	0	10	0
Sidebottom	16	1	69	0	Root	5	2	15	0
Patterson	14	0	71	0	Brophy	2	0	6	0
Pyrah	20	2	120	3	Lyth	1	1	0	0
Rashid	16	2	44	3					
Root	6	3	12	1					

Umpires: I J Gould and S J O'Shaughnessy   Scorers: J T Potter and L B Hewes

Nottinghamshire v. Yorkshire
Bairstow makes it a double

It was a quiet first day as Yorkshire made 291 off 96 overs. Lyth and Sayers put on 101 up to lunch, but both were out soon afterwards.

Root batted very well as he and Gale consolidated the innings, and Bairstow came in when Gale was caught by a vigilant Vokes at leg-slip.

Anyone arriving on the second morning had the prospect of witnessing maiden centuries for Root and Bairstow, who were on 89 and 50. Root was caught by Read on 95 — but Bairstow not only made his century...he gave us a double-century to celebrate.

It was the first time a Yorkshire player had made his first first-class century a double since Major Booth on May 22, 1911, at Worcester, almost 100

JONATHAN BAIRSTOW
First of a kind for 100 years

years ago. Damien Martyn and Ian Harvey began with double-centuries for Yorkshire, but they already had made centuries elsewhere.

It was an excellent innings from Bairstow. He has a good, straight defence, and his off-side driving, especially through extra-cover, was outstanding. He is taller now, and he hits the ball hard, as demonstrated by his straight sixes. He got through his nervous 80s with some trepidation — but treated the 90s with casual nonchalance, hitting Patel for three successive fours and a single. The double-century depended on Sidebottom's support in a ninth-wicket stand of 151. It was surprising that Sidebottom took all of the last over before tea leaving Bairstow on 199, but he hit Patel for a leg-side six straight afterwards. Nottinghamshire had a hard time, although Franks took four wickets. They were without Shreck and Pattinson, while injury restricted Adams.

Yorkshire's bowlers reduced Nottinghamshire to 269-8, still needing 115 to save the follow-on, Pyrah and Rashid taking three wickets apiece, but Phillips and Adams frustratingly put on 114 for the ninth wicket, with Phillips unbeaten on 71, to deny any hope of a positive result. The match ended in over-rate resuscitation.

LV County Championship Division 1
Yorkshire v. Hampshire

Played at Headingley Carnegie, Leeds, on May 11, 12, 13 and 14, 2011
Match drawn at 6.28pm on the Fourth Day

Toss won by Yorkshire   Yorkshire 9 points; Hampshire 6 points
Close of play: First Day, Yorkshire 304-7 (Bresnan 82*, Shahzad 42*); Second Day, Hampshire 189-6 (Ervine 16*, Cork 6*); Third Day, Yorkshire 62-3 (Gale 16*, Bairstow 1*)

First Innings	YORKSHIRE	Second Innings	
A Lyth, b Cork	2	c Pothas b Cork	4
J J Sayers, lbw b Griffiths	4	c Pothas b Griffiths	7
J E Root, run out (Ervine)	35	c Pothas b Cork	31
* A W Gale, c Pothas b Ervine	15	c Dawson b Kabir Ali	20
§ J M Bairstow, b Cork	83	b Kabir Ali	1
G L Brophy, b Kabir Ali	12	not out	37
A U Rashid, c Vince b Kabir Ali	18	c Adams b Cork	9
T T Bresnan, c Pothas b Kabir Ali	87	c Dawson b Kabir Ali	17
A Shahzad, c Dawson b Cork	48	c Dawson b Kabir Ali	5
R J Sidebottom, not out	25	not out	19
S A Patterson, b Cork	9		
Extras lb 12, w 1,nb 4	17	Extras b 1, lb 6, w 2, nb 6	15
Total	355	Total (8 wkts dec)	165

Bonus points — Yorkshire 3, Hampshire 2   110-over score: 317-8

FoW: 1-6 (Sayers), 2-6 (Lyth), 3-48 (Gale), 4-78 (Root), 5-99 (Brophy), 6-143 (Rashid)
1st   7-205 (Bairstow), 8-313 (Bresnan), 9-335 (Shahzad), 10-355 (Patterson)
FoW: 1-4 (Lyth), 2-22 (Sayers), 3-56 (Root), 4-67 (Gale), 5-68 (Bairstow)
2nd   6-87 (Rashid), 7-127 (Bresnan), 8-133 (Shahzad)

	O	M	R	W		O	M	R	W
Cork	37.4	8	75	5	Cork	19	5	51	3
Griffiths	23	6	91	1	Griffiths	11	1	39	1
Kabir Ali	30	10	73	2	Kabir Ali	16	2	43	4
Ervine	18	4	56	1	Briggs	10	2	25	0
Briggs	16	1	48	0					

First Innings	HAMPSHIRE	Second Innings	
J H K Adams, c Bairstow b Bresnan	26	c Root b Bresnan	4
L A Dawson, lbw b Shahzad	19	lbw b Bresnan	2
J G Myburgh, c Bairstow b Shahzad	64	lbw b Sidebottom	1
N D McKenzie, c Lyth b Shahzad	13	lbw b Bresnan	0
J M Vince, lbw b Shahzad	14	c Rashid b Patterson	22
§ N Pothas, b Sidebottom	9	b Patterson	13
S M Ervine, lbw b Bresnan	23	c Gale b Rashid	55
* D G Cork, c Root b Sidebottom	11	lbw b Rashid	22
Kabir Ali, c Patterson b Shahzad	16	not out	5
D R Briggs, lbw b Sidebottom	0	not out	6
D A Griffiths, not out	6		
Extras b 4, lb 10, w 11, nb 6	31	Extras b 5, lb 4, nb 14	23
Total	232	Total (8 wkts)	153

Bonus points — Hampshire 1, Yorkshire 3

FoW: 1-42 (Dawson), 2-69 (Adams), 3-97 (McKenzie), 4-119 (Vince), 5-154 (Pothas)
1st   6-176 (Myburgh), 7-197 (Cork), 8-216 (Ervine), 9-217 (Briggs), 10-232 (Kabir Ali)
FoW: 1-6 (Dawson), 2-7 (Adams), 3-7 (Myburgh), 4-7 (McKenzie), 5-35 (Vince)
2nd   6-54 (Pothas), 7-127 (Cork), 8-130 (Ervine)

	O	M	R	W		O	M	R	W
Sidebottom	22	5	45	3	Sidebottom	12	5	32	1
Bresnan	22	7	41	2	Bresnan	10	3	18	3
Patterson	11	2	32	0	Patterson	11	4	19	2
Shahzad	21.3	4	65	5	Shahzad	14	0	53	0
Rashid	6	0	35	0	Rashid	12	5	22	2

Umpires: J W Lloyds and N A Mallender   Scorers: J T Potter and A E Weld

Another we should have won

CLOSING FOR THE KILL: Yorkshire need two more

Yorkshire should have won and probably would have done had Bresnan not been injured after taking 3-18 with accurate bowling which Shahzad could not replicate. They established their superiority with a first-innings 355: they were 143-6 when Rashid was out, and Root was unfortunate to be run out backing up. Bairstow, batting with confidence after Trent Bridge, and an obdurate Bresnan started the recovery, and after Bairstow's dismissal Shahzad joined Bresnan in a partnership of 108.

It was slow at times, but invaluable in compiling a good first-innings score. Cork's spirited bowling, whole-hearted attitude and remarkable agility for a man approaching 40 drew widespread admiration; Kabir Ali, returning after a long absence, bowled 30 energetic overs, and Griffiths's pace and promise were not reflected in his analysis. Cork took 5-71 in 37.4 overs, but bowled all morning, conceding 15 from 17.

Yorkshire's seam bowlers kept the pressure on, and only Myburgh exceeded 50. Shahzad bowled very well, taking 5-65, but so did the other three without reward. The third day was rain-affected, but Yorkshire lost wickets and Root was out in poor light immediately before a long break. Yorkshire struggled towards 165 as Cork and Kabir Ali bowled well, and they declared just after lunch.

Hampshire were soon 7-4, thanks to Bresnan, with three wickets, and Sidebottom. Vince fell to Patterson at 35, well caught by Rashid, and Pothas was bowled by one that kept low. Hampshire gradually restored their innings as Cork and Ervine took control. Rashid had Cork lbw and induced a surprisingly wild shot from Ervine, which left Hampshire eight down with 13 overs remaining, but Kabir Ali and Briggs survived.

LV County Championship Division 1
Lancashire v. Yorkshire

Played at Aigburth, Liverpool, on May 18, 19, 20 and 21, 2011
Lancashire won by 6 wickets at 6.17pm on the Fourth Day

Toss won by Lancashire
Lancashire 22 points; Yorkshire 2 points
Close of play: First Day, Lancashire 56-1 (Horton 39*, Brown 14*); Second Day, Lancashire 327-8 (Procter 234*, Anderson 4*); Third Day, Yorkshire 131-2 (Sayers 51*, Gale 47*)

YORKSHIRE

First Innings		Second Innings	
A Lyth, lbw b Chapple	4	c and b Chapple	9
J J Sayers, c Croft b Anderson	53	c Horton b Keedy	75
J E Root, lbw b Maharoof	4	lbw b Maharoof	15
* A W Gale, b Keedy	31	c Anderson b Keedy	60
G S Ballance, c Chilton b Keedy	6	b Keedy	57
A U Rashid, c and b Keedy	14	st Cross b Croft	52
§ S M Guy, b Maharoof	8	c Anderson b Keedy	7
R J Sidebottom, not out	7	b Keedy	8
S A Patterson, lbw b Maharoof	1	c Croft b Anderson	2
M A Ashraf, b Maharoof	4	lbw b Keedy	0
O J Hannon-Dalby, lbw b Keedy	0	not out	6
Extras b 6, lb 3	9	Extras b 2, lb 9, nb 6	17
Total	141	Total	308

Bonus points — Lancashire 3

FoW 1st: 1-9 (Lyth), 2-30 (Root), 3-95 (Sayers), 4-105 (Gale), 5-106 (Ballance), 6-129 (Guy), 7-129 (Rashid), 8-130 (Patterson), 9-140 (Ashraf), 10-141 (Hannon-Dalby)

FoW 2nd: 1-13 (Lyth), 2-48 (Root), 3-163 (Gale), 4-190 (Sayers), 5-278 (Rashid), 6-287 (Guy), 7-300 (Ballance), 8-301 (Sidebottom), 9-301 (Ashraf), 10-308 (Patterson)

	O	M	R	W		O	M	R	W
Anderson	16	6	27	1		25.3	8	50	1
Chapple	11	5	9	1		14	7	22	1
Keedy	23.3	4	44	4		54	10	133	6
Maharoof	16	4	35	4		9	2	39	1
Procter	7	1	17	0		26	8	41	1
Croft						2	0	12	0

LANCASHIRE

First Innings		Second Innings	
P J Horton, c Guy b Rashid	93	c Lyth b Rashid	18
S C Moore, lbw b Patterson	1	c and b Rashid	19
K R Brown, lbw b Patterson	19	(6) not out	6
M J Chilton, c Lyth b Moin Ashraf	77		
S J Croft, b Root	41	(3) c Ballance b Sidebottom	28
L A Procter, lbw b Patterson	23		
§ G D Cross, lbw b Root	0	(4) c Patterson b Rashid	11
M F Maharoof, b Sidebottom	34	(5) not out	31
* G Chapple, lbw b Sidebottom	18		
J M Anderson, not out	5		
G Keedy, b Patterson	0		
Extras b 9, lb 5, nb 4	18	Extras b 1, w 5, nb 2	8
Total	329	Total (4 wkts)	121

Bonus points — Lancashire 3, Yorkshire 2
110-over score: 309-7

FoW 1st: 1-9 (Moore), 2-69 (Brown), 3-150 (Horton), 4-240 (Chilton), 5-244 (Croft), 6-244 (Cross), 7-299 (Mararoof), 8-321 (Chapple), 9-329 (Procter), 10-329 (Keedy)

FoW 2nd: 1-39 (Horton), 3-64 (Cross), 4-85 (Croft)

	O	M	R	W		O	M	R	W
Patterson	24.5	8	51	4	Sidebottom	7	0	58	1
Sidebottom	21	7	48	2	Patterson	4	0	28	0
Rashid	30	4	94	1	Rashid	3.2	0	34	3
Ashraf	11	2	50	1					
Hannon-Dalby	13	1	37	0					
Root	15	4	35	2					

Umpires: N L Bainton and R K Illingworth

Scorers: J T Potter and D M White

Lancashire v. Yorkshire

Red Rose blast way to the top

Yorkshire were playing their first Championship match at Aigburth without six of their senior players: McGrath, Brophy, Bairstow, Shahzad, Bresnan and Pyrah.

The pitch looked damp, greenish brown in colour, and a bleak wind off the Mersey suggested favourable conditions for bowlers. Yorkshire lost the toss, and Lancashire's bowlers took full advantage as Anderson and especially Chapple found swing and movement. The ball turned for Keedy on the first morning.

JOE SAYERS: Resolute half-centuries in both innings

Sayers and Gale put Yorkshire in a good position until Croft took an excellent low catch to dismiss Sayers. Gale was bowled by Keedy, and Yorkshire's long tail rapidly succumbed to Keedy and Maharoof.

Lancashire found batting more favourable on Thursday. Their objective was to gain as large a lead as possible, and they took no risks. Horton and Chilton provided a solid foundation, and it was a surprise when Horton fell just short of his century, caught by Guy — restored in the absence of both wicket-keepers. Gale set intelligent defensive fields, and Patterson bowled with skill and perseverance. Root showed his promise as an off-spinner, but Lancashire's 329 gave a lead of 188.

Yorkshire had to bat to save the game...and almost did so. Sayers and Gale added 115 for the third wicket after early aggression from Anderson, much of it verbal, and Chapple. The resolute Sayers, handicapped by injury, made a valuable 75, and had a good match. Both Ballance, with his first 50, and Rashid batted well, but Keedy, an experienced left-armer, bowled 54 overs and took six wickets. Salvation appeared possible at tea until Keedy took three wickets in seven balls. Patterson and Hannon-Dalby hung on for 14 overs, but Lancashire were then left to make 121 off 15 overs in an exciting final session.

They got them through adventurous hitting by Croft and Maharoof, whose two massive sixes were decisive. Yorkshire regained some credit in difficult circumstances, but Lancashire went to the top of the table.

LV County Championship Division 1
Somerset v. Yorkshire

Played at The County Ground, Taunton, on May 24, 25, 26 and 27, 2011

Somerset won by 10 wickets at 5.15pm on the Fourth Day

Toss won by Yorkshire   Somerset 24 points; Yorkshire 6 points

Close of play: First Day, Somerset 7-0 (Trescothick 1*, Suppiah 5*); Second Day, Somerse 389-6 (Hildreth 49*, Gregory 13*); Third Day, Yorkshire 249-6 (Bairstow 80*, Rashid 0*)

	First Innings	YORKSHIRE		Second Innings	
A Lyth,	c Hildreth b Hussain		39	c Buttler b Hussain	14
J E Root,	c Trescothick b Hussain		19	b Gregory	67
A McGrath,	c Buttler b Trego		9	lbw b Kirby	4
* A W Gale,	c Buttler b Kirby		30	lbw b Trego	50
§ J M Bairstow,	b Willoughby		136	c Buttler b Willoughby	80
G S Ballance,	c Buttler b Willoughby		61	c Trescothick b Suppiah	7
A U Rashid,	lbw b Willoughby		0	(8) not out	51
A Shahzad,	lbw b Kirby		27	(9) run out (sub [J Lintott])	11
R J Sidebottom,	c Buttler b Hussain		5	(10) b Kirby	2
S A Patterson,	not out		11	(7) lbw b Suppiah	0
O J Hannon-Dalby,	c Buttler b Kirby		0	c Hildreth b Hussain	2
	Extras lb 10, w 3, nb 8		21	Extras b 10, lb 17, w 2, nb 4	33
	Total		358	Total	321

Bonus points — Yorkshire 4, Somerset 3

FoW: 1-56 (Root), 2-67 (McGrath), 3-75 (Lyth), 4-138 (Gale), 5-305 (Bairstow), 6-305
1st (Rashid), 7-322 (Ballance), 8-331 (Sidebottom), 9-350 (Shahzad), 10-358 (Hannon-Dalby)

FoW: 1-37 (Lyth), 2-46 (McGrath), 3-117 (Gale), 4-224 (Trego), 5-245 (Ballance), 6-245
2nd (Patterson), 7-249 (Bairstow), 8-284 (Shahzad), 9-296 (Sidebottom), 10-321 (Hannon-Dalby)

	O	M	R	W		O	M	R	W
Willoughby	23	3	90	3	Willoughby	23	1	66	1
Kirby	23	8	54	3	Kirby	25	9	67	2
Hussain	21	3	87	3	Hussain	20	5	67	2
Trego	12	1	79	1	Trego	19	4	42	1
Gregory	5	0	23	0	Suppiah	14	4	26	2
Suppiah	6	1	15	0	Gregory	6	0	26	1

	First Innings	SOMERSET		Second Innings	
* M E Trescothick,	c Lyth b Sidebottom		189	not out	151
A V Suppiah,	c Patterson b Rashid		95	not out	67
N R D Compton,	c Bairstow b Shahzad		4		
A W R Barrow,	c Bairstow b Rashid		10		
J C Hildreth,	c Bairstow b Rashid		87		
P D Trego,	lbw b Sidebottom		0		
§ J C Buttler,	b Gale b Patterson		7		
L Gregory,	b Sidebottom		17		
G Hussain,	c Bairstow b Hannon-Dalby		4		
S P Kirby,	lbw b Rashid		6		
C M Willoughby,	not out		0		
	Extras b 9, lb 8, w 4, nb 12		33	Extras w 6, nb 4	10
	Total		452	Total (0 wkts)	228

Bonus points — Somerset 5, Yorkshire 2   110-over score: 421-7

FoW: 1-257 (Suppiah), 2-272 (Compton), 3-301 (Barrow), 4-343 (Trescothick), 5-343 (Trego)
1st 6-366 (Buttler), 7-394 (Gregory), 8-422 (Hussain), 9-448 (Kirby), 10-452 (Hildreth)

	O	M	R	W		O	M	R	W
Shahzad	21	1	92	1	Sidebottom	7	0	37	0
Sidebottom	27	4	66	3	Shahzad	3	0	16	0
Patterson	26	4	69	1	Hannon-Dalby	8	0	30	0
Hannon-Dalby	23	2	91	0	Rashid	10.1	0	88	0
Rashid	19.2	3	100	4	Patterson	4	0	17	0
Root	3	0	17	0	Root	8	0	40	0

Umpires: M A Gough and N J Llong   Scorers: J T Potter and G A Stickley

Trescothick 340 in the match

JONATHAN BAIRSTOW
Second excellent century

Two outstanding batting performances from Trescothick on a good pitch with a fast outfield enabled Somerset to inflict on Yorkshire their worst ever 10-wicket defeat.

His devastating 189 in the first innings earned his side a 94-run lead, and his 151 not out dominated an unbroken opening stand of 228 with Suppiah in the second.

Bairstow and Ballance batted with assurance on the first day after Yorkshire had made an indifferent start. Yorkshire were 305-4 when Willoughby removed Ballance and Rashid in quick succession, and the last six wickets went down for 53.

Bairstow played another excellent innings to reach his second century for Yorkshire, but the loyal Willoughby, former Yorkshire fast bowler Kirby and Hussain — recruited from Gloucestershire with Kirby — held Yorkshire to fewer than they might have expected. Buttler, from King's College, Taunton, a successor to Bairstow as schoolboy cricketer of the year, held five catches behind the stumps.

Trescothick batted almost all day for his 189 with powerful drives and two straight sixes, but credit should also be given to the adhesive Suppiah, who supported him in opening stands of 257 and 228 and was unfortunate to be dismissed for 95 in his first innings. Yorkshire's bowlers hit back, and but for Hildreth they might have achieved parity. Sidebottom took his 500th first-class wicket with Trescothick his victim. Yorkshire's second innings was inconsistent, and despite the efforts of Bairstow, Root and Rashid they had not made enough to save the game.

Somerset required 228 off 51 overs, which Trescothick and Suppiah duly compiled. Trescothick might have been run out, but he was otherwise imperious in reaching his second century of the match. The Yorkshire bowling lacked guile and penetration, so Somerset moved inexorably to their third successive victory at Taunton against them.

LV County Championship Division 1
Sussex v. Yorkshire

Played at The County Ground, Hove, on May 29, 30 and 31 and June 1, 2011

Match drawn at 5.49pm on the Fourth Day

Toss won by Yorkshire

Sussex 10 points, Yorkshire 5 points

Close of play: First Day, Sussex 295-2 (Wells 143*, Goodwin 108 *); Second Day, Yorkshire 21-0 (Root 6*, Sayers 6*); Third Day, Yorkshire 2nd innings 29-2 (McGrath 8*

SUSSEX

L W P Wells, run out (Shahzad/Patterson)		174
C D Nash, lbw b Shahzad		16
J S Gatting, c Sayers b Patterson		9
M W Goodwin, not out		274
* M H Yardy, run out (Hannon-Dalby)		16
§ A J Hodd, not out		32
W D Parnell		
K O Werners		
M S Panesar	Did not bat	
J E Anyon		
Amjad Khan		
Extras b 9, lb 11, w 5, nb 2		27
Total (4 wkts dec)		548

Bonus points — Sussex 4, Yorkshire 0

110-over score: 359-2

E C Joyce replaced J S Gatting from the Third Day onwards

FoW: 1-39 (Nash), 2-78 (Gatting), 3-382 (Wells), 4-448 (Yardy)

	O	M	R	W
Shahzad	31	2	145	1
Sidebottom	22	6	45	0
Patterson	32	10	76	1
Hannon-Dalby	25	3	62	0
Rashid	35.4	2	187	0
Root	4	0	11	0
McGrath	1	0	2	0

YORKSHIRE

	First Innings		Second Innings	
J E Root, b Parnell		70	lbw b Nash	20
J J Sayers, c Joyce b Amjad Khan		6	c Joyce b Parnell	0
A McGrath, b Amjad Khan		4	lbw b Panesar	44
* A W Gale, b Parnell		0	b Panesar	26
§ J M Bairstow, c Yardy b Anyon		28	c Nash b Panesar	76
G S Ballance, lbw b Panesar		25	not out	73
A U Rashid, lbw b Wernars		24	c Joyce b Panesar	27
A Shahzad, c Wernars b Panesar		32	lbw b Amjad Khan	1
R J Sidebottom, c Hodd b Parnell		0	b Panesar	3
S A Patterson, c Wernars		53	not out	2
O J Hannon-Dalby, not out		0		
Extras b 9, lb 10, w 2, nb 10		31	Extras b 16, lb 14, w 5, nb 7	42
Total		273	Total (8 wkts)	314

Bonus points — Yorkshire 2, Sussex 3

FoW: 1-22 (Sayers), 2-28 (McGrath), 3-33 (Gale), 4-72 (Bairstow), 5-109 (Ballance)
1st 6-164 (Rashid), 7-198 (Root), 8-198 (Sidebottom), 9-273 (Shahzad), 10-273 (Patterson)
FoW: 1-9 (Sayers), 2-29 (Root), 3-82 (McGrath), 4-115 (Gale), 5-193 (Bairstow)
2nd 6-261 (Rashid), 7-278 (Shahzad), 8-289 (Sidebottom)

	O	M	R	W		O	M	R	W
Parnell	22	3	60	4	Parnell	16	3	60	1
Amjad Khan	23	4	61	2	Amjad Khan	19	6	43	1
Anyon	13	0	61	1	Anyon	20	2	58	0
Panesar	27	9	59	2	Nash	12	3	19	1
Wernars	8.5	5	13	2	Panesar	36.3	11	89	5
					Wells	3	0	15	0

Umpires: R A Kettleborough and N A Mallender

Scorers: J T Potter and M J Charman

Sussex v. Yorkshire
Gary holds the balance...

A huge innings from Goodwin, an excellent one from young Wells and some profligate Yorkshire bowling enabled Sussex to declare on 548-4 just before tea on the second day.

Yorkshire then regained some esteem as they eventually saved the match with most credit going to Ballance, particularly, and to Bairstow.

Luke Wells, 20, son of Alan Wells, hit a most impressive 143 not out on the first day after Gale had asked Sussex to bat on a breezy, cloudy seaside morning. Nash and Gatting were soon dismissed, but Goodwin joined Wells, and Yorkshire had no further success.

The left-handed Wells scored his third century of the season, and Goodwin reached his hun-

GARY BALLANCE
Wins battle to survive

dred just before the close. Yorkshire's bowling had been reasonably competent on Sunday, but it deteriorated on Monday as Goodwin moved from 108 to 274 after Wells had been run out for 174. Goodwin in this mood is irrepressible; he had 37 boundaries, twice hitting Rashid for three successive fours and moving past his 235 against Yorkshire at Arundel. It was the third highest score ever against Yorkshire after WG Grace's 318 at Cheltenham and Matthew Wood's 297 at Taunton.

Yorkshire had a little over two days to save the game. Despite a determined 70 from Root and a career-best 53 by Patterson they managed only 273 in their first innings. Parnell bowled with deceptive speed, and the Sussex attack had the upper hand. When Root and Sayers fell just before the close on Tuesday the situation was ominous for the last day. McGrath batted well as he and Gale gave Yorkshire a steady start, but Yorkshire were 118-4 at lunch.

Bairstow and Ballance came together, Bairstow more aggressive and Ballance dedicated to survival: he played a most responsible innings to avert any prospect of defeat, with dogged assistance from Rashid and Patterson who survived the last 12 overs with him. Panesar bowled a good, long spell, taking 5-89, but Yorkshire earned the draw.

LV County Championship Division 1
Durham v. Yorkshire

Played at Durham ICG, Chester-le-Street, on June 18, 19, 20 and 21, 2011

Match drawn at 4.53pm on the Fourth Day

Toss won by Durham   Durham 11 points, Yorkshire 5 points
Close of play: First Day, No play; Second Day, Yorkshire 170-9 (Shahzad 9*, Patterson 7*)
Third Day, Yorkshire 13-0 (Lyth 4*, Root 4*)

	First Innings	YORKSHIRE		Second Innings	
A Lyth, c Di Venuto b Onions			0	st Mustard b Blackwell	69
J E Root, c Borthwick b Harmison			27	lbw b Onions	28
A McGrath, lbw b Thorp			3	c Mustard b Harmison	0
* A W Gale, c Borthwick b Onions			9	not out	101
§ J M Bairstow, c Collingwood b Onions			38	run out (Benkenstein/Blackwell)	6
G S Ballance, b Harmison			0	not out	53
A U Rashid, c Mustard b Collingwood			47		
R M Pyrah, run out (Borthwick/Mustard)			18		
A Shahzad, not out			18		
R J Sidebottom, c Mustard b Collingwood			3		
S A Patterson, c Mustard b Harmison			12		
Extras b 1, lb 6, w 1, nb 2			10	Extras b 12, lb 2, w 3, nb 6	23
Total			185	Total (4 wkts dec)	280

Bonus points — Durham 3

FoW: 1-0 (Lyth), 2-9 (McGrath), 3-28 (Gale), 4-70 (Root), 5-76 (Ballance)
1st 6-90 (Bairstow), 7-148 (Rashid), 8-149 (Pyrah), 9-152 (Sidebottom), 10-185 (Patterson)
2nd: 1-50 (Root), 2-59 (McGrath), 3-154 (Lyth), 4-160 (Bairstow)

	O	M	R	W		O	M	R	W
Onions	22	5	75	3	Onions	19	5	61	1
Thorp	11	3	38	1	Thorp	17	3	47	0
Harmison	12.1	4	27	3	Harmison	12	3	51	1
Collingwood	6	1	22	2	Blackwell	17	2	50	1
Blackwell	8	2	16	0	Borthwick	11	2	45	0
					Benkenstein	6	1	12	0

DURHAM

M J Di Venuto, c Rashid b Shahzad		5
W R Smith, c Rashid b Patterson		13
G J Muchall, c Lyth b Sidebottom		55
P D Collingwood, c Lyth b Root		108
D M Benkenstein, c Bairstow b Patterson		5
I D Blackwell, c Lyth b Patterson		28
* § P Mustard, c Lyth b Rashid		70
S G Borthwick, not out		67
C D Thorp, c Patterson b Rashid		29
G Onions, not out		11
S J Harmison	Did not bat	
Extras b 3, lb 2, w 1, nb 6, p 5		17
Total (8 wkts dec)		408

Bonus points — Durham 5, Yorkshire 2

FoW: 1-7 (Di Venuto), 2-54 (Smith), 3-86 (Muchall), 4-91 (Benkenstein), 5-141 (Blackwell)
6-254 (Mustard, 7-319 (Collingwood), 8-387 (Thorp)

	O	M	R	W
Sidebottom	14.5	1	71	1
Shahzad	9	0	63	1
Pyrah	11	1	47	0
Patterson	18	2	82	3
Rashid	18	1	98	2
Root	6	1	33	1
McGrath	1	0	4	0

Umpires: M J D Bodenham and R T Robinson   Scorers: J T Potter and B Hunt

Gale saves it with a century

SKIPPER ANDREW GALE
Took the responsibility

There was no play on the first day, and on Sunday Yorkshire were in trouble at 170-9 after only 53 overs had been possible.

Lyth was out in the first over as Durham welcomed Onions back after a long-term injury and he justified their confidence with three wickets — adding Gale and Bairstow to Lyth.

McGrath again showed his vulnerability as he was lbw. There was resistance from Root and Bairstow, but then only Rashid played with merit. Onions, Thorp, Harmison and Collingwood bowled Yorkshire out for 185 on a pitch that encouraged pace and movement off the seam.

Shahzad had Di Venuto caught by Rashid in the slips, and Smith soon followed. Muchall made a rapid 55, but he and Benkenstein lost their wickets, reducing Durham to 91-4.

Durham regained the initiative. Collingwood, playing his fourth Championship match in five years because of England commitments, was his obdurate self, holding up one end while Mustard, who was dropped three times and also recalled when the umpires reversed an lbw decision, made 70. Mustard and Borthwick held the tail together after Collingwood's dismissal to give the home side maximum batting points in 77.5 overs. On a day when six catches were missed, including Mustard first ball, Lyth took four — he is an accomplished slip fielder, but he would be outstanding in any position.

The last day tested the durability of Yorkshire's batting and their capacity to defy a Durham side which had won its last three Championship matches. Lyth made a good 69 before he was stumped off Blackwell, but Gale took responsibility to ensure survival as he made an invaluable 101 to put Yorkshire well in the lead. Credit should be given to Ballance, still seeking to establish his place, for a calm, mature contribution to a fifth-wicket stand of 120 which saved it for Yorkshire.

LV County Championship Division 1
Yorkshire v. Worcestershire

Played at North Marine Road, Scarborough, on July 11, 12, 13 and 14, 2011
Yorkshire won by 6 wickets at 11.57am on the Fourth Day

Toss won by Yorkshire   Yorkshire 21 points; Worcestershire 3 points
Close of play: First Day, Yorkshire 135-5 (Gale 68*, Ballance 0*); Second Day, Worcestershi
82-4 (Mitchell 38*, Cameron 1*;); Third Day, Yorkshire 80-3 (Root 31*, Bairstow 12*)

First Innings	WORCESTERSHIRE		Second innings	
* D K H Mitchell, c Lyth b Bresnan	....	7	b Pyrah	5!
M G Pardoe, lbw b Sidebottom	.....	0	c Bresnan b Sidebottom	2
V S Solanki, c Bairstow b Pyrah	.....	18	lbw b Shahzad	3(
M M Ali, c Lyth b Shahzad	.....	4	run out (McGrath)	(
A N Kervezee, lbw b Pyrah	.....	7	c Bairstow b Pyrah	1(
J G Cameron, c Ballance b Sidebottom	....	10	c Rashid b Shahzad	1£
G M Andrew, c McGrath b Sidebottom	....	40	c Bairstow b Pyrah	5;
§ B J M Scott, c Rashid b Bresnan	....	26	b Shahzad	£
Saeed Ajmal, not out	....	27	c Bairstow b Pyrah	4;
J D Shantry, c Ballance b Bresnan	....	6	not out	4;
A Richardson, c Bairstow b Bresnan	....	0	b Sidebottom	3(
Extras b 4, lb 12, w 5, nb 2		23	Extras b 13, lb 12, w 1	2(
Total		168	Total	332

Bonus points — Yorkshire 3   Over-rate deduction 2 points

FoW: 1-11 (Pardoe), 2-11 (Mitchell), 3-33 (Solanki), 4-33 (Ali), 5-41 (Kerveze
1st   6-59 (Cameron), 7-114 (Andrew), 8-152 (Scott), 9-168 (Shantry), 10-168 (Richardson
FoW: 1-3 (Pardoe), 2-48 (Solanki), 3-57 (Ali), 4-79 (Kervezee), 5-112 (Cameron
2nd   6-142 (Mitchell), 7-171 (Scott), 8-216 (Andrew), 9-270 (Ajmal), 10-332 (Richardson

	O	M	R	W		O	M	R	W
Sidebottom	14	4	40	2	Sidebottom	15.5	0	53	2
Bresnan	14	1	64	4	Bresnan	27	8	79	0
Shahzad	12	4	20	1	Pyrah	21	1	91	4
Pyrah	14	5	28	2	Shahzad	21	6	77	3
					McGrath	2	0	6	0
					Rashid	4	3	1	0

First Innings	YORKSHIRE		Second Innings	
A Lyth, c Scott b Shantry	.....	9	run out (Richardson)	1(
J E Root, run out (Richardson)	.....	0	not out	52
A McGrath, lbw b Richardson	.....	32	lbw b Richardson	6(
* A W Gale, lbw b Richardson	.....	72	st Scott b Saeed Ajmal	17
§ J M Bairstow, lbw b Saeed Ajmal	.....	16	st Scott b Saeed Ajmal	3:
R M Pyrah, run out (Cameron/Scott)	.....	0		
G S Ballance, lbw b Richardson	.....	51	(6) not out	8
T T Bresnan, b Andrew	.....	41		
A U Rashid, lbw b Shantry	.....	14		
A Shahzad, c Richardson b Saeed Ajmal	.....	70		
R J Sidebottom, not out	.....	28		
Extras b 6, lb 24, nb 4		34	Extras b 8, lb 1	9
Total		367	Total (4 wkts)	135

Bonus points — Yorkshire 4, Worcestershire 3

FoW: 1-4 (Root), 2-15 (Lyth), 3-107 (McGrath), 4-132 (Bairstow), 5-133 (Pyrah
1st   6-143 (Gale), 7-235 (Bresnan), 8-254 (Ballance), 9-258 (Rashid), 10-367 (Shahzad
2nd: 1-13 (Lyth), 2-29 (McGrath), 3-94 (Gale), 4-118 (Bairstow)

	O	M	R	W		O	M	R	W
Richardson	28	9	66	3	Richardson	16	6	25	1
Shantry	28	9	66	2	Shantry	11.3	1	44	0
Andrew	14	0	87	1	Saeed Ajmal	19	2	53	2
Saeed Ajmal	30.1	4	100	2	Andrew	2	0	4	0
Mitchell	4	0	12	0					
Ali	3	0	6	0					

Umpires: R J Bailey and N L Bainton   Scorers: J T Potter and N D Smith

Victory — but get a move on

Fifteen wickets fell on a blustery first day, although two were run out. Worcestershire batted first — and Yorkshire took six wickets for 59 runs with all four seam bowlers contributing.

Bairstow, capped before play started, caught Solanki off Pyrah, who also dismissed Kervezee. Andrew, Scott and Saeed Ajmal brought respectability to Worcestershire before Sidebottom and Bresnan reasserted Yorkshire's superiority

YORKSHIRE STRIKE: Ajmal Shahzad celebrates the second-innings wicket of James Cameron

to dismiss them for 168 in this relegation contest. Root was run out backing up without facing a ball, and Lyth followed. McGrath and Gale appeared to have added solidity until the hard-working Richardson had McGrath lbw, and Bairstow and Pyrah fell — Pyrah to a smart run-out.

Gale was out early on the second morning, and the match was equally balanced. First a sensible partnership of 92 between Bresnan and Ballance, and then a remarkable last-wicket stand of 109 by Shahzad and Sidebottom gave Yorkshire a lead of 199.

Shahzad seized the initiative with exhilarating hitting, while Sidebottom was his accomplice with a wide, straight bat. Shahzad's favourite shot was his powerful on-drive, one of which landed in the gutter on the tea-room roof and another scattered the cognoscenti alongside the Press Box. He hit beautifully through the covers off the back foot.

Worcestershire lost middle-order wickets as skipper Mitchell batted on with a hand injury to play a resolute innings. Andrew and Ajmal added runs, and there was another last-wicket stand between Shantry and Richardson— who had a good match with his lively swing bowling, ran out Lyth and caught Sidebottom on the boundary to end the 10th-wicket stand. Yorkshire needed 135, and Root' responsible innings ensured victory despite the loss of four wickets. Yorkshire lost two points for a slow over rate, negating the gains from the last-wicket stand.

LV County Championship Division 1
Yorkshire v. Lancashire

Played at Headingley Carnegie, Leeds, on July 20, 21, 22 and 23, 2011
Lancashire won by 23 runs at 1.56pm on the Fourth Day

Toss won by Yorkshire | Lancashire 22 points, Yorkshire 4 points
Close of play: First Day, Lancashire 304-7 (Chapple 25*, Mahmood 27*); Second Day, Lancashire 33-3 (Chilton 3*); Third Day, Yorkshire 136-6 (Gale 28*, Sidebottom 0*)

	First Innings	LANCASHIRE	Second Innings	
P J Horton, c Bairstow b Shahzad	36		c McGrath b Bresnan	2
S C Moore, lbw b Sidebottom	0		c McGrath b Bresnan	0
K R Brown, c Rudolph b Sidebottom	22		c Bairstow b Shahzad	27
M J Chilton, c McGrath b Sidebottom	33		lbw b Pyrah	10
S J Croft, b Shahzad	54		b Bresnan	8
T C Smith, c Bairstow b Wardlaw	51		lbw b Sidebottom	4
§ G D Cross, lbw b Shahzad	30		lbw b Bresnan	19
* G Chapple, run out (McGrath)	30		c Bairstow b Pyrah	5
S I Mahmood, b Shahzad	27		b Rashid	50
K W Hogg, c Bairstow b Sidebottom	17		run out (Bresnan/Bairstow)	52
G Keedy, not out	1		not out	3
Extras b 13, lb 14	27		Extras b 5, lb 9	14
Total	328		Total	194

Bonus points — Lancashire 3, Yorkshire 3

FoW: 1-7 Moore, 2-41 (Brown), 3-83 (Horton), 4-116 (Chilton), 5-193 (Croft)
1st 6-235 (Smith), 7-251 (Cross), 8-305 (Mahmood), 9-324 (Chapple), 10-328 (Hogg)
FoW: 1-2 (Horton), 2-3 (Moore), 3-33 (Brown), 4-50 (Croft), 5-50 (Chilton)
2nd 6-66 (Smith), 7-71 (Chapple), 8-87 (Cross), 9-167 (Mahmood), 10-194 (Hogg)

	O	M	R	W		O	M	R	W
Sidebottom	22.2	4	68	4	Bresnan	24	8	50	4
Wardlaw	13	0	68	1	Sidebottom	12	2	54	1
Shahzad	24	4	61	3	Shahzad	13	4	47	1
Pyrah	22	7	51	1	Pyrah	11	4	26	2
Rashid	11	2	53	0	Rashid	4	3	2	1
					Root	1	0	1	0

	First Innings	YORKSHIRE	Second Innings	
J E Root, c Cross b Hogg	0		(2) c Horton b Chapple	14
J A Rudolph, c Chilton b Hogg	12		(1) lbw b Mahmood	35
A McGrath, c Smith b Mahmood	15		lbw b Hogg	19
* A W Gale, lbw b Hogg	0		lbw b Chapple	47
§ J M Bairstow, lbw b Hogg	7		b Chapple	16
G S Ballance, lbw b Hogg	0		c Smith b Keedy	0
A U Rashid, lbw b Smith	3		(9) not out	48
A Shahzad, c Cross b Mahmood	4		(10) c Cross b Hogg	22
R M Pyrah, c Chilton b Smith	117		(11) lbw b Keedy	14
R J Sidebottom, lbw b Chapple	52		(8) c Smith b Chapple	16
T T Bresnan, not out	19		(7) c Smith b Chapple	11
Extras lb 8, nb 2	10		Extras b 1, lb 10, w 1, nb 6	18
Total	239		Total	260

Bonus points — Yorkshire 1, Lancashire 3

T T Bresnan replaced I Wardlaw after lunch on the Second Day

FoW: 1-3 (Root), 2-22 (Rudolph), 3-22 (Gale), 4-32 (Bairstow), 5-32 (Ballance)
1st 6-35 (Rashid), 7-44 (Shahzad), 8-45 (McGrath), 9-199 (Sidebottom), 10-239 (Pyrah)
FoW: 1-41 (Root), 2-80 (McGrath), 3-84 (Rudolph), 4-118 (Bairstow), 5-119 (Ballance)
2nd 6-134 (Bresnan), 7-164 (Sidebottom), 8-177 (Gale), 9-230 (Shahzad), 10-260 (Pyrah)

	O	M	R	W		O	M	R	W
Chapple	16	4	43	1	Chapple	26	3	71	5
Hogg	15	1	62	5	Hogg	17	1	62	2
Smith	10.4	5	24	2	Smith	6	3	12	0
Mahmood	14	1	64	2	Mahmood	12	1	53	1
Keedy	13	2	38	0	Keedy	15.5	2	51	2

Umpires: N A Mallender and G Sharp | Scorers: J T Potter and A West

NIGEL PULLAN'S Special Report on Yorkshire's 3,000th
Championship fixture — a *Roses* clash to live in legend

Pyrah all-time century hero

**RICHARD PYRAH: One of
the best ever in adversity**

This was Yorkshire's 3,000th
Championship fixture, and an
enthralling *Roses* match was
graced by an outstanding innings
from Pyrah and some excellent
bowling from Hogg and Chapple.

Lancashire's consistent performance in their first innings
finally gave them the advantage,
but Yorkshire's determination
with bat and ball almost brought
about an unexpected reversal of
fortune. It was a testament to the
qualities of the four-day first-
class game.

Lancashire were invited to bat
first but, despite some skilful
bowling by Sidebottom,
Yorkshire's attack did not take
full advantage of helpful conditions, and the dropping of Croft
at slip was significant.

When he was bowled just
before tea in poor light Croft had
made 54, and Lancashire's recovery was under way as important
contributions from all the lower-
order raised the total to 328.
Wardlaw on his debut dismissed
Smith, but was expensive.

Thursday morning saw a dra-
matic batting collapse, and Yorkshire were 45-8 just after lunch. Hogg
and Chapple bowled extremely well up to the interval, and while Hogg
deserved his five wickets Chapple was most unfortunate not to take one.
They bowled a fuller length than Yorkshire, much straighter, so that
when the ball moved the batsmen were in trouble.

Six wickets were down at lunch and Chapple, probably contemplat-
ing the follow-on, opened the afternoon session with Smith and
Mahmood. Hogg, grandson of Sonny Ramadhin, tall, fast and accurate,

BOUNCED AND BOWLED: Tim Bresnan gives Steven Croft the full works in Lancashire's second innings

strengthened his position at the top of the national bowling averages. A seemed lost for Yorkshire as Pyrah hit a six to put up the 50 and a fou off consecutive balls after he had been joined by Sidebottom.

Pyrah proceeded to play an innings of 117, which was surely one of the best ever seen for Yorkshire, given the adverse circumstances i which it began. He showed great skill and composure, defending res olutely but attacking wherever possible to hit three sixes and 12 fours. I would not have been achieved without Sidebottom's dogged participa tion with another valuable innings for his county, and they set a recor partnership of 154 for the ninth wicket at Headingley.

Sidebottom was out with Pyrah on 97, and spectators did not know whether Bresnan or Wardlaw would emerge from the pavilion as las man. Bresnan had driven from the England camp at Lord's during th partnership...and he appeared to reassure Pyrah and to see him to a maid en Championship hundred, which was accomplished with a fine cover drive. Together they added another 40 runs.

Yorkshire were still 89 behind on first innings, but Bresnan quickly dismissed Horton, Moore and Croft, and Lancashire subsided to 87-8 only 176 ahead. Hogg and Mahmood set about the bowling, each mak ing important fifties and leaving Yorkshire 284 to make to win. Chapple Lancashire's outstanding captain, was determined that they would no do so, and he bowled 26 overs, taking 5-71 while suffering discomfor from his hip injury. He was loyally supported by Keedy and Hogg.

Yet Yorkshire kept going, and at the close on Friday they were 136-6 still needing 148 with only four wickets remaining on Saturday morn

SAFE AS HOUSES: The returning Jacques Rudolph looks on as Anthony McGrath holds a sharp chance from Mark Chilton in Lancashire's first innings

ing. Sidebottom's employment as nightwatchman and all-rounder Bresnan's return from Lord's meant that the noble Pyrah would probably have to bat at No. 11. Rashid and Shahzad played well, and Shahzad was unfortunate to glove a catch to Cross, so when Pyrah arrived at the crease to join Rashid the last-wicket pair needed 54 to win.

It was a tall order, but Lancashire must have had some palpitations as the score mounted before Keedy trapped a disappointed Pyrah lbw to complete a second 2011 *Roses* success for Lancashire in their quest for the Championship. Thirty years ago to the day I was sitting in the stand behind Bob Willis as he bowled out Australia in the 1981 Test.

Lightning did not strike twice, and Lancashire deserved to win, but we had seen an excellent contest that will live long in the memory.

LV County Championship Division 1
Hampshire v. Yorkshire

Played at The Rose Bowl, West End, Southampton on August 2, 3, 4 and 5, 2011
Match drawn at 5pm on the Fourth Day

Toss won by Yorkshire — Hampshire 9 points, Yorkshire 6 points
Close of play: First Day, Yorkshire 318-3 (McGrath 65*, Ballance 50*); Second Day, Hampshire 116-2 (Carberry 37*, McKenzie 30); Third Day, Hampshire 291-2 (Carberry 148*, McKenzie 95*)

YORKSHIRE

First Innings		Second Innings	
J A Rudolph, c Cork b Imran Tahir	99	not out	27
J J Sayers, c Bates b Wood	8	not out	7
* A W Gale, c Vince b Imran Tahir	54		
A McGrath, c Adams b Ervine	115		
G S Ballance, b Briggs	76		
§ G L Brophy, c and b Imran Tahir	53		
A U Rashid, c McKenzie b Imran Tahir	38		
A Shahzad, c Wood b Imran Tahir	18		
R M Pyrah, st Bates b Briggs	6		
D J Wainwright, c Dawson b Imran Tahir	6		
R J Sidebottom, not out	9		
Extras b 15, lb 18, w 1, nb 16	50	Extras b 2, lb 4	6
Total	532	Total (0 wkts)	40

Bonus points — Yorkshire 3, Hampshire 1   110-over score: 333-3

FoW: 1st: 1-20 (Sayers), 2-149 (Gale), 3-204 (Rudolph), 4-361 (Ballance), 5-431 (McGrath), 6-478 (Brophy), 7-501 (Rashid), 8-514 (Pyrah), 9-518 (Shahzad), 10-532 (Wainwright)

	O	M	R	W		O	M	R	W
Cork	16	2	57	0	Wood	2	0	4	0
Wood	24	11	67	1	Ervine	2	0	16	0
Imran Tahir	49.5	2	132	6	Imran Tahir	4	1	14	0
Ervine	14	3	65	1	Briggs	3	3	0	0
Briggs	51	10	127	2					
Dawson	15	1	46	0					
Carberry	2	0	5	0					

HAMPSHIRE

J H K Adams, c Brophy b Wainwright		29
L A Dawson, c Brophy b Sidebottom		13
M A Carberry, not out		300
N D McKenzie, c Ballance b Wainwright		237
S M Ervine, not out		0
J M Vince		
§ M D Bates		
* D G Cork	Did not bat	
D R Briggs		
C P Wood		
Imran Tahir		
Extras b 12, lb 2, nb 6		20
Total (3 wkts dec)		599

Bonus points — Hampshire 5   110-over score: 401-2

FoW: 1-38 (Dawson), 2-59 (Adams), 3-582 (McKenzie)

	O	M	R	W
Shahzad	19	2	79	0
Sidebottom	18	1	71	1
Pyrah	15	2	74	0
Wainwright	44.5	11	150	2
Rashid	39	3	146	0
Sayers	5	1	16	0
McGrath	4	1	10	0
Rudolph	6	0	28	0
Ballance	2	0	11	0

Umpires: J H Evans and R A Kettleborough   Scorers: J T Potter and A E Weld

523 stand floors Yorkshire

ANTHONY McGRATH: Return to form

The most memorable feature of this match was an outstanding partnership of 523 for the third wicket between Carberry and McKenzie.

It broke numerous records. as detailed in the Championship Factfile.

It was the third-highest partnership ever in the Championship, exceeded only by the Yorkshire opening stands of 555 by Holmes and Sutcliffe at Leyton in 1932 and 554 by Tunnicliffe and Brown at Chesterfield in 1898. Carberry made a magnificent 300 not out, and when Wainwright had McKenzie caught by Ballance the South African Test player had reached a career-best 237. The stand also demonstrated the limitations of the Yorkshire bowlers.

Yorkshire spent almost two days scoring 532. Rudolph set a fine example with an excellent innings curtailed only by a brilliant catch from Cork when he was on 99. McGrath made a welcome return to form with an important century, and he received good support from Ballance. Yet Yorkshire gained only three batting points. Hampshire's spinners, the left-arm Briggs and leg-spinner Imran Tahir bowled 51 and 49.2 overs during two hot days, and Imran earned his 6-132. Wood took an impressive leaping catch to dismiss Shahzad.

Gale's men had to bowl Hampshire out twice to win this important relegation match. They removed Adams and Dawson, but their objective gradually receded as Carberry and McKenzie transformed the innings. On a cloudy third day they proceeded diligently to 291...and on the last day they batted on because no declaration could have made this a viable contest. Carberry had suffered a serious illness, and the triple-hundred to mark his return to first-class cricket was the second-highest score against Yorkshire behind WG Grace's 318 at Cheltenham 135 years ago. It is interesting to recall that after their previous match at the Rose Bowl the hosts were docked eight points for producing an unsatisfactory pitch.

LV County Championship Division 1
Yorkshire v. Sussex

Played at North Marine Road, Scarborough, on August 17, 18, 19 and 20, 2011

Match drawn at 6.11pm on the Fourth Day

Toss won by Sussex   Yorkshire 9 points, Sussex 9 points

Close of play: First Day, Sussex 335-5 (Yardy 126*, Wernars 16*); Second Day, Yorkshire 251-4 (Root 111*, Balance 45*); Third Day, Yorkshire 126-3 (Goodwin 30*, Anyon 1*)

SUSSEX

	First Innings		Second Innings	
E C Joyce, c Bairstow b Pyrah		45	c Bairstow b Sidebottom	42
C D Nash, lbw b Sidebottom		10	lbw b Patterson	32
L W P Wells, c McGrath b Sidebottom		0	c Bairstow b Rashid	20
M W Goodwin, c McGrath b Sidebottom		7	c Bairstow b Rashid	35
* M H Yardy, c Bairstow b Sidebottom		130	(6) c sub (DJ Wainwright) b Rashid	122
§ B C Brown, c Bairstow b Sidebottom		108	(7) not out	16
K O Wernars, b Pyrah		26	(8) not out	1
W D Parnell, c Sidebottom b Pyrah		8		
Amjad Khan, lbw b Rashid		16	(5) b Rashid	53
J E Anyon, not out		11		
M S Panesar, lbw b Rashid		9		
Extras b 4, lb 16, w 6, nb 2		28	Extras b 2, lb 6, nb 4	12
Total		398	Total (6 wkts dec)	333

Bonus points — Sussex 4, Yorkshire 2   110-over score: 375-8

FoW: 1-15 (Nash), 2-15 (Wells), 3-27 (Goodwin), 4-90 (Joyce), 5-288 (Brown)
1st   6-339 (Yardy), 7-362 (Parnell), 8-363 (Wernars), 9-384 (Khan), 10-398 (Panesar)
FoW: 1-62 (Joyce), 2-87 (Nash), 3-121 (Wells), 4-150 (Goodwin), 5-303 (Anyon)
2nd   6-328 (Yardy)

	O	M	R	W		O	M	R	W
Sidebottom	27	9	53	5	Sidebottom	17	8	44	1
Ashraf	15	1	69	0	Pyrah	6	1	21	0
Patterson	18	3	71	0	Patterson	16	3	53	1
Pyrah	24	5	64	3	Ashraf	9	1	50	0
Rashid	24.1	0	82	2	Rashid	31	3	121	4
McGrath	4	0	20	0	Root	8	0	36	0
Root	5	1	19	0					

YORKSHIRE

	First Innings		Second Innings	
* J A Rudolph, c Yardy b Parnell		1	c Goodwin b Nash	120
J J Sayers, lbw b Parnell		8	c Goodwin b Amjad Khan	84
J E Root, c Amjad Khan b Parnell		160	(7) not out	7
A McGrath, lbw b Amjad Khan		29	(5) c Wells b Parnell	17
§ J M Bairstow, c Yardy b Anyon		33	(3) c Parnell b Panesar	26
G S Ballance, c Goodwin b Anyon		87	(4) lbw b Parnell	15
A U Rashid, c Wernars b Panesar		12	(6) not out	4
R M Pyrah, c Joyce b Amjad Khan		8	(6) c Wells b Amjad Khan	19
R J Sidebottom, c Wernars b Amjad Khan		1		
S A Patterson, not out		2		
M A Ashraf, c Yardy b Amjad Khan		4		
Extras b 24, lb 7, w 2, nb 10		43	Extras b 10, lb 8, nb 2	20
Total		388	Total (6 wkts)	312

Bonus points — Yorkshire 4, Sussex 2   110-over score: 373-6

FoW: 1-6 (Rudolph), 2-29 (Sayers), 3-81 (McGrath), 4-156 (Bairstow), 5-345 (Root)
1st   6-356 (Ballance), 7-374 (Rashid), 8-378 (Pyrah), 9-383 (Sidebottom), 10-388 (Ashraf)
FoW: 1-174 (Rudolph), 2-206 (Bairstow), 3-236 (Ballance), 4-270 (McGrath), 5-300 (Pyrah)
2nd   6-303 (Sayers)

	O	M	R	W		O	M	R	W
Parnell	20	2	86	3	Parnell	11	0	67	2
Anyon	29	5	91	2	Anyon	8	2	33	0
Amjad Khan	28	7	70	4	Panesar	18	2	88	1
Wernars	6	0	25	0	Wells	6	0	39	0
Panesar	34	13	71	1	Wernars	3	1	19	0
Wells	5	1	14	0	Nash	5	1	33	1
					Amjad Khan	3	0	15	2

Umpires: N G B Cook and T E Jesty   Scorers: J T Potter and P Elford

Yorkshire v. Sussex

Joe Root arrives with 160

This was a good match on an attractive, refurbished seaside ground with Sussex, marginally superior with the bat, facing the possibility of defeat after a brave Yorkshire batting performance on the last afternoon.

It featured Sussex captain Yardy's achievement of two centuries and Root's maiden first-class hundred at the age of 20.

Yardy dominated the opening day, leading a Sussex recovery after Sidebottom had reduced them to 90-4 at lunch. Despite an unusual stance, his batting technique proved impregnable, and he took advantage of bowling on or outside his leg stump.

The Sussex innings was also rejuvenated by a pugnacious display of hitting from young wicket-keeper Brown, who made an enterprising century.

Yorkshire took the remaining five Sussex wickets next morning, but then lost two to Parnell.

JOE ROOT: Pensive after catch that caused concern

Root's was an outstanding innings, combining skilful defence and patience with impressive attacking strokes, ending the day on 111. He found a reliable partner in Ballance as next day he advanced to 160 and Ballance to 87 before a collapse left Yorkshire 10 behind Sussex. Root's dismissal was controversial, as Amjad Khan may not have had full control over the ball before he threw it in the air, but the umpires ruled in his favour. Yardy made another century on the last day and Anyon a career-best 53 as Sussex set Yorkshire 344 in a minimum of 51 overs.

Yorkshire responded to this well judged declaration with an opening stand of 174 from Sayers and Rudolph, who went on to 126. Yorkshire increased the scoring rate as the innings developed, but the target proved just beyond them. Possibly, the openers might have attacked sooner, but if they had not built a platform the run chase would not have been feasible. The target was down to 44 with the last four overs to play, but Amjad Khan dismissed Pyrah and Sayers to end their hopes.

LV County Championship Division 1
Yorkshire v. Warwickshire

Played at Headingley Carnegie, Leeds, on August 23, 24 and 25, 2011
Warwickshire won by an innings and 58 runs at 5.20pm on the Third Day

Toss won by Yorkshire   Warwickshire 23 points, Yorkshire 4 point
Close of play: First Day, Yorkshire 297 all out; Second Day, Warwickshire 340-6 (Chanderpa
167*, Barker 33*)

First Innings	YORKSHIRE		Second Innings	
* J A Rudolph, lbw b Barker	24		c Ambrose b Barker	
J J Sayers, b Barker	47		lbw b Barker	2
J E Root, lbw b Wright	29		c Westwood b Barker	
A McGrath, c Chopra b Wright	8		c Ambrose b Wright	
G S Ballance, c Westwood b Metters	57		lbw b Wright	
§ G L Brophy, c Metters b Barker	19		b Wright	1
A U Rashid, c Chanderpaul b Metters	21		b Wright	
R M Pyrah, b Barker	18		c Troughton b Barker	2
D J Wainwright, lbw b Metters	32		not out	2
R J Sidebottom, c Ambrose b Carter	11		c Chopra b Wright	
S A Patterson, not out	1		b Carter	1
Extras b 6, lb 10, w 2, nb 12	30		Extras b 4, lb 6	1
Total	297		Total	12

Bonus points — Yorkshire 2, Warwickshire 3

FoW: 1-40 (Rudolph), 2-120 (Root), 3-120 (Sayers), 4-134 (McGrath), 5-191 (Brophy), 6-2
1st   (Rashid), 7-242 (Ballance), 8-260 (Pyrah), 9-292 (Sidebottom), 10-297 (Wainwrigh
FoW: 1-0 (Rudolph), 2-20 (Root), 3-25 (McGrath), 4-25 (Ballance), 5-47 (Broph
2nd   6-47 (Sayers), 7-85 (Pyrah), 8-87 (Rashid), 9-91 (Sidebottom), 10-127 (Patters

	O	M	R	W		O	M	R	W
Barker	23	2	73	4	Barker	14	4	56	4
Carter	25	6	75	1	Carter	9.5	2	19	1
Wright	21	8	65	2	Wright	11	3	31	
Maddy	15	5	37	0	Metters	3	0	11	0
Metters	10.2	0	31	3					

WARWICKSHIRE

V Chopra, b Patterson	1	
I J Westwood, lbw b Sidebottom	3	
L J Evans, c Brophy b Wainwright	30	
S Chanderpaul, c Brophy b Patterson	193	
* J O Troughton, c Brophy b Pyrah	27	
§ T R Ambrose, c Rudolph b Wainwright	66	
D L Maddy, lbw b Wainwright	12	
K H D Barker, c Rashid b Root	85	
N M Carter, st Brophy b Root	40	
C L Metters, c Pyrah b Root	9	
C J C Wright, not out	13	
Extras b 1, lb 2	3	
Total	482	

Bonus points — Warwickshire 4, Yorkshire 2   110 over score: 367-6

FoW: 1-1 (Chopra), 2-5 (Westwood), 3-47 (Evans), 4-115 (Troughton), 5-226 (Ambros
     6-264 (Maddy), 7-383 (Chanderpaul), 8-458 (Barker), 9-463 (Carter), 10-482 (Metter

	O	M	R	W
Sidebottom	25	11	48	1
Patterson	29	7	99	2
Pyrah	26	7	98	1
Wainwright	24	4	111	3
Rashid	25	3	90	0
Root	9.3	1	33	3

Umpires: S C Gale and D J Millns   Scorers: J T Potter and D E Wainwright

Yorkshire v. Warwickshire

Inexplicable batting collapse

ONE DOWN: Patterson celebrates the wicket of Chopra

Decisive victory gave impetus to the visitors' Championship challenge — but brought relegation closer for Yorkshire.

The first day was evenly contested, but the second was dominated by Chanderpaul's long innings and the third saw Yorkshire's inexplicable collapse after Barker and Chanderpaul had looked so assured and the wicket so docile in the morning.

Yorkshire faced a lively attack led by the left-handed Barker with his high action and Wright who had arrived on loan from Essex, with Devonian left-arm spinner Metters also bowling well.

Most Yorkshire batsmen made a contribution, but nobody achieved the necessary long innings. Ballance and Sayers survived the longest, and a total of 297 was a fair reflection of the first day's play.

Warwickshire's response may have been similar but for the durability of Chanderpaul, the West Indian Test batsman: he has a remarkable front-on stance, as if receiving the bowling from square-leg, but he adjusts before the ball is received and takes maximum advantage of any wayward bowling either side of the wicket. Ambrose made an enterprising 66, and Chanderpaul and Barker added 119 for the seventh wicket. Warwickshire batted well on the third morning, but Chanderpaul just missed a double century as Brophy caught him off Patterson.

Yorkshire were expected to survive the two afternoon sessions to earn a draw, but they were put out for 127 as Barker again took four wickets and Wright five. No batsman showed the necessary skill or resolution to build the longer innings required. The loss of Rudolph in Barker's first over and the rapid dismissal of Root and then McGrath and Ballance without scoring left Yorkshire 25-4. The middle-order collapsed to Wright, but a last-wicket stand of 36 gave some respectability to the total. It was a most disappointing batting performance.

Played at Edgbaston, Birmingham, on August 31 and September 1, 2 and 3, 2011
Match drawn at 5.20pm on the Fourth Day

Toss won by Warwickshire   Warwickshire 9 points, Yorkshire 8 point

Close of play: First Day, Yorkshire 254-8 (Sidebottom 8*, Patterson 0*); Second Da
Warwickshire 281-6 (Ambrose 68*); Third Day, Yorkshire 319-5 (Ballance 92*, Rashid 62

First Innings		YORKSHIRE	Second Innings	
J E Root, b Clarke	18		lbw b Metters	4*
* J J Sayers, c Clarke b Metters	84		c Chopra b Wright	2.
A Lyth, lbw b Metters	74		lbw b Wright	(
A McGrath, c Clarke b Wright	8		lbw b Wright	5'
§ J M Bairstow, c Clarke b Metters	1		c Barker b Metters	2
G S Ballance, c Metters b Woakes	13		c Troughton b Woakes	11
A U Rashid, c Clarke b Barker	6		c Troughton b Wright	8.
A Shahzad, c Porterfield b Clarke	15		not out	1.
R J Sidebottom, c Ambrose b Clarke	19		c Metters b Woakes	1.
S A Patterson, not out	15		not out	(
M A Ashraf, c Ambrose b Clarke	0			
Extras b 5, lb 13, nb 4	28		Extras lb 14, nb 2	1(
Total	281		Total (8 wkts dec)	38!

Bonus points — Yorkshire 2, Warwickshire 3

FoW: 1-48 (Root), 2-182 (Sayers), 3-197 (McGrath), 4-208 (Bairstow), 5-209 (Lyt
1st   6-228 (Rashid), 7-230 (Ballance), 8-252 (Shahzad), 9-281 (Sidebottom, 10-281 (Ashra
FoW: 1-42 (Sayers), 2-46 (Lyth), (3-96 Root), 4-152 (Bairstow), 5-170 (McGrat
2nd   6-358 (Ballance), 7-361 (Rashid), 8-381 (Sidebottom)

	O	M	R	W		O	M	R	W
Barker	21	6	50	1	Woakes	26	2	91	2
Woakes	21	8	42	1	Barker	14	2	49	0
Wright	27	7	69	1	Wright	26	4	102	4
Clarke	19.5	4	55	4	Clarke	11	2	35	0
Metters	18	2	47	3	Metters	22	4	94	2

First Innings		WARWICKSHIRE	Second Innings	
V Chopra, c Bairstow b Shahzad	7		c Bairstow b Shahzad	5
I J Westwood, c Lyth b Sidebottom	55		lbw b Rashid	31
W T S Porterfield, c McGrath b Sidebottom	0		c Bairstow b Patterson	47
S Chanderpaul, c Bairstow b Sidebottom	110		not out	56
* J O Troughton, c Bairstow b Ashraf	18		not out	62
§ T R Ambrose, c Balance b Sidebottom	69			
C L Metters, lbw b Sidebottom	4			
R Clarke, lbw b Shahzad	23			
C R Woakes, c Bairstow b Ashraf	5			
K H D Barker, c Bairstow b Ashraf	0			
C J C Wright, not out	5			
Extras b 3, lb 16, w 3	22		Extras b 5, lb 8	13
Total	318		Total (3 wkts)	214

Bonus points — Warwickshire 3, Yorkshire 3

FoW: 1-26 (Chopra), 2-27 (Porterfield), 3-94 (Westwood), 4-137 (Troughton), 5-272 (Chanderpaul
1st   6-281 (Metters), 7-282 (Ambrose), 8-287 (Woakes), 9-301 (Barker), 10-318 (Clark
2nd   1-5 (Chopra), 2-87 (Westwood), 3-89 (Porterfield)

	O	M	R	W		O	M	R	W
Sidebottom	21	6	43	5	Sidebottom	9.2	2	30	0
Shahzad	20	3	76	2	Shahzad	10	0	36	1
Ashraf	21	4	71	3	Rashid	19	0	64	1
Patterson	14	1	47	0	Ashraf	7	1	25	0
Rashid	18	2	51	0	Patterson	8	2	20	1
Root	2	0	11	0	Root	3	0	16	0

Umpires: J H Evans and P J Hartley   Scorers: J T Potter and D E Wainwright

Yorkshire in relegation zone

A second fixture in succession against Warwickshire gave Yorkshire the chance to redeem themselves at an impressively redeveloped Edgbaston.

The batting was considerably better, with a welcome maiden Championship century from Ballance and good contributions from Sayers, Lyth and Rashid.

The bowling also improved, especially Sidebottom, who took five wickets, but they could not bowl Warwickshire out twice. Once again the obdurate Chanderpaul presented an insurmountable obstacle.

Yorkshire made an encouraging start as Sayers and Lyth added 132 for the second wicket — but Warwickshire took the last nine wickets for 99 runs, led by Clarke, who also took four catches, and Metters, who dismissed Bairstow and Lyth in four balls.

Yorkshire took four top-order wickets, but when Ambrose joined Chanderpaul they added 135, so Warwickshire had a narrow lead.

GARY BALLANCE
First Yorkshire century

Chanderpaul made his second century against Yorkshire in just over a week, cautious at first but dominant later, while Ambrose was briskly efficient. Sidebottom led the attack with 5-43 off 21 overs.

Yorkshire stumbled at first despite McGrath's return to form, but the third day belonged to Ballance, who after a commendably consistent summer reached 92 and went on to his first century for Yorkshire, batting with skill and composure at a critical time. Rashid batted as well as he has all season to reach 82, so Yorkshire set Warwickshire a target of 348. Once Chanderpaul and Troughton came together the bowlers were unable to break through, and despite some effort to tempt the batting side to take some risks in an effort to win, bad light claimed the last 20 overs and blacked out any prospect of the decisive result both sides needed. Yorkshire were now in one of the relegation places, 14 points behind Worcestershire, having played a game more.

LV County Championship Division 1
Yorkshire v. Somerset

Played at Headingley Carnegie, Leeds, on September 7, 8, 9 and 10, 2011
Yorkshire won by 6 wickets at 4.13pm on the Fourth Day

Toss won by Yorkshire   Yorkshire 19 points, Somerset 5 points
Close of play: First Day, Somerset 140-4 (Barrow 55*, Butler 43*); Second Da[y]
Yorkshire 20-0 (Root 15*, Sayers 2*); Third Day, Somerset 124-6 (Meschede 39*, Thomas 25[*])

SOMERSET

First Innings		Second Innings	
A W R Barrow, c McGrath b Sidebottom	69	c Bairstow b Sidebottom	1
A V Suppiah, b Shahzad	8	lbw b Sidebottom	12
C R Jones, b Ashraf	31	lbw b Sidebottom	
J C Hildreth, b Ashraf	0	c McGrath b Ashraf	
§ J C Buttler, b Pyrah	52	lbw b McGrath	25
P D Trego, b Shahzad	31	c Ballance b Sidebottom	13
C A J Meschede, c Bairstow b Sidebottom	0	b Shahzad	3
* A C Thomas, b Rashid	49	c Lyth b Sidebottom	28
A J Dibble, lbw b Sidebottom	0	(10) not out	
M Kartik, lbw b Sidebottom	5	(9) c Bairstow b Sidebottom	
S P Kirby, not out	15	lbw b Sidebottom	
Extras lb 5	5	Extras lb 2, w 2, nb 2	
Total	265	Total	132

Bonus points — Somerset 2, Yorkshire 3

FoW: 1st: 1-14 (Suppiah), 2-86 (Jones), 3-88 (Hildreth), 4-151 (Buttler), 5-178 (Barrow)
6-178 (Meschede), 7-202 (Trego), 8-205 (Dibble), 9-215 (Kartik), 10-265 (Thoma[s])
FoW: 2nd: 1-18 (Barrow), 2-21 (Jones), 3-26 (Suppiah), 4-26 (Hildreth), 5-46 (Trego)
6-78 (Buttler), 7-130 (Thomas), 8-130 (Meschede), 9-132 (Kartik), 10-132 (Kirb[y])

	O	M	R	W		O	M	R	W
Sidebottom	19	3	61	4	Sidebottom	13.5	3	37	7
Shahzad	19	3	74	2	Shahzad	11	3	22	1
Pyrah	15	1	59	1	Ashraf	6	0	28	1
Ashraf	17	5	49	2	Pyrah	4	1	8	0
Rashid	4	0	17	1	McGrath	9	1	14	1
					Rashid	5	0	21	0

YORKSHIRE

First Innings		Second Innings	
J E Root, lbw b Thomas	17	lbw b Thomas	46
* J J Sayers, lbw b Kirby	3	c Trego b Kartik	35
A Lyth, c Buttler b Thomas	52	c Suppiah b Kartik	3
A McGrath, c Hildreth b Kirby	0	c Buttler b Kirby	44
§ J M Bairstow, c Suppiah b Dibble	16	not out	53
G S Ballance, c Buttler b Thomas	13	not out	4
A U Rashid, b Kirby	10		
R M Pyrah, not out	31		
A Shahzad, c Barrow b Thomas	6		
R J Sidebottom, c Hildreth b Kartik	27		
M A Ashraf, lbw b Thomas	0		
Extras b 1, lb 9, nb 10	20	Extras b 5, lb 9, nb 6	20
Total	195	Total (4 wkts)	205

Bonus points — Somerset 3

FoW: 1st: 1-23 (Root), 2-23 (Sayers), 3-25 (McGrath), 4-60 (Bairstow), 5-106 (Ballance)
6-121 (Rashid), 7-123 (Lyth), 8-133 (Shahzad), 9-186 (Sidebottom), 10-195 (Ashra[f])
FoW: 2nd: 1-85 (Root), 2-98 (Lyth), 3-103 (McGrath), 4-201 (McGrath)

	O	M	R	W		O	M	R	W
Kirby	16	4	65	3	Kirby	15.3	4	61	1
Thomas	22.4	3	66	5	Thomas	16	3	53	1
Trego	4	1	14	0	Trego	2	1	2	0
Dibble	8	2	26	1	Dibble	8	1	31	0
Kartik	7	3	14	1	Kartik	18	5	44	2

Umpires: T E Jesty and R T Robinson   Scorers: J T Potter and G A Stickley

Great, Siddy, but down we go

OUT: Ryan Sidebottom (11-98) wins his appeal against Arul Suppiah

The first day was much reduced by rain, so at 140-3 neither side had gained any advantage.

Barrow, 19, opening the innings in the absence of Trescothick, made a resolute 69, but wickets fell around him. Again rain curtailed Thursday's play, with Somerset 265 all out and Barrow batting into a sunlit evening.

By contrast Buttler, another of Somerset's home-grown young players, demonstrated his attacking qualities with a succession of boundaries. The Yorkshire attack, led by Sidebottom, worked their way through until a last-wicket stand of 50 by Thomas, their captain, and Kirby, once of Yorkshire, gave them a respectable 265.

Thomas now showed his skills as a fast-medium bowler with good control and movement, and Kirby bowled with his customary enthusiasm and tenacity. Yorkshire were dependent on a 50 from Lyth and a late stand between Pyrah and Sidebottom to finish only 70 behind the visitors. Sidebottom now gave his best display of the summer, taking a career-best 7-37, culminating in 4-2 in 12 balls, to end an excellent season, in which he took 62 first-class wickets and bowled 465.5 overs. Yorkshire required 203 to win, and it was by no means assured despite a sound opening stand from Sayers and Root. Bairstow's speciality is beating the clock, and he was joined by McGrath to steer Yorkshire to their third win of the season.

The points gained were insufficient to save Yorkshire from relegation. They finished eighth: below Worcestershire, whom they had beaten twice, and above Hampshire. If they had won at Headingley against Nottinghamshire and Hampshire this may have been avoided. Generally, the bowlers could not get first-class sides out twice, and while there were some good individual batting performances there were some inexplicable collapses. Most members, I suspect, will still endorse the policy of playing young cricketers developed by the county's coaches.

LV COUNTY CHAMPIONSHIP 2011

DIVISION 1

	P	W	L	D	BAT	BOWL	Pen.	Point
					Bonus Points			
1 Lancashire (Div 1, 4)	16	10	4	2	37	44	1.0	246
2 Warwickshire (Div 1, 6)	16	9	4	3	46	45	9.0	235
3 Durham (Div 1, 5)	16	8	4	4	47	45	0.0	232
4 Somerset (Div 1, 2)	16	6	7	3	45	39	0.0	189
5 Sussex (Div 2, 1)	16	6	6	4	34	40	0.0	182
6 Nottinghamshire (Div 1, 1)	16	5	6	5	35	43	0.0	173
7 Worcestershire (Div 2, 2)	16	4	11	1	31	44	0.0	142
8 Yorkshire (Div 1, 3)*	**16**	**3**	**6**	**7**	**34**	**37**	**2.0**	**138**
9 Hampshire (Div 1, 7)*	16	3	6	7	30	36	8.0	127

Pen. 1 point deducted for each over short in a match based on a rate of 16 overs per hour
* Relegated to Division 2 for 2012

DIVISION 2

	P	W	L	D	BAT	BOWL	Pen.	Points
					Bonus Points			
1 Middlesex (Div 2, 8)*	16	8	2	6	50	44	0.0	240
2 Surrey (Div2, 7)*	16	8	4	4	43	44	0.0	227
3 Northamptonshire (Div 2, 6)	16	7	2	7	48	45	0.0	226
4 Gloucestershire (Div 2, 5)	16	6	5	5	41	47	1.0	198
5 Derbyshire (Div 2, 9)	16	5	6	5	42	44	0.0	181
6 Glamorgan (Div 2, 3)	16	5	6	5	44	40	1.0	178
7 Essex (Div 1, 9)	16	4	4	8	29	44	2.0	159
8 Kent (Div 1, 8)	16	5	9	2	30	42	9.0	149
9 Leicestershire (Div 2, 4)	16	1	11	4	24	36	0.0	88

Pen. 1 point deducted for each over short in a match based on a rate of 16 overs per hour
* Promoted to Division 1 for 2012
Warwickshire, Hampshire and Kent had 8 points deducted for poor pitches

(2010 positions in brackets)

LV COUNTY CHAMPIONSHIP

SCORING OF POINTS — 2011

a) For a win, 16 points plus any points scored in the first innings.

b) In a tie, each side to take eight points plus any points scored in the first innings.

c) In a drawn match, each side to take three points plus any points scored in the first innings.

d) If the scores are equal in a drawn match, the side batting in the fourth innings to score eight points plus any points scored in the first innings, and the opposing side to score three points plus any points scored in the first innings.

e) **First Innings Points** (awarded only for performances **in the first 110 overs** of each first innings, and retained whatever the result of the match).

   (i) A maximum of five batting points to be available as under:—

      200 to 249 runs —　1 point
      250 to 299 runs —　2 points
      300 to 349 runs —　3 points
      350 to 399 runs —　4 points
      400 runs or over —　5 points

   (ii) A maximum of three bowling points to be available as under: —

      3 to 5 wickets taken —　1 point
      6 to 8 wickets taken —　2 points
      9 to 10 wickets taken — 3 points

f) The two sides with the highest aggregate of points gained at the end of the season shall be Champions of their respective division. Should any side in the Championship table be equal on points the side with most wins will have priority.

LV COUNTY CHAMPIONSHIP

Played 16   Won 3   Lost 6   Drawn 7

BATTING AND FIELDING

(Qualification 10 completed innings)

Player	M.	I.	N.O.	Runs	H.S.	Avge	100s	50s	ct/st
J M Bairstow	13	24	2	1015	205	46.13	2	6	43/0
G S Ballance	11	21	4	717	111	42.17	1	8	6
A W Gale	12	22	3	769	145*	40.47	2	4	3
J E Root	15	30	4	937	160	36.03	1	4	5
J J Sayers	10	20	1	581	84	30.57	0	5	4
A Lyth	11	22	1	553	74	26.33	0	6	20
R M Pyrah	11	16	1	376	117	25.06	1	1	2
A U Rashid	16	26	3	556	82	24.17	0	3	9
Ajmal Shahzad	10	15	2	307	70	23.61	0	1	0
A McGrath	12	23	0	485	115	21.08	1	1	12
R J Sidebottom	16	25	6	389	61	20.47	0	2	2
S A Patterson	11	16	6	130	53	13.00	0	1	4
Also played									
J A Rudolph	4	8	1	318	120	45.42	1	1	2
G L Brophy	7	11	3	355	177*	44.37	1	1	7/1
T T Bresnan	3	5	1	175	87	43.75	0	1	1
D J Wainwright	3	5	1	84	32	21.00	0	0	0
S M Guy	1	2	0	15	8	7.50	0	0	1/0
Moin A Ashraf	6	8	1	21	8*	3.00	0	0	0
O J Hannon-Dalby	4	7	2	10	6*	2.00	0	0	0
I Wardlaw	1	0	0	0	—	—	—	—	0

BOWLING

(Qualification 10 wickets)

Player	Overs	Mdns	Runs	Wkts	Avge	Best	5wI	10wM
T T Bresnan	97	27	252	13	19.38	4-50	0	0
R J Sidebottom	467.4	107	1364	62	22.00	7-37	3	1
R M Pyrah	266.4	54	956	29	32.96	5-58	1	0
Ajmal Shahzad	272.2	42	1025	25	41.00	5-65	1	0
A U Rashid	448.3	56	1692	39	43.38	6-77	2	1
S A Patterson	294.5	55	973	21	46.33	4-51	0	0
Moin A Ashraf	135	23	498	10	49.80	3-71	0	0
Also bowled								
J E Root	84.3	13	319	7	45.57	3-33	0	0
A McGrath	21	2	56	1	56.00	1-14	0	0
D J Wainwright	92.5	18	336	5	67.20	3-111	0	0
I Wardlaw	13	0	68	1	68.00	1-68	0	0
O J Hannon-Dalby	97	7	325	2	162.50	1-28	0	0
J A Rudolph	6	0	28	0	—	0-28	0	0
J J Sayers	5	1	16	0	—	0-16	0	0
G L Brophy	2	0	6	0	—	0- 6	0	0
A Lyth	2	1	10	0	—	0- 0	0	0
G S Ballance	2	0	11	0	—	0-11	0	0

MCC University Match (First-Class)
Durham MCCU v. Yorkshire

Played at The Racecourse Ground, Durham, on April 27, 28 and 29, 2011
Yorkshire won by 10 wickets at 4.58pm on the Third Day
Toss won by Durham MCCU

Close of play: First Day, Yorkshire 118-0 (Ballance 72*, Sayers 39*); Second Day, Durham MCCU 110- (Westley 28*, Masood 16*)

DURHAM MCCU

	First Innings		Second Innings	
C R Jones,	b Wainwright	69	b Shahzad	0
L E Durandt,	c Gibson b Hannon-Dalby	11	lbw b Ashraf	3
G P Smith,	b Wainwright	22	c Gibson b Shahzad	18
* T Westley,	lbw b Wainwright	17	c Sayers b Shahzad	127
Shan Masoon Khan,	b Wainwright	6	c Ballance b Randhawa	3
R A C Shah,	c Geldart b Wainwright	13	b Randhawa	1
L A Blackaby,	b Sayers	17	c Gibson b Wainwright	0
L A Patel,	lbw b Sayers	19	c Gibson b Hannon-Dalby	32
§ J J Atkinson,	lbw b Sayers	5	c Gibson b Shahzad	17
N Watkins,	c Gibson b Wainwright	0	b Shahzad	4
J D Salt,	not out	0	not out	1
Extras	b 5, lb 7, w 5	17	b 9, lb 9, w 1, nb 6	25
Total		196		287

FoW: 1st 1-26 (Durandt), 2-81 (Smith), 3-122 (Westley), 4-135 (Jones), 5-144 (Masood Khan), 6-161 (Shah), 7-190 (Patel), 8-191 (Blackaby), 9-192 (Watkins), 10-196 (Atkinson)

FoW: 2nd 1-0 (Jones), 2-51 (Smith), 3-68 (Durandt), 4-147 (Masood), 5-161 (Shah), 6-16 (Blackaby), 7-235 (Patel), 8-278 (Atkinson), 9-284 (Watkins), 10-287 (Westley)

First Innings	O	M	R	W		O	M	R	W
Shahzad	14	4	30	0	Shahzad	15.1	0	61	5
Hannon-Dalby	11	2	33	1	Hannon-Dalby	13	1	40	1
Lilley	10	3	31	0	Wainwright	25	1	75	1
Ashraf	9	2	27	0	Ashraf	14	3	36	1
Wainwright	26	12	40	6	Lilley	3	1	3	0
Randhawa	3	1	8	0	Randhawa	18	3	54	2
Sayers	8.2	2	15	3					

YORKSHIRE

	First Innings		Second Innings	
G S Ballance,	c Atkinson b Salt	72	not out	73
* J J Sayers,	c Atkinson b Westley	139	not out	53
C J Geldart,	lbw b Westley	34		
A Z Lees,	c and b Watkins	0		
A E Lilley,	lbw b Watkins	0		
A Shahzad,	b Watkins	13		
D J Wainwright,	c Smith b Blackaby	62		
G S Randhawa,	lbw b Watkins	5		
M A Ashraf,	b Westley	6		
O J Hannon-Dalby,	c and b Watkins	0		
§ B P Gibson,	not out	1		
Extras	b 8, lb 10, w 1, nb 4	23	lb 2, w 1	3
Total		355	Total (0 wkts)	129

FoW: 1st 1-118 (Ballance), 2-172 (Geldart), 3-180 (Lees), 4-180 (Lilley), 5-198 (Shahzad), 6-32 (Wainwright), 7-342 (Randhawa), 8-352 (Sayers), 9-353 (Hannon-Dalby), 10-355 (Ashraf)

	O	M	R	W		O	M	R	W
Salt	21	5	71	1	Salt	5	0	22	0
Shan Masoon Khan	7	0	35	0	Shah Masoon Khan	6	2	25	0
Durandt	4	1	20	0	Westley	7	0	33	0
Westley	29	7	64	3	Watkins	6	0	41	0
Blackaby	14	1	41	1	Durandt	0.5	0	6	0
Watkins	29	2	88	5					
Patel	9	2	18	0					

Umpires: R J Evans and P J Hartley   Scorers: J T Potter and J D Davidson

Durham MCCU v. Yorkshire
Youngest of the young ones

BARNEY GIBSON
Opened with five catches

Durham MCCU have first-class status for their matches against the counties.

Barney Gibson was in the Yorkshire team as wicket-keeper and, as he was born on March 31, 1996, he was making his debut at the age of 15 years and 27 days.

This was a record for Yorkshire by some margin as Paul Jarvis was the previous youngest at 16 years and 75 days at Hove in 1981.

Daffodil-covered *Wisden*, despite its 1,648 pages, has no juvenile records, but the Who's Who of Cricketers on Page 1,196 states that left-arm bowler Charles Robertson Young played for Hampshire at Gravesend in 1867 at 15 years and 131 days.

Other notably youthful Yorkshire first-class debutants have included Doug Padgett at 16 years and 320 days against Somerset at Taunton in 1951, Chris Old at 17 years 228 days against Hampshire at Portsmouth in 1966 and Gary Ramsden at 17 years 76 days against Derbyshire at Derby, who played only once.

Yorkshire bowled Durham out for 196 with Jones making 69, Wainwright taking 6-40 and Gibson two catches. Ballance and Sayers gave Yorkshire an excellent start at the Racecourse Ground before Ballance was out for 72. Sayers went on to 139 in just under six hours, which was encouraging after his long absence. It was also very necessary, as only Wainwright with 62 was able to succeed against a University attack in which Watkins, from Abingdon School, took 5-88 and Westley 3-64. Westley, who is on the Essex staff and played for their Second Eleven at 15 years and 88 days, continued in good form when Durham batted again, and made a good 127.

Left-arm spin debutant Randhawa took two wickets, while Shahzad, returning to county duties after England's winter tours, took 5-61 as Gibson took four more catches. Yorkshire had to score more runs than they anticipated, but Ballance and Sayers put on 129 to see them home.

ALL FIRST-CLASS MATCHES

Played 17   Won 4   Lost 6   Drawn 7

BATTING AND FIELDING

(Qualification 10 completed innings)

Player	M.	I.	N.O.	Runs	H.S.	Avge	100s	50s	ct/st
G S Ballance	12	23	5	862	111	47.88	1	10	7
J M Bairstow	13	24	2	1015	205	46.13	2	6	43/0
A W Gale	12	22	3	769	145*	40.47	2	4	3
J J Sayers	11	22	2	773	139	38.65	1	6	5
J E Root	15	30	4	937	160	36.03	1	4	5
A Lyth	11	22	1	553	74	26.33	0	6	20
R M Pyrah	16	16	1	376	117	25.06	1	1	2
A U Rashid	16	26	3	556	82	24.17	0	3	9
Ajmal Shahzad	11	16	2	320	70	22.85	0	1	0
A McGrath	12	23	0	485	115	21.08	1	1	12
R J Sidebottom	16	25	6	389	61	20.47	0	2	2
S A Patterson	11	16	6	130	53	13.00	0	1	4

Also played

Player	M.	I.	N.O.	Runs	H.S.	Avge	100s	50s	ct/st
J A Rudolph	4	8	1	318	120	45.42	1	1	2
G L Brophy	7	11	3	355	177*	44.37	1	1	7/1
T T Bresnan	3	5	1	175	87	43.75	0	1	1
C J Geldart	1	1	0	34	34	34.00	0	0	1
D J Wainwright	4	6	1	146	62	29.20	0	1	0
S M Guy	1	2	0	15	8	7.50	0	0	1/0
G S Randhawa	1	1	0	5	5	5.00	0	0	0
Moin A Ashraf	7	9	1	27	8*	3.37	0	0	0
O J Hannon-Dalby	5	8	2	10	6*	1.66	0	0	0
A E Lilley	1	1	0	0	0	0.00	0	0	0
A Z Lees	1	1	0	0	0	0.00	0	0	0
B P Gibson	1	1	1	1	1*	—	0	0	6/0
I Wardlaw	1	0	0	—	—	—	0	0	0

BOWLING

(Qualification 10 wickets)

Player	Overs	Mdns	Runs	Wkts	Avge	Best	5wI	10wM
T T Bresnan	97	27	252	13	19.38	4-50	0	0
R J Sidebottom	467.4	107	1364	62	22.00	7-37	3	1
R M Pyrah	266.4	54	956	29	32.96	5-58	1	0
Ajmal Shahzad	301.3	46	1116	30	37.20	5-61	2	0
D J Wainwright	143.5	31	451	12	37.58	6-40	1	0
A U Rashid	448.3	56	1692	39	43.38	6-77	2	1
S A Patterson	294.5	55	973	21	46.33	4-51	0	0
T L Best	198	20	793	18	44.05	4-86	0	0
Moin A Ashraf	158	22	561	11	51.00	3-71	0	0

Also bowled

Player	Overs	Mdns	Runs	Wkts	Avge	Best	5wI	10wM
J J Sayers	13.2	3	31	3	10.33	3-15	0	0
G S Randhawa	21	4	62	2	31.00	2-54	0	0
J E Root	84.3	13	319	7	45.57	3-33	0	0
A McGrath	21	2	56	1	56.00	1-14	0	0
I Wardlaw	13	0	68	1	68.00	1-68	0	0
O J Hannon-Dalby	121	10	398	4	99.50	1-28	0	0
A E Lilley	13	4	34	0	—	0- 3	0	0
J A Rudolph	6	0	28	0	—	0-28	0	0
G L Brophy	2	0	6	0	—	0- 6	0	0
A Lyth	2	1	10	0	—	0- 0	0	0
G S Ballance	2	0	11	0	—	0-11	0	0

Other First-Class Match
England Lions v. Sri Lanka A

Played at North Marine Road, Scarborough, on August 2, 3, 4 and 5, 2011

Match drawn at 5.32pm on the Fourth Day

Toss won by England Lions

Close of play: First Day, Sri Lanka A 27-0 (Warnapura 22*, Thirimanna 5*): Second Day, Sri Lanka A 329-8 (Senanayaka 12*, Alvitigala 11*); Third Day, England Lions 182-3 (Taylor 15*, Kieswetter 24*)

ENGLAND LIONS

First Innings		Second Innings	
J E Root, lbw b Premaratna	10	c Thirimanne b Serasinghe	66
A D Hales, c Silva b Premaratna	50	c Karunaratna b Senanayaka	42
R S Bopara, c Silva b Alvitigala	19	c Karunaratna b Senanayaka	25
* J W A Taylor, lbw b Serasinghe	76	b Serasinghe	98
§ C Kieswetter, c Karunaratna b Senanayaka	0	c Perera b Senanayake	32
J M Bairstow, c Serasinghe b Kulasekara	50	not out	109
S R Patel, c Karunaratna b Senanayaka	52	not out	27
S G Borthwick, c Karunaratna b Senanayaka	3		
J A R Harris, not out	7		
S C Meaker, b Senanayaka	12		
J W Dernbach, c Warnapura b Senanayaka	1		
Extras (b 10, lb 1, w 1, nb 7)	19	Extras (b 5, lb 2, w 5, nb 4)	16
Total (81 overs)	299	Total (5 wkts dec, 104 overs)	415

FoW: 1-25 (Root), 2-73 (Bopara), 3-99 (Hales), 4-100 (Kieswetter), 5-207 (Bairstow)
1st 6-275 (Patel), 7-277 (Taylor), 8-281 (Borthwick), 9-295 (Meaker), 10-299 (Dernbach)
2nd 1-98 (Hales), 2-143 (Bopara), 3-143 (Root), 4-214 (Kieswetter), 5-360 (Taylor)

	O	M	R	W		O	M	R	W
Kulasekara	17	1	73	1	Kulasekara	17	3	71	0
Alvitigala	18	1	70	1	Premaratna	15	1	67	0
Premaratna	14	2	51	2	Senanayaka	11	2	35	0
Senanayaka	17	3	47	5	Alvitigala	39	3	160	3
Thirimanna	7	0	30	0	Serasinghe	22	3	75	2
Serasinghe	8	1	17	1					

SRI LANKA A

First Innings		Second Innings	
S M Warnapura, lbw b Dernbach	34	not out	79
H D R L Thirimanna, lbw b Meaker	22	not out	36
F D M Karunaratna, c Bairstow b Harris	43		
* § J K Silva, c Kieswetter b Harris	89		
P B B Rajapaksha, c Taylor b Dernbach	76		
P S C Serasinghe, run out	13		
K J Perera, c Kieswetter b Dernbach	1		
C K B Kulasekara, lbw b Harris	4		
S M S M Senanayaka, c Kieswetter b Meaker	38		
K G Alvitigala, c Kieswetter b Meaker	36		
W G H N Premaratne, not out	0		
Extras (b 21, lb 4, nb 8)	33	Extras (b 4, w 1, nb 7)	12
Total (102.3 overs)	389	Total (0 wkts, 28 overs)	127

FoW: 1-60 (Warnapura), 2-73 (Thirimanna), 3-145 (Karunaratna), 4-292 (Rajapaksha), 5-304 (Silva), 6-305 (Perera), 7-308 (Serasinghe), 8-325 (Kulasekara), 9-386 (Alvitigala) 10-389 (Senanayaka)

	O	M	R	W		O	M	R	W
Dernbach	26	5	104	3	Dernbach	4	1	11	0
Harris	28	4	97	3	Harris	3	1	6	0
Meaker	13.3	5	37	3	Borthwick	11	1	44	0
Bopara	9	1	41	0	Meaker	5	1	42	0
Borthwick	17	2	57	0	Bopara	2	0	14	0
Patel	9	0	28	0	Patel	3	1	6	0

Umpires: N G B Cook and J W Lloyds   Scorers: M Snook and H Clayton

NOTE: K J Perera kept wicket during England Lions' second innings.

CLYDESDALE BANK 40
HIGHLIGHTS OF 2011

Totals of 250 and over (3)

    302-4   v. Sussex at Scarborough (won)
    275-4   v. Middlesex at Lord's (won)
    254-7   v. Kent at Canterbury (won)

Match aggregates of 500 and over (2)

    528   Yorkshire (275-4) defeated Middlesex (253) by 22 runs at Lord's
    569   Yorkshire (302-4) defeated Sussex (267) by 35 runs at Scarborough

Century Partnerships (6)

For the 1st wicket (1)

    142   J A Rudolph and A Lyth   v. Sussex at Scarborough

For the 2nd wicket (1)

    113   J A Rudolph and J M Bairstow   v. Sussex at Scarborough

For the 3rd wicket (3)

    124   A W Gale and J E Root   v. Kent at Canterbury
    122   J M Bairstow and J E Root   v. Worcestershire at Leeds
    105   J M Bairstow and A McGrath   v. Middlesex at Lord's

For the 4th wicket (1)

    111   A Lyth and G S Ballance   v. Middlesex at Leeds

Centuries (3)

    J M Bairstow (1)
        114   v. Middlesex at Lord's
    A W Gale (1)
        112   v. Kent at Canterbury
    J A Rudolph (1)
        132*   v. Sussex at Scarborough

4 wickets in an innings (1)

    S A Patterson (1)
        4 for 28 v. Worcestershire at Worcester

3 catches in an innings (1)

    A W Gale (1)
        3   v. Kent at Leeds

3 dismissals in an innings (3)

    J M Bairstow (1)
        3 (2ct, 1st) v. Netherlands at Amsterdam
    G L Brophy (1)
        3 (2ct, 1st) v. Kent at Canterbury
    S M Guy (1)
        3 (2ct, 1st) v. Worcestershire at Worcester

Debuts (4)

List A cricket: M A Ashraf, O J Hannon-Dalby, A Z Lees and I Wardlaw

Clydesdale Bank 40 Matches Played by Yorkshire in 2011

*Captain
§Wicket Keeper

WINNERS

SURREY, who beat Somerset by 5 wickets *(D/L method)*

PREVIOUS WINNERS		*Yorkshire's Position*
		1st Group B
2010	Warwickshire	

NATIONAL LEAGUE

PREVIOUS WINNERS		*Yorkshire's Position*
1999	Lancashire	5th Div 1
2000	Gloucestershire	2nd Div 1
2001	Kent	6th Div 1
2002	Glamorgan	4th Div 1
2003	Surrey	8th Div 1
2004	Glamorgan	4th Div 2
2005	Essex	8th Div 2
2006	Essex	9th Div 2
2007	Worcestershire	6th Div 2
2008	Sussex	2nd Div2
2009	Sussex	7th Div1

SUNDAY LEAGUE

PREVIOUS WINNERS		*Yorkshire's Position*	PREVIOUS WINNERS		*Yorkshire's Position*
1969	Lancashire	8th	1984	Essex	=13th
1970	Lancashire	14th	1985	Essex	6th
1971	Worcestershire	15th	1986	Hampshire	8th
1972	Kent	4th	1987	Worcestershire	=13th
1973	Kent	2nd	1988	Worcestershire	8th
1974	Leicestershire	=6th	1989	Lancashire	11th
1975	Hampshire	=5th	1990	Derbyshire	6th
1976	Kent	15th	1991	Nottinghamshire	7th
1977	Leicestershire	=13th	1992	Middlesex	15th
1978	Hampshire	7th	1993	Glamorgan	9th
1979	Somerset	=4th	1994	Warwickshire	5th
1980	Warwickshire	=14th	1995	Kent	12th
1981	Essex	=7th	1996	Surrey	3rd
1982	Sussex	16th	1997	Warwickshire	10th
1983	Yorkshire	1st	1998	Lancashire	9th

Match-By-Match Reports	DAVE CALDWELL
Scorecards	JOHN POTTER
Pictures	SIMON WILKINSON
	VAUGHN RIDLEY

Played at Headingley Carnegie, Leeds, on April 24, 2011

Netherlands won by 2 runs

Toss won by Netherlands
Netherlands 2 points, Yorkshire 0 points

NETHERLANDS

E S Szwarczynski, c Brophy b Shahzad	....	15
§ W Barresi, b Sidebottom	....	2
T L W Cooper, b Rashid	....	32
M R Swart, b Pyrah	....	13
T N de Grooth, run out (Rashid)	....	7
* P W Borren, lbw Rashid	....	18
B P Kruger, c Lyth b Root	....	11
S Mott, not out	....	50
Mudassar Bukhari, c Rashid b Sidebottom	....	25
T J Heggelman, not out	....	3
P M Seelaar	Did not bat	
Extras b 5, lb 4, w 5		14
Total (8 wkts, 40 overs)	....	190

FoW: 1-4 (Barresi), 2-22 (Szwarczynski), 3-49 (Swart), 4-68 (Cooper), 5-72 (de Grooth),
6-101 (Borren), 7-112 (Kruger), 8-173 (Bukhari)

	O	M	R	W
Shahzad	8	0	48	1
Sidebottom	8	0	29	2
Pyrah	8	1	31	1
Patterson	4	0	34	0
Rashid	8	0	20	2
Root	4	0	19	1

YORKSHIRE

* A W Gale, c Cooper b Bukhari	....	9
A Lyth, c and b Mott	....	2
J E Root, c Cooper b Borren	....	5
A McGrath, lbw b Bukhari	....	0
J M Bairstow, c Swart b Kruger	....	7
§ G L Brophy, c Swart b Borren	....	7
R M Pyrah, c Szwarczynski b Bukhari	....	69
A Shahzad, c Bukhari b Seelaar	....	11
A U Rashid, not out	....	42
R J Sidebottom, run out (Borren/Barresi)	....	29
S A Patterson	Did not bat	
Extras lb 1, w 4, nb 2		7
Total (9 wkts, 40 overs)	....	188

FoW: 1-15 (Lyth), 2-15 (Gale), 3-15 (McGrath). 4-27 (Bairstow), 5-27 (Root),
6-54 (Brophy), 7-79 (Shahzad), 8-147 (Pyrah), 9-188 (Sidebottom)

	O	M	R	W
Mott	8	1	43	1
Mudassar Bukhari	8	1	26	3
Kruger	5	1	24	1
Borren	8	0	39	2
Seelaar	8	0	41	1
Swart	3	0	14	0

Umpires: S A Garratt and P Willey
Scorers: J T Potter and R F Onstein

Dutch courage shocks

The Netherlands shocked Yorkshire as they won this tense opening fixture by two runs to conclude a dismal weekend for the hosts after their capitulation against Nottinghamshire in the County Championship.

The thrilling finish was not on the cards after Yorkshire had slumped to 79-7 chasing 191.

The White Rose top order made a disastrous start to their reply on a slow pitch as Bukhari's gentle seam bowling reduced them to 27-5, the first five all out for single figures.

Had it not been for an eighth-wicket stand of 68 in 12 overs between Pyrah and Rashid the contest would have been over long before the last ball.

Pyrah contributed a career-best 69 from 82 balls with six boundaries, and Rashid offered good support with excellent running between the wickets before Pyrah

Out of the ground: Richard Pyrah celebrates the wicket of Michael Swart

fell at 147. Carnegie needed 44 from four overs, and some lusty blows, in particular from Sidebottom, took them to within 19 of victory with six balls to go. The first ball yielded a scampered single, giving Sidebottom the strike: he launched a huge six over long-on...a dot ball and a quick two followed. The last-but-one ball disappeared on to the rugby-stand roof, leaving four to get off the last delivery. Sidebottom was run out going for a second run, and the spirited fightback fell just short. Rashid was unbeaten on 42, Sidebottom crashing 29 in 14 balls.

Yorkshire caused the Dutch plenty of problems with the moving ball. Sidebottom bowled Barresi in his first over, while Szwarczynski was caught behind off Shahzad for 15. Two more quick wickets fell, Rashid and Pyrah taking one apiece, and the Dutch were 68-4. At 112-7 Yorkshire were looking to finish them off in timely fashion, but a sixth-wicket stand of 61 between Mott and Bukhari in nigh on eight overs propelled them to a competitive total. Mott was unbeaten with a fine half-century from 46 balls, and Rashid was the pick for Yorkshire with 2-20.

Clydesdale Bank 40 — Group A
Yorkshire v. Derbyshire

Played at Headingley Carnegie, Leeds, on May 2, 2011

Derbyshire won by 52 runs

Toss won by Derbyshire

Derbyshire 2 points, Yorkshire 0 points

DERBYSHIRE

U T Khawaja, b Shahzad		20
C F Hughes, b Sidebottom		11
W J Durston, c Shahzad b Pyrah		95
G M Smith, b Sidebottom		30
W L Madsen, st Brophy b Rashid		66
J L Clare, lbw b Pyrah		1
P S Jones, c Brophy b Pyrah		8
G T Park, c Pyrah b Rashid		2
* § L D Sutton, not out		2
J Needham, not out		1
T D Groenewald	Did not bat	
Extras lb 1, w 8		9
Total (8 wkts, 40 overs)		245

FoW: 1-26 (Hughes), 2-42 (Khawaja), 3-138 (Smith), 4-203 (Durston), 5-205 (Clare) 6-223 (Jones), 7-238 (Park), 8-242 (Madsen)

	O	M	R	W
Sidebottom	8	0	38	2
Shahzad	8	1	42	1
Pyrah	8	0	41	3
Rashid	8	0	57	2
Wainwright	6	0	48	0
Root	2	0	18	0

YORKSHIRE

* A W Gale, c and b Durston		74
A Lyth, c Park b Groenewald		15
J E Root, lbw b Durston		45
J M Bairstow, c Madsen b Hughes		4
§ G L Brophy, c Madsen b Durston		5
J J Sayers, c Park b Jones		12
R M Pyrah, c Sutton b Clare		3
A Shahzad, lbw b Jones		1
A U Rashid, not out		12
D J Wainwright, c Khawaja b Jones		6
R J Sidebottom, c Khawaja b Clare		8
Extras b 1, lb 5, w 2		8
Total (39 overs)		193

FoW: 1-35 (Lyth), 2-125 (Root), 3-138 (Bairstow), 4-145 (Gale), 5-156 (Brophy), 6-164 (Pyrah), 7-167 (Shahzad), 8-168 (Sayers), 9-177 (Wainwright), 10-193 (Sidebottom),

	O	M	R	W
Durston	7	0	25	3
Jones	7	0	38	3
Groenewald	4	0	21	1
Clare	8	0	28	2
Needham	5	0	32	0
Hughes	8	0	43	1

TV Man of the Match: W J Durston

Umpires: N G B Cook and J H Evans   Scorers: J T Potter and J M Brown

Third Umpire: M J Saggers

Yorkshire v. Derbyshire
Yorkshire struggle to fire

Durston starred with an exceptional all-round performance against a lacklustre Yorkshire who struggled to fire with either bat or ball.

Derbyshire got off to a promising start as left-hand openers Khawaja and Hughes put on 26 before Sidebottom bowled Hughes and Shahzad castled Khawaja with a beauty. 42-2.

Durston and Smith started to rebuild as

Inside-out hands: Joe Root takes the bowlers on, but the reverse-sweep was to end his knock of 45

the bowlers applied good pressure, giving the batsmen little width, Smith very much playing anchor in a stand of 96 before Sidebottom bowled him for a conservative 30 from 44 balls. Durston was now in full flow, spinners Wainwright and Rashid in particular feeling his wrath...but just as a deserved century was nearing Shahzad took a superb catch at short-third-man off Pyrah to leave him five runs short. It was an innings that spanned 99 balls and put his side into a commanding position at 203-4. Pyrah added two late wickets as runs and dismissals came thick and fast in the closing overs. Madsen, the main aggressor, smashed 66 in 41 balls, Derbyshire closing on a challenging 245.

Lyth left at 35 from the first seven overs, and Yorkshire consolidated with Root and Gale playing in resolute fashion. Runs did dry up as Derbyshire's fielding and bowling started to get a grip, and the hosts struggled to wrestle the initiative away from the Falcons. Root and Gale added 90 in 18 overs, but Root, 45, was trapped in front trying an ill advised reverse sweep against Durston. Bairstow followed 13 runs later, holing out to long off, and the pressure increased.

The game-defining moment came with Yorkshire on 145, as Gale drove hard back to Durston, who took a superb low return catch. Gale had made 74 from 86 deliveries, with four fours and two sixes, but the run rate had slipped. With two new batsmen in the task looked less than achievable. Yorkshire almost apologetically gave it up with poor shot selection against accurate bowling and athletic outcricket. Durston completed an excellent day, following his 95 with 3-25 in seven overs.

Clydesdale Bank 40 — Group A
Kent v. Yorkshire

Played at St Lawrence Ground, Canterbury, on May 8, 2011
Yorkshire won by 93 runs

Toss won by Yorkshire   Yorkshire 2 points, Kent 0 points

YORKSHIRE

* A W Gale, run out (Ball/Jones)	112
J M Bairstow, c Stevens b Ball	26
A Lyt, c Jones b Ball	0
J E Root, c Mahmood b Tredwell	43
§ G L Brophy, lbw b Mahmood	28
T T Bresnan, b Coles	9
A Shahzad, c Blake b Mahmood	7
R M Pyrah, retired hurt	0
A U Rashid, not out	7
R J Sidebottom, not out	3
D J Wainwright Did not bat	
Extras b 3, lb 4, w 8, nb 4	19
Total (7 wkts, 40 overs)	254

FoW: 1-40 (Bairstow), 2-40 (Lyt), 3-164 (Root), 4-221 (Brophy), 5-232 (Bresnan), 6-240 (Gale), [7-243 (Pyrah retired hurt)], 7-250 (Shahzad)

	O	M	R	W
Ball	5	0	33	2
Azhar Mahmood	8	1	57	2
Coles	8	0	65	1
Stevens	6	0	24	0
Tredwell	8	0	33	1
Shaw	4	0	27	0
van Jaarsveld	1	0	8	0

KENT

S A Northeast, c Brophy b Sidebottom	3
* R W T Key, c Rashid b Bresnan	18
M van Jaarsveld, c Wainwright b Sidebottom	0
D I Stevens, b Rashid	39
A J Blake, c Brophy b Sidebottom	19
§ G O Jones, b Bresnan	15
Azhar Mahmood, c Rashid b Shahzad	13
J C Tredwell, b Wainwright	25
M T Coles, st Brophy b Rashid	11
A J Ball, not out	2
S A Shaw, c Wainwright b Root	0
Extras lb 4, w 8, nb 4	16
Total	161

FoW: 1-13 (Northeast), 2-13 (van Jaarsveld), 3-46 (Key), 4-74 (Blake), 5-101 (Stevens), 6-116 (Jones), 7-122 (Mahmood), 8-156 (Coles), 9-160 (Tredwell), 10-161 (Shaw)

	O	M	R	W
Sidebottom	4	0	19	2
Bresnan	7	0	34	2
Shahzad	7	0	43	1
Rashid	8	0	30	3
Wainwright	5	0	30	1
Root	0.4	0	1	1

Umpires: R J Bailey and N G C Cowley   Scorers: J T Potter and B L Rodwell

Gale shoots down Spitfires

Gale led from the front with a fine century as Yorkshire got their *CB40* season up and running after two abject performances.

They opted to bat, and the skipper Gale and Bairstow got the proceedings off to a flier with 40 in 21 minutes before Bairstow fell to a splendid catch by Stevens off Ball.

One over later Lyth was caught behind first ball to the

ANDREW GALE: Piloted Yorkshire home with century in 105 balls

same bowler, and Yorkshire needed to regroup. Not that you would have thought it as Gale continued undeterred, striking the ball cleanly on both sides of the wicket. Gale and Root played beautifully in a partnership of 124 in 21 overs: Yorkshire's skipper was the chief run-maker, but Root's 43 in 57 deliveries should not be left without praise. Gale's 50 arrived in 61 balls, his second 50 in 44 balls — sandwiched in between Root's dismissal when he offered a simple catch, reverse-sweeping Tredwell.

Yorkshire's total could have been more significant than the 254 they actually achieved, had they not lost four quick middle-order wickets and endured the worrying sight of the in-form Pyrah leaving the field after being struck on the knee while batting.

Kent in reply never really recovered from losing two wickets at 13. The second was the dangerous Van Jaarsveld, cutting high into the hands off third-man Wainwright to give Sidebottom two wickets in as many balls. Key tamely offered a catch to mid-wicket Rashid with the score on 46, and Blake was next to go for 19, caught behind by Brophy off Rashid. A glimmer of hope arrived as Stevens counter-attacked, but after rattling up 39 he was clean bowled advancing down the track to Rashid, and the Spitfires were badly holed. Rashid and Bresnan were the pick of Yorkshire's attack with five wickets between them, but Root finished it in the 32nd over with Kent 93 runs adrift.

Played at Headingley Carnegie, Leeds, on May 18, 2011

Kent won by 2 wickets

Toss won by Kent   Kent 2 points, Yorkshire 0 points

YORKSHIRE

* A W Gale, b Azhar Mahmood		34
§ J M Bairstow, b Stevens		22
A Lyth, c Stevens b Blake		40
J E Root, b Stevens		6
G S Ballance, run out (Northeast/Jones)		47
L J Hodgson, lbw b Blake		0
A Shahzad, not out		59
A U Rashid, c Key b Coles		3
D J Wainwright, not out		8
R J Sidebottom		
S A Patterson	Did not bat	
Extras lb 2, w 7, nb 2		11
Total (7 wkts, 40 overs)		230

FoW: 1-48 (Gale), 2-60 (Bairstow), 3-77 (Root), 4-145 (Lyth), 5-145 (Hodgson), 6-167 (Ballance), 7-179 (Rashid)

	O	M	R	W
Azhar Mahmood	8	1	45	1
Shaw	4	0	33	0
Stevens	8	1	27	2
Coles	8	0	58	1
Tredwell	7	0	33	0
Riley	3	0	19	0
Blake	2	1	13	2

KENT

S A Northeast, c Gale b Sidebottom		15
* R W T Key, lbw b Patterson		12
M T Coles, c Root b Hodgson		47
M van Jaarsveld, b Shahzad		74
D I Stevens, c Shahzad b Rashid		1
A J Blake, c Gale b Patterson		19
§ G O Jones, c Gale b Shahzad		39
Azhar Mahmood, b Patterson		0
J C Tredwell, not out		12
S A Shaw, not out		4
A E N Riley	Did not bat	
Extras lb 4, w 3, nb 2		9
Total (8 wkts, 39.4 overs)		232

FoW: 1-27 (Northeast), 2-44 (Key), 3-99 (Coles), 4-101 (Stevens), 5-137 (Blake), 6-195 (van Jaarsveld), 7-197 (Mahmood), 8-227 (Jones)

	O	M	R	W
Shahzad	7.4	0	63	2
Sidebottom	8	0	32	1
Patterson	8	0	45	3
Rashid	6	0	31	1
Hodgson	7	1	39	1
Wainwright	3	0	18	0

Umpires: J W Lloyds and N A Mallender   Scorers: J T Potter and J C Foley

The Spitfires shoot back

Lucky escape: Skipper Andrew Gale is dropped by bowler Ashley Shaw during his innings of 34

It really was a game of two halves for all-rounder Shahzad.

First, he savaged Kent's bowlers with a brutal, unbeaten 59 in Yorkshire's 230.

Then his radar was found wanting as he had the ball in his hand with the game in Yorkshire's grip.

At 175-5 after 32 overs Shahzad came back to find van Jaarsveld in uncompromising mood: he was despatched for five consecutive boundaries before he hit the stumps to end van Jaarsveld's knock of 74 in 65 balls.

This had put Kent in pole position, but Yorkshire's bowlers began to find control and some movement, Patterson in particular providing a cool head under pressure. Kent needed four from the last over: Shahzad returned...and celebrated first ball as Jones lobbed a catch to the off-side, where Gale pounced. Then two dot balls...Shaw clubbed the fourth to the mid-wicket fence and victory.

Earlier, Yorkshire found the going a little tough, especially after Gale left in the seventh over at 48. Runs in the middle overs were a scarcity, and despite a well constructed 68 for the fourth wicket from Ballance and Lyth the hosts looked likely to fall a long way short of 200. A typically accurate spell from Stevens was followed by Blake, who saw Lyth cut hard into backward point's hands and then trapped Hodgson in front. Shahzad and Ballance collided, leaving the young left-hander a long way out after making a fine 47. Shahzad and Wainwright repaired some of the damage with a cracking 33 off the last 10 balls, and Shahzad's 59 in 34 balls with eight fours and three sixes was a personal best.

Clydesdale Bank 40 — Group A
Worcestershire v. Yorkshire

Played at New Road, Worcester, on May 22, 2011

Yorkshire won by 7 wickets

Toss won by Worcestershire   Yorkshire 2 points, Worcestershire 0 points

WORCESTERSHIRE

* M M Ali, c Guy b Patterson	9
V S Solanki, b Hannon-Dalby	4
A N Kervezee, c Guy b Hannon-Dalby	12
N D Pinner, st Guy b Patterson	2
J G Cameron, c Ballance b Patterson	51
A Kapil, lbw b Rashid	44
G M Andrew, c Lyth b Patterson	3
§ B J M Scott, c Wainwright b Rashid	7
S H Choudhry, not out	8
C D Whelan, b Hodgson	6
J D Shantry, not out	2
Extras lb 4, w 3	7
Total (9 wkts, 40 overs)	155

FoW: 1-14 (Solanki), 2-14 (Ali), 3-26 (Pinner), 4-30 (Kervezee), 5-118 (Kap
6-129 (Andrew), 7-137 (Cameron), 8-138 (Scott), 9-150 (Whelan)

	O	M	R	W
Hannon-Dalby	6	1	22	2
Patterson	8	2	28	4
Hodgson	5	0	14	1
Wainwright	8	0	27	0
Rashid	8	0	41	2
Root	5	1	19	0

YORKSHIRE

* A W Gale, c Shantry b Ali	56
G S Ballance, st Scott b Choudhry	27
A Lyth, run out (Kervezee/Scott)	49
J E Root, not out	11
G L Brophy, not out	0
§ S M Guy	
A U Rashid	
L J Hodgson Did not bat	
O J Hannon-Dalby	
D J Wainwright	
S A Patterson	
Extras b 4, lb 5, w 4	13
Total (3 wkts, 36.3 overs)	156

FoW: 1-59 (Ballance), 2-132 (Gale), 3-154 (Lyth)

	O	M	R	W
Shantry	6	0	20	0
Andrew	4.3	0	23	0
Whelan	5	1	20	0
Ali	8	0	38	1
Choudhry	8	1	25	1
Kapil	5	1	21	0

Umpires: R J Bailey and M A Gough   Scorers: J T Potter and N D Smith

Worcestershire v. Yorkshire

Medium-pacers heal wound

Medium-pace duo Hannon-Dalby and Patterson gave Yorkshire just the fillip required after their agonising *Roses* defeat the day before.

Yorkshire lost the toss, but the seam attack got straight to work on a slow track offering a hint of lateral movement.

Hannon-Dalby struck first, bowling Royals skipper Solanki for four, but Patterson snapped up

OLIVER HANNON-DALBY: Just the fillip to lift the pricked *White Rose*

two more — thank in no small part to emergency wicket-keeper Simon Guy, who played because of Bairstow's England call-up and Brophy's injury. Guy took a superb catch standing up to despatch Ali, followed by swift work to stump Pinner down the leg-side and reduce the hosts to 26-3. It became 30-4 as Guy took Kervezee regulation-style off Hannon-Dalby. A useful 88 from Cameron and Kapil gave Worcestershire some hope of posting a target of substance, but Rashid trapped Kapil lbw for 14. Andrew came and went before top-scorer Cameron departed for an 89-ball 51, neatly taken in the deep by Ballance to give Patterson his fourth scalp. Worcester rather limped along to 155-9 from their 40 overs, Patterson finishing with 4-28 and Hannon-Dalby 2-22.

With a small total to defend, Worcestershire needed early wickets: an opening stand of 59 between the in-form skipper Gale and the promoted Ballance was not what the Royals hosts were looking for. Both batsmen were in good touch, Ballance timing the ball well on both sides of the wicket before the introduction of promising slow left-armer Choudhry. The young spinner showed good control and flight in his eight overs, tempting Ballance out of his ground to be stumped by Scott for a 37-ball 27. Gale started to drop anchor after a good start, allowing Lyth to free his arms: this pair added 73 before Gale miscued Ali to Shantry after compiling 56 from 89 deliveries. Lyth advanced to 49 with minimal fuss, but going for a highly dangerous second run brought about his demise, leaving Root and Brophy to seal the victory.

Clydesdale Bank 40 — Group A
Yorkshire v. Middlesex

Played at Headingley Carnegie, Leeds, on July 17, 2011
Start delayed by rain — match reduced to 31 over per side
Middlesex won by 6 wickets

Toss won by Middlesex   Middlesex 2 points, Yorkshire 0 points

YORKSHIRE

* A W Gale, c and b Crook	....	15
J J Sayers, c Malan b Collymore	....	0
A Lyth, c Dexter b Collymore	....	52
A McGrath, run out (Crook)	....	1
G S Ballance, c Newman b Dexter	....	71
§ J M Bairstow, c Crook b Collymore	....	33
A Shahzad, b Dexter	....	0
R M Pyrah, not out	....	2
A Rashid, not out	....	0
R J Sidebottom		
B W Sanderson	Did not bat	
Extras b 1, lb 1, w 16, nb4	....	22
Total (7 wkts, 31 overs)	....	196

FoW: 1-1 (Sayers), 2-36 (Gale), 3-41 (McGrath), 4-152 (Ballance), 5-159 (Lyth), 6-169 (Shahzad), 7-194 (Bairstow)

	O	M	R	W
Collymore	6	0	52	3
Finn	6	1	38	0
Murtagh	7	0	30	0
Crook	6	0	37	1
Dexter	5	0	26	2
Dalrymple	1	0	11	0

MIDDLESEX

S A Newman, c Sidebottom b Sanderson	....	33
D J Malan, c Bairstow b Rashid	....	31
P R Stirling, b Sidebottom	....	57
C J L Rogers, c Sidebottom b Shahzad	....	51
* N J Dexter, not out	....	7
J W M Dalrymple, not out	....	8
§ J A Simpson		
C D Collymore		
S P Crook	Did not bat	
T J Murtagh		
S T Finn		
Extras b 6, lb 1, w 3	....	10
Total (4 wkts, 30 overs)	....	197

FoW: 1-59 (Newman), 2-64 (Malan), 3-180 (Stirling), 4-182 (Rogers)

	O	M	R	W
Shahzad	6	0	34	1
Sidebottom	7	0	39	1
Pyrah	4	0	33	0
Sanderson	6	0	36	1
Rashid	6	0	38	1
McGrath	1	0	11	0

Umpires: D J Millns and R T Robinson   Scorers: J T Potter and D K Shelley

Panthers and thunderers

GARY BALLANCE
Scintillating with Lyth

A scintillating stand between Ballance and Lyth, which produced 111 runs at a thunderous rate, could not prevent Yorkshire being well beaten in this rain-affected tussle.

Yorkshire showed little or no attacking intent while limping to 53-3 from the first 16 overs, but they added a remarkable 143 in the next 15 of a match cut to 31 overs a side.

Sayers fell in the first over, wicket-keeper Dexter making a hash of a regulation catch — only to see the ball deflected into the waiting hands of Malan at first slip.

Gale followed after a real struggle for this usually fluent opener, and McGrath continued his dismal trot with a run-out from a direct hit.

Ballance and Lyth found the going tough as the home supporters grew restless — but suddenly Ballance took the attack apart, thrashing Finn for 17 in one over and despatching Crook to all parts for 22 in the next. The 100 partnership was up in 83 balls before Ballance, who appeared nigh on invincible, holed out to Newman off Dexter for a superb 71 in 53 balls.

Lyth was next to go, taken in the deep for 52 from 73 deliveries, and the scene was set for Bairstow, who hit Collymore for three successive sixes before falling at the fourth attempt to a fine catch by Dexter on the fence. Collymore's over cost 27 runs, and Bairstow had cracked up 33 from 15 balls.

Early wickets must have brought Yorkshire victory...McGrath put down a straightforward slip chance, and Middlesex Panthers were seldom in trouble. Newman and Malan got away to a rapid start before Middlesex were pegged back slightly, but Stirling and Rogers combined effortlessly to put on 116 in 13 overs: Stirling made 57 in 37 balls, Rogers 51 from 44. Panthers eased over the line with an over remaining.

153

Clydesdale Bank 40 — Group A
Sussex v. Yorkshire

Played at The County Ground, Hove, on July 27, 2011
Sussex won by 76 runs

Toss won by Sussex   Sussex 2 points, Yorkshire 0 points

SUSSEX

E C Joyce, c Shahzad b Sidebottom		7
C D Nash, b Pyrah		79
L Vincent, lbw b Rashid		21
M W Goodwin, c and b Wainwright		22
*M H Yardy, c Bairstow b Rashid		15
L W P Wells, b Wainwright		17
§ B C Brown, not out		50
Rana Naved-ul-Hasan, b Shahzad		4
Naved Arif Gondal, not out		17
C J Liddle		
M S Panesar	Did not bat	
Extras lb 5, w 9		14
Total (7 wkts, 40 overs)		246

FoW: 1-16 (Joyce), 2-66 (Vincent), 3-111 (Goodwin), 4-150 (Yardy), 5-164 (Nash), 6-178 (Wells), 7-187 (Rana Naved-ul-Hasan)

	O	M	R	W
Sidebottom	8	0	57	1
Shahzad	8	0	56	1
Rashid	8	0	35	2
Pyrah	7	0	48	1
Wainwright	8	0	37	2
Sayers	1	0	8	0

YORKSHIRE

*A W Gale, lbw b Naved Arif Gondal		0
J J Sayers, st Brown b Panesar		25
A Lyth, c Goodwin b Rana Naved-ul-Hasan		33
J A Rudolph, b Yardy		35
G S Ballance, c Vincent b Nash		8
§ J M Bairstow, c Rana Naved-ul-Hasan b Yardy		43
A Shahzad, b Rana Naved-ul-Hasan		0
R M Pyrah, run out (Vincent/Brown)		12
A U Rashid, lbw b Yardy		0
R J Sidebottom, c Vincent b Yardy		0
D J Wainwright, not out		0
Extras lb 2, w 12		14
Total (34.3 overs)		170

FoW: 1-0 (Gale), 2-65 (Lyth), 3-76 (Sayers), 4-95 (Ballance), 5-139 (Rudolph), 6-14. (Shahzad), 7-166 (Pyrah), 8-166 (Rashid), 9-170 (Sidebottom), 10-170 (Bairstow)

	O	M	R	W
Naved Arif Gondal	6	0	29	1
Liddle	3	0	24	0
Rana Naved-ul-Hasan	6	0	34	2
Panesar	8	0	36	1
Nash	8	0	35	1
Yardy	3.3	0	10	4

TV Man of the Match: C D Nash

Umpires: N G C Cowley and J F Steele   Scorers: J T Potter and M J Charman

Third Umpire: D J Millns

Bairstow braves the Sharks

JONATHAN BAIRSTOW: Mission impossible, but that's entertainment

The Sharks kept their jaws clamped on the group's top spot with convincing performance against a far from impressive and visibly jaded Yorkshire.

The visitors clawed their way back into the game after Nash had seemingly put Sussex into pole position, but their bowling and fielding crumbled during the batting power play.

With Naved-ul-Hasan seventh out at 187 Sussex probably would have settled for 215. Instead, young Ben Brown struck a savage maiden one-day 50, which took them to near 250, always likely to be a stiff target on a slow pitch. Brown, dropped by Wainwright off the first ball of the 39th over from Sidebottom, produced some clean hitting as the over yielded 23 and his 50 came in 30 balls.

Nash had been the main thorn in Yorkshire's side earlier, sharing in useful stands with Vincent, Goodwin and Yardy, before Pyrah bowled him for 79 from 84 balls. Yorkshire's two best bowlers were spinners Rashid and Wainwright, who both bowled accurately but were let down at times by some sloppy outcricket.

Skipper Gale departed on the fourth ball of the innings, lbw to a marginal decision off Arif, but Sayers and Lyth regrouped: this pair added 55, both looking in good, positive form, but once Lyth was taken on the deep-square-leg fence for 33 and Sayers stumped by the impressive Brown for 25 the run chase started to look hopeless. Ballance left at 95, while Rudolph struggled to 35 before he was bowled by Yardy.

Only Bairstow was left to attempt the unlikely: he hammered an entertaining 43 from 44 balls, but he, too, was to fall to Yardy's left-arm darts as the England one-day spinner took the last two wickets in successive deliveries of the 35th over to finish with 4-10 from 3.3 overs.

Clydesdale Bank 40 — Group A
Netherlands v. Yorkshire

Played at VRA Ground, Amstelveen, Amsterdam, on July 31, 2011
Netherlands won by 4 wickets

Toss won by Yorkshire   Netherlands 2 points, Yorkshire 0 points

YORKSHIRE

* A W Gale, c Gruijters b Borren		16
J J Sayers, c Gruijters b Mott		1
A Lyth, c Seelaar b Bukhari		1
§ J M Bairstow, b Borren		4
G S Ballance, run out (Diepeveen)		24
A U Rashid, c Szwarczynski b Mott		43
A Shahzad, c de Grooth b Seelaar		12
R M Pyrah, c Diepeveen b Bukhari		7
D J Wainwright, not out		3
B W Sanderson, c Barresi b Bukhari		2
I Wardlaw, run out (Diepeveen)		1
Extras b 1, lb 1, w 7		9
Total (39.1 overs)		123

FoW: 1-11 (Sayers), 2-12 (Lyth), 3-20 (Bairstow), 4-46 (Gale), 5-60 (Ballance), 6-8? (Shahzad), 7-113 (Rashid), 8-115 (Pyrah), 9-118 (Sanderson), 10-123 (Wardlaw)

	O	M	R	W
Mudassar Bukhari	8	0	28	3
Mott	8	3	18	2
Borren	7.1	0	24	2
Heggelman	5	1	13	0
Swart	7	0	23	0
Seelaar	4	0	15	1

NETHERLANDS

§ W Barresi, run out (Wainwright/Bairstow)		21
E S Szwarczynski, c Bairstow b Shahzad		0
Mudassar Bukhari, c Sanderson b Rashid		27
M R Swart, st Bairstow b Wainwright		4
W P Diepeveen, c Lyth b Wainwright		22
* P W Borren, c Bairstow b Shahzad		34
T N de Grooth, not out		4
T G J Gruijters, not out		0
S Mott		
T J Heggelman	Did not bat	
P M Seelaar		
Extras b 2, lb 6, w 4, nb 2		14
Total (6 wkts, 27.3 overs)		126

FoW: 1-3 (Szwarczynski), 2-55 (Barresi), 3-61 (Mudassar Bukhari), 4-77 (Swart), 5-12? (Diepeveen), 6-122 (Borren)

	O	M	R	W
Shahzad	6	1	22	2
Sanderson	4	1	12	0
Pyrah	2	0	18	0
Wardlaw	4	0	15	0
Rashid	6	1	24	1
Wainwright	5.3	1	27	2

Umpires: M J D Bodenham and J F Steele   Scorers: J T Potter and R F Onstein

Double Dutch disaster

ADIL RASHID
Top score and wicket

Yorkshire's dismal season in all formats took another nosedive as a dreadful batting display gave former whipping boys the Netherlands their second victory over the *White Rose* in 2011.

Opting to bat, Yorkshire were in the mire from the off: Sayers edged to second slip while Lyth played a poor shot and was caught by Seelaar. Bairstow was bowled by Borren, and it was 20-3 in the ninth over.

Gale steadied the ship momentarily, but the runs did not come, and the skipper's dogged rearguard ended at 46 as he edged behind to give Borren his second scalp. Rashid and Ballance advanced the total to 60, but Ballance was run out for 24 going for a suicidal single. Despite Rashid's best efforts the 100 did not arrive until the 35th over, and once the leg-spinner was out for a top-score 43, turning a full toss straight to mid-wicket, the innings subsided to a wholly unacceptable 123.

Szwarczynski was caught behind off his first ball when the hosts replied, but Barresi and Bukhari steadied the ship with a stand of 52 in a little under 10 overs. The situation may have been different had Gale not spilled two catches at the expense of Sanderson and Wardlaw to keep Bukhari there.

Two quick wickets redressed the balance to make it 77-4, and Rashid's introduction caused some problems for the Dutchmen. Gale dropped a third chance at mid-wicket to reprieve Diepeveen. Borren remained positive at the other end, and these two almost saw their side over the line — only to fall in quick succession with a couple of runs needed. de Grooth hit them off with over 12 overs to go to condemn Yorkshire to a defeat that Cricket Director Martyn Moxon condemned as totally unacceptable. Yorkshire's batting and fielding was, without question, a huge disappointment, especially for the loyal band of fans who made the trip.

Clydesdale Bank 40 — Group A
Middlesex v. Yorkshire

Played at Lord's on August 10, 2011
Yorkshire won by 22 runs

Toss won by Middlesex   Yorkshire 2 points, Middlesex 0 points

YORKSHIRE

* A W Gale, c Simpson b Collymore		0
A Rudolph, c Stirling b Crook		40
§ J M Bairstow, b Dexter		114
A McGrath, c Dalrymple b Murtagh		63
G S Ballance, not out		34
A Shahzad, not out		15
A U Rashid		
R M Pyrah		
D J Wainwright	Did not bat	
R J Sidebottom		
B W Sanderson		
Extras lb 3, w 6		9
Total (4 wkts, 40 overs)		275

FoW: 1-0 (Gale), 2-85 (Rudolph), 3-190 (McGrath), 4-228 (Bairstow)

	O	M	R	W
Collymore	7	1	55	1
Murtagh	8	0	59	1
Dexter	8	0	55	1
Crook	8	1	46	1
Dalrymple	2	0	11	0
Smith	7	0	46	0

MIDDLESEX

S A Newman, b Sidebottom		4
D L Malan, lbw b Rashid		14
P R Stirling, c Pyrah b Wainwright		68
C J L Rogers, lbw b Rashid		11
* N J Dexter, c Wainwright b Rashid		27
J W M Dalrymple, run out (Bairstow)		14
§ J A Simpson, run out (Rudolph/Wainwright)		12
S P Crook, c Gale b Sidebottom		61
T M J Smith, c Sidebottom b Pyrah		27
T J Murtagh, c Ballance b Pyrah		6
C D Collymore, not out		1
Extras lb 3, w 5		8
Total		253

FoW: 1-4 (Newman), 2-47 (Malan), 3-77 (Rogers), 4-124 (Stirling), 5-132 (Dexter), 6-14 (Dalrymple), 7-160 (Simpson), 8-226 (Smith), 9-248 (Crook), 10-253 (Murtagh)

	O	M	R	W
Sidebottom	7	0	59	2
Shahzad	5	0	34	0
Rashid	8	0	43	3
Pyrah	5	0	42	2
Wainwright	8	1	26	1
Rudolph	2	0	14	0
Sanderson	3	0	32	0

Umpires: M A Gough and S J O'Shaughnessy   Scorers: J T Potter and D K Shelley

Bairstow blitz on Lord's

JONATHAN BAIRSTOW
Maiden one-day century

Carnegie dented the Panthers' semi-final hopes with an excellent victory in this high-scoring encounter. Bairstow completed his first one-day 100 at the 25th attempt, and Yorkshire were always that one step too far, despite a spirited run chase.

The match received the police go-ahead during the morning after the rioting that dominated the national and international news, but instead of turning out under lights the players emerged at midday.

Bairstow entered to the fifth ball after Gale was taken at slip for a duck. Rudolph played superbly in a partnership of 85 in 15 overs before holing out in the covers for 40 off 50 balls.

McGrath, 63, showed some much-needed confidence in his 60-ball stay for a stand of 105 with Bairstow, who was blazing a trail at the other end. The young batsman raced to his 50 in 47 balls, and he was in full flow when he played across the line to Dexter after making a magnificent 114 from 87 balls, with nine fours and three sixes. Ballance finished the innings with a well executed 34 in 24 deliveries to leave Middlesex with a big ask.

Sidebottom bowled Newman early, but Irish batsman Stirling took the ight to Yorkshire. Wickets were going down at the other end as Stirling crashed the ball to all parts for his 68 from 47 balls, 46 of his runs coming in boundaries. His stylish knock ended with a smart catch by Pyrah lose on the off-side to Wainwright. Middlesex slumped to 160-7 before Crook enjoyed a do-or-die eighth-wicket stand of 66 in 11 overs with Smith. The game fell away from the Panthers as Smith, 27, and then Crook — who hammered a valiant 61 from 40 balls — were dismissed y Pyrah and Sidebottom, the innings closing after 38 overs.

Derbyshire v. Yorkshire

Played at Queen's Park, Chesterfield, on August 14, 2011
Derbyshire won by 6 wickets

Toss won by Yorkshire   Derbyshire 2 points, Yorkshire 0 point

YORKSHIRE

* J A Rudolph, st Poynton b Knight	75
J J Sayers, c Poynton b Park	23
A Lyth, b Smith	16
A McGrath, c Park b Smith	6
G S Ballance, not out	81
§ G L Brophy, c Hughes b Groenewald	6
A U Rashid, c Guptill b Park	17
D J Wainwright, run out (Park/Groenewald)	0
S A Patterson, not out	0
M A Ashraf	
O J Hannon-Dalby Did not bat	
Extras b 1, lb 5, w 4	10
Total (7 wkts, 40 overs)	234

FoW: 1-61 (Sayers), 2-105 (Lyth), 3-115 (McGrath), 4-147 (Rudolph), 5-165 (Brophy), 6-217 (Rashid), 7-228 (Wainwright)

	O	M	R	W
Groenewald	8	0	54	1
Durston	4	0	31	0
Footitt	4	0	41	0
Whiteley	3	0	16	0
Park	5	0	21	2
Knight	8	0	35	1
Smith	8	0	30	2

DERBYSHIRE

C F Hughes, c Hannon-Dalby b Wainwright	38
M J Guptill, not out	103
W J Durston, b Rashid	20
* W L Madsen, c Wainwright b Patterson	28
G M Smith, c Ashraf b Patterson	1
R A Whiteley, not out	31
G T Park	
§ T Poynton	
T C Knight Did not bat	
T D Groenewald	
M H A Footitt	
Extras b 5, w 7, nb 2	14
Total (4 wkts, 33.4 overs)	235

FoW: 1-82 (Hughes), 2-114 (Durston), 3-171 (Madsen), 4-178 (Smith)

	O	M	R	W
Hannon-Dalby	3.4	0	34	0
Ashraf	5	0	48	0
Rashid	6	0	44	1
Patterson	7	0	29	2
Wainwright	6	0	45	1
McGrath	6	0	30	0

Umpires: M J D Bodenham and P Willey   Scorers: J T Potter and J M Brown

Derbyshire v. Yorkshire

Neighbours...yet another loss

Yorkshire turned in a below-par performance in front of a bumper Chesterfield crowd, with New Zealand opener Guptill the star as he crashed an unbeaten century in 83 deliveries.

Carnegie opted to bat on what looked a belter of a track, Rudolph and Sayers combining nicely in an opening partnership of 61 in under 40 minutes before Sayers was snapped up down the leg side for 23.

Rudolph raced to his 50 in 46 balls, but he became a little tied down and the runs dried up. Lyth and then McGrath also struggled to negoti-

GARY BALLANCE: Superb form

ate the spin and medium-pace attack. Rudolph finally departed for 75 from 81 balls as he tried hit young spinner Knight down the ground, only to be stumped by some distance. Brophy miscued to Hughes at mid-off, and Yorkshire were in danger of not reaching 200. Ballance was in superb form as he took his growing reputation up another notch with an unbeaten 81 in 65 deliveries. The visitors helped themselves to 52 from the last four overs to post what looked like a decent total.

This notion was given short shrift as Guptill and Hughes combined effortlessly to crack up 82 in next to no time and leave Yorkshire a mountain to climb. Wainwright bagged Hughes with his first delivery to get the vital breakthrough, taken in the deep by Hannon-Dalby for 38, and Durston was next to fall, bowled by Rashid for 20. Guptill remained unperturbed, completing his 50 in 34 balls with shots on both sides of the wicket as Yorkshire's bowling and fielding became more ragged and lacking in intensity. Patterson brought some cheer for the travelling support with two quick wickets, but Guptill reached his hundred and an easy win for his side with six overs to spare, leaving Yorkshire with yet another deserved defeat against their near neighbours.

Clydesdale Bank 40 — Group A
Yorkshire v. Sussex

Played at North Marine Road, Scarborough, on August 21, 2011
Yorkshire won by 35 runs

Toss won by Sussex   Yorkshire 2 points, Sussex 0 points

YORKSHIRE

* J A Rudolph, not out		132
A Lyth, b Panesar		73
J M Bairstow, c Vincent b Parnell		52
§ G L Brophy, b Liddle		7
G S Ballance, b Panesar		14
A McGrath, not out		6
A U Rashid		
D J Wainwright		
S A Patterson	Did not bat	
M A Ashraf		
O J Hannon-Dalby		
Extras lb 10, w 4, nb 4		18
Total (4 wkts, 40 overs)		302

FoW: 1-142 (Lyth), 2-255 (Bairstow), 3-280 (Brophy), 4-296 (Ballance)

	O	M	R	W
Liddle	6	0	48	1
Naved Arif Gondal	7	0	57	0
Parnell	8	0	48	2
Yardy	7	0	56	0
Panesar	8	0	49	1
Nash	4	0	34	0
Total (36.5 overs)				

SUSSEX

E C Joyce, c Hannon-Dalby b Rashid		21
C D Nash, c Bairstow b Patterson		3
L Vincent, c Ballance b Hannon-Dalby		35
M W Goodwin, c Rashid b Patterson		9
* M H Yardy, b Rashid		53
J S Gatting, c and b Wainwright		19
§ B C Brown, run out (Bairstow/Brophy)		60
W D Parnell, c Brophy b Rashid		47
Naved Arif Gondal, c Ballance b Hannon-Dalby		8
C J Liddle, b Ashraf		6
M S Panesar, not out		1
Extras lb 2, w 3		5
Total (36.5 overs)		267

FoW: 1-22 (Joyce), 2-36 (Nash), 3-52 (Goodwin), 4-80 (Vincent), 5-136 (Gatting), 6-160 (Yardy), 7-227 (Parnell), 8-247 (Arif), 9-259 (Liddle), 10-267 (Brown)

	O	M	R	W
Hannon-Dalby	7	0	53	2
Patterson	6	0	37	2
Rashid	8	0	64	3
Wainwright	8	0	59	1
Ashraf	7.5	0	52	1

Umpires: N G B Cook and T E Jesty   Scorers: J T Potter and P Elford

Rudolph revenge on Sharks

JACQUES RUDOLPH: 132 not out was his seventh century at resort

Returning hero Rudolph ran up his second hundred in as many days as Yorkshire inflicted a rare defeat on group leaders Sussex in front of another packed resort crowd.

Rudolph, fresh from a near match-winning 120 in the Championship match the day before, was in exquisite touch with an unbeaten 132 from 112 deliveries — his seventh century at Scarborough.

The South African shared an opening stand of 142 in 22 overs with Lyth who, too, was in irrepressible form: the Whitby-born left-hander produced a lovely innings which combined touch, placement and power in equal measure as he cruised to 73 in 68 balls. Lyth had a slice of luck as Panesar spilled a simple chance behind square in the first over, but after that blemish neither looked troubled.

Panesar did get his man — a little later than he would have wished, as he bowled Lyth on the sweep. Bairstow, clearly a man high in form and confidence, joined Rudolph and the pair eased into another century partnership. Bairstow had 52 from 45 balls when he was expertly taken by Vincent at long-off. 255-2. Brophy fell early, but Ballance added a few scintillating late boundaries to take Carnegie over the 300 mark.

Joyce made a positive start against Hannon-Dalby, and a close finish could have been in the offing, but three fairly quick wickets ensured that the Sharks were always kept in check, despite some spirited and entertaining knocks from the middle-order. Patterson took two wickets in a useful opening burst, although runs did continue to flow at both ends.

Vincent looked in fine fettle until he was third out, brilliantly taken by Ballance in the deep off Hannon-Dalby. Wainwright took a hard return catch to dismiss Gatting after he had added 56 with Yardy...who continued on his way to 50 from 39 balls, but then tried to carve Rashid away and was bowled. Parnell with 47 from 28 balls and Brown with 60 from 51 added 67 in quick time to leave Yorkshire more than a little worried, but once Parnell was caught at the wicket they could close the game out.

Clydesdale Bank 40 — Group A
Yorkshire v. Worcestershire

Played at Headingley Carnegie, Leeds, on August 29, 2011

Yorkshire won by 6 wickets

Toss won by Yorkshire   Yorkshire 2 points, Worcestershire 2 points

WORCESTERSHIRE

M M Ali, c Bairstow b Ashraf		26
J K Manuel, c Root b Patterson		32
A N Kervezee, lbw b Hannon-Dalby		21
J G Cameron, c Hannon-Dalby b Wainwright		5
* D K H Mitchell, not out		81
A Kapil, c Shahzad b Wainwright		20
G M Andrew, c Lyth b Shahzad		11
§ B J M Scott, not out		22
B L D'Oliveira		
J D Shantry	Did not bat	
N L Harrison		
Extras b 1, lb 4, w 7		12
Total (6 wkts, 40 overs)		230

FoW: 1-56 (Ali), 2-72 (Manuel), 3-89 (Cameron), 4-90 (Kervezee), 5-147 (Kapil), 6-170 (Andrew)

	O	M	R	W
Shahzad	8	0	45	1
Hannon-Dalby	5	0	35	1
Patterson	7	0	51	1
Ashraf	5	0	29	1
Wainwright	8	0	33	2
Root	7	0	32	0

YORKSHIRE

A Lyth, c Ali b Harrison		33
* J J Sayers, c Cameron b Harrison		10
§ J M Bairstow, c D'Oliveira b Kapil		80
J E Root, c Mitchell b D'Oliveira		62
G S Ballance, not out		25
A Z Lees, not out		12
O J Hannon-Dalby		
D J Wainwright		
S A Patterson	Did not bat	
A Shahzad		
M A Ashraf		
Extras lb 5, w 4		9
Total (4 wkts, 38.1 overs)		231

FoW: 1-32 (Sayers), 2-51 (Lyth), 3-173 (Bairstow), 4-204 (Root)

	O	M	R	W
Shantry	7.1	0	42	0
Harrison	8	1	43	2
Andrew	7	0	35	0
D'Oliveira	6	0	40	1
Ali	3	0	24	0
Mitchell	2	0	12	0
Kapil	5	0	30	1

Umpires: M J D Bodenham and S C Gale   Scorers: J T Potter and N D Smith

Young ones condemn Royals

Bairstow struck an aggressive 80, with good support from Root, as Carnegie condemned the Royals to bottom spot. Bairstow used only 67 balls, hitting six fours and four sixes, and his side chased down the required 231 with 11 balls remaining.

Yorkshire gave a debut to Academy graduate Alex Lees, 18, while Royals handed a first appearance to leg-spinner Brett D'Oliveira, son of Damian and grandson of the late Basil.

Acting Yorkshire skipper Sayers decided to field, but he was soon in contemplative

Nice catch: Yorkshire's Ajmal Shahzad holds Aneesh Kapil

mood as the first pair raced to 56 in a little over 40 balls before Ashraf struck in his first over, Ali edging behind to Bairstow for 26. Manuel soon followed, comfortably taken by Root on the off-side fence off Patterson for 32, and when Cameron and Kervezee fell in quick succession, leaving Worcestershire 90-4, Yorkshire were looking to wrap up the innings swiftly. Mitchell and Kapil had other ideas, adding 57 until Kapil, 20, was caught on the sweep by Shahzad to give Wainwright a deserved wicket. Mitchell continued with a variety of partners to finish unbeaten on 81 from 80 deliveries, his partnership of 60 for the unbroken seventh wicket with Scott taking Royals to a challenging 230.

Lyth looked in fine form as he reached 33 from 31 deliveries, but both he and Sayers went to the fast-medium Harrison, and Yorkshire were 51-2. This brought together Bairstow and Root, who went about their business in no-nonsense fashion: Root played anchor while Bairstow blazed away, and Carnegie were well ahead of the asking rate as Bairstow laid waste to Harrison, ruining the young bowler's analysis as one over went for 17 runs. The total had advanced to 173 when Bairstow played one cavalier shot too many and was pouched by D'Oliveira on the cover boundary. Root took anchor once more as Ballance played his shots — but Root edged to slip Mitchell to give D'Oliveira his maiden wicket. Lees struck his second ball for four, and Ballance finished the proceedings with a six off Shantry to give young Yorkshire an excellent win.

Clydesdale Bank 40

FINAL TABLES 2011

GROUP A

		P	W	L	T	NR/A	PTS	NRR
1	Sussex Sharks (A1) *	12	8	4	0	0	16	1.070
2	Middlesex Panthers (B6)	12	8	4	0	0	16	0.213
3	Derbyshire Falcons (B4)	12	6	5	1	0	13	-0.079
4	Kent Spitfires (C2)	12	6	6	0	0	12	-0.017
5	Netherlands (B7)	12	5	5	1	1	12	-0.361
6	**Yorkshire Carnegie (B1**	**12**	**5**	**7**	**0**	**0**	**10**	**-0.147**
7	Worcestershire Royals (A5)	12	2	9	0	1	5	-0.710

GROUP B

		P	W	L	T	NR/A	PTS	NRR
1	Surrey Lions) (A3) *	12	10	1	0	1	21	1.047
2	Durham Dynamos (C5) *	12	9	2	0	1	19	0.901
3	Northamptonshire Steelbacks (B5)	12	6	6	0	0	12	-0.304
4	Hampshire Royals (C4)	12	5	6	0	1	11	0.224
5	Warwickshire Bears (C1)	12	5	7	0	0	10	-0.274
6	Leicestershire Foxes (C6)	12	2	8	0	2	6	-0.833
7	Scottish Saltires (C7)	12	2	9	0	1	5	-0.857

GROUP C

		P	W	L	T	NR/A	PTS	NRR
1	Somerset (A1) *	12	9	2	0	1	19	1.008
2	Nottinghamshire Outlaws (C3)	12	7	4	0	1	15	0.260
3	Essex Eagles (B2)	12	6	3	0	3	15	0.255
4	Lancashire Lightning (A4)	12	6	5	0	1	13	-0.172
5	Glamorgan Dragons (A7)	12	4	5	0	3	11	0.161
6	Gloucestershire Gladiators (B3)	12	4	8	0	0	8	-0.488
7	Unicorns (A6)	12	1	10	0	1	3	-0.640

* Qualified for Semi-Finals

(2010 positions in brackets)

YORKSHIRE AVERAGES 2011

CLYDESDALE BANK 40

Played 12   Won 5   Lost 7

BATTING AND FIELDING
(Qualification 4 completed innings)

Player	M.	I.	N.O.	Runs	H.S.	Avge	100s	50s	ct/st
G S Ballance	9	9	3	331	81*	55.16	0	2	4
M Bairstow	10	10	0	385	114	38.50	1	2	6/1
A W Gale	9	9	0	316	112	35.11	1	2	4
E Root	6	6	1	172	62	34.40	0	1	2
A U Rashid	11	8	4	124	43	31.00	0	0	4
A Lyth	11	11	0	314	73	28.54	0	2	4
R M Pyrah	7	6	2	93	69	23.25	0	1	2
A McGrath	5	5	1	76	63	19.00	0	1	0
Ajmal Shahzad	9	8	2	105	59*	17.50	0	1	4
J Sayers	6	6	0	71	25	11.83	0	0	0
G L Brophy	6	6	1	53	28	10.60	0	0	5/2

Also played

Player	M.	I.	N.O.	Runs	H.S.	Avge	100s	50s	ct/st
A Rudolph	4	4	1	282	132*	94.00	1	1	0
R J Sidebottom	7	4	1	40	29	13.33	0	0	3
T T Bresnan	1	1	0	9	9	9.00	0	0	0
D J Wainwright	10	5	3	17	8*	8.50	0	0	7
B W Sanderson	3	1	0	2	2	2.00	0	0	1
I Wardlaw	1	1	0	1	1	1.00	0	0	0
L J Hodgson	2	1	0	0	0	0.00	0	0	0
A Z Lees	1	1	1	12	12*	—	0	0	0
S A Patterson	6	1	1	0	0*	—	0	0	0
S M Guy	1	0	0	—	—	—	0	0	2/1
Moin A Ashraf	3	0	0	0	—	—	0	0	1
O J Hannon-Dalby	4	0	0	0	—	—	0	0	3

BOWLING
(Qualification 4 wickets)

Player	Overs	Mdns	Runs	Wkts	Avge	Best	4wI	RPO
S A Patterson	40	2	224	12	18.66	4-28	1	5.60
A U Rashid	80	1	427	21	20.33	3-30	0	5.33
R J Sidebottom	50	0	273	11	24.81	2-19	0	5.46
O J Hannon-Dalby	21.4	1	144	5	28.80	2-22	0	6.64
R M Pyrah	34	1	213	7	30.42	3-41	0	6.26
D J Wainwright	65.3	2	350	10	35.00	2-27	0	5.34
Ajmal Shahzad	63.4	2	387	10	38.70	2-22	0	6.07

Also bowled

Player	Overs	Mdns	Runs	Wkts	Avge	Best	4wI	RPO
T T Bresnan	7	0	34	2	17.00	2-34	0	4.85
L J Hodgson	12	1	53	2	26.50	1-14	0	4.41
J E Root	18.4	1	89	2	44.50	1- 1	0	4.76
Moin A Ashraf	17.5	0	129	2	64.50	1-29	0	7.23
B W Sanderson	13	1	80	1	80.00	1-36	0	6.15
A McGrath	7	0	40	0	—	0-10	0	5.71
I Wardlaw	4	0	15	0	—	0-15	0	3.75
J A Rudolph	2	0	14	0	—	0-14	0	7.00
J J Sayers	1	0	8	0	—	0- 8	0	8.00

Second NatWest Series One-Day International
England v. Sri Lanka

Played at Headingley Carnegie, Leeds, on July 1, 2011

Sri Lanka won by 69 runs

Toss won by England

SRI LANKA

D P M D Jayawardene, st Kieswetter b Swann		144
* T M Dilshan, run out (Broad)		9
L D C Chandimal, run out (Anderson)		5
§ K C Sangakkara, st Kieswetter b Swann		69
A D Mathews, not out		46
K M D N Kulasekara, c Pietersen b Bresnan		13
B M A J Mendis, not out		7
S H T Kandamby		
R A S Lakmal		
S Randiv	Did not bat	
S L Malinga		
Extras lb 5, w 11		16
Total (5 wkts, 50 over)		309

FoW: 1-15 (Dilshan), 2-45 (Chandimal), 3-204 (Sangakkara), 4-271 (Jayawardene) 5-296 (Kulasekara)

	O	M	R	W
Anderson	10	0	44	0
Bresnan	9	0	70	1
Broad	10	0	70	0
Dernbach	9	0	63	0
Swann	10	0	42	2
Pietersen	2	0	15	0

ENGLAND

* A N Cook, c Mathews b Randiv	48
§ C Kieswetter, c Kulasekara b Lakmal	25
I J L Trott, b Lakmal	39
K P Pietersen, c Malinga b Mendis	13
E J G Morgan, st Sangakkara b Radiv	52
I R Bell, c Lakmal b Kulasekara	35
T T Bresnan, c Chandimal b Randiv	2
S C J Broad, st Sangakkara b Mendis	1
G P Swann, not out	13
J M Anderson, b Malinga	0
J W Dernbach, c Kulasekara b Lakmal	5
Extras lb 1, w 6	7
Total (45.5 overs)	240

FoW: 1-53 (Kieswetter), 2-85 (Cook), 3-113 (Pietersen), 4-144 (Trott), 5-201 (Morgan) 6-204 (Bresnan), 7-206(Broad), 8-232 (Bell), 9-233(Malinga), 10-240 (Dernbach)

	O	M	R	W
Dilshan	4	0	29	0
Kulasekara	9	0	39	1
Malinga	8	0	41	1
Lakmal	7.5	0	43	3
Randiv	9	0	43	3
Mendis	6	0	31	2
Mathews	2	0	13	0

Man of the Match: D P M D Jayawardene

Umpires: B F Bowden and R A Kettleborough   Scorers: J T Potter and M Snook
Third Umpire: N J Llong   Fourth Umpire: R J Bailey   Match Referee: A G Hurst

A mirror image

In a congratulatory message to Lancashire Chief Executive Jim Cumbes on the Red Rose winning the LV County Championship in 2011 Yorkshire Vice-President and Club statistician Roy Wilkinson made the following comparison:

In their second innings at Hove in 1959 Sussex batted deep into the final afternoon, being all out for 311 — leaving Yorkshire to score 215 to win. With minutes to spare the runs were made in 28.3 overs at 7.64 per over.

Yorkshire won the Championship.

In their second innings at Taunton in 2011 Somerset batted deep into the final afternoon, being all out for 310 — and leaving Lancashire to score 211 to win. With minutes to spare the runs were made in 29.1 overs at 7.3 per over.

Lancashire won the match and the Championship.

Books raise £4,500

The second-hand bookstall at Headingley Carnegie Cricket Ground, run by Geoff Holmes and Vivien Stone, raised £4,500 last year in aid of the John Featherstone Memorial Foundation. Takings were down on 2010 due to there being no Test match at Headingley, but Geoff said he expected them to be up again this year in view of the Second Test between England and South Africa being staged on the ground from August 2 to 6 in addition to the third NatWest one-day international between England and South Africa on June 22.

Trevor honoured

Yorkshire CCC member Trevor Constantine received the Order of Mercy medal in recognition of his 15 years of voluntary work at Bradford Royal Infirmary. Trevor, chairman and treasurer of the Friends of BRI, received his medal from Lord Linfield, president of the Order of Mercy, in a ceremony at the Mansion House in London on June 1.

FRIENDS LIFE t20
HIGHLIGHTS OF 2011

Win by 8 wickets (1)

Yorkshire (128-2) beat Derbyshire (127-7) at Derby

Totals of 175 and over (1)

178-4   v. Lancashire at Leeds (won)

Match aggregates of 350 and over (2)

377   Nottinghamshire (215-6) defeated Yorkshire (162-8) by 53 runs at Nottingham

365   Leicestershire (191-4) defeated Yorkshire (174-9) by 18 runs *D/L method*
       at Leeds

4 wickets in an innings (3)

R M Pyrah (2)

5 for 16   v. Durham at Scarborough
4 for 21   v. Worcestershire at Leeds

A U Rashid (1)

4 for 26   v. Lancashire at Leeds

Debuts (2)

t20 cricket: J E Root and I Wardlaw

Don't tell him, Pike

A giant pike, 46 inches long and weighing 37 pounds, caught by Major Booth in the River Wye in 1910, is the subject of a legal battle in Worcester, reported *The Times*. The stuffed fish in a glass case was given to Hereford Museum by Major's widow in 1960, the Yorkshire and England all-rounder having been killed on the Somme in 1916. |In 1980, when an angler asked to see this phenomenon, the Museum realised it was missing. The owner of the Portobello Inn has evidence that the fish has been hanging in his skittle alley since at least 1969. The museum has asked for its return.

Friends Life
t20 in 2011

WINNERS

Leicestershire, who beat Somerset by 18 runs

PREVIOUS WINNERS

2003 **Surrey**, who beat Warwickshire by 9 wickets
2004 **Leicestershire,** who beat Surrey by 7 wickets
2005 **Somerset,** who beat Lancashire by 7 wickets
2006 **Leicestershire,** who beat Nottinghamshire by 4 runs
2007 **Kent,** who beat Gloucestershire by 4 wickets
2008 **Middlesex,** who beat Kent by 3 run
2009 **Sussex,** who beat Somerset by 64 runs
2010 **Hampshire**, who beat Somerset by losing fewer wickets
with the scores level

NORTH GROUP

		P	W	L	T	NR	PTS	NRR
1	Nottinghamshire Outlaws (2) *	16	11	2	0	3	25	1.087
2	Leicestershire Foxes (7) *	16	10	2	0	4	24	0.541
3	Lancashire Lightning (3) *	16	9	5	1	1	20	0.459
4	Durham Dynamos (8) *	16	6	6	0	4	16	0.678
5	Worcestershire Royals (9)	16	6	7	0	3	15	-0.089
6	**Yorkshire Carnegie (6)**	**16**	**6**	**7**	**0**	**3**	**15**	**-0.548**
7	Derbyshire Falcons (5)	16	4	8	1	3	12	-0.489
8	Warwickshire Bears (1)	16	4	10	0	2	10	-0.598
9	Northamptonshire Steelbacks (4)	16	2	11	0	3	7	-0.912

SOUTH GROUP

		P	W	L	T	NR	PTS	NRR
1	Hampshire Royals (4) * §	16	11	2	0	3	23	1.093
2	Sussex Sharks (3) *	16	9	5	0	2	20	0.061
3	Kent Spitfires (7) *	16	9	5	0	2	20	-0.205
4	Somerset (1) *	16	7	4	1	4	19	0.978
5	Surrey Lions (5)	16	7	6	0	3	17	0.131
6	Essex Eagles (2)	16	7	7	0	2	16	-0.086
7	Glamorgan Dragons (8)	16	5	9	0	2	12	0.045
8	Gloucestershire Gladiators (9)	16	4	11	0	1	9	-0.473
9	Middlesex Panthers (6)	16	2	12	1	1	6	-1.247

* Qualified for the Quarter-Finals
§ Deducted two points for a poor pitch in 2010

(2010 divisional positions in brackets)

Match-By-Match Reports	DAVE CALDWELL
Scorecards	JOHN POTTER
Pictures	SIMON WILKINSON
	VAUGHN RIDLEY

Friends Life t20 — North Group
Yorkshire v. Warwickshire

Played at Headingley Carnegie, Leeds, on June 3, 2011
Warwickshire won by 5 wickets

Toss won by Warwickshire   Warwickshire 2 points, Yorkshire 0 points

YORKSHIRE

* A W Gale, run out (Piolet/Ambrose)	54
J M Bairstow, c Barker b Miller	11
A Lyth, c Patel b Maddy	33
A McGrath, b Maddy	28
J E Root, c Barker b Carter	7
§ G L Brophy, c Barker b Maddy	1
A U Rashid, c Clarke b Carter	6
R M Pyrah, not out	13
R J Sidebottom, c Clarke b Barker	3
D J Wainwright	
S A Patterson Did not bat	
Extras lb 2, w 1, nb 2	5
Total (8 wkts, 20 overs)	161

FoW: 1-52 (Bairstow), 2-82 (Gale), 3-122 (Lyth), 4-130 (McGrath), 5-136 (Brophy) 6-136 (Root), 7-151 (Rashid), 8-161 (Sidebottom)

	O	M	R	W
Carter	4	0	34	2
Miller	2	0	25	1
Clarke	2	0	18	0
Barker	3	0	28	1
Patel	3	0	17	0
Piolet	4	0	27	0
Maddy	2	0	10	3

WARWICKSHIRE

V Chopra, lbw b Rashid	4
N M Carter, c Brophy b Wainwright	27
W T S Porterfield, lbw b Rashid	64
* J O Troughton, lbw b Root	18
D L Maddy, c Brophy b Rashid	0
§ T R Ambrose, not out	26
R Clarke, not out	21
K H D Barker	
S A Piolet	
J S Patel Did not bat	
A S Miller	
Extras lb 1, w 3	4
Total (5 wkts, 17.5 overs)	164

FoW: 1-4 (Chopra), 2-75 (Carter), 3-116 (Porterfield), 4-116 (Maddy), 5-122 (Troughton)

	O	M	R	W
Rashid	4	0	28	3
Sidebottom	3	0	28	0
Patterson	3.5	0	40	0
Pyrah	3	0	33	0
Wainwright	2	0	22	1
Root	2	0	12	1

Man of the Match: W T S Porterfield

Umpires: J W Lloyds and D J Millns   Scorers: J T Potter and D E Wainwright

Yorkshire v. Warwickshire
Trapped by the Bears

ANDREW GALE: Cruel fall of skipper in imperious form

A gruelling 15 days on the road ended with Yorkshire back on home turf with very little t20 preparation.

Skipper Gale and Bairstow set about the Bears' experienced attack with renewed vim and vigour — the first 50 coming before five overs had been completed. Bairstow mistimed a forcing shot, and was taken by Barker at short-third-man.

Gale looked in imperious form, finding the boundary with consummate ease; his off-side play in particular looked in fine fettle, and Lyth proved a good foil until disaster struck at 82. Lyth sent his partner back while going for a second run: Gale slipped and, despite a valiant dive, was well short of his ground to end a captain's innings of 54.

The tide now turned as Warwickshire's outcricket and miserly bowling proved too much for a middle-order missing the "enforcer" counties often need in the middle to late overs. Lyth fell for 33 in the deep, and McGrath was yorked by Maddy for 28. The boundaries dried up, and the Bears turned the screw: some of their fielding was a joy, typified by Clarke's stunning catch to remove Sidebottom off the last ball which appeared to be sailing for six.

Yorkshire limped to 161-8, a total many feared to be insufficient. So it proved, despite Rashid's quick success against Chopra, sweeping across the line in the first over. The visitors were seldom in trouble: Carter, 37, was his usual combative self, while Porterfield was sublime in his shot placement. The pair added 71 in no little time, and a mid-innings wobble, again spearheaded by Rashid, was not enough. The run rate of a little over six was negotiated with ease by Ambrose and Clarke, and Bears reached the target with 13 balls to spare.

Friends Life t20 — North Group
Nottinghamshire v. Yorkshire

Played at Trent Bridge, Nottingham, on June 5, 2011
Nottinghamshire won by 53 runs

Toss won by Nottinghamshire   Nottinghamshire 2 points, Yorkshire 0 points

NOTTINGHAMSHIRE

A D Hales, c Pyrah b Sidebottom		10
M H Wessels, b Sidebottom b Rashid		4
A C Voges, c Root b McGrath		74
* D J Hussey, c Root b Wainwright		28
S R Patel, c Patterson b McGrath		52
§ C M W Read, not out		34
S J Mullaney, c Wainwright b McGrath		5
S L Elstone, not out		5
B J Phillips		
D J Pattinson	Did not bat	
A Cater		
Extras w 1, nb 2		3
Total (6 wkts, 20 overs)		215

FoW: 1-5 (Wessels), 2-23 (Hales), 3-76 (Hussey), 4-170 (Voges), 5-174 (Patel), 6-191 (Mullaney)

	O	M	R	W
Rashid	3	0	41	1
Sidebottom	4	0	35	1
Patterson	3	0	35	0
Wainwright	3	0	23	1
Pyrah	4	0	42	0
Root	1	0	22	0
McGrath	2	0	17	3

YORKSHIRE

* A W Gale, b Phillips		17
J M Bairstow, c Mullaney b Patel		31
A Lyth, c Mullaney b Carter		43
A McGrath, lbw b Carter		9
§ G L Brophy, c Elstone b Patel		4
J E Root, c Hussey b Pattinson		8
R M Pyrah, c Hussey b Pattinson		9
A U Rashid, c Elstone b Phillips		7
R J Sidebottom, not out		12
D J Wainwright, not out		6
S A Patterson	Did not bat	
Extras lb 7, w 5, nb 4		16
Total (8 wkts, 20 overs)		162

FoW: 1-44 (Gale), 2-74 (Bairstow), 3-114 (Lyth), 4-114 (McGrath), 5-125 (Brophy), 6-127 (Root), 7-134 (Rashid), 8-145 (Pyrah)

	O	M	R	W
Pattinson	4	0	32	2
Phillips	4	0	31	2
Carter	4	0	38	2
Patel	4	0	27	2
Mullaney	4	0	27	0

Man of the Match: S R Patel

Umpires: S A Garratt and P J Hartley   Scorers: J T Potter and L B Hewes

Yorkshire bowlers hammered

ADAM LYTH: Top scorer against record odds

The Outlaws proved why they are many people's tip to go all the way this year with a routine victory against a below par Yorkshire.

They hammered an impressive 215 from their 20 overs — a record for the East Midlands outfit — with superb half-centuries from Patel and Voges, the No. 3 in particular making batting look easy with an explosive 74 from 46 balls.

The Aussie's innings paled in comparison with Patel — whose 52 came from a paltry 23 balls. Rashid once again had a wicket in his first over, Wessels trapped in front third ball, and Hales fell in the power play to former teammate Sidebottom, when he was neatly taken by Pyrah at point.

McGrath cheered the travelling Yorkshire supporters with three late wickets for 17 in two overs, but Read continued his liking for Yorkshire with an unbeaten 34.

Yorkshire were roundly dispatched to all parts, and Wainwright was the only bowler who was able to show any signs of keeping his economy rate down to manageable levels.

Yorkshire's reply was always going to rely heavily on the opening partnership of Bairstow and Gale, and the signs looked promising as 33 runs were gathered in four overs until Gale was castled by an excellent yorker from Phillips and a familiar pattern was presented.

Carnegie struggled once the pace was taken off the ball, boundaries became elusive and the running between the wickets hesitant. Bairstow was dismissed in the deep for 31, top-scorer Lyth was caught for a 27-ball 43, and McGrath was trapped in front next ball. With seven overs remaining the contest was as good as over. Yorkshire's innings subsided and finished 53 runs shy of their target with eight wickets down, Patel completing an excellent day with 2-27 from his allocation.

175

Friends Life t20 — North Group
Yorkshire v. Worcestershire

Played at Headingley Carnegie, Leeds, on June 9, 2011
Yorkshire won by 2 runs

Toss won by Yorkshire   Yorkshire 2 points, Worcestershire 0 points

YORKSHIRE

* A W Gale, c Solanki b Shakib al Hasan	....	29
J M Bairstow, lbw b Ali	....	24
A Lyth, c Ali b Choudhry	....	13
A McGrath, c Shantry b Andrew	....	21
§ G L Brophy, c Mitchell b Andrew	....	18
G S Ballance, c Scott b Andrew	....	9
A U Rashid, not out	....	13
R M Pyrah, c and b Shakib al Hasan	....	5
R J Sidebottom, not out	....	16
D J Wainwright		
S A Patterson	Did not bat	
Extras b 1, lb 1, w 2		4
Total (7 wkts, 20 overs)	....	152

FoW: 1-40 (Gale), 2-64 (Lyth), 3-73 (Bairstow), 4-99 (McGrath), 5-114 (Ballance)
6-125 (Brophy), 7-131 (Pyrah)

	O	M	R	W
Wright	2	0	17	0
Shantry	3	0	24	0
Shakib al Hasan	4	0	32	2
Ali	3	0	19	1
Choudhry	4	0	28	1
Andrew	4	0	30	3

WORCESTERSHIRE

M M Ali, c Sidebottom b Rashid	....	1
V S Solanki, c Patterson b Pyrah	....	28
A N Kervezee, lbw b Rashid	....	0
Shakib al Hasan, b Pyrah	....	3
J G Cameron, c Rashid b Pyrah	....	28
* D K H Mitchell, b Rashid	....	15
G M Andrew, not out	....	60
§ B J M Scott, c and b Pyrah	....	0
S H Choudhry, not out	....	5
D G Wright		
J D Shantry	Did not bat	
Extras b 2, lb 5, w 3	....	10
Total (7 wkts, 20 overs)	....	150

FoW: 1-11 (Ali), 2-12 (Kervezee), 3-36 (Solanki), 4-37 (Shakib al Hasan), 5-67 (Mitchell)
6-126 (Cameron), 7-133 (Scott)

	O	M	R	W
Rashid	4	0	19	3
Sidebottom	4	0	17	0
Patterson	4	0	37	0
Pyrah	4	0	21	4
Wainwright	3	0	36	0
McGrath	1	0	13	0

Man of the Match: R M Pyrah

Umpires: R T Robinson and G Sharp   Scorers: J T Potter and N D Smith

Pyrah pick of the victors

REVERSE SWEEP: Bairstow confounds the fielders

Yorkshire got this part of their season off the ground at the third attempt in a nail-biting encounter. They set the Royals a target of 153, and it looked as though a home win was only a few overs away as the visitors slumped to 67-5 and some distance from the required run rate. Then the unlikely pairing of Cameron and Andrew added 59 in six overs before Cameron was caught by Rashid off Pyrah for 26. Scott left next ball to a smart return catch by Pyrah, but the aggressive Andrew was still there.

Twelve were needed off the last over as Sidebottom producing a master class in death bowling. A scrambled bye from the last-but-one ball got Andrew off strike, and Worcester needed a boundary off the final delivery. A fine yorker put paid to that, and the Royals could manage only a bye. Pyrah and Rashid, as was so often the case last season, were the pick of the attack, contributing the seven wickets between them for 40 runs. Sidebottom, miserly in his return, conceded only 17 from his four overs, but Wainwright and Patterson were very much put to the sword. Left-hander Andrew finished with 60 from only 26 balls.

Yorkshire had once again enjoyed an excellent start, spearheaded as ever by skipper Gale, who contributed 29 to the opening stand of 40 before miscuing to mid-on. Lyth was caught for 13 in the deep after the 50 had come up within six overs. Bairstow was trapped playing to leg for 24 in 27 balls, and from this point the wickets fell consistently. Batsmen looked to get themselves set, but the innings never caught fire after the promising start. The decision to open with the two main enforcers is clearly putting too much pressure on the middle-order.

Friends Life t20 — North Group
Lancashire v. Yorkshire

Played at Old Trafford, Manchester, on June 10, 2011
Yorkshire won by 2 wickets

Toss won by Yorkshire   Yorkshire 2 points, Lancashire 0 points

LANCASHIRE

S C Moore, run out (Ballance/Gale)	....	34
T C Smith, lbw b Rashid	....	0
* S J Croft, c Lyth b Rashid	....	6
P J Horton, c Rashid b Azeem Rafiq	....	11
§ G D Cross, b Azeem Rafiq	....	4
J Clark, c Ballance b Azeem Rafiq	....	1
K R Brown, not out	....	34
L A Procter, not out	....	25
S D Parry		
G Keedy	Did not bat	
S C Kerrigan		
Extras b 1, lb 5, w 1,	....	7
Total (7 wkts, 20 overs)	....	122

FoW: 1-1 (Smith), 2-22 (Croft), 3-44 (Horton), 4-52 (Cross), 5-58 (Clark), 6-62 (Moore)

	O	M	R	W
Rashid	4	0	29	2
Sidebottom	4	0	29	0
Pyrah	4	0	28	0
Wainwright	4	0	15	0
Azeem Rafiq	4	0	15	3

YORKSHIRE

* A W Gale, c Brown b Smith	....	16
J M Bairstow, c Horton b Smith	....	10
A Lyth, b Keedy	....	28
A McGrath, c Moore b Procter	....	18
A U Rashid, run out (Procter/Cross)	....	9
§ G L Brophy, c Croft b Procter	....	0
G S Ballance, c Brown b Procter	....	14
R M Pyrah, run out (Croft/Parry)	....	6
Azeem Rafiq, not out	....	11
R J Sidebottom, not out	....	3
D J Wainwright	Did not bat	
Extras lb 2, w 6	....	8
Total (8 wkts, 19.4 overs)	....	123

FoW: 1-18 (Gale), 2-34 (Bairstow), 3-71 (Lyth), 4-75 (McGrath), 5-75 (Brophy), 6-96 (Ballance), 7-107 (Pyrah), 8-108 (Rashid)

	O	M	R	W
Smith	3.4	0	34	2
Kerrigan	4	0	25	0
Parry	4	0	23	0
Keedy	4	0	17	1
Procter	4	0	22	3

Man of the Match: Azeem Rafiq

Umpires: S C Gale and P J Hartley   Scorers: J T Potter and A West
Third Umpire: A Hicks

Rafiq scoops up the points

AZEEM RAFIQ: Man of the Match with three wickets

A thrilling contest went the *White Rose* way — but it looked as though Gale's team had thrown away the points until the Man of the Match Azeem Rafiq took control.

Batting first on an overcast evening, Lancashire were soon on the back foot. Smith was trapped playing a reverse-sweep to Rashid first ball, and Croft was taken easily by Lyth after miscuing the same bowler for six.

The introduction of Rafiq brought instant rewards. The young off-spinner in his first game of the season had Horton caught by Rashid, bowled Cross and tempted Clark to hole out to Ballance.

Lancashire 58-5, which became 62-6 when Moore was run out for 34 from 37 deliveries. Brown and Procter held firm, and slowly eased the home side into a position if not of power, then of relief. They added an unbeaten 60, and a respectable 122 was reached when it had looked as though 100 would be a tall order.

Gale and Bairstow offered simple catches, reducing their side to 34-2, but a steady partnership of 33 between Lyth and McGrath appeared to have Carnegie coasting to victory. The script was turned on its head by Procter, who followed Keedy's wicket of Lyth for 28 by having McGrath mistime to Moore for 18. Procter snared Brophy first ball, thanks to a fine catch at wide gully by Croft, and Ballance was taken in the deep. Pyrah fell short of an ill advised second run, and Rafiq joined Rashid, who was run out for nine. Rafiq scooped his first ball for three; Sidebottom pushed a single, and 11 were needed off the last over. Sidebottom gave the strike to his young partner, who tried his scoop shot again...and missed. Rafiq tried it again...four runs this time...three balls left. The field blocked fine-leg. Smith put it around off-stump, and Rafiq reversed his scoop over short-third-man for the winning boundary.

179

Yorkshire v. Northamptonshire

At Headingley Carnegie, Leeds, on June 12, 2011
Match abandoned without a ball bowled
Yorkshire 1 point, Northamptonshire 1 point

Yorkshire v. Lancashire

Played at Headingley Carnegie, Leeds, on June 17, 2011
Yorkshire won by 11 runs

Toss won by Lancashire   Yorkshire 2 points, Lancashire 0 points

YORKSHIRE

* A W Gale, c Moore b Smith		60
§ J M Bairstow, lbw b Keedy		32
A Lyth, c and b Mahmood		45
G S Ballance, not out		25
A Shahzad, c Cross b Hogg		11
R M Pyrah, not out		1
A McGrath		
A U Rashid		
R J Sidebottom	Did not bat	
Azeem Rafiq		
J E Root		
Extras lb 2, w 2		4
Total (4 wkts, 20 overs)		178

FoW: 1-69 (Bairstow), 2-134 (Gale), 3-164 (Lyth), 4-177 (Shahzad)

	O	M	R	W
Procter	2	0	21	0
Smith	3	0	41	1
Mahmood	4	0	20	1
Hogg	3	0	35	1
Parry	4	0	29	0
Keedy	4	0	30	1

LANCASHIRE

S C Moore, run out (Root)	9
T C Smith, c and b Rashid	16
* S J Croft, b Azeem Rafiq	24
K R Brown, c Azeem Rafiq b Rashid	35
S I Mahmood, lbw b Azeem Rafiq	1
§ G D Cross, lbw b Rashid	30
J Clark, run out (Bairstow)	38
L A Procter, lbw b Rashid	0
K W Hogg, b Shahzad	1
S D Parry, b Sidebottom	5
G Keedy, not out	1
Extras lb 4, w 1, nb 2	7
Total (19.1 overs)	167

FoW: 1-25 (Moore), 2-27 (Smith), 3-65 (Croft), 4-67 (Mahmood), 5-118 (Cross), 6-119 (Brown), 7-120 (Procter), 8-123 (Hogg), 9-137 (Parry), 10-167 (Clark)

	O	M	R	W
Rashid	4	0	26	4
Sidebottom	3.1	0	25	1
Pyrah	4	0	48	0
Shahzad	4	0	35	1
Azeem Rafiq	4	0	29	2

Man of the Match: A W Gale

Umpires: M J D Bodenham and S A Garratt   Scorers: J T Potter and A West

Gale makes it a *Roses* double

ANDREW GALE: Superb 60 set up victory for the spinners

Rashid and Rafiq spun Yorkshire to another thrilling victory against the old enemy with five balls remaining in front of a 13,000 Headingley Carnegie crowd.

Chasing 179 to win, Lancashire were in serious trouble as Rafiq, the hero of the week before, grabbed two wicket in his first over, while Rashid picked up three in five balls seemingly to set up a routine victory.

Clark threw his hand up and lashed the normally economical Pyrah for 24 in the last-but-one over. This propelled the *Red Rose* to 12 runs from victory in the last over with one wicket left.

Keedy failed to get a bat on Sidebottom's first ball, and they went for a bye, but Bairstow was on hand to run out Clark for 38 from 18 deliveries. Rashid contributed 4-28, Rafiq adding to his rising stock with an excellent 2-29, but skipper Gale scooped the Man of the Match award with a superb 60.

Yorkshire, put in to bat, got off to their best start so far, Gale and Bairstow striking the ball sweetly to rattle up 69 in eight overs. Gale went after Procter, while his partner took a distinct liking to Smith, hitting the medium-pacer for two fours and a huge six in quick succession. Mahmood established some control, but Keedy provided the breakthrough when Bairstow was trapped in front on the reverse-sweep after racing to 32 in 19 balls. Lyth kept up the run rate with his captain, and they put on 65 in under eight overs before Gale hit a full toss to Moore at mid-off to end his knock of 60 off 46 balls, with six fours and a six.

Lyth gave a return catch to Mahmood, failing to pick the paceman's slower ball, but his 45 in 33 balls boosted Yorkshire's charge towards their highest score of the tournament to date, and Ballance added a breezy unbeaten 25. Mahmood was the pick of the attack with 1-20.

Friends Life t20 — North Group
Yorkshire v. Derbyshire

Played at Headingley Carnegie, Leeds, on June 22, 2011
Derbyshire won by 12 runs

Toss won by Derbyshire

Derbyshire 2 points, Yorkshire 0 points

DERBYSHIRE

M J Guptill, run out (Rafiq/Bairstow)		1
W J Durston, lbw b Shahzad		5
C F Hughes, b Azeem Rafiq		32
W L Madsen, not out		61
G T Park, st Bairstow b Patterson		31
R A Whiteley, not out		17
* § L D Sutton		
J L Clare		
P S Jones	Did not bat	
T D Groenewald		
T C Knight		
Extras b 1, lb 1, w 1, nb 2		5
Total (4 wkts, 20 overs)		152

FoW: 1-1 (Guptill), 2-15 (Durston), 3-68 (Hughes), 4-127 (Park)

	O	M	R	W
Rashid	4	0	24	0
Shahzad	4	0	27	1
Patterson	4	0	34	1
Pyrah	4	0	32	0
Azeem Rafiq	4	0	33	1

YORKSHIRE

* A W Gale, st Sutton b Durston		2
§ J M Bairstow, c Durston b Hughes		16
A Lyth, c Guptill b Groenewald		17
A McGrath, run out (Madsen/Sutton)		6
J E Root, not out		46
G S Ballance, c Guptill b Jones		46
A Shahzad, not out		0
R M Pyrah		
A U Rashid		
Azeem Rafiq	Did not bat	
S A Patterson		
Extras lb 1, w 6		7
Total (5 wkts, 20 overs)		140

FoW: 1-5 (Gale), 2-31 (Lyth), 3-38 (McGrath), 4-53 (Bairstow), 5-135 (Ballance)

	O	M	R	W
Durston	2	0	16	1
Clare	3	0	20	0
Groenewald	4	0	25	1
Hughes	4	0	25	1
Knight	4	0	27	0
Jones	3	0	26	1

Man of the Match: W L Madsen

Umpires: S C Gale and M A Gough   Scorers: J T Potter and J M Brown
Third Umpire: S J O'Shaughnessy

Yorkshire v. Derbyshire

Victory charge comes too late

Yorkshire's recent good run came to an end after Ballance and Root had left their charge a little later than needed in pursuit of a challenging yet perfectly achievable total.

They added 83 for the fifth wicket, but despite some late blows from Ballance the inexperienced pair let the rate creep to unmanageable levels and, with some big hitters un tapped, they paid the price.

Yorkshire started brightly as Guptill was run out for a single when Rafiq's throw from the leg-side to Bairstow despatched the dangerous Kiwi.

Shahzad had Durston

FIELDING ACE: Yorkshire's Pyrah stops a certain four off his own bowling from Madsen

bw for five, and Derbyshire were struggling at 15-2 with nearly four overs completed. Hughes, normally a free-scoring striker, found it hard at first as Yorkshire kept disciplined lines, but Madsen at the other end kept the board moving without any undue risks. Hughes was bowled by the energised Rafiq, but Park and Madsen cut loose to take their side to a decent total. Madsen top-scored with 61 from 48 balls, but he could manage only three boundaries.

Yorkshire's reply started in poor style as Gale, so often the rock on which their one-day innings is built, was dismissed for two, Sutton completing some superb glove work to provide Durston with the wicket. Lyth and Bairstow then struggled to time the ball with any conviction as Derbyshire's mixture of slow bowlers and medium-pacers showed superb control, backed up with energetic outcricket marshalled by the effervescent Park. In fairness to Root and Ballance, the rate had slipped long before their arrival, and both of their inning showed great maturity. Ballance made 46 from 32 balls and Root finished unbeaten with a 41-ball 46, but with wickets in hand their push for the line was delayed that over too many, leaving their side a long way adrift at the death.

183

Friends Life t20 — North Group
Warwickshire v. Yorkshire

Played at Edgbaston, Birmingham, on June 24, 2011

No result

Toss won by Yorkshire   Yorkshire 1 point, Warwickshire 1 point

WARWICKSHIRE

I J L Trott, run out (Gale/Rashid)	1
N M Carter, b Azeem Rafiq	25
W T S Porterfield, c Azeem Rafiq b Pyrah	34
D L Maddy, b Shahzad	9
* J O Troughton, not out	49
R Clarke, b Pyrah	8
§ T R Ambrose, not out	5
A G Botha	
K H D Barker	
S A Piolet	Did not bat
J S Patel	
Extras lb 1, w 6	7
Total (5 wkts, 18 overs)	138

FoW: 1-1 (Trott), 2-53 (Carter), 3-70 (Maddy), 4-87 Porterfield), 5-110 (Clarke

	O	M	R	W
Rashid	4	0	26	0
Bresnan	3	0	27	1
Shahzad	3	0	25	1
Azeem Rafiq	4	0	26	1
Pyrah	3	0	21	2
McGrath	1	0	12	0

YORKSHIRE

* A W Gale	
§ J M Bairstow	
A Lyth	
A McGrath	
G S Ballance	
J E Root	Did not bat
A Shahzad	
R M Pyrah	
Azeem Rafiq	
A U Rashid	
T T Bresnan	

Umpires: J H Evans and S J O'Shaughnessy   Scorers: J T Potter and D E Wainwright

Warwickshire v. Yorkshire

Yorkshire thwarted by rain

It was a disappointing evening for fans and players alike after constant drizzle almost from the first ball halted proceedings with the Bears 38-5 and the match intriguingly poised.

Umpires Evans and O'Shaughnessy were as fair as they could be in keeping the players out for as long as possible in the conditions.

By the time the match was abandoned some 90 minutes later there were very few spectators in the ground to hear the announcement.

All the pre-match

AJMAL SHAHZAD: Defied slippery surface to seize scalp of Maddy

talk was of the returning Bresnan and a rare appearance for Trott in Warwickshire colours in front of the resplendent new pavilion which, while not open to the public, looked complete bar the shouting.

Gale won the toss, and not surprisingly opted to field. He was soon celebrating a star wicket as Trott was left mid-pitch in a terrible mix-up with Carter. Gale's throw from square-leg ran out the England batsman for a single. Bresnan and Shahzad were struggling on the slippery surface, and Carter and Porterfield profited from some wayward seam bowling until off-spinner Rafiq made the vital breakthrough.

Rafiq bowled Carter for 25 as he advanced down the wicket, and Maddy's castle was wrecked by a very quick full delivery from Shahzad. Porterfield had made 34 from 26 deliveries when he was neatly taken by Rafiq in the deep off Pyrah with the score on 87, and Troughton was looking dangerous as he made his way to an excellent 49 from 30 balls before play had to be brought to an untimely end.

Friends Life t20 — North Group
Worcestershire v. Yorkshire

Played at New Road, Worcester, on June 26, 2011
Worcestershire won by 41 runs

Toss won by Worcestershire   Worcestershire 2 points, Yorkshire 0 point

WORCESTERSHIRE

M M Ali, c Azeem Rafiq b Pyrah		40
V S Solanki, c Rashid b Shahzad		8
A N Kervezee, c Azeem Rafiq b Rashid		56
Shakib al Hasan, c McGrath b Pyrah		5
J G Cameron, c Pyrah b Shahzad		55
G M Andrew, c Pyrah b Shahzad		2
* D K H Mitchell, not out		11
§ B J M Scott, c Lyth b Bresnan		1
S H Choudhry, not out		1
Saeed Ajmal		
J D Shantry	Did not bat	
Extras b 2, lb 1, w 1		4
Total (7 wkts, 20 overs)		183

FoW: 1-30 (Solanki), 2-55 (Ali), 3-70 (Shakib), 4-147 (Kervezee), 5-164 (Andrew), 6-170 (Cameron), 7-171 (Scott)

	O	M	R	W
Rashid	4	0	37	1
Bresnan	4	0	47	1
Shahzad	4	0	30	3
Pyrah	4	0	36	2
Azeem Rafiq	4	0	30	0

YORKSHIRE

* A W Gale, c Cameron b Andrew		20
§ J M Bairstow, c Scott b Shantry		1
A Lyth, st Scott b Shakib		12
A McGrath, b Shakib		4
J E Root, c Scott c Shakib		26
A Shahzad, c Cameron b Shakib		9
G S Ballance, c Andrew b Shantry		26
T T Bresnan, not out		25
A U Rashid, st Scott b Saeed Ajmal		2
R M Pyrah, c Scott b Andrew		10
Azeem Rafiq, c Saeed Ajmal b Andrew		0
Extras b 5, lb 1, w 1		7
Total (18.5 overs)		142

FoW: 1-3 (Bairstow), 2-29 (Gale), 3-37 (McGrath), 4-38 (Lyth), 5-49 (Shahzad), 6-86 (Ballance), 7-112 (Root), 8-131 (Rashid), 9-142 (Pyrah), 10-142 (Azeem Rafiq)

	O	M	R	W
Shantry	3	0	29	2
Andrew	2.5	0	17	3
Shakib al Hasan	4	0	31	4
Saeed Ajmal	3	0	17	1
Ali	4	0	28	0
Choudhry	2	0	14	0

Man of the Match: Shakib al Hasan

Umpires: M R Benson and J F Steele   Scorers: J T Potter and N D Smith

Worcestershire v. Yorkshire
Dogged by inconsistencies

JOE ROOT: Mounted recovery with fellow freshman Gary Ballance

The inconsistencies that have dogged Yorkshire since this competition's inception reared their heads again in a resounding defeat against the spirited and much in form Royals.

The hosts got away to a useful start as Moeen Ali powered his way to 40 off 20 balls, despite losing skipper Solanki early on for eight.

Pyrah, Yorkshire's best bowler on the day, had Ali pouched by Rafiq at mid-wicket, reducing the Royals to 55-2, which became 70-3 when the same bowler saw Shakib neatly taken by McGrath at point. Worcestershire charged on, with Kervezee, 56, and Cameron, 55, sharing a scintillating stand of 77 in 50 deliveries. Yorkshire's bowling and outcricket became ragged. Bresnan, still feeling his way back after injury, found the going tough, conceding 47 runs in his four overs.

Worcestershire's 183 seemed at least 20-30 runs more than Yorkshire would be comfortable chasing — a view that seemed to be shared by a rueful skipper Gale as his side left the field. Carnegie's batsmen were soon in trouble as the top four all perished within the power-play overs. The Royals' joy was evident as the prized scalps of Gale and Bairstow were captured from top edges. Shakib followed with the wickets of McGrath, clean bowled for four, and Lyth two balls later, stumped a considerable distance from safety for 12.

Ballance and Root mounted a recovery of sorts, contributing 26 apiece, but it was a forlorn hope. Yorkshire were well behind the required rate after key wickets had gone down early. A spirited knock from Bresnan, 25, moved Yorkshire to a slightly more respectable 142, but the damage had alreadybeen done. Worcestershire's young slow left-arm bowler, Shakib, finished with career-best figures of 4-31, the ever reliable Andrew contributed 3-17, and the Royals romped home to a resounding 41 run victory.

Friends Life t20 — North Group
Leicestershire v. Yorkshire

Played at Grace Road, Leicester, on June 29, 2011

Leicestershire won by 8 wickets

Toss won by Leicestershire   Leicestershire 2 points, Yorkshire 0 points

YORKSHIRE

* A W Gale, c White b Gurney	67
J J Sayers, b Hoggard	18
A Lyth, c Jefferson b McDonald	13
§ J M Bairstow, c Nixon b McDonald	1
G S Ballance, b McDonald	9
A Shahzad, c Jefferson b Cobb	20
R M Pyrah, lbw b Abdul Razzaq	1
R J Sidebottom, run out (Abdul Razzaq)	2
J E Root, b Gurney	4
Azeem Rafiq, not out	1
A U Rashid, b Gurney	1
Extras lb 4, w 3	7
Total (20 overs)	144

FoW: 1-38 (Sayers), 2-73 (Lyth), 3-79 (Bairstow), 4-101 (Ballance), 5-128 (Shahzad), 6-130 (Pyrah), 7-132 (Sidebottom), 8-141 (Gale), 9-142 (Root), 10-144 (Rashid)

	O	M	R	W
Abdul Razzaq	4	0	38	1
Gurney	4	0	26	3
Hoggard	2	0	20	1
Henderson	4	0	22	0
McDonald	4	0	18	3
Cobb	2	0	16	1

LEICESTERSHIRE

J J Cobb, c Sidebottom b Pyrah		46
A B McDonald, not out		59
W I Jefferson, c and b Pyrah		5
J W A Taylor, not out		33
J du Toit		
Abdul Razzaq		
§ P A Nixon		
W A White	Did not bat	
C W Henderson		
* M J Hoggard		
H F Gurney		
Extras b 1, lb2, w1		4
Total (2 wkts, 16.2 overs)		147

FoW:- 1-74 (Cobb), 2-84 (Jefferson)

	O	M	R	W
Rashid	4	0	30	0
Sidebottom	2.2	0	21	0
Shahzad	3	0	43	0
Azeem Rafiq	3	0	25	0
Pyrah	4	0	25	2

Man of the Match: A B McDonald

Umpires: R A Kettleborough and R T Robinson   Scorers: J T Potter and G A York

Third Umpire: G Sharp

Leicestershire v. Yorkshire

Foxes too hot to handle

Foxes overseas star Andrew McDonald produced a superb all-round display to quash any notion that Yorkshire could go home with two points.

Yorkshire started brightly again after being put in — this time the recalled Sayers was the foil for the explosive Gale. The left-handed duo took the score to 38 before Sayers was bowled by Hoggard for 18 off 13 deliveries, and Lyth and Gale took it to 73, only to see complete collapse and some ordinary batting at best.

Once more Yorkshire were 20-30 runs short of a competitive total. McDonald did the damage with his accurate medium pace, claiming the vital wickets of Lyth, Bairstow and Ballance for 18.

Gale was the only Yorkshire batsmen to show real resistance, but with wickets tumbling around him the skipper's shots became less risky as he tried to hold one end. Shahzad showed intent with 20 from 11 balls including a siz-

ANDREW GALE: Where would we be without him?

able six off Cobb, but Gale finally fell, taken deep on the leg-side off the impressive young left-arm seam bowler Gurney, for 67 in 46 balls with six boundaries. One wondered where Yorkshire would be without him.

Leicestershire set about their target with vim and vigour, the combination of Cobb and McDonald proving too hot for Carnegie's attack to handle. Cobb made a swashbuckling 46 from 25 balls, with the out-of-sorts England hopeful Shahzad conceding 43 runs in his three overs. Pyrah had Cobb taken neatly by Sidebottom, and followed this with the wicket of Jefferson: the dependable medium-pacer took a superb return catch to finish with his side's best figures of 2-25. McDonald, who had been playing second fiddle, now came into his own and to time the ball sweetly. Taylor weighed in with a typically frenetic 33 not out, while his Australian teammate came in with 59 from 47 deliveries.

Foxes were home with nearly four overs to spare.

189

Friends Life t20 — North Group
Northamptonshire v. Yorkshire

Played at The County Ground, Northampton, on July 1, 2011

Yorkshire won by 12 runs

Toss won by Northamptonshire   Yorkshire 2 points, Northamptonshire 0 points

YORKSHIRE

* A W Gale, c Daggett b Evans	....	7
J J Sayers, c O'Brien b Daggett	....	44
A Lyth, c Middlebrook b Hall	....	30
§ J M Bairstow, b Hall	....	5
G S Ballance, c O'Brien b Hall	....	10
J E Root, c Wakely b Botha	....	8
A Shahzad, b Middlebrook	....	12
A U Rashid, c O'Brien b Daggett	....	5
R M Pyrah, lbw b Hall	....	0
Azeem Rafiq, not out	....	10
R J Sidebottom, run out (Wakely)	....	6
Extras b 2, lb 4, w 1	....	7
Total (20 overs)	....	144

FoW: 1-16 (Gale), 2-87 (Lyth), 3-93 (Sayers), 4-97 (Bairstow), 5-106 (Root), 6-12● (Shahzad), 7-127 (Ballance), 8-127 (Pyrah), 9-129 (Rashid), 10-144 (Sidebottom

	O	M	R	W
Brooks	3	0	19	0
Evans	3	0	25	1
Middlebrook	3	0	30	1
Botha	3	0	19	1
Daggett	4	0	22	2
Hall	4	0	23	4

NORTHAMPTONSHIRE

R A White, lbw b Pyrah	....	12
B M Shafayat, lbw b Shahzad	....	0
§ N J O'Brien, c Rafiq b Sidebottom	....	1
A G Wakely, c Ballance b Pyrah	....	38
R I Newton, lbw b Sidebottom	....	37
J Botha, run out (Sidebottom)	....	11
J D Middlebrook, not out	....	9
* A J Hall, b Shahzad	....	10
J A Brooks, not out	....	9
L M Daggett		
L Evans	Did not bat	
Extras lb 1, w 4	....	5
Total (7 wkts, 20 overs)	....	132

FoW: 1-0 (Shafayat), 2-4 (O'Brien), 3-27 (White), 4-76 (Wakely), 5-103 (Botha) 6-103 (Newton), 7-120 (Hall)

	O	M	R	W
Sidebottom	4	1	18	2
Shahzad	4	0	22	2
Pyrah	4	0	32	2
Azeem Rafiq	4	0	30	0
Rashid	4	0	29	0

Man of the Match: J J Sayers

Umpires: S A Garratt and T E Jesty   Scorers: M E Woolley and A C Kingston

Northamptonshire v. Yorkshire

Yorkshire seamers do the job

For the second game in succession Yorkshire capitulated after a promising start — and for the second time in succession they totalled 144.

This time they were indebted to rock-bottom Northamptonshire, who were never seriously in the run chase.

Put in again, Yorkshire were soon without skipper Gale, who lobbed a simple catch to Daggett at mid-on. Sayers and Lyth produced a pleasing partnership, Lyth starting to strike the ball with much-needed confidence.

The stand of 71 ended in the 11th over when Lyth, after an 18-ball 30, gave Hall the first of his four wickets, taken comfortably at mid-off by Middlebrook. Sayers edged Daggett behind for a well constructed 44 from 84 balls, and Yorkshire were 93-3.

As was so often the case this season the middle-order found the pressure of forcing the pace too great. Wickets toppled regularly, and four went down for nine runs, Hall and Daggett turning in the excellent figures of 4-23 and 2-22.

It was the turn of Yorkshire's pacemen to step up to the plate as Sidebottom and Shahzad produced an excellent opening burst: Shafayat was trapped in front for a duck, and it was not until the 10th ball that

RYAN SIDEBOTTOM
Stepped up to the plate

Steelbacks celebrated their first run. With four on the board O'Brien made a needless swipe to mid-off to give Sidebottom his first scalp, and White made slow progress to 12 before Pyrah pinned him in front. Wakeley and Newton made a steady if unspectacular stand of 49 before Wakeley gave a catch to Ballance off Pyrah for 38. Botha was unfortunately run out at the non-striker's end while backing up, and Sidebottom grabbed the key wicket of Newton, lbw for 37, two balls later. Yorkshire's seam attack showed good discipline in the final stages, ensuring that their opponents were always just too far from the run rate.

Friends Life t20 — North Group
Yorkshire v. Nottinghamshire

Played at Headingley Carnegie, Leeds, on July3, 2011

Nottinghamshire won by 6 wickets

Toss won by Yorkshire

Nottinghamshire 2 points, Yorkshire 0 points

YORKSHIRE

* A W Gale, c Fletcher b Adams	....	62
J J Sayers, c Wessels b Fletcher	....	2
A Lyth, run out (Pattinson)	....	16
A McGrath, c Read b White	....	6
G S Ballance, run out (White/Read)	....	3
§ J M Bairstow, not out	....	41
A Shahzad, not out	....	15
R M Pyrah		
A U Rashid		
Azeem Rafiq	Did not bat	
I Wardlaw		
Extras lb 3, w 2, nb 2	....	7
Total (5 wkts, 20 overs)	....	152

FoW: 1-10 (Sayers), 2-42 (Lyth), 3-67 (McGrath), 4-74 (Ballance), 5-107 (Gale

	O	M	R	W
Pattinson	3	0	45	0
Fletcher	4	0	24	1
Adams	3	0	27	1
White	4	0	23	1
Voges	2	0	12	0
Mullaney	4	0	18	0

NOTTINGHAMSHIRE

Tamim Iqbal, c Lyth b Wardlaw	....	47
A D Hales, c McGrath b Pyrah	....	24
M H Wessels, c Lyth b Wardlaw	....	27
* A C Voges, b Azeem Rafiq	....	2
§ C M W Read, not out	....	26
S L Elstone, not out	....	21
G G White		
S J Mullaney		
A R Adams	Did not bat	
D J Pattinson		
L J Fletcher		
Extras lb 1, w 8	....	9
Total (4 wkts, 18.1 overs)	....	156

FoW: 1-41 (Hales), 2-102 (Wessels), 3-102 (Tamim Iqbal), 4-105 ((Voges)

	O	M	R	W
Rashid	4	0	34	0
Shahzad	3	0	27	0
Wardlaw	3.1	0	17	2
Pyrah	4	0	38	1
Azeem Rafiq	4	0	39	1

Man of the Match: Tamim Iqbal

Umpires: N G B Cook and G Sharp

Scorers: J T Potter and L B Hewes

Yorkshire v. Nottinghamshire
Outlaws kill knockout hopes

Ups and downs...the flying bails mean that Darren Pattinson's smart throw was run out Yorkshire's Adam Lyth

Any hopes of Yorkshire appearing in the knock-out stages all but evaporated in this one-sided affair.

They won the toss, opted for first use, and Sayers was taken supremely one-handed at short-extra by Wessels for two.

Lyth and Gale looked untroubled as they moved to 62 at an excellent rate until Lyth was run out by Pattinson for 16. McGrath, who seemed in no sort of form, inside-edged to White and was caught at the wicket, and Ballance ran himself out to leave Yorkshire teetering on 57-4. Captain Gale once again led by example, striking his fourth half-century of the tournament as he received valuable support from Bairstow, now batting in the middle-order where his attributes are so much better suited. The boundaries were hard to find as the medium-pacers took control, and Gale perished on 62 from 55 balls, caught behind square off Adams. Bairstow seized the moment: he launched Pattinson for two mammoth sixes — and survived being caught of a no-ball in his entertaining 41 from 26 balls. Shahzad proved solid company for Bairstow with 15 from 10 deliveries, but the overwhelming feeling of the 5,000-strong crowd was that Yorkshire were 20 runs short.

Nottinghamshire Outlaws coasted to victory. Hales and Iqbal went along brightly until Hales was caught for 24 off 19 balls. Iqbal was joined by Wessels, and the pair with vastly contrasting styles took the game away from Yorkshire with a stand of 61. Debutant Iain Wardlaw, 26, was handed the ball, and the fast-medium right-armer, plucked straight from the Bradford league, picked up his first wicket as Wessels was caught in the deep for 27. Still at 102, Wardlaw was celebrating again when Iqbal was taken at long-on for 47 from 37 deliveries.

Yorkshire's hopes were elevated further as Voges was bowled at 105 reverse-sweeping Rafiq, but Read and Elstone saw Outlaws to victory in the 19th over with no further alarms in unbeaten stand of 51. Wardlaw finished with 2-17 from 3.1 overs, easily his side's best analysis.

Friends Life t20 — North Group
Yorkshire v. Leicestershire

Played at Headingley Carnegie, Leeds, on July 6, 2011
Leicestershire won by 18 runs (D/L method)

Toss won by Yorkshire   Leicestershire 2 points, Yorkshire 0 points

LEICESTERSHIRE

J J Cobb, c Sidebottom b Pyrah	....	26
* A B McDonald, not out	....	96
W I Jefferson, c Sidebottom b Wainwright	....	28
Abdul Razzaq, c Lyth b Sidebottom	....	16
J du Toit, c Bairstow b Shahzad	....	2
W A White, not out	....	12
M A G Boyce		
§ P A Nixon		
C W Henderson	Did not bat	
J K H Naik		
H F Gurney		
Extras b 4, lb 1, w 6	....	11
Total (4 wkts, 19 overs)		191

Rain stopped play at 88-1 off 9.3 overs — 1 over lost

FoW: 1-58 (Cobb), 2-105 (Jefferson), 3-157 (Abdul Razzaq), 4-164 (du Toit)

	O	M	R	W
Rashid	4	0	58	0
Sidebottom	4	0	45	1
Shahzad	4	0	33	1
Pyrah	3	0	26	1
Wainwright	4	0	24	1

D/L target to win: 193 runs off 19 overs

YORKSHIRE

* A W Gale, c and b Cobb	....	20
J J Sayers, c Abdul Razzaq b Henderson	....	27
A Shahzad, b Gurney	....	15
A Lyth, c McDonald b White	....	10
§ G L Brophy, c McDonald b Henderson	....	22
G S Ballance, st Nixon b Naik	....	25
J M Bairstow, c Cobb b Abdul Razzaq	....	25
R M Pyrah, c Cobb b Naik	....	0
A U Rashid, c McDonald b Naik	....	0
R J Sidebottom, not out	....	11
D J Wainwright, not out	....	5
Extras b 2, lb 2, w 8, nb 2	....	14
Total (9 wkts, 19 overs)	....	174

FoW: 1-34 (Gale), 2-53 (Shahzad), 3-75 (Lyth), 4-87 (Sayers), 5-103 (Brophy), 6-145 (Ballance), 7-146 (Pyrah), 8-147 (Rashid), 9-162 (Bairstow)

	O	M	R	W
Abdul Razzaq	4	0	44	1
Gurney	4	0	19	1
Cobb	1	0	14	1
White	3	0	27	1
Henderson	4	0	35	2
McDonald	2	0	28	0
Naik	1	0	3	3

Man of the Match: A B McDonald

Umpires: N G C Cowley and P J Hartley   Scorers: JT Potter and G A York

Starts without a finish

The Foxes confirmed their place in the quarter-finals after a *Duckworth/Lewis* adjustment to Yorkshire's target.

The game, which was cut to 19 overs per side after a first-innings rain break, was always within Foxes' grip after McDonald's superb 6 not out had propelled them to an imposing 191-4.

McDonald's brutal knock took only 7 balls, with nine fours and three sixes, and the commanding Aussie's opening partner, Cobb, was in equally impressive form as they raced to 0 in 23 balls.

Eight runs later Cobb holed out to mid-off. Rain started

Top-scorer: Joe Sayers returns the Foxes' fire as Paul Nixon looks on

to fall, and the players went off in the 10th over for a 45-minute delay. Jefferson struck the ball sweetly on the resumption to reach 28 before Wainwright — Yorkshire's best bowler on the day — induced a miss-hit. Two more wickets fell before McDonald found an accomplice in White, and the last two overs yielded 28 runs off a dispirited Yorkshire.

Yorkshire's batsmen got in, but failed to go on to match-winning scores. Gale, Sayers and Brophy had 20s, while No. 3 Shahzad made 15 in seven balls. Bairstow and Ballance hammered 42 in four overs for the sixth wicket, but 48 were needed from the last four. Naik's first ball had Ballance stumped for 25, and Pyrah and Rashid followed to give Naik 3-3 from his only over. Bairstow fell for 25 as Yorkshire petered out.

The team sheets for Yorkshire's no-result fixture at The Emirates Durham ICG on July 8 appear at the end of these match reports.

195

Friends Life t20 — North Group
Yorkshire v. Durham

Played at North Marine Road, Scarborough, on July 10, 2011

Yorkshire won by 3 wickets

Toss won by Yorkshire

Yorkshire 2 points, Durham 0 point

DURHAM

§ P Mustard, c Wainwright b Pyrah	....	18
G J Muchall, c Wainwright b Pyrah		5
I D Blackwell, c Gale b Sanderson	....	2
D A Miller, c Ballance b Rashid	....	54
P D Collingwood, c Rashid b Pyrah	....	1
* D M Benkenstein, b Pyrah	....	33
G R Breese, c Brophy b Pyrah	....	0
L E Plunkett, run out (Pyrah/Brophy)		12
S G Borthwick, not out	....	6
M E Claydon		
C Rushworth	Did not bat	
Extras b 1, lb 4, w 6, nb 2		13
Total (8 wkts, 20 overs)	....	144

FoW: 1-28 (Mustard), 2-32 (Blackwell), 3-33 (Muchall), 4-39 (Collingwood), 5-1 (Benkenstein), 6-116 (Breese), 7-133 (Miller), 8-144 (Plunkett)

	O	M	R	W
Wardlaw	4	0	21	0
Sanderson	4	0	27	1
Pyrah	4	0	16	5
Wainwright	4	0	39	0
Rashid	4	0	36	1

YORKSHIRE

* A W Gale, c Benkenstein b Plunkett	....	34
J J Sayers, c Breese b Collingwood	....	20
A Lyth, c Breese b Benkenstein	....	5
§ G L Brophy, c Breese b Collingwood	....	0
G S Ballance, c Mustard b Rushworth	....	48
J M Bairstow, c Breese b Benkenstein	....	6
A U Rashid, b Borthwick	....	7
R M Pyrah, not out	....	17
D J Wainwright, not out	....	3
B W Sanderson		
I Wardlaw	Did not bat	
Extras lb 3, w 7	....	10
Total (7 wkts, 19.3 over)	....	150

FoW: 1-42 (Sayers), 2-56 (Gale), 3-58 (Brophy), 4-68 (Lyth), 5-83 (Bairstow) 6-115 (Rashid), 7-132 (Ballance)

	O	M	R	W
Rushworth	4	0	35	1
Claydon	3.3	0	48	0
Collingwood	4	0	15	2
Plunkett	2	0	25	1
Benkenstein	4	0	14	2
Breese	1	0	5	0
Borthwick	1	0	5	1

Man of the Match: R M Pyrah

Umpires: R J Bailey and N L Bainton

Scorers: J T Potter and B Hunt

Yorkshire v. Durham

Herculean Pyrah unchained

A capacity crowd celebrated North Marine Road's first *t20* action with an exciting White Rose victory inspired by Pyrah's Herculean all-round performance.

Coming on first change, the medium-pacer picked up a career-best 5-16, a best bowling performance for either side in a Yorkshire *t20* fixture.

Openers Mustard and Muchall made a bright start with 28 in four overs before Pyrah's introduction, but Mustard chipped to Wainwright at mid-wicket, and his partner fell to the same combi-

RICHARD PYRAH: Career-best five-for and big hits at the death

nation. Sanderson and Rashid captured the key wickets of Blackwell and Collingwood before Pyrah was back in action: he bowled Benkenstein for 33 after a partnership of 77 with Miller; Breese edged his first ball behind, and Plunkett would have provided the Dewsbury-born all-rounder with a hat-trick but for a thin edge onto his pads. South African Miller made 54 from 41 balls before cutting Rashid to backward-point, Durham closing on 144.

This was still a tough total to chase on a slow pitch, but left-handers Gale and Sayers amassed 42 in the first five overs before Sayers gave Breese the first of four catches after completing a rapid 20. Gale was in ominous form before he fell to Plunkett for a 19-ball 34, but there was then a mini-collapse: Lyth departed for five, Brophy first ball, and it was 68-4. Ballance batted superbly as wickets fell, and he was on 48 in the last-but-one over with the total 132 when Rushworth forced the edge and Mustard took it. This left Pyrah on strike in the last over and former Yorkshire fast bowler Claydon with the ball. A boundary and a towering six settled the argument with three balls remaining — leaving Durham's quarter-final hopes in serious jeopardy.

Friends Life t20 — North Group
Derbyshire v. Yorkshire

Played at The County Ground, Derby, on July 15, 2011

Yorkshire won by 8 wickets

Toss won by Derbyshire   Yorkshire 2 points, Derbyshire 0 points

DERBYSHIRE

W J Durston, lbw b Bresnan		10
M J Guptill, b Pyrah		46
G M Smith, lbw b Sanderson		3
W L Madsen, c Lyth b Pyrah		29
R A Whiteley, b Sanderson		12
C F Hughes, c Bairstow b Sanderson		2
J L Clare, b Sanderson		0
A L Hughes, not out		11
P S Jones, not out		10
* § L D Sutton		
M L Turner	Did not bat	
Extras lb 2, nb 2		4
Total (7 wkts, 20 overs)		127

FoW: 1-13 (Durston), 2-32 (Smith), 3-90 (Madsen), 4-90 (Guptill), 5-93 (C F Hughes), 6-93 (Clare), 7-109 (Whiteley)

	O	M	R	W
Wardlaw	4	0	27	0
Bresnan	4	0	32	1
Sanderson	4	0	21	4
Wainwright	4	0	26	0
Pyrah	4	0	19	2

YORKSHIRE

* A W Gale, lbw b Whiteley		30
J J Sayers, lbw b C F Hughes		43
A Lyth, not out		41
J E Root, not out		7
G S Ballance		
§ J M Bairstow		
T T Bresnan		
R M Pyrah	Did not bat	
D J Wainwright		
I Wardlaw		
B W Sanderson		
Extras lb 2, w 5		7
Total (2 wkts, 18 overs)		128

FoW: 1-52 (Gale), 2-95 (Sayers)

	O	M	R	W
Jones	4	0	28	0
Turner	1	0	18	0
Whiteley	2	0	16	1
A L Hughes	3	0	24	0
Smith	4	0	20	0
C F Hughes	4	0	21	1

Man of the Match: B W Sanderson

Umpires: J W Lloyds and P Willey   Scorers: J T Potter and J M Brown

Derbyshire v. Yorkshire

The Yorkshire stranglers

ADAM LYTH: Four fours in one over

Yorkshire cantered to victory after their hosts had struggled to post an imposing target, thanks to fine seam bowling from Sanderson and Pyrah, backed up by excellent outcricket.

Straight from the off Yorkshire took a stranglehold on proceedings. Durston and Smith left early to Bresnan and Sanderson, and despite a solid 58 in 10 overs between Guptill and Madsen the home side could not get the run rate much over six.

Pyrah struck twice in two balls to remove both at 90, and three runs later Sanderson repeated the trick, forcing the edge from Hughes and cleaning up Clare. Derbyshire managed only 34 in the last five overs, Sanderson coming in with 4-21 and Pyrah 2-19.

Yorkshire's reply was far from circumspect, with Gale and Sayers quick to seize the initiative. The 50 was up by the sixth over, Gale racing to a 22-ball 30 with five boundaries before Whiteley trapped him in front. Sayers continued his encouraging *t20* form with a top-score 43 from 38 deliveries before he was lbw working the ball to leg: his reinvention as a one-day opening batsmen had surprised many, but it made sense as the fielding restrictions allowed the steady left-hander to work the gaps and prove the perfect foil for Gale. Lyth and Root took Yorkshire over the line in the 18th over with no alarms, Lyth taking four boundaries of Jones's last over to finish with an unbeaten 41.

Yorkshire's *t20* campaign had been woefully short of the consistency needed. The batting often produced good starts, but the absence of a proven finisher was evident. The bowling relied heavily on Pyrah and Rashid, with too few stepping up to the mark when they had an off day.

Friends Life t20 — North Group
Durham v. Yorkshire

At Durham ICG, Chester-le-Street, on July 8, 2011

No Result

Toss won by Yorkshire

Yorkshire 1 point, Durham 1 point

The teams were announced, and the players took to the field, but rain fell and prevented the match from starting

DURHAM

§ P Mustard
G J Muchall
I D Blackwell
* D M Benkenstein
P D Collingwood
G Onions
G R Breese
S G Borthwick
M E Claydon
L E Plunkett
C Rushworth

YORKSHIRE

* A W Gale
J J Sayers
A Lyth
§ G L Brophy
G S Ballance
J M Bairstow
R M Pyrah
A U Rashid
A Shahzad
D J Wainwright
I Wardlaw

Umpires: J H Evans and P J Hartley

Scorers: J T Potter and B Hunt

YORKSHIRE AVERAGES 2011

FRIENDS LIFE t20

Played 16   Won 6   Lost 7   No result 2   Abandoned 1

BATTING AND FIELDING

(Qualification 4 completed innings)

Player	M.	I.	N.O.	Runs	H.S.	Avge	100s	50s	ct/st
A W Gale	15	13	0	418	67	32.15	0	4	1
J J Sayers	7	6	0	154	44	25.66	0	0	0
A Lyth	15	13	1	306	45	25.50	0	0	6
G S Ballance	13	10	1	215	48	23.88	0	0	3
J E Root	9	7	2	106	46*	21.20	0	0	2
J M Bairstow	15	12	1	203	41*	18.45	0	0	2/1
A Shahzad	9	7	2	82	20	16.40	0	0	0
A McGrath	9	7	0	92	28	13.14	0	0	2
R M Pyrah	15	10	3	62	17*	8.85	0	0	5
G L Brophy	7	6	0	45	22	7.50	0	0	3/0
A U Rashid	14	9	1	50	13*	6.25	0	0	5

Also played

Azeem Rafiq	8	4	3	22	11*	22.00	0	0	5
R J Sidebottom	8	7	4	53	16*	17.66	0	0	5
T T Bresnan	3	1	1	25	25*	—	0	0	0
D J Wainwright	8	3	3	14	6*	—	0	0	3
S A Patterson	4	0	0	0		—	0	0	2
I Wardlaw	4	0	0	0		—	0	0	0
B W Sanderson	2	0	0	0		—	0	0	0

BOWLING

(Qualification 4 wickets)

Player	Overs	Mdns	Runs	Wkts	Avge	Best	4wI	RPO
B W Sanderson	8	0	48	5	9.60	4-21	1	6.00
R M Pyrah	53	0	417	21	19.85	5-16	2	7.86
A Shahzad	29	0	242	9	26.88	3-30	0	8.34
A U Rashid	51	0	417	15	27.80	4-26	1	8.17
Azeem Rafiq	31	0	227	8	28.37	3-15	0	7.32
Sidebottom	28.3	1	218	5	43.60	2-18	0	7.64

Also bowled

A McGrath	4	0	42	3	14.00	3-17	0	10.50
I Wardlaw	11.1	0	65	2	32.50	2-17	0	5.82
J E Root	3	0	34	1	34.00	1-12	0	11.33
T T Bresnan	11	0	106	2	53.00	1-32	0	9.63
D J Wainwright	24	0	185	3	61.66	1-22	0	7.70
S A Patterson	14.5	0	146	1	146.00	1-34	0	9.84

Second Eleven 2011

PLAYERS WHO APPEARED FOR YORKSHIRE SECOND ELEVEN IN 2011
(excluding First Eleven capped players)

Player	Date of Birth	Birthplace	Type
J A R Blain *	January 4, 1979	Edinburgh	RHB/RMF
J E Lee *	December 23, 1988	Sheffield	LHB/RFM
O J Hannon-Dalby *	June 20, 1989	Halifax	RHB/RFM
G S Ballance *	November 22, 1989	Harare, Zimbabwe	LHB/LB
Azeem Rafiq *	February 27, 1991	Karachi, Pakistan	RHB/OB
B W Sanderson *	January 3, 1989	Sheffield	RHB/RMF
J E Root *	December 30, 1990	Sheffield	RHB/OB
L J Hodgson	June 29, 1986	Middlesbrough	RHB/RFM
M A Ashraf*	January 5, 1992	Bradford	RHB/RF
C J Geldart	December 17, 1991	Huddersfield	LHB/RM
J B Hargreaves	December 6, 1991	Huddersfield	RHB/RFM
G S Randhawa*	January 25, 1992	Huddersfield	LHB/SLA
W T Root	August 5, 1992	Sheffield	LHB/OB
A Z Lees*	April 14, 1993	Halifax	LHB/LB
J M Hughes	November 17, 1992	Pontefract	LHB/SLA
A E Lilley	April 17, 1992	Halifax	RHB/LM
J C Wainman	January 25, 1993	Harrogate	RHB/LM
I Wardlaw	June 29, 1985	Dewsbury	RHB/LM
B P Gibson	March 31, 1996	Leeds	RHB/WK
E Wilson	July 7, 1994	Huddersfield	LHB/WK
G S Ross	October 29, 1993	Leeds	LHB/OB
J H Tattersall	May 11, 1991	Knaresborough	RHB/WK
J A Leaning	October 18, 1993	Bristol	RHB/RMF
J J Stuart	January 28, 1992	Doncaster	RHB/RMF
D M Hodgson	February 26, 1990	Northallerton	RHB/WK
D F Girling	September 26, 1992	Edgware	RHB/RMF
G J Rudolph	March 2, 1988	Pretoria, South Africa	RHB/LB
M R Good	May 20, 1993	Leeds	RHB
J A Tattersall	December 15, 1994	Knaresborough	RHB/LB
O G Jackson	January 11, 1993	Doncaster	LHB/SLA

* Second Eleven cap

SECOND ELEVEN HIGHLIGHTS OF 2011

CHAMPIONSHIP

Century Partnerships (6)
For the 2nd wicket (3)

198	J E Root and A Z Lees	v. Derbyshire at Stamford Bridge
170	C J Geldart and A Z Lees	v. Nottinghamshire at Barnsley
119	A Lyth and G J Rudolph	v. Leicestershire at Hinckley

For the 3rd wicket (1)

147	A McGrath and A Z Lees	v. MCC Universities at York

For the 4th wicket (1)

145	A McGrath and J A Leaning	v. MCC Universities at York

For the 7th wicket (1)

104	J A Leaning and G S Randhawa	v. Worcestershire at Worcester

Centuries (7)
A McGrath (2)

186	v. MCC Universities at York
122	v. Lancashire at Stamford Bridge

J E Root (2)

126	v. Derbyshire at Stamford Bridge
103*	v. MCC Universities at York

C J Geldart (1)

110	v Nottinghamshire at Barnsley

A Lyth (1)

103	v. Leicestershire at Hinckley

J A Leaning (1)

150*	v. Worcestershire at Worcester

Four dismissals in an innings
G L Brophy (2)

5 (4ct, 1st)	v. Lancashire at Stamford Bridge
4 (4ct)	v. Northamptonshire at Headingley

E Wilson (1)

4 (2ct, 2st)	v. Nottinghamshire at Barnsley

TROPHY

Century Partnerships (3)
For the 1st wicket (2)

147	G S Balance and C J Geldart	v. v Derbyshire at Derby
137	A Lyth and J J Sayers	v. Northamptonshire at Pudsey

For the 3rd wicket (1)

156	C J Geldart and G L Brophy	v. Lancashire at Bingley

Centuries (1)
G S Balance (1)

129	v Nottinghamshire at Headingley

4 wickets in an innings (3)
O J Hannon-Dalby (1)

5-29	v Worcestershire at Worcester

A E Lilley (1)

4-28	v. Leicestershire at Leicester

I Wardlaw (1)

4-51	v Northamptonshire at Pudsey

Four dismissals in an innings
J H Tattersall (1)

4 (4ct)	v. Warwickshire at Knowle

DEBUTS (12)
B P Gibson, D F Girling, M R Good, D M Hodgson, O G Jackson, J A Leaning. G S Ross, G J Rudolph, J J Stuart, J A Tattersall, J H Tattersall and E Wilson

Second Eleven Championship
Yorkshire v. Nottinghamshire

Played at Shaw Lane, Barnsley, on May 4, 5 and 6, 2011

Nottinghamshire won by 9 wickets at 5.45pm on the Third Day

Toss won by Nottinghamshire   Nottinghamshire 24 points; Yorkshire 4 points
Close of play: First Day, Yorkshire 4-1 (Geldart 0*); Second Day, Yorkshire (second innings) 104-1 (Geldart 65*, Lees 29*)

First Innings	NOTTINGHAMSHIRE		Second Innings	
A Patel, c Sanderson b Lee		103	not out	17
S K W Wood, c Wilson b Lee		85	c and Hannon-Dalby	0
M H Wessels, st Wilson b Ballance		170	not out	25
* A D Brown, c Ballance b Hodgson		55		
S L Elstone, c Wilson b Wainwright		2		
M C Robson, b Hodgson		23		
T C Rowe, lbw b Ballance		2		
§ A Shafique, st Wilson b Wainwright		3		
G P W Bacon, not out		0		
B A Hutton, c and b Wainwright		0		
J T Ball, c Lee b Wainwright		0		
Extras (b 16, lb 10, w 2, nb 10)		38	Extras (b 12, lb 2)	14
Total (101 overs)		481	Total (1 wkt, 8 overs)	56

Twelfth man: D J Pattinson, who took no part in the match

FoW: 1-202 (Wood), 2-205 (Patel), 3-340 (Brown), 4-347 (Elstone), 5-467 (Robson)
1st   6-476 (Wessels), 7-479 (Rowe), 8-481 (Shafique), 9-481 (Hutton), 10-481 (Ball)
2nd   1-7 (Wood)

	O	M	R	W		O	M	R	W
Hannon-Dalby	14	1	87	0	Hannon-Dalby	4	1	26	1
Lee	18	2	69	2	Lee	4	0	16	0
Lilley	10	1	46	0					
Hodgson	19	2	93	2					
Wainwright	29	6	95	4					
Sanderson	7	0	45	0					
Ballance	4	0	20	2					

First Innings	YORKSHIRE		Second Innings	
G S Ballance, b Ball		4	lbw b Hutton	4
C J Geldart, run out		4	c Bacon b Wood	110
A Z Lees, lbw b Bacon		11	b Patel	77
L J Hodgson, c Shafique b Patel		5	c Wessels b Wood	0
A E Lilley, lbw b Bacon		0	lbw b Patel	2
D J Wainwright, lbw b Bacon		0	lbw b Wood	29
J B Hargreaves, c Shafique b Ball		33	b Patel	47
§ E Wilson, lbw b Patel		57	c Elstone b Ball	15
J E Lee, b Patel		25	c Elstone b Patel	7
B W Sanderson, not out		28	c and b Patel	7
O J Hannon-Dalby, c Shafique b Wood		0	not out	9
Extras (b 3, lb 2, nb 2)		17	Extras (b 25, lb 19, w 1)	45
Total (62.2 overs)		184	Total (119.1 overs)	352

*Twelfth man: * J A R Blain*

FoW: 1-4 (Ballance), 2-13 (Geldart), 3-27 (Lees), 4-27 (Lilley), 5-27 (Wainwright)
1st   6-27 (Hodgson), 7-118 (Hargreaves), 8-138 (Wilson), 9-169 (Lee), 10-184 (Hannon-Dalby)
FoW: 1-13 (Ballance), 2-183 (Geldart), 3-183 (Hodgson), 4-186 (Lilley), 5-251 (Wainwright)
2nd   6-253 (Lees), 7-284 (Wilson), 8-295 (Lee), 9-314 (Sanderson), 10-352 (Hargreaves)

	O	M	R	W		O	M	R	W
Ball	13	2	40	2	Ball	21	7	58	1
Hutton	11	6	15	0	Hutton	21.1	5	65	2
Bacon	7	2	16	3	Patel	35	14	53	4
Patel	16	5	38	3	Bacon	12	1	54	0
Wood	9	0	31	1	Wood	27	7	74	3
Elstone	7	1	29	0	Elstone	3	1	4	0

Umpires: G D Lloyd and D M Koch

Scorers: M Snook and R Marshall

Second Eleven Championship
Warwickshire v. Yorkshire

Played at Bull's Head Ground, Coventry, on May 18, 19 and 20, 2011

Warwickshire won by 7 wickets at 4.39pm on the Third Day

Toss won by Yorkshire

Warwickshire 23 points; Yorkshire 5 points

Close of play: First Day, Warwickshire 43-0 (Westwood 28*, Evans 10*); Second Day, Yorkshire 01-1 (Geldart 51*, McGrath 24*)

YORKSHIRE

First Innings		Second Innings	
C J Geldart, b Barker	20	c Johnson b Getkate	59
G S Ross, c Johnson b Barker	10	c Piolet b Barker	16
A McGrath, c Getkate b Milnes	26	lbw b Piolet	79
L J Hodgson, c Piolet b Barker	0	c Piolet b Barker	0
B Hargreaves, b Barker	4	c Piolet b Barker	2
A Leaning, b Barker	51	c Johnson b Piolet	21
S J H Tattersall, lbw b Barker	31	b Allin	1
E Lee, b Barker	0	c Javid b Allin	5
G S Randhawa, c Johnson b Burton	7	c Evans b Javid	7
B W Sanderson, c Johnson b Piolet	15	lbw b Barker	0
Wardlaw, not out	4	not out	6
Extras (b 4, lb 12, w 8, nb 4)	28	Extras (b 8, lb 3, w 4, nb 8)	23
Total (65.4 overs)	196	Total (70.2 overs)	219

Twelfth man: *J A R Blain

FoW: 1-30 (Geldart), 2-33 (Ross), 3-37 (Hodgson), 4-43 (Hargreaves), 5-67 (McGrath),
1st 6-137 (Tattersall), 7-137 (Lee), 8-154 (Leaning), 9-182 (Randhawa), 10-196 (Sanderson)
FoW: 1-35 (Ross), 2-110 (Geldart), 3-111 (Hodgson), 4-119 (Hargreaves), 5-177 (Leaning),
2nd 6-178 (Tattersall), 7-188 (Lee), 8-211 (McGrath), 9-213 (Randhawa), 10-219 (Sanderson)

	O	M	R	W		O	M	R	W
Barker	21	6	43	7	Barker	12.2	3	26	4
Allin	12	3	33	0	Allin	12	2	42	2
Milnes	14	2	54	1	Milnes	5	0	27	0
Piolet	8.4	2	21	1	Piolet	22	5	60	2
Getkate	6	1	23	0	Javid	11	3	23	1
Burton	4	1	6	1	Westwood	1	0	3	0
					Getkate	7	1	27	1

WARWICKSHIRE

First Innings		Second Innings	
* I J Westwood, c Tattersall b Sanderson	47	c Geldart b Randhawa	20
L J Evans, c Tattersall b Sanderson	20	b Wardlaw	24
J P Webb, c Lee b Sanderson	10	b Ross	29
§ R M Johnson, c Wardlaw b Lee	41	not out	22
A Javid, lbw b Randhawa	69	not out	10
K H D Barker, b Sanderson	19		
F R J Coleman, c Leaning b Ross	11		
S A Piolet, b Wardlaw	21		
T W Allin, b Ross	9		
T P Milnes, b Wardlaw	24		
T R H Burton, not out	3		
Extras (b 9, lb 13, w 2)	24	Extras (b 8, lb 5)	13
Total (100 overs)	298	Total (3 wkts, 25.4 overs)	118

Twelfth man: S C Getkate

FoW: 1-76 (Evans), 2-81 (Westwood), 3-94 (Webb), 4-150 (Johnson), 5-225 (Javed)
1st 6-225 (Barker), 7-242 (Coleman), 8-258 (Allin), 9-195 (Piolet), 10-298 (Milnes)
2nd 1-44 (Evans), 2-60 (Westwood), 3-102 (Webb)

	O	M	R	W		O	M	R	W
Lee	21	7	61	1	Lee	4	0	17	0
Wardlaw	22	8	53	2	Wardlaw	6	3	14	1
Randhawa	18	8	35	1	Hodgson	3	0	7	0
Sanderson	15	3	25	4	Ross	2.4	0	17	1
Hodgson	11	1	51	0	Randhawa	6	0	32	1
Blain	4	0	24	0	Sanderson	4	0	18	0
Ross	9	1	27	2	Hodgson	11	1	51	0
					Blain	4	0	24	0
					Ross	9	1	27	2

Umpires: A Hicks and M D Gumbley

Scorers: M Snook and S Smith

Second Eleven Championship
Yorkshire v. Derbyshire

Played at Low Catton Road, Stamford Bridge, on June 14, 15 and 16, 2011

Match drawn at 5pm on the Third Day

Toss won by Yorkshire

Close of play: First Day, Derbyshire 49-1 (Lineker 29*, Turner 2*); Second Day, Yorkshire 74 (Azeem Rafiq 34, Sayers 36)

Yorkshire 11 points; Derbyshire 11 points

	First Innings		YORKSHIRE	Second Innings	
J E Root, c Lineker b Burgoyne		126			
J J Sayers, c Burgoyne b Footitt		5	b Sanderson		6
A Z Lees, c Lineker b Liburd		96	b Burgoyne		4
G S Ross, b Burgoyne		5	c Lineker b Sanderson		1
Azeem Rafiq, c Hughes b Sanderson		52	(1) retired, not out		34
§ E Wilson, c and b Liburd		12	(7) c Poynton b Burgoyne		4
G S Randhawa, c Palladino b Liburd		13	(8) c Borrington b Lineker		4
B W Sanderson, c and b Sanderson		0	(9) c Turner b Lineker		0
M A Ashraf, not out		10	(10) c Liburd b Sanderson		4
O J Hannon-Dalby, c Borrington b Sanderson		0	(11) not out		8
L J Hodgson			(6) b Taylor		86
J A Leaning	Did not bat		(5) c Poynton b Lineker		44
Extras (b 4, lb 6, w 4, nb 2)		16	Extras (b 8, w 2, nb 2)		12
Total (9 wkts dec, 88.3 overs)		335	Total (9 wkts all out, 99 overs)		314

Twelfth man: * J A R Blain

FoW: 1-29 (Sayers), 2-227 (Root), 3-238 (Ross), 4-258 (Lees), 5-286 (Wilson)
1st 6-324 (Azeem Rafiq), 7-325 (Randhawa), 8-327 (Sanderson), 9-335 (Hannon-Dalby)
FoW: 1-118 (Sayers), 2-156 (Ross), 3-175 (Lees), 4-253 (Leaning), 5-260 (Wilson)
2nd 6-267 (Randhawa), 7-269 (Sanderson), 8-282 (Ashraf), 9-314 (Hodgson)

	O	M	R	W		O	M	R	W
Palladino	14	2	42	0	Palladino	10	1	23	0
Footitt	13.3	3	34	1	Wilson	10	2	40	0
Wilson	8	0	49	0	Taylor	8	1	36	1
Hughes	9	5	27	0	Burgoyne	18	1	53	2
Burgoyne	20	1	76	2	Sanderson	31	5	93	3
Sanderson	10.3	1	47	3	Liburd	9	0	36	0
Liburd	13.3	0	50	3	Lineker	13	2	25	3

	First Innings		DERBYSHIRE	Second Innings	
M S Lineker, c Sayers b Hannon-Dalby		40	(2) not out		5
P M Borrington, c Ross b Azeem Rafiq		12	(1) b Hannon-Dalby		2
K Turner, b Ashraf		5	not out		0
A L Hughes, c and b Randhawa		42			
§ T Poynton, c Sayers b Ashraf		1			
S S W Liburd, c Wilson b Sanderson		23			
C M Durham, lbw b Randhawa		43			
P Burgoyne, c Leaning b Randhawa		77			
A P Palladino, b Ross		136			
M J Wilson, c Hannon-Dalby b Randhawa		24			
T Taylor, not out		4			
Extras (b 2, lb 6, w 6, nb 8)		22	Extras (lb 2)		2
Total (94.1 overs)		429	Total (1 wkt, 5 overs)		9

Twelfth man: M Sanderson

FoW: 1-31 (Borrington), 2-54 (Turner), 3-66 (Lineker), 4-69 (Poynton), 5-120 (Liburd)
1st 6-150 (Hughes), 7-253 (Durham), 8-264 (Burgoyne), 9-330 (Wilson), 10-429 (Palladino)
2nd 1-8 (Borrington)

	O	M	R	W		O	M	R	W
Hannon-Dalby	22	2	82	1	Hannon-Dalby	3	1	3	1
Ashraf	18	3	84	2	Ashraf	2	1	4	0
Azeem Rafiq	13	2	48	1					
Ross	3.1	0	15	1					
Hodgson	7	0	37	0					
Sanderson	12	1	77	1					
Randhawa	19	2	78	4					

Umpires: A G B Wharf and I J Dixon

Scorers: M Snook and T M Cottam

NOTES: For Yorkshire, J E Root was injured while batting in the first innings, and was replaced by J A Leaning. Azeem Rafiq was called up for First XI duties at the start of the Third Day.
For Derbyshire, M H A Footitt was injured while bowling his 14th over, and was replaced by T Taylor. S S W Liburd completed Footitt's over.

Second Eleven Championship
Durham v. Yorkshire

Played at Feethams, Darlington, on June 21, 22 and 23, 2011

Match drawn. Rain prevented any play on the Third Day

Toss won by Yorkshire   Durham 10 points; Yorkshire 7 points

Close of play: First Day, rain stopped play. Durham 73-3 (Breese 28*, Claydon 11*); Second Day, rain stopped play. Yorkshire 1-0 (Lees 0*, Sayers 0*)

YORKSHIRE

First Innings		Second Innings	
A Z Lees, b Rushworth	0	not out	0
J Sayers, not out	56	not out	0
W T Root, c Richardson b Claydon	1		
§ G L Brophy, b Rushworth	0		
L J Hodgson, c Richardson b Rushworth	1		
D J Wainwright, c Tye b Brathwaite	5		
G S Randhawa, c Richardson b Davies	1		
I Wardlaw, lbw b Davies	2		
B W Sanderson, lbw b Claydon	9		
M A Ashraf, b Rushworth	4		
O J Hannon-Dalby, lbw b Rushworth	0		
Extras (lb 11, w 1)	12	Extras (lb 1)	1
Total (38.5 overs)	91	Total (0 wkts, 2 overs)	1

*Twelfth man: * J A R Blain*

FoW: 1-0 (Lees), 2-5 (Root), 3-6 (Brophy), 4-18 (Hodgson), 5-47 (Wainwright) 6-48 (Randhawa), 7-54 (Wardlaw), 8-82 (Sandersonb), 9-91 (Ashraf), 10-91 (Hannon-Dalby)

	O	M	R	W		O	M	R	W
Rushworth	11.5	3	20	5	Rushworth	1	1	0	0
Claydon	10	3	14	2	Claydon	1	1	0	0
Brathwaite	6	1	13	1					
Davies	7	2	17	2					
Harmison	3	1	14	0					
Breese	1	0	2	0					

DURHAM

M D Stoneman, c and b Ashraf	8
B A Raine, b Wainwright	20
*G R Breese, c Brophy b Wardlaw	28
§ M J Richardson, c Lees b Randhawa	6
B W Harmison, b Ashraf	91
R D Pringle, c Lees b Wardlaw	11
R Shahzad, lbw b Wardlaw	0
M E Claydon, b Wainwright	31
A J Tye, lbw b Wainwright	16
R M R Brathwaite, c and b Wainwright	15
C Rushworth, not out	9
Extras (b 2, lb 8, w 2, nb 4)	16
Total (68.1 overs)	251

Twelfth man: A M Davies

FoW: 1-26 (Stoneman), 2-47 (Raine), 3-60 (Richardson), 4-73 (Breese), 5-129 (Pringle) 6-137 (Shahzad), 7-206 (Claydon), 8-214 (Tye), 9-242 (Harmison), 10-251 (Brathwaite)

	O	M	R	W
Hannon-Dalby	13	0	42	0
Ashraf	14	3	48	2
Sanderson	12	4	32	0
Wainwright	13.1	1	43	4
Randhawa	4	1	10	1
Wardlaw	8	2	40	3
Hodgson	4	0	26	0

Umpires: B V Taylor and J W Crockatt   Scorers: M Snook and R V Hilton

Second Eleven Championship
Yorkshire v. MCC Universities

Played at Clifton Park, York, on July 5, 6 and 7, 2011

Match drawn at 5.08pm on the Third Day

Toss won by Yorkshire   Yorkshire 9 points; MCC Universities 6 points
Close of play: First Day, Yorkshire 403-6 (Hodgson 0*); Second Day, MCC Universities 225-5 (Bendon 3*, Woolley 18*)

First Innings	YORKSHIRE		Second Innings	
J E Root, c Durandt b Reece	41		not out	103
C J Geldart, c Woolley b Turnbull	26		lbw b Turnbull	24
*A McGrath, c Bendon b Moore	186		c Bell b Reece	11
A Z Lees, c and b Bendon	79		not out	28
J A Leaning, lbw b Woolley	40			
J J Stuart, c Bell b Woolley	19			
§ D M Hodgson, not out	0			
G S Randhawa				
I Wardlaw				
M A Ashraf	Did not bat			
O J Hannon-Dalby				
Extras (b 2, lb 2, w 6, nb 2)	12		Extras (b 3, lb 4)	7
Total (6 wkts dec, 103.4 overs)	403		Total (2 wkts dec, 27 overs)	173

Twelfth man : J C Wainman

FoW: 1-54 (Geldart), 2-89 (Root), 3-236 (Lees), 4-381 (leaning), 5-393 (McGrath), 6-403 (Stuart)
1st
2nd   1-77 (Geldart, 2-96 (McGrath)

	O	M	R	W		O	M	R	W
Turnbull	17	3	79	1	Turnbull	8	0	24	1
Wilson	9	2	32	0	Wilson	3	0	33	0
Woolley	13.4	2	56	2	Reece	10	2	49	1
Reece	16	3	67	1	Woolley	4	0	29	0
Moore	9	3	20	1	Bush	2	0	31	0
Watkins	12	0	52	0					
Bush	12	2	49	0					
Ransley	8	0	20	0					
Bendon	7	0	24	1					

First Innings	MCC UNIVERSITIES		Second Innings (following on)	
L E Durandt, c Hodgson b Wardlaw	66		c Hodgson b Hannon-Dalby	7
B J Ackland, c Lees b Wainman	89		lbw b Ashraf	24
H Bush, c McGrath b Wardlaw	1		c Geldart b Randhawa	17
R A L Moore, c Root b Randhawa	22		not out	39
L M Reece, c Hannon-Dalby b Root	12		not out	6
D S Bendon, not out	3			
*R J J Woolley, not out	18			
§ D W Bell				
S M Ransley				
P T Turnbull	Did not bat			
A D Wilson				
Extras (b 7, lb 4, w 1, nb 2)	14		Extras (lb 3, nb 2)	5
Total (5 wkts dec, 65 overs)	225		Total (3 wkts, 37 overs)	98

Twelfth man: N A T Watkins

FoW: 1-112 (Durandt), 2-122 (Bush), 3-180 (Moore), 4-204 (Reece), 5-204 (Ackland)
2nd   1-32 (Durandt), 2-36 (Ackland), 3-84 (Bush)

	O	M	R	W		O	M	R	W
Hannon-Dalby	13	2	44	0	Hannon-Dalby	8	2	21	1
Wardlaw	9	2	22	2	Wardlaw	9	2	37	0
Ashraf	12	5	29	0	Ashraf	9	5	12	1
Wainman	9	0	58	0	Wainman	6	1	19	0
Randhawa	17	4	54	1	Randhawa	5	2	6	1
Root	5	2	7	1					

Umpires: I Dawood and G Parker   Scorers: M Snook and A Gowlett

Second Eleven Championship
Yorkshire v. Lancashire

Played at Low Catton Road, Stamford Bridge, on July 26, 27 and 28, 2011

Lancashire won by 3 wickets at 5.26pm on the Third Day

Toss won by Yorkshire — Lancashire 23 points; Yorkshire 8 points

Close of play: First Day, Lancashire 30-2 (Thompson 8*, Bentley 3*); Second Day, Yorkshire 140-3 (Brophy 5*, Lees 0*)

YORKSHIRE

	First Innings		Second Innings	
J E Root,	c Agathangelou b Newby	45	b Newby	64
C J Geldart,	run out	29	c Davies b Newby	15
A McGrath,	c Davies b Newby	122	c Agathangelou b Caunce	54
§ G L Brophy,	c Reece b Newby	5	c Clark b Newby	32
A Z Lees,	c Bailey b Lilley	53	lbw b Parry	0
A E Lilley,	lbw b Caunce	2	c and b Newby	5
G S Randhawa,	c Davies b Newby	21	not out	16
* S A Patterson,	lbw b Caunce	16	c Davies b Newby	4
I Wardlaw,	c Caunce b Newby	12	(10) c Agathangelou b Parry	5
M A Ashraf,	not out	3	(9) c Agathangelou b Newby	0
O J Hannon-Dalby,	lbw b Caunce	0	c Newby b Lilley	5
	Extras (b 2, lb 2, nb 4)	8	Extras (b 6, w 1, nb 8)	15
	Total (89.3 overs)	316	Total (62.2 overs)	215

Twelfth man: J C Wainman

FoW: 1-62 (Geldart), 2-107 (Root), 3-121 (Brophy), 4-212 (Lees), 5-257 (Lilley), 6-273 (McGrath),
1st 7-288 (Randhawa), 8-302 (Wardlaw), 9-316 (Patterson), 10-316 (Hannon-Dalby)
FoW: 1-31 (Geldart), 2-128 (Root), 3-138 (McGrath), 4-144 (Lees), 5-169 (Lilley),
2nd 6-178 (Brophy), 7-190 (Patterson), 8-190 (Ashraf), 9-200 (Wardlaw), 10-215 (Hannon-Dalby)

	O	M	R	W		O	M	R	W
Newby	20	3	71	5	Newby	20	7	67	6
Cheetham	19	5	70	0	Cheetham	7	1	25	0
Caunce	15.3	2	47	3	Caunce	12	3	42	1
Bailey	11	2	48	0	Bailey	0	0	15	0
Reece	1	0	7	0	Parry	18	4	47	2
Parry	18	2	35	0	Lilley	3.2	1	13	1
Lilley	5	0	34	1					

LANCASHIRE

	First Innings		Second Innings	
A P Agathangelou,	c Hannon-Dalby b Wardlaw	8	b Randhawa	64
L R Reece,	c Brophy b Hannon-Dalby	3	c Lees b Ashraf	21
H Thompson,	c Root b Wardlaw	32	(8) c Root b Randhawa	2
L N Bentley,	b Newby	24	(3) lbw b Ashraf	45
J Clark,	c Brophy b Hannon-Dalby	97	(4) c McGrath b Randhawa	0
* S D Parry,	c Patterson b Randhawa	88	(5) c Root b Randhawa	27
O J Newby,	c Lilley b Randhawa	9	(6) b Ashraf	16
§ A L Davies,	c Brophy b Randhawa	5	(7) not out	35
A M Lilley,	c Brophy b Randhawa	4	not out	29
T Bailey,	st Brophy b Patterson	2		
S P Cheetham,	not out	0		
	Extras (b 1, lb 15)	16	Extras (lb 6, nb 2)	8
	Total (79.3 overs)	288	Total (7 wkts, 60.1 overs)	247

Twelfth man: N T Caunce

FoW: 1-14 (Reece), 2-16 (Agathangelou), 3-74 (Thompson), 4-76 (Bentley), 5-262 (Clark),
1st 6-274 (Newby), 7-282 (Parry), 8-286 (Davies), 9-286 (Lilley), 10-288 (Bailey)
FoW: 1-60 (Reece), 2-125 (Agathangelou), 3-125 (Clark), 4-147 (Bentley), 5-179 (Parry),
2nd 6-179 (Newby), 7-182 (Thompson)

	O	M	R	W		O	M	R	W
Wardlaw	12	3	38	2	Wardlaw	9	0	62	0
Hannon-Dalby	15	5	42	2	Hannon-Dalby	7.1	2	24	0
Randhawa	17.3	3	75	4	Ashraf	12	1	46	3
Patterson	10	3	40	1	Patterson	9	2	33	0
Ashraf	12	3	40	1	Randhawa	22	4	68	4
Wainman	6	3	18	0	Root	1	0	8	0
McGrath	1	0	2	0					
Lilley	6	1	17	0					

Umpires: M A Eggleston and D M Koch

Scorers: M Snook and D M White

Second Eleven Championship
Yorkshire v. Northamptonshire

Played at Headingley Carnegie Cricket Ground, Leeds, on August 10, 11 and 12, 2011
Match drawn. Bad light ended play at 4.42pm on the Third Day

Toss won by Yorkshire   Northamptonshire 7 points; Yorkshire 6 points
Close of play: First Day, rain stopped play — Northamptonshire 27-0 (Keogh 11*, Reynoldson 13*); Second Day, bad light and rain stopped play — Northamptonshire 293-7 (Lucas 14*, Burton 3*)

Yorkshire forfeited their first innings, Northamptonshire their second

NORTHAMPTONSHIRE — First Innings

R I Keogh, c Randhawa b Ashraf		43
A M Reynoldson, c Brophy b Patterson		52
P L Mommsen, c Hodgson b Girling		76
D J G Sales, b Patterson		1
* § D Murphy, c Brophy b Hannon-Dalby		48
D J Willey, c Brophy b Girling		29
C A L Davis, c Ashraf b Girling		15
D S Lucas, not out		17
D A Burton, c Brophy b Ashraf		9
B M R Akram		
S Sweeney	Did not bat	
Extras (b 5, lb 3, nb 6)		14
Total (8 wkts dec, 87 overs)		304

Twelfth man: T Brett

FoW: 1-102 (Reynoldson), 2-102 (Keogh), 3-103 (Sales), 4-216 (Murphy), 5-241 (Mommsen), 6-274 (Willey), 7-281 (Davis), 8-304 (Burton)

	O	M	R	W
Wardlaw	16	2	64	0
Hannon-Dalby	16	2	35	1
Patterson	16	4	54	2
Ashraf	15	2	55	2
Girling	12	3	39	3
Randhawa	12	1	49	0

YORKSHIRE — Second Innings

A Lyth, b Burton		38
* J J Sayers, c Murphy b Burton		2
A Z Lees, c Mommsen b Sweeney		8
§ G L Brophy, not out		65
D M Hodgson, lbw b Brett		0
D F Girling, c Sales b Burton		0
G S Randhawa, not out		16
C J Geldart		
S A Patterson		
M A Ashraf	Did not bat	
I Wardlaw		
Extras (w 1, nb 8)		9
Total (5 wkts, 53 overs)		138

Twelfth man : O J Hannon-Dalby

FoW: 1-19 (Sayers), 2-37 (Lees), 3-84 (Lyth), 4-87 (Hodgson), 5-110 (Girling)

	O	M	R	W
Burton	18	6	34	3
Lucas	11	3	21	0
Sweeney	10	1	37	1
Davis	3	0	9	0
Brett	11	1	37	1

Umpires: S J Malone and G Parker   Scorers: M Snook and M E Woolley

Played at Leicester Road, Hinckley, on August 17, 18 and 19, 2011

Match tied at 6.04pm on the Third Day

Toss won by Leicestershire   Leicestershire 14 points; Yorkshire 12 points

Close of play: First Day, Leicestershire 377-9 (Eckersley 133*, Wyatt 16*); Second Day, Yorkshire 148-5 (Hodgson 21*, Lilley 4*)

	First Innings	LEICESTERSHIRE	Second Innings	
P S P Handscomb, c Brophy b Lilley		42	(2) c Randhawa b Wardlaw	14
W S Jones, c Wainman b Hannon-Dalby		15	(1) not out	37
*J du Toit, lbw b Randhawa		28	not out	15
Kadeer Ali, c Rudolph b Lyth		2		
§ E J Eckersley, not out		133		
L J Hill, c Lees b Randhawa		4		
R M L Taylor, lbw b Blain		55		
L J Kinch, c Brophy b Hannon-Dalby		46		
W MacVicar, b Lilley		8		
T J Wells, c Hodgson b Randhawa		16		
A C F Wyatt, not out		16		
Extras (b 5, lb 5, nb 2)		12	Extras (b 1, lb 5)	6
Total (9 wkts dec, 104 overs)		377	Total (1 wkt dec, 10 overs)	72

Twelfth man: J S Sykes

FoW: 1-29 (Jones), 2-80 (Handscomb), 3-86 (Kadeer Ali), 4-92 (du Toit), 5-96 (Hill)
1st   6-213 (Taylor), 7-294 (Kinch), 8-309 (MacVicar), 9-338 (Wells)
2nd   1-38 (Handscomb)

	O	M	R	W		O	M	R	W
Hannon-Dalby	20	5	57	2	Hannon-Dalby.	3	0	24	0
Wardlaw	15	0	57	0	Wardlaw	3	0	16	1
Wainman	13	1	45	0	Wainman	2	0	6	0
Lilley	15	2	41	2	Lilley	2	0	20	0
Randhawa	20	2	96	3					
Lyth	16	2	59	1					
Blain	5	0	12	1					

	First Innings	YORKSHIRE	Second Innings	
A Lyth, c Jones b Sykes		54	c Eckersley b Sykes	103
A Z Lees, lbw b Wyatt		8	b Taylor	9
G J Rudolph, lbw b Sykes		13	c Jones b Kadeer Ali	44
§ G L Brophy, c Eckersley b Wyatt		21	c Wells b Sykes	67
M R Good, c Sykes b Kinch		15	b Sykes	2
D M Hodgson, not out		21	c MacVicar b Sykes	16
A E Lilley, not out		4	lbw b Sykes	11
G S Randhawa			c du Toit b Wyatt	14
I Wardlaw			b Sykes	23
J C Wainman	Did not bat		not out	1
O J Hannon-Dalby			lbw b Wyatt	0
Extras (b 4, lb 2, w 6)		12	Extras (b 7, lb 4)	11
Total (5 wkts dec, 60.3 overs)		148	Total (82.4 overs)	301

*Twelfth man: * J A R Blain*

FoW: 1-20 (Lees), 2-57 (Rudolph), 3-93 (Lyth), 4-105 (Brophy), 5-137 (Good)
2nd   1-24 (Lees), 2-143 (Rudolph), 3-169 (Lyth), 4-181 (Good), 5-213 (Hodgson)
     6-234 (Lilley), 7-251 (Randhawa), 8-297 (Brophy), 9-298(Wardlaw), 10-301 (Hannon-Dalby)

	O	M	R	W		O	M	R	W
Wyatt	14	5	38	2	Wyatt	20.4	4	74	2
Taylor	8	2	20	0	Taylor	10	5	30	1
Wells	11	3	31	0	Sykes	26	2	107	6
Sykes	20	9	41	2	Wells	4	0	14	0
Kadeer Ali	5	1	7	0	Jones	5	0	18	0
Kinch	2.3	0	5	1	MacVicar	5	2	10	0
					Kadeer Ali	12	0	37	1

Umpires : P K Baldwin and P R Pollard   Scorers: M Snook and D Ayriss

Second Eleven Championship
Worcestershire v. Yorkshire

Played at New Road, Worcester, on August 23, 24 and 25, 2011
Worcestershire won by 6 wickets at 5.38pm on the Third Day

Toss won by Yorkshire   Worcestershire 23 points; Yorkshire 8 points
Close of play: First Day, Worcestershire 31-1 (Pardoe 25*, Pinner 6*); Second Day, rain stopped play — Worcestershire 268-9 (Cox 71*)

First Innings	YORKSHIRE		Second Innings	
A Lyth, c Blofield b Shantry	71		c Blofield b Manuel	25
A Z Lees, lbw b Russell	35		c Pinner b D'Oliveira	78
J A Leaning, not out	150		not out	42
G S Ross, b Shantry	0		not out	16
§ D M Hodgson, lbw b Shantry	0			
E Wilson, c Cox b Underhill	15			
A E Lilley, lbw b Russell	5			
G S Randhawa, c Cox b Russell	26			
I Wardlaw, c Russell b Shantry	0			
J C Wainman, b Shantry	1			
O J Hannon-Dalby Did not bat				
Extras (b 4, lb 6, w 17, nb 2)	29		Extras (w 3)	3
Total (9 wkts, 92.5 overs)	332		Total (2 wkts dec, 13.2 overs)	164

Twelfth man: * J A R Blain

FoW: 1-98 (Lees), 2-119 (Lyth), 3-119 (Ross), 4-123 (Hodgson), 5-165 (Wilson)
1st   6-170 (Lilley), 7-274 (Randhawa), 8-312 (Wardlaw), 9-332 (Wainman)
2nd   1-62 (Lyth), 2-128 (Lees)

	O	M	R	W		O	M	R	W
Shantry	23.5	6	63	5	Cox	4	0	62	0
Sweeney	13	0	95	0	Manuel	6.2	0	74	1
Underhill	12	4	41	0	D'Oliveira	3	0	28	1
Russell	16	5	52	3					
Blofield	19	3	39	0					
D'Oliveira	6	0	25	0					
Leach	3	1	7	0					

First Innings	WORCESTERSHIRE		Second Innings	
M G Pardoe, c Ross b Randhawa	47		c Lilley b Ross	88
J K Manuel, c Wainman b Wardlaw	4		c and b Hannon-Dalby	0
* N D Pinner, c Hodgson b Hannon-Dalby	10		c Lilley b Ross	81
W T Root, c Lilley b Randhawa	18		c and b Ross	1
J Leach, c Lilley b Ross	48		not out	38
B L D'Oliveira, lbw b Hannon-Dalby	37		not out	11
§ O B Cox, not out	71			
A D Blofield, c Lees b Hannon-Dalby	14			
J D Shantry, c Hodgson b Wardlaw	0			
S Sweeney, lbw b Hannon-Dalby	16			
C J Russell Did not bat				
Extras (lb 3, nb 4)	7		Extras (b 2, lb 9, w 1)	12
Total (9 wkts, 68.4 overs)	268		Total (4 wkts, 47.1 overs)	231

Twelfth man: T Underhill

FoW: 1-0 (Manuel), 2-39 (Pinner), 3-70 (Root), 4-109 (Pardoe), 5-133 (Leach)
1st   6-222 (D'Oliveira), 7-236 (Blofield), 8-237 (Shantry), 9-268 (Sweeney)
2nd   1-5 (Manuel), 2-169 (Pinner), 3-175 (Root), 4-202 (Pardoe)

	O	M	R	W		O	M	R	W
Hannon-Dalby	20.4	5	68	4	Hannon-Dalby	11	4	37	1
Wardlaw	17	3	72	2	Wardlaw	10	1	28	0
Randhawa	17	3	65	2	Wainman	3	0	18	0
Wainman	7	2	31	0	Randhawa	12	1	66	0
Ross	2	0	9	1	Ross	7.1	1	39	3
Lilley	1	1	20	0	Lilley	4	0	32	0

Umpires: P Willey and D J Gower   Scorers: M Snook and Mrs D E Pugh

NOTES: For Worcestershire, N D Pinner kept wicket in Yorkshire's second innings

SECOND ELEVEN CHAMPIONSHIP 2011

FINAL

Warwickshire (384 and 150-4) beat Glamorgan (215 and 317) by 6 wickets

GROUP A FINAL TABLE

		P	W	L	D	Tied	Bat	Bowl	Pen.	Points
1	Warwickshire (1)	9	6	2	1	0	25	32	0	156
2	Leicestershire (4)	9	4	2	2	1	29	26	0	133
3	Lancashire (3)	9	4	1	4	0	26	29	0	131
4	Durham (2)	9	4	3	3	0	24	29	0	126
5	Nottinghamshire (7)	9	3	3	3	0	32	33	0	122
6	Worcestershire (6)	9	3	2	4	0	21	31	0	112
7	Derbyshire (9)	9	2	3	4	0	22	35	0	101
8	Northamptonshire (—)	9	1	4	4	0	22	24	0	74
9	MCC Universities (—)	9	1	5	3	0	25	21	0	71
10	Yorkshire (8)	9	0	4	4	1	18	32	0	70

GROUP B FINAL TABLE

		P	W	L	D	Tied	Bat	Bowl	Pen.	Points
1	Glamorgan((—)	9	5	1	3	0	32	31	0	152
2	Middlesex (6)	9	4	1	4	0	30	34	0	140
3	Essex (8)	9	4	3	2	0	20	36	1	125
4	Hampshire (9)	9	4	4	1	0	31	28	2	124
5	Somerset (2)	9	3	1	5	0	28	30	0.5	120.5
6	Sussex (4)	9	3	1	5	0	27	29	4	115
7	Surrey (1)	9	2	2	5	0	23	35	3.5	101.5
8	MCC Young Cricketers (—)	9	2	3	4	0	25	28	0.5	96.5
9	Kent (10)	9	1	6	2	0	16	29	0	67
10	Gloucestershire (3)	9	0	6	3	0	13	31	0	53

(2010 group positions in brackets)

SECOND ELEVEN CHAMPIONS

(In the seasons in which Yorkshire have competed. The Championship has been split into two groups since 2009, the group winners playing off for the Championship.)

Season	Champions	Yorkshire's Position	Season	Champions	Yorkshire's Position
1959	Gloucestershire	7th	1992	Surrey	5th
1960	Northamptonshire	14th	1993	Middlesex	3rd
1961	Kent	11th	1994	Somerset	2nd
1975	Surrey	4th	1995	Hampshire	5th
1976	Kent	5th	1996	Warwickshire	4th
1977	**Yorkshire**	**1st**	1997	Lancashire	2nd
1978	Sussex	5th	1998	Northamptonshire	9th
1979	Warwickshire	3rd	1999	Middlesex	14th
1980	Glamorgan	5th	2000	Middlesex	5th
1981	Hampshire	11th	2001	Hampshire	2nd
1982	Worcestershire	14th	2002	Kent	3rd
1983	Leicestershire	2nd	**2003**	**Yorkshire**	**1st**
1984	**Yorkshire**	**1st**	2004	Somerset	8th
1985	Nottinghamshire	12th	2005	Kent	10th
1986	Lancashire	5th	2006	Kent	3rd
1987	**Yorkshire** and Kent	**1st**	2007	Sussex	10th
1988	Surrey	9th	2008	Durham	5th
1989	Middlesex	9th	2009	Surrey	A 2nd
1990	Sussex	17th	2010	Surrey	A 8th
1991	**Yorkshire**	**1st**	2011	Warwickshire	A 10th

Played 9   Won 0   Tied 1   Drawn 4   Lost 4

BATTING AND FIELDING

(Qualification 5 innings)

Player	M.	I.	N.O.	Runs	H.S.	Avge	100s	50s	ct/st
J E Root	3	5	1	379	126	94.75	2	1	4
J A Leaning	3	6	2	348	150*	87.00	1	1	2
A McGrath	3	6	0	478	186	79.66	2	2	2
A Lyth	3	5	0	291	103	58.20	1	2	0
J J Sayers	3	5	2	123	60	41.00	0	2	2
A Z Lees	8	15	2	530	96	40.76	0	5	6
G L Brophy	4	6	1	190	67	38.00	0	2	11/1
C J Geldart	5	8	0	287	110	35.87	1	1	2
E Wilson	3	5	0	103	57	20.60	0	1	3/2
G S Randhawa	8	10	2	124	26	15.50	0	0	3
L J Hodgson	4	6	0	92	86	15.33	0	1	0
D M Hodgson	4	5	2	37	21*	12.33	0	0	6/0
G S Ross	4	6	1	58	16*	11.60	0	0	3
I Wardlaw	7	7	2	52	23	10.40	0	0	1
B W Sanderson	4	7	1	59	28*	9.83	0	0	1
M A Ashraf	5	5	2	21	10*	7.00	0	0	2
A E Lilley	4	7	1	29	11	4.83	0	0	5
O J Hannon-Dalby	6	8	2	22	9*	3.66	0	0	5

Also played

Player	M.	I.	N.O.	Runs	H.S.	Avge	100s	50s	ct/st
Azeem Rafiq	1	2	1	86	52	86.00	0	1	0
G J Rudolph	1	2	0	57	44	28.50	0	0	1
J B Hargreaves	2	4	0	86	47	21.50	0	0	0
J J Stuart	1	1	0	19	19	19.00	0	0	0
J H Tattersall	1	2	0	32	31	16.00	0	0	2/0
D J Wainwright	2	3	0	34	29	11.33	0	0	2
S A Patterson	2	2	0	20	16	10.00	0	0	1
J E Lee	2	4	0	37	25	9.25	0	0	2
M R Good	1	2	0	17	15	8.50	0	0	0
G S Ballance	1	2	0	8	4	4.00	0	0	1
J C Wainman	4	2	1	2	1*	2.00	0	0	2
W T Root	1	1	0	1	1	1.00	0	0	0
D F Girling	1	1	0	0	0	0.00	0	0	0

BOWLING

(Qualification 10 wickets)

Player	Overs	Mdns	Runs	Wkts	Avge	Best	5wI	10wM
G S Randhawa	169.3	31	634	22	28.81	4-68	0	0
M A Ashraf	94	23	318	11	28.90	3-46	0	0
I Wardlaw	136	26	503	13	38.69	3-40	0	0
O J Hannon-Dalby	169.5	32	592	14	42.28	4-68	0	0

Also bowled

Player	Overs	Mdns	Runs	Wkts	Avge	Best	5wI	10wM
G S Ballance	4	0	20	2	10.00	2-20	0	0
D F Girling	12	3	39	3	13.00	3-39	0	0
G S Ross	24	2	107	8	13.37	3-39	0	0
J E Root	6	2	15	1	15.00	1-7	0	0
D J Wainwright	42.1	7	138	8	17.25	4-43	0	0
J A R Blain	9	0	36	1	36.00	1-12	0	0
B W Sanderson	50	8	197	5	39.40	4-25	0	0
S A Patterson	35	9	127	3	42.33	2-54	0	0
Azeem Rafiq	13	2	48	1	48.00	1-48	0	0
J E Lee	47	9	163	3	54.33	2-69	0	0
A Lyth	16	2	59	1	59.00	1-59	0	0
A E Lilley	42	5	176	2	88.00	2-41	0	0
L J Hodgson	44	3	214	2	107.00	2-93	0	0
J C Wainman	46	7	195	1	195.00	1-58	0	0
A McGrath	1	0	2	0	—	—	0	0

Second Eleven Trophy
Yorkshire v. Nottinghamshire

Played at Headingley Carnegie Cricket Ground, Leeds, on May 3, 2011

Nottinghamshire won by 4 wickets at 5.23pm

oss won by Yorkshire   Nottinghamshire 2 points; Yorkshire 0 points

YORKSHIRE

G S Ballance, c Robson b Elstone	129
C J Geldart, b Patel	65
A Z Lees, not out	20
L J Hodgson, not out	5
A E Lilley	
D J Wainwright	
§ E Wilson	
G S Randhawa	Did not bat
J E Lee	
O J Hannon-Dalby	
* J A R Blain	
Extras (b 3, lb 4, w 5)	12
Total (2 wkts, 40 overs)	231

oW: 1-147 (Geldart), 2-224 (Ballance)

	O	M	R	W
Ball	7	1	38	0
Hutton	8	0	65	0
Bacon	5	0	25	0
Wood	8	0	36	0
Patel	8	0	40	1
Elstone	4	0	20	1

NOTTINGHAMSHIRE

A Patel, st Wilson b Wainwright	77
* A D Brown, c Wainwright b Hannon-Dalby	3
M H Wessels, b Hodgson	38
S K W Wood, c Wainwright b Randhawa	11
S L Elstone, c Lilley b Wainwright	52
J T Ball, b Wainwright	8
M C Robson, not out	9
T Rowe, not out	7
§ A Shafique	
B A Hutton	Dd not bat
G P W Bacon	
Extras (b 4, lb 8, w 13, nb 2)	27
Total (6 wkts, 38.5 overs)	232

oW: 1-7 (Brown), 2-78 (Wessels), 3-121 (Wood), 4-181 (Patel), 5-294 (Ball)
6-215 (Elstone)

	O	M	R	W
Hannon-Dalby	5.5	1	26	1
Lee	7	0	56	0
Hodgson	7	0	38	1
Lilley	4	0	30	0
Wainwright	8	0	32	3
Randhawa	7	0	38	1

mpires: G D Lloyd and H Fidler   Scorers : M Snook and R Marshall

Warwickshire v. Yorkshire

Played at Station Road, Knowle, on May 17, 2011
Yorkshire won by 62 runs at 4.38pm

Toss won by Yorkshire

Yorkshire 2 points; Warwickshire 0 point

YORKSHIRE

C J Geldart, c and b Barker	12
G S Ross, b Burton	32
A McGrath, b Getkate	14
L J Hodgson, b Burton	30
J B Hargreaves, b Westwood	16
§ J H Tattersall, c Johnson b Westwood	3
J E Lee, c and b Westwood	3
G S Randhawa, not out	16
B W Sanderson, b Allin	4
I Wardlaw, b Barker	11
* J A R Blain, b Barker	6
Extras (lb 6, w 13, nb 2)	21
Total (37.3 overs)	168

FoW: 1-14 (Geldart), 2-47 (McGrath), 3-75 (Ross), 4-112 (Hargreaves), 5-118 (Tattersa
6-125 (Lee), 7-131 (Hodgson), 8-143 (Sanderson), 9-160 (Wardlaw), 10-168 (Bla

	O	M	R	W
Barker	6.3	0	26	3
Allin	8	0	37	1
Getkate	4	0	23	1
Piolet	4	0	17	0
Burton	8	0	35	3
Westwood	7	0	24	2

WARWICKSHIRE

J P Webb, c McGrath b Wardlaw	10
L J Evans, c Tattersall b Lee	1
K H D Barker, c Tattersall b Sanderson	38
* I J Westwood, c Randhawa b Lee	5
A Javid, c Tattersall b Lee	0
§ R M Johnson, lbw b Hodgson	0
S A Piolet, b Sanderson	1
F R J Coleman, b Randhawa	9
T W Allin, c Tattersall b Randhawa	22
T R H Burton, lbw b Hodgson	8
S C Getkate, not out	0
Extras (lb 9, w 3)	12
Total (24.2 overs)	106

FoW: 1-10 (Evans), 2-32 (Webb), 3-40 (Westwood), 4-40 (Javid), 5-65 (Johnso
6-65 (Barker), 7-66 (Piolet), 8-93 (Allin), 9-100 (Coleman), 10-106 (Burto

	O	M	R	W
Lee	6	1	28	3
Wardlaw	5	1	24	1
Hodgson	5.2	0	14	2
Sanderson	5	0	22	2
Randhawa	3	0	9	2

Umpires: A Hicks and Mansoor Qureshi

Scorers : M Snook and S Smith

Second Eleven Trophy
Yorkshire v. Unicorns A

Played at Centre Vale, Todmorden, on June 3, 2011

Unicorns A won by 169 runs at 4.52pm

Toss won by Unicorns A   Unicorns A 2 points; Yorkshire 0 points

UNICORNS A

J R A Campbell, c Hodgson b Hannon-Dalby		18
J E Ord, c Hodgson b Ross		97
C P J Wootton, c Wilson b Blain		48
S M Park, c Randhawa b Hodgson		60
A Chishti, c Lilley b Sanderson		15
Amar Rashid, b Hannon-Dalby		4
§ J I Pope, not out		27
R G Querl, c Sanderson b Wainman		3
L E Beavan, b Wainman		0
* C Brown		
A Syddall	Did not bat	
Extras (b 4, lb 3, w 11)		18
Total (8 wkts, 40 overs)		290

FoW: 1-39 (Chapman), 2-160 (Wootton), 3-202 (Ord), 4-254 (Park), 5-254 (Chishti) 6-272 (Amar Rashid), 7-283 (Querl), 8-290 (Beavan)

	O	M	R	W
Hannon-Dalby	5	0	36	2
Wainman	4	0	41	2
Hodgson	8	0	51	1
Sanderson	6	1	51	1
Ross	6	0	53	1
Randhawa	8	0	36	0
Blain	3	0	15	1

YORKSHIRE

A Z Lees, b Syddall	3
G S Ross, c Park b Querl	5
J A Leaning, c Pope b Querl	1
L J Hodgson, c Pope b Syddall	6
§ E Wilson, c Beavan b Brown	16
A E Lilley, c Wootton b Brown	45
G S Randhawa, c Campbell b Beavan	10
B W Sanderson, c Beavan b Chishti	22
J C Wainman, b Chishti	6
O J Hannon-Dalby, b Beavan	0
* J A R Blain, not out	0
Extras (lb 3, w 4)	7
Total (29.1 overs)	121

FoW: 1-3 (Lees), 2-4 (Leaning), 3-17 (Hodgson), 4-17 (Ross), 5-66 (Wilson), 6-90 (Lilley) 7-93 (Randhawa), 8-121 (Sanderson), 9-121 (Wainman), 10-121 (Hannon-Dalby)

	O	M	R	W
Querl	6	1	16	2
Syddall	3	0	9	2
Amar Rashid	8	0	47	0
Brown	8	0	30	2
Beavan	3.1	0	14	2
Chishti	1	0	2	2

Umpires: M A Eggleston and B W Reidy   Scorers: M Snook and A C S Gibbs

Second Eleven Trophy
Yorkshire v. Derbyshire

Played at Windy Hill Lane, Marske-by-the-Sea, on June 13, 2011

*Match abandoned — no result. The match was abandoned when a damp patch on the
pitch caused the ball to behave unpredictably*

Toss won by Yorkshire   Yorkshire 1 point; Derbyshire 1 point

YORKSHIRE

J E Root, not out		12
J J Sayers, c Poynton b Palladino		0
§ G L Brophy, not out		8
A Z Lees		
L J Hodgson		
Azeem Rafiq		
G S Randhawa	Did not bat	
B W Sanderson		
M A Ashraf		
O J Hannon-Dalby		
* J A R Blain		
Extras (w 2)		2
Total (1 wkt, 8 overs)		22

FoW: 1-2 (Sayers)

	O	M	R	W
Footitt	4	0	8	0
Palladino	4	0	14	1

DERBYSHIRE

M S Lineker
P M Borrington
K Turner
§ T Poynton
A L Hughes
S S W Liburd
* J Needham
P Burgoyne
A P Palladino
M L Turner
M H A Footitt

Umpires: A G B Wharf and G Wood   Scorers: M Snook and T M Cottam

Second Eleven Trophy
Durham v. Yorkshire

Played at Feethams, Darlington, on June 20, 2011
Durham won by 6 wickets at 5.01pm

Toss won by Yorkshire   Durham 2 points; Yorkshire 0 points

YORKSHIRE

A Z Lees, c Richardson b Brathwaite	....	12
J J Sayers, c Harmison b Davies	....	16
§ G L Brophy, c Harmison b Brathwaite	....	30
W T Root, c Pringle b Brathwaite	....	10
L J Hodgson, c Richardson b Brathwaite	....	1
D J Wainwright, not out	....	43
Azeem Rafiq, c Harmison b Shahzad	....	1
I Wardlaw, b Raine	....	8
B W Sanderson, lbw b Shahzad	....	0
* J A R Blain, not out	....	18
O J Hannon-Dalby	Did not bat	
Extras (b 2, lb 2, w 9, nb 2)	....	15
Total (8 wkts, 40 overs)		154

FoW: 1-26 (Sayers), 2-30 (Lees), 3-59 (Root), 4-65 (Hodgson), 5-78 (Brophy)
6-81 (Azeem Rafiq), 7-101 (Wardlaw), 8-102 (Sanderson)

	O	M	R	W
Rushworth	7	1	48	0
Davies	6	1	18	1
Brathwaite	8	2	27	4
Breese	8	0	19	0
Shahzad	7	0	20	2
Raine	4	0	18	1

DURHAM

M D Stoneman, b Hannon-Dalby	....	2
K K Jennings, c Brophy b Wardlaw	....	1
B A Raine, c Sayers b Azeem Rafiq	....	33
B W Harmison, not out	....	83
* G R Breese, c Root b Azeem Rafiq	....	3
§ M J Richardson, not out	....	29
R D Pringle		
R Shahzad		
R M R Brathwaite	Did not bat	
C Rushworth		
A M Davies		
Extras (w 7)	....	7
Total (4 wkts, 33.4 overs)	....	158

FoW: 1-3 (Stoneman), 2-Jennings), 3-70 (Raine), 4-76 (Breese)

	O	M	R	W
Hannon-Dalby	5	1	24	1
Wardlaw	4	0	13	1
Sanderson	5	0	21	0
Azeem Rafiq	8	0	32	2
Wainwright	7.4	0	36	0
Hodgson	4	0	32	0

Umpires: B V Taylor and H Evans   Scorers: M Snook and R V Hilton

Second Eleven Trophy
Yorkshire v. Lancashire

Played at Wagon Lane, Bingley, on July 26, 2011
Lancashire won by 7 wickets at 5.19pm

Toss won by Yorkshire

Lancashire 2 points; Yorkshire 0 poin

YORKSHIRE

J E Root, lbw b Newby	12
C J Geldart, c Bentley b Prior	85
A Z Lees, b Newby	0
§ G L Brophy, c Reece b Cheetham	81
D M Hodgson, lbw b Parry	15
A E Lilley, b Lilley	11
G S Randhawa, c Davies b Cheetham	11
* S A Patterson, c Agathangelou b Newby	1
I Wardlaw, c Agathangelou b Newby	6
M A Ashraf, c Agathangelou b Newby	1
O J Hannon-Dalby, not out	1
Extras (lb 10, w 4)	14
Total (38.5 overs)	238

FoW: 1-31 (Root), 2-31 (Lees), 3-187 (Brophy), 4-191 (Geldart), 5-212 (Hodgson), 6-2 (Lilley), 7-230 (Patterson), 8-231 (Randhawa), 9-232 (Ashraf), 10-238 (Wardla

	O	M	R	W
Newby	7.5	0	39	5
Cheetham	7	0	37	2
Cauce	6	0	41	0
Parry	8	0	55	2
Lilley	8	0	36	1
Woolley	2	0	20	0

LANCASHIRE

A P Agathangelou, run out		70
L N Bentley, b Lilley		66
L R Reece, c Brophy b Root		75
J Clark, not out		21
* S D Parry, not out		0
O J Newby		
§ A L Davies		
A M Lilley	Did not bat	
R J J Woolley		
N T Caunce		
S P Cheetham		
Extras (w 5, nb 4)		9
Total (3 wkts, 35.5 overs)		241

FoW: 1-123 (Agathangelou), 2-184 (Bentley), 3-237 (Clark)

	O	M	R	W
Wardlaw	5	0	30	0
Hannon-Dalby	4	0	32	0
Patterson	6	0	38	0
Ashraf	4.5	0	35	0
Randhawa	5	0	33	0
Root	7	0	49	1
Lilley	4	0	24	1

Umpires: S J Malone and K Fergusson

Scorers: M Snook and D M White

Second Eleven Trophy
Yorkshire v. Northamptonshire

Played at The Britannia Cricket Ground, Pudsey, on August 9, 2011
Yorkshire won by 37 runs at 5.34pm

Toss won by Yorkshire   Yorkshire 2 points; Northamptonshire 0 points

YORKSHIRE

A Lyth, c Mommsen b Burton		70
*J J Sayers, c Davis b Reynoldson		68
J E Root, c Mommsen b Sweeney		27
§ G L Brophy, b Lucas		23
C J Geldart, c Mommsen b Sweeney		30
A E Lilley, lbw b Lucas		1
D F Girling, not out		12
G S Randhawa, not out		0
S A Patterson		
I Wardlaw	Did not bat	
O J Hannon-Dalby		
Extras (b 1, lb 3, w 7, nb 2)		13
Total (6 wkts, 40 overs)		244

FoW: 1-137 (Sayers), 2-158 (Lyth), 3- 189 (Root), 4-198 (Brophy), 5-200 (Lilley)
6-243 (Geldart)

	O	M	R	W
Burton	7	0	51	1
Lucas	8	0	32	2
Sweeney	8	0	57	2
Davis	3	0	15	0
Mommsen	3	0	20	0
Brett	6	0	33	0
Reynoldson	5	0	32	1

NORTHAMPTONSHIRE

D J Willey, lbw b Root	25
A M Reynoldson, c Root b Girling	36
P L Mommsen, lbw b Patterson	0
C A L Davis, c Brophy b Patterson	0
* § D Murphy, b Wardlaw	73
R I Keogh, c Lyth b Girling	0
D S Lucas, b Wardlaw	54
B M R Akram, b Wardlaw	1
D A Burton, run out	1
S Sweeney, not out	3
T Brett, b Wardlaw	0
Extras (lb 8, w 4, nb 2)	14
Total (37 overs)	207

FoW: 1-52 (Willey), 2-53 (Mommsen), 3-53 (Davis), 4-72 (Reynoldson), 5-72 (Keogh)
6-185 (Murphy), 7-187 (Akram), 8-190 (Burton), 9-207 (Lucas), 10-207 (Brett)

	O	M	R	W
Hannon-Dalby	4	0	32	0
Wardlaw	8	0	51	4
Patterson	7	0	42	2
Root	5	0	17	1
Girling	4	0	12	2
Lilley	4	0	30	0
Randhawa	5	0	15	0

Umpires: S J Malone and I J Dixon   Scorers: M Snook and M E Woolley

Second Eleven Trophy
Leicestershire v. Yorkshire

Played at Grace Road, Leicester, on August 16, 2011
Leicestershire won by 2 wickets at 5.53pm

Toss won by Leicestershire   Leicestershire 2 points; Yorkshire 0 points

YORKSHIRE

A Lyth, c du Toit b Malik		21
* A Z Lees, c Sykes b Gurney		65
G J Rudolph, lbw b Wyatt		4
M R Good, lbw b Sykes		3
J J Stuart, b Sykes		12
§ D M Hodgson, run out		33
A E Lilley, not out		9
G S Randhawa		
I Wardlaw		
J C Wainman	Did not bat	
O J Hannon-Dalby		
Extras (lb 10, w 21)		31
Total (6 wkts, 37 overs)		178

FoW: 1-46 (Lyth), 2-67 (Rudolph), 3-73 (Good), 4-102 (Stuart), 5-157 (Lees)
6-178 (Hodgson)

	O	M	R	W
Gurney	8	0	43	1
Malik	7	0	40	1
Sykes	8	2	30	2
Wyatt	6	0	28	1
Taylor	5	0	16	0
Kadeer Ali	3	0	11	0

LEICESTERSHIRE

* W S Jones, lbw b Hannon-Dalby		4
P S P Handscomb, c and b Lilley		23
Kadeer Ali, c Hodgson b Wardlaw		2
J du Toit, b Wardlaw		0
§ E J Eckersley, not out		94
R M L Taylor, c Lyth b Lilley		0
L J Kinch, c Hodgson b Lilley		2
M N Malik, b Lilley		4
H F Gurney, run out		0
A C F Wyatt, not out		32
J S Sykes	Did not bat	
Extras (lb 6, w 9, nb 4)		19
Total (8 wkts, 37 overs)		180

FoW: 1-5 (Jones), 2-15 (Kadeer Ali), 3-15 (du Toit), 4-70 (Handscomb), 5-70 (Taylor)
6-74 (Kinch), 7-80 (Malik), 8-80 (Gurney)

	O	M	R	W
Hannon-Dalby	8	0	37	1
Wardlaw	7	1	39	2
Wainman	8	2	24	0
Lilley	6	0	28	4
Randhawa	5	0	33	0
Lyth	2	0	13	0

Umpires: S A Garratt and I M Armitage   Scorers: M Snook and D Ayriss

Second Eleven Trophy
Worcestershire v. Yorkshire

Played at New Road, Worcester, on August 22, 2011
Yorkshire won by 23 runs at 5.20pm

Toss won by Yorkshire   Yorkshire 2 points; Worcestershire 0 points

YORKSHIRE

A Lyth, c Cox b Shantry	0
A Z Lees, c Pinner b Root	32
J A Leaning, lbw b Russell	27
J A Tattersall, lbw b D'Oliveira	13
§ D M Hodgson, not out	88
E Wilson, st Cox b Root	35
A E Lilley, st Cox b Blofield	6
G S Randhawa, run out	1
I Wardlaw	
O J Hannon-Dalby Did not bat	
* J A R Blain	
Extras (b 1, lb 7, w 14)	22
Total (7 wkts, 40 overs)	224

FoW: 1-0 (Lyth), 2-61 (Lees), 3-75 (Leaning), 4-96 (Tattersall), 5-194 (Wilson)
6-223 (Lilley), 7-224 (Randhawa)

	O	M	R	W
Shantry	8	2	46	1
Sweeney	3	0	19	0
Russell	7	0	54	1
Root	6	0	28	2
D'Oliveira	8	0	27	1
Blofield	8	0	42	1

WORCESTERSHIRE

M G Pardoe, c Leaning b Wardlaw	5
J K Manuel, c Leaning b Hannon-Dalby	16
* N D Pinner, lbw b Waradlaw	4
W T Root, b Hannon-Dalby	1
T C Fell, b Hannon-Dalby	77
B L D'Oliveira, lbw b Blain	14
§ O B Cox, c Hannon-Dalby b Randhawa	35
A D Blofield, not out	26
J D Shantry, c Hodgson b Wardlaw	1
S Sweeney, b Wardlaw	1
C J Russell, b Hannon-Dalby	6
Extras (lb 5, w 8, nb 2)	15
Total (38.2 overs)	201

FoW: 1-13 (Pardoe), 2-17 (Pinner), 3-26 (Manuel), 4-34 (Root), 5-70 (D'Oliveira)
6-126 (Cox), 7-185 (Fell), 8-189 (Shantry), 9-191 (Sweeney), 10-201 (Russell)

	O	M	R	W
Hannon-Dalby	7.2	0	29	5
Wardlaw	8	0	47	3
Lilley	5	0	22	0
Blain	5	1	16	1
Randhawa	8	0	44	1
Tattersall	3	0	23	0
Lyth	2	0	15	0

Umpires: M A Eggleston and R Murphy   Scorers: M Snook and Mrs D E Pugh

SECOND ELEVEN TROPHY 2011

ZONE A – FINAL TABLE

		P	W	L	Tie	No result	Pen.	Net run rate	Points
1	Nottinghamshire (1)	9	9	0	0	0	0	0.686	18
2	Lancashire (2)	9	8	1	0	0	0	0.916	16
3	Durham (4)	9	6	3	0	0	0	0.082	12
4	Leicestershire (6)	9	5	4	0	0	0	-0.106	10
5	Worcestershire (7)	9	4	5	0	0	0	0.005	8
6	Yorkshire (5)	9	3	5	0	1	0	-0.392	7
7	Unicorns A (—)	9	3	6	0	0	0	0.852	6
8	Warwickshire (8)	9	3	6	0	0	0	-0.699	6
9	Derbyshire (9)	9	1	6	0	2	0	-0.571	4
10	Northamptonshire (—) ...	9	1	7	0	1	0	-0.980	3

ZONE B – FINAL TABLE

		P	W	L	Tie	No result	Pen.	Net run rate	Points
1	Somerset (9)	9	6	1	2	0	0	0.649	14
2	Glamorgan (—)	9	6	3	0	0	0	0.037	12
3	Kent (8)	9	5	3	0	1	0	0.664	11
4	Middlesex (1)	9	5	3	0	1	0	0.547	11
5	Sussex (5)	9	5	4	0	0	0	0.202	10
6	Hampshire (4)	9	4	3	0	2	0	0.017	10
7	Surrey (3)	9	3	4	1	1	0	-0.436	8
8	MCC Young Cricketers (—) .	9	3	6	0	0	0	-0.862	6
9	Essex (2)	9	2	6	0	1	0	-0.667	5
10	Gloucestershire (10)	9	1	7	1	0	0	-0.093	3

(2010 zone positions in brackets)

SEMI-FINALS

Nottinghamshire beat Glamorgan by 36 runs. Lancashire beat Somerset by 4 wickets

FINAL

Nottinghamshire beat Lancashire by 4 wickets

PREVIOUS WINNERS

1986	**Northamptonshire**, who beat Essex by 14 runs
1987	**Derbyshire**, who beat Hampshire by 7 wickets
1988	**Yorkshire**, who beat Kent by 7 wickets
1989	**Middlesex**, who beat Kent by 6 wickets
1990	**Lancashire**, who beat Somerset by 8 wickets
1991	**Nottinghamshire**, who beat Surrey by 8 wickets
1992	**Surrey**, who beat Northamptonshire by 8 wickets
1993	**Leicestershire**, who beat Sussex by 142 runs
1994	**Yorkshire**, who beat Leicestershire by 6 wickets
1995	**Leicestershire**, who beat Gloucestershire by 3 runs
1996	**Leicestershire**, who beat Durham by 46 runs
1997	**Surrey**, who beat Gloucestershire by 3 runs
1998	**Northamptonshire**, who beat Derbyshire by 5 wickets
1999	**Kent**, who beat Hampshire by 106 runs.
2000	**Leicestershire**, who beat Hampshire by 25 runs.
2001	**Surrey**, who beat Somerset by 6 wickets
2002	**Kent**, who beat Hampshire by 5 wickets
2003	**Hampshire**, who beat Warwickshire by 8 wickets
2004	**Worcestershire**, who beat Essex by 8 wickets
2005	**Sussex**, who beat Nottinghamshire by 6 wickets
2006	**Warwickshire**, who beat Yorkshire by 93 runs
2007	**Middlesex**, who beat Somerset by 1 run
2008	**Hampshire**, who beat Essex by 7 runs
2009	**Yorkshire, who** beat Lancashire by 2 wickets
2010	**Essex**, who beat Lancashire by 14 runs

SECOND ELEVEN TROPHY
AVERAGES 2011

Played 9   Won 3   Lost 5   Abandoned 1

BATTING AND FIELDING
(Qualification 3 innings)

Player	M.	I.	N.O.	Runs	H.S.	Avge	100s	50s	ct/st
D M Hodgson	3	3	1	136	88*	68.00	0	1	3/0
C J Geldart	4	4	0	192	85	48.00	0	2	0
G L Brophy	4	4	1	142	81	47.33	0	1	3/0
A Lyth	3	3	0	91	70	30.33	0	1	2
J Sayers	3	3	0	84	68	28.00	0	1	1
A Z Lees	7	6	1	132	65	26.40	0	1	0
J E Root	3	3	1	51	27	25.50	0	0	1
A R Blain	6	3	2	24	18*	24.00	0	0	0
A E Lilley	6	5	1	72	45	18.00	0	0	3
L J Hodgson	5	4	1	42	30	14.00	0	0	2
G S Randhawa	8	5	2	38	16*	12.66	0	0	2
B W Sanderson	4	3	0	26	22	8.66	0	0	1
Wardlaw	6	3	0	25	11	8.33	0	0	0
Also played									
G S Ballance	1	1	0	129	129	129.00	1	0	0
E Wilson	3	2	0	51	35	25.50	0	0	1/1
G S Ross	2	2	0	37	32	18.50	0	0	0
B Hargreaves	1	1	0	16	16	16.00	0	0	0
A Leaning	2	2	0	28	27	14.00	0	0	2
A McGrath	1	1	0	14	14	14.00	0	0	1
A Tattersall	1	1	0	13	13	13.00	0	0	0
J Stuart	1	1	0	12	12	12.00	0	0	0
W T Root	1	1	0	10	10	10.00	0	0	1
J C Wainman	2	1	0	6	6	6.00	0	0	0
G J Rudolph	1	1	0	4	4	4.00	0	0	0
J E Lee	2	1	0	3	3	3.00	0	0	0
H Tattersall	1	1	0	3	3	3.00	0	0	4/0
M R Good	1	1	0	3	3	3.00	0	0	1
O J Hannon-Dalby	8	2	1	1	1*	1.00	0	0	1
Azeem Rafiq	2	1	0	1	1	1.00	0	0	0
M A Ashraf	2	1	0	1	1	1.00	0	0	0
S A Patterson	2	1	0	1	1	1.00	0	0	0
D J Wainwright	2	1	1	43	43*	—	0	0	2
D F Girling	1	1	1	12	12*	—	0	0	1

BOWLING
(Qualification 5 wickets)

Player	Overs	Mdns	Runs	Wkts	Avge	Best	4wI
Wardlaw	37	2	204	11	18.54	4-51	1
O J Hannon-Dalby	39.1	2	216	10	21.60	5-29	1
A E Lilley	23	0	134	5	26.80	4-28	1
Also bowled							
L J Hodgson	24	0	135	4	33.75	2-14	0
G S Randhawa	41	0	208	4	52.00	2-9	0
D J Wainwright	15.4	0	68	3	22.66	3-32	0
J E Lee	13	1	84	3	28.00	3-28	0
B W Sanderson	16	1	94	3	31.33	2-22	0
D F Girling	4	0	12	2	6.00	2-12	0
J A R Blain	8	1	31	2	15.50	1-15	0
Azeem Rafiq	8	0	32	2	16.00	2-32	0
J C Wainman	12	2	65	2	32.50	2-41	0
J E Root	12	0	66	2	33.00	1-17	0
S A Patterson	13	0	80	2	40.00	2-42	0
G S Ross	6	0	53	1	53.00	1-53	0
M A Ashraf	4.5	0	35	0	—	—	0
A Lyth	4	0	28	0	—	—	0
J A Tattersall	3	0	23	0	—	—	0

Second Eleven Twenty20
Yorkshire v. Derbyshire

Played at Headingley Carnegie Cricket Ground, Leeds, on May 25, 2011

Derbyshire won by 2 wickets at 2.06pm

Toss won by Derbyshire   Derbyshire 2 points; Yorkshire 0 points

YORKSHIRE

A Z Lees, run out	. . . .	12
G S Ross, c Durham b Hughes	. . . .	15
J A Leaning, c Poynton b Whiteley	. . . .	37
L J Hodgson, c Footitt b Burgoyne	. . . .	10
§ E Wilson, st Poynton b Needham	. . . .	7
A E Lilley, c Footitt b Knight	. . . .	8
J E Lee, b Knight	. . . .	0
G S Randhawa, run out	. . . .	6
B W Sanderson, not out	. . . .	12
J C Wainman, not out	. . . .	1
* J A R Blain	Did not bat	
Extras (w 5)	. . . .	5
Total (8 wkts, 20 overs)	. . . .	113

FoW: 1-15 (Lees), 2-39 (Ross), 3-57 (Hodgson), 4-70 (Wilson), 5-89 (Leaning), 6-93 (Lilley), 7-93 (Lee), 8-102 (Randhawa)

	O	M	R	W
Knight	4	0	25	2
Footitt	3	0	7	0
Hughes	2	0	9	1
Whiteley	3	0	39	1
Burgoyne	4	0	17	1
Needham	4	0	16	1

DERBYSHIRE

M S Lineker, c Blain b Hodgson	. . . .	7
P M Borrington, b Hodgson	. . . .	19
§ T Poynton, b Hodgson	. . . .	10
A L Hughes, b Ross	. . . .	14
R A Whiteley, c Randhawa b Hodgson	. . . .	0
* J Needham, c Wainman b Ross	. . . .	23
M Fletcher, lbw b Ross	. . . .	0
P Burgoyne, c Wilson b Ross	. . . .	15
C M Durham, not out	. . . .	22
T C Knight, not out	. . . .	2
M H A Footitt	Did not bat	
Extras (lb 6)	. . . .	6
Total (8 wkts, 19.3 overs)	. . . .	118

FoW: 1-24 (Lineker), 2-36 (Poynton), 3-43 (Borrington), 4-43 (Whiteley), 5-66 (Hughes), 6-66 (Fletcher), 7-79 (Needham), 8-108 (Burgoyne)

	O	M	R	W
Lee	2.3	0	14	0
Wainman	2	0	17	0
Hodgson	4	0	13	4
Randhawa	4	0	28	0
Ross	4	0	20	4
Sanderson	3	0	20	0

Umpires: M J Saggers and I J Dixon   Scorers: M Snook and T M Cottam

Second Eleven Twenty20
Yorkshire v. Derbyshire

Played at Headingley Carnegie Cricket Ground, Leeds, on May 25, 2011
Derbyshire won by 7 wickets at 5.16pm

Toss won by Derbyshire

Derbyshire 2 points; Yorkshire 0 points

YORKSHIRE

A Z Lees, c Knight b Footitt	....	7
G S Ross, c Poynton b Sheikh	....	8
J A Leaning, run out	....	25
L J Hodgson, st Poynton b Burgoyne	....	26
§ E Wilson, not out	....	19
A E Lilley, b Hughes	....	2
J E Lee, not out	....	3
G S Randhawa		
B W Sanderson		
J C Wainman	Did not bat	
* J A R Blain		
Extras (b 1, lb 3, w 4)	....	8
Total (5 wkts, 20 overs)	....	98

FoW: 1-18 (Ross), 2-19 (Lees), 3-65 (Leaning), 4-81 (Hodgson), 5-84 (Lilley)

	O	M	R	W
Knight	4	0	18	0
Footitt	4	1	11	2
Sheikh	2	0	11	2
Needham	4	0	21	0
Hughes	3	0	16	0
Burgoyne	3	0	17	0

DERBYSHIRE

P M Borrington, b Randhawa	....	27
M S Lineker, b Ross	....	27
§ T Poynton, b Randhawa	....	3
A L Hughes, not out	....	12
R A Whiteley, not out	....	21
* J Needham		
M Fletcher		
P Burgoyne	Did not bat	
A Sheikh		
T C Knight		
M H A Footitt		
Extras (w 12)	....	12
Total (3 wkts, 17 overs)	....	102

FoW: 1-60 (Borrington), 2-66 (Lineker), 3-74 (Poynton)

	O	M	R	W
Lee	3	0	22	0
Wainman	2	0	11	0
Sanderson	2	0	7	0
Hodgson	2	0	16	0
Randhawa	4	0	11	2
Ross	4	0	35	1

Umpires: M J Saggers and I J Dixon

Scorers: M Snook and T M Cottam

Second Eleven Twenty20
Yorkshire v. Nottinghamshire

Played at Headingley Carnegie Cricket Ground, Leeds, on May 26, 2011

Nottinghamshire won by 8 wickets at 2.05pm

Toss won by Yorkshire   Nottinghamshire 2 points; Yorkshire 0 points

YORKSHIRE

A Z Lees, run out	....	14
G S Ross, b Weightman	....	41
J A Leaning, b Carter	....	19
L J Hodgson, run out	....	6
§ D M Hodgson, not out	....	8
A E Lilley, not out	....	15
G S Randhawa		
J A Tattersall		
B W Sanderson	Did not bat	
I Wardlaw		
* J A R Blain		
Extras (b 1, lb 1, w 8)	....	10
Total (4 wkts, 19 overs)	....	113

FoW: 1-30 (Lees), 2-81 (Ross), 3-86 (Leaning), 4-97 (L J Hodgson)

	O	M	R	W
Carter	4	0	23	1
Ball	4	0	24	0
Hutton	2	0	6	0
Bacon	2	0	8	0
Elstone	4	0	29	0
Wood	1	0	13	0
Weightman	2	0	8	1

NOTTINGHAMSHIRE

§ S Kelsall, st D M Hodgson b Randhawa	....	22
J T Ball, c Lees b Sanderson	....	11
S L Elstone, not out	....	73
S K W Wood, not out	....	7
O J D Swann		
M C Robson		
A Tillcock		
M W Weightman	Did not bat	
B A Hutton		
G P W Bacon		
* A Carter		
Extras (lb 1, w 3)	....	4
Total (2 wkts, 15.4 overs)	....	117

FoW: 1-26, Ball, 2-78 (Kelsall)

	O	M	R	W
Sanderson	3	0	22	1
Wardlaw	3	0	14	0
L J Hodgson	2	0	14	0
Blain	2	0	19	0
Randhawa	3	0	22	1
Ross	2.4	0	25	0

Umpires: M J Saggers and G Parker   Scorers: M Snook and R Marshall

Second Eleven Twenty20
Yorkshire v. Nottinghamshire

Played at Headingley Carnegie Cricket Ground, Leeds, on May 26, 2011
Match abandoned, no result at 4.58pm

Toss won by Yorkshire   Yorkshire 1 point; Nottinghamshire 1 point

YORKSHIRE

A Z Lees, not out	....	65
G S Ross, run out	....	33
J A Leaning, not out	....	32
L J Hodgson		
§ D M Hodgson		
A E Lilley		
G S Randhawa	Did not bat	
J A Tattersall		
B W Sanderson		
I Wardlaw		
* J A R Blain		
Extras (lb 3, w 4, pen 5)	....	12
Total (1 wkt, 14 overs)	....	142

FoW: 1-48 (Ross)

	O	M	R	W
Ball	3	0	24	0
Hutton	3	0	31	0
Bacon	2	0	22	0
Weightman	2	0	21	0
Wood	2	0	14	0
Tilcock	2	0	22	0

NOTTINGHAMSHIRE

T Rowe, not out	....	6
S K W Wood, not out	....	11
O J D Swann		
S L Elstone		
M C Robson		
A Tillcock		
M W Weightman	Did not bat	
* § S Kelsall		
B A Hutton		
G P W Bacon		
J T Ball		
Extras (w 1)	....	1
Total (0 wkts, 3 overs)	....	18

	O	M	R	W
Sanderson	2	0	10	0
Wardlaw	1	0	8	0

Umpires: M J Saggers and G Parker   Scorers: M Snook and R Marshall

Second Eleven Twenty20
Lancashire v. Yorkshire

At Station Road, Neston, on May 30, 2011
Match abandoned without a ball being bowled
Yorkshire 1 point; Lancashire 1 point

Lancashire v. Yorkshire

Played at Station Road, Neston, on May 30, 2011
Lancashire won by 28 runs at 5.58pm

Toss won by Yorkshire   Lancashire 2 points; Yorkshire 0 points

LANCASHIRE

J Clark, c Blain b Wardlaw	1
A P Agathangelou, c Sanderson b Wainman	4
L N Bentley, b Sanderson	29
W Chapples, b Wainman	2
* S D Parry, b L J Hodgson	7
§ A L Davies, b Sanderson	14
S C Kerrigan, not out	7
A M Lilley, c Lees b L J Hodgson	2
N T Caunce, b L J Hodgson	0
S P Cheetham not out	1
G T Griffiths	Did not bat
Extras (lb 2, w 10)	12
Total (8 wkts, 10 overs)	79

FoW: 1-3 (Clark), 2-6 (Agathangelou), 3-9 (Chapples), 4-37 (Parry), 5-69 (Bentley)
6-70 (Davis), 7-77 (Lilley), 8-77 (Caunce)

	O	M	R	W
Wardlaw	2	0	16	1
Wainman	2	0	14	2
L J Hodgson	2	0	10	3
Randhawa	2	0	25	0
Sanderson	2	0	12	2

YORKSHIRE

A Z Lees, c Bentley b Caunce	0
G S Ross, b Caunce	3
J A Leaning, lbw b Griffiths	10
L J Hodgson, st Davies b Parry	6
§ D M Hodgson, run out	7
A E Lilley, st Davies b Parry	3
G S Randhawa, b Caunce	10
B W Sanderson, c Cheetham b Griffiths	1
J C Wainman, not out	3
I Wardlaw, c Bentley b Griffiths	1
* J A R Blain, run out	1
Extras (b 1, lb 3, w 2)	6
Total (9.4 overs)	51

FoW: 1-4 (Ross), 2-5 (Lees), 3-15 (L J Hodgson), 4-26 (D M Hodgson), 5-30 (Lilley)
6-37 (Leaning), 7-39 (Sanderson), 8-46 (Randhawa), 9-49 (Wardlaw), 10-51 (Blain)

	O	M	R	W
Cheetham	2	0	7	0
Caunce	2	0	11	3
Parry	2	0	10	2
Kerrigan	2	0	11	0
Griffiths	1.4	0	8	3

Umpires: P J Hartley and H Evans   Scorers: M Snook and C Rimmer

Second Eleven Twenty20
Durham v. Yorkshire

Played at Riverside, Chester-le-Street, on June 6, 2011
Durham won by 4 wickets at 2.09pm

Toss won by Yorkshire   Durham 2 points; Yorkshire 0 points

YORKSHIRE

G S Ballance, c Brathwaite b Smith	0
J J Sayers, c Tye b Coyne	56
A Z Lees, c Borthwick b Brathwaite	45
J A Leaning, not out	25
L J Hodgson, not out	8

Azeem Rafiq
§ E Wilson
G S Randhawa   Did not bat
M A Ashraf
O J Hannon-Dalby
* J A R Blain

Extras (lb 3, w 4)	7
Total (3 wkts, 20 overs)	141

FoW: 1-0 (Ballance), 2-84 (Sayers), 3-129 (Lees)

	O	M	R	W
Smith	4	1	17	1
Coyne	4	0	18	0
Tye	4	0	24	1
Brathwaite	2	0	17	1
Raine	2	0	29	0
Borthwick	3	0	25	0
Coetzer	1	0	8	0

DURHAM

M D Stoneman, c Leaning b Hannon-Dalby	12
K J Coetzer, c and b Hannon-Dalby	2
W R Smith, not out	57
S G Borthwick, lbw b Azeem Rafiq	8
B W Harmison, lbw b Azeem Rafiq	16
* § M J Richardson, c Sayers b Hodgson	17
B A Raine, c Wilson b Ashraf	4
K K Jennings, not out	7

J J Coyne
A J Tye   Did not bat
R M R Brathwaite

Extras (b 2, lb 6, w 9, nb 2)	19
Total (6 wkts, 20 overs)	142

FoW: 1-12 (Coertzer), 2-26 (Stoneman), 3-42 (Borthwick), 4-71 (Harmison), 5-109 (Richardson), 6-133 (Raine)

	O	M	R	W
Hannon-Dalby	3	0	13	2
Ashraf	3	0	25	1
Hodgson	3	0	20	1
Blain	3	0	25	0
Azeem Rafiq	4	0	22	2
Randhawa	4	0	29	0

Umpires: J H Evans and J W Crockatt   Scorers: M Snook and R V Hilton

Second Eleven Twenty20
Durham v. Yorkshire

Played at Riverside, Chester-le-Street, on June 6, 2011
Durham won by 8 wickets at 5.25pm

Toss won by Durham

Durham 2 points; Yorkshire 0 points

YORKSHIRE

A Z Lees, c Tye b Coyne	....	10
J J Sayers, b Brathwaite	....	26
J A Leaning, b Brathwaite	....	11
Azeem Rafiq, c Coetzer b Borthwick	....	12
G S Ballance, b Smith	....	2
L J Hodgson, c Borthwick b Smith	....	16
§ E Wilson, c Jennings b Coetzer	....	16
G S Randhawa, not out	....	24
M A Ashraf, run out	....	1
O J Hannon-Dalby, run out	....	6
* J A R Blain, b Brathwaite	....	2
Extras (b 1, lb 3, w 9)	....	13
Total (20 overs)	....	139

FoW: 1-23 (Lees), 2-50 (Sayers), 3-53 (Leaning), 4-69 (Azeem Rafiq), 5-69 (Leaning)
6-101 (Hodgson), 7-105 (Wilson), 8-110 (Ashraf), 9-134 (Hannon-Dalby), 10-139 (Blain)

	O	M	R	W
Smith	4	0	15	2
Tye	2	0	22	0
Coyne	3	0	26	1
Brathwaite	4	0	29	3
Borthwick	4	0	22	1
Coetzer	3	0	21	1

DURHAM

M D Stoneman, c Azeem Rafiq b Hannon-Dalby	....	76
K J Coetzer, b Blain	....	41
W R Smith, not out	....	15
B A Raine, not out	....	3
B W Harmison		
* § M J Richardson		
S G Borthwick		
K K Jennings	Did not bat	
J J Coyne		
A J Tye		
R M R Brathwaite		
Extras (lb 2, w 3)	....	5
Total (2 wkts, 18.3 overs)	....	140

FoW: 1-114 (Coetzer), 2-129 (Stoneman)

	O	M	R	W
Hannon-Dalby	3.3	0	28	1
Ashraf	4	0	28	0
Randhawa	4	0	32	0
Hodgson	2	0	14	0
Azeem Rafiq	3	0	24	0
Blain	2	0	12	1

Umpires: J H Evans and J W Crockatt

Scorers: M Snook and R V Hilton

SECOND ELEVEN
TWENTY20 2011

(Two matches played against the same opponents
at the same venue on the same day)

ZONE A – FINAL TABLE

		P	W	L	Tie	No result	Pen.	Net run rate	Points
1	Leicestershire	8	5	2	1	0	0	0.202	11
2	Middlesex	8	4	2	1	1	0	0.385	10
3	Northamptonshire	8	4	4	0	0	0	0.131	8
4	Unicorns A	8	3	4	0	1	0	-0.121	7
5	Essex	8	2	6	0	0	0	-0.539	4

ZONE B – FINAL TABLE

		P	W	L	Tie	No result	Pen.	Net run rate	Points
1	Durham	8	6	2	0	0	0	0.874	12
2	Derbyshire	8	6	2	0	0	0	0.451	12
3	Lancashire	8	3	4	0	1	0	-0.050	7
4	Nottinghamshire	8	3	4	0	1	0	-0.653	7
5	**Yorkshire**	**8**	**0**	**6**	**0**	**2**	**0**	**-0.925**	**2**

ZONE C – FINAL TABLE

		P	W	L	Tie	No result	Pen.	Net run rate	Points
1	Gloucestershire	8	6	1	0	1	0	2.811	13
2	Glamorgan	8	4	3	0	1	0	0.084	9
3	Worcestershire	8	4	4	0	0	0	-0.130	8
4	Somerset	8	2	5	0	1	0	-0.946	5
5	Warwickshire	8	2	5	0	1	0	-1.384	5

ZONE D – FINAL TABLE

		P	W	L	Tie	No result	Pen.	Net run rate	Points
1	Sussex	8	4	2	0	2	0	1.612	10
2	Hampshire	8	5	3	0	0	0	1.140	10
3	Kent	8	4	4	0	0	0	-0.416	8
4	MCC Young Cricketers	8	2	4	0	2	0	-0.671	6
5	Surrey	8	3	5	0	0	0	-1.493	6

SEMI-FINALS

Durham beat Gloucestershire by 7 wickets. Sussex beat Leicestershire by 62 runs

FINAL

Sussex beat Durham by 24 runs

SECOND ELEVEN TWENTY20
AVERAGES 2011

Played 8   Won 0   Lost 6   Abandoned 2

BATTING AND FIELDING
(Qualification 3 innings)

Player	M.	I.	N.O.	Runs	H.S.	Avge	100s	50s	ct/st
J A Leaning	8	7	2	159	37	31.80	0	0	1
A Z Lees	8	7	1	153	65*	25.50	0	1	2
E Wilson	4	3	1	42	19*	21.00	0	0	2/0
G S Ross	6	5	0	100	41	20.00	0	0	0
G S Randhawa	8	3	1	40	24*	20.00	0	0	1
L J Hodgson	8	6	1	72	26	14.40	0	0	0
A E Lilley	5	4	1	28	15*	9.33	0	0	0
Also played									
J J Sayers	2	2	0	82	56	41.00	0	1	1
D M Hodgson	4	2	1	15	8*	15.00	0	0	0/1
B W Sanderson	6	2	1	13	12*	13.00	0	0	1
Azeem Rafiq	2	1	0	12	12	12.00	0	0	1
O J Hannon-Dalby	2	1	0	6	6	6.00	0	0	1
J E Lee	2	2	1	3	3*	3.00	0	0	0
J A R Blain	8	2	0	3	2	1.50	0	0	2
G S Ballance	2	2	0	2	2	1.00	0	0	0
I Wardlaw	4	1	0	1	1	1.00	0	0	0
M A Ashraf	2	1	0	1	1	1.00	0	0	0
J C Wainman	4	2	2	4	3*	—	0	0	1

BOWLING
(Qualification 5 wickets)

Player	Overs	Mdns	Runs	Wkts	Avge	Best	4wI
L J Hodgson	15	0	87	8	10.88	4-13	1
G S Ross	10.4	0	80	5	16.00	4-20	0
Also bowled							
O J Hannon-Dalby	6	0	41	3	13.67	2-13	0
J C Wainman	6	0	42	2	21.00	2-14	0
Azeem Rafiq	7	0	46	2	23.00	2-22	0
B W Sanderson	12	0	71	3	23.67	2-12	0
I Wardlaw	6	0	38	1	38.00	1-16	0
G S Randhawa	21	0	147	3	49.00	2-11	0
M A Ashraf	7	0	53	1	53.00	1-25	0
J A R Blain	7	0	56	1	56.00	1-12	0
J E Lee	5.3	0	36	0	—	—	0

Played at Weetwood Cricket Ground, Leeds, on April 13, 2011

Durham won by 2 wickets at 5.46pm

Toss won by Yorkshire

YORKSHIRE

G S Ballance, b Brathwaite	1
C J Geldart, lbw b Smith	91
A Z Lees, st Richardson b Breese	49
L J Hodgsosn, b Brathwaite	37
D J Wainwright, c Rushworth b Jennings	8
Azeem Rafiq, not out	9
A E Lilley, b Brathwaite	1
J E Lee, not out	6
G S Randhawa	
O J Hannon-Dalby Did not bat	
§ B P Gibson	
Extras (b 1, lb 9, w 21, nb 2)	33
Total (6 wkts, 50 overs)	235

Twelfth man: * J A R Blain

FoW: 1-6 (Ballance), 2-147 (Lees), 3-181 (Geldart), 4-192 (Wainwright), 5-220 (Hodgson)
6-226 (Lilley)

	O	M	R	W
Brathwaite	8	1	35	3
Rushworth	7	1	30	0
Harmison	4	0	25	0
Wood	5	0	29	0
Breese	10	0	33	1
Smith	10	0	38	1
Jennings	6	0	35	1

DURHAM

W R Smith, c Ballance b Lee	11
K J Coetzer, lbw b Randhawa	68
§ M J Richardson, c Lees b Hannon-Dalby	1
B W Harmison, c Gibson b Azeem Rafiq	89
* G R Breese, c Geldart b Azeem Rafiq	6
M A Wood, not out	31
B A Raine, st Gibson b Azeem Rafiq	5
K K Jennings, c and b Azeem Rafiq	1
P Coughlin, run out	1
C Rushworth, not out	5
R M R Brathwaite Did not bat	
Extras (b 1, lb 4, w 14)	19
Total (8 wkts, 49 overs)	237

Twelfth man: J Killeen

FoW: 1-26 (Smith), 2-27 (Richardson), 3-166 (Coetzer), 4-191 (Breese), 5-199 (Harmison)
6-211 (Raine), 7-220 (Jennings), 8-222 (Coughlin)

	O	M	R	W
Hannon-Dalby	7	0	24	1
Lee	8	0	41	1
Hodgson	6	0	23	0
Lilley	3	0	13	0
Wainwright	10	0	56	0
Azeem Rafiq	10	0	45	4
Randhawa	5	0	30	1

Umpires: I J Dixon and J A Gomersall   Scorers: M Snook and R V Hilton

Other Second Eleven Match
Yorkshire v. Durham

Played at Weetwood Cricket Ground, Leeds, on April 14, 2011

Yorkshire won by 8 wickets at 5.32pm

Toss won by Yorkshire

DURHAM

B A Raine, c Gibson b Lee	0
K J Coetzer, c Gibson b Wainman	0
K K Jennings, c Ballance b Azeem Rafiq	41
B W Harmison, lbw b Lee	4
* G R Breese, c Blain b Randhawa	72
M A Wood, b Azeem Rafiq	1
P Coughlin, c Geldart b Randhawa	10
§ C J Pearce, lbw b Randhawa	5
C Rushworth, c and b Randhawa	12
R M R Brathwaite, not out	3
C T Harding, lbw b Hodgson	2
Extras (b 1, lb 2, w 10)	13
Total (44.4 overs)	163

Twelfth man: J Killeen

FoW: 1-0 (Raine), 2-0 (Coetzer), 3-7 (Harmison), 4-93 (Jennings), 5-95 (Wood), 6-118 (Coughlin), 7-126 (Pearce), 8-154 (Breese), 9-154 (Rushworth), 10-163 (Harding)

	O	M	R	W
Lee	6	1	21	2
Wainman	6	1	13	1
Hodgson	6.4	1	19	1
Lilley	1	0	6	0
Blain	6	0	23	0
Azeem Rafiq	10	2	37	2
Randhawa	9	0	41	4

YORKSHIRE

G S Ballance, c Jennings b Rushworth		14
J J Sayers, not out		69
C J Geldart, lbw b Killeen		21
A Z Lees, not out		41
L J Hodgson		
D J Wainwright		
Azeem Rafiq		
A E Lilley	Did not bat	
J E Lee		
G S Randhawa		
§ B P Gibson		
Extras (b 9, lb 7, w 3)		19
Total (2 wkts, 39.2 overs)		164

Twelfth man: * J A R Blain

FoW: 1-18 (Ballance), 2-71 (Lees)

	O	M	R	W
Brathwaite	7	1	29	0
Rushworth	8	3	20	1
Harding	6	0	23	0
Killeen	5	0	18	1
Breese	4	1	11	0
Wood	5	0	30	0
Coughlin	4.2	0	17	0

Umpires: S Boulton and P M McFarlane   Scorers: M Snook and R V Hilton

Other Second Eleven Match
Derbyshire v. Yorkshire

Played at Christ Church Meadows, Belper, on April 19, 20 and 21, 2011

Derbyshire won by 1 wicket at 5.54pm on the Third Day

Toss won by Yorkshire

Close of play: First Day, Derbyshire 15-0 (Lineker 10*, Park 3*); Second Day, Yorkshire 93-1 (Ballance 48*, Geldart 20*)

YORKSHIRE

First Innings		Second Innings	
G S Ballance, c Poynton b Whiteley	15	not out	101
J J Sayers, c Needham b Knight	128	c Park b Ahmed Mehraj	7
C J Geldart, c Lineker b Needham	49	c Durham b Park	31
A Z Lees, c Poynton b Needham	27	c Lineker b Needham	1
L J Hodgson, c Lineker b Knight	38	not out	17
Azeem Rafiq, c Needham b Whiteley	24		
A E Lilley, not out	16		
J E Lee, not out	23		
G S Randhawa			
J C Wainman	Did not bat		
§ B P Gibson			
Extras (b 1, lb 9, w 5, nb 8)	23	Extras (b 6, lb 3, w 11, nb 17)	37
Total (6 wkts dec, 100 overs)	343	Total (3 wkts dec, 39 overs)	194

Twelfth man: * J A R Blain

FoW: 1-23 (Ballance), 2-160 (Geldart), 3-222 (Lees), 4-251 (Sayers), 5-279 (Azeem Rafiq)
1st 6-312 (Hodgson)
2nd 1-44 (Sayers), 2-155 (Lees), 3-158 (Hodgson)

	O	M	R	W		O	M	R	W
Sheikh	6	0	41	0	Sheikh	6	0	38	0
Whiteley	12	5	25	2	Cotton	6	2	16	0
Cotton	9	2	33	0	Ahmed Mehraj	7	0	44	1
Ahmed Mehraj	8	2	30	0	Knight	5	0	10	0
Knight	26	3	95	2	Usman Muzzafer	3	0	11	0
Needham	25	5	75	2	Park	6	0	28	1
Usman Muzzafer	14	2	34	0	Needham	6	0	38	1

DERBYSHIRE

First Innings		Second Innings	
M S Lineker, c Azeem Rafiq b Wainman	39	(2) c Lilley b Lee	0
G T Park, lbw b Lee	6	(1) not out	165
A C Williamson, c Geldart b Lee	5	run out	4
§ T Poynton, run out	25		
A L Hughes, c Ballance b Lee	90	(4) run out	0
M Fletcher, lbw b Randhawa	52	(5) c Gibson b Randhawa	1
* J Needham, c Wainman b Azeem Rafiq	27	c Gibson b Wainman	38
Ahmed Mehraj, c Azeem Rafiq b Randhawa	3	c Gibson b Randhawa	0
T C Knight, not out	11	b Randawa	21
A Sheikh, c Blain b Randhawa	0	b Azeem Rafiq	1
B Cotton		not out	0
§ C M Durham	Did not bat	(6) c Sayers b Randhawa	36
Extras (b 1, lb 3, w 1)	5	Extras (b 6, lb 5, w 1)	12
Total (9 wkts dec, 87.4 overs)	263	Total (9 wkts, 77.1 overs)	278

Twelfth man: Usman Muzzafer

FoW: 1-23 (Park), 2-34 (Williamson), 3-77 (Lineker), 4-78 (Poynton), 5-186 (Fletcher)
1st 6-238 (Needham), 7-252 (Ahmed Mehraj), 8-258 (Highes), 9-258 (Sheikh)
FoW: 1-7 (Lineker), 2-12 (Williamson), 3-23 (Hughes), 4-30 (Fletcher), 5-90 (Durham)
2nd 6-173 (Needham), 7-174 (Ahmed Mehraj), 8-236 (Knight), 9-257 (Sheikh)

	O	M	R	W		O	M	R	W
Lee	19	3	58	3	Lee	6	0	33	1
Wainman	11	3	30	1	Wainman	7	3	8	1
Azeem Rafiq	21	6	50	1	Azeem Rafiq	28.1	4	94	1
Randhawa	16.4	2	53	3	Randhawa	27	6	98	4
Hodgson	11	2	32	0	Hodgson	9	1	34	0
Lilley	9	3	36	0					

Umpires: P K Baldwin and N R Roper

Scorers: M Snook and T M Cottam

NOTES: For Derbyshire, R A Whiteley was called up for First Eleven duties at the start of the Second Day. He was replaced by M Fletcher. T Poynton was called up for First Eleven duties during the evening session of the Second Day. G T Park kept wicket for the remainder of the session, in which role he caught J J Sayers. C M Durham took over wicket-keeping duties for the Third Day

A Kent-Northamptonshire XII v. Yorkshire

Played at Worsley Bridge Road, Beckenham, on May 9, 10, 11 and 12, 2011
Yorkshire won by 174 runs at 4.50pm on the Fourth Day
Toss won by Yorkshire

Close of play: First day, Yorkshire 334-5 (Lees 177*, Wilson 25*); Second Day, Kent-Northamptonshire 145-3 (Howgego 54*, Keogh 13*); Third Day, Yorkshire 184-2 (Ballance 101*, Wainwright 46*)

First Innings	YORKSHIRE	Second Innings	
G S Ballance, lbw b Baker	75	c Neale b Day	109
C J Geldart, c Lucas b Willey	3	c Keogh b Neale	22
A Z Lees, c & Billings b Baker	204	lbw b Burns	4
D J Wainwright, lbw b Burns	27	not out	73
J B Hargreaves, lbw b Neale	5	not out	23
A E Lilley, lbw b Burns	0		
§ E Wilson, c Burns b Neale	52		
G S Randhawa, b Burton	12		
B W Sanderson, c Piesley b Burns	44		
* J A R Blain, not out	35		
O J Hannon-Dalby, not out	3		
Extras (b 3, lb 7, w 4, nb 16)	40	Extras (b 1, lb 8, w 3)	12
Total (9 wkts dec, 142 overs)	500	Total (3 wkts dec, 44 overs)	243

FoW: 1-4 (Geldart), 2-135 (Ballance), 3-220 (wainwright), 4-255 (Hargreaves), 5-260 (Lilley)
1st   6-391 (Wilson), 7-403 (Lees), 8-417 (Randhawa), 9-492 (Sanderson)
2nd   1-80 (Geldart), 2-85 (Lees), 3-199 (Ballance)

	O	M	R	W		O	M	R	W
Lucas	18	4	52	0	Burton	7	0	50	0
Willey	13.5	2	60	1	Baker	4	0	22	0
Day	9	1	54	0	Burns	17	0	83	1
Baker	29	6	105	2	Day	7	1	27	1
Neale	34	6	112	2	Neale	7	0	38	1
Burns	20	4	49	3	Keogh	1	0	7	0
Piesley	4.1	0	12	0	Piesley	1	0	7	0
Burton	14	3	36	1					

First Innings	KENT-NORTHAMPTONSHIRE	Second Innings	
B H N Howgego, c Lees b Hannon-Dalby	180	c Wilson b Hannon-Dalby	12
C D Piesley, c Wilson b Hannon-Dalby	23	c Ballance b Randhawa	18
R I Newton, lbw b Hannon-Dalby	23	b Wainwright	52
* § S W Billings, lbw b Blain	40	c Geldart b Hannon-Dalby	35
R I Keogh, c Wilson b Hannon-Dalby	13	c Ballance b Hannon-Dalby	1
C R G Vernon, b Wainwright	13	lbw b Wainwright	3
D J Willey, c Ballance b Randhawa	13	lbw b Sanderson	35
G C Baker, c and b Wainwright	3	c Geldart b Wainwright	0
D J Burns, not out	33	lbw b Randhawa	1
D A Burton, not out	6	not out	13
A Neale	Did not bat	c Ballance b Sanderson	8
Extras (b 14, lb 10, w 13, nb 8)	45	Extras (b 10, lb 2, w 7, nb 4)	23
Total (8 wkts dec, 116 overs)	368	Total (63.5 overs)	201

Twelfth man: J H Day

FoW: 1-8 (Piesley), 2-43 (Newton), 3-127 (Billings), 4-145 (Keogh), 5-199 (Vernon)
1st   6-255 (Willey), 7-282 (Baker), 8-352 (Howgego)
FoW: 1-32 (Howgego), 2-51 (Piesley), 3-105 (Newton), 4-132 (Keogh), 5-133 (Billings)
2nd   6-139 (Vernon), 7-151 (Baker), 8-168 (Burns), 9-191 (Willey), 10-201 (Neale)

	O	M	R	W		O	M	R	W
Hannon-Dalby	25	3	77	4	Hannon-Dalby	12	1	45	3
Sanderson	15	0	61	0	Sanderson	7.5	0	24	2
Blain	12	2	38	1	Randhawa	19	6	36	2
Wainwright	32	13	57	2	Blain	4	0	31	0
Randhawa	22	6	54	1	Wainwright	21	7	53	3
Lilley	6	1	17	0					
Hargreaves	4	0	40	0					

Umpires: A G B Wharf and R L Collins   Scorers: M Snook and C A Booth

NOTE: For Kent-Northamptonshire, D S Lucas was called up for First Eleven duties on the Second Day. He was replaced by D A Burton.

Other Second Eleven Match
Yorkshire v. Ireland A

Played at St George's Road, Harrogate, on July 13, 14 and 15, 2011
Yorkshire won by an innings and 75 runs at 11.51am on the Third Day

Toss won by Ireland A

Close of play: First Day, Yorkshire 174-1 (Lees 59*, Brophy 101*): Second Day, Ireland A 120-3 (Shannon 20*, McDonnell 19*)

IRELAND A

	First Innings			Second Innings	
C Dougherty, lbw b Ashraf	18		run out		30
T D L Fisher, b L J Hodgson	29		c Brophy b Wainman		25
J N K Shannon, c D M Hodgson b Wardlaw	31		(4) b Wainman		20
N J McDonnell, lbw b Wainman	6		(5) b Lilley		53
* A D Poynter, b Wainman	35		(6) lbw b Wainman		4
S R Thompson, c D M Hodgson b Ashraf	21		(7) lbw b Wainman		0
J D Hall, lbw b Ashraf	0		(3) c and b Wainwright		15
§ R D McCann, not out	40		c Lees b Ashraf		13
L T Nelson, c Brophy b Hannon-Dalby	20		c Wainman b Ashraf		0
G J McCarter, lbw b Hannon-Dalby	0		c Wainman b Lilley		20
E J Richardson, run out	30		not out		1
Extras (b 6, lb 14, nb 10)	30		Extras (b 4, lb 13, nb 4)		21
Total (63.4 overs)	260		Total (54 overs)		202

FoW: 1-29 (Dougherty), 2-86 (Shannon), 3-90 (Fisher), 4-104 (McDonnell), 5-153 (Thompson)
1st 6-155(Hall), 7-155 (Poynter), 8-213 (Nelson), 9-213 (McCarter), 10-260 (Richardson)
FoW: 1-66 (Dougherty), 2-66 (Fisher), 3-94 (Hall), 4-120 (Shannon), 5-130 (Poynter)
2nd 6-130 (Thompson), 7-175 (McCann), 8-177 (Nelson), 9-197 (McDonnell), 10-202 (McCarter)

	O	M	R	W		O	M	R	W
Hannon-Dalby	15	2	47	2	Hannon-Dalby	13	3	47	0
Wardlaw	11	1	38	1	Ashraf	10	1	39	2
Ashraf	16	3	44	3	Wainman	9	3	26	4
L J Hodgson	5	0	26	1	Wardlaw	5	2	11	0
Wainman	9	3	42	2	Wainwright	8	1	32	1
Wainwright	7	2	39	0	Randhawa	4	2	9	0
Randhawa	0.4	0	4	0	Lilley	5	0	21	2

YORKSHIRE

A Z Lees, c Dougherty b McCarter	138
J J Sayers, c Eaglestone b McCarter	0
§ G L Brophy, lbw b Eaglestone	118
D J Wainwright, c Dougherty b Richardson	180
D M Hodgson, c Fisher b Thompson	19
L J Hodgson, lbw b Richardson	15
G S Randhawa, not out	14
I Wardlaw, c Hall b Richardson	9
M A Ashraf	
J C Wainman	Did not bat
O J Hannon-Dalby	
Extras (b 5, lb 13, w 4, nb 22)	44
Total (7 wkts dec, 116.4 overs)	537

Twelfth man: * J A R Blain

FoW: 1-2 (Sayers), 2-205 (Brophy), 3-385 (Lees), 4-434 (D M Hodgson), 5-513 (Wainwright)
6-513 (L J Hodgson), 7-537 (Wardlaw)

	O	M	R	W
Eaglestone	23	2	99	1
McCarter	24	4	80	2
Thompson	14	1	83	1
Richardson	20.4	1	106	3
Nelson	20	1	77	0
Poynter	5	0	21	0
Hall	10	1	53	0

Umpires: R J Evans and H Evans   Scorer: M Snook

NOTES: For Yorkshire, D F Girling and A E Lilley replaced J J Sayers, D J Wainwright and I Wardlaw, who were called up for First Eleven duties on the Third Day.

Played at Weetwood, Leeds, on August 31 and September 1 and 2, 2011

Yorkshire won by 72 runs at 2.15pm on the Third Day

Toss won by MCC Young Cricketers

Close of play: First Day, MCC Young Cricketers 56-2 (Lewis 15*, Hose 5*); Second Day, Yorkshire 169-9 (Wardlaw 21*, Jackson 0*)

YORKSHIRE	First Innings		Second Innings	
A Z Lees, c Dobb b Porter	15	(2) c Garside b Porter	19
G J Rudolph, lbw b Barrett	40	(1) c and b Barrett	43
§ G L Brophy, c Ballard Garside	28	c Marsh b Porter	15
D M Hodgson, c Hose b Dobb	86	c Marsh b Barrett	0
J J Stuart, b Dobb	0	(6) c Marsh b Garside	9
G S Randhawa, lbw b Dobb	2	(7) c Southgate b Dobb	22
O J Hannon-Dalby, c Lewis b Clarke	13	(8) b Barrett	14
M R Good, lbw b Hampton	8	(5) lbw b Garside	8
I Wardlaw, c Marsh b Hampton	4	c Marsh b Barrett	25
* J A R Blain, not out	39	lbw b Barrett	0
O G Jackson, not out	12	not out	5
Extras (b 10, lb 3, nb 19)	32	Extras (b 6, lb 5, w 9, nb 2)	22
Total (9 wkts dec, 80 overs)	269	Total (48.5 overs)	182

FoW: 1-44 (Lees), 2-99 (Brophy), 3-106 (Rudolph), 4-107 (Stuart), 5-123 (Randhawa)
1st 6-175 (Hannon-Dalby), 7-196 (Good), 8-200 (Wardlaw), 9-228 (Hodgson)

FoW: 1-47 (Lees), 2-82 (Brophy), 3-82 (Rudolph), 4-83 (Hodgson), 5-104 (Good)
2nd 6-119 (Stuart), 7-129 (Randhawa), 8-(Hannon-Dalby), 9-151 (Blain), 10-182 (Wardlaw)

	O	M	R	W		O	M	R	W
Hampton	14	2	50	2	Hampton	4	0	15	0
Barrett	12	4	15	1	Barrett	10.5	2	35	5
Porter	12	0	42	1	Garside	12	4	30	2
Garside	14	3	58	1	Porter	8	3	32	2
Dobb	19	4	67	3	Dobb	10	4	35	1
Clarke	25	5	75	2	Clarke	4	0	24	0

MCC YOUNG CRICKETERS	First Innings		Second Innings	
T P Lewis, b Hannon-Dalby	17	c Brophy b Wardlaw	7
*O M Ali, c Blain b Wardlaw	16	lbw b Wardlaw	0
J A Southgate, lbw b Hannon-Dalby	17	c Brophy b Hannon-Dalby	0
A Hose, b Hannon-Dalby	18	c Brophy b Wardlaw	23
E C Ballard, c Brophy b Hannon-Dalby	0	c Wardlaw b Jackson	44
A D Clarke, c Jackson b Randhawa	8	b Randhawa	16
§ C R J Marsh, b Randhawa	25	lbw b Blain	1
C A Barrett, b Jackson	63	c Brophy b Wardlaw	17
A Dobb, lbw b Randhawa	9	not out	35
K A Garside, c Good b Randhawa	2	lbw b Wardlaw	0
J A Porter, not out	23	c Blain b Randhawa	8
Extras (b 6, lb 7, nb 4)	17	Extras (b 5, lb 6, nb 2)	13
Total (78.1 overs)	215	Total (33.3 overs)	164

Twelfth man: T R G Hampton

FoW: 1-20 (Ali), 2-44 (Southgate), 3-73 (Lewis), 4-73 (Ballard), 5-76 (Hose)
1st 6-90 (Clarke), 7-123 (Marsh), 8-157 (Dobb), 9-165 (Garside), 10-215 (Barrett)

FoW: 1-0 (Ali), 2-3 (Sothgate), 3-7 (Lewis), 4-44 (Hose), 5-72 (Clarke)
2nd 6-83 (Marsh), 7-118 (Barrett), 8-118 (Ballard), 9-123 (Garside), 10-164 (Porter)

	O	M	R	W		O	M	R	W
Hannon-Dalby	22	5	46	4	Hannon-Dalby	7	3	15	1
Wardlaw	16	2	58	1	Wardlaw	11	1	82	5
Randhawa	23	9	56	4	Blain	4	1	12	1
Jackson	10.1	3	18	1	Randhawa	5.3	1	16	2
Stuart	7	1	24	0	Jackson	6	1	28	1

Umpires: A Hicks and D M Koch   Scorers: M Snook and K N Hutchinson

NOTES: For Yorkshire, A E Lilley and J C Wainman were nominated, but they were injured before play began. They were replaced by the nominated Twelfth Man, O G Jackson, and M R Good.

YORKSHIRE ECB COUNTY PREMIER LEAGUE 2011

	P	CW	IW1	IW2	IW3	IL1	IL2	IL3	CL	T	C	A	Points
*													
York	26	15	0	4	0	0	1	0	2	1	2	1	158
Rotherham Town . .	26	10	0	2	5	0	0	0	5	0	2	2	134
Cleethorpes	26	9	1	0	5	0	2	1	0	4	0		122
Yorkshire Academy	**2**	**11**	**0**	**1**	**2**	**0**	**0**	**5**	**3**	**0**	**4**	**0**	**118**
Sheffield Collegiate	26	10	0	2	2	0	0	1	8	0	2	1	113
Scarborough	26	7	0	3	2	2	2	2	3	0	3	2	107
Castleford	26	7	1	3	1	0	0	3	6	1	3	1	102
Barnsley	26	5	0	2	5	0	0	6	5	1	1	1	92
Harrogate	26	4	2	0	5	0	3	1	7	1	3	0	90
Appleby Frodingham	26	6	0	1	4	0	0	1	11	0	2	1	87
Sheffield United . .	26	5	0	0	1	2	4	4	7	0	2	1	63
Driffield Town	26	4	0	1	0	0	2	2	13	2	1	1	54
Hull	26	1	0	0	3	0	0	3	14	0	4	1	41
Doncaster Town . . .	26	2	0	0	1	0	5	7	8	0	1	2	36

* P = Played; CW = Complete win (8 points); IW1 = Incomplete win (6 points); IW2 = Incomplete win (6 points); IW3 = Incomplete win (6 points); IL1 = Incomplete loss (2 points); IL2 = Incomplete loss 1 (1 point); IL3 = Incomplete loss (0 points); CL = Complete loss (0 points); T = Tied (4 points); C = Cancelled (3 points); A = Abandoned (3 points).

Yorkshire League Cup: Winners: **Yorkshire Academy.** Runners-up:Scarborough.

YORKSHIRE ACADEMY BATTING IN ECB LEAGUE AND CUP

Player	M.	I.	N.O.	Runs	H.S.	Avge	100s	50s	ct/st
A Lees	23	22	6	1097	112	68.56	2	11	10
G Ross	27	23	3	783	90	41.21	0	7	10
H Chadwick	17	10	5	200	70	40.00	0	0	12/3
J Leaning	27	25	6	754	85	39.68	0	4	13
J Tattersall	27	22	4	479	61	26.61	0	2	9
E Wilson	23	14	4	242	65	24.20	0	1	10
W Rhodes	11	8	2	133	36	22.16	0	0	2
J McNichol	14	13	2	223	33*	20.27	0	0	1
J Blain	11	4	2	21	10*	10.50	0	0	3
D Girling	17	10	1	79	25	8.78	0	0	3
B Coad	24	9	4	42	10	8.40	0	0	1
J Wainman	20	6	0	33	11	5.50	0	0	2

Also batted: A McGrath 107, 90; J Shaw 0*, 1, 10, ct 1; A Leyshon 0*, 1*, 2*, ct 3; A Lilley 33*, 9, 20*, ct 2; A Shahzad 12, 9; A Robinson 0, 2*; J Moxon 2, 2, ct 1; C Free 0

YORKSHIRE ACADEMY BOWLING IN ECB LEAGUE AND CUP

Player	Overs	Mdns	Runs	Wkts	Avge	Best	5wI
A Lilley	45	9	144	15	9.60	7-15	1
J Wainman	164.2	39	438	37	11.86	4-12	0
B Coad	153.3	44	455	27	16.85	6-31	1
J Tattersall	135.3	14	470	26	18.07	5-59	1
J Blain	54.2	11	174	9	19.33	4-37	0
A Robinson	39.5	6	147	7	21.00	2-14	0
J McNichol	19	1	87	4	21.75	3-24	0
G Ross	131.4	19	478	20	23.90	3-20	0
S Patterson	14	7	75	3	25.00	2-14	0
W Rhodes	34	7	103	4	25.75	3-14	0
D Girling	120.5	14	348	12	29.00	4-23	0
J Shaw	32	12	112	4	28.00	2-12	0
A Leyshon	104.1	11	356	12	29.67	4-40	0
J Moxon	65	11	288	9	32.00	3-36	0

Also bowled: A Shahzad 20-3-63-1, A McGrath 4-0-12-1, C Free 4-0-12-0, J Leaning 3-0-15-0, M Fisher 13-2-37-1

RECORDS SECTION

(All records in this section relate to First-Class Yorkshire matches only — except where otherwise stated)

HONOURS

County Champions (32)
1867, 1870, 1893, 1896, 1898, 1900, 1901, 1902, 1905, 1908, 1912, 1919, 1922, 1923, 1924, 1925, 1931, 1932, 1933, 1935, 1937, 1938, 1939, 1946, 1959, 1960, 1962, 1963, 1966, 1967, 1968, 2001.

Joint Champions (2)
1869, 1949

Promoted to Division 1
2005

Gillette Cup Winners (2)
1965, 1969

Cheltenham & Gloucester Trophy (1)
2002

Benson & Hedges Cup Winners (1)
1987

John Player Special League Winners (1)
1983

Fenner Trophy Winners (3)
1972, 1974, 1981

Asda Challenge Winners (1)
1987

Ward Knockout Cup (1)
1989

Joshua Tetley Festival Trophy (7)
1991, 1992 (Joint), 1993, 1994, 1996, 1997 and 1998

Tilcon Trophy Winners (2)
1978 and 1988

Pro-Arch Trophy (1)
2007-08

Second Eleven Champions (4)
1977, 1984, 1991, 2003

Joint Champions (1)
1987

Minor Counties Champions (5)
1947, 1957, 1958, 1968, 1971

Under-25 Competition Winners (3)
1976, 1978, 1987

Bain Clarkson Trophy Winners (2)
1988 and 1994

Second Eleven Trophy (1)
2009

YORKSHIRE'S CHAMPIONSHIP CAPTAINS

1867 to 2001

R Iddison (2)	1867, 1870
Lord Hawke (8)	1893, 1896, 1898, 1900, 1901, 1902, 1905, 1908
Sir Archibald White (1)	1912
D C F Burton (1)	1919
G Wilson (3)	1922, 1923, 1924
A W Lupton (1)	1925
F E Greenwood (2)	1931, 1932
A B Sellers (6)	1933, 1935, 1937, 1938, 1939, 1946
J R Burnet (1)	1959
J V Wilson (2)	1960, 1962
D B Close (4)	1963, 1966, 1967, 1968
D Byas (1)	2001

Joint Champions

R Iddison (1)	1869
N W D Yardley (1)	1949

RECORDS SECTION INDEX

	Page
Champion Counties since 1873	245
Season-by-Season Record of all First-Class Matches	247
Analysis of Results	248
Highest Match Aggregates	251
Lowest Match Aggregates	251
Large Margins of Victory	252
Heavy Defeats	254
Narrow Victories and Narrow Defeats	255
High Fourth Innings Scores	256
Tie Matches	257
Highest Scores By and Against Yorkshire	257
Lowest Scores By and Against Yorkshire	259
Individual Innings of 150 and over	261
Centuries By Current Yorkshire Players	271
Centuries Including Highest Score	273
Summary of Centuries For and Against Yorkshire	276
Four Centuries in One Innings	277
Century in Each Innings	278
Highest Individual Scores For and Against Yorkshire	278
Carrying Bat Through Completed Innings	282
2,000 Runs in a Season and 1,000 Runs in a Season	283
Batsmen who have scored centuries for and against Yorkshire	287
Batsmen who have scored over 10,000 Runs	288
Record Partnerships For and Against Yorkshire	289
Highest Partnerships for each Wicket	290
Fifteen Wickets or More in a Match	298
Ten Wickets in an Innings	300
Eight Wickets or More in an Innings	300
Six Wickets in an Innings at Less than Four Runs Each	305
Four Wickets in Four Balls	308
Best Bowling Analyses in a Match For and Against Yorkshire	309
Best Bowling Analyses in an Innings For and Against Yorkshire	311
Hat Tricks	313
200 Wickets in a Season and 100 Wickets in a Season	314
Bowlers who have Taken over 500 Wickets	316
Bowling Unchanged in a Match	316
Most Catches in an Innings	317
Most Catches in a Match/A Season/A Career	317
Most Dismissals in an Innings/A Match/A Season/A Career	318
The Double (All First-Class Matches)	319
Yorkshire Test Cricketers	321
Centuries for England	325
10 Wickets in a Match for England	327
Test Match Hat Tricks	330
Test Matches at Leeds, 1899-2010	337
Yorkshire One-Day International Cricketers	346
Limited-Overs International Matches at Leeds, 1973-2011	348
List of Yorkshire Players and Career Records	352
Friends Provident Trophy/Cheltenham & Gloucester/Gillette Cup/NatWest Trophy	375
Benson & Hedges Cup Records	385
Clydesdale Bank 40, Pro40, National and Sunday League Records	389
All Limited-Overs Career Records	399
Yorkshire Twenty20 International Cricketers	402
Twenty20 Cup Records	403
Second Eleven Records	407

CHAMPION COUNTIES SINCE 1873

		Yorkshire's Position			Yorkshire's Position
1873	{ Gloucestershire / Nottinghamshire }	7th	1925	**Yorkshire**	**1st**
1874	Gloucestershire	4th	1926	Lancashire	2nd
1875	Nottinghamshire	4th	1927	Lancashire	3rd
1876	Gloucestershire	3rd	1928	Lancashire	4th
1877	Gloucestershire	7th	1929	Nottinghamshire	2nd
1878	Middlesex	6th	1930	Lancashire	3rd
1879	Nottinghamshire/Lancashire	6th	**1931**	**Yorkshire**	**1st**
1880	Nottinghamshire	5th	**1932**	**Yorkshire**	**1st**
1881	Lancashire	3rd	**1933**	**Yorkshire**	**1st**
1882	Nottinghamshire/Lancashire	3rd	1934	Lancashire	5th
1883	Nottinghamshire	2nd	**1935**	**Yorkshire**	**1st**
1884	Nottinghamshire	3rd	1936	Derbyshire	3rd
1885	Nottinghamshire	2nd	**1937**	**Yorkshire**	**1st**
1886	Nottinghamshire	4th	**1938**	**Yorkshire**	**1st**
1887	Surrey	3rd	**1939**	**Yorkshire**	**1st**
1888	Surrey	2nd	**1946**	**Yorkshire**	**1st**
1889	{ Surrey/Lancashire / Nottinghamshire }	7th	1947	Middlesex	7th
1890	Surrey	3rd	1948	Glamorgan	4th
1891	Surrey	8th	**1949**	**Yorkshire**/Middlesex	**1st**
1892	Surrey	6th	1950	Lancashire/Surrey	3rd
1893	**Yorkshire**	**1st**	1951	Warwickshire	2nd
1894	Surrey	2nd	1952	Surrey	2nd
1895	Surrey	3rd	1953	Surrey	12th
1896	**Yorkshire**	**1st**	1954	Surrey	2nd
1897	Lancashire	4th	1955	Surrey	2nd
1898	**Yorkshire**	**1st**	1956	Surrey	7th
1899	Surrey	3rd	1957	Surrey	3rd
1900	**Yorkshire**	**1st**	1958	Surrey	11th
1901	**Yorkshire**	**1st**	**1959**	**Yorkshire**	**1st**
1902	**Yorkshire**	**1st**	**1960**	**Yorkshire**	**1st**
1903	Middlesex	3rd	1961	Hampshire	2nd
1904	Lancashire	2nd	**1962**	**Yorkshire**	**1st**
1905	**Yorkshire**	**1st**	**1963**	**Yorkshire**	**1st**
1906	Kent	2nd	1964	Worcestershire	5th
1907	Nottinghamshire	2nd	1965	Worcestershire	4th
1908	**Yorkshire**	**1st**	**1966**	**Yorkshire**	**1st**
1909	Kent	3rd	**1967**	**Yorkshire**	**1st**
1910	Kent	8th	**1968**	**Yorkshire**	**1st**
1911	Warwickshire	7th	1969	Glamorgan	13th
1912	**Yorkshire**	**1st**	1970	Kent	4th
1913	Kent	2nd	1971	Surrey	13th
1914	Surrey	4th	1972	Warwickshire	10th
1919	**Yorkshire**	**1st**	1973	Hampshire	14th
1920	Middlesex	4th	1974	Worcestershire	11th
1921	Middlesex	3rd	1975	Leicestershire	2nd
1922	**Yorkshire**	**1st**	1976	Middlesex	8th
1923	**Yorkshire**	**1st**	1977	Kent/Middlesex	12th
1924	**Yorkshire**	**1st**	1978	Kent	4th
			1979	Essex	7th
			1980	Middlesex	6th
			1981	Nottinghamshire	10th

		Yorkshire's Position			*Yorkshire's Position*
1982	Middlesex	10th	1997	Glamorgan	6th
1983	Essex	17th	1998	Leicestershire	3rd
1984	Essex	14th	1999	Surrey	6th
1985	Middlesex	11th	2000	Surrey	3rd
1986	Essex	10th	**2001**	**Yorkshire**	**1st**
1987	Nottinghamshire	8th	2002	Surrey	9th
1988	Worcestershire	13th	2003	Sussex	Div 2, 4th
1989	Worcestershire	16th	2004	Warwickshire	Div 2, 7th
1990	Middlesex	10th	2005	Nottinghamshire	Div 2, 3rd
1991	Essex	14th	2006	Sussex	Div 1, 6th
1992	Essex	16th	2007	Sussex	Div 1, 6th
1993	Middlesex	12th	2008	Durham	Div 1, 7th
1994	Warwickshire	13th	2009	Durham	Div 1, 7th
1995	Warwickshire	8th	2010	Nottinghamshire	Div 1, 3rd
1996	Leicestershire	6th	2011	Lancashire	Div 1, 8th

SEASON-BY-SEASON RECORD OF ALL FIRST-CLASS
MATCHES PLAYED BY YORKSHIRE 1863-2011

Season	Played	Won	Lost	Drawn	Abd§	Season	Played	Won	Lost	Drawn	Abd§
1863	4	2	1	1		1921	30	17	5	8	
1864	7	2	4	1		1922	33	20	2	11	
1865	9	—	7	2		1923	35	26	1	8	
1866	3	—	2	1		1924	35	18	4	13	
1867	7	7	—	—		1925	36	22	—	14	
1868	7	4	3	—		1926	35	14	—	21	1
1869	5	4	1	—		1927	34	11	3	20	1
1870	7	6	—	1		1928	32	9	—	23	
1871	7	3	3	1		1929	35	11	2	22	
1872	10	2	7	1		1930	34	13	3	18	2
1873	13	7	5	1		1931	33	17	1	15	1
1874	14	10	3	1		1932	32	21	2	9	2
1875	12	6	4	2		1933	36	21	5	10	
1876	12	5	3	4		1934	35	14	7	14	
1877	14	2	7	5		1935	36	24	2	10	
1878	20	10	7	3		1935-6	3	1	—	2	
1879	17	7	5	5		1936	35	14	2	19	
1880	20	6	8	6		1937	34	22	3	9	1
1881	20	11	6	3		1938	36	22	2	12	
1882	24	11	9	4		1939	34	23	4	7	1
1883	19	10	2	7		1945	2	—	—	2	
1884	20	10	6	4		1946	31	20	1	10	
1885	21	8	3	10		1947	32	10	9	13	
1886	21	5	8	8		1948	31	11	6	14	
1887	20	6	5	9		1949	33	16	3	14	
1888	20	7	7	6		1950	34	16	6	12	1
1889	16	3	11	2	1	1951	35	14	3	18	
1890	20	10	4	6		1952	34	17	3	14	
1891	17	5	11	1	2	1953	35	7	7	21	
1892	19	6	6	7		1954	35	16	3	16*	
1893	23	15	5	3		1955	33	23	6	4	
1894	28	18	6	4	1	1956	35	11	7	17	
1895	31	15	10	6		1957	34	16	5	13	1
1896	32	17	6	9		1958	33	10	8	15	2
1897	30	14	7	9		1959	35	18	8	9	
1898	30	18	3	9		1960	38	19	7	12	
1899	34	17	4	13		1961	39	19	5	15	
1900	32	19	1	12		1962	37	16	5	16	
1901	35	23	2	10	1	1963	33	14	4	15	
1902	31	15	3	13	1	1964	33	12	4	17	
1903	31	16	5	10		1965	33	12	4	17	
1904	32	10	2	20	1	1966	32	16	6	10	1
1905	33	21	4	8		1967	31	16	5	10	2
1906	33	19	6	8		1968	32	13	4	15	
1907	31	14	5	12	2	1969	29	4	7	18	
1908	33	19	—	14		1970	26	10	5	11	
1909	30	12	5	13		1971	27	5	8	14	
1910	31	11	8	12		1972	21	4	5	12	1
1911	32	16	9	7		1973	22	3	5	14*	
1912	35	14	3	18	1	1974	22	6	7	9	1
1913	32	16	5	11		1975	21	11	1	9	
1914	31	16	4	11	2	1976	22	7	7	8	
1919	31	12	5	14		1977	23	7	5	11	1
1920	30	17	6	7		1978	24	10	3	11	1

Season	Played	Won	Lost	Drawn	Abd§	Season	Played	Won	Lost	Drawn	Abe
1979	22	6	3	13	1	1995-6	2	2	—	—	
1980	24	5	4	15		1996	19	8	5	6	
1981	24	5	9	10		1997	20	7	4	9	
1982	22	5	1	16	1	1998	19	9	3	7	
1983	23	1	5	17	1	1999	17	8	6	3	
1984	24	5	4	15		2000	18	7	4	7	
1985	25	3	4	18	1	2001	16	9	3	4	
1986	25	4	6	15		2002	16	2	8	6	
1986-7	1	—	—	1		2003	17	4	5	8	
1987	24	7	4	13	1	2004	16	3	4	9	
1988	24	5	6	13		2005	17	6	1	10	
1989	22	3	9	10		2006	16	3	6	7	
1990	24	5	9	10		2007	17	5	4	8	
1991	24	4	6	14		2008	16	2	5	9	
1991-2	1	—	1	—		2009	17	2	2	13	
1992	22	4	6	12	1	2010	18	6	2	10	
1992-3	1	—	—	1		2011	17	4	6	7	
1993	19	6	4	9			3515	1478	645	1392	38
1994	20	7	6	7							
1995	20	8	8	4		*Includes one tie in each season.					

§ All these matches were abandoned without a ball being bowled, except Yorkshire v Kent
Harrogate, 1904, which was abandoned under Law 9. The two in 1914 and the one in 1939 were
abandoned because of war. All these matches are excluded from the total played.

Of the 1,478 matches won, 506 have been by an innings margin, 81 by 200 runs or more, and
130 by 10 wickets. Of the 645 matches lost, 108 have been by an innings margin, 12 by 200 runs
or more and 34 by 10 wickets.

ANALYSIS OF RESULTS VERSUS ALL FIRST-CLASS
TEAMS 1863-2011

COUNTY CHAMPIONSHIP

Opponents	Played	Won	Lost	Drawn	Tied
Derbyshire	201	101	19	81	—
Durham	28	12	7	9	—
Essex	158	83	25	50	—
Glamorgan	109	52	13	44	—
Gloucestershire	198	100	43	55	—
Hampshire	163	72	19	72	—
Kent	198	84	39	75	—
Lancashire	253	74	52	127	—
Leicestershire	164	83	15	65	1
Middlesex	225	78	54	92	1
Northamptonshire	138	65	26	47	—
Nottinghamshire	246	87	47	112	—
Somerset	165	89	22	54	—
Surrey	238	85	67	86	—
Sussex	193	83	32	78	—
Warwickshire	182	80	31	71	—
Worcestershire	138	68	21	49	—
Cambridgeshire	8	3	4	1	—
Total	3005	1299	536	1168	2

OTHER FIRST-CLASS MATCHES

Opponents	Played	Won	Lost	Drawn	Tied
Derbyshire	2	1	1	0	—
Essex	2	2	0	0	—
Hampshire	1	0	0	1	—
Lancashire	12	5	3	4	—
Leicestershire	2	1	1	0	—
Middlesex	1	1	0	0	—
Nottinghamshire	2	1	1	0	—
Surrey	1	0	0	1	—
Sussex	2	0	0	2	—
Warwickshire	2	0	0	2	—
Totals	27	11	6	10	—
Australians	55	6	19	30	—
Indians	14	5	1	8	—
New Zealanders	10	2	0	8	—
Pakistanis	4	1	0	3	—
South Africans	17	1	3	13	—
Sri Lankans	3	0	0	3	—
West Indians	17	3	7	7	—
Zimbabweans	2	0	1	1	—
Bangladesh A	1	1	0	0	—
India A	2	0	0	2	—
Pakistan A	1	1	0	0	—
South Africa A	1	0	0	1	—
Totals	127	20	31	76	—
Cambridge University/U C C E	88	42	17	29	—
Canadians	1	1	0	0	—
Combined Services	1	0	0	1	—
Durham MCCU	1	1	0	0	—
England XI's	6	1	2	3	—
Hon. M.B. Hawke's XI	1	0	1	0	—
International XI	1	1	0	0	—
Ireland	3	3	0	0	—
Jamaica	3	1	0	2	—
Liverpool and District*	3	2	1	0	—
Loughborough UCCE	2	1	0	1	—
MCC	153	54	39	60	—
Mashonaland	1	1	0	0	—
Matebeleland	1	1	0	0	—
Minor Counties	1	1	0	0	—
Oxford University	44	21	3	20	—
Philadelphians	1	0	0	1	—
Rest of England	16	4	5	7	—
Royal Air Force	1	0	0	1	—
Scotland**	11	7	0	4	—
South of England	2	1	0	1	—
C. I. Thornton's XI	5	2	0	3	—
United South of England	1	1	0	0	—
Western Province	2	0	1	1	—
Windward Islands	1	0	0	1	—
Zingari	6	2	3	1	—
Totals	356	148	72	136	—
Grand Totals	3515	1478	645	1390	2

*Matches played in 1889, 1891, 1892 and 1893 are excluded. **Match played in 1878 is included

ABANDONED MATCHES (38)

1889	v. MCC at Lord's	1939	v. MCC at Scarborough (due to war)
1891 (2)	v. MCC at Lord's	1950	v. Cambridge University
	v. MCC at Scarborough		at Cambridge
1894	v. Kent at Bradford	1957	v. West Indians at Bradford
1901	v. Surrey at The Oval	1958 (2)	v. Nottinghamshire at Hull
1902	v. Leicestershire at Leicester (AR)		v. Worcestershire at Bradford
1904	v. Kent at Harrogate (Law 9	1966	v. Oxford University at Oxford
	— now Law 10)	1967 (2)	v. Leicestershire at Leeds
1907 (2)	v. Derbyshire at Sheffield		v. Lancashire at Manchester
	v. Nottinghamshire at Huddersfield	1972	v. Australians at Bradford
1912	v. Surrey at Sheffield	1974	v. Hampshire at Bournemouth
1914 (2)	v. England at Harrogate (due to war)	1977	v. Gloucestershire at Bristol
	v. MCC at Scarborough (due to war)	1978	v. Pakistan at Bradford
1926	v. Nottinghamshire at Leeds	1979	v. Nottinghamshire at Sheffield (AP)
1927	v. Kent at Bradford	1982	v. Nottinghamshire at Harrogate
1930 (2)	v. Derbyshire at Chesterfield*	1983	v. Middlesex at Lord's
	v. Northamptonshire at Harrogate*	1985	v. Essex at Sheffield (AP)
1931	v. Sussex at Hull	1987	v. Sussex at Hastings
1932 (2)	v. Derbyshire at Chesterfield	1992	v. Oxford University at Oxford
	v. Kent at Sheffield		
1937	v. Cambridge University at Bradford		

*Consecutive matches

ANALYSIS OF RESULTS ON GROUNDS IN YORKSHIRE USED IN 2011

FIRST-CLASS MATCHES

Ground	Played	Won	Lost	Drawn	Tied
Leeds					
Headingley 1891-2011	417	157 (37.65%)	77 (18.47%)	183 (43.88%)	0 (0.0%)
Scarborough					
North Marine Road 1874-2011	243	96 (39.51%)	34 (13.99)	113 (46.50%)	0 (0.0%)

Leeds, June 1955

The struggle between the two leading sides in the country drew over 60,000 people, and the atmosphere resembled that of a Test match. Surrey struggled hard to preserve their record, but were beaten for the first time in 16 consecutive games. The gates were locked on Saturday, when 35,000 saw Surrey fight back after losing their first eight wickets for 119.

Wisden on Yorkshire

HIGHEST MATCH AGGREGATES – OVER 1350 RUNS

Runs	Wkts	
1665	33	Yorkshire (351 and 481) lost to Warwickshire (601:9 dec and 232:4) by 6 wkts at Birmingham, 2002
1606	31	Yorkshire (438 and 363:5 dec) lost to Somerset (326 and 479:6) by 4 wkts at Taunton, 2009
1479	28	Yorkshire (405 and 333:4 dec) lost to Somerset (377 and 364:4) by 6 wkts at Taunton , 2010
1473	17	Yorkshire (600:4 dec. and 231:3 dec.) drew with Worcestershire (453:5 dec. and 189:5) at Scarborough, 1995.
1442	29	Yorkshire (501:6 dec. and 244:6 dec.) beat Lancashire (403:7 dec. and 294) by 48 runs at Scarborough, 1991.
1439	32	Yorkshire (536:8 dec. and 205:7 dec.) beat Glamorgan (482: 7 dec. and 216) by 43 runs at Cardiff, 1996.
1431	32	Yorkshire (388 and 312:6) drew with Sussex (398 and 333:6 dec) at Scarborough, 2011
1417	33	Yorkshire (422 and 193:7) drew with Glamorgan (466 and 336:6 dec) at Colwyn Bay, 2003
1406	37	Yorkshire (354 and 341:8) drew with Derbyshire (406 and 305:9 dec) at Derby, 2004
1400	32	Yorkshire (299 and 439: 4 dec.) drew with Hampshire (296 and 366:8) at Southampton, 2007
1393	35	Yorkshire (331 and 278) lost to Kent (377 and 407:5 dec) by 175 runs at Maidstone, 1994.
1390	34	Yorkshire (431:8 dec and 265:7) beat Hampshire (429 and 265) by 3 wkts at Southampton, 1995.
1376	33	Yorkshire (531 and 158:3) beat Lancashire (373 and 314) by 7 wkts at Leeds, 2001
1376	20	Yorkshire (677: 7 dec.) drew with Durham (518 and 181:3 dec.) at Leeds, 2006
1374	36	Yorkshire (594: 9 dec. and 266:7 dec.) beat Surrey (344 and 170) by 346 runs at The Oval, 2007
1373	36	Yorkshire (520 and 114:6) drew with Derbyshire (216 and 523) at Derby, 2005
1364	35	Yorkshire (216 and 433) lost to Warwickshire (316 and 399:5 dec.) by 66 runs at Birmingham, 2006
1359	25	Yorkshire (561 and 138:3 dec.) drew with Derbyshire (412:4 dec. and 248:8) at Sheffield, 1996.
1359	30	Yorkshire (358 and 321) lost to Somerset (452 and 228:0) by 10 wickets at Taunton, 2011
1353	18	Yorkshire (377:2 dec. and 300:6) beat Derbyshire (475:7 dec. and 201:3 dec.) by 4 wkts at Scarborough, 1990.

LOWEST MATCH AGGREGATES – UNDER 225 RUNS IN A COMPLETED MATCH

Runs	Wkts	
165	30	Yorkshire (46 and 37:0) beat Nottinghamshire (24 and 58) by 10 wkts at Sheffield, 1888.
175	29	Yorkshire (104) beat Essex (30 and 41) by an innings and 33 runs at Leyton, 1901.
182	15	Yorkshire (4:0 dec. and 88.5) beat Northamptonshire (4:0 dec. and 86) by 5 wkts at Bradford, 1931.
193	29	Yorkshire (99) beat Worcestershire (43 and 51) by an innings and 5 runs at Bradford, 1900.
219	30	Yorkshire (113) beat Nottinghamshire (71 and 35) by an innings and 7 runs at Nottingham, 1881.
222	32	Yorkshire (98 and 14:2) beat Gloucestershire (68 and 42) by 8 wkts at Gloucester, 1924.
223	40	Yorkshire (58 and 51) lost to Lancashire (64 and 50) by 5 runs at Manchester, 1893.

LOWEST MATCH AGGREGATES – UNDER 325 RUNS
IN A MATCH IN WHICH ALL 40 WICKETS FELL

Runs	Wkts	
223	40	Yorkshire (58 and 51) lost to Lancashire (64 and 50) by 5 runs at Manchester, 1893.
288	40	Yorkshire (55 and 68) lost to Lancashire (89 and 76) by 42 runs at Sheffield, 1872.
295	40	Yorkshire (71 and 63) lost to Surrey (56 and 105) by 27 runs at The Oval, 1886.
303	40	Yorkshire (109 and 77) beat Middlesex (63 and 54) by 69 runs at Lord's, 1891.
318	40	Yorkshire (96 and 96) beat Lancashire (39 and 87) by 66 runs at Manchester, 1874.
318	40	Yorkshire (94 and 104) beat Northamptonshire (61 and 59) by 78 runs at Bradford, 1955.
319	40	Yorkshire (84 and 72) lost to Derbyshire (106 and 57) by 7 runs at Derby, 1878.
320	40	Yorkshire (98 and 91) beat Surrey (72 and 59) by 58 runs at Sheffield, 1893.
321	40	Yorkshire (88 and 37) lost to I Zingari (103 and 93) by 71 runs at Scarborough, 1877.
321	40	Yorkshire (80 and 67) lost to Derbyshire (129 and 45) by 27 runs at Sheffield, 1879.

LARGE MARGINS OF VICTORY – BY AN INNINGS
AND OVER 250 RUNS

Inns and 397 runs	Yorkshire (548:4 dec.) beat Northamptonshire (58 and 93) at Harrogate, 1921
Inns and 387 runs	Yorkshire (662) beat Derbyshire (118 and 157) at Chesterfield, 1898.
Inns and 343 runs	Yorkshire (673:8 dec) beat Northamptonshire (184 and 146) at Leeds, 2003
Inns and 321 runs	Yorkshire (437) beat Leicestershire (58 and 58) at Leicester, 1908.
Inns and 314 runs	Yorkshire (356:8 dec) beat Northamptonshire (27 and 15) at Northampton, 1908. (Yorkshire's first match v. Northamptonshire).
Inns and 313 runs	Yorkshire (555:1 dec) beat Essex (78 and 164) at Leyton, 1932.
Inns and 307 runs	Yorkshire (681:5 dec.) beat Sussex (164 and 210) at Sheffield, 1897.
Inns and 302 runs	Yorkshire (660) beat Leicestershire (165 and 193) at Leicester, 1896.
Inns and 301 runs	Yorkshire (499) beat Somerset (125 and 73) at Bath, 1899.
Inns and 294 runs	Yorkshire (425:7 dec.) beat Gloucestershire (47 and 84) at Bristol, 1964.

LARGE MARGINS OF VICTORY – BY AN INNINGS
AND OVER 250 RUNS *(Continued)*

ns and 284 runs   Yorkshire (467:7 dec) beat Leicestershire (111 and 72)
at Bradford, 1932.

ns and 282 runs   Yorkshire (481:8 dec) beat Derbyshire (106 and 93)
at Huddersfield, 1901.

ns and 280 runs   Yorkshire (562) beat Leicestershire (164 and 118)
at Dewsbury, 1903.

ns and 271 runs   Yorkshire (460) beat Hampshire (128 and 61) at Hull, 1900.

ns and 271 runs   Yorkshire (495:5 dec) beat Warwickshire (99 and 125)
at Huddersfield, 1922.

ns and 266 runs   Yorkshire (352) beat Cambridgeshire (40 and 46)
at Hunslet, 1869.

ns and 260 runs   Yorkshire (521: 7dec.) beat Worcestershire (129 and 132)
at Leeds, 2007.

ns and 258 runs   Yorkshire (404:2 dec) beat Glamorgan (78 and 68)
at Cardiff, 1922.
(Yorkshire's first match v. Glamorgan).

ns and 256 runs   Yorkshire (486) beat Leicestershire (137 and 93)
at Sheffield, 1895.

ns and 251 runs   Yorkshire (550) beat Leicestershire (154 and 145)
at Leicester, 1933.

LARGE MARGINS OF VICTORY – BY OVER 300 RUNS

89 runs   Yorkshire (368 and 280:1 dec) beat Somerset (125 and 134)
at Bath, 1906.

70 runs   Yorkshire (194 and 274) beat Hampshire (62 and 36)
at Leeds, 1904.

51 runs   Yorkshire (280 and 331) beat Northamptonshire (146 and 114)
at Northampton, 1947.

46 runs   Yorkshire (594: 9 dec. and 266: 7 dec.) beat Surrey (344 and 179)
at The Oval, 2007.

28 runs   Yorkshire (186 and 318:1 dec) beat Somerset (43 and 133)
at Bradford, 1930.

28 runs   Yorkshire (280 and 277:7 dec) beat Glamorgan (104 and 105)
at Swansea, 2001

20 runs   Yorkshire (331 and 353:9 dec) beat Durham (150 and 214)
at Chester-le-Street, 2004.

08 runs   Yorkshire (89 and 420) beat Warwickshire (72 and 129)
at Birmingham, 1921.

LARGE MARGINS OF VICTORY – BY 10 WICKETS
(WITH OVER 100 RUNS SCORED IN THE 4th INNINGS)

4th Innings

167:0 wkt	Yorkshire (247 and 167:0) beat Northamptonshire 233 and 180) at Huddersfield, 1948.
147:0 wkt	Yorkshire (381 and 147:0) beat Middlesex (384 and 142) at Lord's, 1896.
142:0 wkt	Yorkshire (304 and 142:0) beat Sussex (254 and 188) at Bradford, 1887.
139:0 wkt	Yorkshire (163:9 dec and 139:0) beat Nottinghamshire (234 and 67) at Leeds, 1932.
138:0 wkt	Yorkshire (293 and 138:0) beat Hampshire (251 and 179) at Southampton, 1897.
132:0 wkt	Yorkshire (328 and 132:0) beat Northamptonshire (281 and 175) at Leeds, 2005
129:0 wkt	Yorkshire (355 and 129:0) beat Durham MCCU (196 and 287) at Durham, 2011
127:0 wkt	Yorkshire (258 and 127:0) beat Cambridge University (127 and 257) at Cambridge, 1930.
119:0 wkt	Yorkshire (109 and 119:0) beat Essex (108 and 119) at Leeds, 1931.
118:0 wkt	Yorkshire (121 and 118:0) beat MCC (125 and 113) at Lord's, 1883.
116:0 wkt	Yorkshire (147 and 116:0) beat Hampshire (141 and 120) at Bournemouth, 1930.
114:0 wkt	Yorkshire (135 and 114:0) beat Hampshire (71 and 176) at Bournemouth, 1948.

HEAVY DEFEATS – BY AN INNINGS
AND OVER 250 RUNS

Inns and 272 runs	Yorkshire (78 and 186) lost to Surrey (536) at The Oval, 1898.
Inns and 261 runs	Yorkshire (247 and 89) lost to Sussex (597: 8 dec.) at Hove, 2007.
Inns and 255 runs	Yorkshire (125 and 144) lost to All England XI (524) at Sheffield, 1865.

HEAVY DEFEATS – BY OVER 300 RUNS

324 runs	Yorkshire (247 and 204) lost to Gloucestershire (291 and 484) at Cheltenham, 1994.
305 runs	Yorkshire (119 and 51) lost to Cambridge University (312 and 163) at Cambridge, 1906.

HEAVY DEFEATS – BY 10 WICKETS
(WITH OVER 100 RUNS SCORED IN THE 4th INNINGS)

th Innings

28:0 wkt	Yorkshire (358 and 321) lost to Somerset (452 and 228:0) at Taunton, 2011
48:0 wkt	Yorkshire (83 and 216) lost to Lancashire (154 and 148:0) at Manchester, 1875.
19:0 wkt	Yorkshire (92 and 109) lost to Nottinghamshire (86 and 119:0 wkt) at Leeds, 1989.
08:0 wkt	Yorkshire (236 and 107) lost to Hampshire (236 and 108:0 wkt) at Southampton, 2008
00:0 wkt	Yorkshire (95 and 91) lost to Gloucestershire (88 and 100:0) at Bristol, 1956.

NARROW VICTORIES – BY 1 WICKET

Yorkshire (70 and 91:9) beat Cambridgeshire (86 and 74) at Wisbech, 1867.
Yorkshire (91 and 145:9) beat MCC (73 and 161) at Lord's, 1870.
Yorkshire (265 and 154:9) beat Derbyshire (234 and 184) at Derby, 1897.
Yorkshire (177 and 197:9) beat MCC (188 and 185) at Lord's, 1899.
Yorkshire (391 and 241:9) beat Somerset (349 and 281) at Taunton, 1901.
Yorkshire (239 and 168:9) beat MCC (179 and 226) at Scarborough, 1935.
Yorkshire (152 and 90:9) beat Worcestershire (119 and 121) at Leeds, 1946.
Yorkshire (229 and 175:9) beat Glamorgan (194 and 207) at Bradford, 1960.
Yorkshire (265.9 dec and 191:9) beat Worcestershire (227 and 227) at Worcester, 1961.
Yorkshire (329:6 dec and 167:9) beat Essex (339.9 dec and 154) at Scarborough, 1979.
Yorkshire (Innings forfeited and 251:9 beat Sussex (195 and 55.1 dec) at Leeds, 1986.
Yorkshire (314 and 150:9) beat Essex (200 and 261) at Scarborough, 1998.

NARROW VICTORIES – BY 5 RUNS OR LESS

By 1 run	Yorkshire (228 and 214) beat Middlesex (206 and 235) at Bradford, 1976.
By 1 run	Yorkshire (383 and inns forfeited) beat Loughborough UCCE (93: 3 dec. and 289) at Leeds, 2007.
By 2 runs	Yorkshire (108 and 122) beat Nottinghamshire (56 and 172) at Nottingham, 1870.
By 2 runs	Yorkshire (304:9 dec and 135) beat Middlesex (225:2 dec and 212) at Leeds, 1985.
By 3 runs	Yorkshire (446:9 dec and 172:4 dec) beat Essex (300:3 dec and 315) at Colchester, 1991.
By 5 runs	Yorkshire (271 and 147:6 dec) beat Surrey (198 and 215) at Sheffield, 1950.
By 5 runs	Yorkshire (151 and 176) beat Hampshire (165 and 157) at Bradford, 1962.
By 5 runs	Yorkshire (376:4 and 106) beat Middlesex (325:8 and 152) at Lord's, 1975
By 5 runs	Yorkshire (323:5 dec and inns forfeited) beat Somerset (inns forfeited and 318) at Taunton, 1986.

NARROW DEFEATS – BY 1 WICKET

Yorkshire (224 and 210) lost to Australian Imperial Forces XI (265 and 170:9) at Leeds, 1985.
Yorkshire (101 and 159) lost to Warwickshire (45 and 216:9) at Scarborough, 1934.
Yorkshire (239 and 184:9 dec.) lost to Warwickshire (125 and 302:9) at Birmingham, 1983.
Yorkshire (289 and 153) lost to Surrey (250:2 dec and 193:9) at Guildford, 1991.
Yorkshire (341 and Inns forfeited) lost to Surrey (39:1 dec and 306:9) at Bradford, 1992.

NARROW DEFEATS – BY 5 RUNS OR LESS

By 1 run   Yorkshire (135 and 297) lost to Essex (139 and 294) at Huddersfield, 1897.
By 1 run   Yorkshire (159 and 232) lost to Gloucestershire (164 and 228) at Bristol, 190
By 1 run   Yorkshire (126 and 137) lost to Worcestershire (101 and 163)
           at Worcester, 1968.
By 1 run   Yorkshire (366 and 217) lost to Surrey (409 and 175) at The Oval, 1995.
By 2 runs   Yorkshire (172 and 107) lost to Gloucestershire (157 and 124)
           at Sheffield, 1913.
By 2 runs   Yorkshire (179:9 dec and 144) lost to MCC (109 and 216) at Lord's, 1957.
By 3 runs   Yorkshire (126 and 181) lost to Sussex (182 and 128) at Sheffield, 1883.
By 3 runs   Yorkshire (160 and 71) lost to Lancashire (81 and 153) at Huddersfield, 1889
By 3 runs   Yorkshire (134 and 158) lost to Nottinghamshire (200 and 95) at Leeds, 1923
By 4 runs   Yorkshire (169 and 193) lost to Middlesex (105 and 261) at Bradford, 1920.
By 5 runs   Yorkshire (58 and 51) lost to Lancashire (64 and 50) at Manchester, 1893.
By 5 runs   Yorkshire (119 and 115) lost to Warwickshire (167 and 72) at Bradford, 1969

HIGH FOURTH INNINGS SCORES – 300 AND OVER

By Yorkshire

To Win: 406:4   beat Leicestershire by 6 wkts at Leicester, 2005.
         400:4   beat Leicestershire by 6 wkts at Scarborough, 2005
         331:8   beat Middlesex by 2 wkts at Lord's, 1910.
         327:6   beat Nottinghamshire by 4 wkts at Nottingham, 1990.*
         323:5   beat Nottinghamshire by 5 wkts at Nottingham, 1977.
         318:3   beat Glamorgan by 7 wkts at Middlesbrough, 1976.
         309:7   beat Somerset by 3 wkts at Taunton, 1984.
         305:8   beat Nottinghamshire by 2 wkts at Worksop, 1982.
         305:3   beat Lancashire by 7 wickets at Manchester, 1994.
         304:4   beat Derbyshire by 6 wkts at Chesterfield, 1959.
         300:4   beat Derbyshire by 6 wkts at Chesterfield, 1981.
         300:6   beat Derbyshire by 4 wkts at Scarborough, 1990.*

To Draw: 341:8   (set 358) drew with Derbyshire at Derby, 2004.
         333:7   (set 369) drew with Essex at Chelmsford, 2010
         316:6   (set 326) drew with Oxford University at Oxford, 1948.
         312:6   (set 344) drew with Sussex at Scarborough 2011
         316:7   (set 320) drew with Somerset at Scarborough, 1990.
         300:5   (set 392) drew with Kent at Canterbury, 2010

To Lose: 433   (set 500) lost to Warwickshire by 66 runs at Birmingham, 200
         380   (set 406) lost to MCC. by 25 runs at Lord's, 1937.
         343   (set 490) lost to Durham by 146 runs at Leeds 2011
         324   (set 485) lost to Northamptonshire by 160 runs at Luton, 1994
         322   (set 344) lost to Middlesex by 21 runs at Lord's, 1996.
         309   (set 400) lost to Middlesex by 90 runs at Lord's 1878.

*Consecutive matches

By Opponents:

To Win: 479:6   Somerset won by 4 wkts at Taunton, 2009
         404:5   Hampshire won by 5 wkts at Leeds, 2006
         392:4   Gloucestershire won by 6 wkts at Bristol, 1948.
         364:4   Somerset won by 6 wickets at Taunton, 2010
         354:5   Nottinghamshire won by 5 wkts at Scarborough, 1990.
         337:4   Worcestershire won by 6 wkts at Kidderminster, 2007.
         334:6   Glamorgan won by 4 wkts at Harrogate, 1955.
         329:5   Worcestershire won by 5 wkts at Worcester, 1979.
         306:9   Surrey won by 1 wkt at Bradford, 1992.
         305:7   Lancashire won by 3 wkts at Manchester, 1980.
         302:9   Warwickshire won by 1 wkt at Birmingham, 1983.

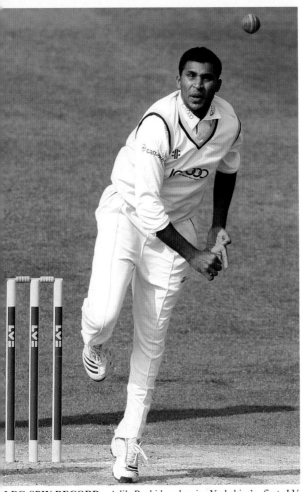

LEG-SPIN RECORD: Adil Rashid, who in Yorkshire's first LV Championship match of 2011 at Worcester returned match figures of 11-114, the best leg-spin match aggregate ever recorded for the county.

PRESIDENT'S DIAMOND: It was on August 18, 1951, that President Raymond Illingworth, second left, made his First Class debut for Yorkshire against Hampshire at Headingley. Clifford Gregg, extreme left, of Yorkshire County Cricket Supporters' Association Committee, secretary Paul Chapman and chairwoman Charlotte Evers are seen presenting Raymond with a framed copy of the scorecard to mark his Diamond Anniversary.

PAST-PRESIDENT'S DIAMOND: It was 60 years since Past-President Bob Appleyard, centre, became one of only four Yorkshiremen to have taken 200 First Class wickets in a season, and the Supporters presented Bob with a framed match-by-match breakdown of his analyses in what was Festival of Britain year. Making the presentation are four association members who watched Bob bowl that season: John Briggs, John Harrison, Pam Martin and Brian Senior.

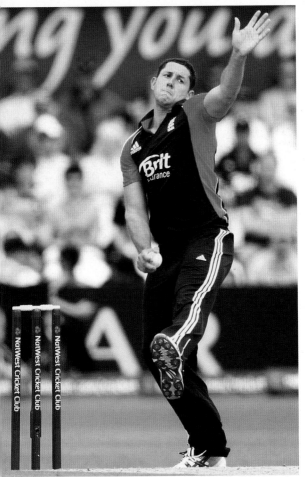

OUR MAN WITH ENGLAND: Yorkshire all-rounder Tim Bresnan in full throttle for the one-day international against Sri Lanka at Headingley Carnegie. Tim took 13 wickets at under 20 apiece in the three Championship matches for which he was available and hit 87 against Hampshire.

READING THE GAME: Chairman of Yorkshire Players' Association and former left-hand opening batsman Bryan Stott with Audrey Woodhouse at the opening of The Anthony Woodhouse Library in the Yorkshire Cricket Centre at Headingley Carnegie. The late Tony Woodhouse, Audrey's husband, who was Yorkshire's historian for many years and a Vice-President, had a vast collection of cricket books, and Audrey has donated some of them to the Library that will bear his name.

NEW DAWN: 2011 was the first full season in the Carnegie Pavilion at the Kirkstall Lane End of Headingley. *(Photo: YORKSHIRE POST)*

SMASH HIT: Yorkshire captain Andrew Gale goes for a big hit in his innings of 62 against Nottinghamshire Outlaws in the *Friends Life t20* Cup match at Headingley Carnegie. It was his fourth half-century of the campaign, and he was easily his side's leading scorer with 418 runs at 32.15.

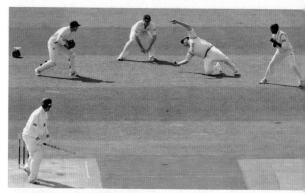

SMART CATCH: Anthony McGrath dives at second slip to hold Nottinghamshire's Paul Franks off Ryan Sidebottom in the LV County Championship match at Headingley Carnegie. **BELOW:** Richard Pyrah, one of Yorkshire's most brilliant fielders, puts everything into this attempt to catch Lancashire's Steven Croft in the *t20* at Headingley.

HAPPY RETURN: South African Jacques Rudolph made a brief but welcome return to the Yorkshire ranks in the second half of the season — and quickly showed that his run-scoring powers had not deserted him. Here he is running to an unbeaten 132 against Sussex in the *CB40* at North Marine Road, Scarborough.

SHALL WE DANCE: Yorkshire off-spinning all-rounder Azeem Rafiq embraces skipper Andrew Gale after bowling Lancashire's Steven Croft in the *t20* Roses match at Headingley Carnegie.

HIGH FOURTH INNINGS SCORES – 300 AND OVER *(Continued)*

By Opponents:

To Draw:

366:8	(set 443) Hampshire drew at Southampton, 2007.
334:7	(set 339) MCC. drew at Scarborough, 1911.
322:9	(set 334) Middlesex drew at Leeds, 1988.
317:6	(set 355) Nottinghamshire drew at Nottingham, 1910.
300:9	(set 314) Northamptonshire drew at Northampton, 1990.

To Lose:

370	(set 539) Leicestershire lost by 168 runs at Leicester, 2001
319	(set 364) Gloucestershire lost by 44 runs at Leeds, 1987.
318	(set 324) Somerset lost by 5 runs at Taunton, 1986.
315	(set 319) Essex lost by 3 runs at Colchester, 1991.
314	(set 334) Lancashire lost by 19 runs at Manchester, 1993.
310	(set 417) Warwickshire lost by 106 runs at Scarborough, 1939.
306	(set 413) Kent lost by 106 runs at Leeds, 1952.
300	(set 330) Middlesex lost by 29 runs at Sheffield, 1930.

TIE MATCHES

Yorkshire (351:4 dec and 113) tied with Leicestershire (328 and 136) at Huddersfield, 1954.
Yorkshire (106:9 dec and 207) tied with Middlesex (102 and 211) at Bradford, 1973.

HIGHEST SCORES BY AND AGAINST YORKSHIRE

Yorkshire versus: —

	By Yorkshire:	**Against Yorkshire:**
Derbyshire:		
In Yorkshire:	570 at Leeds, 2005	491 at Bradford, 1949
Away:	662 at Chesterfield, 1898	523 at Derby, 2005
Durham:		
In Yorkshire:	677:7 dec. at Leeds, 2006	518 at Leeds, 2006
Away:	448 at Chester-le-Street, 2003	481 at Chester-le-Street, 2007
Essex:		
In Yorkshire:	516 at Scarborough, 2010	622:8 dec. at Leeds, 2005
Away:	555:1 dec. at Leyton, 1932	521 at Leyton, 1905
Glamorgan:		
In Yorkshire:	580:9 dec at Scarborough, 2001	498 at Leeds, 1999
Away:	536:8 dec. at Cardiff, 1996	482:7 dec. at Cardiff, 1996
Gloucestershire:		
In Yorkshire:	504:7 dec. at Bradford, 1905	411 at Leeds, 1992
Away:	494 at Bristol, 1897	574 at Cheltenham, 1990
Hampshire:		
In Yorkshire:	493:1 dec. at Sheffield, 1939	498:6 dec at Scarborough, 2010
Away	585:3 dec at Portsmouth 1920	599:3 at Southampton, 2011
Kent:		
In Yorkshire:	550:9 dec. at Scarborough, 1995	486 at Scarborough, 2007
Away:	559 at Canterbury, 1887	580: 9 dec. at Maidstone, 1998
Lancashire:		
In Yorkshire:	590 at Bradford, 1887	517 at Leeds, 2007.
Away:	528:8 dec. at Manchester, 1939	537 at Manchester, 2005
Leicestershire:		
In Yorkshire	562 { at Scarborough, 1901 / at Dewsbury, 1903	681:7 dec. at Bradford, 1996
Away:	660 at Leicester, 1896	425 at Leicester, 1906

Yorkshire versus: —

	By Yorkshire:	Against Yorkshire:
Middlesex:		
In Yorkshire:	575:7 dec. at Bradford, 1899	527 at Huddersfield, 1887
Away:	538:6 dec. at Lord's, 1925	488 at Lord's, 1899
Northamptonshire:		
In Yorkshire:	673:8 dec. at Leeds, 2003	517:7 dec. at Scarborough, 1999
Away:	523:8 dec. at Wellingborough, 1949	531:4 at Northampton, 1996
Nottinghamshire:		
In Yorkshire:	562 at Bradford, 1899	545:7 dec at Leeds, 2010
Away	534:9 dec at Nottingham, 2011	490 at Nottingham, 1897
Somerset:		
In Yorkshire:	525:4 dec. at Leeds, 1953	630 at Leeds, 1901
Away:	589:5 dec at Bath, 2001	592 at Taunton, 1892
Surrey:		
In Yorkshire:	582:7 dec. at Sheffield, 1935	510 at Leeds, 2002
Away:	704 at The Oval, 1899	560:6 dec. at The Oval, 1933
Sussex:		
In Yorkshire:	681:5 dec. at Sheffield, 1897	566 at Sheffield, 1937
Away:	522:7 dec. at Hastings, 1911	597:8 dec. at Hove, 2007
Warwickshire:		
In Yorkshire	561:7 dec at Scarborough 2007	482 at Leeds, 2011
Away:	887 at Birmingham, 1896	601:9 dec. at Birmingham, 2002
	(Highest score by a First-Class county)	
Worcestershire:		
In Yorkshire:	600: 4 dec. at Scarborough, 1995	453:5 dec. at Scarborough, 1995
Away:	560:6 dec. at Worcester, 1928	456:8 at Worcester, 1904
Australians:		
In Yorkshire:	377 at Sheffield, 1953	470 at Bradford, 1893
Indians:		
In Yorkshire:	385 at Hull, 1911	490:5 dec. at Sheffield, 1946
New Zealanders:		
In Yorkshire:	419 at Bradford, 1965	370:7 dec. at Bradford, 1949
Pakistanis:		
In Yorkshire:	433:9 dec. at Sheffield, 1954	356 at Sheffield, 1954
South Africans:		
In Yorkshire:	579 at Sheffield, 1951	454:8 dec at Sheffield, 1951
Sri Lankans:		
In Yorkshire:	314:8 dec. at Leeds, 1991	422:8 dec. at Leeds, 1991
West Indians:		
In Yorkshire:	312:5 dec. at Scarborough, 1973	426 at Scarborough, 1995
Zimbabweans:		
In Yorkshire:	298:9 dec at Leeds, 1990	235 at Leeds, 2000
Cambridge University:		
In Yorkshire:	359 at Scarborough, 1967	366 at Leeds, 1998
Away:	540 at Cambridge, 1938	425:7 at Cambridge, 1929
Durham MCCU:		
Away:	355 at Durham, 2011	287 at Durham, 2011
Loughborough MCCU:		
In Yorkshire:	383:6 dec at Leeds, 2007	289 at Leeds, 2007

HIGHEST SCORES BY AND AGAINST YORKSHIRE *(Continued)*

Yorkshire versus: —

MCC:

	By Yorkshire:	**Against Yorkshire:**
In Yorkshire:	557:8 dec. at Scarborough, 1933	478:8 at Scarborough, 1904
Away:	528:8 dec. at Lord's, 1919	488 at Lord's, 1919

Oxford University:

In Yorkshire:	173 at Harrogate, 1972	190:6 dec at Harrogate, 1972
Away:	468:6 dec. at Oxford, 1978	422:9 dec. at Oxford, 1953

LOWEST SCORES BY AND AGAINST YORKSHIRE

Yorkshire versus:

Derbyshire:

	By Yorkshire:	**Against Yorkshire:**
In Yorkshire:	50 at Sheffield, 1894	20 at Sheffield, 1939
Away:	44 at Chesterfield, 1948	26 at Derby, 1880

Durham:

In Yorkshire:	93 at Leeds, 2003	125 at Harrogate, 1995
Away:	108 at Durham, 1992	74 at Chester-le-Street, 1998

Essex:

In Yorkshire:	31 at Huddersfield, 1935	52 at Harrogate, 1900
Away:	98 at Leyton, 1905	30 at Leyton, 1901

Glamorgan:

In Yorkshire:	83 at Sheffield, 1946	52 at Hull, 1926
Away:	92 at Swansea, 1956	48 at Cardiff, 1924

Gloucestershire:

In Yorkshire:	61 at Leeds, 1894	36 at Sheffield, 1903
Away:	35 at Bristol, 1959	42 at Gloucester, 1924

Hampshire:

In Yorkshire:	23 at Middlesbrough, 1965	36 at Leeds, 1904
Away:	96 at Bournemouth, 1971	36 at Southampton, 1898

Kent:

In Yorkshire:	30 at Sheffield, 1865	39 { at Sheffield, 1882 / at Sheffield, 1936
Away:	62 at Maidstone, 1889	63 at Canterbury, 1901

Lancashire:

In Yorkshire:	33 at Leeds, 1924	30 at Holbeck, 1868
Away:	51 { at Manchester, 1888 / at Manchester, 1893	39 at Manchester, 1874

Leicestershire:

	By Yorkshire:	**Against Yorkshire:**
In Yorkshire:	93 at Leeds, 1935	34 at Leeds, 1906
Away:	47 at Leicester, 1911	57 at Leicester, 1898

Middlesex:

In Yorkshire:	45 at Leeds, 1898	45 at Huddersfield, 1879
Away:	43 at Lord's, 1888	49 at Lord's in 1890

Northamptonshire:

In Yorkshire:	85 at Sheffield, 1919	51 at Bradford, 1920
Away	64 at Northampton, 1959	15 at Northampton, 1908 (and 27 in first innings)

Nottinghamshire:

In Yorkshire:	32 at Sheffield, 1876	24 at Sheffield, 1888
Away:	43 at Nottingham, 1869	13 at Nottingham, 1901 (second smallest total by a First-Class county)

LOWEST SCORES BY AND AGAINST YORKSHIRE *(continued)*

Yorkshire versus:

Somerset:	**By Yorkshire:**	**Against Yorkshire:**
In Yorkshire:	73 at Leeds, 1895	43 at Bradford, 1930
Away:	83 at Wells, 1949	35 at Bath, 1898
Surrey:		
In Yorkshire:	54 at Sheffield, 1873	31 at Holbeck, 1883
Away:	26 at The Oval, 1909	44 at The Oval, 1935
Sussex:		
In Yorkshire:	61 at Dewsbury, 1891	20 at Hull, 1922
Away:	42 at Hove, 1922	24 at Hove, 1878
Warwickshire:		
In Yorkshire:	49 at Huddersfield, 1951	35 at Sheffield, 1979
Away:	54 at Birmingham, 1964	35 at Birmingham, 1963
Worcestershire:		
In Yorkshire:	62 at Bradford, 1907	24 at Huddersfield, 1903
Away:	72 at Worcester, 1977	65 at Worcester, 1925
Australians:		
In Yorkshire:	48 at Leeds, 1893	23 at Leeds, 1902
Indians:		
In Yorkshire:	146 at Bradford, 1959	66 at Harrogate, 1932
New Zealanders:		
In Yorkshire:	189 at Harrogate, 1931	134 at Bradford, 1965
Pakistanis:		
In Yorkshire:	137 at Bradford, 1962	150 at Leeds, 1967
South Africans:		
In Yorkshire:	113 at Bradford, 1907	76 at Bradford, 1951
Sri Lankans:		
In Yorkshire:	Have not been dismissed. Lowest is 184:1 dec at Leeds, 1991	287:5 dec at Leeds, 1988
West Indians:		
In Yorkshire:	50 at Harrogate, 1906	58 at Leeds, 1928
Zimbabweans:		
In Yorkshire:	124 at Leeds, 2000	68 at Leeds, 2000
Cambridge University:		
In Yorkshire:	110 at Sheffield, 1903	39 at Sheffield, 1903
Away:	51 at Cambridge, 1906	30 at Cambridge, 1928
Durham MCCU:		
Away	355 at Durham, 2011	196 at Durham, 2011
Loughborough MCCU:		
In Yorkshire	348:5 dec at Leeds, 2010	289 at Leeds, 2007
MCC:		
In Yorkshire:	46 { at Scarborough, 1876 / at Scarborough, 1877	31 at Scarborough, 1877
Away:	44 at Lord's, 1880	27 at Lord's, 1902
Oxford University:		
In Yorkshire:	Have not been dismissed. Lowest is 115:8 at Harrogate, 1972	133 at Harrogate, 1972
Away:	141 at Oxford, 1949	46 at Oxford, 1956

INDIVIDUAL INNINGS OF 150 AND OVER

A complete list of all First-class Centuries up to and including 2007 is to be found in the 2008 edition

J M BAIRSTOW (1)

105	v Nottinghamshire	Nottingham	2011

W BARBER (7)

162	v Middlesex	Sheffield	1932
168	v MCC	Lord's	1934
148	v Kent	Leeds	1934
191	v Sussex	Leeds	1935
155	v Surrey	Sheffield	1935
158	v Kent	Sheffield	1936
157	v Surrey	Sheffield	1938

M G BEVAN (2)

153*	v Surrey	The Oval	1995
160*	v Surrey	Middlesbrough	1996

H D BIRD (1)

181*	v Glamorgan	Bradford	1959

R J BLAKEY (3)

204*	v Gloucestershire	Leeds	1987
196	v Oxford University	Oxford	1991
223*	v Northamptonshire	Leeds	2003

G BLEWETT (1)

190	v Northamptonshire	Scarborough	1999

M W BOOTH (1)

210	v Worcestershire	Worcester	1911

G BOYCOTT (32)

165*	v Leicestershire	Scarborough	1963
151	v Middlesex	Leeds	1964
151*	v Leicestershire	Leicester	1964
177	v Gloucestershire	Bristol	1964
164	v Sussex	Hove	1966
220	v Northamptonshire	Sheffield	1967
180*	v Warwickshire	Middlesbrough	1968
260*	v Essex	Colchester (Garrison Ground)	1970
169	v Nottinghamshire	Leeds	1971
233	v Essex	Colchester (Garrison Ground)	1971
182*	v Middlesex	Lord's	1971
169	v Lancashire	Sheffield	1971
151	v Leicestershire	Bradford	1971
204*	v Leicestershire	Leicester	1972
152*	v Worcestershire	Worcester	1975
175*	v Middlesex	Scarborough	1975
201*	v Middlesex	Lord's	1975
161*	v Gloucestershire	Leeds	1976
207*	v Cambridge University	Cambridge	1976
156*	v Glamorgan	Middlesbrough	1976

261

G BOYCOTT *(Continued)*

154	v Nottinghamshire	Nottingham	1977
151*	v Derbyshire	Leeds	1979
167	v Derbyshire	Chesterfield	1979
175*	v Nottinghamshire	Worksop	1979
154*	v Derbyshire	Scarborough	1980
159	v Worcestershire	Sheffield (Abbeydale Park)	1982
152*	v Warwickshire	Leeds	1982
214*	v Nottinghamshire	Worksop	1983
163	v Nottinghamshire	Bradford	1983
169*	v Derbyshire	Chesterfield	1983
153*	v Derbyshire	Harrogate	1984
184	v Worcestershire	Worcester	1985

G L BROPHY (1)

177*	v Worcestershire	Worcester	2011

J T BROWN (8)

168*	v Sussex	Huddersfield	1895
203	v Middlesex	Lord's	1896
311	v Sussex	Sheffield	1897
300	v Derbyshire	Chesterfield	1898
150	v Sussex	Hove	1898
168	v Cambridge University	Cambridge	1899
167	v Australians	Bradford	1899
192	v Derbyshire	Derby	1899

D BYAS (5)

153	v Nottinghamshire	Worksop	1991
156	v Essex	Chelmsford	1993
181	v Cambridge University	Cambridge	1995
193	v Lancashire	Leeds	1995
213	v Worcestershire	Scarborough	1995

D B CLOSE (5)

164	v Combined Services	Harrogate	1954
154	v Nottinghamshire	Nottingham	1959
198	v Surrey	The Oval	1960
184	v Nottinghamshire	Scarborough	1960
161	v Northamptonshire	Northampton	1963

D DENTON (11)

153*	v Australians	Bradford	1905
165	v Hampshire	Bournemouth	1905
172	v Gloucestershire	Bradford	1905
184	v Nottinghamshire	Nottingham	1909
182	v Derbyshire	Chesterfield	1910
200*	v Warwickshire	Birmingham	1912
182	v Gloucestershire	Bristol	1912
221	v Kent	Tunbridge Wells	1912
191	v Hampshire	Southampton	1912
168*	v Hampshire	Southampton	1914
209*	v Worcestershire	Worcester	1920

INDIVIDUAL INNINGS OF 150 AND OVER *(Continued)*

A W GALE (2)

150	v Surrey	The Oval	2008
151*	v Nottinghamshire	Nottingham	2010

P A GIBB (1)

157*	v Nottinghamshire	Sheffield	1935

S HAIGH (1)

159	v Nottinghamshire	Sheffield	1901

L HALL (1)

160	v Lancashire	Bradford	1887

J H HAMPSHIRE (5)

150	v Leicestershire	Bradford	1964
183*	v Sussex	Hove	1971
157*	v Nottinghamshire	Worksop	1974
158	v Gloucestershire	Harrogate	1974
155*	v Gloucestershire	Leeds	1976

I J HARVEY (1)

209*	v Somerset	Leeds	2005

LORD HAWKE (1)

166	v Warwickshire	Birmingham	1896

G H HIRST (15)

186	v Surrey	The Oval	1899
155	v Nottinghamshire	Scarborough	1900
214	v Worcestershire	Worcester	1901
153	v Leicestershire	Dewsbury	1903
153	v Oxford University	Oxford	1904
152	v Hampshire	Portsmouth	1904
157	v Kent	Tunbridge Wells	1904
341	v Leicestershire	Leicester (Aylestone Road)	1905
232*	v Surrey	The Oval	1905
169	v Oxford University	Oxford	1906
158	v Cambridge University	Cambridge	1910
156	v Lancashire	Manchester	1911
218	v Sussex	Hastings	1911
166*	v Sussex	Hastings	1913
180*	v MCC	Lord's	1919

P HOLMES (16)

302*	v Hampshire	Portsmouth	1920
150	v Derbyshire	Chesterfield	1921
277*	v Northamptonshire	Harrogate	1921
209	v Warwickshire	Birmingham	1922
220*	v Warwickshire	Huddersfield	1922
199	v Somerset	Hull	1923
315*	v Middlesex	Lord's	1925
194	v Leicestershire	Hull	1925
159	v Hampshire	Southampton	1925
180	v Gloucestershire	Gloucester	1927
175*	v New Zealanders	Bradford	1927
179*	v Middlesex	Leeds	1928

P HOLMES *(Continued)*

275	v Warwickshire	Bradford	1928
285	v Nottinghamshire	Nottingham	1929
250	v Warwickshire	Birmingham	1931
224*	v Essex	Leyton	1932

L HUTTON (31)

196	v Worcestershire	Worcester	1934
163	v Surrey	Leeds	1936
161	v MCC	Lord's	1937
271*	v Derbyshire	Sheffield	1937
153	v Leicestershire	Hull	1937
180	v Cambridge University	Cambridge	1938
158	v Warwickshire	Birmingham	1939
280*	v Hampshire	Sheffield	1939
151	v Surrey	Leeds	1939
177	v Sussex	Scarborough	1939
183*	v Indians	Bradford	1946
171*	v Northamptonshire	Hull	1946
197	v Glamorgan	Swansea	1947
197	v Essex	Southend-on-Sea	1947
270*	v Hampshire	Bournemouth	1947
176*	v Sussex	Sheffield	1948
155	v Sussex	Hove	1948
167	v New Zealanders	Bradford	1949
201	v Lancashire	Manchester	1949
165	v Sussex	Hove	1949
269*	v Northamptonshire	Wellingborough	1949
156	v Essex	Colchester (Castle Park)	1950
153	v Nottinghamshire	Nottingham	1950
156	v South Africans	Sheffield	1951
151	v Surrey	The Oval	1951
194*	v Nottinghamshire	Nottingham	1951
152	v Lancashire	Leeds	1952
189	v Kent	Leeds	1952
178	v Somerset	Leeds	1953
163	v Combined Services	Harrogate	1954
194	v Nottinghamshire	Nottingham	1955

R A HUTTON (1)

189	v Pakistanis	Bradford	1971

R ILLINGWORTH (2)

150	v Essex	Colchester (Castle Park)	1959
162	v Indians	Sheffield	1959

Hon F S JACKSON (3)

160	v Gloucestershire	Sheffield	1898
155	v Middlesex	Bradford	1899
158	v Surrey	Bradford	1904

P A JAQUES (5)

243	v Hampshire	Southampton (Rose Bowl)	2004
173	v Glamorgan	Leeds	2004
176	v Northamptonshire	Leeds	2005
219	v Derbyshire	Leeds	2005
172	v Durham	Scarborough	2005

INDIVIDUAL INNINGS OF 150 AND OVER *(Continued)*

R KILNER (5)

169	v Gloucestershire	Bristol	1914
206*	v Derbyshire	Sheffield	1920
166	v Northamptonshire	Northampton	1921
150	v Northamptonshire	Harrogate	1921
150	v Middlesex	Lord's	1926

F LEE (1)

165	v Lancashire	Bradford	1887

D S LEHMANN (13)

177	v Somerset	Taunton	1997
163*	v Leicestershire	Leicester	1997
182	v Hampshire	Portsmouth	1997
200	v Worcestershire	Worcester	1998
187*	v Somerset	Bath	2001
252	v Lancashire	Leeds	2001
193	v Leicestershire	Leicester	2001
216	v Sussex	Arundel	2002
187	v Lancashire	Leeds	2002
150	v Warwickshire	Birmingham	2006
193	v Kent	Canterbury	2006
172	v Kent	Leeds	2006
339	v Durham	Leeds	2006

E I LESTER (5)

186	v Warwickshire	Scarborough	1949
178	v Nottinghamshire	Nottingham	1952
157	v Cambridge University	Hull	1953
150	v Oxford University	Oxford	1954
163	v Essex	Romford	1954

M LEYLAND (17)

191	v Glamorgan	Swansea	1926
204*	v Middlesex	Sheffield	1927
247	v Worcestershire	Worcester	1928
189*	v Glamorgan	Huddersfield	1928
211*	v Lancashire	Leeds	1930
172	v Middlesex	Sheffield	1930
186	v Derbyshire	Leeds	1930
189	v Middlesex	Sheffield	1932
153	v Leicestershire	Leicester (Aylestone Road)	1932
166	v Leicestershire	Bradford	1932
153*	v Hampshire	Bournemouth	1932
192	v Northamptonshire	Leeds	1933
210*	v Kent	Dover	1933
263	v Essex	Hull	1936
163*	v Surrey	Leeds	1936
167	v Worcestershire	Stourbridge	1937
180*	v Middlesex	Lord's	1939

E LOCKWOOD (1)

208	v Kent	Gravesend	1883

INDIVIDUAL INNINGS OF 150 AND OVER (Continued)

J D LOVE (4)

163	v Nottinghamshire	Bradford	1976
170*	v Worcestershire	Worcester	1979
161	v Warwickshire	Birmingham	1981
154	v Lancashire	Manchester	1981

F A LOWSON (10)

155	v Kent	Maidstone	1951
155	v Worcestershire	Bradford	1952
166	v Scotland	Glasgow	1953
259*	v Worcestershire	Worcester	1953
165	v Sussex	Hove	1954
164	v Essex	Scarborough	1954
150*	v Kent	Dover	1954
183*	v Oxford University	Oxford	1956
154	v Somerset	Taunton	1956
154	v Cambridge University	Cambridge	1957

R G LUMB (2)

159	v Somerset	Harrogate	1979
165*	v Gloucestershire	Bradford	1984

A McGRATH (7)

165	v Lancashire	Leeds	2002
174	v Derbyshire	Derby	2004
165*	v Leicestershire	Leicester	2005
173*	v Worcestershire	Leeds	2005
158	v Derbyshire	Derby	2005
188*	v Warwickshire	Birmingham	2007
211	v Warwickshire	Birmingham	2009

D R MARTYN (1)

238	v Gloucestershire	Leeds	2003

A METCALFE (7)

151	v Northamptonshire	Luton	1986
151	v Lancashire	Manchester	1986
152	v MCC	Scarborough	1987
216*	v Middlesex	Leeds	1988
162	v Gloucestershire	Cheltenham	1990
150*	v Derbyshire	Scarborough	1990
194*	v Nottinghamshire	Nottingham	1990

A MITCHELL (7)

189	v Northamptonshire	Northampton	1926
176	v Nottinghamshire	Bradford	1930
177*	v Gloucestershire	Bradford	1932
150*	v Worcestershire	Worcester	1933
158	v MCC	Scarborough	1933
152	v Hampshire	Bradford	1934
181	v Surrey	Bradford	1934

F MITCHELL (2)

194	v Leicestershire	Leicester	1899
162*	v Warwickshire	Birmingham	1901

INDIVIDUAL INNINGS OF 150 AND OVER *(Continued)*

M D MOXON (14)

153	v Lancashire	Leeds	1983
153	v Somerset	Leeds	1985
168	v Worcestershire	Worcester	1985
191	v Northamptonshire	Scarborough	1989
162*	v Surrey	The Oval	1989
218*	v Sussex	Eastbourne	1990
200	v Essex	Colchester (Castle Park)	1991
183	v Gloucestershire	Cheltenham	1992
171*	v Kent	Leeds	1993
161*	v Lancashire	Manchester	1994
274*	v Worcestershire	Worcester	1994
203*	v Kent	Leeds	1995
213	v Glamorgan	Cardiff (Sophia Gardens)	1996
155	v Pakistan 'A'	Leeds	1997

E OLDROYD (5)

151*	v Glamorgan	Cardiff	1922
194	v Worcestershire	Worcester	1923
162*	v Glamorgan	Swansea	1928
168	v Glamorgan	Hull	1929
164*	v Somerset	Bath	1930

D E V PADGETT (1)

161*	v Oxford University	Oxford	1959

R PEEL (2)

158	v Middlesex	Lord's	1889
210*	v Warwickshire	Birmingham	1896

A U RASHID (1)

157*	v Lancashire	Leeds	2009

W RHODES (8)

196	v Worcestershire	Worcester	1904
201	v Somerset	Taunton	1905
199	v Sussex	Hove	1909
176	v Nottinghamshire	Harrogate	1912
152	v Leicestershire	Leicester (Aylestone Road)	1913
167*	v Nottinghamshire	Leeds	1920
267*	v Leicestershire	Leeds	1921
157	v Derbyshire	Leeds	1925

P E ROBINSON (2)

150*	v Derbyshire	Scarborough	1990
189	v Lancashire	Scarborough	1991

J E ROOT (1)

160	v Sussex	Scarborough	2011

J W ROTHERY (1)

161	v Kent	Dover	1908

J A RUDOLPH (5)

220	v Warwickshire	Scarborough	2007
155	v Somerset	Taunton	2008
198	v Worcestershire	Leeds	2009
191	v Somerset	Taunton	2009
228*	v Durham	Leeds	2010

INDIVIDUAL INNINGS OF 150 AND OVER *(Continued)*

H RUDSTON (1)

164	v Leicestershire	Leicester (Aylestone Rd)	1904

J J SAYERS (3)

187	v Kent	Tunbridge Wells	2007
173	v Warwickshire	Birmingham	2009
152	v Somerset	Taunton	2009

A B SELLERS (1)

204	v Cambridge University	Cambridge	1936

K SHARP (2)

173	v Derbyshire	Chesterfield	1984
181	v Gloucestershire	Harrogate	1986

P J SHARPE (4)

203*	v Cambridge University	Cambridge	1960
152	v Kent	Sheffield	1960
197	v Pakistanis	Leeds	1967
172*	v Glamorgan	Swansea	1971

G A SMITHSON (1)

169	v Leicestershire	Leicester	1947

W B STOTT (2)

181	v Essex	Sheffield	1957
186	v Warwickshire	Birmingham	1960

H SUTCLIFFE (39)

174	v Kent	Dover	1919
232	v Surrey	The Oval	1922
213	v Somerset	Dewsbury	1924
160	v Sussex	Sheffield	1924
255*	v Essex	Southend-on-Sea	1924
235	v Middlesex	Leeds	1925
206	v Warwickshire	Dewsbury	1925
171	v MCC	Scarborough	1925
200	v Leicestershire	Leicester (Aylestone Road)	1926
176	v Surrey	Leeds	1927
169	v Nottinghamshire	Bradford	1927
228	v Sussex	Eastbourne	1928
150	v Northamptonshire	Northampton	1929
150*	v Essex	Dewsbury	1930
173	v Sussex	Hove	1930
173*	v Cambridge University	Cambridge	1931
230	v Kent	Folkestone	1931
183	v Somerset	Dewsbury	1931
195	v Lancashire	Sheffield	1931
187	v Leicestershire	Leicester (Aylestone Road)	1931
153*	v Warwickshire	Hull	1932
313	v Essex	Leyton	1932
270	v Sussex	Leeds	1932
182	v Derbyshire	Leeds	1932
194	v Essex	Scarborough	1932
205	v Warwickshire	Birmingham	1933
177	v Middlesex	Bradford	1933

INDIVIDUAL INNINGS OF 150 AND OVER *(Continued)*

H SUTCLIFFE (Continued)

174	v Leicestershire	Leicester (Aylestone Road)	1933
152	v Cambridge University	Cambridge	1934
166	v Essex	Hull	1934
203	v Surrey	The Oval	1934
187*	v Worcestershire	Bradford	1934
200*	v Worcestershire	Sheffield	1935
212	v Leicestershire	Leicester (Aylestone Road)	1935
202	v Middlesex	Scarborough	1936
189	v Leicestershire	Hull	1937
165	v Lancashire	Manchester	1939
234*	v Leicestershire	Hull	1939
175	v Middlesex	Lord's	1939

W H H SUTCLIFFE (3)

171*	v Worcestershire	Worcester	1952
181	v Kent	Canterbury	1952
161*	v Glamorgan	Harrogate	1955

K TAYLOR (8)

168*	v Nottinghamshire	Nottingham	1956
159	v Leicestershire	Sheffield	1961
203*	v Warwickshire	Birmingham	1961
178*	v Oxford University	Oxford	1962
163	v Nottinghamshire	Leeds	1962
153	v Lancashire	Manchester	1964
160	v Australians	Sheffield	1964
162	v Worcestershire	Kidderminster	1967

T L TAYLOR (1)

156	v Hampshire	Harrogate	1901

J TUNNICLIFFE (2)

243	v Derbyshire	Chesterfield	1898
158	v Worcestershire	Worcester	1900

G ULYETT (1)

199*	v Derbyshire	Sheffield	1887

M P VAUGHAN (7)

183	v Glamorgan	Cardiff (Sophia Gardens)	1996
183	v Northamptonshire	Northampton	1996
161	v Essex	Ilford	1997
177	v Durham	Chester-le-Street	1998
151	v Essex	Chelmsford	1999
153	v Kent	Scarborough	1999
155*	v Derbyshire	Leeds	2000

E WAINWRIGHT (3)

171	v Middlesex	Lord's	1897
153	v Leicestershire	Leicester	1899
228	v Surrey	The Oval	1899

INDIVIDUAL INNINGS OF 150 AND OVER *(Continued)*

W WATSON (7)

153*	v Surrey	The Oval	1947
172	v Derbyshire	Scarborough	1948
162*	v Somerset	Leeds	1953
163	v Sussex	Sheffield	1955
174	v Lancashire	Sheffield	1955
214*	v Worcestershire	Worcester	1955
162	v Northamptonshire	Harrogate	1957

C WHITE (6)

181	v Lancashire	Leeds	1996
172*	v Worcestershire	Leeds	1997
186	v Lancashire	Manchester	2001
183	v Glamorgan	Scarborough	2001
161	v Leicestershire	Scarborough	2002
173*	v Derbyshire	Derby	2003

B B WILSON (2)

150	v Warwickshire	Birmingham	1912
208	v Sussex	Bradford	1914

J V WILSON (7)

157*	v Sussex	Leeds	1949
157	v Essex	Sheffield	1950
166*	v Sussex	Hull	1951
223*	v Scotland	Scarborough	1951
154	v Oxford University	Oxford	1952
230	v Derbyshire	Sheffield	1952
165	v Oxford University	Oxford	1956

M J WOOD (5)

200*	v Warwickshire	Leeds	1998
157	v Northamptonshire	Leeds	2003
207	v Somerset	Taunton	2003
155	v Hampshire	Scarborough	2003
202*	v Bangladesh 'A'	Leeds	2005

N W D YARDLEY (2)

177	v Derbyshire	Scarborough	1947
183*	v Hampshire	Leeds	1951

YOUNUS KHAN (2)

202*	v Hampshire	Southampton (Rose Bowl)	2007
217*	v Kent	Scarborough	2007

CENTURIES BY CURRENT PLAYERS

**A complete list of all First-class Centuries up to and including 2007
is to be found in the 2008 edition**

AZEEM RAFIQ (1)

100	v Worcestershire	Worcester	2009

J M BAIRSTOW (2)

205	Nottinghamshire	Nottingham	2011
136	Somerset	Taunton	2011

G S BALLANCE (1)

111	v Warwickshire	Birmingham	2011

T T BRESNAN (2)

116	v Surrey	The Oval	2007
101*	v Warwickshire	Scarborough	2007

G L BROPHY (3)

100*	v Hampshire	Southampton	2007
103	v Warwickshire	Leeds	2010
177*	v Worcestershire	Worcester	2011

A W GALE (11)

149	v Warwickshire	Scarborough	2006
138	v Hampshire	Leeds	2008
150	v Surrey	The Oval	2008
136	v Lancashire	Manchester	2008
101	v Worcestershire	Worcester	2009
121	v Lancashire	Manchester	2009
101	v Somerset	Leeds	2010
135	v Essex	Scarborough	2010
151*	v Nottinghamshire	Nottingham	2010
145*	v Nottinghamshire	Leeds	2011
101*	v Durham	Chester-le-Street	2011

A LYTH (4)

132	v Nottinghamshire	Nottingham	2008
142	v Somerset	Taunton	2010
133	v Hampshire	Southampton	2010
100	v Lancashire	Manchester	2010

A McGRATH (32)

101	v Kent	Canterbury	1996
137	v Hampshire	Harrogate	1996
105*	v Oxford University	Oxford	1997
141	v Worcestershire	Leeds	1997
142*	v Middlesex	Leeds	1999
133	v Kent	Canterbury	2000
116*	v Surrey	The Oval	2001
165	v Lancashire	Leeds	2002
127*	v Glamorgan	Colwyn Bay	2003
126	v Durham	Chester-le-Street	2004
174	v Derbyshire	Derby	2004
109	v Derbyshire	Leeds	2004
165*	v Leicestershire	Leicester	2005
133*	v Durham	Chester-le-Street	2005

271

A McGRATH *(Continued)*

134	v Derbyshire	Leeds	2005
173*	v Worcestershire	Leeds	2005
158	v Derbyshire	Derby	2005
123*	v Kent	Canterbury	2006
127	v Hampshire	Leeds	2006
140*	v Durham	Chester-le-Street	2006
102	v Lancashire	Manchester	2006
100	v Kent	Tunbridge Wells	2007
188*	v Warwickshire	Birmingham	2007
120	v Kent	Scarborough	2007
144	v Kent	Canterbury	2008
128	v Somerset	Scarborough	2008
120	v Worcestershire	Leeds	2009
211	v Warwickshire	Birmingham	2009
105	v Durham	Leeds	2010
112	v Essex	Scarborough	2010
124*	v Durham	Chester-le-Street	2010
115	v Hampshire	Southampton	2011

R M PYRAH *(3)*

106	v Loughborough UCCE	Leeds	2007
134*	v Loughborough MCCU	Leeds	2010
117	v Lancashire	Leeds	2011

A U RASHID *(4)*

108	v Worcestershire	Kidderminster	2007
111	v Sussex	Hove	2008
117*	v Hampshire	Basingstoke	2009
157*	v Lancashire	Leeds	2009

J E ROOT *(1)*

160	v Sussex	Scarborough	2011

J A RUDOLPH *(18)*

122	v Surrey	The Oval	2007
129*	v Worcestershire	Leeds	2007
111	v Durham	Chester-le-Street	2007
220	v Warwickshire	Scarborough	2007
104*	v Nottinghamshire	Leeds	2008
121	v Surrey	The Oval	2008
155	v Somerset	Taunton	2008
129	v Kent	Canterbury	2008
146	v Kent	Scarborough	2008
198	v Worcestershire	Leeds	2009
191	v Somerset	Taunton	2009
127	v Lancashire	Manchester	2009
149	v Nottinghamshire	Nottingham	2009
228*	v Durham	Leeds	2010
106	v Essex	Chelmsford	2010
141	v Nottinghamshire	Leeds	2010
100	v Durham	Chester-le-Street	2010
120	v Sussex	Scarborough	2011

J J SAYERS (9)

104	v Leicestershire	Scarborough	2005
115	v Bangladesh 'A'	Leeds	2005
122*	v Middlesex	Scarborough	2006
149*	v Durham	Leeds	2007
123	v Worcestershire	Leeds	2007
187	v Kent	Tunbridge Wells	2007
173	v Warwickshire	Birmingham	2009
152	v Somerset	Taunton	2009
139	v Durham MCCU	Durham	2011

D J WAINWRIGHT (2)

104*	v Sussex	Hove	2008
102*	v Warwickshire	Scarborough	2009

CENTURIES

(Including highest score)

112	H Sutcliffe	313	v Essex	at Leyton	1932
103	G Boycott	260*	v Essex	at Colchester (Garrison Gd)	1970
85	L Hutton	280*	v Hampshire	at Sheffield	1939
62	M Leyland	263	v Essex	at Hull	1936
61	D Denton	221	v Kent	at Tunbridge Wells	1912
60	P Holmes	315*	v Middlesex	at Lord's	1925
56	G H Hirst	341	v Leicestershire	at Leicester (Aylestone Rd)	1905
46	W Rhodes	267*	v Leicestershire	at Leeds	1921
41	M D Moxon	274*	v Worcestershire	at Worcester	1994
39	A Mitchell	189	v Northamptonshire	at Northampton	1926
37	E Oldroyd	194	v Worcestershire	at Worcester	1923
34	J H Hampshire	183*	v Sussex	at Hove	1971
33	D B Close	198	v Surrey	at The Oval	1960
32	A McGrath	211	v Warwickshire	at Birmingham	2009
30	F A Lowson	259*	v Worcestershire	at Worcester	1953
29	D E V Padgett	161*	v Oxford University	at Oxford	1959
29	J V Wilson	230	v Derbyshire	at Sheffield	1952
28	D Byas	213	v Worcestershire	at Scarborough	1995
27	W Barber	255	v Surrey	at Sheffield	1935
26	D S Lehmann	339	v Durham	at Leeds	2006
26	W Watson	214*	v Worcestershire	at Worcester	1955
25	A A Metcalfe	216*	v Middlesex	at Leeds	1988
24	E I Lester	186	v Warwickshire	at Scarborough	1949
23	J T Brown	311	v Sussex	at Sheffield	1897
23	P J Sharpe	203*	v Cambridge University	at Cambridge	1960
22	R J Lumb	165*	v Gloucestershire	at Bradford	1984
22	J Tunnicliffe	243	v Derbyshire	at Chesterfield	1898
21	Hon F S Jackson	160	v Gloucestershire	at Sheffield	1898
20	M P Vaughan	183	v Glamorgan	at Cardiff (Sophia Gardens)	1996
	and	183	v Northamptonshire	at Northampton	1996
19	C White	186	v Lancashire	at Manchester	2001
18	J A Rudolph	228*	v Durham	at Leeds	2010
18	E Wainwright	228	v Surrey	at The Oval	1899
17	W B Stott	186	v Warwickshire	at Birmingham	1960
17	N W D Yardley	183*	v Hampshire	at Leeds	1951
16	K Taylor	203*	v Warwickshire	at Birmingham	1961
16	M J Wood	207	v Somerset	at Taunton	2003

15	R Kilner	206*	v Derbyshire	at Sheffield	1920
15	G Ulyett	199*	v Derbyshire	at Sheffield	1887
15	B B Wilson	208	v Sussex	at Bradford	1914
14	R Illingworth	162	v Indians	at Sheffield	1959
13	J D Love	170*	v Worcestershire	at Worcester	1979
12	R J Blakey	223*	v Northamptonshire	at Leeds	2003
12	H Halliday	144	v Derbyshire	at Chesterfield	1950
11	A W Gale	151*	v Nottinghamshire	at Nottingham	2010
11	K Sharp	181	v Gloucestershire	at Harrogate	1986
10	C W J Athey	134	v Derbyshire	at Derby	1982
10	Lord Hawke	166	v Warwickshire	at Birmingham	1896
10	F Mitchell	194	v Leicestershire	at Leicester	1899
9	D L Bairstow	145	v Middlesex	at Scarborough	1980
9	M G Bevan	160*	v Surrey	at Middlesbrough	1996
9	L Hall	160	v Lancashire	at Bradford	1887
9	J J Sayers	187	v Kent	at Tunbridge Wells	2007
8	W Bates	136	v Sussex	at Hove	1886
8	M J Lumb	144	v Middlesex	at Southgate	2006
8	T L Taylor	156	v Hampshire	at Harrogate	1901
7	J B Bolus	146*	v Hampshire	at Portsmouth	1960
7	P A Jaques	243	v Hampshire	at Southampton (Rose Bowl)	2004
7	E Robinson	135*	v Leicestershire	at Leicester (Aylestone Rd)	1921
7	P E Robinson	189	v Lancashire	at Scarborough	1991
6	E Lockwood	208	v Kent	at Gravesend	1883
6	R Peel	210*	v Warwickshire	at Birmingham	1896
6	W H H Sutcliffe	181	v Kent	at Canterbury	1952
5	C M Old	116	v Indians	at Bradford	1974
4	I Grimshaw	129*	v Cambridge University	at Sheffield	1885
4	S Haigh	159	v Nottinghamshire	at Sheffield	1901
4	S N Hartley	114	v Gloucestershire	at Bradford	1982
4	R A Hutton	189	v Pakistanis	at Bradford	1971
4	A Lyth	142	v Somerset	at Taunton	2010
4	A U Rashid	157*	v Lancashire	at Leeds	2009
4	A B Sellers	204	v Cambridge University	at Cambridge	1936
3	G L Brophy	177*	v Worcestershire	at Worcester	2011
3	P Carrick	131*	v Northamptonshire	at Northampton	1980
3	A J Dalton	128	v Middlesex	at Leeds	1972
3	A Drake	147*	v Derbyshire	at Chesterfield	1911
3	F Lee	165	v Lancashire	at Bradford	1887
3	G G Macaulay	125*	v Nottinghamshire	at Nottingham	1921
3	R Moorhouse	113	v Somerset	at Taunton	1896
3	R M Pyrah	134*	v Loughborough MCCU	at Leeds	2010
3	J W Rothery	161	v Kent	at Dover	1908
3	J Rowbotham	113	v Surrey	at The Oval	1873
3	T F Smailes	117	v Glamorgan	at Cardiff	1938
3	Younus Khan	217*	v Kent	at Scarborough	2007
2	J M Bairstow	205	v Nottinghamshire	at Nottingham	2011
2	M W Booth	210	v Worcestershire	at Worcester	1911
2	T T Bresnan	116	v Surrey	at The Oval	2007
2	D C F Burton	142*	v Hampshire	at Dewsbury	1919
2	K R Davidson	128	v Kent	at Maidstone	1934
2	P A Gibb	157*	v Nottinghamshire	at Sheffield	1935
2	P J Hartley	127*	v Lancashire	at Manchester	1988

2	I J Harvey	209*	v Somerset	at Leeds	2005
2	C Johnson	107	v Somerset	at Sheffield	1973
2	S A Kellett	125*	v Derbyshire	at Chesterfield	1991
2	N Kilner	112	v Leicestershire	at Leeds	1921
2	B Parker	138*	v Oxford University	at Oxford	1997
2	A Sellers	105	v Middlesex	at Lord's	1893
2	E Smith (Morley)	129	v Hampshire	at Bradford	1899
2	G A Smithson	169	v Leicestershire	at Leicester	1947
2	G B Stevenson	115*	v Warwickshire	at Birmingham	1982
2	F S Trueman	104	v Northamptonshire	at Northampton	1963
2	C Turner	130	v Somerset	at Sheffield	1936
2	D J Wainwright	104*	v Sussex	at Hove	2008
2	T A Wardall	106	v Gloucestershire	at Gloucester (Spa Ground)	1892
1	Azeem Rafiq	100	v Worcestershire	at Worcester	2009
1	G S Ballance	111	v Warwickshire	at Birmingham	2011
1	A T Barber	100	v England XI	at Sheffield	1929
1	H D Bird	181*	v Glamorgan	at Bradford	1959
1	T J D Birtles	104	v Lancashire	at Sheffield	1914
1	G S Blewett	190	v Northamptonshire	at Scarborough	1999
1	M T G Elliott	127	v Warwickshire	at Birmingham	2002
1	T Emmett	104	v Gloucestershire	at Clifton	1873
1	G M Fellows	109	v Lancashire	at Manchester	2002
1	J N Gillespie	123*	v Surrey	at The Oval	2007
1	D Gough	121	v Warwickshire	at Leeds	1996
1	A K D Gray	104	v Somerset	at Taunton	2003
1	A P Grayson	100	v Worcestershire	at Worcester	1994
1	F E Greenwood	104*	v Glamorgan	at Hull	1929
1	G M Hamilton	125	v Hampshire	at Leeds	2000
1	W E Harbord	109	v Oxford University	at Oxford	1930
1	R Iddison	112	v Cambridgeshire	at Hunslet	1869
1	W G Keighley	110	v Surrey	at Leeds	1951
1	R A Kettleborough				
		108	v Essex	at Leeds	1996
1	B Leadbeater	140*	v Hampshire	at Portsmouth	1976
1	D R Martyn	238	v Gloucestershire	at Leeds	2003
1	J T Newstead	100*	v Nottinghamshire	at Nottingham	1908
1	R B Richardson	112	v Warwickshire	at Birmingham	1993
1	J E Root	160	v Sussex	at Scarborough	2011
1	H Rudston	164	v Leicestershire	at Leicester (Aylestone Road)	1904
1	A Sidebottom	124	v Glamorgan	at Cardiff (Sophia Gardens)	1977
1	I G Swallow	114	v MCC	at Scarborough	1987
1	S R Tendulkar	100	v Durham	at Durham	1992
1	J Thewlis	108	v Surrey	at The Oval	1868
1	C T Tyson	100*	v Hampshire	at Southampton	1921
1	H Verity	101	v Jamaica	at Kingston (Sabina Park)	1935/36
1	A Waddington	114	v Worcestershire	at Leeds	1927
1	W A I Washington				
		100*	v Surrey	at Leeds	1902
1	H Wilkinson	113	v MCC	at Scarborough	1904
1	W H Wilkinson	103	v Sussex	at Sheffield	1909
1	E R Wilson	104*	v Essex	at Bradford	1913
1	A Wood	123*	v Worcestershire	at Sheffield	1935
1	J D Woodford	101	v Warwickshire	at Middlesbrough	1971

| FOR YORKSHIRE | | | | AGAINST YORKSHIRE | | |
Total	In Yorkshire	Away		Total	In Yorkshire	Away
105	62	43	Derbyshire	54	25	29
20	9	11	Durham	16	10	6
74	33	41	Essex	45	20	25
68	38	30	Glamorgan	23	13	10
85	41	44	Gloucestershire	52	27	25
86	35	51	Hampshire	54	23	31
80	36	44	Kent	58	28	30
109	56	53	Lancashire	112	58	54
94	51	43	Leicestershire	44	22	22
89	45	44	Middlesex	84	36	48
77	33	44	Northamptonshire	52	25	27
118	55	63	Nottinghamshire	81	32	49
93	47	46	Somerset	56	20	36
111	47	64	Surrey	104	37	67
87	41	46	Sussex	70	31	39
101	35	66	Warwickshire	71	27	44
72	30	42	Worcestershire	40	14	26
1	1	—	Cambridgeshire	—	—	—
1470	**695**	**775**	**Totals**	**1016**	**448**	**568**
9	9	—	Australians	16	16	—
9	9	—	Indians	7	7	—
8	8	—	New Zealanders	3	3	—
5	5	—	Pakistanis	1	1	—
9	9	—	South Africans	7	7	—
5	5	—	Sri Lankans	1	1	—
5	5	—	West Indians	6	6	—
1	1	—	Zimbabweans	—	—	—
3	3	—	Bangladesh 'A'	1	1	—
—	—	—	India 'A'	1	1	—
1	1	—	Pakistan 'A'	1	1	—
45	1	44	Cambridge University	20	2	18
2	2	—	Combined Services	—	—	—
1	—	1	Durham MCCU	1	—	1
4	3	1	England XI's	3	2	1
—	—	—	International XI	1	1	—
1	—	1	Ireland	—	—	—
3	—	3	Jamaica	3	—	3
1	—	1	Liverpool & District	—	—	—
2	2	—	Loughborough MCCU	1	1	—
1	—	1	Mashonaland	—	—	—
2	—	2	Matebeleland	1	—	1
52	38	14	MCC	52	34	18
39	—	39	Oxford University	11	—	11
6	—	6	Rest of England	15	—	15
9	5	4	Scotland	1	—	1
3	3	—	C I Thornton's XI	4	4	—
—	—	—	Western Province	1	—	1
1	1	—	I Zingari	1	1	—
227	**110**	**117**	**Totals**	**161**	**91**	**70**
1697	**805**	**892**	**Grand Totals**	**1177**	**539**	**638**

FOUR CENTURIES IN ONE INNINGS

		F S Jackson	117
		E Wainwright	126
1896	v. Warwickshire	Lord Hawke	166
	at Birmingham	R Peel	*210

(First instance in First-Class cricket)

THREE CENTURIES IN ONE INNINGS

1884	v. Cambridge University	L Hall	116
	at Cambridge	W Bates	133
		I Grimshaw	115
1887	v. Kent	G Ulyett	124
	at Canterbury	L Hall	110
		F Lee	119
1897	v. Sussex	J T Brown	311
	at Sheffield	J Tunnicliffe	147
		E Wainwright	*104
1899	v. Middlesex	F S Jackson	155
	at Bradford	D Denton	113
		F Mitchell	121
1904	v. Surrey	D Denton	105
	at The Oval	G H Hirst	104
		J Tunnicliffe	*139
1919	v. Gloucestershire	H Sutcliffe	118
	at Leeds	D Denton	122
		R Kilner	*115
1925	v. Glamorgan	P Holmes	130
	at Huddersfield	H Sutcliffe	121
		E Robinson	*108
1928	v. Middlesex	P Holmes	105
	at Lord's	E Oldroyd	108
		A Mitchell	105
1928	v. Essex	H Sutcliffe	129
	at Leyton	P Holmes	136
		M Leyland	*133
1929	v. Glamorgan	E Oldroyd	168
	at Hull	W Barber	114
		F E Greenwood	*104
1933	v. MCC	H Sutcliffe	107
	at Scarborough	A Mitchell	158
		M Leyland	133
1936	v. Surrey	H Sutcliffe	129
	at Leeds	L Hutton	163
		M Leyland	*163
1937	v. Leicestershire	H Sutcliffe	189
	at Hull	L Hutton	153
		M Leyland	*118
1947	v. Leicestershire	L Hutton	137
	at Leicester	N W D Yardley	100
		G.A Smithson	169
1971	v. Oxford University	J H Hampshire	*116
	at Oxford	R A Hutton	101
		A J Dalton	111

THREE CENTURIES IN ONE INNINGS *(Continued)*

		G Boycott	141
1975	v. Gloucestershire	R G Lumb	101
	at Bristol	J H Hampshire	.........*106
		M D Moxon	130
1995	v. Cambridge University	D Byas	181
	at Cambridge	M G Bevan	.........*113
		M J Wood	102
2001	v. Leicestershire	M J Lumb	122
	at Leeds	D S Lehmann	104
		C White	183
2001	v. Glamorgan	M J Wood	124
	at Scarborough	D Byas	104
		J A Rudolph	122
2007	v. Surrey	T T Bresnan	116
	at The Oval	J N Gillespie	.........*123

CENTURY IN EACH INNINGS

D Denton	107 and 109*	v. Nottinghamshire at Nottingham, 1906
G H Hirst	111 and 117*	v. Somerset at Bath, 1906
D Denton	133 and 121	v. MCC at Scarborough, 1908
W Rhodes	128 and 115	v. MCC at Scarborough, 1911
P Holmes	126 and 111*	v. Lancashire at Manchester, 1920
H Sutcliffe	107 and109*	v. MCC at Scarborough, 1926
H Sutcliffe	111 and 100*	v. Nottinghamshire at Nottingham, 1928
E I Lester	126 and 142	v. Northamptonshire at Northampton, 1947
L Hutton	197 and 104	v. Essex at Southend, 1947
E I Lester	125* and 132	v. Lancashire at Manchester, 1948
L Hutton	165 and 100	v. Sussex at Hove, 1949
L Hutton	103 and 137	v. MCC at Scarborough, 1952
G Boycott	103 and 105	v. Nottinghamshire at Sheffield, 1966
G Boycott	163 and 141*	v. Nottinghamshire at Bradford, 1983
M D Moxon	123 and 112*	v. Indians at Scarborough, 1986
A A Metcalfe	194* and 107	v. Nottinghamshire at Nottingham, 1990
M P Vaughan	100 and 151	v. Essex at Chelmsford, 1999
Younus Khan	106 and 202*	v. Hampshire at Southampton, 2007

HIGHEST INDIVIDUAL SCORES
FOR AND AGAINST YORKSHIRE

Highest For Yorkshire:
341 G H Hirst v. Leicestershire at Leicester, 1905
Highest Against Yorkshire:
318* W G Grace for Gloucestershire at Cheltenham, 1876

Yorkshire versus:

Derbyshire	*For Yorkshire:*	300 — J T Brown at Chesterfield, 1898
	Against:	219 — J D Eggar at Bradford, 1949
Most Centuries	*For Yorkshire:*	G Boycott 9
	Against:	K J Barnett and W Storer 4 each
Durham	*For Yorkshire:*	339 — D S Lehmann at Leeds, 2006
	Against:	184 — M J di Venuto at Chester-le-Street, 2008
Most Centuries	*For Yorkshire:*	A McGrath 5
	Against:	M J Di Venuto 4
Essex	*For Yorkshire:*	313 — H Sutcliffe at Leyton, 1932
	Against:	219* — D J Insole at Colchester, 1949
Most Centuries	*For Yorkshire:*	H Sutcliffe 9
	Against:	F L Fane, K W R Fletcher, G A Gooch and D J Insole 3 each

Yorkshire versus

Glamorgan	*For Yorkshire:*	213 — M D Moxon at Cardiff, 1996
	Against:	202* — H Morris at Cardiff, 1996
Most Centuries	*For Yorkshire:*	G Boycott, P Holmes and H Sutcliffe 5 each
	Against:	H Morris 5
Gloucestershire	*For Yorkshire:*	238 — D R Martyn at Leeds, 2003
	Against:	318* — W G Grace at Cheltenham, 1876
Most Centuries	*For Yorkshire:*	G Boycott 6
	Against:	W G Grace 9
Hampshire	*For Yorkshire:*	302* — P Holmes at Portsmouth, 1920
	Against:	300* — M A Carberry at Southampton, 2011
Most Centuries	*For Yorkshire:*	H Sutcliffe 6
	Against:	C P Mead 10
Kent	*For Yorkshire:*	248 — W Barber at Leeds, 1934.
	Against:	207 — D P Fulton at Maidstone, 1998
Most Centuries	*For Yorkshire:*	A McGrath 6
	Against:	F E Woolley 5
Lancashire	*For Yorkshire:*	252 — D S Lehmann at Leeds, 2001
	Against:	225 — G D Lloyd at Leeds, 1997 (Non-Championship)
		206 — S G Law at Leeds, 2007
Most Centuries	*For Yorkshire:*	G Boycott and H Sutcliffe 9 each
	Against:	M A Atherton and C H Lloyd 6 each.
Leicestershire	*For Yorkshire:*	341— G H Hirst at Leicester, 1905
	Against:	218— J J Whitaker at Bradford, 1996
Most Centuries	*For Yorkshire:*	H Sutcliffe 10
	Against:	J J Whitaker and C J B Wood 5 each
Middlesex	*For Yorkshire:*	315* — P Holmes at Lord's, 1925
	Against:	243* — A J Webbe at Huddersfield, 1887
Most Centuries	*For Yorkshire:*	P Holmes and H Sutcliffe 7 each
	Against:	M W Gatting 8
Northamptonshire	*For Yorkshire:*	277* — P Holmes at Harrogate, 1921
	Against:	235 — A J Lamb at Leeds, 1990
Most Centuries	*For Yorkshire:*	H Sutcliffe 5
	Against:	W Larkins 5
Nottinghamshire	*For Yorkshire:*	285 — P Holmes at Nottingham, 1929
	Against:	251* — D J Hussey at Leeds, 2010
Most Centuries	*For Yorkshire:*	G Boycott 15
	Against:	R T Robinson 6
Somerset	*For Yorkshire:*	213 — H Sutcliffe at Dewsbury, 1924
	Against:	297 — M J Wood at Taunton, 2005
Most Centuries	*For Yorkshire:*	G Boycott 6
	Against:	L C H Palairet, IVA. Richards, M E Trescothick 5 each
Surrey	*For Yorkshire:*	255 — W Barber at Sheffield, 1935
	Against:	273 — T W Hayward at The Oval, 1899
Most Centuries	*For Yorkshire:*	H Sutcliffe 9
	Against:	J B Hobbs 8

Yorkshire versus

Sussex	*For Yorkshire:*	311 — J T Brown at Sheffield, 1897
	Against:	274* — M W Goodwin at Hove, 2011
Most Centuries	*For Yorkshire:*	L Hutton 8
	Against:	C B Fry 7
Warwickshire	*For Yorkshire:*	275 — P Holmes at Bradford, 1928
	Against:	225 — D P Ostler at Birmingham, 2002
Most Centuries	*For Yorkshire:*	G Boycott and H Sutcliffe 8 each
	Against:	D L Amiss, H E Dollery, R B Khanhai and W G Quaife 4 each.
Worcestershire	*For Yorkshire:*	274* — M D Moxon at Worcester, 1994
	Against:	259 — D Kenyon at Kidderminster, 1956
Most Centuries	*For Yorkshire:*	M Leyland 6
	Against:	D Kenyon and G M Turner 5 each
Australians	*For Yorkshire:*	167 — J T Brown at Bradford, 1899
	Against:	193* — B C Booth at Bradford, 1964
Most Centuries	*For Yorkshire:*	G Boycott and D Denton 2 each
	Against:	N C O'Neill 2
Indians	*For Yorkshire:*	183* — L Hutton at Bradford, 1946
	Against:	244* — V S Hazare at Sheffield, 1946
Most Centuries	*For Yorkshire:*	M D Moxon 2
	Against:	V S Hazare, VMankad, PR Umrigar D K Gaekwad, G A Parkar and R Lamba 1 each
New Zealanders	*For Yorkshire:*	175 — P Holmes at Bradford, 1927
	Against:	126 — W M Wallace at Bradford, 1949
Most Centuries	*For Yorkshire:*	L Hutton and DB Close 2 each
	Against:	H G Vivian, WM Wallace and J G Wright 1 each
Pakistanis	*For Yorkshire:*	197 — P J Sharpe at Leeds, 1967
	Against:	139 — A H Kardar at Sheffield, 1954
Most Centuries	*For Yorkshire:*	P J Sharpe 2
	Against:	A H Kardar 1
South Africans	*For Yorkshire:*	156 — L Hutton at Sheffield, 1951
	Against:	168 — I J Seidle at Sheffield, 1929
Most Centuries	*For Yorkshire:*	L Hutton 2
	Against:	H B Cameron, J D Lindsay, B Mitchell, D P B Morkel, I J Seidle, L J Tancred, C B van Ryneveld 1 each
Sri Lankans	*For Yorkshire:*	132 — M D Moxon at Leeds, 1988
	Against:	112 — S A R Silva at Leeds, 1988
Most Centuries	*For Yorkshire:*	K Sharp 2
	Against:	S A R Silva 1
West Indians	*For Yorkshire:*	112* — D Denton at Harrogate, 1906
	Against:	164 — S F A Bacchus at Leeds, 1980
Most Centuries	*For Yorkshire:*	M G Bevan, D Denton, L Hutton, R G Lumb and A A Metcalfe 1 each
	Against:	S F A Bacchus, C O Browne, S Chanderpaul P A Goodman, C L Hooper and G St A Sobers 1 each

Yorkshire versus

Zimbabweans	*For Yorkshire:*	113 — M D Moxon at Leeds, 1990
	Against:	89 — G J Whittall at Leeds, 2000
Most Centuries	*For Yorkshire:*	M D Moxon 1
	Against:	None
Cambridge	*For Yorkshire:*	207* — G Boycott at Cambridge, 1976
University	*Against:*	171* — G L Jessop at Cambridge, 1899
		171 — P B H May at Cambridge, 1952
Most Centuries	*For Yorkshire:*	H Sutcliffe 4
	Against:	G M Kemp 2
Durham MCCU	*For Yorkshire:*	139 — J J Sayers at Durham, 2011
	Against:	127 — T Westley at Durham, 2011
Most Centuries	*For Yorkshire:*	J J Sayers 1
	Against:	T Westley 1
Loughborough MCCU	*For Yorkshire:*	134* — R M Pyrah at Leeds, 2010
	Against:	107 — C P Murtagh
Most Centuries	*For Yorkshire:*	R M Pyrah 2
	Against:	C P Murtagh 1
MCC	*For Yorkshire:*	180* — G H Hirst at Lord's, 1919
	Against:	214 — E H Hendren at Lord's, 1919
Most Centuries	*For Yorkshire:*	L Hutton 8
	Against:	R E S Wyatt 5
Oxford University	*For Yorkshire:*	196 — R J Blakey at Oxford, 1991
	Against:	201— J E Raphael at Oxford, 1904
Most Centuries	*For Yorkshire:*	M Leyland 4
	Against:	A A Baig and Nawab of Pataudi (Jun.) 2 each

J B Hobbs scored 11 centuries against Yorkshire – the highest by any individual (8 for Surrey and 3 for the Rest of England).

Three players have scored 10 centuries against Yorkshire – W G Grace (9 for Gloucestershire and 1 for MCC). E H Hendren (6 for Middlesex, 3 for MCC and 1 for the Rest of England) and C P Mead (all 10 for Hampshire).

They'll think me daft

He was only 13 years old, trudging off in the February snow of 1930 to his first net session at Headingley. In his pocket was the letter Yorkshire CCC had sent him. It was addressed to Mr Leonard Hutton. In his right hand was a kitbag containing his Harrow-sized Herbert Sutcliffe bat. He said he felt very little — "small in a sheepish sort of way"— as he walked along the slushy streets of Leeds. "They'll think me daft," he said, talking to himself, "going to play cricket in winter".

Duncan Hamilton: Wisden on Yorkshire

CARRYING BAT THROUGH A COMPLETED INNINGS

Batsman	Score	Total	Against	Season
G R Atkinson	30*	73	Nottinghamshire at Bradford	1865
L Hall	31*	94	Sussex at Hove	1878
L Hall	124*	331	Sussex at Hove	1883
L Hall	128*	285	Sussex at Huddersfield	1884
L Hall	32*	81	Kent at Sheffield	1885
L Hall	79*	285	Surrey at Sheffield	1885
L Hall	37*	96	Derbyshire at Derby	1885
L Hall	50*	173	Sussex at Huddersfield	1886
L Hall	74*	172	Kent at Canterbury	1886
G Ulyett	199*	399	Derbyshire at Sheffield	1887
L Hall	119*	334	Gloucestershire at Dewsbury	1887
L Hall	82*	218	Sussex at Hove	1887
L Hall	34*	104	Surrey at The Oval	1888
L Hall	129*	461	Gloucestershire at Clifton	1888
L Hall	85*	259	Middlesex at Lord's	1889
L Hall	41*	106	Nottinghamshire at Sheffield	1891
W Rhodes	98*	184	MCC at Lord's	1903
W Rhodes	85*	152	Essex at Leyton	1910
P Holmes	145*	270	Northamptonshire at Northampton	1920
H Sutcliffe	125*	307	Essex at Southend	1920
P Holmes	175*	377	New Zealanders at Bradford	1927
P Holmes	110*	219	Northamptonshire at Bradford	1929
H Sutcliffe	104*	170	Hampshire at Leeds	1932
H Sutcliffe	114*	202	Rest of England at The Oval	1933
H Sutcliffe	187*	401	Worcestershire at Bradford	1934
H Sutcliffe	135*	262	Glamorgan at Neath	1935
H Sutcliffe	125*	322	Oxford University at Oxford	1939
L Hutton	99*	200	Leicestershire at Sheffield	1948
L Hutton	78*	153	Worcestershire at Sheffield	1949
F A Lowson	76*	218	MCC at Lord's	1951
W B Stott	144*	262	Worcestershire at Worcester	1959
D E V Padgett	115*	230	Gloucestershire at Bristol	1962
G Boycott	114*	297	Leicestershire at Sheffield	1968
G Boycott	53*	119	Warwickshire at Bradford	1969
G Boycott	182*	320	Middlesex at Lord's	1971
G Boycott	138*	232	Warwickshire at Birmingham	1971
G Boycott	175*	360	Nottinghamshire at Worksop	1979
G Boycott	112*	233	Derbyshire at Sheffield	1983
G Boycott	55*	183	Warwickshire at Leeds	1984
G Boycott	55*	131	Surrey at Sheffield	1985
M J Wood	60*	160	Somerset at Scarborough	2004
J J Sayers	122*	326	Middlesex at Scarborough	2006
J J Sayers	149*	414	Durham at Leeds	2007

43 instances, of which L Hall (14 times), G Boycott (8) and H Sutcliffe (6) account for 28 between them.

The highest percentage of an innings total is 61.17 by H. Sutcliffe (104* v. Hampshire at Leeds in 1932) but P Holmes was absent ill, so only 9 wickets fell.

Other contributions exceeding 55% are:

59.48%	G Boycott	(138* v. Warwickshire at Birmingham, 1971)
56.87%	G Boycott	(182* v. Middlesex at Lord's, 1971)
56.43%	H Sutcliffe	(114* v. Rest of England at The Oval, 1933)
55.92%	W Rhodes	(85* v. Essex at Leyton, 1910)

2,000 RUNS IN A SEASON

Batsman	Season	M	I	NO	Runs	HS	Avge	100s
G H Hirst	1904	32	44	3	2257	157	55.04	8
D Denton	1905	33	52	2	2258	172	45.16	8
G H Hirst	1906	32	53	6	2164	169	46.04	6
D Denton	1911	32	55	4	2161	137*	42.37	6
D Denton	1912	36	51	4	2088	221	44.23	6
P Holmes	1920	30	45	6	2144	302*	54.97	7
P Holmes	1925	35	49	9	2351	315*	58.77	6
H Sutcliffe	1925	34	48	8	2236	235	55.90	7
H Sutcliffe	1928	27	35	5	2418	228	80.60	11
P Holmes	1928	31	40	4	2093	275	58.13	6
H Sutcliffe	1931	28	33	8	2351	230	94.04	9
H Sutcliffe	1932	29	41	5	2883	313	80.08	12
M Leyland	1933	31	44	4	2196	210*	54.90	7
A Mitchell	1933	34	49	10	2100	158	53.84	6
H Sutcliffe	1935	32	47	3	2183	212	49.61	8
L Hutton	1937	28	45	6	2448	271*	62.76	8
H Sutcliffe	1937	32	52	5	2054	189	43.70	4
L Hutton	1939	29	44	5	2316	280*	59.38	10
L Hutton	1947	19	31	2	2068	270*	71.31	10
L Hutton	1949	26	44	6	2640	269*	69.47	9
F A Lowson	1950	31	54	5	2067	141*	42.18	5
D E V Padgett	1959	35	60	8	2158	161*	41.50	4
W B Stott	1959	32	56	2	2034	144*	37.66	3
P J Sharpe	1962	36	62	8	2201	138	40.75	7
G Boycott	1971	18	25	4	2221	233	105.76	11
A A Metcalfe	1990	23	44	4	2047	194*	51.17	6

1,000 RUNS IN A SEASON

Batsman		Runs scored	Runs scored	Runs scored
C W J Athey	(2)	1113 in 1980	1339 in 1982	—
D L Bairstow	(3)	1083 in 1981	1102 in 1983	1163 in 1985
J M Bairstow	(1)	1015 in 2011	—	—
W Barber	(8)	1000 in 1932	1595 in 1933	1930 in 1934
		1958 in 1935	1466 in 1937	1455 in 1938
		1501 in 1939	1170 in 1946	—
M G Bevan	(2)	1598 in 1995	1225 in 1996	—
R J Blakey	(5)	1361 in 1987	1159 in 1989	1065 in 1992
		1236 in 1994	1041 in 2002	—
J B Bolus	(2)	1245 in 1960	1970 in 1961	—
M W Booth	(2)	1189 in 1911	1076 in 1913	—
G Boycott	(19)	1628 in 1963	1639 in 1964	1215 in 1965
		1388 in 1966	1530 in 1967	1004 in 1968
		1558 in 1970	2221 in 1971	1156 in 1972
		1478 in 1974	1915 in 1975	1288 in 1976
		1259 in 1977	1074 in 1978	1160 in 1979
		1913 in 1982	1941 in 1983	1567 in 1984
		1657 in 1985	—	—
J T Brown	(9)	1196 in 1894	1260 in 1895	1755 in 1896
		1634 in 1897	1641 in 1898	1375 in 1899
		1181 in 1900	1627 in 1901	1291 in 1903
D Byas	(5)	1557 in 1991	1073 in 1993	1297 in 1994
		1913 in 1995	1319 in 1997	—
D B Close	(13)	1192 in 1952	1287 in 1954	1131 in 1955
		1315 in 1957	1335 in 1958	1740 in 1959
		1699 in 1960	1821 in 1961	1438 in 1962
		1145 in 1963	1281 in 1964	1127 in 1965
		1259 in 1966	—	—

Batsman	Runs scored	Runs scored	Runs scored
K R Davidson .... (1)	1241 in 1934	—	—
D Denton .... (20)	1028 in 1896	1357 in 1897	1595 in 1899
	1378 in 1900	1400 in 1901	1191 in 1902
	1562 in 1903	1919 in 1904	2258 in 1905
	1905 in 1906	1128 in 1907	1852 in 1908
	1765 in 1909	1106 in 1910	2161 in 1911
	2088 in 1912	1364 in 1913	1799 in 1914
	1213 in 1919	1324 in 1920	—
A Drake .... (2)	1487 in 1911	1029 in 1913	—
A P Grayson .... (1)	1046 in 1994	—	—
S Haigh .... (1)	1031 in 1904	—	—
L Hall .... (1)	1120 in 1887	—	—
H Halliday .... (4)	1357 in 1948	1484 in 1950	1351 in 1952
	1461 in 1953	—	—
J H Hampshire .... (12)	1236 in 1963	1280 in 1964	1424 in 1965
	1105 in 1966	1244 in 1967	1133 in 1968
	1079 in 1970	1259 in 1971	1124 in 1975
	1303 in 1976	1596 in 1978	1425 in 1981
Lord Hawke .... (1)	1005 in 1895	—	—
G H Hirst .... (19)	1110 in 1896	1248 in 1897	1546 in 1899
	1752 in 1900	1669 in 1901	1113 in 1902
	1535 in 1903	2257 in 1904	1972 in 1905
	2164 in 1906	1167 in 1907	1513 in 1908
	1151 in 1909	1679 in 1910	1639 in 1911
	1119 in 1912	1431 in 1913	1655 in 1914
	1312 in 1919	—	—
P Holmes .... (14)	1876 in 1919	2144 in 1920	1458 in 1921
	1614 in 1922	1884 in 1923	1610 in 1924
	2351 in 1925	1792 in 1926	1774 in 1927
	2093 in 1928	1724 in 1929	1957 in 1930
	1431 in 1931	1191 in 1932	—
L Hutton .... (12)	1282 in 1936	2448 in 1937	1171 in 1938
	2316 in 1939	1322 in 1946	2068 in 1947
	1792 in 1948	2640 in 1949	1581 in 1950
	1554 in 1951	1956 in 1952	1532 in 1953
R Illingworth .... (5)	1193 in 1957	1490 in 1959	1029 in 1961
	1610 in 1962	1301 in 1964	—
F S Jackson .... (4)	1211 in 1896	1300 in 1897	1442 in 1898
	1468 in 1899	—	—
P A Jaques .... (2)	1118 in 2004	1359 in 2005	—
S A Kellett .... (2)	1266 in 1991	1326 in 1992	—
R Kilner .... (10)	1586 in 1913	1329 in 1914	1135 in 1919
	1240 in 1920	1137 in 1921	1132 in 1922
	1265 in 1923	1002 in 1925	1021 in 1926
	1004 in 1927	—	—
D S Lehmann .... (5)	1575 in 1997	1477 in 2000	1416 in 2001
	1136 in 2002	1706 in 2006	—
E I Lester .... (6)	1256 in 1948	1774 in 1949	1015 in 1950
	1786 in 1952	1380 in 1953	1330 in 1954
M Leyland .... (17)	1088 in 1923	1203 in 1924	1560 in 1925
	1561 in 1926	1478 in 1927	1554 in 1928
	1407 in 1929	1814 in 1930	1127 in 1931
	1821 in 1932	2196 in 1933	1228 in 1934
	1366 in 1935	1621 in 1936	1120 in 1937
	1640 in 1938	1238 in 1939	—

atsman	Runs scored	Runs scored	Runs scored
D Love	(2) 1161 in 1981	1020 in 1983	—
A Lowson	(8) 1678 in 1949	2067 in 1950	1607 in 1951
	1562 in 1952	1586 in 1953	1719 in 1954
	1082 in 1955	1428 in 1956	
1 J Lumb	(1) 1038 in 2003	—	—
. G Lumb	(5) 1002 in 1973	1437 in 1975	1070 in 1978
	1465 in 1979	1223 in 1980	—
. Lyth	(1) 1509 in 2010	—	—
. McGrath	(3) 1425 in 2005	1293 in 2006	1219 in 2010
A Metcalfe	(6) 1674 in 1986	1162 in 1987	1320 in 1988
	1230 in 1989	2047 in 1990	1210 in 1991
. Mitchell	(10) 1320 in 1928	1633 in 1930	1351 in 1932
	2100 in 1933	1854 in 1934	1530 in 1935
	1095 in 1936	1602 in 1937	1305 in 1938
	1219 in 1939	—	—
. Mitchell	(2) 1678 in 1899	1801 in 1901	—
. Moorhouse	(1) 1096 in 1895	—	—
4 D Moxon	(11) 1016 in 1984	1256 in 1985	1298 in 1987
	1430 in 1988	1156 in 1989	1621 in 1990
	1669 in 1991	1314 in 1992	1251 in 1993
	1458 in 1994	1145 in 1995	—
. Oldroyd	(10) 1473 in 1921	1690 in 1922	1349 in 1923
	1607 in 1924	1262 in 1925	1197 in 1926
	1390 in 1927	1304 in 1928	1474 in 1929
	1285 in 1930	—	—
▶ E V Padgett	(12) 1046 in 1956	2158 in 1959	1574 in 1960
	1856 in 1961	1750 in 1962	1380 in 1964
	1220 in 1965	1194 in 1966	1284 in 1967
	1163 in 1968	1078 in 1969	1042 in 1970
. Peel	(1) 1193 in 1896	—	—
W Rhodes	(17) 1251 in 1904	1353 in 1905	1618 in 1906
	1574 in 1908	1663 in 1909	1355 in 1910
	1961 in 1911	1030 in 1912	1805 in 1913
	1325 in 1914	1138 in 1919	1329 in 1921
	1368 in 1922	1168 in 1923	1030 in 1924
	1256 in 1925	1071 in 1926	—
. Robinson	(2) 1104 in 1921	1097 in 1929	—
. E Robinson	(3) 1173 in 1988	1402 in 1990	1293 in 1991
A Rudolph	(4) 1078 in 2007	1292 in 2008	1366 in 2009
	1375 in 2010	—	—
J Sayers	(1) 1150 in 2009	—	—
. B Sellers	(1) 1109 in 1938	—	—
. Sharp	(1) 1445 in 1984	—	—
J Sharpe	(10) 1039 in 1960	1240 in 1961	2201 in 1962
	1273 in 1964	1091 in 1965	1352 in 1967
	1256 in 1968	1012 in 1969	1149 in 1970
	1320 in 1973	—	—
W B Stott	(5) 1362 in 1957	1036 in 1958	2034 in 1959
	1790 in 1960	1409 in 1961	—

Batsman		Runs scored	Runs scored	Runs scored
H Sutcliffe	(21)	†1839 in 1919	1393 in 1920	1235 in 192
		1909 in 1922	1773 in 1923	1720 in 192
		2236 in 1925	1672 in 1926	1814 in 192
		2418 in 1928	1485 in 1929	1636 in 193
		2351 in 1931	2883 in 1932	1986 in 193
		1511 in 1934	2183 in 1935	1295 in 193
		2054 in 1937	1660 in 1938	1416 in 193

† First season in First-Class cricket – The record for a debut season.

Batsman		Runs scored	Runs scored	Runs scored
W H H Sutcliffe	(1)	1193 in 1955	—	—
K Taylor	(6)	1306 in 1959	1107 in 1960	1494 in 196
		1372 in 1962	1149 in 1964	1044 in 196
T L Taylor	(2)	1236 in 1901	1373 in 1902	—
S R Tendulkar	(1)	1070 in 1992	—	—
J Tunnicliffe	(12)	1333 in 1895	1368 in 1896	1208 in 189
		1713 in 1898	1434 in 1899	1496 in 190
		1295 in 1901	1274 in 1902	1650 in 190
		1096 in 1905	1232 in 1906	1195 in 190
C Turner	(1)	1153 in 1934	—	—
G Ulyett	(4)	1083 in 1878	1158 in 1882	1024 in 188
		1285 in 1887	—	—
M P Vaughan	(4)	1066 in 1994	1235 in 1995	1161 in 199
		1161 in 1998	—	—
E Wainwright	(3)	1492 in 1897	1479 in 1899	1044 in 190
W A I Washington	(1)	1022 in 1902	—	—
W Watson	(8)	1331 in 1947	1352 in 1948	1586 in 195
		1350 in 1953	1347 in 1954	1564 in 195
		1378 in 1956	1455 in 1957	—
W H Wilkinson	(1)	1282 in 1908	—	—
B B Wilson	(5)	1054 in 1909	1455 in 1911	1453 in 191
		1533 in 1913	1632 in 1914	—
B B Wilson	(5)	1054 in 1909	1455 in 1911	1453 in 191
J V Wilson	(12)	1460 in 1949	1548 in 1950	1985 in 195
		1349 in 1952	1531 in 1953	1713 in 195
		1799 in 1955	1602 in 1956	1287 in 195
		1064 in 1960	1018 in 1961	1226 in 196
A Wood	(1)	1237 in 1935	—	—
M J Wood	(4)	1080 in 1998	1060 in 2001	1432 in 200
		1005 in 2005	—	—
N W D Yardley	(4)	1028 in 1939	1299 in 1947	1413 in 194
		1031 in 1950	—	—

PLAYERS WHO HAVE SCORED CENTURIES
FOR AND AGAINST YORKSHIRE

layer		For	Venue	Season
: W J Athey (5)	114*	Gloucestershire	Bradford	1984
0 for Yorkshire)	101	Gloucestershire	Gloucester	1985
	101*	Gloucestershire	Leeds	1987
	112	Sussex	Scarborough	1993
	100	Sussex	Eastbourne	1996
M G Bevan (1)	142	Leicestershire	Leicester	2002
9 for Yorkshire)				
B Bolus (2)	114	Nottinghamshire	Bradford	1963
7 for Yorkshire)	138	Derbyshire	Sheffield	1973
B Close (1)	102	Somerset	Taunton	1971
33 for Yorkshire)				
1 T G Elliott (1)	125	Glamorgan	Leeds	2004
1 for Yorkshire)				
A Gibb (1)	107	Essex	Brentwood	1951
2 for Yorkshire)				
A Jaques (1)	222	Northamptonshire	Northampton	2003
7 for Yorkshire)				
N Kilner (2)	119	Warwickshire	Hull	1932
2 for Yorkshire)	197	Warwickshire	Birmingham	1933
J Sharpe (1)	126	Derbyshire	Chesterfield	1976
23 for Yorkshire)				

Pudsey power

Eighty first-class cricketers appeared in the (Bradford) League in 1943, and crowd records were broken on all grounds. More than 10,000 saw Pudsey St Lawrence, for whom Len Hutton made 64, defeat Brighouse. The Pudsey club also won promotion to Division A. Eddie Paynter and Hutton both scored more than 600 runs, and Arthur Booth and George Pope of Spen Victoria headed the bowling, taking more than 70 wickets.

Roy Genders, 1952

BATSMEN WHO HAVE SCORED OVER 10,000 RUNS

Player	M	I	NO	Runs	HS	Av'ge	100s
H Sutcliffe	602	864	96	38558	313	50.20	112
D Denton	676	1058	61	33282	221	33.38	61
G Boycott	414	674	111	32570	260*	57.85	103
G H Hirst	717	1050	128	32024	341	34.73	56
W Rhodes	883	1195	162	31075	267*	30.08	46
P Holmes	485	699	74	26220	315*	41.95	60
M Leyland	548	720	82	26180	263	41.03	62
L Hutton	341	527	62	24807	280*	53.34	85
D B Close	536	811	102	22650	198	31.94	33
J H Hampshire	456	724	89	21979	183*	34.61	34
J V Wilson	477	724	75	20548	230	31.66	29
D E V Padgett	487	774	63	20306	161*	28.55	29
J Tunnicliffe	472	768	57	19435	243	27.33	22
M D Moxon	277	476	42	18973	274*	43.71	41
A Mitchell	401	550	69	18189	189	37.81	39
P J Sharpe	411	666	71	17685	203*	29.72	23
E Oldroyd	383	509	58	15891	194	35.23	37
J T Brown	345	567	41	15694	311	29.83	23
W Barber	354	495	48	15315	255	34.26	27
R Illingworth	496	668	131	14986	162	27.90	14
D Byas	268	449	42	14398	213	35.37	28
G Ulyett	355	618	31	14157	199*	24.11	15
R J Blakey	339	541	84	14150	223*	30.96	12
W Watson	283	430	65	13953	214*	38.22	26
F A Lowson	252	404	31	13897	259*	37.25	30
A McGrath	228	388	26	13443	211	37.13	32
Lord Hawke	510	739	91	13133	166	20.26	10
R Kilner	365	478	46	13018	206*	30.13	15
D L Bairstow	429	601	113	12985	145	26.60	9
K Taylor	303	505	35	12864	203*	27.37	16
N W D Yardley	302	420	56	11632	183*	31.95	17
R G Lumb	239	395	30	11525	165*	31.57	22
E Wainwright	352	545	30	11092	228	21.53	18
S Haigh	513	687	110	10993	159	19.05	4
E I Lester	228	339	27	10616	186	34.02	24
A A Metcalfe	184	317	19	10465	216*	35.11	25
C White	221	350	45	10376	186	34.01	19
Hon F S Jackson	207	328	22	10371	160	33.89	21
J D Love	247	388	58	10263	170*	31.10	13

RECORD PARTNERSHIPS FOR YORKSHIRE

1st wkt	555	P Holmes (224*) and H Sutcliffe (313) v. Essex at Leyton, 1932
2nd wkt	346	W Barber (162) and M Leyland (189) v. Middlesex at Sheffield, 1932
3rd wkt	346	J J Sayers (173) and A McGrath (211) v. Warwickshire at Birmingham, 2009
4th wkt	358	D S Lehmann (339) and M J Lumb (98) v. Durham at Leeds, 2006
5th wkt	340	E Wainwright (228) and G H Hirst (186) v. Surrey at The Oval, 1899
6th wkt	276	M Leyland (191) and E Robinson (124*) v. Glamorgan at Swansea, 1926
7th wkt	254	W Rhodes (135) and D C F Burton (142*) v. Hampshire at Dewsbury, 1919
8th wkt	292	R Peel (210*) and Lord Hawke (166) v. Warwickshire at Birmingham, 1896
9th wkt	246	T T Bresnan (116) and J N Gillespie (123*) v. Surrey at The Oval, 2007
10th wkt	149	G Boycott (79) and G B Stevenson (115*) v. Warwickshire at Birmingham, 1982

RECORD PARTNERSHIPS AGAINST YORKSHIRE

1st wkt	372	R R Montgomerie (127) and M B Loye (205) for Northamptonshire at Northampton, 1996
2nd wkt	417	K J Barnett (210*) and TA Tweats (189) for Derbyshire at Derby, 1997
3rd wkt	523	M A Carberry (300*) and N D McKenzie (237) for Hampshire at Southampton, 2011
4th wkt	447	R Abel (193) and T Hayward (273) for Surrey at The Oval, 1899
5th wkt	261	W G Grace (318*) and W O Moberley (103) for Gloucestershire at Cheltenham, 1876
6th wkt	294	D R Jardine (157) and P G H Fender (177) for Surrey at Bradford, 1928
7th wkt	315	D M Benkenstein (151) and O D Gibson (155) for Durham at Leeds, 2006
8th wkt	178	A P Wells (253*) and B T P Donelan (59) for Sussex at Middlesbrough, 1991
9th wkt	233	I J L Trott (161*) and J S Patel (120) for Warwickshire at Birmingham, 2009
10th wkt	132	A Hill (172*) and M Jean-Jacques (73) for Derbyshire at Sheffield, 1986

CENTURY PARTNERSHIPS FOR THE FIRST WICKET IN BOTH INNINGS

128	108	G Ulyett (82 and 91) and L Hall (87 and 37) v. Sussex at Hove, 1885
		(First instance in First-Class cricket)
138	147*	J T Brown (203 and 81*) and J Tunnicliffe (62 and 63*) v. Middlesex at Lord's, 1896
		(Second instance in First-Class cricket)
105	265*	P Holmes (51 and 127*) and H Sutcliffe (71 and 131*) v. Surrey at The Oval, 1926
184	210*	P Holmes (83 and 101*) and H Sutcliffe (111 and 100*) v. Nottinghamshire at Nottingham, 1928
110	117	L Hutton (95 and 86) and W Watson (34 and 57) v. Lancashire at Manchester, 1947
122	230	W B Stott (50 and 114) and K Taylor (79 and 140) v. Nottinghamshire at Nottingham, 1957
136	138	J B Bolus (108 and 71) and K Taylor (89 and 75) v. Cambridge University at Cambridge, 1962
105	105	G Boycott (38 and 64) and K Taylor (85 and 49) v. Leicestershire at Leicester, 1963
116	112*	K Taylor (45 and 68) and J H Hampshire (68 and 67*) v. Oxford University at Oxford, 1964
104	104	G Boycott (117 and 49*) and R G Lumb (47 and 57) v. Sussex at Leeds, 1974
134	185*	M D Moxon (57 and 89*) and A A Metcalfe (216* and 78*) v. Middlesex at Leeds, 1988
118	129*	G S Ballance (72 and 73*) and J J Sayers (139 and 53*) v. Durham MCCU at Durham, 2011

CENTURY PARTNERSHIPS FOR THE FIRST WICKET IN BOTH INNINGS BUT WITH CHANGE OF PARTNER

109		W H H Sutcliffe (82) and F A Lowson (46)
	143	W H H Sutcliffe (88) and W Watson (52) v. Canadians at Scarborough, 1954
109		G Boycott (70) and R G Lumb (44)
	135	G Boycott (74) and JH Hampshire (58) v. Northamptonshire at Bradford, 197

CENTURY PARTNERSHIPS

FIRST WICKET (Qualification 200 runs)

555	P Holmes (224*) and H Sutcliffe (313) v. Essex at Leyton, 1932
554	J T Brown (300) and J Tunnicliffe (243) v. Derbyshire at Chesterfield, 1898
378	J T Brown (311) and J Tunnicliffe (147) v. Sussex at Sheffield, 1897
362	M D Moxon (213) and M P Vaughan (183) v. Glamorgan at Cardiff, 1996
351	G Boycott (184) and M D Moxon (168) v. Worcestershire at Worcester, 1985
347	P Holmes (302*) and H Sutcliffe (131) v. Hampshire at Portsmouth, 1920
323	P Holmes (125) and H Sutcliffe (195) v. Lancashire at Sheffield, 1931
315	H Sutcliffe (189) and L Hutton (153) v. Leicestershire at Hull, 1937
315	H Sutcliffe (116) and L Hutton (280*) v. Hampshire at Sheffield, 1939
309	P Holmes (250) and H Sutcliffe (129) v. Warwickshire at Birmingham, 1931
309	C White (186) and M J Wood (115) v. Lancashire at Manchester, 2001
290	P Holmes (179*) and H Sutcliffe (104) v. Middlesex at Leeds, 1928
288	G Boycott (130*) and R G Lumb (159) v. Somerset at Harrogate, 1979
286	L Hutton (156) and F A Lowson (115) v. South Africans at Sheffield, 1951
282	M D Moxon (147) and A A Metcalfe (151) v. Lancashire at Manchester, 1986
281*	W B Stott (138*) and K Taylor (130*) v. Sussex at Hove, 1960
279	P Holmes (133) and H Sutcliffe (145) v. Northamptonshire at Northampton, 1919
274	P.Holmes (199) and H Sutcliffe (139) v. Somerset at Hull, 1923
274	P Holmes (180) and H Sutcliffe (134) v. Gloucestershire at Gloucester, 1927
272	P Holmes (194) and H Sutcliffe (129) v. Leicestershire at Hull, 1925
272	M J Wood (202*) and J J Sayers (115) v. Bangladesh 'A' at Leeds, 2005
268	P Holmes (136) and H Sutcliffe (129) v. Essex at Leyton, 1928
267	W Barber (248) and L Hutton (70) v. Kent at Leeds, 1934
265*	P Holmes (127*) and H Sutcliffe (131*) v. Surrey at The Oval, 1926
264	G Boycott (161*) and R G Lumb (132) v. Gloucestershire at Leeds, 1976
253	P Holmes (123) and H Sutcliffe (132) v. Lancashire at Sheffield, 1919
248	G Boycott (163) and A A Metcalfe (122) v. Nottinghamshire at Bradford, 1983
245	L Hutton (152) and F A Lowson (120) v. Lancashire at Leeds, 1952
244	J A Rudolph (149) and J J Sayers (86) v Nottinghamshire at Nottingham, 2009
241	P Holmes (142) and H Sutcliffe (123*) v. Surrey at The Oval, 1929
240	G Boycott (233) and P J Sharpe (92) v. Essex at Colchester, 1971
238*	P Holmes (126*) and H Sutcliffe (105*) v. Cambridge University at Cambridge, 1923
236	G Boycott (131) and K Taylor (153) v. Lancashire at Manchester, 1964
235	P Holmes (130) and H Sutcliffe (132*) v. Glamorgan at Sheffield, 1930
233	G Boycott (141*) and R G Lumb (90) v. Cambridge University at Cambridge, 1973
233	H Halliday (116) and W Watson (108) v. Northamptonshire at Northampton, 1948
231	M P Vaughan (151) and D Byas (90) v. Essex at Chelmsford, 1999
230	H Sutcliffe (129) and L Hutton (163) v. Surrey at Leeds, 1936
230	W B Stott (114) and K Taylor (140*) v. Nottinghamshire at Nottingham, 1957
228	H Halliday (90) and J V Wilson (223*) v. Scotland at Scarborough, 1951
228	G Boycott (141) and R G Lumb (101) v. Gloucestershire at Bristol, 1975
227	P Holmes (110) and H Sutcliffe (119) v. Leicestershire at Leicester, 1928
225	R G Lumb (101) and C W J Athey (125*) v. Gloucestershire at Sheffield, 1980
224	C W J Athey (114) and J D Love (104) v. Warwickshire at Birmingham, 1980

CENTURY PARTNERSHIPS *(Continued)*

222	W B Stott (141) and K Taylor (90) v. Sussex at Bradford, 1958
221	P Holmes (130) and H Sutcliffe (121) v. Glamorgan at Huddersfield, 1925
221	M D Moxon (141) and A A Metcalfe (73) v. Surrey at The Oval, 1992
219	P Holmes (102) and A Mitchell (130*) v. Somerset at Bradford, 1930
218	M Leyland (110) and H Sutcliffe (235) v. Middlesex at Leeds, 1925
218	R G Lumb (145) and M D Moxon (111) v. Derbyshire at Sheffield, 1981
210*	P Holmes (101*) and H Sutcliffe (100*) v. Nottinghamshire at Nottingham, 1928
210	G Boycott (128) and P J Sharpe (197) v. Pakistanis at Leeds, 1967
209	F A Lowson (115) and D E V Padgett (107) v. Scotland at Hull, 1956
208	A Mitchell (85) and E Oldroyd (111) v. Cambridge University at Cambridge, 1929
207	A Mitchell (90) and W Barber (107) v. Middlesex at Lord's, 1935
206	G Boycott (118) and R G Lumb (87) v. Glamorgan at Bradford, 1978
204	M D Moxon (66) and A A Metcalfe (162) v. Gloucestershire at Cheltenham, 1990
203	L Hutton (119) and F A Lowson (83) v. Somerset at Huddersfield, 1952
203	M D Moxon (117) and S A Kellett (87) v. Somerset at Middlesbrough, 1992
203	M D Moxon (134) and M P Vaughan (106) v. Matebeleland at Bulawayo, 1996
200*	P Holmes (107*) and H Sutcliffe (80*) v. Oxford University at Oxford, 1930

Note: P Holmes and H Sutcliffe shared 69 century opening partnerships for Yorkshire;
G Boycott and R G Lumb 29; L Hutton and F A Lowson 22; M D Moxon and A A Metcalfe 21;
J T Brown and J Tunnicliffe 19; H Sutcliffe and L Hutton 15, and L Hall and G Ulyett 12.

SECOND WICKET (Qualification 200 runs)

346	W Barber (162) and M Leyland (189) v. Middlesex at Sheffield, 1932
343	F A Lowson (183*) and J V Wilson (165) v. Oxford University at Oxford, 1956
333	P Holmes (209) and E Oldroyd (138*) v. Warwickshire at Birmingham, 1922
314	H Sutcliffe (255*) and E Oldroyd (138) v. Essex at Southend-on-Sea, 1924
305	J W.Rothery (134) and D Denton (182) v. Derbyshire at Chesterfield, 1910
302	W Watson (172) and J V Wilson (140) v. Derbyshire at Scarborough, 1948
301	P J Sharpe (172*) and D E V Padgett (133) v. Glamorgan at Swansea, 1971
288	H Sutcliffe (165) and A Mitchell (136) v. Lancashire at Manchester, 1939
280	L Hall (160) and F Lee (165) v. Lancashire at Bradford, 1887
266*	K Taylor (178*) and D E V Padgett (107*) v. Oxford University at Oxford, 1962
261*	L Hutton (146*) and J V Wilson (110*) v. Scotland at Hull, 1949
260	R G Lumb (144) and K Sharp (132) v. Glamorgan at Cardiff, 1984
258	H Sutcliffe (230) and E Oldroyd (93) v. Kent at Folkestone, 1931
253	B B Wilson (150) and D Denton (200*) v. Warwickshire at Birmingham, 1912
248	H Sutcliffe (200) and M. Leyland (116) v. Leicestershire at Leicester, 1926
244	P. Holmes (138) and E Oldroyd (151*) v. Glamorgan at Cardiff, 1922
243	G Boycott (141) and J D Love (163) v. Nottinghamshire at Bradford, 1976
243	C White (183) and M J Wood (124) v. Glamorgan at Scarborough, 2001
237	H Sutcliffe (118) and D Denton (122) v. Gloucestershire at Leeds, 1919
237	M D Moxon (132) and K Sharp (128) v. Sri Lankans at Leeds, 1988
236	F A Lowson (112) and J V Wilson (157) v. Essex at Leeds, 1950
235	M D Moxon (130) and D Byas (181) v. Cambridge University at Cambridge, 1995
230	L Hutton (180) and A Mitchell (100) v. Cambridge University at Cambridge, 1938
230	M P Vaughan (109) and B Parker (138*) v. Oxford University at Oxford, 1997.
227	M J Wood (102) and M J Lumb (122) v. Leicestershire at Leeds, 2001
225	H Sutcliffe (138) and E Oldroyd (97) v. Derbyshire at Dewsbury, 1928
223	M D Moxon (153) and R J Blakey (90) v. Somerset at Leeds, 1985
222	H Sutcliffe (174) and D Denton (114) v. Kent at Dover, 1919
219	F S Jackson (155) and D Denton (113) v. Middlesex at Bradford, 1899
217	R G Lumb (107) and J D Love (107) v. Oxford University at Oxford, 1978
216	M P Vaughan (105) and D Byas (102) v. Somerset at Bradford, 1994

215	A W Gale (136) and A McGrath (99) v. Lancashire at Manchester, 2008
211	J A Rudolph (141) and A McGrath (80) v Nottinghamshire at Leeds, 2010
207	P A Jaques (115) and A McGrath (93) v. Essex at Chelmsford, 2004
206	J Tunnicliffe (102) and F S Jackson (134*) v. Lancashire at Sheffield, 1898
206	H Sutcliffe (187) and M Leyland (90) v. Leicestershire at Leicester, 1931
205	H Sutcliffe (174) and A Mitchell (95) v. Leicestershire at Leicester, 1933
205	G Boycott (148) and P J Sharpe (108) v. Kent at Sheffield, 1970
203	A T Barber (100) and E Oldroyd (143) v. An England XI at Sheffield, 1919
203	J J Sayers (187) and A McGrath (100) v. Kent at Tunbridge Wells, 2007
202*	W Rhodes (115*) and G H Hirst (117*) v. Somerset at Bath, 1906
202	G Boycott (113) and C W J Athey (114) v. Northamptonshire at Northampton, 1978

THIRD WICKET (Qualification 200 runs)

346	J J Sayers (173) and A McGrath (211) v. Warwickshire at Birmingham, 2009
323*	H Sutcliffe (147*) and M Leyland (189*) v. Glamorgan at Huddersfield, 1928
317	A McGrath (165) and D S Lehmann (187) v. Lancashire at Leeds, 2002
310	A McGrath (134) and P A Jaques (219) v. Derbyshire at Leeds, 2005
301	H Sutcliffe (175) and M Leyland (180*) v. Middlesex at Lord's, 1939
293*	A A Metcalfe (150*) and P E Robinson (150*) v. Derbyshire at Scarborough, 1990
269	D Byas (101) and R J Blakey (196) v. Oxford University at Oxford, 1991
258*	J T Brown (134*) and F Mitchell (116*) v. Warwickshire at Bradford, 1901
252	D E V Padgett (139*) and D B Close (154) v. Nottinghamshire at Nottingham, 1959
249	D E V Padgett (95) and D B Close (184) v. Nottinghamshire at Scarborough, 1960
248	C Johnson (102) and J H Hampshire (155*) v. Gloucestershire at Leeds, 1976
247	P Holmes (175*) and M Leyland (118) v. New Zealanders at Bradford, 1927
244	D E V Padgett (161*) and D B Close (144) v. Oxford University at Oxford, 1959
240	L Hutton (151) and M Leyland (95) v. Surrey at Leeds, 1939
237	J A Rudolph (198) and A McGrath (120) v. Worcestershire at Leeds, 2009
236	H Sutcliffe (107) and R Kilner (137) v. Nottinghamshire at Nottingham, 1920
236	M J Wood (94) and D S Lehmann (200) v. Worcestershire at Worcester, 1998
234*	D Byas (126*) and A McGrath (105*) v. Oxford University at Oxford, 1997.
233	L Hutton (101) and M Leyland (167) v. Worcestershire at Stourbridge, 1937
230	D Byas (103) and M J Wood (103) v. Derbyshire at Leeds, 1998
229	L Hall (86) and R Peel (158) v. Middlesex at Lord's, 1889
228	A Mitchell (142) and M Leyland (133) v. Worcestershire at Sheffield, 1933
228	W Barber (141) and M Leyland (71) v. Surrey at The Oval, 1939
228	J V Wilson (132*) and D E V Padgett (115) v. Warwickshire at Birmingham, 1955
226	D E V Padgett (117) and D B Close (198) v. Surrey at The Oval, 1960
224	J V Wilson (110) and D B Close (114) v. Cambridge University at Cambridge, 1955
224	G Boycott (140*) and K Sharp (121) v. Gloucestershire at Cheltenham, 1983
221	A Mitchell (138) and M Leyland (134) v. Nottinghamshire at Bradford, 1933
219	L Hall (116) and W Bates (133) v. Cambridge University at Cambridge, 1884
218	J A Rudolph (127) and A W Gale (121) v. Lancashire at Manchester, 2009
217	A McGrath (144) and J A Rudolph (129) v. Kent at Canterbury, 2008
216	R G Lumb (118) and J H Hampshire (127) v. Surrey at The Oval, 1975
215	A Mitchell (73) and M Leyland (139) v. Surrey at Bradford, 1928
213	E Oldroyd (168) and W Barber (114) v. Glamorgan at Hull, 1928
208	J V Wilson (157*) and E I Lester (112) v. Sussex at Leeds, 1949
206	A McGrath (105) and J A Rudolph (228*) v Durham at Leeds, 2010
205*	E Oldroyd (122*) and M Leyland (100*) v. Hampshire at Harrogate, 1924
205	F S Jackson (124) and D Denton (112) v. Somerset at Taunton, 1897
205	D E V Padgett (83) and D B Close (128) v. Somerset at Bath, 1959
204	M P Vaughan (113) and A McGrath (70) v. Essex at Scarborough, 2001
203	D Denton (132) and J Tunnicliffe (102) v. Warwickshire at Birmingham, 1905
203	A A Metcalfe (216*) and P E Robinson (88) v. Middlesex at Leeds, 1988
201	J Tunnicliffe (101) and T L Taylor (147) v. Surrey at The Oval, 1900

CENTURY PARTNERSHIPS *(Continued)*

THIRD WICKET (Qualification 200 runs) *(Continued)*

201	H Sutcliffe (87) and W Barber (130) v. Leicestershire at Leicester, 1938
200	M D Moxon (274*) and A P Grayson (100) v. Worcestershire at Worcester, 1994

FOURTH WICKET (Qualification 175 runs)

358	D S Lehmann (339) and M J Lumb (98) v. Durham at Leeds, 2006
330	M J Wood (116) and D R Martyn (238) v. Gloucestershire at Leeds, 2003
312	D Denton (168*) and G H Hirst (146) v. Hampshire at Southampton, 1914
299	P Holmes (277*) and R Kilner (150) v. Northamptonshire at Harrogate, 1921
272	D Byas (138) and A McGrath (137) v. Hampshire at Harrogate, 1996
271	B B Wilson (208) and W Rhodes (113) v. Sussex at Bradford, 1914
259	A Drake (115) and G H Hirst (218) v. Sussex at Hastings, 1911
258	J Tunnicliffe (128) and G H Hirst (152) v. Hampshire at Portsmouth, 1904
258	P E Robinson (147) and D Byas (117) v. Kent at Scarborough, 1989
249	W B Stott (143) and G Boycott (145) v. Lancashire at Sheffield, 1963
247*	R G Lumb (165*) and S N Hartley (104*) v. Gloucestershire at Bradford, 1984
247	M Leyland (263) and L Hutton (83) v. Essex at Hull, 1936
238	D S Lehmann (216) and M J Lumb (92) v. Sussex at Arundel, 2002
233	D Byas (120) and P E Robinson (189) v. Lancashire at Scarborough, 1991.
226	W H Wilkinson (89) and G H Hirst (140) v. Northamptonshire at Hull, 1909
225	C H Grimshaw (85) and G H Hirst (169) v. Oxford University at Oxford, 1906
212	B B Wilson (108) and G H Hirst (166*) v. Sussex at Hastings, 1913
212	G Boycott (260*) and J H Hampshire (80) v. Essex at Colchester, 1970
211	J V Wilson (120) and W Watson (108) v. Derbyshire at Harrogate, 1951
210*	A Mitchell (150*) and M Leyland (117*) v. Worcestershire at Worcester, 1933
210	E I. Lester (178) and W Watson (97) v. Nottinghamshire at Nottingham, 1952
207	D Byas (213) and C White (107*) v. Worcestershire at Scarborough, 1995
206	J A Rudolph (121) and A W Gale (150) v. Surrey at The Oval, 2008
205*	G Boycott (151*) and P J Sharpe (79*) v. Leicestershire at Leicester, 1964
205	E Oldroyd (121) and R Kilner (117) v. Lancashire at Dudley, 1922
205	W Watson (162*) and E I Lester (98) v. Somerset at Leeds, 1953
201*	J H Hampshire (105*) and D B Close (101*) v. Surrey at Bradford, 1965
200	W H H Sutcliffe (181) and L Hutton (120) v. Kent at Canterbury, 1952
200	J V Wilson (92) and W Watson (122) v. Somerset at Taunton, 1950
198	A A Metcalfe (138) and D Byas (95) v. Warwickshire at Leeds, 1989
197	N W D Yardley (177) and A Coxon (58) v. Derbyshire at Scarborough, 1947
196	M D Moxon (130) and D L Bairstow (104) v. Derbyshire at Harrogate, 1987
193	A Drake (85) and G H Hirst (156) v. Lancashire at Manchester, 1911
192	J V Wilson (132) and W Watson (105) v. Essex at Bradford, 1955
191	M Leyland (114) and C Turner (63) v. Essex at Ilford, 1938
188	H Myers (60) and G H Hirst (158) v. Cambridge University at Cambridge, 1910
187	E Oldroyd (168) and F E Greenwood (104*) v. Glamorgan at Hull, 1929
187	K Taylor (203*) and W B Stott (57) v. Warwickshire at Birmingham, 1961
186	D S Lehmann (193) and D Byas (100) v. Leicestershire at Leicester, 2001
184	J H Hampshire (96) and R Illingworth (100*) v. Leicestershire at Sheffield, 1968
182*	E I Lester (101*) and W Watson (103*) v. Nottinghamshire at Bradford, 1952
180*	G Boycott (207*) and B Leadbeater (50*) v. Cambridge University at Cambridge, 1976
180	J Tunnicliffe (139*) and G H Hirst (108) v. Surrey at The Oval, 1904
179	J H Hampshire (179) and S N Hartley (63) v. Surrey at Harrogate, 1981
179	M D Moxon (171*) and R J Blakey (71) v. Kent at Leeds, 1993
178	E I Lester (186) and J V Wilson (71) v. Warwickshiire at Scarborough, 1949
177	J D Love (105*) and J H Hampshire (89) v. Lancashire at Manchester, 1980
175	L Hutton (177) and W Barber (84) v. Sussex at Scarborough, 1939
175	A McGrath (188*) and J A Rudolph (82) v. Warwickshire at Birmingham, 2007

CENTURY PARTNERSHIPS *(Continued)*

FIFTH WICKET (Qualification 150 runs)

340	E Wainwright (228) and G H Hirst (186) v. Surrey at The Oval, 1899
329	F Mitchell (194) and E Wainwright (153) v. Leicestershire at Leicester, 1899
276	W Rhodes (104*) and R Kilner (166) v. Northamptonshire at Northampton, 1921
273	L Hutton (270*) and N W D Yardley (136) v. Hampshire at Bournemouth, 1947
245*	H Sutcliffe (107*) and W Barber (128*) v. Northamptonshire at Northampton, 1939
229	D S Lehmann (193) and C White (79) v. Kent at Canterbury, 2006
217	D B Close (140*) and R Illingworth (107) v. Warwickshire at Sheffield, 1962
198	E Wainwright (145) and R Peel (111) v. Sussex at Bradford, 1896
198	W Barber (168) and K R Davidson (101*) v. MCC at Lord's, 1934
196*	R Kilner (115*) and G H Hirst (82*) v. Gloucestershire at Leeds, 1919
195	M J Lumb (93) and C White (173*) v. Derbyshire at Derby, 2003
194*	Younus Khan (202*) and G L Brophy (100*) v. Hampshire at Southampton, 2007
193	A Mitchell (189) and W Rhodes (88) v. Northamptonshire at Northampton, 1926
193	J D Love (106) and S N Hartley (108) v. Oxford University at Oxford, 1985
192	C W J Athey (114*) and J D Love (123) v. Surrey at The Oval, 1982
191*	L Hutton (271*) and C Turner (81*) v. Derbyshire at Sheffield, 1937
191	M G Bevan (105) and A A Metcalfe (100) v. West Indians at Scarborough, 1995
190*	R J Blakey (204*) and J D Love (79*) v. Gloucestershire at Leeds, 1987
189	J E Root (160) and G S Ballance (87) v. Sussex at Scarborough 2011
188	D E V Padgett (146) and J V Wilson (72) v. Sussex at Middlesbrough, 1960
187	J V Wilson (230) and H Halliday (74) v. Derbyshire at Sheffield, 1952
185	G Boycott (104*) and K Sharp (99) v. Kent at Tunbridge Wells, 1984
182	E Lockwood (208) and E Lumb (40) v. Kent at Gravesend, 1882
182	B B Wilson (109) and W Rhodes (111) v. Sussex at Hove, 1910
182	D B Close (164) and J V Wilson (55) v. Combined Services at Harrogate, 1954
181	A A Metcalfe (149) and J D Love (88) v. Glamorgan at Leeds, 1986
177	Hon F S Jackson (87) and G H Hirst (232*) v. Surrey at The Oval, 1905
176	L Hutton (176*) and A Coxon (72) v. Sussex at Sheffield, 1948
175	A Drake (108) and R Kilner (77) v. Cambridge University at Cambridge, 1913
173	H Sutcliffe (206) and R Kilner (124) v. Warwickshire at Dewsbury, 1925
170	W Rhodes (157) and R Kilner (87) v. Derbyshire at Leeds, 1925
170	J V Wilson (130*) and N W D Yardley (67) v. Lancashire at Manchester, 1954
169	W Watson (147) and A B Sellers (92) v. Worcestershire at Worcester, 1947
168	A T Barber (63) and A Mitchell (122*) v. Worcestershire at Worcester, 1929
167	J M Bairstow (136) and G S Ballance (61) v. Somerset at Taunton 2011
165	E Oldroyd (143) and W Rhodes (110) v. Glamorgan at Leeds, 1922
165	K Sharp (100*) and P Carrick (73) v. Middlesex at Lord's, 1980
164	A A Metcalfe (151) and D L Bairstow (88) v. Northamptonshire at Luton, 1986
159*	J D Love (170*) and D L Bairstow (52*) v. Worcestershire at Worcester, 1979
159	D B Close (128) and R Illingworth (74) v. Lancashire at Sheffield, 1959
159	J H Hampshire (183*) and C Johnson (53) v. Sussex at Hove, 1971
158*	G Boycott (153*) and P E Robinson (74*) v. Derbyshire at Harrogate, 1984
157	T L Taylor (135*) and G H Hirst (72) v. An England XI at Hastings, 1901
157	G H Hirst (142) and F Smith (51) v. Somerset at Bradford, 1903
157	W Barber (87) and N W D Yardley (101) v. Surrey at The Oval, 1937
156	A McGrath (158) and I J Harvey (103) v. Derbyshire at Derby, 2005
153	S N Hartley (87) and M D Moxon (112*) v. Indians at Scarborough, 1986
152	J H Hampshire (83) and S N Hartley (106) v. Nottinghamshire at Nottingham, 1981
151*	G H Hirst (102*) and R Kilner (50*) v. Kent at Bradford, 1913
151	G H Hirst (120) and F Smith (55) v. Kent at Leeds, 1903
151	W Rhodes (57) and R Kilner (90) v. Nottinghamshire at Nottingham, 1925

CENTURY PARTNERSHIPS *(Continued)*

SIXTH WICKET (Qualification 150 runs)

276	M Leyland (191) and E Robinson (124*) v. Glamorgan at Swansea, 1926
252	C White (181) and R J Blakey (109*) v. Lancashire at Leeds, 1996
233	M W Booth (210) and G H Hirst (100) v. Worcestershire at Worcester, 1911
229	W Rhodes (267*) and N Kilner (112) v. Leicestershire at Leeds, 1921
225	E Wainwright (91) and Lord Hawke (127) v. Hampshire at Southampton, 1899
217*	H Sutcliffe (200*) and A Wood (123*) v. Worcestershire at Sheffield, 1935
214	W Watson (214*) and N W D Yardley (76) v. Worcestershire at Worcester, 1955
205	G H Hirst (125) and S Haigh (159) v. Nottinghamshire at Sheffield, 1901
200	D Denton (127) and G H Hirst (134) v. Essex at Bradford, 1902
198	M Leyland (247) and W Rhodes (100*) v. Worcestershire at Worcester, 1928
190	W Rhodes (126) and M Leyland (72) v. Middlesex at Bradford, 1923
190	J A Rudolph (122) and A U Rashid (86) v. Surrey at The Oval, 2007
188	W Watson (174) and R Illingworth (53) v. Lancashire at Sheffield, 1955
188	M P Vaughan (161) and R J Blakey (92) v. Essex at Ilford, 1997.
188	G S Ballance (111) and A U Rashid (82) v. Warwickshire at Birmingham 2011
184	R Kilner (104) and M W Booth (79) v. Leicestershire at Leeds, 1913
183	G H Hirst (131) and E Smith (129) v. Hampshire at Bradford, 1899
183	W Watson (139*) and R Illingworth (78) v. Somerset at Harrogate, 1956
178*	D Denton (108*) and G H Hirst (112*) v. Lancashire at Manchester, 1902
178*	N W D Yardley (100*) and R Illingworth (71*) v. Gloucestershire at Bristol, 1955
178	E Robinson (100) and D C F Burton (83) v. Derbyshire at Hull, 1921
178	H Sutcliffe (135) and P A Gibb (157*) v. Nottinghamshire at Sheffield, 1935
175	G M Fellows (88) and R J Blakey (103) v. Warwickshire at Birmingham, 2002
174	D S Lehmann (136) and G M Hamilton (73) v. Kent at Maidstone, 1998
172	A J Dalton (119*) and D L Bairstow (62) v. Worcestershire at Dudley, 1971
170	A W Gale (101) and T T Bresnan (97) v. Worcestershire at Worcester, 2009
169	W Barber (124) and H Verity (78*) v. Warwickshire at Birmingham, 1933
169	R Illingworth (162) and J Birkenshaw (37) v. Indians at Sheffield, 1959
166	E Wainwright (116) and E Smith (61) v. Kent at Catford, 1900
166	D B Close (161) and F S Trueman (104) v. Northamptonshire at Northampton, 1963
162*	G Boycott (220*) and J G Binks (70*) v. Northamptonshire at Sheffield, 1967
161*	D L Bairstow (100*) and P Carrick (59*) v. Middlesex at Leeds, 1983
159*	D S Lehmann (187*) and R J Blakey (78*) v. Somerset at Bath, 2001
156	W Rhodes (82*) and E Robinson (94) v. Derbyshire at Chesterfield, 1919
154	C Turner (84) and A Wood (79) v. Glamorgan at Swansea, 1936
153*	J A Rudolph (92*) and A U Rashid (73*) v. Worcestershire at Kidderminster, 2007
153	J A Rudolph (69*) and J M Bairstow (81) v. Warwickshire at Birmingham, 2010
151	D Denton (91) and W Rhodes (76) v. Middlesex at Sheffield, 1904
151	G Boycott (152*) and P Carrick (75) v. Warwickshire at Leeds, 1982
150	G Ulyett (199*) and J M Preston (93) v. Derbyshire at Sheffield, 1887

SEVENTH WICKET (Qualification 125 runs)

254	W Rhodes (135) and D C F Burton (142*) v. Hampshire at Dewsbury, 1919
247	P Holmes (285) and W Rhodes (79) v. Nottinghamshire at Nottingham, 1929
215	E Robinson (135*) and D C F Burton (110) v. Leicestershire at Leicester, 1921
185	E Wainwright (100) and G H Hirst (134) v. Gloucestershire at Bristol, 1897
183	G H Hirst (341) and H Myers (57) v. Leicestershire at Leicester, 1905
183	J A Rudolph (220) and T T Bresnan (101*) v. Warwickshire at Scarborough, 2007
180	C Turner (130) and A Wood (97) v. Somerset at Sheffield, 1936
168	G L Brophy (99) and A U Rashid (157*) v. Lancashire at Leeds, 2009
170	G S Blewett (190) and G M Hamilton (84*) v. Northamptonshire at Scarborough, 1999
166	R Peel (55) and I Grimshaw (122*) v. Derbyshire at Holbeck, 1886
162	E Wainwright (109) and S Haigh (73) v. Somerset at Taunton, 1900
162	R J Blakey (90) and R K J Dawson (87) v. Kent at Canterbury, 2002
162	A W Gale (149) and G L Brophy (97) v. Warwickshire at Scarborough, 2006

161	R G Lumb (118) and C M Old (89) v. Worcestershire at Bradford, 1980
160	J Tunnicliffe (158) and D Hunter (58*) v. Worcestershire at Worcester, 1900
157*	F A Lowson (259*) and R Booth (53*) v. Worcestershire at Worcester, 1953
155	D Byas (122*) and P Carrick (61) v. Leicestershire at Leicester.1991.
154*	G H Hirst (76*) and J T Newstead (100*) v. Nottinghamshire at Nottingham, 1908
148	J Rowbotham (113) and J Thewlis (50) v. Surrey at The Oval, 1873
147	E Wainwright (78) and G Ulyett (73) v. Somerset at Taunton, 1893
147	M P Vaughan (153) and R J Harden (64) v. Kent at Scarborough, 1999
143	C White (135*) and A K D Gray (60) v. Durham at Chester-le-Street, 2003
141	G H Hirst (108*) and S Haigh (48) v. Worcestershire at Worcester, 1905
141	J H Hampshire (149*) and J G Binks (72) v. MCC at Scarborough, 1965
140	E Wainwright (117) and S Haigh (54) v. CI Thornton's XI at Scarborough, 1900
140	D Byas (67) and P J Hartley (75) v. Derbyshire at Chesterfield, 1990
138	D Denton (78) and G H Hirst (103*) v. Sussex at Leeds, 1905
136	GH Hirst (93) and S Haigh (138) v. Warwickshire at Birmingham, 1904
136	E Robinson (77*) and A Wood (65) v. Glamorgan at Scarborough, 1931
133*	W Rhodes (267*) and M Leyland (52*) v. Leicestershire at Leeds, 1921
133*	E I Lester (86*) and A B Sellers (73*) v. Northamptonshire at Northampton, 1948
133	D Byas (100) and P W Jarvis (80) v. Northamptonshire at Scarborough, 1992
132	W Rhodes (196) and S Haigh (59*) v. Worcestershire at Worcester, 1904
131*	D L Bairstow (79*) and A Sidebottom (52*) v. Oxford University at Oxford, 1981
130	P J Sharpe (64) and J V Wilson (134) v. Warwickshire at Birmingham, 1962
128	W Barber (66) and T F Smailes (86) v. Cambridge University at Cambridge, 1938
128	D B Close (88*) and A Coxon (59) v. Essex at Leeds, 1949
126	E Wainwright (171) and R Peel (46) v. Middlesex at Lord's, 1897
126	W Rhodes (91) and G G Macaulay (63) v. Hampshire at Hull, 1925
126	J C Balderstone (58) and J G Binks (95) v. Middlesex at Lord's, 1964
126	J M Bairstow (70) and A U Rashid (59) v. Kent at Canterbury, 2010
125	A B Sellers (109) and T F Smailes (65) v. Kent at Bradford, 1937

EIGHTH WICKET (Qualification 125 runs)

292	R Peel (210*) and Lord Hawke (166) v. Warwickshire at Birmingham, 1896
238	I J Harvey (209*) and T T Bresnan (74) v. Somerset at Leeds, 2005
192*	W Rhodes (108*) and G G Macaulay (101*) v. Essex at Harrogate, 1922
192	A U Rashid (117*) and A Shahzad (78) v. Hampshire at Basingstoke, 2009
180	W Barber (191) and T F Smailes (89) v. Sussex at Leeds, 1935
165	S Haigh (62) and Lord Hawke (126) v. Surrey at The Oval, 1902
163	G G Macaulay (67) and A Waddington (114) v. Worcestershire at Leeds, 1927
159	E Smith (95) and W Rhodes (105) v. MCC at Scarborough, 1901
157	A Shahzad (88) and D J Wainwright (85*) v. Sussex at Hove, 2009
152	W Rhodes (98) and J W Rothery (70) v. Hampshire at Portsmouth, 1904
151	W Rhodes (201) and Lord Hawke (51) v. Somerset at Taunton, 1905
151	R J Blakey (80*) and P J Hartley (69) v. Sussex at Eastbourne, 1996
149	G L Brophy (177*) and R J Sidebottom (61) v. Worcestershire at Worcester 2011
147	J P G Chadwick (59) and F S Trueman (101) v. Middlesex at Scarborough, 1965
146	S Haigh (159) and Lord Hawke (89) v. Nottinghamshire at Sheffield, 1901
144	G L Brophy (85) and D J Wainwright (102*) v. Warwickshire at Scarborough, 2009
138	E Wainwright (100) and Lord Hawke (81) v. Kent at Tonbridge, 1899
137	E Wainwright (171) and Lord Hawke (75) v. Middlesex at Lord's, 1897
135	P W Jarvis (55) and P J Hartley (69) v. Nottinghamshire at Scarborough, 1992
133	R Illingworth (61) and F S Trueman (74) v. Leicestershire at Leicester, 1955
132	G H Hirst (103) and E Smith (59) v. Middlesex at Sheffield, 1904
132	W Watson (119) and J H Wardle (65) v. Leicestershire at Leicester, 1949
131	P E Robinson (85) and P Carrick (64) v. Surrey at Harrogate, 1990
130	E Smith (98) and Lord Hawke (54) v. Lancashire at Leeds, 1904
128	H Verity (96*) and T F Smailes (77) v. Indians at Bradford, 1936
128	D L Bairstow (145) and G B Stevenson (11) v. Middlesex at Scarborough, 1980

CENTURY PARTNERSHIPS *(Continued)*

127	E Robinson (70*) and A Wood (62) v. Middlesex at Leeds, 1928
126	R Peel (74) and E Peate (61) v. Gloucestershire at Bradford, 1883
126	M W Booth (56) and E R Wilson (104*) v. Essex at Bradford, 1913
126	J D Middlebrook (84) and C E W Silverwood (70) v. Essex at Chelmsford, 2001
126	M J Lumb (115*) and D Gough (72) v. Hampshire at Southampton, 2003

NINTH WICKET (Qualification 100 runs)

246	T T Bresnan (116) and J N Gillespie (123*) v. Surrey at The Oval, 2007
192	G H Hirst (130*) and S Haigh (85) v. Surrey at Bradford, 1898
179	R A Hutton (189) and G A Cope (30*) v. Pakistanis at Bradford, 1971
176*	R Moorhouse (59*) and G H Hirst (115*) v. Gloucestershire at Bristol, 1894
173	S Haigh (85) and W Rhodes (92*) v. Sussex at Hove, 1902
167	H Verity (89) and T F Smailes (80) v. Somerset at Bath, 1936
162	W Rhodes (94*) and S Haigh (84) v. Lancashire at Manchester, 1904
161	E Smith (116*) and W Rhodes (79) v. Sussex at Sheffield, 1900
154	R M Pyrah (117) and R J Sidebottom (52) v.Lancashire at Leeds 2011
151	J M Bairstow (205) and R J Sidebottom (45*) v. Nottinghamshire at Nottingham 2011
150	Azeem Rafiq (100) and M J Hoggard (56*) v. Worcestershire at Worcester, 2009
149*	R J Blakey (63*) and A K D Gray (74*) v. Leicestershire at Scarborough, 2002
149	G H Hirst (232*) and D Hunter (40) v. Surrey at The Oval, 1905
146	G H Hirst (214) and W Rhodes (53) v. Worcestershire at Worcester, 1901
144	T T Bresnan (91) and J N Gillespie (44) v. Hampshire at Leeds, 2006
140	A U Rashid (111) and D J Wainwright (104) v. Sussex at Hove, 2008
136	R Peel (210*) and G H Hirst (85) v. Warwickshire at Birmingham, 1896
125*	L Hutton (269*) and A Coxon (65*) v. Northamptonshire at Wellingborough, 1949
124	P J Hartley (87*) and P W Jarvis (47) v. Essex at Chelmsford, 1986
120	G H Hirst (138) and W Rhodes (38) v. Nottinghamshire at Nottingham, 1899
119	A B Sellers (80*) and E P Robinson (66) v. Warwickshire at Birmingham, 1938
118	S Haigh (96) and W Rhodes (44) v. Somerset at Leeds, 1901
114	E Oldroyd (194) and A Dolphin (47) v. Worcestershire at Worcester, 1923
114	N Kilner (102*) and G G Macaulay (60) v. Gloucestershire at Bristol, 1923
113	G G Macaulay (125*) and A Waddington (44) v. Nottinghamshire at Nottingham, 1921
113	A Wood (69) and H.Verity (45*) v. MCC at Lord's, 1938
112	G H Hirst (78) and Lord Hawke (61*) v. Essex at Leyton, 1907
109	Lees Whitehead (60) and W Rhodes (81*) v. Sussex at Harrogate, 1899
108	A McGrath (133*) and C E W Silverwood (80) v. Durham at Chester-le-Street, 2005
105	J V Wilson (134) and A G Nicholson (20*) v. Nottinghamshire at Leeds, 1962
105	C M Old (100*) and H P Cooper (30) v. Lancashire at Manchester, 1978
105	C White (74*) and J D Batty (50) v. Gloucestershire at Sheffield, 1993
104	L Hall (129*) and R Moorhouse (86) v. Gloucestershire at Clifton, 1888
100	G Pollitt (51) and Lees Whitehead (54) v. Hampshire at Bradford, 1899

TENTH WICKET (Qualification 100 runs)

149	G Boycott (79) and G B Stevenson (115*) v. Warwickshire at Birmingham, 1982
148	Lord Hawke (107*) and D Hunter (47) v. Kent at Sheffield, 1898
144	A Sidebottom (124) and A L Robinson (30*) v. Glamorgan at Cardiff, 1977
121	J T Brown (141) and D Hunter (25*) v. Liverpool & District at Liverpool, 1894
118	Lord Hawke (110*) and D Hunter (41) v. Kent at Leeds, 1896
113	P J Hartley (88*) and R D Stemp (22) v. Middlesex at Lord's, 1994
110	C E W. Silverwood (45*) and R D Stemp (65) v. Durham at Chester-le-Street, 1996
109	A Shahzad (70) and R J Sidebottom (28*) v. Worcestershire at Scarborough, 2011
108	Lord Hawke (79) and Lees Whitehead (45*) v. Lancashire at Manchester, 1903
108	G Boycott (129) and M K Bore (37*) v. Nottinghamshire at Bradford, 1973
106	A B Sellers (79) and D V Brennan (30) v. Worcestershire at Worcester, 1948
103	A Dolphin (62*) and E Smith (49) v. Essex at Leyton, 1919
102	D Denton (77*) and D Hunter (45) v. Cambridge University at Cambridge, 1895

FIFTEEN WICKETS OR MORE IN A MATCH

A complete list of 12, 13 and 14 wickets in a match up to and including 2007 is to be found in the 2008 edition

W E BOWES (1)

16 for 35 (8 for 18 and 8 for 17) v. Northamptonshire at Kettering, 1935

A DRAKE (1)

15 for 51 (5 for 16 and 10 for 35) v. Somerset at Weston-super-Mare, 1914

T EMMETT (1)

16 for 38 (7 for 15 and 9 for 23) v. Cambridgeshire at Hunslet, 1869

G H HIRST (1)

15 for 63 (8 for 25 and 7 for 38) v. Leicestershire at Hull, 1907

R ILLINGWORTH (1)

15 for 123 (8 for 70 and 7 for 53) v. Glamorgan at Swansea, 1960

R PEEL (1)

15 for 50 (9 for 22 and 6 for 28) v. Somerset at Leeds, 1895

W RHODES (1)

15 for 56 (9 for 28 and 6 for 28) v. Essex at Leyton, 1899

H VERITY (4)

17 for 91 (8 for 47 and 9 for 44) v. Essex at Leyton, 1933
15 for 129 (8 for 56 and 7 for 73) v. Oxford University at Oxford, 1936
15 for 38 (6 for 26 and 9 for 12) v. Kent at Sheffield, 1936
15 for 100 (6 for 52 and 9 for 48) v. Essex at Westcliffe-on-Sea, 1936

J H WARDLE (1)

16 for 112 (9 for 48 and 7 for 64) v. Sussex at Hull, 1954

TEN WICKETS IN A MATCH
(including best analysis)

61	W Rhodes	15 for	56	v Essex	at Leyton	1899
48	H Verity	17 for	91	v Essex	at Leyton	1933
40	G H Hirst	15 for	63	v Leicestershire	at Hull	1907
31	G G Macaulay	14 for	92	v Gloucestershire	at Bristol	1926
28	S Haigh	14 for	43	v Hampshire	at Southampton	1898
27	R Peel	14 for	33	v Nottinghamshire	at Sheffield	1888
25	W E Bowes	16 for	35	v Northamptonshire	at Kettering	1935
25	J H Wardle	16 for	112	v Sussex	at Hull	1954
22	E Peate	14 for	77	v Surrey	at Huddersfield	1881
20	F S Trueman	14 for	123	v Surrey	at The Oval	1960
19	T Emmett	16 for	38	v Cambridgeshire	at Hunslet	1869
17	R Appleyard	12 for	43	v Essex	at Bradford	1951
15	E Wainwright	14 for	77	v Essex	at Bradford	1896
11	R Illingworth	15 for	123	v Glamorgan	at Swansea	1960
10	A Waddington	13 for	48	v Northamptonshire	at Northampton	1920
9	M W Booth	14 for	160	v Essex	at Leyton	1914
9	R Kilner	12 for	55	v Sussex	at Hove	1924
8	W Bates	11 for	47	v Nottinghamshire	at Nottingham	1881
8	G Freeman	13 for	60	v Surrey	at Sheffield	1869
7	E P Robinson	13 for	115	v Lancashire	at Leeds	1939
7	D Wilson	13 for	52	v Warwickshire	at Middlesbrough	1967

6 G A Cope	12 for 116	v Glamorgan	at Cardiff (Sophia Gardens)	1968
6 A Hill	12 for 59	v Surrey	at The Oval	1871
6 T F Smailes	14 for 58	v Derbyshire	at Sheffield	1939
5 P Carrick	12 for 89	v Derbyshire	at Sheffield (Abbeydale Pk)	1983
5 J M Preston	13 for 63	v MCC	at Scarborough	1888
5 E Robinson	12 for 95	v Northamptonshire	at Huddersfield	1927
4 J T Newstead	11 for 72	v Worcestershire	at Bradford	1907
3 T W Foster	11 for 93	v Liverpool & District	at Liverpool	1894
3 G P Harrison	11 for 76	v Kent	at Dewsbury	1883
3 F S Jackson	12 for 80	v Hampshire	at Southampton	1897
3 P W Jarvis	11 for 92	v Middlesex	at Lord's	1986
3 S P Kirby	13 for 154	v Somerset	at Taunton	2003
3 A G Nicholson	12 for 73	v Glamorgan	at Leeds	1964
3 R K Platt	10 for 87	v Surrey	at The Oval	1959
3 A Sidebottom	11 for 64	v Kent	at Sheffield (Abbeydale Pk)	1980
3 G Ulyett	12 for 102	v Lancashire	at Huddersfield	1889
2 T Armitage	13 for 46	v Surrey	at Sheffield	1876
2 R Aspinall	14 for 65	v Northamptonshire	at Northampton	1947
2 J T Brown (Darfield)	12 for 109	v Gloucestershire	at Huddersfield	1899
2 R O Clayton	12 for 104	v Lancashire	at Manchester	1877
2 D B Close	11 for 116	v Kent	at Gillingham	1965
2 M J Cowan	12 for 87	v Warwickshire	at Birmingham	1960
2 A Coxon	10 for 57	v Derbyshire	at Chesterfield	1949
2 D Gough	10 for 80	v Lancashire	at Leeds	1995
2 G M Hamilton	11 for 72	v Surrey	at Leeds	1998
2 P J Hartley	11 for 68	v Derbyshire	at Chesterfield	1995
2 R A Hutton	11 for 62	v Lancashire	at Manchester	1971
2 E Leadbeater	11 for 162	v Nottinghamshire	at Nottingham	1950
2 M A Robinson	12 for 124	v Northamptonshire	at Harrogate	1993
2 M Ryan	10 for 77	v Leicestershire	at Bradford	1962
2 E Smith (Morley)	10 for 97	v MCC	at Scarborough	1893
2 R J Sidebottom	11 for 43	v Kent	at Leeds	2000
2 G B Stevenson	11 for 74	v Nottinghamshire	at Nottingham	1980
2 S Wade	11 for 56	v Gloucestershire	at Cheltenham	1886
2 E R Wilson	11 for 109	v Sussex	at Hove	1921
1 A B Bainbridge	12 for 111	v Essex	at Harrogate	1961
1 J Birkenshaw	11 for 134	v Middlesex	at Leeds	1960
1 A Booth	10 for 91	v Indians	at Bradford	1946
1 H P Cooper	11 for 96	v Northamptonshire	at Northampton	1976
1 A Drake	15 for 51	v Somerset	at Weston-Super-Mare	1914
1 L Greenwood	11 for 71	v Surrey	at The Oval	1867
1 P M Hutchison	11 for 102	v Pakistan 'A'	at Leeds	1997
1 L Hutton	10 for 101	v Leicestershire	at Leicester (Aylestone Rd)	1937
1 R Iddison	10 for 68	v Surrey	at Sheffield	1864
1 M Leyland	11 for 94	v Leicestershire	at Leicester (Aylestone Rd)	1933
1 J D Middlebrook	10 for 170	v Hampshire	at Southampton	2000
1 F W Milligan	12 for 110	v Sussex	at Sheffield	1897
1 H Myers	12 for 192	v Gloucestershire	at Dewsbury	1904
1 C M Old	11 for 46	v Gloucestershire	at Middlesbrough	1969
1 D Pickles	12 for 133	v Somerset	at Taunton	1957
1 A U Rashid	11 for 114	v Worcestershire	at Worcester	2011
1 W Ringrose	11 for 135	v Australians	at Bradford	1905
1 C E W Silverwood	12 for 148	v Kent	at Leeds	1997
1 W Slinn	12 for 53	v Nottinghamshire	at Nottingham	1864
1 J Waring	10 for 63	v Lancashire	at Leeds	1966
1 F Wilkinson	10 for 129	v Hampshire	at Bournemouth	1938
1 A C Williams	10 for 66	v Hampshire	at Dewsbury	1919

TEN WICKETS IN AN INNINGS

Bowler			Year
A Drake	10 for 35	v. Somerset at Weston-super-Mare	1914
H Verity	10 for 36	v. Warwickshire at Leeds	1931
*H Verity	10 for 10	v. Nottinghamshire at Leeds	1932
T F Smailes	10 for 47	v. Derbyshire at Sheffield	1939

*Includes the hat trick.

EIGHT WICKETS OR MORE IN AN INNINGS

(Ten wickets in an innings also listed above)

A complete list of seven wickets in an innings up to and including 2007 is to be found in the 2008 edition

R APPLEYARD (1)

8 for 76 v. MCC at Scarborough, 1951

R ASPINALL (1)

8 for 42 v. Northamptonshire at Northampton, 1947

W BATES (2)

8 for 45 v. Lancashire at Huddersfield, 1878
8 for 21 v. Surrey at The Oval, 1879

M W BOOTH (4)

8 for 52 v. Leicestershire at Sheffield, 1912
8 for 47 v. Middlesex at Leeds, 1912
8 for 86 v. Middlesex at Sheffield, 1913
8 for 64 v. Essex at Leyton, 1914

W E BOWES (9)

8 for 77 v. Leicestershire at Dewsbury, 1929
8 for 69 v. Middlesex at Bradford, 1930
9 for 121 v. Essex at Scarborough, 1932
8 for 62 v. Sussex at Hove, 1932
8 for 69 v. Gloucestershire at Gloucester, 1933
8 for 40 v.Worcestershire at Sheffield, 1935
8 for 18 v. Northamptonshire at Kettering, 1935
8 for 17 v. Northamptonshire at Kettering, 1935
8 for 56 v. Leicestershire at Scarborough, 1936

J T BROWN (Darfield) (1)

8 for 40 v. Gloucestershire at Huddersfield, 1899

P CARRICK (2)

8 for 33 v. Cambridge University at Cambridge, 1973
8 for 72 v. Derbyshire at Scarborough, 1975

R O CLAYTON (1)

8 for 66 v. Lancashire at Manchester, 1877

D B CLOSE (2)

8 for 41 v. Kent at Leeds, 1959
8 for 43 v. Essex at Leeds, 1960

H P COOPER (1)

8 for 62 v. Glamorgan at Cardiff, 1975

G A COPE (1)

8 for 73 v. Gloucestershire at Bristol, 1975

M J COWAN (1)

9 for 43 v. Warwickshire at Birmingham, 1960

A COXON (1)

8 for 31 v. Worcestershire at Leeds, 1946

A DRAKE (2)

8 for 59 v. Gloucestershire at Sheffield, 1913
10 for 35 v. Somerset at Weston-super-Mare, 1914

T EMMETT (8)

9 for 34 v. Nottinghamshire at Dewsbury, 1868
9 for 23 v. Cambridgeshire at Hunslet, 1869
8 for 31 v. Nottinghamshire at Sheffield, 1871
8 for 46 v. Gloucestershire at Clifton, 1877
8 for 16 v. MCC at Scarborough, 1877
8 for 22 v. Surrey at The Oval, 1881
8 for 52 v. MCC at Scarborough, 1882
8 for 32 v. Sussex at Huddersfield, 1884

S D FLETCHER (1)

8 for 58 v. Essex at Sheffield, 1988

T W FOSTER (1)

9 for 59 v. MCC at Lord's, 1894

G FREEMAN (2)

8 for 11 v. Lancashire at Holbeck, 1868
8 for 29 v. Surrey at Sheffield, 1869

L GREENWOOD (1)

8 for 35 v. Cambridgeshire at Dewsbury, 1867

S HAIGH (5)

8 for 78 v. Australians at Bradford, 1896
8 for 35 v. Hampshire at Harrogate, 1896
8 for 21 v. Hampshire at Southampton, 1898
8 for 33 v. Warwickshire at Scarborough, 1899
9 for 25 v. Gloucestershire at Leeds, 1912

P J HARTLEY (2)

8 for 111 v. Sussex at Hove, 1992
9 for 41 v. Derbyshire at Chesterfield, 1995

G H HIRST (8)

8 for 59 v. Warwickshire at Birmingham, 1896
8 for 48 v. Australians at Bradford, 1899
8 for 25 v. Leicestershire at Hull, 1907
9 for 45 v. Middlesex at Sheffield, 1907
9 for 23 v. Lancashire at Leeds, 1910
8 for 80 v. Somerset at Sheffield, 1910
9 for 41 v. Worcestershire at Worcester, 1911
9 for 69 v. MCC at Lord's, 1912

R ILLINGWORTH (5)

8 for 69 v. Surrey at The Oval, 1954
9 for 42 v. Worcestershire at Worcester, 1957
8 for 70 v. Glamorgan at Swansea, 1960
8 for 50 v. Lancashire at Manchester, 1961
8 for 20 v. Worcestershire at Leeds, 1965

R KILNER (2)

8 for 26 v. Glamorgan at Cardiff, 1923
8 for 40 v. Middlesex at Bradford, 1926

S P KIRBY (1)

8 for 80 v. Somerset at Taunton, 2003

E LEADBEATER (1)

8 for 83 v. Worcestershire at Worcester, 1950

M LEYLAND (1)

8 for 63 v. Hampshire at Huddersfield, 1938

G G MACAULAY (3)

8 for 43 v. Gloucestershire at Bristol, 1926
8 for 37 v. Derbyshire at Hull, 1927
8 for 21 v. Indians at Harrogate, 1932

H MYERS (1)

8 for 81 v. Gloucestershire at Dewsbury, 1904

A G NICHOLSON (2)

9 for 62 v. Sussex at Eastbourne, 1967
8 for 22 v. Kent at Canterbury, 1968

E PEATE (6)

8 for 24 v. Lancashire at Manchester, 1880
8 for 30 v. Surrey at Huddersfield, 1881
8 for 69 v. Sussex at Hove, 1881
8 for 32 v. Middlesex at Sheffield, 1882
8 for 5 v. Surrey at Holbeck, 1883
8 for 63 v. Kent at Gravesend, 1884

R PEEL (6)

8 for 12 v. Nottinghamshire at Sheffield, 1888
8 for 60 v. Surrey at Sheffield, 1890
8 for 54 v. Cambridge University at Cambridge, 1893
9 for 22 v. Somerset at Leeds, 1895
8 for 27 v. South of England XI at Scarborough, 1896
8 for 53 v. Kent at Halifax, 1897

J M PRESTON (2)

8 for 27 v. Sussex at Hove, 1888
9 for 28 v. MCC at Scarborough, 1888

W RHODES (18)

9 for 28 v. Essex at Leyton, 1899
8 for 38 v. Nottinghamshire at Nottingham, 1899
8 for 68 v. Cambridge University at Cambridge, 1900
8 for 43 v. Lancashire at Bradford, 1900
8 for 23 v. Hampshire at Hull, 1900
8 for 72 v. Gloucestershire at Bradford, 1900
8 for 28 v. Essex at Harrogate, 1900
8 for 53 v. Middlesex at Lord's, 1901
8 for 55 v. Kent at Canterbury, 1901
8 for 26 v. Kent at Catford, 1902
8 for 87 v. Worcestershire at Worcester, 1903
8 for 61 v. Lancashire at Bradford, 1903
8 for 90 v. Warwickshire at Birmingham, 1905
8 for 92 v. Northamptonshire at Northampton, 1911
8 for 44 v. Warwickshire at Bradford, 1919
8 for 39 v. Sussex at Leeds, 1920
8 for 48 v. Somerset at Huddersfield, 1926
9 for 39 v. Essex at Leyton, 1929

W RINGROSE (1)

9 for 76 v. Australians at Bradford, 1905

E ROBINSON (3)

9 for 36 v. Lancashire at Bradford, 1920
8 for 32 v. Northamptonshire at Huddersfield, 1927
8 for 13 v. Cambridge University at Cambridge, 1928

E P ROBINSON (2)

8 for 35 v. Lancashire at Leeds, 1939
8 for 76 v. Surrey at The Oval, 1946

M A ROBINSON (1)

9 for 37 v. Northamptonshire at Harrogate, 1993

A SIDEBOTTOM (1)

8 for 72 v. Leicestershire at Middlesbrough, 1986

T F SMAILES (2)

8 for 68 v. Glamorgan at Hull, 1938
10 for 47 v. Derbyshire at Sheffield, 1939

G B STEVENSON (2)

8 for 65 v. Lancashire at Leeds, 1978
8 for 57 v. Northamptonshire at Leeds, 1980

F S TRUEMAN (8)

8 for 70 v. Minor Counties at Lord's, 1949
8 for 68 v. Nottinghamshire at Sheffield, 1951
8 for 53 v. Nottinghamshire at Nottingham, 1951
8 for 28 v. Kent at Dover, 1954
8 for 84 v. Nottinghamshire at Worksop, 1962
8 for 45 v. Gloucestershire at Bradford, 1963
8 for 36 v. Sussex at Hove, 1965
8 for 37 v. Essex at Bradford, 1966

H VERITY (20)

9 for 60 v. Glamorgan at Swansea, 1930
10 for 36 v. Warwickshire at Leeds, 1931
8 for 33 v. Glamorgan at Swansea, 1931
8 for 107 v. Lancashire at Bradford, 1932
8 for 39 v. Northamptonshire at Northampton, 1932
10 for 10 v. Nottinghamshire at Leeds, 1932
8 for 47 v. Essex at Leyton, 1933
9 for 44 v. Essex at Leyton, 1933
9 for 59 v. Kent at Dover, 1933
8 for 28 v. Leicestershire at Leeds, 1935
8 for 56 v. Oxford University at Oxford, 1936
8 for 40 v. Worcestershire at Stourbridge, 1936
9 for 12 v. Kent at Sheffield, 1936
9 for 48 v. Essex at Westcliff-on-Sea, 1936
8 for 42 v. Nottinghamshire at Bradford, 1936
9 for 43 v. Warwickshire at Leeds, 1937
8 for 80 v. Sussex at Eastbourne, 1937
8 for 43 v. Middlesex at The Oval, 1937
9 for 62 v. MCC at Lord's, 1939
8 for 38 v. Leicestershire at Hull, 1939

A WADDINGTON (3)

8 for 34 v. Northamptonshire at Leeds, 1922
8 for 39 v. Kent at Leeds, 1922
8 for 35 v. Hampshire at Bradford, 1922

E WAINWRIGHT (3)

8 for 49 v. Middlesex at Sheffield, 1891
9 for 66 v. Middlesex at Sheffield, 1894
8 for 34 v. Essex at Bradford, 1896

J H WARDLE (4)

8 for 87 v. Derbyshire at Chesterfield, 1948
8 for 26 v. Middlesex at Lord's, 1950
9 for 48 v. Sussex at Hull, 1954
9 for 25 v. Lancashire at Manchester, 1954

C WHITE (1)

8 for 55 v. Gloucestershire at Gloucester, 1998

A C WILLIAMS (1)

9 for 29 v. Hampshire at Dewsbury, 1919

R WOOD (1)

8 for 45 v. Scotland at Glasgow, 1952

SIX WICKETS IN AN INNINGS AT LESS THAN FOUR RUNS EACH

A complete list of 5 wickets at less than 4 runs each up to and including 2007 is to be found in the 2008 edition

R APPLEYARD (2)

6 for 17 v. Essex at Bradford, 1951
6 for 12 v. Hampshire at Bournemouth, 1954

T ARMITAGE (1)

6 for 20 v. Surrey at Sheffield, 1876

R ASPINALL (1)

6 for 23 v. Northamptonshire at Northampton, 1947

W BATES (5)

6 for 11 v. Middlesex at Huddersfield, 1879
6 for 22 v. Kent at Bradford, 1881
6 for 17 v. Nottinghamshire at Nottingham, 1881
6 for 12 v. Kent at Sheffield, 1882
6 for 19 v. Lancashire at Dewsbury, 1886

A BOOTH (1)

6 for 21 v. Warwickshire at Birmingham, 1946

W E BOWES (4)

6 for 17 v. Middlesex at Lord's, 1934
6 for 16 v. Lancashire at Bradford, 1935
6 for 20 v. Gloucestershire at Sheffield, 1936
6 for 23 v. Warwickshire at Birmingham, 1947

J T BROWN (Darfield) (1)

6 for 19 v. Worcestershire at Worcester, 1899

R.O CLAYTON (1)

6 for 20 v. Nottinghamshire at Sheffield, 1876

A COXON (1)

6 for 17 v. Surrey at Sheffield, 1948

T EMMETT (6)

6 for 7 v. Surrey at Sheffield, 1867
6 for 13 v. Lancashire at Holbeck, 1868
6 for 21 v. Middlesex at Scarborough, 1874
6 for 12 v. Derbyshire at Sheffield, 1878
6 for 19 v. Derbyshire at Bradford, 1881
6 for 22 v. Australians at Bradford, 1882

H FISHER (1)

6 for 11 v. Leicestershire at Bradford, 1932

SIX WICKETS IN AN INNINGS AT LESS THAN FOUR
RUNS EACH *(Continued)*

S HAIGH (10)

6 for 18 v. Derbyshire at Bradford, 1897
6 for 22 v. Hampshire at Southampton, 1898
6 for 21 v. Surrey at The Oval, 1900
6 for 23 v. Cambridge University at Cambridge, 1902
6 for 19 v. Somerset at Sheffield, 1902
6 for 22 v. Cambridge University at Sheffield, 1903
6 for 21 v. Hampshire at Leeds, 1904
6 for 21 v. Nottinghamshire at Sheffield, 1905
6 for 13 v. Surrey at Leeds, 1908
6 for 14 v. Australians at Bradford, 1912

A HILL (2)

6 for 9 v. United South of England XI at Bradford, 1874
6 for 18 v. MCC at Lord's, 1881

G H HIRST (7)

6 for 23 v. MCC at Lord's, 1893
6 for 20 v. Lancashire at Bradford, 1906
6 for 12 v. Northamptonshire at Northampton, 1908
6 for 7 v. Northamptonshire at Northampton, 1908
6 for 23 v. Surrey at Leeds, 1908
6 for 23 v. Lancashire at Manchester, 1909
6 for 20 v. Surrey at Sheffield, 1909

R ILLINGWORTH (2)

6 for 15 v. Scotland at Hull, 1956
6 for 13 v. Leicestershire at Leicester, 1963

F S JACKSON (1)

6 for 19 v. Hampshire at Southampton, 1897

R KILNER (5)

6 for 22 v. Essex at Harrogate, 1922
6 for 13 v. Hampshire at Bournemouth, 1922
6 for 14 v. Middlesex at Bradford, 1923
6 for 22 v. Surrey at Sheffield, 1923
6 for 15 v. Hampshire at Portsmouth, 1924

G G MACAULAY (10)

6 for 10 v. Warwickshire at Birmingham, 1921
6 for 3 v. Derbyshire at Hull, 1921
6 for 8 v. Northamptonshire at Northampton, 1922
6 for 12 v. Glamorgan at Cardiff, 1922
6 for 18 v. Northamptonshire at Bradford, 1923
6 for 19 v. Northamptonshire at Northampton, 1925
6 for 22 v. Leicestershire at Leeds, 1926
6 for 11 v. Leicestershire at Hull, 1930
6 for 22 v. Leicestershire at Bradford, 1933
6 for 22 v. Middlesex at Leeds, 1934

SIX WICKETS IN AN INNINGS AT LESS THAN FOUR
RUNS EACH *(Continued)*

E PEATE (5)

6 for 14 v. Middlesex at Huddersfield, 1879
6 for 12 v. Derbyshire at Derby, 1882
6 for 13 v. Gloucestershire at Moreton-in-Marsh, 1884
6 for 16 v. Sussex at Huddersfield, 1886
6 for 16 v. Cambridge University at Sheffield, 1886

R PEEL (4)

6 for 21 v. Nottinghamshire at Sheffield, 1888
6 for 19 v. Australians at Huddersfield, 1888
6 for 22 v. Gloucestershire at Bristol, 1891
6 for 19 v. Leicestershire at Scarborough, 1896

A C RHODES (1)

6 for 19 v. Cambridge University at Cambridge, 1932

W RHODES (12)

6 for 21 v. Somerset at Bath, 1898
6 for 16 v. Gloucestershire at Bristol, 1899
6 for 4 v. Nottinghamshire at Nottingham, 1901
6 for 15 v. MCC at Lord's, 1902
6 for 16 v. Cambridge University at Cambridge, 1905
6 for 9 v. Essex at Huddersfield, 1905
6 for 22 v. Derbyshire at Glossop, 1907
6 for 17 v. Leicestershire at Leicester, 1908
6 for 13 v. Sussex at Hove, 1922
6 for 23 v. Nottinghamshire at Leeds, 1923
6 for 22 v. Cambridge University at Cambridge, 1924
6 for 20 v. Gloucestershire at Dewsbury, 1927

W RINGROSE (1)

6 for 20 v. Leicestershire at Dewsbury, 1903

R J SIDEBOTTOM (1)

6 for 16 v. Kent at Leeds, 2000

W SLINN (1)

6 for 19 v. Nottinghamshire at Nottingham, 1864

G B STEVENSON(1)

6 for 14 v. Warwickshire at Sheffield, 1979

F S TRUEMAN (4)

6 for 23 v. Oxford University at Oxford, 1955
6 for 23 v. Oxford University at Oxford, 1958
6 for 18 v. Warwickshire at Birmingham, 1963
6 for 20 v. Leicestershire at Sheffield, 1968

H VERITY (5)

6 for 11 v. Surrey at Bradford, 1931
6 for 21 v. Glamorgan at Swansea, 1931
6 for 12 v. Derbyshire at Hull, 1933
6 for 10 v. Essex at Ilford, 1937
6 for 22 v. Hampshire at Bournemouth, 1939

SIX WICKETS IN AN INNINGS AT LESS THAN FOUR
RUNS EACH *(Continued)*

A WADDINGTON (2)

6 for 21 v. Northamptonshire at Harrogate, 1921
6 for 21 v. Northamptonshire at Northampton, 1923

S WADE (1)

6 for 18 v. Gloucestershire at Dewsbury, 1887

E WAINWRIGHT (4)

6 for 16 v. Sussex at Leeds, 1893
6 for 23 v. Sussex at Hove, 1893
6 for 18 v. Sussex at Dewsbury, 1894
6 for 22 v. MCC at Scarborough, 1894

J H WARDLE (8)

6 for 17 v. Sussex at Sheffield, 1948
6 for 10 v. Scotland at Edinburgh, 1950
6 for 12 v. Gloucestershire at Hull, 1950
6 for 20 v. Kent at Scarborough, 1950
6 for 23 v. Somerset at Sheffield, 1951
6 for 21 v. Glamorgan at Leeds, 1951
6 for 18 v. Gloucestershire at Bristol, 1951
6 for 6 v. Gloucestershire at Bristol, 1955

D WILSON (3)

6 for 22 v. Sussex at Bradford, 1963
6 for 15 v. Gloucestershire at Middlesbrough, 1966
6 for 22 v. Middlesex at Sheffield, 1966

FOUR WICKETS IN FOUR BALLS

A Drake v. Derbyshire at Chesterfield, 1914

FOUR WICKETS IN FIVE BALLS

F S Jackson v. Australians at Leeds, 1902
A Waddington v. Northamptonshire at Northampton, 1920
G G Macaulay v. Lancashire at Manchester, 1933
P J Hartley v. Derbyshire at Chesterfield, 1995
D Gough v. Kent at Leeds, 1995
J D Middlebrook v. Hampshire at Southampton, 2000

BEST BOWLING ANALYSES IN A MATCH
FOR AND AGAINST YORKSHIRE

Best For Yorkshire:
17 for 91 (8 for 47 and 9 for 44) H Verity v Essex at Leyton, 1933

Against Yorkshire:
17 for 91 (9 for 62 and 8 for 29) H Dean for Lancashire at Liverpool, 1913
(non-championship)

County Championship
16 for 114 (8 for 48 and 8 for 66) G Burton for Middlesex at Sheffield, 1888

Yorkshire versus:

Derbyshire	*For Yorkshire:*	14 for 58 (4 for 11 and 10 for 47) T F Smailes at Sheffield, 1939
	Against:	13 for 65 (7 for 33 and 6 for 32) W Mycroft at Sheffield, 1879
Most 10 wickets in a match	*For Yorkshire:*	P Carrick and E Peate 4 each
	Against:	W Mycroft 3
Durham	*For Yorkshire:*	10 for 101 (6 for 57 and 4 for 44) M A Robinson at Durham, 1992
	Against:	10 for 144 (7 for 81 and 3 for 63) O D Gibson at Chester-le-Street, 2007
Most 10 wickets in a match	*For Yorkshire:*	M A Robinson 1
	Against:	G R Breese and O D Gibson 1 each
Essex	*For Yorkshire:*	17 for 91 (8 for 47 and 9 for 44) H Verity at Leyton, 1933
	Against:	14 for 127 (7 for 37 and 7 for 90) W Mead at Leyton, 1899
Most 10 wickets in a match	*For Yorkshire:*	W Rhodes 7
	Against:	J K Lever, W Mead 2 each
Glamorgan	*For Yorkshire:*	15 for 123 (8 for 70 and 7 for 53) R Illingworth at Swansea. 1960
	Against:	12 for 76 (7 for 30 and 5 for 46) D J Shepherd at Cardiff, 1957
Most 10 wickets in a match	*For Yorkshire:*	H Verity 5
	Against:	D J Shepherd, J S Pressdee 1 each
Gloucestershire	*For Yorkshire:*	14 for 64 (7 for 58 and 7 for 6) R Illingworth at Harrogate, 1967
	Against:	15 for 79 (8 for 33 and 7 for 46) W G Grace at Sheffield, 1872
Most 10 wickets in a match	*For Yorkshire:*	W Rhodes 8
	Against:	E G Dennett 5
Hampshire	*For Yorkshire:*	14 for 43 (8 for 21 and 6 for 22) S Haigh at Southampton, 1898
	Against:	12 for 145 (7 for 78 and 5 for 67) D Shackleton at Bradford, 1962
Most 10 wickets in a match	*For Yorkshire:*	W Rhodes, E Robinson, H Verity 3 each
	Against:	A S Kennedy 3

Yorkshire versus

Kent	*For Yorkshire:*	15 for 38 (6 for 26 and 9 for 12) H Verity at Sheffield, 1936
	Against:	13 for 48 (5 for 13 and 8 for 35) A Hearne at Sheffield, 1885
Most 10 wickets *in a match*	*For Yorkshire:*	E Peate and J H Wardle 4 each
	Against:	C Blythe 6
Lancashire	*For Yorkshire:*	14 for 80 (6 for 56 and 8 for 24) E Peate at Manchester, 1880
	Against:	17 for 91 (9 for 62 and 8 for 29) H Dean at Liverpool, 1913 (non-championship) 14 for 90 (6 for 47 and 8 for 43) R Tattersall at Leeds, 1956 (championship)
Most 10 wickets *in a match*	*For Yorkshire:*	T Emmett 5
	Against:	J Briggs 8
Leicestershire	*For Yorkshire:*	15 for 63 (8 for 25 and 7 for 38) G H Hirst at Hull, 1907
	Against:	12 for 139 (8 for 85 and 4 for 54) A D Pougher at Leicester, 1895
Most 10 wickets *in a match*	*For Yorkshire:*	G H Hirst 5
	Against:	A D Pougher 2
Middlesex	*For Yorkshire:*	13 for 94 (6 for 61 and 7 for 33) S Haigh at Leeds, 1900
	Against:	16 for 114 (8 for 48 and 8 for 66) G Burton at Sheffield, 1888
Most 10 wickets *in a match*	*For Yorkshire:*	W Rhodes 5
	Against:	J T Hearne 7
Northamptonshire	*For Yorkshire:*	16 for 35 (8 for 18 and 8 for 17) W E Bowes at Kettering, 1935
	Against:	15 for 31 (7 for 22 and 8 for 9) G E Tribe at Northampton, 1958
Most 10 wickets *in a match*	*For Yorkshire:*	W E Bowes, G G Macaulay, H Verity, A Waddington 3 each
	Against:	G E Tribe 3
Nottinghamshire	*For Yorkshire:*	14 for 33 (8 for 12 and 6 for 21) R Peel at Sheffield, 1888
	Against:	14 for 94 (8 for 38 and 6 for 56) F Morley at Nottingham, 1878
Most 10 wickets *in a match*	*For Yorkshire:*	G H Hirst 5
	Against:	F Morley, J C Shaw 4 each
Somerset	*For Yorkshire:*	15 for 50 (9 for 22 and 6 for 28) R Peel at Leeds, 1895
	Against:	15 for 71 (6 for 30 and 9 for 41) L C Braund at Sheffield, 1902
Most 10 wickets *in a match*	*For Yorkshire:*	G H Hirst 7
	Against:	L C Braund 3

BEST BOWLING ANALYSES IN A MATCH
FOR AND AGAINST YORKSHIRE *(continued)*

Yorkshire versus

Surrey	*For Yorkshire:*	14 for 77 (6 for 47 and 8 for 30)
		E Peate at Huddersfield, 1881
	Against:	15 for 154 (7 for 55 and 8 for 99)
		T Richardson at Leeds, 1897
Most 10 wickets	*For Yorkshire:*	W Rhodes 7
in a match	*Against:*	G A Lohmann, T Richardson 6 each
Sussex	*For Yorkshire:*	16 for 112 (9 for 48 and 7 for 64)
		J H Wardle at Hull, 1954
	Against:	12 for 110 (6 for 71 and 6 for 39)
		G R Cox at Sheffield, 1907
Most 10 wickets	*For Yorkshire:*	R Peel, E Wainwright 3 each
in a match	*Against:*	Twelve players 1 each
Warwickshire	*For Yorkshire:*	14 for 92 (9 for 43 and 5 for 49)
		H Verity at Leeds, 1937
	Against:	12 for 55 (5 for 21 and 7 for 34)
		T W Cartwright at Bradford, 1969
Most 10 wickets	*For Yorkshire:*	S Haigh 4
in a match	*Against:*	E F Field 4
Worcestershire	*For Yorkshire:*	14 for 211 (8 for 87 and 6 for 124)
		W Rhodes at Worcester, 1903
	Against:	13 for 76 (4 for 38 and 9 for 38)
		J A Cuffe at Bradford, 1907
Most 10 wickets	*For Yorkshire:*	S Haigh, G G Macaulay 4 each
in a match	*Against:*	N Gifford 2
Australians	*For Yorkshire:*	13 for 149 (8 for 48 and 5 for 101)
		G H Hirst at Bradford, 1899
	Against:	13 for 170 (6 for 91 and 7 for 79)
		J M Gregory at Sheffield, 1919
Most 10 wickets	*For Yorkshire:*	S Haigh 2
in a match	*Against:*	C V Grimmett, F R Spofforth, C T B Turner,
		H Trumble 2 each

BEST BOWLING ANALYSES IN AN INNINGS
FOR AND AGAINST YORKSHIRE

Best For Yorkshire:
10 for 10 H Verity v Nottinghamshire at Leeds, 1932

Against Yorkshire:
10 for 37 C V Grimmett for Australians at Sheffield, 1930
(non-championship)

County Championship
10 for 51 H Howell for Warwickshire at Birmingham, 1923

Yorkshire versus:

Derbyshire	*For Yorkshire:*	10 for 47	T F Smailes at Sheffield, 1939
	Against:	9 for 27	J J Hulme at Sheffield, 1894
Most 5 wickets	*For Yorkshire:*	S Haigh, E Peat, W Rhodes 11 each	
in an innings	*Against:*	W Mycroft 10	

Yorkshire versus

Durham

	For Yorkshire:	6 for 37	R D Stemp at Durham, 1994
		6 for 37	J N Gillespie at Chester-le-Street, 2006
	Against:	7 for 58	J Wood at Leeds, 1999
Most 5 wickets	For Yorkshire:	D Gough and M J Hoggard 2 each	
in an innings	Against:	G R Breese, S J E Brown, S J Harmison and G Onions 2 each	

Essex

	For Yorkshire:	9 for 28	W Rhodes at Leyton, 1899
	Against:	8 for 44	F G Bull at Bradford, 1896
Most 5 wickets	For Yorkshire:	W Rhodes 18	
in an innings	Against:	W Mead 14	

Glamorgan

	For Yorkshire:	9 for 60	H Verity at Swansea, 1930
	Against:	9 for 43	J S Pressdee at Swansea, 1965
Most 5 wickets	For Yorkshire:	H Verity 12	
in an innings	Against:	D J Shepherd 6	

Gloucestershire

	For Yorkshire:	9 for 25	S Haigh at Leeds, 1912
	Against:	9 for 36	C W L Parker at Bristol, 1922
Most 5 wickets	For Yorkshire:	W Rhodes 22	
in an innings	Against:	T W J Goddard 17	

Hampshire

	For Yorkshire:	9 for 29	A C Williams at Dewsbury, 1919
	Against:	8 for 49	O W Herman at Bournemouth, 1930
Most 5 wickets	For Yorkshire:	G H Hirst 10	
in an innings	Against:	A S Kennedy 10	

Kent

	For Yorkshire:	9 for 12	H Verity at Sheffield, 1936
	Against:	8 for 35	A Hearne at Sheffield, 1885
Most 5 wickets	For Yorkshire:	W Rhodes 12	
in an innings	Against:	A P Freeman 14	

Lancashire

	For Yorkshire:	9 for 23	G H Hirst at Leeds, 1910
	Against:	9 for 41	A Mold at Huddersfield, 1890
Most 5 wickets	For Yorkshire:	T Emmett 15	
in an innings	Against:	J Briggs 19	

Leicestershire

	For Yorkshire:	8 for 25	G H Hirst at Hull, 1907
	Against:	9 for 63	C T Spencer at Huddersfield, 1954
Most 5 wickets	For Yorkshire:	G H Hirst 15	
in an innings	Against:	H A Smith 7	

Middlesex

	For Yorkshire:	9 for 45	G H Hirst at Sheffield 1907
	Against:	9 for 57	F A Tarrant at Leeds, 1906
Most 5 wickets	For Yorkshire:	W Rhodes 18	
in an innings	Against:	J T Hearne 21	

Northamptonshire

	For Yorkshire:	9 for 37	M A Robinson at Harrogate, 1993
	Against:	9 for 30	A E Thomas at Bradford, 1920
Most 5 wickets	For Yorkshire:	G G Macaulay 14	
in an innings	Against:	G E Tribe, W Wells 7 each	

Nottinghamshire

	For Yorkshire:	10 for 10	H Verity at Leeds, 1932
	Against:	8 for 32	J C Shaw at Nottingham, 1865
Most 5 wickets	For Yorkshire:	W Rhodes 17	
in an innings	Against:	F Morley 17	

BEST BOWLING ANALYSES IN AN INNINGS
FOR AND AGAINST YORKSHIRE *(continued)*

Yorkshire versus

Somerset

	For Yorkshire:	10 for 35	A Drake at Weston-super-Mare, 1914
	Against:	9 for 41	L C Braund at Sheffield, 1902
Most 5 wickets	For Yorkshire:	G H Hirst 16	
in an innings	Against:	E J Tyler 8	

Surrey

	For Yorkshire:	8 for 5	E Peate at Holbeck, 1883
	Against:	9 for 47	T Richardson at Sheffield, 1893
Most 5 wickets	For Yorkshire:	W Rhodes 17	
in an innings	Against:	W Southerton 19	

Sussex

	For Yorkshire:	9 for 48	J H Wardle at Hull, 1954
	Against:	9 for 34	James Langridge at Sheffield, 1934
Most 5 wickets	For Yorkshire:	W Rhodes 14	
in an innings	Against:	G R Cox, J A Snow 6 each	

Warwickshire

	For Yorkshire:	10 for 36	H Verity at Leeds, 1930
	Against:	10 for 51	H Howell at Birmingham, 1923
Most 5 wickets	For Yorkshire:	W Rhodes 18	
in an innings	Against:	E F Field, W E Hollies 7 each	

Worcestershire

	For Yorkshire:	9 for 41	G H Hirst at Worcester, 1911
	Against:	9 for 38	J A Cuffe at Bradford, 1907
Most 5 wickets	For Yorkshire:	S Haigh, W Rhodes 11 each	
in an innings	Against:	R T D Perks 7	

Australians

	For Yorkshire:	9 for 76	W Ringrose at Bradford, 1905
	Against:	10 for 37	C V Grimmett at Sheffield, 1930
Most 5 wickets	For Yorkshire:	R Peel 7	
in an innings	Against:	F R Spofforth 7	

HAT-TRICKS

G Freeman v. Lancashire at Holbeck, 1868
G Freeman v. Middlesex at Sheffield, 1868
A Hill v. United South of England XI at Bradford, 1874
A Hill v. Surrey at The Oval, 1880
E Peate v. Kent at Sheffield, 1882
G Ulyett v. Lancashire at Sheffield, 1883
E Peate v. Gloucestershire at Moreton-in-Marsh, 1884
W Fletcher v. MCC at Lord's, 1892
E Wainwright v. Sussex at Dewsbury, 1894
G H Hirst v. Leicestershire at Leicester, 1895
J T Brown v. Derbyshire at Derby, 1896
R Peel v. Kent at Halifax, 1897
S Haigh v. Derbyshire at Bradford, 1897
W Rhodes v. Kent at Canterbury, 1901
S Haigh v. Somerset at Sheffield, 1902
H A Sedgwick v. Worcestershire at Hull, 1906
G Deyes v. Gentlemen of Ireland at Bray, 1907
G H Hirst v. Leicestershire at Hull, 1907
J T Newstead v. Worcestershire at Bradford, 1907
S Haigh v. Lancashire at Manchester, 1909
M W Booth v. Worcestershire at Bradford, 1911
A Drake v. Essex at Huddersfield, 1912

M W Booth v. Essex at Leyton, 1912
A Drake v. Derbyshire at Chesterfield, 1914 (4 in 4)
W Rhodes v. Derbyshire at Derby, 1920
A Waddington v. Northamptonshire at Northampton, 1920 (4 in 5)
G G Macaulay v. Warwickshire at Birmingham, 1923
E Robinson v. Sussex at Hull, 1928
G G Macaulay v. Leicestershire at Hull, 1930
E Robinson v. Kent at Gravesend, 1930
H Verity v. Nottinghamshire at Leeds, 1932
H Fisher v. Somerset at Sheffield, 1932 (all lbw)
G G Macaulay v. Glamorgan at Cardiff, 1933
G G Macaulay v. Lancashire at Manchester, 1933 (4 in 5)
M.Leyland v. Surrey at Sheffield, 1935
E Robinson v. Kent at Leeds, 1939
A Coxon v. Worcestershire at Leeds, 1946
F S Trueman v. Nottinghamshire at Nottingham, 1951
F S Trueman v. Nottinghamshire at Scarborough, 1955
R Appleyard v. Gloucestershire at Sheffield, 1956
F S.Trueman v. MCC at Lord's, 1958
D Wilson v. Nottinghamshire at Middlesbrough, 1959
F S Trueman v. Nottinghamshire at Bradford, 1963
D Wilson v. Nottinghamshire at Worksop, 1966
D Wilson v. Kent at Harrogate, 1966
G A Cope v. Essex at Colchester, 1970
A L Robinson v. Nottinghamshire at Worksop, 1974
P W Jarvis v. Derbyshire at Chesterfield, 1985
P J Hartley v. Derbyshire at Chesterfield, 1995 (4 in 5)
D Gough v. Kent at Leeds, 1995 (4 in 5)
C White v. Gloucestershire at Gloucester, 1998
M J Hoggard v. Sussex at Hove, 2009

52 Hat-Tricks: G G Macaulay and F S Trueman took four each, S Haigh and D Wilson three each. There have been seven hat-tricks versus Kent and Nottinghamshire, and six versus Derbyshire.

200 WICKETS IN A SEASON

Bowler	Season	Overs	Maidens	Runs	Wickets	Average
W Rhodes	1900	1366.4	411	3054	240	12.72
W Rhodes	1901	1455.3	474	3497	233	15.00
G H Hirst	1906	1111.1	262	3089	201	15.36
G G Macaulay	1925	1241.2	291	2986	200	14.93
R Appleyard†	1951	1323.2	394	2829	200	14.14

† First full season in First-Class cricket.

100 WICKETS IN A SEASON

Bowler		Wickets taken	Wickets taken	Wickets taken
R Appleyard	(3)	200 in 1951	141 in 1954	110 in 1956
A Booth	(1)	111 in 1946	—	
M W Booth	(3)	104 in 1912	167 in 1913	155 in 1914
W E Bowes	(8)	117 in 1931	168 in 1932	130 in 1933
		109 in 1934	154 in 1935	113 in 1936
		106 in 1938	107 in 1939	—

100 WICKETS IN A SEASON *(Continued)*

Bowler	Wickets taken	Wickets taken	Wickets taken
D B Close .... (2)	105 in 1949	114 in 1952	—
A Coxon .... (2)	101 in 1949	129 in 1950	—
A Drake .... (2)	115 in 1913	158 in 1914	—
T Emmett .... (1)	112 in 1886	—	—
S Haigh .... (10)	100 in 1898	160 in 1900	154 in 1902
	102 in 1903	118 in 1904	118 in 1905
	161 in 1906	120 in 1909	100 in 1911
	125 in 1912		
G H Hirst .... (12)	150 in 1895	171 in 1901	121 in 1903
	114 in 1904	100 in 1905	201 in 1906
	169 in 1907	164 in 1908	138 in 1910
	130 in 1911	113 in 1912	100 in 1913
R Illingworth .... (5)	103 in 1956	120 in 1961	116 in 1962
	122 in 1964	105 in 1968	—
R Kilner .... (4)	107 in 1922	143 in 1923	134 in 1924
	123 in 1925	—	—
G G Macaulay .... (10)	101 in 1921	130 in 1922	163 in 1923
	184 in 1924	200 in 1925	133 in 1926
	130 in 1927	117 in 1928	102 in 1929
	141 in 1933	—	—
J T Newstead .... (1)	131 in 1908	—	—
A G Nicholson .... (2)	113 in 1966	101 in 1967	—
E Peate .... (3)	131 in 1880	133 in 1881	165 in 1882
R Peel .... (6)	118 in 1888	132 in 1890	106 in 1892
	134 in 1894	155 in 1895	108 in 1896
W Rhodes .... (22)	141 in 1898	153 in 1899	240 in 1900
	233 in 1901	174 in 1902	169 in 1903
	118 in 1904	158 in 1905	113 in 1906
	164 in 1907	100 in 1908	115 in 1909
	105 in 1911	117 in 1914	155 in 1919
	156 in 1920	128 in 1921	100 in 1922
	127 in 1923	102 in 1926	111 in 1928
	100 in 1929		
E Robinson .... (1)	111 in 1928	—	—
E P Robinson .... (4)	104 in 1938	120 in 1939	149 in 1946
	108 in 1947	—	—
T F Smailes .... (4)	105 in 1934	125 in 1936	120 in 1937
	104 in 1938	—	—
F S Trueman .... (8)	129 in 1954	140 in 1955	104 in 1959
	150 in 1960	124 in 1961	122 in 1962
	121 in 1965	107 in 1966	—
H Verity .... (9)	169 in 1931	146 in 1932	168 in 1933
	100 in 1934	199 in 1935	185 in 1936
	185 in 1937	137 in 1938	189 in 1939
A Waddington .... (5)	100 in 1919	140 in 1920	105 in 1921
	132 in 1922	105 in 1925	—
E Wainwright .... (3)	114 in 1893	157 in 1894	102 in 1896
J H Wardle .... (10)	148 in 1948	100 in 1949	172 in 1950
	122 in 1951	169 in 1952	126 in 1953
	122 in 1954	159 in 1955	146 in 1956
	106 in 1957	—	—
D Wilson .... (3)	100 in 1966	107 in 1968	101 in 1969

BOWLERS WHO HAVE TAKEN OVER 500 WICKETS

Player	M	Runs	Wkts	Av'ge	Best
W Rhodes	883	57634	3598	16.01	9 for 28
G H Hirst	717	44716	2481	18.02	9 for 23
S Haigh	513	29289	1876	15.61	9 for 25
G G Macaulay	445	30554	1774	17.22	8 for 21
F S Trueman	459	29890	1745	17.12	8 for 28
H Verity	278	21353	1558	13.70	10 for 10
J H Wardle	330	27917	1539	18.13	9 for 25
R Illingworth	496	26806	1431	18.73	9 for 42
W E Bowes	301	21227	1351	15.71	9 for 121
R Peel	318	20638	1311	15.74	9 for 22
T Emmett	299	15465	1216	12.71	9 for 23
D Wilson	392	22626	1104	20.49	7 for 19
P Carrick	425	30530	1018	29.99	8 for 33
E Wainwright	352	17744	998	17.77	9 for 66
D B Close	536	23489	967	24.29	8 for 41
Emmott Robinson	413	19645	893	21.99	9 for 36
A G Nicholson	.282	17296	876	19.74	9 for 62
R Kilner	365	14855	857	17.33	8 for 26
A Waddington	255	16203	835	19.40	8 for 34
T F Smailes	262	16593	802	20.68	10 for 47
E Peate	154	9986	794	12.57	8 for 5
Ellis P Robinson	208	15141	735	20.60	8 for 35
C M Old	222	13409	647	20.72	7 for 20
R Appleyard	133	9903	642	15.42	8 for 76
W Bates	202	10692	637	16.78	8 for 21
G A Cope	230	15627	630	24.80	8 for 73
P J Hartley	195	17438	579	30.11	9 for 41
A Sidebottom	216	13852	558	24.82	8 for 72
M W Booth	144	11017	557	19.17	8 for 47
A Hill	140	7002	542	12.91	7 for 14
Hon F S Jackson	207	9690	506	19.15	7 for 42

BOWLERS UNCHANGED IN A MATCH

(IN WHICH THE OPPONENTS WERE DISMISSED TWICE)

There have been 31 instances. The first and most recent are listed below.
A complete list is to be found in the 2008 edition.

First: L Greenwood (11 for 71) and G Freeman (8 for 73) v. Surrey
at The Oval, 1867
Yorkshire won by an innings and 111 runs

Most Recent: E Robinson (8 for 65) and G G Macaulay (12 for 50) v. Worcestershire
at Leeds, 1927
Yorkshire won by an innings and 106 runs

FIELDERS (IN MATCHES FOR YORKSHIRE)

MOST CATCHES IN AN INNINGS

5	E P Robinson v. Leicestershire at Bradford, 1938
5	J Tunnicliffe v. Leicestershire at Leeds, 1897
5	J Tunnicliffe v. Leicestershire at Leicester, 1900
5	J Tunnicliffe v. Leicestershire at Scarborough, 1901
5	A B Sellers v. Essex at Leyton, 1933
5	D Wilson v. Surrey at The Oval, 1969
5	R G Lumb v. Gloucestershire at Middlesbrough, 1972

MOST CATCHES IN A MATCH

7	J Tunnicliffe v. Leicestershire at Leeds, 1897
7	J Tunnicliffe v. Leicestershire at Leicester, 1900
7	A B Sellers v Essex at Leyton, 1933
7	E P Robinson v. Leicestershire at Bradford, 1938
7	D Byas v. Derbyshire at Leeds, 2000

MOST CATCHES IN A SEASON

70	J Tunnicliffe in 1901
70	P J Sharpe in 1962
61	J Tunnicliffe in 1895
60	J Tunnicliffe in 1904
59	J Tunnicliffe in 1896
57	J V Wilson in 1955
54	J V Wilson in 1961
53	J V Wilson in 1957
51	J V Wilson in 1951

MOST CATCHES IN A CAREER

665	J Tunnicliffe (1.40 per match)
586	W Rhodes (0.66 per match)
564	D B Close (1.05 per match)
525	P J Sharpe (1.27 per match)
520	J V Wilson (1.09 per match)
518	G H Hirst (0.72 per match)

Ballance hits double ton

Gary Ballance continued the excellent form he showed for Yorkshire in 2011 by returning to Zimbabwe and scoring his maiden first-class double century for Mid West Rhinos against Southern Rocks at Masvingo Sports Club in the second round of the Logan Cup on October 3-5. Ballance hit 20 fours and two sixes off the 336 balls he faced, and he put on 341 for the third wicket with Zimbabwe one-day international batsman Malcolm Waller. Rhinos won by an innings and 215 runs.

WICKET-KEEPERS IN MATCHES FOR YORKSHIRE

MOST DISMISSALS IN AN INNINGS

7	(7ct)	D L Bairstow v. Derbyshire at Scarborough, 1982
6	(6ct)	J Hunter v. Gloucestershire at Gloucester, 1887
6	(5ct,1st)	D Hunter v. Surrey at Sheffield, 1891
6	(6ct)	D Hunter v. Middlesex at Leeds, 1909
6	(2ct,4st)	W R Allen v. Sussex at Hove, 1921
6	(5ct,1st)	J G Binks v. Lancashire at Leeds, 1962
6	(6ct)	D L Bairstow v. Lancashire at Manchester, 1971
6	(6ct)	D L Bairstow v. Warwickshire at Bradford, 1978
6	(5ct,1st)	D L Bairstow v. Lancashire at Leeds, 1980
6	(6ct)	D L Bairstow v. Derbyshire at Chesterfield, 1984
6	(6ct)	R J Blakey v. Sussex at Eastbourne, 1990
6	(5ct,1st)	R J Blakey v. Gloucestershire at Cheltenham, 1992
6	(5ct,1st)	R J Blakey v. Glamorgan at Cardiff, 1994
6	(6ct)	R J Blakey v. Glamorgan at Leeds, 2003
6	(6ct)	G L Brophy v. Durham at Chester-le-Street, 2009

MOST DISMISSALS IN A MATCH

11	(11ct)	D L Bairstow v. Derbyshire at Scarborough, 1982
		(Equalled World Record)
9	(9ct)	J.Hunter v. Gloucestershire at Gloucester, 1887
9	(8ct,1st)	A Dolphin v. Derbyshire at Bradford, 1919
9	(9ct)	D L Bairstow v. Lancashire at Manchester, 1971
9	(9ct)	R J Blakey v. Sussex at Eastbourne, 1990
8	(2ct,6st)	G Pinder v. Lancashire at Sheffield, 1872
8	(2ct,6st)	D Hunter v. Surrey at Bradford, 1898
8	(7ct,1st)	A Bairstow v. Cambridge University at Cambridge, 1899
8	(8ct)	A Wood v. Northamptonshire at Huddersfield, 1932
8	(8ct)	D L Bairstow v. Lancashire at Leeds, 1978
8	(7ct,1st)	D L Bairstow v. Derbyshire at Chesterfield, 1984
8	(6ct,2st)	D L Bairstow v. Derbyshire at Chesterfield, 1985
8	(8ct)	R J Blakey v. Hampshire at Southampton, 1989
8	(8ct)	R J Blakey v. Northamptonshire at Harrogate, 1993

MOST DISMISSALS IN A SEASON MOST DISMISSALS IN A CAREER

107	(96ct,11st)	J G Binks, 1960	1186	(863ct,323st)	D Hunter (2.29 per match)
94	(81ct,13st)	JG Binks, 1961	1044	(872ct,172st)	J G Binks (2.12 per match)
89	(75ct,14st)	A Wood, 1934	1038	(907ct,131st)	D L Bairstow (2.41 per match)
88	(80ct,8st)	J G Binks, 1963	855	(612ct,243st)	A Wood (2.09 per match)
86	(70ct,16st)	J G Binks, 1962	829	(569ct,260st)	A Dolphin (1.94 per match)
82	(52ct,30st)	A Dolphin, 1919	824	(768ct, 56st)	R J Blakey (2.43 per match)
80	(57ct,23st)	A. Wood, 1935			

YORKSHIRE PLAYERS WHO HAVE
COMPLETED THE "DOUBLE"

(all First-Class matches)

Player	Year	Runs	Average	Wickets	Average
M W Booth (1)	1913	1,228	27.28	181	18.46
D B Close (2)	†1949	1,098	27.45	113	27.87
	1952	1,192	33.11	114	24.08
A Drake (1)	1913	1,056	23.46	116	16.93
S Haigh (1)	1904	1,055	26.37	121	19.85
G H Hirst (14)	1896	1,122	28.20	104	21.64
	1897	1,535	35.69	101	23.22
	1901	1,950	42.39	183	16.38
	1903	1,844	47.28	128	14.94
	1904	2,501	54.36	132	21.09
	1905	2,266	53.95	110	19.94
	††1906	2,385	45.86	208	16.50
	1907	1,344	28.38	188	15.20
	1908	1,598	38.97	114	14.05
	1909	1,256	27.30	115	20.05
	1910	1,840	32.85	164	14.79
	1911	1,789	33.12	137	20.40
	1912	1,133	25.75	118	17.37
	1913	1,540	35.81	101	20.13
R Illingworth (6)	1957	1,213	28.20	106	18.40
	1959	1,726	46.64	110	21.46
	1960	1,006	25.79	109	17.55
	1961	1,153	24.53	128	17.90
	1962	1,612	34.29	117	19.45
	1964	1,301	37.17	122	17.45
F S Jackson (1)	1898	1,566	41.21	104	15.67
R Kilner (4)	1922	1,198	27.22	122	14.73
	1923	1,404	32.24	158	12.91
	1925	1,068	30.51	131	17.92
	1926	1,187	37.09	107	22.52
R Peel (1)	1896	1,206	30.15	128	17.50
W Rhodes (16)	1903	1,137	27.07	193	14.57
	1904	1,537	35.74	131	21.59
	1905	1,581	35.93	182	16.95
	1906	1,721	29.16	128	23.57
	1907	1,055	22.93	177	15.57
	1908	1,673	31.56	115	16.13
	1909	2,094	40.26	141	15.89
	1911	2,261	38.32	117	24.07
	1914	1,377	29.29	118	18.27
	1919	1,237	34.36	164	14.42
	1920	1,123	28.07	161	13.18
	1921	1,474	39.83	141	13.27
	1922	1,511	39.76	119	12.19
	1923	1.321	33.02	134	11.54
	1924	1,126	26.18	109	14.46
	1926	1,132	34.30	115	14.86
T F Smailes (1)	1938	1,002	25.05	113	20.84
E Wainwright (1)	1897	1,612	35.82	101	23.06

† First season in First-Class cricket.
†† The only instance in First-Class cricket of 2,000 runs and 200 wickets in a season.

H Sutcliffe (194) and M Leyland (45) hit 102 off six consecutive overs for Yorkshire v. Essex at Scarborough in 1932.

From 1898 to 1930 inclusive, Wilfred Rhodes took no less than 4,187 wickets, and scored 39,969 runs in First-Class cricket at home and abroad, a remarkable record. He also took 100 wickets and scored 1,000 in a season 16 times, and G H Hirst 14 times.

Of players with a qualification of not less than 50 wickets, Wilfred Rhodes was first in bowling in First-Class cricket in 1900, 1901, 1919, 1920, 1922, 1923 and 1926; Schofield Haigh in 1902, 1905, 1908 and 1909; Mr E R Wilson in 1921; G G Macaulay in 1924; H Verity in 1930, 1933, 1935, 1937 and 1939; W E Bowes in 1938; A Booth in 1946; R Appleyard in 1951 and 1955, and F S Trueman in 1952 and 1963.

The highest aggregate of runs made in one season in First-Class cricket by a Yorkshire player is 3,429 by L Hutton in 1949. This total has been exceeded three times, viz: D C S Compton 3,816 and W J Edrich 3,539 in 1947, and 3,518 by T Hayward in 1906. H Sutcliffe scored 3,336 in 1932.

Three players have taken all 10 Yorkshire wickets in an innings. G Wootton, playing for All England XI at Sheffield in 1865, took all 10 wickets for 54 runs. H Howell performed the feat for Warwickshire at Edgbaston in 1923 at a cost of 51 runs; and C V Grimmett, Australia, took all 10 wickets for 37 runs at Sheffield in 1930.

The match against Sussex at Dewsbury on June 7th and 8th, 1894, was brought to a summary conclusion by a remarkable bowling performance on the part of Edward Wainwright. In the second innings of Sussex, he took the last five wickets in seven balls, including the "hat trick". In the whole match he obtained 13 wickets for only 38 runs.

M D Moxon has the unique distinction of scoring a century in each of his first two First-Class matches in Yorkshire — 116 (2nd inns.) v. Essex at Leeds and 111 (1st inns.) v. Derbyshire at Sheffield, June 1981).

In the Yorkshire v. Norfolk match — played on the Hyde Park Ground, Sheffield, on July 14th to 18th, 1834 — 851 runs were scored in the four innings, of which no fewer than 128 were extras: 75 byes and 53 wides. At that time wides were not run out, so that every wide included in the above total represents a wide actually bowled. This particular achievement has never been surpassed in the annals of county cricket.

L Hutton reached his 1,000 runs in First-Class cricket in 1949 as early as June 9th.

W Barber reached his 1,000 runs in 1934 on June 13th. P Holmes reached his 1,000 in 1925 on June 16th, as also did H Sutcliffe in 1932. J T Brown reached his 1,000 in 1899 on June 22nd. In 1905, D Denton reached his 1,000 on June 26th; and in 1906 G H Hirst gained the same total on June 27th.

In 1912, D Denton scored over 1,000 runs during July, while M Leyland and H Sutcliffe both scored over 1,000 runs in August 1932.

L Hutton scored over 1,000 in June and over 1,000 runs in August in 1949.

H Verity took his 100th wicket in First-Class cricket as early as June 19th in 1936 and on June 27th in 1935. In 1900, W Rhodes obtained his 100th wicket on June 21st, and again on the same date in 1901, while G H Hirst obtained his 100th wicket on June 28th, 1906.

In 1930, Yorkshiremen (H Sutcliffe and H Verity) occupied the first places by English players in the batting and the bowling averages of First-Class cricket, which is a record without precedent. H Sutcliffe was also first in the batting averages in 1931 and 1932.

G Boycott was the first player to have achieved an average of over 100 in each of two English seasons. In 1971, he scored 2,503 runs for an average of 100.12, and in 1979 he scored 1,538 runs for an average of 102.53.

FIRST-CLASS MATCHES BEGUN AND FINISHED IN ONE DAY

Yorkshire v. Somerset, at Huddersfield, July 9th, 1894.
Yorkshire v. Hampshire, at Southampton, May 27th, 1898.
Yorkshire v. Worcestershire, at Bradford, May 7th, 1900

For England

YORKSHIRE TEST CRICKETERS 1877-2012 (Correct to January 6, 2012)

Player	M.	I	NO	Runs	HS.	Av'ge.	100s	50s	Balls	R	W	Av'ge	Best	5wI	10wM	c/st
APPLEYARD, R ...1954-56	9	9	6	51	19*	17.00	—	—	1596	554	31	17.87	5-51	1	—	4
ARMITAGE, T ...1877	2	3	0	33	21	11.00	—	—	12	15	0	—	—	—	—	—
ATHEY, C W J ...1980-88	23	41	1	919	123	22.97	1	4	—	—	—	—	—	—	—	13
BAIRSTOW, D L ...1979-81	4	7	1	125	59	20.83	—	1	—	—	—	—	—	—	—	12/1
BARBER, W ...1935	2	4	0	83	44	20.75	—	—	2	0	1	0.00	1-0	—	—	1
BATES, W ...1881-87	15	26	2	656	64	27.33	—	5	2364	821	50	16.42	7-28	4	1	9
BINKS, J G ...1964	2	4	0	91	55	22.75	—	1	—	—	—	—	—	—	—	8/—
BLAKEY, R J ...1993	2	4	0	7	6	1.75	—	—	—	—	—	—	—	—	—	2/—
BOOTH, M W ...1913-14	2	2	0	46	32	23.00	—	—	312	130	7	18.57	4-49	—	—	—
BOWES, W E ...1932-46	15	11	5	28	10*	4.66	—	—	3655	1519	68	22.33	6-33	6	—	2
†BOYCOTT, G ...1964-82	108	193	23	8114	246*	47.72	22	42	944	382	7	54.57	3-47	—	—	33
BRENNAN, D V ...1951	2	2	0	16	16	8.00	—	—	—	—	—	—	—	—	—	—/1
BRESNAN, T T ...2009-11	10	8	1	318	91	45.42	—	3	2031	968	41	23.60	5-48	1	—	3
BROWN, J T ...1894-99	8	16	3	470	140	36.15	1	1	35	22	0	—	—	—	—	7
†CLOSE, D B ...1949-76	22	37	2	887	70	25.34	—	4	1212	532	18	29.55	4-35	—	—	24
COPE, G A ...1977-78	3	3	0	40	22	13.33	—	—	864	277	8	34.62	3-102	—	—	1
COXON, A ...1948	1	2	0	19	19	9.50	—	—	378	172	3	57.33	2-90	—	—	—
DAWSON, R K J ...2002-03	7	13	3	114	19*	11.40	—	—	1116	677	11	61.54	4-134	—	—	3
DENTON, D ...1905-10	11	22	1	424	104	20.19	1	1	—	—	—	—	—	—	—	8
DOLPHIN, A ...1921	1	2	0	1	1	0.50	—	—	—	—	—	—	—	—	—	1/—
EMMETT, T ...1877-82	7	13	1	160	48	13.33	—	—	728	284	9	31.55	7-68	1	—	9
GIBB, P A ...1938-46	8	13	0	581	120	44.69	2	3	—	—	—	—	—	—	—	3/1
GOUGH, D ...1994-2003	58	86	18	855	65	12.57	—	2	11821	6503	229	28.39	6-42	9	—	13
GREENWOOD, A ...1877	2	4	0	77	49	19.25	—	—	—	—	—	—	—	—	—	2

Player	M.	I	NO	Runs	HS.	Av'ge.	100s	50s	Balls	R	W	Av'ge	Best	5wI	10wM	c/st
HAIGH, S 1899-1912	11	18	3	113	25	7.53	—	—	1294	622	24	25.91	6-11	1	—	8
HAMILTON, G.M. 1999	1	2	0	0	0	0.00	—	—	90	63	0	—	—	—	—	—
HAMPSHIRE, J H ...1969-75	8	16	1	403	107	26.86	1	2	—	—	—	—	—	—	—	9
†HAWKE, LORD ...1896-99	5	8	1	55	30	7.85	—	—	—	—	—	—	—	—	—	3
HILL, A 1877	2	4	2	101	49	50.50	—	—	340	130	7	18.57	4-27	—	—	1
HIRST, G H ...1897-1909	24	38	3	790	85	22.57	—	5	3967	1770	59	30.00	5-48	3	—	18
HOGGARD, M J .2000-2008	67	92	27	473	38	7.27	—	—	13909	7564	248	30.50	7-61	7	1	24
HOLMES, P ...1921-32	7	14	1	357	88	27.46	—	4	—	—	—	—	—	—	—	3
HUNTER, J ...1884-85	5	7	2	93	39*	18.60	—	—	—	—	—	—	—	—	—	8/3
†HUTTON, L ...1937-55	79	138	15	6971	364	56.67	19	33	260	232	3	77.33	1-2	—	—	57
HUTTON, R A 1971	5	8	2	219	81	36.50	—	2	738	257	9	28.55	3-72	—	—	9
†ILLINGWORTH, R .1958-73	61	90	11	1836	113	23.24	2	5	11934	3807	122	31.20	6-29	3	—	45
†JACKSON, Hon F S1893-1905	20	33	4	1415	144*	48.79	5	6	1587	799	24	33.29	5-52	1	—	10
JARVIS, P W ...1988-93	9	15	2	132	29*	10.15	—	—	1912	965	21	45.95	4-107	—	—	2
KILNER, R 1924-26	9	8	1	233	74	33.28	—	2	2368	734	24	30.58	4-51	—	—	6
LEADBEATER, E .1951-52	2	2	0	40	38	20.00	—	—	289	218	2	109.00	1-38	—	—	3
LEYLAND, M ...1928-38	41	65	5	2764	187	46.06	9	10	1103	585	6	97.50	3-91	—	—	13
LOWSON, F A ...1951-55	7	13	0	245	68	18.84	—	2	—	—	—	—	—	—	—	5
McGRATH, A ...2003	4	5	0	201	81	40.20	—	2	102	56	4	14.00	3-16	—	—	3
MACAULAY, G G ..1923-33	8	10	4	112	76	18.66	—	1	1701	662	24	27.58	5-64	1	—	5
MILLIGAN, F W ...1899	2	4	0	58	38	14.50	—	—	45	29	0	—	—	—	—	1
MITCHELL, A ...1933-36	6	10	0	298	72	29.80	—	2	6	4	0	—	—	—	—	9
*MITCHELL, F ...1899	2	4	0	88	41	22.00	—	—	—	—	—	—	—	—	—	2
MOXON, M D ...1986-89	10	17	1	455	99	28.43	—	3	48	30	0	—	—	—	—	10
OLD, C M ...1972-81	46	66	9	845	65	14.82	—	2	8858	4020	143	28.11	7-50	4	—	22

YORKSHIRE TEST CRICKETERS 1877-2012 (Continued)

Player	M.	I	NO	Runs	HS.	Av'ge	100s	50s	Balls	R	W	Av'ge	Best	5wI	10wM	c/st
PADGETT, D E V 1960	2	4	0	51	31	12.75	—	—	12	8	0	—	—	—	—	—
PEATE, E 1881-86	9	14	8	70	13	11.66	—	—	2096	682	31	22.00	6-85	2	—	2
PEEL, R 1884-96	20	33	4	427	83	14.72	—	3	5216	1715	101	16.98	7-31	5	1	17
RHODES, W 1899-1930	58	98	21	2325	179	30.19	2	11	8231	3425	127	26.96	8-68	6	1	60
SHARPE, P J 1963-69	12	21	4	786	111	46.23	1	4	—	—	—	—	—	—	—	17
SHAHZAD, A 2010	1	1	0	5	5	5.00	—	—	102	63	4	15.75	3-45	—	—	2
SIDEBOTTOM, A 1985	1	1	0	2	2	2.00	—	—	112	65	1	65.00	1-65	—	—	—
SIDEBOTTOM, R J .2001-10	22	31	11	313	31	15.65	—	—	4812	2231	79	28.24	7-47	5	—	5
SILVERWOOD, CEW 1997-2003	6	7	3	29	10	7.25	—	—	828	444	11	40.36	5-91	1	—	2
SMAILES, T F 1946	1	—	—	25	25	25.00	—	—	120	62	3	20.66	3-44	—	—	—
SMITHSON, G A 1948	2	3	0	70	35	23.33	—	—	—	—	—	—	—	—	—	—
†STANYFORTH, R T 1927-28	4	6	1	13	6*	2.60	—	—	—	—	—	—	—	—	—	7/2
STEVENSON, G B ..1980-81	2	2	1	28	27*	28.00	—	—	312	183	5	36.60	3-111	—	—	—
SUTCLIFFE, H 1924-35	54	84	9	4555	194	60.73	16	23	—	—	—	—	—	—	—	23
TAYLOR, K 1959-64	3	5	0	57	24	11.40	—	—	12	6	0	—	—	—	—	1
TRUEMAN, F S 1952-65	67	85	14	981	39*	13.81	—	—	15178	6625	307	21.57	8-31	17	3	64
ULYETT, G 1877-90	25	39	0	949	149	24.33	1	7	2627	1020	50	20.40	7-36	1	—	19
†VAUGHAN M P .1999-2008	82	147	9	5719	197	41.44	18	18	978	561	6	93.50	2-71	—	—	44
VERITY, H 1931-39	40	44	12	669	66*	20.90	—	3	11173	3510	144	24.37	8-43	5	2	30
WADDINGTON, A .1920-21	2	4	0	16	7	4.00	—	—	276	119	1	119.00	1-35	—	—	1
WAINWRIGHT, E .1893-98	5	9	2	132	49	14.66	—	—	127	73	0	—	—	—	—	2
WARDLE, J H 1948-57	28	41	8	653	66	19.78	—	2	6597	2080	102	20.39	7-36	5	1	12
WATSON, W 1951-59	23	37	3	879	116	25.85	2	3	—	—	—	—	—	—	—	8
WHITE, C 1994-2002	30	50	7	1052	121	24.46	1	5	3959	2220	59	37.62	5-32	3	—	14
WILSON, C E M 1899	2	4	1	42	18	14.00	—	—	—	—	—	—	—	—	—	—

For England

YORKSHIRE TEST CRICKETERS 1877-2012 (Continued)

Player	M.	I	NO	Runs	HS.	Av'ge	100s	50s	Balls	R	W	Av'ge	Best	5wI	10wM	c/st
WILSON, D 1964-71	6	7	1	75	42	12.50	—	—	1472	466	11	42.36	2-17	—	—	1
WILSON, E R 1921	1	2	0	10	5	5.00	—	1	123	36	3	12.00	2-28	—	—	—
WOOD, A 1938-39	4	5	1	80	53	20.00	—	1	—	—	—	—	—	—	—	10/1
†YARDLEY, N W D ...1938-50	20	34	2	812	99	25.37	—	4	1662	707	21	33.66	3-67	—	—	14

†Captained England
*Also represented and captained South Africa

For South Africa

Player	M.	I	NO	Runs	HS.	Av'ge	100s	50s	Balls	R	W	Av'ge	Best	5wI	10wM	c/st
†MITCHELL, F 1912	3	6	0	28	12	4.66	—	—	—	—	—	—	—	—	—	—

†Captained South Africa

Overseas Players
(Qualification: 20 first-class matches for Yorkshire)

For Australia

Player	M.	I	NO	Runs	HS.	Av'ge	100s	50s	Balls	R	W	Av'ge	Best	5wI	10wM	c/st
BEVAN, M G 1994-98	18	30	3	785	91	29.07	—	6	1285	703	29	24.24	6-82	1	1	8
GILLESPIE, J N 1996-2006	71	93	28	1218	201*	18.73	1	2	14234	6770	259	26.13	7-37	8	—	27
JAQUES, P A 2005-2008	11	19	0	902	150	47.47	3	6	—	—	—	—	—	—	—	7
LEHMANN, D S ...1999-2004	27	42	2	1798	177	44.95	5	10	974	412	15	27.46	3-42	—	—	11

For South Africa

Player	M.	I	NO	Runs	HS.	Av'ge	100s	50s	Balls	R	W	Av'ge	Best	5wI	10wM	c/st
RUDOLPH, J A 2003-11/12	40	71	8	2238	222*	35.52	5	9	664	432	4	108.00	1-1	—	—	24

For West Indies

Player	M.	I	NO	Runs	HS.	Av'ge	100s	50s	Balls	R	W	Av'ge	Best	5wI	10wM	c/st
RICHARDSON, R B 1983-84/95	86	146	12	5949	194	44.39	16	27	66	18	0	—	—	—	—	90

CENTURIES FOR ENGLAND

C W J ATHEY (1)
123 v Pakistan at Lord's, 1987

G BOYCOTT (22)

113	v. Australia at The Oval, 1964	112	v West Indies at Port-of-Spain, 1974
117	v. South Africa at Port Elizabeth, 1965	107	v. Australia at Nottingham, 1977
246*	v. India at Leeds, 1967	191	v. Australia at Leeds, 1977
116	v. West Indies at Georgetown, 1968	100*	v. Pakistan at Hyderabad, 1978
128	v. West Indies at Manchester, 1969	131	v. New Zealand at Nottingham, 1978
106	v. West Indies at Lord's, 1969	155	v. India at Birmingham, 1979
142*	v. Australia at Sydney, 1971	125	v. India at The Oval, 1979
119*	v. Australia at Adelaide, 1971	128*	v. Australia at Lord's, 1980
121*	v. Pakistan at Lord's, 1971	104*	v. West Indies at St John's, 1981
112	v. Pakistan at Leeds, 1971	137	v. Australia at The Oval, 1981
115	v. New Zealand at Leeds, 1973	105	v. India at Delhi, 1981

J T BROWN (1)
140 v. Australia at Melbourne, 1895

D DENTON (1)
104 v. South Africa at Old Wanderers, Johannesburg, 1910

P A GIBB (2)
106 v. South Africa at Old Wanderers, Johannesburg, 1938
120 v. South Africa at Kingsmead, Durban, 1939

J H HAMPSHIRE (1)
107 v. West Indies at Lord's, 1969

L HUTTON (19)

100	v. New Zealand at Manchester, 1937	206	v. New Zealand at The Oval, 1949
100	v. Australia at Nottingham, 1938	202*	v. West Indies at The Oval, 1950
364	v. Australia at The Oval, 1938	156*	v. Australia at Adelaide, 1951
196	v. West Indies at Lord's, 1939	100	v. South Africa at Leeds, 1951
165*	v. West Indies at The Oval, 1939	150	v. India at Lord's, 1952
122*	v. Australia at Sydney, 1947	104	v. India at Manchester, 1952
100	v. South Africa at Leeds, 1947	145	v. Australia at Lord's, 1953
158	v. South Africa at Ellis Park, J'b'rg, 1948	169	v. West Indies at Georgetown, 1954
123	v. South Africa at Ellis Park, J'b'rg, 1949	205	v. West Indies at Kingston, 1954
101	v. New Zealand at Leeds, 1949		

R ILLINGWORTH (2)
113 v. West Indies at Lord's, 1969
107 v. India at Manchester, 1971

Hon. F S JACKSON (5)

103	v. Australia at The Oval, 1893	144*	v. Australia at Leeds, 1905
118	v. Australia at The Oval, 1899	113	v. Australia at Manchester, 1905
128	v. Australia at Manchester, 1902		

M LEYLAND (9)

137	v. Australia at Melbourne, 1929	161	v. South Africa at The Oval, 1935
102	v. South Africa at Lord's, 1929	126	v. Australia at Woolloongabba,
109	v. Australia at Lord's, 1934		Brisbane, 1936
153	v. Australia at Manchester, 1934	111*	v. Australia at Melbourne, 1937
110	v. Australia at The Oval, 1934	187	v. Australia at The Oval, 1938

CENTURIES FOR ENGLAND

W RHODES (2)

179 v. Australia at Melbourne, 1912
152 v. South Africa at Old Wanderers, Johannesburg, 1913

P J SHARPE (1)

111 v. New Zealand at Nottingham, 1969

H SUTCLIFFE (16)

122	v. South Africa at Lord's, 1924	114	v. South Africa at Birmingham, 1929
115	v. Australia at Sydney, 1924	100	v. South Africa at Lord's, 1929
176	v. Australia at Melbourne, 1925 (1st Inns)	104	v. South Africa at The Oval, 1929 (1st inns)
127	v. Australia at Melbourne, 1925 (2nd Inns)	109*	v. South Africa at The Oval, 1929 (2nd inns)
143	v. Australia at Melbourne, 1925	161	v. Australia at The Oval, 1930
161	v. Australia at The Oval, 1926	117	v. New Zealand at The Oval, 1931
102	v. South Africa at Old Wanderers, Jbg.1927	109*	v. New Zealand at Manchester, 1931
135	v. Australia at Melbourne, 1929	194	v. Australia at Sydney, 1932

G ULYETT (1)

149 v. Australia at Melbourne, 1882

M P VAUGHAN (18)

120	v. Pakistan at Manchester, 2001	105	v. Sri Lanka at Kandy, 2003
115	v. Sri Lanka at Lord's, 2002	140	v. West Indies at Antigua, 2004
100	v. India at Lord's, 2002	103	v. West Indies at Lord's (1st inns) 2004
197	v. India at Nottingham, 2002	101*	v. West Indies at Lord's (2nd inns) 2004
195	v. India at The Oval, 2002	120	v. Bangladesh at Lord's, 2005
177	v. Australia at Adelaide, 2002	166	v. Australia at Manchester,2005
145	v. Australia at Melbourne, 2002	103	v. West Indies at Leeds, 2007
183	v. Australia at Sydney, 2003	124	v. India at Nottingham, 2007
156	v. South Africa at Birmingham, 2003	106	v. New Zealand at Lord's, 2008

W WATSON (2)

109 v. Australia at Lord's, 1953   116 v. West Indies at Kingston, 1954

C WHITE (1)

121 v. India at Ahmedabad, 2001

Summary of the Centuries

versus	Total	In England	Away
Australia	40	21	19
Bangladesh	1	1	0
India	12	10	2
New Zealand	9	9	—
Pakistan	5	4	1
South Africa	18	10	8
Sri Lanka	2	1	1
West Indies	17	10	7
Totals	104	66	38

For Australia

J N GILLESPIE (1)

201* v. Bangladesh at Chittagong, 2006

P A JAQUES (3)

100 v. Sri Lanka at Brisbane, 2007   108 v. West Indies at Bridgetown, 2008
150 v. Sri Lanka at Hobart, 2007

D S LEHMANN (5)

160	v. West Indies at Port of Spain, 2003	129	v. Sri Lanka at Galle, 2004
110	v. Bangladesh at Darwin, 2003	153	v. Sri Lanka at Columbo, 2004
177	v. Bangladesh at Cairns, 2003		

10 WICKETS IN A MATCH FOR ENGLAND

W BATES (1)
14 for 102 (7 for 28 and 7 for 74) v. Australia at Melbourne, 1882

M J HOGGARD (1)
12 for 205 (5 for 144 and 7 for 61) v. South Africa at Johannesburg, 2005

R PEEL (1)
11 for 68 (7 for 31 and 4 for 37) v. Australia at Mancester, 1888

Note: The scorebook for the Australia v. England Test match at Sydney in February 1888
shows that the final wicket to fall was taken by W Attewell, and not by Peel

Peel therefore took 9, and not 10 wickets, in the match

His career totals have been amended to take account of this alteration

W RHODES (1)
15 for 124 (7 for 56 and 8 for 68) v. Australia at Melbourne, 1904

R J SIDEBOTTOM (1)
10 for 139 (4 for 90 and 6 for 49) v. New Zealand at Hamilton, 2008

F S TRUEMAN (3)
11 for 88 (5 for 58 and 6 for 30) v. Australia at Leeds, 1961
11 for 152 (6 for 100 and 5 for 52) v. West Indies at Lord's, 1963*
12 for 119 (5 for 75 and 7 for 44) v. West Indies at Birmingham, 1963*

consecutive Tests

H VERITY (2)
11 for 153 (7 for 49 and 4 for 104) v. India at Chepauk, Madras, 1934
15 for 104 (7 for 61 and 8 for 43) v. Australia at Lord's, 1934

J H WARDLE (1)
12 for 89 (5 for 53 and 7 for 36) v. South Africa at Cape Town, 1957

Summary of Ten Wickets in a Match

versus	Total	In England	Away
Australia	5	3	2
India	1	—	1
New Zealand	1	—	1
Pakistan	—	—	—
South Africa	2	—	2
Sri Lanka	—	—	—
West Indies	2	2	—
Totals	11	5	6

For Australia

M G BEVAN (1)
10 for 113 (4 for 31and 6 for 82) v. West Indies at Adelaide, 1997

5 WICKETS IN AN INNINGS FOR ENGLAND

R APPLEYARD (1)
5 for 51 v. Pakistan at Nottingham, 1954

W BATES (4)
7 for 28 v. Australia at Melbourne, 1882   5 for 31 v. Australia at Adelaide, 1884
7 for 74 v. Australia at Melbourne, 1882   5 for 24 v. Australia at Sydney, 1885

327

5 WICKETS IN AN INNINGS FOR ENGLAND *(Continued)*

W E BOWES (6)

6 for 34	v. New Zealand at Auckland, 1933	5 for 100v. South Africa at Manchester, 1935
6 for 142	v. Australia at Leeds, 1934*	5 for 49 v. Australia at The Oval, 1938
5 for 55	v. Australia at The Oval, 1934*	6 for 33 v. West Indies at Manchester, 1939

*consecutive Test matches

T T BRESNAN (1))

5 for 48 v. India at Nottingham, 2011

T EMMETT (1)

7 for 68 v. Australia at Melbourne, 1879

D GOUGH (9)

6 for 49	v. Australia at Sydney, 1995	5 for 70 v. South Africa at Johannesburg, 1999
5 for 40	v.New Zealand at Wellington, 1997	5 for 109 v. West Indies at Birmingham, 2000
5 for 149	v. Australia at Leeds, 1997	5 for 61 v. Pakistan at Lord's, 2001
6 for 42	v.South Africa at Leeds, 1998	5 for 103 v. Australia at Leeds, 2001
5 for 96	v. Australia at Melbourne, 1998	

S HAIGH (1)

6 for 11 v. South Africa at Cape Town, 1909

G H HIRST (3)

5 for 77	v. Australia at The Oval, 1902	5 for 58 v. Australia at Birmingham, 1909
5 for 48	v. Australia at Melbourne, 1904	

M J HOGGARD (7)

7 for 63	v. New Zealand at Christchurch, 2002	5 for 73 v. Bangladesh at Chester-le-Street, 2005
5 for 92	v. Sri Lanka at Birmingham, 2002	6 for 57 v. India at Nagpur, 2006
5 for 144	v. South Africa at Johannesburg, 2005*	7 for 109 v. Australia at Adelaide, 2006
7 for 61	v. South Africa at Johannesburg, 2005*	

*Consecutive Test innings

R ILLINGWORTH (3)

6 for 29	v. India at Lord's, 1967	5 for 70 v. India at The Oval, 1971
6 for 87	v. Australia at Leeds, 1968	

Hon F S JACKSON (1)

5 for 52 v. Australia at Nottingham, 1905

G G MACAULAY (1)

5 for 64 v. South Africa at Cape Town, 1923

C M OLD (4)

5 for 113	v. New Zealand at Lord's, 1973	6 for 54v. New Zealand at Wellington, 1978
5 for 21	v. India at Lord's, 1974	7 for 50 v. Pakistan at Birmingham, 1978

E PEATE (2)

5 for 43 v. Australia at Sydney, 18826 for 85 v. Australia at Lord's, 1884

R PEEL (5)

5 for 51 v. Australia at Adelaide, 1884	6 for 67 v. Australia at Sydney, 1894
5 for 18 v. Australia at Sydney, 1888	6 for 23 v. Australia at The Oval, 1896
7 for 31 v. Australia at Manchester, 1888	

W RHODES (6)

7 for 17 v. Australia at Birmingham, 1902	7 for 56 v. Australia at Melbourne, 1904*
5 for 63 v. Australia at Sheffield, 1902	8 for 68 v. Australia at Melbourne, 1904*
5 for 94 v. Australia at Sydney, 1903*	5 for 83 v. Australia at Manchester, 1909

5 WICKETS IN AN INNINGS FOR ENGLAND *(Continued)*

C E W SILVERWOOD (1)

5 for 91 v. South Africa, at Cape Town, 2000

R J SIDEBOTTOM (5)

5 for 88	v. West Indies at Chester-le-Street, 2007	7 for 47 v. New Zealand at Napier, 2008
6 for 49	v. New Zealand at Hamilton, 2008	6 for 47 v. New Zealand at Nottingham, 2008
5 for 105	v. New Zealand at Wellington, 2008	

F S TRUEMAN (17)

8 for 31	v. India at Manchester, 1952	6 for 31 v. Pakistan at Lord's, 1962
5 for 48	v. India at The Oval, 1952	5 for 62 v. Australia at Melbourne, 1963
5 for 90	v. Australia at Lord's, 1956	7 for 75 v. New Zealand at Christchurch, 1963
5 for 63	v. West Indies at Nottingham, 1957	6 for 100 v. West Indies at Lord's, 1963*
5 for 31	v. New Zealand at Birmingham, 1958	5 for 52 v. West Indies at Lord's, 1963*
5 for 35	v. West Indies at Port-of-Spain, 1960	5 for 75 v. West Indies at Birmingham, 1963*
5 for 27	v. South Africa at Nottingham, 1960	7 for 44 v. West Indies at Birmingham, 1963*
5 for 58	v. Australia at Leeds, 1961*	5 for 48 v. Australia at Lord's, 1964
6 for 30	v. Australia at Leeds, 1961*	

G ULYETT (1)

7 for 36 v. Australia at Lord's, 1884

H VERITY (5)

5 for 33	v. Australia at Sydney, 1933	8 for 43 v. Australia at Lord's, 1934*
7 for 49	v. India at Chepauk, Madras, 1934	5 for 70 v. South Africa at Cape Town, 1939
7 for 61	v. Australia at Lord's, 1934*	

J H WARDLE (5)

7 for 56	v. Pakistan at The Oval, 1954	7 for 36 v. South Africa at Cape Town, 1957*
5 for 79	v. Australia at Sydney, 1955	5 for 61 v. South Africa at Kingsmead,
5 for 53	v. South Africa at Cape Town, 1957*	Durban, 1957*

C WHITE (3)

5 for 57 v. West Indies at Leeds, 2000   5 for 32 v. West Indies at The Oval, 2000

5 for 127 v. Australia at Perth, 2002

*consecutive Test innings

Summary of Five Wickets in an Innings

versus	Total	In England	Away
Australia	42	22	20
Bangladesh	1	1	—
India	7	5	2
India	8	6	2
New Zealand	11	3	8
Pakistan	5	5	—
South Africa	13	3	10
Sri Lanka	1	1	
West Indies	11	10	1
Totals	92	51	41

For Australia

M G BEVAN (1)

6 for 82 v.   West Indies at Adelaide, 1997

5 WICKETS IN AN INNINGS

For Australia *(Continued)*

J N GILLESPIE (8)

5 for 54	v.	South Africa at Port Elizabeth, 1997
7 for 37	v.	England at Leeds, 1997
5 for 88	v.	England at Perth, 1998
5 for 89	v.	West Indies at Adelaide, 2000
6 for 40	v.	West Indies at Melbourne, 2000
5 for 53	v.	England at Lord's, 2001
5 for 39	v.	West Indies at Georgetown, 2003
5 for 56	v.	India at Nagpur, 2004

HAT-TRICKS

W Bates v. Australia at Melbourne, 1882
D Gough v. Australia at Sydney, 1998
M J Hoggard v. West Indies at Bridgetown, 2004
R J Sidebottom v. New Zealand at Hamilton, 2008

FOUR WICKETS IN FIVE BALLS

C M Old v. Pakistan at Birmingham, 1978

THREE WICKETS IN FOUR BALLS

R Appleyard v. New Zealand at Auckland, 1955
D Gough v. Pakistan at Lord's, 2001

YORKSHIRE PLAYERS WHO PLAYED ALL THEIR TEST CRICKET AFTER LEAVING YORKSHIRE

For England

Player	M.	I	NO	Runs	HS.	Av'ge	100s	50s	Balls	R	W	Av'ge	Best	5wI	10wM	c/st
BALDERSTONE, J C ...1976	2	4	1	39	35	9.75	—	—	96	80	1	80.00	1:80	—	—	1
BATTY, G J ...2003	2	7	1	136	38	22.66	—	—	992	504	8	63.00	3:55	—	—	—
BIRKENSHAW, J ...1973-74	5	7	0	148	64	21.14	—	1	1017	469	13	36.07	5:57	1	—	3
BOLUS, J B ...1963-64	7	12	0	496	88	41.33	—	4	18	16	0	—	—	—	—	2
†PARKIN, C H ...1920-24	10	16	3	160	36	12.30	—	—	2095	1128	32	35.25	5:38	2	—	3
RHODES, S J ...1994-95	11	17	5	294	65*	24.50	—	1	—	—	—	—	—	—	—	46/3
†SUGG, F H ...1888	2	2	0	55	31	27.50	—	—	—	—	—	—	—	—	—	1
WARD, A ...1893-95	7	13	0	487	117	37.46	1	3	—	—	—	—	—	—	—	6
WOOD, B ...1972-78	12	21	0	454	90	21.61	—	2	98	50	0	—	—	—	—	—

For South Africa

Player	M.	I	NO	Runs	HS.	Av'ge	100s	50s	Balls	R	W	Av'ge	Best	5wI	10wM	c/st
THORNTON, P G ...1902	1	1	1	1	1*	—	—	—	24	20	1	20.00	1:20	—	—	1

†Born outside Yorkshire

CENTURIES FOR ENGLAND

A WARD (1)
117 v. Australia at Sydney, 1894

5 WICKETS IN AN INNINGS FOR ENGLAND

J BIRKENSHAW (1)
5 : 57 v. Pakistan at Karachi, 1973

C H PARKIN (2)
5 : 60 v. Australia at Adelaide, 1921
5 : 38 v. Australia at Manchester, 1921

331

YORKSHIRE'S TEST CRICKET RECORDS

R APPLEYARD

Auckland 1954-55: took 3 wickets in 4 balls as New Zealand were dismissed for the lowest total in Test history (26).

C W J ATHEY

Perth 1986-87: shared an opening stand of 223 with B C Broad – England's highest for any wicket at the WACA Ground.

W BATES

Melbourne 1882-83 (Second Test): achieved the first hat-trick for England when he dismissed P S McDonnell, G Giffen and G J Bonnor in Australia's first innings. Later in the match, he became the first player to score a fifty (55) and take 10 or more wickets (14 for 102) in the same Test.

W E BOWES

Melbourne 1932-33: enjoyed the unique satisfaction of bowling D G Bradman first ball in a Test match (his first ball to him in Test cricket).

G BOYCOTT

Leeds 1967: scored 246 not out off 555 balls in 573 minutes to establish the record England score against India. His first 100 took 341 minutes (316 balls) and he was excluded from the next Test as a disciplinary measure; shared in hundred partnerships for three successive wickets.

Adelaide 1970-71: with J H Edrich, became the third opening pair to share hundred partnerships in both innings of a Test against Australia.

Port-of-Spain 1973-74: first to score 99 and a hundred in the same Test.

Nottingham 1977: with A P E Knott, equalled England v. Australia sixth-wicket partnership record of 215 – the only England v. Australia stand to be equalled or broken since 1938. Batted on each day of the five-day Test (second after M L Jaisimha to achieve this feat).

Leeds 1977: first to score his 100th First Class hundred in a Test; became the fourth England player to be on the field for an entire Test.

Perth: 1978-79: eighth to score 2,000 runs for England against Australia.

Birmingham 1979: emulated K F Barrington by scoring hundreds on each of England's six current home grounds.

Perth: 1979-80: fourth to carry his bat through a completed England.
innings (third v. Australia) and the first to do so without scoring 100; first to score 99 not out in a Test.

Lord's 1981: 100th Test for England – second after M C Cowdrey (1968).

The Oval, 1981: second after Hon F S Jackson to score five hundreds v. Australia in England.

Gained three Test records from M C Cowdrey: exceeded England aggregate of 7,624 runs in 11 fewer Tests (Manchester 1981); 61st fifty – world record (The Oval 1981); 189th innings – world record (Bangalore 1981-82).

Delhi, 4.23p.m. on 23 December 1981: passed G St.A Sobers's world Test record of 8,032 runs, having played 30 more innings and batted over 451 hours (cf. 15 complete five-day Tests); his 22nd hundred equalled the England record.

J T BROWN

Melbourne 1894-95: his 28-minute fifty remains the fastest in Test cricket, and his 95-minute hundred was a record until 1897-98; his third-wicket stand of 210 with A Ward set a Test record for any wicket.

YORKSHIRE'S TEST CRICKET RECORDS *(Continued)*

D B CLOSE

Manchester 1949: at 18 years 149 days he became – and remains – the youngest to represent England.

Melbourne 1950-51: became the youngest (19 years 301 days) to represent England against Australia.

T EMMETT

Melbourne 1878-79: first England bowler to take seven wickets in a Test innings.

P A GIBB

Johannesburg 1938-39: enjoyed a great England debut, scoring 93 and 106 as well as sharing second-wicket stands of 184 and 168 with E Paynter.

Durban 1938-39: shared record England v. South Africa second-wicket stand of 280 with W J Edrich, his 120 in 451 minutes including only two boundaries.

D GOUGH

Sydney 1998-99: achieved the 23rd hat-trick in Test cricket (ninth for England and first for England v. Australia since 1899).

Lord's 2001: took 3 wickets in 4 balls v. Pakistan.

S HAIGH

Cape Town 1898-99: bowled unchanged through the second innings with A E Trott, taking 6 for 11 as South Africa were dismissed for 35 in the space of 114 balls.

J H HAMPSHIRE

Lord's 1969: became the first England player to score 100 at Lord's on his debut in Tests.

A HILL

Melbourne 1876-77: took the first wicket to fall in Test cricket when he bowled N Thompson, and held the first catch when he dismissed T P Horan.

G H HIRST

The Oval: 1902: helped to score the last 15 runs in a match-winning tenth-wicket partnership with W Rhodes.

Birmingham 1909: shared all 20 Australian wickets with fellow left-arm spinner C Blythe (11 for 102).

M J HOGGARD

Bridgetown 2004: became the third Yorkshire player to take a hat-trick in Test cricket (see W Bates and D Gough). It was the 10th hat-trick for England and the third for England versus West Indies.

L HUTTON

Nottingham 1938: scored 100 in his first Test against Australia.

The Oval 1938: his score (364) and batting time (13 hours 17 minutes – the longest innings in English First-Class cricket) remain England records, and were world Test records until 1958. It remains the highest Test score at The Oval. His stand of 382 with M Leyland is the England second-wicket record in all Tests and the highest for any wicket against Australia. He also shared a record England v. Australia sixth-wicket stand of 216 with J Hardstaff Jr. – the first instance of a batsman sharing in two stands of 200 in the same Test innings. 770 runs were scored during his innings (Test record) which was England's 100th century against Australia, and contained 35 fours. England's total of 903 for 7 declared remains the Ashes Test record.

Lord's 1939: added 248 for the fourth wicket with D C S Compton in 140 minutes.

YORKSHIRE'S TEST CRICKET RECORDS *(Continued)*

L HUTTON *(Continued)*

The Oval 1939: shared (then) world-record third-wicket stand of 264 with W R Hammond, which remains the record for England v. West Indies. Hutton's last eight Tests had brought him 1,109 runs.

The Oval 1948: last out in the first innings, he was on the field for all but the final 57 minutes of the match.

Johannesburg 1948-49: shared (then) world-record first-wicket stand of 359 in 310 minutes with C Washbrook on the opening day of Test cricket at Ellis Park; it remains England's highest opening stand in all Tests.

The Oval 1950: scored England's first 200 in a home Test v. West Indies, and remains alone in carrying his bat for England against them; his 202 not out (in 470 minutes) is the highest score by an England batsman achieving this feat.

Adelaide 1950-51: only England batsman to carry his bat throughout a complete Test innings twice, and second after R Abel (1891-92) to do so for any country against Australia.

Manchester 1951: scored 98 not out, just failing to become the first to score his 100th First Class hundred in a Test match.

The Oval 1951: became the only batsman to be out 'obstructing the field' in Test cricket.

1952: first professional to be appointed captain of England in the 20th Century.

The Oval 1953: first captain to win a rubber after losing the toss in all five Tests.

Kingston 1953-54: scored the first 200 by an England captain in a Test overseas.

R ILLINGWORTH

Manchester 1971: shared record England v. India eighth-wicket stand of 168 with P. Lever.

Hon. F S JACKSON

The Oval 1893: his 100 took 135 minutes, and was the first in a Test in England to be completed with a hit over the boundary (then worth only four runs).

The Oval 1899: his stand of 185 with T W Hayward was then England's highest for any wicket in England, and the record opening partnership by either side in England v. Australia Tests.

Nottingham 1905: dismissed M A Noble, C Hill and J Darling in one over (W01W0W).

Leeds 1905: batted 268 minutes for 144 not out – the first hundred in a Headingley Test.

Manchester 1905: first to score five Test hundreds in England.

The Oval 1905: first captain to win every toss in a five-match rubber.

M LEYLAND

Melbourne 1928-29: scored 137 in his first innings against Australia.

1934: first to score three hundreds in a rubber against Australia in England.

Brisbane 1936-37: scored England's only 100 at 'The Gabba' before 1974-75.

The Oval 1938: contributed 187 in 381 minutes to the record Test total of 903 for 7 declared, sharing in England's highest stand against Australia (all wickets) and record second-wicket stand in all Tests: 382 with L Hutton. First to score hundreds in his first and last innings against Australia.

G G MACAULAY

Cape Town 1922-23: fourth bowler (third for England) to take a wicket (G A L Hearne) with his first ball in Test cricket. Made the winning hit in the fourth of only six Tests to be decided by a one-wicket margin.

Leeds 1926: shared a match-saving ninth-wicket stand of 108 with G Geary.

334

YORKSHIRE'S TEST CRICKET RECORDS *(Continued)*

C M OLD

Birmingham 1978: took 4 wickets in 5 balls in his 19th over (0WW no-ball WW1) to emulate the feat of M J C Allom.

R PEEL

Took his 50th wicket in his ninth Test and his 100th in his 20th Test – all against Australia.

W RHODES

Birmingham 1902: his first-innings analysis of 7 for 17 remains the record for all Tests at Edgbaston.

The Oval 1902: helped to score the last 15 runs in a match-winning tenth-wicket partnership with G H Hirst.

Sydney 1903-04: shared record England v. Australia tenth-wicket stand of 130 in 66 minutes with R E Foster.

Melbourne 1903-04: first to take 15 wickets in England v. Australia Tests; his match analysis of 15 for 124 remains the record for all Tests at Melbourne.

Melbourne 1911-12: shared record England v. Australia first-wicket stand of 323 in 268 minutes with J B Hobbs.

Johannesburg 1913-14: took his 100th wicket and completed the first 'double' for England (in 44 matches).

Sydney 1920-21: first to score 2,000 runs and take 100 wickets in Test cricket.

Adelaide 1920-21: third bowler to take 100 wickets against Australia.

The Oval 1926: set (then) record of 109 wickets against Australia.

Kingston 1929-30: ended the world's longest Test career (30 years 315 days) as the oldest Test cricketer (52 years 165 days).

H SUTCLIFFE

Birmingham 1924: shared the first of 15 three-figure partnerships with J B Hobbs at the first attempt.

Lord's 1924: shared stand of 268 with J B Hobbs, which remains the first-wicket record for all Lord's Tests, and was then the England v. South Africa record.

Sydney 1924-25: his first opening stands against Australia with J B Hobbs realised 157 and 110.

Melbourne 1924-25 (Second Test): with J B Hobbs achieved the first instance of a batting partnership enduring throughout a full day's Test match play; they remain the only England pair to achieve this feat, and their stand of 283 in 289 minutes remains the longest for the first wicket in this series. Became the first to score 100 in each innings of a Test against Australia, and the first Englishman to score three successive hundreds in Test cricket.

Melbourne 1924-25 (Fourth Test): first to score four hundreds in one rubber of Test matches; it was his third 100 in successive Test innings at Melbourne. Completed 1,000 runs in fewest Test innings (12) – since equalled.

Sydney 1924-25: his aggregate of 734 runs was the record for any rubber until 1928-29.

The Oval 1926: shared first-wicket stand of 172 with J B Hobbs on a rain-affected pitch.

The Oval 1929: first to score hundreds in each innings of a Test twice; only England batsman to score four hundreds in a rubber twice.

Sydney 1932-33: his highest England innings of 194 overtook J B Hobbs's world record of 15 Test hundreds.

F S TRUEMAN

Leeds 1952: reduced India to 0 for 4 in their second innings by taking 3 wickets in 8 balls on his debut.

Manchester 1952: achieved record England v. India innings analysis of 8 for 31.

The Oval 1952: set England v. India series record with 29 wickets.

F S TRUEMAN *(Continued)*

Leeds 1961: took 5 for 0 with 24 off-cutters at a reduced pace v. Australia.

Lord's 1962: shared record England v. Pakistan ninth-wicket stand of 76 with T W Graveney.

Christchurch 1962-63: passed J B Statham's world Test record of 242 wickets; his analysis of 7 for 75 remains the record for Lancaster Park Tests and for England in New Zealand.

Birmingham 1963: returned record match analysis (12 for 119) against West Indies in England and for any Birmingham Test, ending with a 6 for 4 spell from 24 balls.

The Oval 1963: set England v. West Indies series record with 34 wickets.

The Oval 1964: first to take 300 wickets in Tests.

G ULYETT

Sydney 1881-82: with R G Barlow shared the first century opening partnership in Test cricket (122).

Melbourne 1881-82: his 149 was the first Test hundred for England in Australia, and the highest score for England on the first day of a Test in Australia until 1965-66.

M P VAUGHAN

Scored 1481 runs in 2002 – more than any other England player in a calendar year, surpassing the 1379 scored by D L Amiss in 1979. It was the fourth highest in a calendar year.

Scored 633 runs in the 2002-3 series versus Australia – surpassed for England in a five Test series versus Australia only by W R Hammond, who scored 905 runs in 1928-29, H Sutcliffe (734 in 1924-25), J B Hobbs (662 in 1911-12) and G Boycott (657 in 1970-71), when he played in five of the six Tests.

Scored six Test Match centuries in 2002 to equal the record set for England by D C S Compton in 1947.

Lord's 2004: scored a century in each innings (103 and 101*) versus West Indies and so became the third player (after G A Headley and G A Gooch) to score a century in each innings of a Test match at Lord's.

Lord's 2005: only the second player (J B Hobbs is the other) to have scored centuries in three consecutive Test match innings at Lord's. Scored the 100th century for England by a Yorkshire player.

H VERITY

Lord's 1934: took 14 for 80 on the third day (six of them in the final hour) to secure England's first win against Australia at Lord's since 1896. It remains the most wickets to fall to one bowler in a day of Test cricket in England. His match analysis of 15 for 104 was then the England v. Australia record, and has been surpassed only by J C Laker.

W WATSON

Lord's 1953: scored 109 in 346 minutes in his first Test against Australia.

N W D YARDLEY

Melbourne 1946-47: dismissed D G Bradman for the third consecutive innings without assistance from the field. Became the first to score a fifty in each innings for England and take five wickets in the same match.

Nottingham 1947: shared record England v. South Africa fifth-wicket stand of 237 with D C S Compton.

* * *

Facts adapted by Bill Frindall from his *England Test Cricketers – The Complete Record from 1877* (Collins Willow, 1989). With later additions.

TEST MATCHES AT HEADINGLEY, LEEDS 1899-2010

1899 **Australia 172** (J Worrall 76) and **224** (H Trumble 56, J T Hearne hat-trick). **England 220** (A F A Lilley 55, H Trumble 5 for 60) and **19 for 0 wkt.**
Match drawn
Toss: Australia

1905 **England 301** (Hon F S Jackson 144*) and **295 for 5 wkts dec** (J T Tyldesley 100, T W Hayward 60, W W. Armstrong 5 for 122). **Australia 195** (W W Armstrong 66, A R Warren 5 for 57) and **224 for 7 wkts** (M A Noble 62).
Match drawn
Toss: England

1907 **England 76** (G A Faulkner 6 for 17) and **162** (C B Fry 54). **South Africa 110** (C Blythe 8 for 59) and **75** (C Blythe 7 for 40).
England won by 53 runs
Toss: England

1909 **Australia 188** and **207** (S F Barnes 6 for 63). **England 182** (J Sharp 61, J T Tyldesley 55, C G Macartney 7 for 58) and **87** (A Cotter 5 for 38).
Australia won by 126 runs
Toss: Australia

1912 **England 242** (F E Woolley 57) and **238** (R H Spooner 82, J B Hobbs 55). **South Africa 147** (S F Barnes 6 for 52) and **159**.
England won by 174 runs
Toss: England

1921 **Australia 407** (C G Macartney 115, W W Armstrong 77, C E Pellew 52, J M Taylor 50) and **273 for 7 wkts dec** (T J E Andrew 92). **England 259** (J W H T Douglas 75, Hon L H Tennyson 63, G Brown 57) and **202.**
Australia won by 219 runs
Toss: Australia

1924 **England 396** (E H Hendren 132, H Sutcliffe 83) and **60 for 1 wkt.** **South Africa 132** (H W Taylor 59*, M W Tate 6 for 42) and **323** (H W Taylor 56, R H Catterall 56).
England won by 9 wickets
Toss: England

1926 **Australia 494** (C G Macartney 151, W M Woodfull 141, A J Richardson 100). **England 294** (G G Macaulay 76, C V Grimmett 5 for 88) and **254 for 3 wkts** (H Sutcliffe 94, J B Hobbs 88).
Match drawn
Toss: England

1929 **South Africa 236** (R H Catterall 74, C L Vincent 60, A P Freeman 7 for 115) and **275** (H G Owen-Smith 129). **England 328** (F E Woolley 83, W R Hammond 65, N A Quinn 6 for 92) and **186 for 5 wkts** (F E Woolley 95*).
England won by 5 wickets
Toss: South Africa

1930 **Australia 566** (D G Bradman 334, A F Kippax 77, W M Woodfull 50, M W Tate 5 for 124). **England 391** (W R Hammond 113, C V Grimmett 5 for 135) and **95 for 3 wkts.**
Match drawn
Toss: Australia

1934 **England 200** and **229 for 6 wkts.** **Australia 584** (D G Bradman 304, W H Ponsford 181, W E Bowes 6 for 142).
Match drawn
Toss: England

1935 **England 216** (W R Hammond 63, A Mitchell 58) and **294 for 7 wkts dec** (W R Hammond 87*, A Mitchell 72, D Smith 57). **South Africa 171** (E A B Rowan 62) and **194 for 5 wkts** (B Mitchell 58).
Match drawn
Toss: England

1938 **England 223** (W R Hammond 76, W J O'Reilly 5 for 66) and **123** (.W J O'Reilly 5 for 56). **Australia 242** (D G Bradman 103, B A Barnett 57) and **107 for 5 wkts.**
Australia won by 5 wickets
Toss: England

1947 **South Africa 175** (B Mitchell 53, A Nourse 51) and **184** (A D Nourse 57). **England 317 for 7 wkts dec** (L Hutton 100, C Washbrook 75) and **47 for 0 wkt.**
England won by 10 wickets
Toss: South Africa

1948 **England 496** (C Washbrook 143, W J Edrich 111, L Hutton 81, A V Bedser 79) and **365 for 8 wkts dec** (D C S. Compton 66, C Washbrook 65, L Hutton 57, W J Edrich 54). **Australia 458** (R N Harvey 112, S J E Loxton 93, R R Lindwall 77, K R Miller 58) and **404 for 3 wkts** (A R Morris 182, D G Bradman 173*).
Australia won by 7 wickets
Toss: England

1949 **England 372** (D C S Compton 114, L Hutton 101, T B Burtt 5 for 97, J Cowie 5 for 127) and **267 for 4 wkts dec** (C Washbrook 103*, W J Edrich 70). **New Zealand 341** (F B Smith 96, M P Donnelly 64, T E Bailey 6 for 118) and **195 for 2 wkts** (B Sutcliffe 82, F Smith 54*).
Match drawn   Toss: England

1951 **South Africa 538** (E A B Rowan 236, P N F Mansell 90, C B. van Ryneveld 83, R A McLean 67) and **87 for 0 wkt** (E A B Rowan 60*). **England 505** (P B H May 138, L Hutton 100, T E Bailey 95, F A Lowson 58, A M B Rowan 5 for 174).
Match drawn   Toss: South Africa

1952 **India 293** (V L Manjrekar 133, V S Hazare 89) and 165 (D G Phadkar 64, V S Hazare 56). **England 334** (T W Graveney 71, T G Evans 66, Ghulam Ahmed 5 for 100) and **128 for 3 wkts** (R T Simpson 51).
England won by 7 wickets   Toss: India

1953 **England 167** (T W Graveney 55, R R Lindwall 5 for 54) and **275** (W J Edrich 64, D C S Compton 61). **Australia 266** (R N Harvey 71, G B Hole 53, A V Bedser 6 for 95) and **147 for 4 wkts.**
Match drawn   Toss: Australia

1955 **South Africa 171** and **500** (D J McGlew 133, W R Endean 116*, T L Goddard 74, H J Keith 73). **England 191** (D C S Compton 61) and **256** (P B H May 97, T L Goddard 5 for 69, H J Tayfield 5 for 94).
South Africa won by 224 runs   Toss: South Africa

1956 **England 325** (P B H May 101, C Washbrook 98). **Australia 143** (J C Laker 5 for 58) and **140** (R N Harvey 69, J C Laker 6 for 55).
England won by an innings and 42 runs   Toss: England

1957 **West Indies 142** (P J Loader 6 for 36, including hat-trick) and **132.** **England 279** (P B H May 69, M C Cowdrey 68, Rev D S Sheppard 68, F M M Worrell 7 for 70).
England won by an innings and 5 runs   Toss: West Indies

1958 **New Zealand 67** (J C Laker 5 for 17) and **129** (G A R Lock 7 for 51). **England 267 for 2 wkts dec** (P B H May 113*, C A Milton 104*).
England won by an innings and 71 runs   Toss: New Zealand

1959 **India 161** and **149.** **England 483 for 8 wkts dec** (M C Cowdrey 160, K F Barrington 80, W G A Parkhouse 78, G Pullar 75).
England won by an innings and 173 runs   Toss: India

1961 **Australia 237** (R N Harvey 73, C C McDonald 54, F S Trueman 5 for 58) and **120** (R N Harvey 53, F S Trueman 6 for 30); **England 299** (M C Cowdrey 93, G Pullar 53, A K Davidson 5 for 63) and **62 for 2 wkts.**
England won by 8 wickets   Toss: Australia

1962 **England 428** (P H Parfitt 119, M J Stewart 86, D A Allen 62, Munir Malik 5 for 128). **Pakistan 131** (Alimuddin 50) and **180** (Alimuddin 60, Saeed Ahmed 54).
England won by an innings and 117 runs   Toss: Pakistan

1963 **West Indies 397** (G St A Sobers 102, R B Kanhai 92, J S Solomon 62) and **229** (B F Butcher 78, G St.A Sobers 52). **England 174** (G A R Lock 53, C C Griffith 6 for 36) and **231** (J M Parks 57, D B Close 56).
West Indies won by 221 runs   Toss: West Indies

1964 **England 268** (J M Parks 68, E R Dexter 66, N J N Hawke 5 for 75) and 229 (K F Barrington 85). **Australia 389** (P J P Burge 160, W M Lawry 78) and **111 for 3 wkts** (I R Redpath 58*).
Australia won by 7 wickets   Toss: England

1965 **England 546 for 4 wkts dec** (J H Edrich 310*, K F Barrington 163). **New Zealand 193** (J R Reid 54) and **166** (V Pollard 53, F J Titmus 5 for 19).
England won by an innings and 187 runs   Toss: England

1966 **West Indies 500 for 9 wkts dec** (G.St.A Sobers 174, S M Nurse 137). **England 240** (B L D'Oliveira 88, G.St.A Sobers 5 for 41) and **205** (R W Barber 55, L R Gibbs 6 for 39).
West Indies won by an innings and 55 runs   Toss: West Indies

338

1967 **England 550 for 4 wkts dec** (G Boycott 246*, B L D'Oliveira 109, K F Barrington 93, T W Graveney 59) and **126 for 4 wkts**. **India 164** (Nawab of Pataudi jnr 64) and **510** (Nawab of Pataudi jnr 148, A L Wadekar 91, F M Engineer 87, Hanumant Singh 73).
England won by 6 wickets Toss: England

1968 **Australia 315** (I R Redpath 92, I M Chappell 65) and **312** (I M Chappell 81, K D Walters 56, R Illingworth 6 for 87). **England 302** (R M Prideaux 64, J H Edrich 62, A N Connolly 5 for 72) and **230 for 4 wkts** (J H Edrich 65).
Match drawn Toss: Australia

1969 **England 223** (J H Edrich 79) and **240** (G.St A Sobers 5 for 42). **West Indies 161** and **272** (B F Butcher 91, G S Camacho 71).
England won by 30 runs Toss: England

1971 **England 316** (G Boycott 112, B L D'Oliveira 74) and **264** (B L D'Oliveira 72, D L Amiss 56) **Pakistan 350** (Zaheer Abbas 72, Wasim Bari 63, Mushtaq Mohammad 57) and **205** (Sadiq Mohammad 91).
England won by 25 runs Toss: England

1972 **Australia 146** (K R Stackpole 52) and **136** (D L Underwood 6 for 45). **England 263** (R Illingworth 57, A A Mallett 5 for 114) and **21 for 1 wkt**.
England won by 9 wickets Toss: Australia

1973 **New Zealand 276** (M G Burgess 87, V Pollard 62) and **142** (G M Turner 81, G G Arnold 5 for 27). **England 419** (G Boycott 115, K W R Fletcher 81, R Illingworth 65, RO Collinge 5 for 74).
England won by an innings and 1 run Toss: New Zealand

1974 **Pakistan 285** (Majid Khan 75, Safraz Nawaz 53) and **179**. **England 183** and **238 for 6 wkts** (J H Edrich 70, K W R Fletcher 67*).
Match drawn Toss: Pakistan

1975 **England 288** (D S Steele 73, J H Edrich 62, A W Greig 51, G J Gilmour 6 for 85) and **291** (D S Steele 92). **Australia 135** (P H Edmonds 5 for 28) and **220 for 3 wkts** (R B McCosker 95*, I M Chappell 62).
Match drawn Toss: England

1976 **West Indies 450** (C G Greenidge 115, R C Fredericks 109, I V A Richards 66, L G Rowe 50) and **196** (C L King 58, R G D Willis 5 for 42). **England 387** (A W Greig 116, A P E Knott 116) and **204** (A W Greig 76*).
West Indies won by 55 runs Toss: West Indies

1977 **England 436** (G Boycott 191, A P E Knott 57). **Australia 103** (I T Botham 5 for 21) and **248** (R W Marsh 63).
England won by an innings and 85 runs Toss: England

1978 **Pakistan 201** (Sadiq Mohammad 97). **England 119 for 7 wkts** (Safraz Nawaz 5 for 39).
Match drawn Toss: Pakistan

1979 **England 270** (I T Botham 137). **India 223 for 6 wkts** (S M Gavaskar 78, D B Vengsarkar 65*).
Match drawn Toss: England

1980 **England 143 and 227 for 6 wkts dec** (G A Gooch 55). **West Indies 245**.
Match drawn Toss: West Indies

1981 **Australia 401 for 9 wkts dec** (J Dyson 102, K J Hughes 89, G N Yallop 58, I T Botham 6 for 95) and **111** (R G D Willis 8 for 43). **England 174** (I T Botham 50) and **356** (I T Botham 149*, G R Dilley 56, T M Alderman 5 for 135).
England won by 18 runs Toss: Australia

1982 **Pakistan 275** (Imran Khan 67*, Mudassar Nazar 65, Javed Miandad 54) and **199** (Javed Miandad 52, I T Botham 5 for 74). **England 256** (D I Gower 74, I T Botham 57, Imran Khan 5 for 49) and **219 for 7 wkts** (G Fowler 86).
England won by 3 wickets Toss: Pakistan

1983 **England 225** (C J Tavaré 69, A J Lamb 58, B L Cairns 7 for 74) and **252** (D I Gower 112*, E J Chatfield 5 for 95). **New Zealand 377** (J G Wright 93, B A Edgar 84, R J Hadlee 75) and **103 for 5 wkts** (R G D Willis 5 for 35).
New Zealand won by 5 wickets Toss: New Zealand

339

1984 **England 270** (A J Lamb 100) and **159** (G Fowler 50, M D Marshall 7 for 53). **West Indies 302** (H A Gomes 104*, M A Holding 59, P J W Allott 6 for 61) and **131 for 2 wkts.**
West Indies won by 8 wickets Toss: England

1985 **Australia 331** (A M J Hilditch 119) and **324** (W B Phillips 91, A M J Hilditch 80, K C Wessels 64, J E Emburey 5 for 82). **England 533** (R T Robinson 175, I T Botham 60, P R Downton 54, M W Gatting 53) and **123 for 5 wkts.**
England won by 5 wickets Toss: Australia

1986 **India 272** (D B Vengsarkar 61) and **237** (D B Vengsarkar 102*). **England 102** (R M H Binny 5 for 40) and **128.**
India won by 279 runs Toss: India

1987 **England 136** (D J Capel 53) and **199** (D I Gower 55, Imran Khan 7 for 40). **Pakistan 353** (Salim Malik 99, Ijaz Ahmed 50, N A Foster 8 for 107).
Pakistan won by an innings and 18 runs Toss: England

1988 **England 201** (A J Lamb 64*) and **138** (G A Gooch 50). **West Indies 275** (R A Harper 56, D L Haynes 54, D R Pringle 5 for 95) and **67 for 0 wkt.**
West Indies won by 10 wickets Toss: West Indies

1989 **Australia 601 for 7 wkts dec** (S R Waugh 177*, M A Taylor 136, D M Jones 79, M G Hughes 71, A R Border 66) and **230 for 3 wkts dec** (M A Taylor 60, A R Border 60*). **England 430** (A J Lamb 125, K J Barnett 80, R A Smith 66, T M Alderman 5 for 107) and **191.** (G A Gooch 68, T M Alderman 5 for 44).
Australia won by 210 runs Toss: England

1991 **England 198** (R A Smith 54) and **252** (G A Gooch 154*, C E L Ambrose 6 for 52). **West Indies 173** (I V A Richards 73) and **162** (R B Richardson 68).
England won by 115 runs Toss: West Indies

1992 **Pakistan 197** (Salim Malik 82*) and **221** (Salim Malik 84*, Ramiz Raja 63, N A Mallinder 5 for 50). **England 320** (G A Gooch 135, M A Atherton 76, Waqar Younis 5 for 117) and **99 for 4 wkts.**
England won by 6 wickets Toss: Pakistan

1993 **Australia 653 for 4 wkts dec** (A R Border 200*, S R Waugh 157*, D C Boon 107, M J Slater 67, M E Waugh 52). **England 200** (G A Gooch 59, M A Atherton 55, P R Reiffel 5 for 65) and **305** (A J Stewart 78, M A Atherton 63).
Australia won by an innings and 148 runs Toss: Australia

1994 **England 477 for 9 wkts dec** (M A Atherton 99, A J Stewart 89, G P Thorpe 72, S J Rhodes 65*) and **267 for 5 wkts dec** (G A Hick 110, G P Thorpe 73). **South Africa 447** (P N Kirsten 104, B M McMillan 78, C R Matthews 62*) and **116 for 3 wkts** (G Kirsten 65).
Match drawn Toss: England

1995 **England 199** (M A Atherton 81, I R Bishop 5 for 32) and **208** (G P Thorpe 61). **West Indies 282** (S L Campbell 69, J C Adams 58, B C Lara 53) and **129 for 1 wkt** (C L Hooper 73*).
West Indies won by 9 wickets Toss: West Indies

1996 **Pakistan 448** (Ijaz Ahmed 141, Mohin Khan 105, Salim Malik 55, Asif Mujtaba 51, D G Cork 5 for 113) and **242 for 7 wkts dec** (Inzamam-ul-Haq 65, Ijaz Ahmed sen 52) **England 501** (A J Stewart 170, N V Knight 113, J P Crawley 53).
Match drawn Toss: England

1997 **England 172** (J N. Gillespie 7 for 37) and **268** (N Hussain 105, J P Crawley 72, P R Reiffel 5 for 49). **Australia 501 for 9 wkts dec** (M T G Elliott 199, R T Ponting 127, P R Reiffel 54*, D Gough 5 for 149).
Australia won by an innings and 61 runs Toss: Australia

1998 **England 230** (M A Butcher 116) and **240** (N Hussain 94, S M Pollock 5 for 53, A A Donald 5 for 71). **South Africa 252** (W J. Cronje 57, A R C Fraser 5 for 42) and **195** (J N Rhodes 85, B M McMillan 54, D Gough 6 for 42).
England won by 23 runs Toss: England

2000 **West Indies 172** (R R Sarwan 59*, C White 5 for 57) and **61** (A R Caddick 5 for 14). **England 272** (M P Vaughan 76, G A Hick 59).
England won by an innings and 39 runs Toss: West Indies

340

2001   **Australia 447** (R T Ponting 144, D R Martyn 118, M E Waugh 72, D Gough 5 for 103)
and **176 for 4 wkts dec** (R T Ponting 72). **England 309** (A J Stewart 76*, G D McGrath
7 for 76) and **315 for 4 wkts** (M A Butcher 173*, N Hussain 55).
England won by 6 wickets   Toss: Australia

2002   **India 628 for 8 wkts dec** (S R Tendulkar 193, R S Dravid 148, S C Ganguly 128,
S B Bangar 68). **England 273** (A J Stewart 78*, M P Vaughan 61) and **309**
(N Hussain 110.)
India won by an innings and 46 runs   Toss: India

2003   **South Africa 342** (G Kirsten 130, M Zondeki 59, J A Rudolph 55) and **365** (A J Hall 99*,
G Kirsten 60). **England 307** (M A Butcher 77, M E Trescothick 59, A Flintoff 55) and **209**
(M A Butcher 61, A Flintoff 50, J H Kallis 6 for 54.)
South Africa won by 191 runs   Toss: South Africa

2004   **New Zealand 409** (S P Fleming 97, M H W Papps 86, B B McCullum 54) and **161.**
England 526 (M E Trescothick 132, G O Jones 100, A Flintoff 94, A J Strauss 62)
and **45 for 1 wkt**
England won by 9 wickets   Toss: England

2006   **England 515** (K P Pietersen 135, I R Bell 119, Umar Gul 5 for 123) and **345** (A J Strauss
116, M E Trescothick 58, C M W Reid 55). **Pakistan 538** (Mohammad Yousuf 192,
Younis Khan 173) and **155**.
England won by 167 runs   Toss: England

2007   **England 570 for 7 wkts dec** (K P Pietersen 226, M P Vaughan 103, M J Prior 75).
West Indies 146 and **141** (D J Bravo 52).
England won by an innings and 283 runs   Toss: England

2008   **England 203** and **327** (S C J Broad 67*, A N Cook 60). **South Africa 522** (A B de
Villiers 174, A G Prince 149) and **9 for 0 wkt**.
South Africa won by 10 wickets   Toss: South Africa

2009   **England 102** (P M Siddle 5 for 21) and **263** (G P Swann 62, S C J Broad 61, M G Johnson
5 for 69). **Australia 445** (M J North 110, M J Clarke 93, R T Ponting 78, S R Watson 51,
S C J Broad 6 for 91).
Australia won by an innings and 80 runs   Toss: England

2010   **Australia 88** and **349** (R T Ponting 66, M J Clarke 77, S P D Smith 77).
Pakistan 258 (S R Watson 6-33) and **180-7** (Imran Farhat 67, Azhar Ali 51).
Pakistan won by 3 wickets   Toss: Australia
(This was a Home Test Match for Pakistan)

SUMMARY OF RESULTS

ENGLAND	First played	Last played	Played	Won	Lost	Drawn
v. Australia	1899	2009	24	7	9	8
v. India	1952	2002	6	3	2	1
v. New Zealand	1949	2004	6	4	1	1
v. Pakistan	1962	2006	9	5	1	3
v. South Africa	1907	2008	12	6	3	3
v. West Indies	1957	2007	12	5	6	1
Totals	1899	2009	69	30	22	17

SIX HIGHEST AGGREGATES

Runs	Wkts	
1723	31	in 1948 (England 496 and 365 for 8 wkts dec; Australia 458 and 404 for 3 wkts)
1553	40	in 2006 (England 515 and 345; Pakistan 538 and 155)
1452	30	in 1989 (Australia 601 for 7 wkts dec and 230 for 3 wkts dec; England 430 and 191)
1350	28	in 1967 (England 550 for 4 wkts dec and 126 for 4 wkts; India 164 and 510)
1311	35	in 1985 (Australia 331 and 324; England 533 and 123 for 5 wkts)
1307	28	in 1994 (England 477 and 267 for 5 wkts dec; South Africa 447 and 116 for 3 wkts)

Note: The highest aggregate prior to the Second World War
| 1141 | 37 | in 1921 (Australia 407 and 272 for 7 wkts dec; England 259 and 202) |

SIX LOWEST AGGREGATES

Runs	Wkts	
423	40	in 1907 (England 76 and 162; South Africa 110 and 75)
463	22	in 1958 (New Zealand 67 and 129; England 267 for 2 wkts)
505	30	in 2000 (West Indies 172 and 61; England 272)
553	30	in 1957 (West Indies 142 and 132; England 279)
566	31	in 1972 (Australia 146 and 136; England 263 and 21 for 1 wkt)
608	30	in 1956 (England 325; Australia 143 and 140)

SIX HIGHEST TOTALS

653 for 4 wkts dec	Australia v. England, 1993
608 for 8 wkts dec	India v. England, 2002
601 for 7 wkts dec	Australia v. England, 1989
584	Australia v. England, 1934
570 for 7 wkts dec	England v. West Indies, 2007
566	Australia v. England, 1930

SIX LOWEST TOTALS

61	West Indies v. England, 2000
67	New Zealand v. England, 1958
75	South Africa v. England, 1907
76	England v. South Africa, 1907
87	England v Australia, 1909
88	Australia v. Pakistan, 2010

SIX HIGHEST INDIVIDUAL SCORES

For England

310*	J H Edrich versus New Zealand, 1965
246*	G Boycott versus India, 1967
226	K P Pietersen versus West Indies, 2007
191	G Boycott versus Australia, 1977
175	R T Robinson versus Australia, 1985
173*	M A Butcher versus Australia, 2001

For Australia

334	D G Bradman, 1930
304	D G Bradman, 1934
200*	A R Border, 1993
199	M T G Elliott, 1997
182	A R Morris, 1948
181	W H Ponsford, 1934

For Pakistan

192	Mohammad Yousuf, 2006
173	Younis Khan, 2006
141	Ijaz Ahmed, 1996
105	Moin Khan, 1996
99	Salim Malik, 1987
97	Sadiq Mohammad, 1978

For India

193	S R Tendulkar, 2002
148	Nawab of Pataudi jnr, 1967
148	R S Dravid, 2002
133	V L Manjrekar, 1952
128	S C Gangulay, 2002
102*	D B Vengsarkar, 1986

For South Africa

236	E A B Rowan, 1951
174	A B de Villiers, 2008
149	A G Prince, 2008
133	D J McGlew, 1955
130	G Kirsten, 2003
129	H G Owen-Smith, 1929

For New Zealand

97	S P Fleming, 2004
96	F B Smith, 1949
93	J G Wright, 1983
87	M G Burgess, 1973
86	M H W Papps, 2004
84	B A Edgar, 1983

For West Indies

174	G St.A Sobers, 1966
137	S M Nurse, 1966
115	C G. Greenidge, 1976
109	R C Fredericks, 1976
104*	H A Gomes, 1984
102	G St A Sobers, 1963

HUNDRED BEFORE LUNCH

First day

112*	C G Macartney for Australia, 1926
105*	D G Bradman for Australia, 1930

Third day

102	(from 27* to 129) H G Owen-Smith for South Africa, 1929

CARRYING BAT THROUGH A COMPLETED INNINGS

154* out of 252 G A Gooch, England v. West Indies, 1991

MOST CENTURIES IN AN INNINGS

3	1926	C G Macartney (151), W M Woodfull (141) and A J Richardson for Australia
3	1993	A R Border (200*), S R Waugh (157*) and D C Boon (107) for Australia
3	2002	S R Tendulkar (193), R S Dravid (148) and S C Ganguly (128) for India

MOST CENTURIES IN A MATCH

5	1948	C Washbrook (143) and W J Edrich (111) for England; R N Harvey (112), A R Morris (182) and D G Bradman (173*) for Australia
5	2006	K P Pietersen (135), I R Bell (119) and A J Strauss (116) for England; Younis Khan (173) and Mohammad Yousuf (192) for Pakistan
4	1976	C G Greenidge (115) and R C Fredericks (109) for West Indies; A W Greig (116) and A P E Knott (116) for England
4	1996	Ijaz Ahmed (141) and Moin Khan (105) for Pakistan; A J Stewart (170) and N V Knight (113) for England
4	2002	S R Tendulkar (193), R S Dravid (148) and S C Ganguly (128) for India; N Hussain (110) for England

CENTURY PARTNERSHIPS

For England
(six highest)
For the 1st wicket

168	L Hutton (81) and C Washbrook (143) v. Australia, 1948 (1st inns)
168	G A Gooch (135) and M A Atherton (76) v. Pakistan, 1992
158	M E Trescothick (58) and A J Strauss (116) v. Pakistan, 2006
156	J B Hobbs (88) and H Sutcliffe (94) v. Australia, 1926
153	M E Trescothick (132) and A J Strauss (62) v. New Zealand, 2004
146	W G A Parkhouse (78) and G Pullar (75) v. India, 1959

For all other wickets

369	(2nd wkt) J H Edrich (310*) and K F Barrington (163) v. New Zealand, 1965
252	(4th wkt) G Boycott (246*) and B L D'Oliveira (109) v. India, 1967
194*	(3rd wkt) C A Milton (104*) and P B H May (113*) v. New Zealand, 1958
193	(4th wkt) M C Cowdrey (160) and K F Barrington (80) v. India, 1959
187	(4th wkt) P B H May (101) and C Washbrook (98) v. Australia, 1956
181	(3rd wkt) M A Butcher (173*) and N Hussain (55) v. Australia, 2001

For Australia
(six highest)
For the 1st wkt – none

For all other wickets

388	(4th wkt) W H Ponsford (181) and D G Bradman (304), 1934
332*	(5th wkt) A R Border (200*) and S R Waugh (157*), 1993
301	(2nd wkt) A R Morris (182) and D G Bradman (173*), 1948
268	(5th wkt) M T G Elliott (199) and R T Ponting (127), 1997
235	(2nd wkt) W M Woodfull (141) and C G Macartney (151), 1926
229	(3rd wkt) D G Bradman (334) and A F Kippax (77), 1930

CENTURY PARTNERSHIPS
(in total)
For India

249	(4th wkt) S R Tendulkar (193) and S C Gangulay (128), 2002
222	(4th wkt) V S Hazare (89) and V L Manjrekar (133), 1952
170	(2nd wkt) S B Bangar (68) and R S Dravid (148), 2002
168	(2nd wkt) F M Engineer (87) and A L Wadekar (91), 1967
150	(3rd wkt) R S Dravid (148) and S R Tendulkar (193), 2002
134	(5th wkt) Hanumant Singh (73) and Nawab of Pataudi jnr (148), 1967
105	(6th wkt) V S Hazare (56) and D G Phadkar (64), 1952

For New Zealand

169	(2nd wkt) M H W Papps (86) and S P Fleming (97), 2004
120	(5th wkt) M P Donnelly (64) and F B Smith (96), 1949
116	(2nd wkt) J G Wright (93) and M D Crowe (37), 1983
112	(1st wkt) B Sutcliffe (82) and V J Scott (43), 1949
106	(5th wkt) M G Burgess (87) and V Pollard (62), 1973

For Pakistan

363	(3rd wkt) Younis Khan (173) and Mohammad Yousuf (192), 2006
130	(4th wkt) Ijaz Ahmed (141) and Salim Malik (55), 1996
129	(3rd wkt) Zaheer Abbas (72) and Mushtaq Mohammed (57), 1971
112	(7th wkt) Asif Mujtaba (51) and Moin Khan (105), 1996
110	(2nd wkt) Imran Farhat (67) and Azhar Ali (51), 2010 v. Australia
100	(3rd wkt) Mudassar Nazar (65) and Javed Miandad (54), 1982
100	(4th wkt) Majid Khan (75) and Zaheer Abbas (48), 1974

For South Africa

212	(5th wkt) A G Prince (149) and A B de Villiers (174), 2008
198	(2nd wkt) E A B Rowan (236) C B van Ryneveld (83), 1951
176	(1st wkt) D J McGlew (133) and T L Goddard (74), 1955
150	(8th wkt) G Kirsten (130) and M Zondeki (59), 2003
117	(6th wkt) J N Rhodes (85) and B M McMillan (54), 1998
115	(7th wicket) P N Kirsten (104) and B M McMillan (78), 1994
108	(5th wkt) E A B Rowan (236) and R A McLean (67), 1951
103	(10th wkt) H G Owen-Smith (129) and A J Bell (26*), 1929

For West Indies

265	(5th wkt) S M Nurse (137) and G St A Sobers (174), 1966
192	(1st wkt) R C Fredericks (109) and C G Greenidge (115), 1976
118*	(2nd wkt) C L Hooper (73*) and B C Lara (48*), 1995
143	(4th wkt) R B Kanhai (92) and G St A Sobers (102), 1963
108	(3rd wkt) G S Camacho (71) and B F Butcher (91), 1969
106	(1st wkt) C G Greenidge (49) and D L Haynes (43), 1984

6 BEST INNINGS ANALYSES
For England

8 for 43	R G D Willis v. Australia, 1981
8 for 59	C Blythe v. South Africa, 1907 (1st inns)
8 for 107	N A Foster v. Pakistan, 1987
7 for 40	C Blythe v. South Africa, 1907 (2nd inns)
7 for 51	G A R Lock v. New Zealand, 1958
7 for 115	A P Freeman v. South Africa, 1929

For Australia

7 for 37	J N Gilliespie, 1997
7 for 58	C G Macartney, 1909
7 for 76	G D McGrath, 2001
6 for 33	S R Watson, 2010 v. Pakistan
6 for 85	G J Gilmour, 1975
6 for 135	T M Alderman, 1981

5 WICKETS IN AN INNINGS

For India (2)

5 for 40	R M H Binny, 1986
5 for 100	Ghulam Ahmed, 1952

For New Zealand (5)

7 for 74	B L Cairns, 1983
5 for 74	R O Collinge, 1973
5 for 95	E J Chatfield, 1983
5 for 97	T B Burtt, 1949
5 for 127	J Cowie, 1949

For Pakistan (6)

7 for 40	Imran Khan, 1987
5 for 39	Sarfraz Nawaz, 1978
5 for 49	Imran Khan, 1982
5 for 117	Waqar Younis, 1992
5 for 123	Umar Gul, 2006
5 for 128	Munir Malik, 1962

For South Africa (7)

6 for 17	G A Faulkner, 1907
6 for 92	N A Quinn, 1929
6 for 54	J H Kallis, 2003
5 for 53	S M Pollock, 1998
5 for 69	T L Goddard, 1955
5 for 71	A A Donald, 1998
5 for 94	H J Tayfield, 1955
5 for 174	A M B Rowan, 1951

For West Indies (8)

7 for 53	M D Marshall, 1984
7 for 70	F M Worrell, 1957
6 for 36	C C Griffith, 1963
6 for 39	L R Gibbs, 1996
6 for 52	C E L Ambrose, 1991
5 for 32	I R Bishop, 1995
5 for 41	G.St.A Sobers, 1966
5 for 42	G.St A Sobers, 1969

10 WICKETS IN A MATCH

For England (7)

15 for 99	(8 for 59 and 7 for 40)	C Blythe v. South Africa, 1907
11 for 65	(4 for 14 and 7 for 51)	G A R Lock v. New Zeland, 1958
11 for 88	(5 for 58 and 6 for 30)	F S Trueman v. Australia, 1961
11 for 113	(5 for 58 and 6 for 55)	J C Laker v. Australia, 1956
10 for 82	(4 for 37 and 6 for 45)	D L Underwood v. Australia, 1972
10 for 115	(6 for 52 and 4 for 63)	S F Barnes v. South Africa, 1912
10 for 207	(7 for 115 and 3 for 92)	A P Freeman v. South Africa, 1929

For Australia (3)

11 for 85	(7 for 58 and 4 for 27)	C G Macartney, 1909
10 for 122	(5 for 66 and 5 for 56)	W J O'Reilly, 1938
10 for 151	(5 for 107 and 5 for 44)	T M Alderman, 1989

For New Zealand (1)

10 for 144	(7 for 74 and 3 for 70)	B L Cairns, 1983

For Pakistan (1)

10 for 77	(3 for 37 and 7 for 40)	Imran Khan, 1987

Note: Best bowling in a match for:

India:	7 for 58 (5 for 40 and 2 for 18) R M H Binney, 1986
South Africa:	9 for 75 (6 for 17 and 3 for 58) G A Faulkner, 1907
West Indies:	9 for 81 (6 for 36 and 3 for 45) C C Griffith, 1963

HAT-TRICKS

J T Hearne v. Australia, 1899
P J Loader v. West Indies, 1957

TEST MATCH AT BRAMALL LANE, SHEFFIELD 1902

1902 **Australia 194** (S F Barnes 6 for 49) and **289** (C Hill 119, V T Trumper 62, W Rhodes 5 for 63) **England 145** (J V Saunders 5 for 50, M A Noble 5 for 51) and **195** (A C MacLaren 63, G L Jessop 55, M A Noble 6 for 52).
Australia won by 143 runs Toss: Australia

For England YORKSHIRE ONE-DAY INTERNATIONAL CRICKETERS 1971-2010 (Correct to February 2, 2011)

Player	M	I	NO	Runs	HS	Av'ge	100s	50s	Balls	Runs	W	Av'ge	Best	4wI	Ct/St
ATHEY, C W J ...1980-88	31	30	3	848	142*	31.40	2	4	—	—	—	—	—	—	16
BAIRSTOW, D L ...1979-84	21	20	6	206	23*	14.71	—	—	—	—	—	—	—	—	17/4
BLAKEY, R J ...1992-93	3	2	0	25	25	12.50	—	—	—	—	—	—	—	—	2/1
BOYCOTT, G ...1971-81	36	34	4	1082	105	36.06	1	9	168	105	5	21.00	2-14	—	5
BRESNAN, T T ...2006-11	35	29	11	455	80	25.27	—	1	1713	1523	40	38.07	4-28	1	8
COPE, G A ...1977-78	2	1	1	1	1*	—	—	—	112	35	2	17.50	1-16	—	—
GOUGH, D ...1994-2006	158	87	38	609	46*	12.42	—	—	8422	6154	234	26.29	5-44	10	24
HAMPSHIRE, J H ...1971-72	3	3	1	48	25*	24.00	—	—	—	—	—	—	—	—	—
HOGGARD, M J ...2001-06	26	6	2	17	7	4.25	—	—	1306	1152	32	36.00	5-49	1	5
JARVIS, P W ...1988-93	16	8	2	31	16*	5.16	—	—	879	672	24	28.00	5-35	2	1
LOVE, J D ...1981	3	3	0	61	43	20.33	—	—	—	—	—	—	—	—	1
McGRATH, A ...2003-04	14	12	2	166	52	16.60	—	1	228	175	4	43.75	1-13	—	4
MOXON, M D ...1985-88	8	8	0	174	70	21.75	—	1	—	—	—	—	—	—	5
OLD, C M ...1973-81	32	25	7	338	51*	18.77	—	1	1755	999	45	22.20	4-8	2	8
RASHID, A U ...2009	5	4	1	60	31*	20.00	—	—	204	191	3	63.66	1-16	—	2
ŷSHAHZAD, A ...2010-11	9	6	1	32	9	6.40	—	—	480	394	14	28.14	3-41	—	4
SIDEBOTTOM, R J ...2001-10	25	18	8	133	24	13.30	—	—	1277	1039	29	35.82	3-19	—	6
SILVERWOOD, C E W ...1996-2001	7	4	0	17	12	4.25	—	—	306	244	6	40.66	3-43	—	—
STEVENSON, G B ...1980-81	4	4	3	43	28*	43.00	—	—	192	125	7	17.85	4-33	1	2
VAUGHAN, M P ...2001-07	86	83	10	1982	90*	27.15	—	16	796	649	16	40.56	4-22	1	25
WHITE, C ...1994-2003	51	41	5	568	57*	15.77	—	1	2364	1726	65	26.55	5-21	2	12
For Scotland															
BLAIN, J A R ...1999-2009	33	25	6	284	41	14.94	—	—	1329	1173	41	28.60	5-22	4	8
HAMILTON, G M 1999-2010	38	38	3	1231	119	35.17	2	7	220	160	3	53.33	2-36	—	6/1

YORKSHIRE PLAYERS WHO PLAYED ALL THEIR ONE-DAY INTERNATIONAL CRICKET AFTER LEAVING YORKSHIRE

For England

Player	M	I	NO	Runs	HS	Av'ge	100s	50s	Balls	Runs	W	Av'ge	Best	4wI	Ct/St
BATTY, G J 2002-09	10	8	2	30	17	5.00	—	—	440	366	5	73.20	2-40	—	4
CLOSE, D B 1972	3	3	0	49	43	16.33	—	—	18	21	0	—	—	—	1
GRAYSON, A P 2000-01	2	2	0	6	6	3.00	—	—	90	60	3	20.00	3-40	—	1
ILLINGWORTH, R .1971-72	3	2	0	5	4	2.50	—	—	130	84	4	21.00	3-50	—	1
RHODES, S J 1989-95	9	8	2	107	56	17.83	—	1							9/2
WHARF, A G 2004-05	13	5	3	19	9	9.50	—	—	584	428	18	23.77	4-24	1	1
WOOD, B 1972-82	13	12	2	314	78*	31.40	—	2	420	224	9	24.88	2-14	—	6

Overseas Players

(Qualification: 24 List A matches for Yorkshire)

For Australia

Player	M	I	NO	Runs	HS	Av'ge	100s	50s	Balls	Runs	W	Av'ge	Best	4wI	Ct/St
BEVAN, M G 1994-2004	232	196	67	6912	108*	53.58	6	46	1,966	1655	36	45.97	3-36	—	128
JAQUES, P A 2006-2007	6	6	0	125	94	20.83	1	1	—	—	—	—	—	—	3
LEHMANN, D S . 1996-2005	117	101	22	3078	119	38.96	4	17	1,793	1445	52	27.78	4-7	1	26

For South Africa

Player	M	I	NO	Runs	HS	Av'ge	100s	50s	Balls	Runs	W	Av'ge	Best	4wI	Ct/St
RUDOLPH, J A 2003-06	43	37	6	1157	81	37.32	—	7	24	26	0	—	—	—	11

For West Indies

Player	M	I	NO	Runs	HS	Av'ge	100s	50s	Balls	Runs	W	Av'ge	Best	4wI	Ct/St
RICHARDSON, R B 1983-96	224	217	30	6248	122	33.41	5	44	58	46	1	46.00	1-4	—	75

LIMITED-OVERS INTERNATIONAL MATCHES
AT HEADINGLEY, LEEDS 1973-2011

1973 **West Indies** 181 (54 overs) (R B Kanhai 55). **England** 182 for 9 wkts (54.3 overs)
(M H Denness 66).
England won by 1 wicket   Award: M H Denness

1974 **India** 265 (53.5 overs) (B P Patel 82, A L Wadekar 67). **England** 266 for 6 wkts (51.1
overs) (J H Edrich 90).
England won by 4 wickets   Award: J H Edrich

1975 **Australia** 278 for 7 wkts (60 overs) (R Edwards 80*). **Pakistan** 205 (53 overs) (Majid
Khan 65, Asif Iqbal 53, D K Lillee 5 for 34).
Australia won by 73 runs   Award: D K Lillee

1975 **East Africa** 120 (55.3 overs). **India** 123 for 0 wkt (29.5 overs) (S M Gavaskar 65*
F M Engineer 54*).
India won by 10 wickets   Award: F M Engineer

1975 **England** 93 (36.2 overs) (G J Gilmour 6 for 14). **Australia** 94 for 6 wkts (28.4 overs).
Australia won by 4 wickets   Award: G J Gilmour

1979 **Canada** 139 for 9 wkts (60 overs). **Pakistan** 140 for 2 wkts (40.1 overs) (Sadiq
Mohammed 57*).
Pakistan won by 8 wickets   Award: Sadiq Mohammed

1979 **India** 182 (55.5 overs) (S M Gavaskar 55). **New Zealand** 183 for 2 wkts (57 overs)
(B A Edgar 84*).
New Zealand won by 8 wickets   Award: B A Edgar

1979 **England** 165 for 9 wkts (60 overs). **Pakistan** 151 (56 overs) (Asif Iqbal 51, M
Hendrick 4 for 15)
England won by 14 runs   Award: M Hendrick

1980 **West Indies** 198 (55 overs) (C G Greenidge 78). **England** 174 (51.2 overs) (C J Tavaré
82*).
West Indies won by 24 runs   Award: C J Tavaré

1981 **Australia** 236 for 8 wkts (55 overs) (G M Wood 108). **England** 165 (46.5 overs) (R M
Hogg 4 for 29).
Australia won by 71 runs   Award: G M Wood

1982 **India** 193 (55 overs) (Kapil Dev 60, I T Botham 4 for 56). **England** 194 for 1 wkt
(50.1 overs) (B Wood 78*, C J Tavaré 66).
England won by 9 wickets   Award: B Wood

1983 **West Indies** 252 for 9 wkts (60 overs) (H A Gomes 78). **Australia** 151 (30.3 overs)
(W W Davis 7 for 51).
West Indies won by 101 runs   Award: W W Davis

1983 **Pakistan** 235 for 7 wkts (60 overs) (Imran Khan 102*, Shahid Mahboob 77, A L F de
Mel 5 for 39). **Sri Lanka** 224 (58.3 overs) (S Wettimuny 50, Abdul Qadir 5 for 44).
Pakistan won by 11 runs   Award: Abdul Qadir

1983 **Sri Lanka** 136 (50.4 overs). **England** 137 for 1 wkt (24.1 overs) (G Fowler 81*).
England won by 9 wickets   Award: R G D Willis

1986 **New Zealand** 217 for 8 wkts (55 overs) (J J Crowe 66). **England** 170 (48.2 overs).
New Zealand won by 47 runs   Award: J J Crowe

1988 **England** 186 for 8 wkts (55 overs). **West Indies** 139 (46.3 overs).
England won by 47 runs   Award: D R Pringle

1990 **England** 295 for 6 wkts (55 overs) (R A Smith 128, G A Gooch 55). **New Zealand**
298 for 6 wkts (54.5 overs) (M J Greatbatch 102*, J G Wright 52, A H Jones 51).
New Zealand won by 4 wickets   Award: M J Greatbatch

1990 **England** 229 (54.3 overs) (A J Lamb 56, D I Gower 50). **India** 233 for 4 wkts (53
overs) (S V Manjrekar 82, M Azharuddin 55*).
India won by 6 wickets   Award: A Kumble

348

LIMITED-OVERS INTERNATIONAL MATCHES
AT HEADINGLEY, LEEDS 1973-2011 *(Continued)*

1996 **India 158** (40.2 overs). **England 162 for 4 wkts** (39.3 overs) (G P Thorpe 79*).
England won by 6 wickets   **Award: G P Thorpe**

1997 **Australia 170 for 8 wkts** (50 overs).**England 175 for 4 wkts** (40.1 overs) (G P
Thorpe 75*, A J Hollioake 66*).
England won by 6 wickets.   **Award: G P Thorpe**

1998 **South Africa 205 for 8 wkts** (50 overs) (S M Pollock 56). **England 206 for 3 wkts**
(35 overs) (A D Brown 59, N V Knight 51).
England won by 7 wickets   **Award: A D Brown**

1999 **Pakistan 275 for 8 wkts** (50 overs) (Inzamam-ul-Haq 81, Abdur Razzaq 60). **Australia
265** (49.5 overs) (M G Bevan 61, Wasim Akram 4-40).
Pakistan won by 10 runs   **Award: Inazmam-ul-Haq**

1999 **Zimbabwe 175** (49.3 overs) (M A Goodwin 57). **New Zealand 70 for 3 wkts** (15
overs).
No result   **No Award**

1999 **South Africa 271 for 7 wkts** (50 overs) (H H Gibbs 101, D J Cullinan 50). **Australia
275 for 5 wkts** (49.4 overs) (S R. Waugh 120*, R T Ponting 69).
Australia won by 5 wickets   **Award: S R Waugh**

2001 **England 156 (45.2 overs)** (B C Hollioake 53, Waqar Younis 7 for 36). **Pakistan 153
for 4 wkts** (39.5 overs) (Abdur Razzaq 75).
Pakistan won — England conceding the match following a pitch invasion.
                                                              Award: Waqar Younis

2002 **Sri Lanka 240 for 7 wkts** (32 overs) (S T Jayasuriya 112). **England 241 for 7 wkts**
(31.2 overs) (M E Trescothick 82).
England won by 3 wkts   **Award: S T Jayasuriya**

2003 **England 81 for 4 wkts. Zimbabwe did not bat.**
No result   **No Award**

2004 **West Indies 159** (40.1 overs). **England 160 for 3 wkts** (22 overs) (M E Trescothick 55).
England won by 7 wickets   **Award: S J Harmison**

2005 **Bangladesh 208 for 7 wkts** (50 overs) (Belim 81, A Flintoff 4-29). **England 209
for 5 wkts** (38.5 overs) (A J Strauss 98)
England won by 5 wickets   **Award: A J Strauss**

      Australia 219 for 7 wkts (50 overs) (P D Collingwood 4-34). **England 221 for 1 wkt**
(46 overs) (M E Trescothick 104*, M P Vaughan 59*).
England won by 9 wickets   **Award: M E Trescothick**

2006 **England 321 for 7 wkts** (50 overs) (M E Trescothick 121, S L Malinga 4-44).
Sri Lanka 324 for 2 wkts (37.3 overs) (S T Jayasuriya 152, W U Tharanga 109).
Sri Lanka won by 8 wickets   **Award: S T Jayasuriya**

2007 **India 324 for 6 wkts** (50 overs) (Yuvraj Singh 72, S R Tendulkar 71, S C Ganguly
59, G Gambhir 51). **England 242 for 8 wkts** (39 overs) (P D Collingwood 91*)
India won by 38 runs *(D/L Method)*   **Award: S C Ganguly**

2008 **England 275 for 4 wkts** (50 overs) (K P Pietersen 90*, A Flintoff 78). **South Africa 255**
(J H Kallis 52).
England won by 20 runs   **Award: K P Pietersen**

2009 **England v. West Indies**   **Match abandoned without a ball bowled**

2010 **Pakistan 294 for 8 wkts** (50 overs) (Kamran Akmal 74, Asad Shafiq 50, S C J Broad
4-81). **England 295 for 6 wkts** (A J Strauss 126, I J L Trott 53)
England won by 4 wickets   **Award: A J Strauss**

2011 **Sri Lanka 309 for 5 wkts** (50 overs) (D P M D Jayawardene 144, K C Sangakkara 69)
England 240 all out (E J G Morgan 52)
Sri Lanka won by 69 runs   **Award: D P M D Jayawardene**

SUMMARY OF RESULTS

ENGLAND	Played	Won	Lost
v. Australia	4	2	2
v. Bangladesh	1	1	0
v. India	5	3	2
v. New Zealand	2	0	2
v. Pakistan	3	2	1
v. South Africa	2	2	0
v. Sri Lanka	4	2	2
v. West Indies	4	3	1
v. Zimbabwe	1*	0	0
Totals	26	15	10

*No result. In addition one match v. West Indies abandoned

AUSTRALIA	Played	Won	Lost
v. England	4	2	2
v. Pakistan	2	1	1
v. South Africa	1	1	0
v. West Indies	1	0	1
Totals	8	4	4

BANGLADESH	Played	Won	Lost
v. England	1	0	1
Totals	1	0	1

INDIA	Played	Won	Lost
v. England	5	2	3
v. East Africa	1	1	0
v. New Zealand	1	0	1
Totals	7	3	4

NEW ZEALAND	Played	Won	Lost
v. England	2	2	0
v. India	1	1	0
v. Zimbabwe	1*	0	0
Totals	4	3	0

*No result

PAKISTAN	Played	Won	Lost
v. Australia	2	1	1
v. Canada	1	1	0
v. England	3	1	2
v. Sri Lanka	1	1	0
Totals	7	4	3

SOUTH AFRICA	Played	Won	Lost
v. Australia	1	0	1
v. England	2	0	2
Totals	3	0	3

SRI LANKA	Played	Won	Lost
v. England	4	2	2
v. Pakistan	1	0	1
Totals	5	2	3

SUMMARY OF RESULTS *(Continued)*

WEST INDIES	Played	Won	Lost
v. Australia	1	1	0
v. England	4	1	3
Totals	5	2	3

In addition one match abandoned

ZIMBABWE	Played	Won	Lost
v. England	1*	0	0
v. New Zealand	1*	0	0
Totals	2*	0	0

*No result

CANADA	Played	Won	Lost
v. Pakistan	1	0	1

EAST AFRICA	Played	Won	Lost
v. India	1	0	1

CENTURIES

152	S J Jayasuriya for Sri Lanka v. England, 2006
144	D P M D Jayawardene Sri Lanka v. England, 2011
128	R A Smith for England v. New Zealand, 1990
126	A J Strauss for England v. Pakistan, 2010
121	M E Trescothick for England v. Sri Lanka, 2006
120*	S R Waugh for Australia v. South Africa, 1999
112	S J Jayasuriya for Sri Lanka v. England, 2002
109	W U Tharanga for Sri Lanka v. England, 2006
108	G M Wood for Australia v. England, 1981
104*	M E Trescothick for England v. Australia, 2005
102*	Imran Khan for Pakistan v. Sri Lanka, 1983
102*	M J Greatbatch for New Zealand v. England, 1990
101	H H Gibbs for South Africa v. Australia,1999

4 WICKETS IN AN INNINGS

7 for 36	Waqar Younis for Pakistan v. Pakistan, 2001
7 for 51	W W Davis for West Indies v. Australia, 1983
6 for 14	G J Gilmour for Australia v. England, 1975
5 for 34	D K Lillee for Australia v. England, 1975
5 for 39	A L F de Mel for Sri Lanka v. Pakistan, 1983
5 for 44	Abdul Qadir for Pakistan v. Sri Lanka, 1983
4 for 15	M Hendrick for England v. Pakistan, 1979
4 for 29	R M Hogg for Australia v England, 1981
4 for 29	A Flintoff for England v. Bangladesh, 2005
4 for 34	P D Collingwood for England v. Australia, 2005
4 for 40	Wasim Akram for Pakistan v. Australia, 1999
4 for 44	S L Malinga for Sri Lanka v. England, 2006
4 for 56	I T Botham for England v. India, 1982
4 for 81	S J C Broad for England v. Pakistan, 2010

LIMITED-OVERS INTERNATIONAL MATCHES
AT NORTH MARINE ROAD, SCARBOROUGH 1976-1978

1976 **England 202 for 8 wkts** (55 overs) (G D Barlow 80*, A M E Roberts 4 for 32).
West Indies 207 for 4 wkts (41 overs) (I V A Richards 119*).
West Indies won by 6 wickets   **Award: I V A Richards**

1978 **England 206 for 8 wkts** (55 overs) (G A Gooch 94, B L Cairns 5 for 28).
New Zealand 187 for 8 wkts (55 overs) (B E Congdon 52*).
England won by 19 runs   **Award: G A Gooch**

LIST OF PLAYERS AND CAREER AVERAGES IN ALL FIRST-CLASS MATCHES FOR YORKSHIRE 1863–2011

Based on research by John T Potter, Roy D Wilkinson and the late Anthony Woodhouse

The Editor and Statistics Editor welcome any information which will help in keeping this list up to date. The present compilers do not believe that we should alter the status of matches from that determined at the time they were played. Therefore, these averages include the match versus Gentlemen of Scotland in 1878, and exclude the matches versus Liverpool and District played in 1889, 1891, 1892 and 1893 in line with what appear to be the decisions of the Club at the time.

* Played as an amateur © Awarded County Cap § Born outside Yorkshire

Player	Date of Birth	Date of Death (if known)	First Played	Last Played	M	Inns	NO	Runs	HS	Av'ge	100s	Runs	Wkts	Av'ge	Ct/St
Ackroyd, A *	Aug. 29, 1858	Oct. 3, 1927	1879	1879	1	1	1	2	2*	—	0	7	0	—	—
Allen, S *	Dec. 20, 1893	Oct. 9, 1978	1924	1924	1	1	0	8	6	4.00	0	116	2	58.00	—
Allen, W R	Apr14, 1893	Oct 14, 1950	1921	1925	30	32	10	475	95*	21.59	0	—	—	—	45/21
Ambler, J	Feb 12, 1860	Feb 10 1899	1886	1886	4	7	1	68	25	9.71	0	22	0	—	2
Anderson, G	Jan 20, 1826	Nov 27, 1902	1851	1869	19	31	6	520	99*	20.80	0	—	—	—	19
Anderson, P N	Apr. 28, 1966		1988	1988	1	1	0	0	0	0.00	0	—	—	—	1
Anson, C E *	Oct 14, 1889	Mar 26, 1969	1924	1924	1	2	0	27	14	13.50	0	47	1	47.00	1
Appleton, C *	May15, 1844	Feb 26, 1925	1865	1865	3	6	1	56	18	11.20	0	—	—	—	1
Appleyard, R	© June 27, 1924		1950	1958	133	122	43	679	63	8.59	0	9,903	642	15.42	70
Armitage, C I *	Apr 24, 1849	Apr 24, 1917	1873	1878	3	5	0	26	12	5.20	0	29	0	—	—
Armitage, T	Apr 25, 1848	Sept 21, 1922	1872	1878	52	85	8	1,053	95	13.67	0	1,614	107	15.08	20
Ash, D L	Feb 18, 1944		1965	1965	3	3	0	22	12	7.33	0	22	0	—	—
Ashman, J R	May 20, 1926		1951	1951	1	1	1	0	0*	—	0	116	4	29.00	—
Ashraf, Moin A	© **Jan 5, 1992**		2010	2011	**11**	**13**	**1**	**42**	**10**	**3.50**	**0**	**773**	**22**	**35.13**	**1**
Aspinall, R	© Oct 26, 1918	Aug 16, 1999	1946	1950	36	48	8	763	75*	19.07	0	2,670	131	20.38	18
Aspinall, W	Mar 24, 1858	Not known	1880	1880	2	3	0	16	14	5.33	0	—	—	—	1
Asquith, F T	Feb 5, 1870	Jan 11, 1916	1903	1903	1	1	0	0	0	0.00	0	—	—	—	—
Athey, C W J	© Sept 27, 1957		1976	1983	151	246	21	6,320	134	28.08	10	1,003	21	47.76	144/2
Atkinson, G R	Sept 21, 1830	May 3, 1906	1861	1870	27	38	8	399	44	13.30	0	1,146	54	21.22	14
Atkinson, H	Feb 1, 1881	Dec 22, 1959	1907	1907	1	2	0	0	0	0.00	0	17	0	—	—
Azeem Rafiq	**Feb 27, 1991**		2009	2010	**7**	**8**	**1**	**146**	**100**	**20.85**	**1**	**755**	**15**	**50.33**	**1**
Backhouse, E N	May 13, 1901	Nov 1, 1936	1931	1931	1	1	0	2	2	2.00	0	4	0	—	—
Badger, H D *	Mar 7, 1900	Aug 10, 1975	1921	1922	1	2	0	6	6*	3.00	0	145	6	24.16	1

LIST OF PLAYERS AND CAREER AVERAGES IN ALL FIRST-CLASS MATCHES FOR YORKSHIRE (Continued)

Player	Date of Birth	Date of Death (if known)	First Played	Last Played	M	Inns	NO	Runs	HS	Av'ge	100s	Runs	Wkts	Av'ge	Ct/St
Bainbridge, A B	Oct 15, 1932		1961	1963	5	10	0	93	24	9.30	0	358	20	17.90	3
Baines, F E *	June 18, 1864	Nov 17, 1948	1888	1888	1	1	0	0	0	0.00	0				
Bairstow, A	Aug 14, 1868	Dec 7, 1945	1896	1900	24	24	10	69	12	4.92	0	192	6	32.00	41/18
Bairstow, D L Ⓖ	Sept 1, 1951	Jan 5, 1998	1970	1990	429	601	113	12,985	145	26.60	9				907/131
Bairstow J M Ⓖ	**Sept 26, 1989**		**2009**	**2011**	**41**	**72**	**15**	**2525**	**205**	**44.29**	**2**				**93/5**
Baker, G R	Apr 18, 1862	Feb 6, 1938	1884	1884	7	11	1	42	13	4.20	0	43	0		5
Baker, R *	July 13, 1849	June 21, 1896	1874	1875	3	5	1	45	22	11.25	0	790	37	21.35	3
Balderstone, J C	Nov 16, 1940	Mar 6, 2000	1961	1969	68	81	6	1,332	82	17.76	0				24
§ Ballance G S	**Nov 22, 1989**		**2008**	**2011**	**16**	**30**	**7**	**952**	**111**	**41.39**	**1**	**11**	**0**		**8**
Barber, A T *	June 17, 1905	Mar 10, 1985	1929	1930	42	54	3	1,050	100	20.58	1				40
Barber, W Ⓖ	Apr 18, 1901	Sept 10, 1968	1926	1947	354	495	48	15,315	255	34.26	27	404	14	28.85	169
Barraclough, E S	Mar 30, 1923	May 21, 1999	1949	1950	2	4	2	43	24*	21.50	0	136	4	34.00	
Bates, W	Nov 19, 1855	Jan 8, 1900	1877	1887	202	331	12	6,499	136	20.37	8	10,692	637	16.78	163
Bates, W E Ⓖ	Mar 5, 1884	Jan 17, 1957	1907	1913	113	167	15	2,634	81	17.32	0	57	2	28.50	64
Batty G J	Oct 13, 1977		1997	1997	1	2	0	18	18	9.00	0	70	2	35.00	
Batty, J D	May 15, 1971		1989	1994	64	67	20	703	51	14.95	0	5,286	140	37.75	25
Bayes, G W	Feb 27, 1884	Dec 6, 1960	1910	1921	18	24	11	165	36	12.69	0	1,534	48	31.95	2
Beaumont, H	Oct 14, 1916	Nov. 15, 2003	1946	1947	28	46	6	716	60	17.90	0	236	9	26.22	11
Beaumont, J	Sept 16, 1855	May 1, 1920	1877	1878	5	9	3	60	24	10.00	0	50	2	25.00	
Bedford, H	July 17, 1907	July 5, 1968	1928	1928	5	5	1	57	24	14.25	0	179	8	22.37	1
Bedford, H	Feb 24, 1879	July, 28 1939	1903	1903	2	2	1	38	30*	38.00	0	117	2	58.50	
Bell, J T	June 16, 1895	Aug 8, 1974	1921	1921	7	8	1	125	54	17.85	0				12
Berry, John	Jan 10, 1823	Feb 26, 1895	1849	1867	18	32	2	492	78	16.40	0	149	8	18.62	
Berry, Joseph	Nov 29, 1829	Apr 20, 1894	1861	1874	3	7	3	68	31*	17.00	0				1
Berry, P J	Dec 28, 1966		1986	1990	7	9	8	76	40	76.00	0	401	7	57.28	2
§ Best T L	Aug 26, 1981		2010	2010	2	4	1	56	44*	18.66	0	793	18	44.05	4
Betts, D	Sept 19, 1843	Sept 26, 1902	1873	1874	9	9	0	86	56	9.55	0				
§ Bevan, M G Ⓖ	May 8, 1970		1995	1996	32	56	8	2,823	160*	58.81	9	720	10	72.00	24
Binks, J G Ⓖ	Oct 5, 1935		1955	1969	491	587	128	6,745	95	14.69	0	66	0		872/172
Binns, J Ⓖ	Mar 31, 1870	Dec 8, 1934	1898	1898	1	2	1	4	4	4.00	0				0/3
Bird, H D	Apr 19, 1933		1956	1959	14	25	2	613	181*	26.65	1				3

LIST OF PLAYERS AND CAREER AVERAGES IN ALL FIRST-CLASS MATCHES FOR YORKSHIRE (Continued)

Player	Date of Birth	Date of Death (if known)	First Played	Last Played	M	Inns	NO	Runs	HS	Av'ge	100s	Runs	Wkts	Av'ge	Ct/St
Birkenshaw, J.	Nov 13, 1940		1958	1960	30	42	7	588	42	16.80	0	1,819	69	26.36	21
Birtles, T J D	Oct 26, 1886	Jan 13, 1971	1913	1924	37	57	11	876	104	19.04	1	20			19
Blackburn, J D H *	Oct 27, 1924	Feb 19, 1987	1956	1956	1	2	1	18	15	9.00	0				
Blackburn, J S	Sept 24, 1852	July 8, 1922	1876	1877	6	11	1	102	28	10.20	0	173	7	24.71	4
§ Blackburn, W E *	Nov 24, 1888	June 3, 1941	1919	1920	10	13	6	26	6*	3.71	0	1,113	45	24.73	9
§ Blain J A R	Jan 4, 1979		2004	2010	15	17	3	137	28*	13.70	0	1,312	38	34.52	4
Blake, W	Nov 29, 1854	Not known	1880	1880	2	3	0	44	21	14.66	0	17	1	17.00	
Blakey, R J	© Jan 15, 1967		1985	2003	339	541	84	14,150	223*	30.96	12	68	1	68.00	768/56
Blamires, E	July 31, 1850	Mar 22, 1886	1877	1877	1	2	0	23	17	11.50	0	82	5	16.40	
§ Blewett, G S	© Oct 29, 1971		1999	1999	12	23	2	655	190	31.19	1	212	5	42.40	5
Bloom, G R	Sept 13, 1941		1964	1964	1	1	0	2	2	2.00	0				2
Bocking, H	Dec 10, 1835	Feb 22, 1907	1865	1865	1	1	0	14	11	7.00	0				1
Boden, J G *	Dec 27, 1848	Jan 3, 1928	1878	1878	1	2	0	6	6	6.00	0				
Bolton, B C *	Sept 23, 1862	Nov 18, 1910	1890	1891	4	6	0	25	11	4.16	0	252	13	19.38	1
Bolus, J B	© Jan 31, 1934		1956	1962	107	179	16	4,712	146*	29.26	7	407	13	31.30	45
Booth, A	© Nov 3, 1902	Aug 17, 1974	1931	1947	36	36	16	114	29	5.70	0	1,684	122	13.80	10
Booth, M W	© Dec 10, 1886	July 1, 1916	1908	1914	144	218	31	4,244	210	22.69	2	11,017	557	19.17	114
Booth, P A	Sept 5, 1965		1982	1989	23	29	9	193	33*	9.65	0	1,517	35	43.34	7
Booth, R	Oct 1, 1926		1951	1955	65	76	28	730	53*	15.20	0				79/29
Bore, M K	June 2, 1947		1969	1977	74	78	21	481	37*	8.43	0	4,866	162	30.03	27
Borrill, P D	July 4, 1951		1971	1971	2						0	61	6	12.20	
Bosomworth W E	Mar 8, 1847	June 7, 1891	1872	1880	4	7	1	20	7	3.33	0	140	9	15.55	2
Bottomley, I H *	Apr 9, 1855	Apr 23, 1922	1878	1880	9	12	0	166	32	13.83	0	75	1	75.00	1
Bottomley, T	Dec 26, 1910	Feb 19, 1977	1934	1935	6	7	0	142	51	20.28	0	188	1	188.00	5
Bower, W H	Oct 17, 1857	Jan 31, 1943	1883	1883	1	2	0	10	5	5.00	0				
Bowes, W E	© July 25, 1908	Sept 4, 1987	1929	1947	301	257	117	1,251	43*	8.93	0	21,227	1,351	15.71	118
Boycott, G	© Oct 21, 1940		1962	1986	414	674	111	32,570	260*	57.85	103	665	28	23.75	200
Brackin, J	Jan 5, 1859	Oct 7, 1924	1882	1882	3	6	0	9	9	2.00	0				
Brayshay, P B *	Oct 14, 1916	July 6, 2004	1952	1952	1	3	0	20	13	6.66	0	104	3	34.66	
Brearley, H *	June 26, 1913	Aug 14, 2007	1937	1937	2	2	0	17	9	8.50	0				
Brennan, D V *	© Feb 10, 1920	Jan 9, 1985	1947	1953	204	221	66	1,653	47	10.66	0				280/100

LIST OF PLAYERS AND CAREER AVERAGES IN ALL FIRST-CLASS MATCHES FOR YORKSHIRE (Continued)

Player	Date of Birth	Date of Death (if known)	First Played	Last Played	M	Inns	NO	Runs	HS	Av'ge	100s	Runs	Wkts	Av'ge	Ct/St
Bresnan T T .....©	**Feb 28, 1985**		**2003**	**2011**	87	121	22	2,621	116	26.47	2	7,282	231	**31.52**	**35**
Britton, G	Feb 7, 1843	Jan 3, 1910	1867	1867	1	2	0	3	3	1.50	0				1
Broadbent, A	June 7, 1879	July 19, 1958	1909	1910	3	5	0	66	29	13.20	0	252	5	50.40	1
Broadhead, W B	May 31, 1903	Apr 2, 1986	1929	1929	1	2	0	5	3	2.50	0				1
Broadhurst, M	June 20, 1974		1991	1994	3	3	0	7	6	2.33	0	231	7	33.00	—
§ Brophy G L ......©	**Nov 26, 1975**		**2006**	**2011**	69	109	11	2,965	177*	**30.25**	3	6	0		**168/15**
Brook, J W	Feb 1, 1897		1923	1923	1	1	0	0	0	0.00	0				—
Brooke, B	Mar 3, 1930	Mar.3 1989	1950	1950	2	4	0	16	14	4.00	0	191	2	95.50	1
Broughton, P N	Oct 22, 1935		1956	1956	6	5	2	19	12	6.33	0	365	16	22.81	4
Brown, A	June 10, 1854		1872	1872	2	3	0	9	5	3.00	0	47	3	15.66	—
Brown, J T (Driffield) ....©	Aug 20, 1869	Nov 2, 1900	1889	1904	345	567	41	15,694	311	29.83	23	5,183	177	29.28	188
Brown, J T (Darfield) ....©	Nov 24, 1874	Apr 12, 1950	1897	1903	30	32	3	333	37*	11.48	0	2,071	97	21.35	18
Brown, W	Nov 19, 1876	July 27, 1945	1902	1908	2	2	0	7	7	2.00	0	84	4	21.00	7
Brownhill, T	Oct 10, 1838	Jan 6, 1915	1861	1871	14	20	3	185	25	10.88	0				7
Brumfitt, J *	Feb. 18, 1917	Mar 16, 1987	1938	1938	1	1	0	9	9	9.00	0				—
Buller, J S *	Aug 23, 1909	Aug 7, 1970	1930	1930	1	2	0	5	5	2.50	0				2
Bulmer, J R L	Dec 28, 1859	Jan 20, 1917	1891	1891	1	2	0	0	0*	0.00	0	79	1	79.00	—
Burgess, T	Oct 1, 1859	Feb 22, 1922	1895	1895	2	2	1	0	0*	0.00	0				2
Burgin, E	Jan 4, 1924		1952	1953	12	10	3	92	32	13.14	0	795	31	25.64	—
Burman, J	Oct 5, 1838	May 14, 1900	1867	1867	1	2	1	1	1*	1.00	0				—
Burnet, J R * ....©	Oct 11, 1918	Mar 7, 1999	1958	1959	54	75	6	889	54	12.88	0	26	1	26.00	7
§ Burrows, M	Aug 18, 1855	May 29, 1893	1880	1880	6	10	0	82	23	8.20	0				2
Burton, D C F *	Sept 13, 1887	Sept 24, 1971	1907	1921	104	130	15	2,273	142*	19.76	0				44
Burton, R C *	Apr 11, 1891	Apr 30, 1971	1914	1914	2	2	0	47	47	23.50	0	73	6	12.16	2
Butterfield, E B *	Oct 22, 1848	May 6, 1899	1870	1870	1	2	0	18	10	9.00	0				—
Byas, D .....©	Aug 26, 1963		1986	2001	268	449	42	14,398	213	35.37	28	727	12	60.58	351
Byrom, J L *	July, 20, 1851	Aug 24, 1931	1874	1874	2	4	0	19	11	4.75	0				1
Cammish, J W	May 21, 1921	July 16, 1974	1954	1954	2	1	0	0	0	0.00	0	155	3	51.66	—
Carrick, P ....©	July, 16 1952	Jan 11, 2000	1970	1993	425	543	102	9,994	131*	22.66	3	30,530	1,018	29.99	183
Carter, Rev E S *	Feb 3, 1845	May 23, 1923	1876	1881	14	21	2	210	39*	11.05	0	104	8	13.00	4

LIST OF PLAYERS AND CAREER AVERAGES IN ALL FIRST-CLASS MATCHES FOR YORKSHIRE (Continued)

Player	Date of Birth	Date of Death (if known)	First Played	Last Played	M	Inns	NO	Runs	HS	Av'ge	100s	Runs	Wkts	Av'ge	Ct/St
Cartman, W H	June 20, 1861	Jan 16, 1935	1891	1891	3	6	0	57	30	9.50	0	304	4	76.00	1
Cawthray, G	Sept 28, 1913	Jan 5, 2000	1939	1952	6	9	3	114	30	19.00	0	67	2	33.50	7
Chadwick, J P G	Nov 8, 1934		1960	1965	6	9	3	106	29	17.66	0	17	1	17.00	7
Champion, A	Dec 27, 1851	June 30, 1909	1876	1879	14	23	4	148	80	7.78	0				13/3
Chapman, C A	June 8, 1971		1990	1998	8	13	2	238	62	21.63	0				2
Charlesworth, A P	Feb 19, 1865	May 11, 1926	1894	1895	7	12	1	241	63	21.90	0				
§ Chichester-															
Constable, R C J *	Dec 21, 1890	May 26, 1963	1919	1919	1	1	0	0	0	0.00	0	6	0		
Clarkson, A	Sept 5, 1939		1963	1963	6	8	1	80	30	11.42	0	92	5	18.40	5
Claughton, H M	Dec 24, 1891	Oct 17, 1980	1914	1919	4	6	0	39	15	6.50	0	176	3	58.66	1
§ Clayton, M E	Nov 25, 1982		2005	2005	3	2	0	38	38	19.00	0	263	3	87.66	
§ Clayton, R O	Jan 1, 1844	Nov 26, 1901	1870	1879	70	115	23	992	62	10.78	0	2,478	153	16.19	26
§ Cleary, M F	July 19, 1980		2005	2005	2	2	0	23	23	11.50	0	250	8	31.25	
Clegg, H	Dec 8, 1850		1881	1881	5	8	1	63	25*	9.00	0				2
Clifford, C C	July 5, 1942		1972	1972	11	12	4	39	12*	4.87	0	666	26	25.61	5
Close, D B	⊙ Feb 24, 1931		1949	1970	536	811	102	22,650	198	31.94	33	23,489	967	24.29	564
Clough, G D	May 23, 1978		1998	1998	1	2	0	34	33	17.00	0	11	0		1
Collinson, R W *	Nov 6, 1875	Dec 26, 1963	1897	1897	2	3	0	58	56	19.33	0				
Cooper, H P	Apr 17, 1949		1971	1980	98	107	29	1,159	56	14.85	0	6,327	227	27.87	60
Cooper, P E *	Feb 19, 1885	May 21, 1950	1910	1910	1	2	0	0	0	0.00	0				
Cope, G A	⊙ Feb 23, 1947		1966	1980	230	249	89	2,241	78	14.00	0	15,627	630	24.80	64
Corbett, A M	Nov 25, 1855	Oct 7, 1934	1881	1881	1	2	0	0	0	0.00	0				1
Coverdale, S P	Nov 20, 1954		1973	1980	6	4	0	31	18	7.75	0				11/4
Coverdale, W *	July 8, 1862	Sept 23, 1934	1888	1888	2	2	0	2	2	1.00	0				2
Cowan, M J	June 10, 1933		1953	1962	91	84	48	170	19*	4.72	0	6,389	266	24.01	37
Cownley, J M	Feb 24, 1929	Nov 7, 1998	1952	1952	1	2	1	19	19	19.00	0	119	1	119.00	
Coxon, A	⊙ Jan 18, 1916	Jan 22, 2006	1945	1950	142	182	33	2,747	83	18.43	0	9,528	464	20.53	124
Craven, V J	July 31, 1980		2000	2004	33	55	6	1,206	81*	24.61	0	584	15	38.93	18
Crawford, G H	Dec 15, 1890	June 28, 1975	1914	1926	9	8	0	46	21	5.75	0	541	21	25.76	3
Crawford, M G *	July 30, 1920		1951	1951	1	2	0	22	13	11.00	0				
Creighton, E	July 9, 1859	Feb 17, 1931	1888	1888	4	8	2	33	10	5.50	0	181	10	18.10	1

LIST OF PLAYERS AND CAREER AVERAGES IN ALL FIRST-CLASS MATCHES FOR YORKSHIRE (Continued)

Player	Date of Birth	Date of Death (if known)	First Played	Last Played	M	Inns	NO	Runs	HS	Av'ge	100s	Runs	Wkts	Av'ge	Ct/St
Crick, H	Jan 29, 1910	Feb 10, 1960	1937	1947	8	10	0	88	20	8.80	0	—	—	—	18/4
Crookes, R	Oct 9, 1846	Feb 15, 1897	1879	1879	1	2	1	2	2*	2.00	0	14	—	—	—
Crossland, S M	Aug 16, 1851	April 11, 1906	1883	1886	4	6	2	32	20	8.00	0	—	—	—	3/5
Crowther, A	Aug 1, 1878	June 4, 1946	1905	1905	1	2	0	0	0	0.00	0	—	—	—	1
Cuttell, W	Jan 28, 1835	June 10, 1896	1862	1871	15	27	6	271	56	12.90	0	596	36	16.55	4
Dalton, A J	Mar 14, 1947		1969	1972	21	31	2	710	128	24.48	3	—	—	—	6
§ Darnton, T	Feb 12, 1836	Oct 25, 1874	1864	1868	13	22	1	314	81*	14.95	0	349	12	29.08	3
Davidson, K R	Dec 24, 1905	Dec 25, 1954	1933	1935	30	46	5	1,331	128	32.46	2	—	—	—	18
Dawes, J	Feb 14, 1836	Not known	1865	1865	5	9	2	93	28*	13.28	0	196	5	39.20	3
Dawood, I	July 23, 1976		2004	2005	16	31	9	636	75	26.50	0	—	—	—	46/3
Dawson, E	May 1, 1835	Dec 1, 1888	1863	1874	16	25	1	224	20	9.33	0	—	—	—	5
Dawson, R K J	Aug 4, 1980		2001	2006	72	106	9	2,179	87	22.46	0	6,444	157	41.04	39
Day, A G *	Dec 3, 1850	Mar 6, 1916	1870	1870	1	1	0	0	0	0.00	0	—	—	—	—
Dennis, F	Sept 20, 1865	Oct 16, 1908	1885	1888	6	10	0	78	25	7.80	0	—	—	—	1
Dennis, F	© June 11, 1907	Nov 21, 2000	1928	1933	89	100	28	1,332	67	18.50	0	4,517	156	28.95	58
Dennis, S J	© Oct 18, 1960		1980	1988	67	62	24	338	53*	8.89	0	5,548	173	32.06	19
Denton, D	© July 4, 1874	Feb 16, 1950	1894	1920	676	1,058	61	33,282	221	33.38	61	957	34	28.14	360/1
Denton, J	Feb 3, 1865	July 19, 1946	1887	1888	15	24	1	222	59	9.65	0	15	—	—	6
Dewse, H	Feb 23, 1836	July 8, 1910	1873	1873	1	1	0	12	12	7.00	0	—	—	—	1
Deyes, R D *	Feb 11, 1879	Jan 11, 1963	1905	1907	17	24	0	44	12	2.20	0	944	41	23.02	6
Dick, R D *	Apr 16, 1889	Dec 14, 1983	1911	1911	2	2	1	2	1	2.00	0	37	2	18.50	1
Dobson, A	Feb 22, 1854	Sept 17, 1932	1879	1879	1	3	0	1	1	0.33	0	—	—	—	1
Doidge, M J	July 2, 1970		1990	1990	1	—	—	—	—	—	0	106	—	—	—
Dolphin, A	© Dec 24, 1885	Oct 23, 1942	1905	1927	427	446	157	3,325	66	11.50	0	28	1	28.00	569/260
Douglas, J S	Apr 4, 1903	Dec 27, 1971	1925	1934	23	26	1	125	19	6.94	0	1,310	49	26.73	14
Drake, A	© Apr 16, 1884	Feb 14, 1919	1909	1911	157	244	24	4,789	147*	21.76	3	8,623	479	18.00	93
Drake, J	Sept 1, 1893	May 22, 1967	1923	1924	3	4	1	21	14*	7.00	0	117	1	117.00	2
Driver, J	May 16, 1861	Dec 10, 1946	1889	1889	2	4	1	24	18	8.00	0	—	—	—	2
Dury, T S *	June 12, 1854	Mar 20, 1932	1878	1881	13	24	1	329	46	14.30	0	21	0	—	3
Dyson, W L	Dec 11, 1857	May 1, 1936	1887	1887	2	4	0	8	6	2.00	0	—	—	—	2

LIST OF PLAYERS AND CAREER AVERAGES IN ALL FIRST-CLASS MATCHES FOR YORKSHIRE (Continued)

Player	Date of Birth	Date of Death (if known)	First Played	Last Played	M	Inns	NO	Runs	HS	Av'ge	100s	Runs	Wkts	Av'ge	Ct/St
Earnshaw, W	Sept 20, 1867	Nov 24, 1941	1893	1896	6	7	3	44	23	11.00	0	349	11	31.72	6/2
Eastwood, J	Mar 30, 1848	May 17, 1903	1870	1877	29	51	2	591	68	12.06	0	62	0	—	16
Eckersley, R	Sept 4, 1925		1945	1945	1	1		9	9*		0	—	—	—	—
Elam, F W *	Sept 13, 1871	Mar 19, 1943	1900	1902	2	3		48	28	24.00	0	—	—	—	—
§ Elliott, M T G	Sept 28, 1971		2002	2002	5	10	1	487	127	54.11	1	77	1	77.00	7
Ellis, J E	Nov 10, 1864	Dec 1, 1927	1888	1892	11	15	6	14	4*	1.55	0	—	—	—	11/10
Ellis, S *	Nov 23, 1851	Oct 28, 1930	1880	1880	2	3	0	12	9	4.00	0	—	—	—	2
Elms, J E	Dec 24, 1874	Nov 1, 1951	1905	1905	1	2	0	20	20	10.00	0	28	1	28.00	1
Elstub, C J	Feb 3, 1981		2000	2002	1	2	0	28	18*	28.00	0	356	9	39.55	2
Emmett, T ...©	Sept 3, 1841	June 29, 1904	1866	1888	299	484	65	6,315	104	15.07	1	15,465	1,216	12.71	179
Farrar, A	Apr 29, 1884	Dec 25, 1954	1906	1906	1	1	0	2	2	2.00	0	—	—	—	1
Fearnley, M C	Aug 21, 1936	July 7, 1979	1962	1964	3	4	2	19	11*	9.50	0	133	6	22.16	—
Featherby, W D	Aug 18, 1888	Nov 20, 1958	1920	1920	1							12	0	—	—
Fellows, G M	July 30, 1978		1998	2003	46	71	6	1,526	109	23.47	1	1,202	32	37.56	23
Fidding, K	Oct 13, 1847	June 19, 1992	1938	1946	18	24	6	182	25	10.11	0	—	—	—	24/13
Firth, A *	Sept 3, 1847	Jan 16, 1927	1869	1869	1	1	0	4	4	4.00	0	—	—	—	—
Firth, Rev E B *	Apr 11, 1863	July 25, 1905	1894	1894	1	1	1	1	1*	—	0	—	—	—	1
Firth, J	June 27, 1918	Sept 7, 1981	1949	1950	8	8	3	134	67*	44.66	0	—	—	—	14/2
Fisher, H	Aug 3, 1903	Apr 16, 1974	1928	1936	52	58	14	681	76*	15.47	0	2,621	93	28.18	22
Fisher, I D	Mar 31, 1976		1996	2001	24	32	9	545	68*	23.69	0	1,382	43	32.13	1
Flaxington, S	Oct 14, 1860	Mar 10, 1895	1882	1882	4	8	0	121	57	15.12	0	—	—	—	1
§ Fleming, S P	Apr 1, 1973		2003	2003	7	14	2	469	98	39.08	1	—	—	—	13
Fletcher, S D ...©	June 8, 1964		1983	1991	107	91	31	414	28*	6.90	0	7,966	234	34.04	25
Fletcher, W	Feb 16, 1866	June 1, 1935	1892	1892	5	8	1	80	31*	11.42	0	157	7	22.42	4
Foord, C W	June 11, 1924		1947	1953	51	34	16	114	35	6.33	0	3,412	126	27.07	19
Foster, E	Nov 23, 1873	April 16, 1956	1901	1901	1	1	0	2	2	2.00	0	27	0	—	—
Foster, M J	Sept 17, 1972		1993	1994	5	7	1	165	63*	27.50	0	156	6	25.00	6
§ Foster, T W	Nov 12, 1871	Jan 31, 1947	1894	1895	14	20	5	138	25	9.20	0	952	58	16.41	3
Frank, J *	Dec 17, 1857	Oct 22, 1940	1881	1881	1	2	0	10	7	5.00	0	17	1	17.00	3
Frank R W * ...©	May 29, 1864	Sept 9, 1950	1889	1903	18	28	4	298	58	12.41	0	9			8
Freeman, G ...©	July 27, 1843	Nov 18, 1895	1865	1880	32	54	2	752	53	14.46	0	2,079	209	9.94	16

LIST OF PLAYERS AND CAREER AVERAGES IN ALL FIRST-CLASS MATCHES FOR YORKSHIRE (Continued)

Player	Date of Birth	Date of Death (if known)	First Played	Last Played	M	Inns	NO	Runs	HS	Av'ge	100s	Runs	Wkts	Av'ge	Ct/St
Gale, A W	© Nov 28, 1983		2004	2011	72	118	8	3985	151*	36.22	11	47	1	47.00	29
Geldart, C J	Dec 17, 1991		2010	2011	2	2	0	51	34	25.50	0	—	—	—	1
Gibb, P A *©	July 11, 1913	Dec 7, 1977	1935	1946	36	54	7	1,545	157*	32.87	2	82	3	27.33	25/8
Gibson, B P	Mar 31, 1996 **		2011	2011	1	1	1	—	1*	—	0	—	—	—	6/0
§ Gifkins, C J *	Feb 19, 1856	Jan 31, 1897	1880	1880	1	2	1	30	23	10.00	0	—	—	—	1
Gilbert, C R **	Apr 16, 1984		2007	2007	1	1	0	64	64	64.00	0	11	0	—	1
Gill, F	Sept 3, 1883		1906	1906	2	4	0	18	11	4.50	0	—	—	—	—
§ Gillespie, J N	©April 19, 1975		2006	2007	26	34	11	640	123*	27.82	1	2,013	59	34.11	4
Gillhouley, K	Aug 8, 1934		1961	1961	24	31	8	323	56*	13.45	0	1,702	77	22.10	16
Gough, D	© Sept 18, 1970		1989	2008	146	188	29	2,922	121	18.37	1	12,487	453	27.56	30
Goulder, A	Aug 16, 1907	June 11, 1986	1929	1929	2	1	0	3	3	3.00	0	90	3	30.00	—
§ Gray, A K D	May 19, 1974		2001	2004	18	26	3	649	104	28.21	1	1,357	30	45.23	16
Grayson, A P	Mar 31, 1971		1990	1995	52	80	10	1,958	100	27.97	2	846	13	65.07	36
Greenwood, A	Aug 20, 1847	Feb 12, 1889	1869	1880	95	166	8	2,762	91	17.93	0	9	—	—	33
Greenwood, F E *	Sept 28, 1905	July 30, 1963	1929	1932	57	66	8	1,458	104*	25.13	1	36	2	18.00	37
Greenwood, L	July 13, 1834	Nov 1, 1909	1861	1874	50	84	12	885	83	12.29	0	1,615	85	19.00	24
Grimshaw, C H	May 12, 1880	Sept 25, 1947	1904	1908	54	75	4	1,219	129*	17.92	1	221	7	31.57	42
Grimshaw, I	May 4, 1857	Jan 18, 1911	1880	1887	125	194	14	3,354	129*	18.63	4	8	0	—	76/3
Guy S M	Nov 17, 1978		2000	2011	37	52	6	742	52*	16.13	0	—	—	—	98/12
Haggas, S	Apr 18, 1856	Mar 14, 1926	1878	1882	31	47	3	478	43	10.86	0	—	—	—	10
Haigh S	© Mar 19, 1871	Feb 27, 1921	1895	1913	513	687	110	10,993	159	19.05	4	29,289	1,876	15.61	276
Hall, B	Sept 16, 1929	Feb 27, 1989	1952	1952	1	1	0	14	10	7.00	0	55	1	55.00	1
Hall, C H	Apr 5, 1906	Dec 11, 1976	1928	1934	23	22	9	67	15*	5.15	0	1,226	45	27.24	11
§ Hall, J	Nov 11, 1815	Apr 17, 1888	1844	1863	1	2	0	4	3	2.00	0	—	—	—	2
Hall, L	© Nov 1, 1852	Nov 19, 1915	1873	1894	275	477	58	9,757	160	23.28	9	781	15	52.06	173
Halliday, H	Feb 9, 1920	Aug 27, 1967	1938	1953	182	279	18	8,361	144	32.03	12	3,119	101	30.88	140
Halliley, C	Dec 5, 1852	Mar 23, 1929	1872	1872	1	1	0	27	27	27.00	0	—	—	—	2
Hamer, C	Dec 8, 1916	Nov 3, 1993	1938	1938	3	5	0	27	17	5.40	0	64	1	64.00	2
§ Hamilton, G M	© Sept 16, 1974		1994	2003	73	108	18	2,228	125	24.75	1	5,479	222	24.68	25

** At 15 years and 27 days on April 27, the First Day of Yorkshire's match v. Durham MCCU, he became the youngest ever English First Class cricketer.

LIST OF PLAYERS AND CAREER AVERAGES IN ALL FIRST-CLASS MATCHES FOR YORKSHIRE (Continued)

Player	Date of Birth	Date of Death (if known)	First Played	Last Played	M	Inns	NO	Runs	HS	Av'ge	100s	Runs	Wkts	Av'ge	Ct/St
Hampshire, A W	Oct 18, 1950		1975	1975	1	2	0	18	17	9.00	0	109	5	21.80	—
Hampshire, J	Oct 5, 1913	May 23, 1997	1937	1937	3	2	0	5	5	2.50	0	—	—	—	1
Hampshire, J H	Feb 10, 1941		1961	1981	456	724	89	21,979	183*	34.61	34	1,108	24	46.16	368
◎ **Hannon-Dalby A J**	**Jun 20, 1989**		**2008**	**2011**	**23**	**24**	**9**	**40**	**11***	**2.66**	**0**	**1884**	**39**	**48.30**	**1**
§ Harden, W E *	Dec 15, 1908	July 28, 1992	1929	1935	16	21	1	411	109	20.55	1	—	—	—	7
§ Harden, R J	Aug 16, 1965		1999	2000	12	22	3	439	69	23.10	0	—	—	—	2
Hardisty, C H	Dec 10, 1885		1906	1909	38	55	5	991	84	19.82	0	—	—	—	18
Hargreaves, H S	Mar 22, 1913	Mar 2, 1968	1934	1938	18	20	6	51	9	3.64	0	1,145	55	20.81	8
Harris, W	Nov 21, 1861	May 23, 1923	1884	1887	4	8	2	45	25	7.50	0	18	0	—	3
◎ Harrison, G P	Feb 11, 1862	Sept 14, 1940	1883	1892	59	87	26	407	28	6.67	0	3,276	226	14.49	36
Harrison, H	Jan 26, 1885	Feb 11, 1962	1907	1907	2	1	1	4	4*	—	0	39	2	19.50	1
Harrison, W H	May 27, 1863	July 15, 1939	1888	1888	3	6	1	12	7	2.40	0	—	—	—	1
◎ Hart, H W *	Sept 21, 1859	Nov 2, 1895	1888	1888	2	2	0	6	6	3.00	0	32	2	16.00	—
Hart, P R	Jan 12, 1947		1981	1981	3	5	0	23	11	4.60	0	140	2	70.00	1
Hartington, H E	Sept 18, 1881	Feb 16, 1950	1910	1911	10	14	4	51	16	8.50	0	764	23	33.21	2
◎ Hartley, P J	Apr 18, 1960		1985	1997	195	237	51	3,844	127*	20.66	0	17,438	579	30.11	60
Hartley, S N	Mar 18, 1956		1978	1988	133	199	27	4,193	114	24.37	2	2,052	42	48.85	47
§ Harvey, I J	Apr 10, 1972		2004	2005	20	31	2	1,045	209*	36.03	2	831	37	22.45	12
Hatton, A G	Mar 25, 1937		1960	1961	3	1	1	4	4*	—	0	202	6	33.66	1
§ Hawke, Lord *	Aug 16, 1860	Oct 10, 1938	1881	1911	510	739	91	13,133	166	20.26	10	16	0	—	159
Hayley, H	Feb 22, 1860	June 3, 1922	1884	1898	7	12	1	122	24	11.09	0	48	0	—	—
Haywood, W J	Feb 25, 1841	Jan 7, 1912	1872	1878	1	2	0	7	7	3.50	0	14	1	14.00	3
Hicks, J	Dec 10, 1850	June 10, 1912	1876	1876	15	25	3	313	66	14.22	0	17	0	—	—
Higgins, J	Mar 13, 1877	July 19, 1954	1901	1905	9	14	5	93	28*	10.33	0	—	—	—	10/3
Hill, A	Nov 14, 1843	Aug 29, 1910	1871	1882	140	223	25	1,705	49	8.61	0	7,002	542	12.91	91
◎ Hill, H *	Nov 29, 1858	Aug 14, 1935	1888	1891	14	27	2	337	34	13.48	0	—	—	—	10
Hill, L G *	Nov 2, 1860	Aug 27, 1940	1882	1882	1	2	0	13	13	6.50	0	—	—	—	1
Hirst, E T *	May 6, 1857	Oct 26, 1914	1877	1888	21	33	2	328	87*	10.58	0	3	0	—	1
◎ Hirst, G H	Sept 7, 1871	Oct 24, 1933	1891	1921*	717	1,050	128	32,024	341	34.73	56	44,716	2,481	18.02	518
Hirst, T H	May 21, 1865	Apr 3, 1927	1899	1899	2	3	1	5	5*	2.50	0	27	0	—	—

LIST OF PLAYERS AND CAREER AVERAGES IN ALL FIRST-CLASS MATCHES FOR YORKSHIRE (Continued)

Player	Date of Birth	Date of Death (if known)	First Played	Last Played	M	Inns	NO	Runs	HS	Av'ge	100s	Runs	Wkts	Av'ge	Ct/St
Hodgson, G	July 24, 1938		1964	1964	1	1	0	4	4	4.00	0				0/2
Hodgson, I	Nov 15, 1828	Nov 24, 1867	1855	1866	21	35	14	164	21*	7.80	0	1,537	88	17.46	11
Hodgson, L J	Jun 29, 1986		2009	2010	3	3	0	99	34	33.00	0	158	2	79.00	—
Hodgson, P	Sept 21, 1935		1954	1956	13	6	2	33	8*	8.25	0	648	22	29.45	6
Hoggard, M J	© Dec 31, 1976		1996	2009	102	120	34	956	89*	11.11	0	8,956	331	27.05	23
Holdsworth, W E N	Sept 17, 1928		1952	1953	27	26	12	111	22*	7.92	0	1,598	53	30.15	7
Holgate, G	June 23, 1839	July 11, 1895	1865	1867	12	19	0	174	38	9.15	0				17/1
Holmes, P	Nov 25, 1886	Sept 3, 1971	1913	1933	485	699	74	26,220	315*	41.95	60	124	1	124.00	319
Horner, N F	May 10, 1926	Dec 24, 2003	1950	1950	2	4	0	114	43	28.50	0				1
Houseman, I J	Oct 12, 1969		1989	1991	2	2	1	7	7	7.00	0	311	3	103.66	0/1
Hoyle, T H	Mar 19, 1884	June 2, 1953	1919	1919	1	2	0	7	5	3.50	0				—
Hudson, B	June 29, 1852	Nov 11, 1901	1880	1880	1	3	0	13	5	3.25	0				2
Hunter, D	© Feb 23, 1860	Jan 11, 1927	1888	1909	517	681	323	4,177	58*	11.66	0	43	0	—	863/323
Hunter, J	Aug 3, 1855	Jan 4, 1891	1878	1888	143	213	61	1,183	60*	7.78	0				207/102
Hutchison, P M	© June 9, 1977		1996	2001	39	39	23	287	30	11.68	0	3,244	143	22.68	8
Hutton, L	© June 23, 1916	Sept, 6, 1990	1934	1955	341	527	62	24,807	280*	53.34	85	4,221	154	27.40	278
Hutton, R A	© Sept 6, 1942		1962	1974	208	292	45	4,986	189	20.18	4	10,254	468	21.91	160
Iddison, R	Sept 15, 1834	Mar 19, 1890	1855	1876	72	108	15	1,916	112	20.60	0	1,540	102	15.09	70
Illingworth, R	© June 8, 1932		1951	1983	496	668	131	14,986	162	27.90	14	26,806	1,431	18.73	286
§ Imran Tahir	Mar 27, 1979		2007	2007	1	2	0	5	5	2.50	0	141	0	—	—
Ingham, P G	Sept 28, 1956		1979	1981	8	14	0	290	64	20.71	0				—
Inglis, J W	Oct 19, 1979		2000	2000	1	2	0	4	2	2.00	0				—
§ Inzamam-ul-Haq	Mar 3, 1970		2007	2007	3	4	0	89	51	22.25	0				5
Jackson, Hon F S *	© Nov 21, 1870	Mar 9, 1947	1890	1907	207	328	22	10,371	160	33.89	21	9,690	506	19.15	129
Jackson, S R *	July 15, 1859	July 19, 1941	1891	1891	1	2	0	9	9	4.50	0				—
Jacques, T A	Feb 19, 1905	Feb 23, 1995	1927	1936	28	20	7	162	35*	12.46	0	1,786	57	31.33	12
Jakeman, F	Jan 10, 1920	May 18, 1986	1946	1947	10	16	3	262	51	18.71	0				3
James, B	Apr 23, 1934		1954	1954	4	5	3	22	11*	11.00	0	228	8	28.50	—
§ Jaques, P A	**© May 3, 1979**		**2004**	**2005**	**24**	**42**	**2**	**2,477**	**243**	**61.92**	**7**	**37**	**0**	**—**	**25**

LIST OF PLAYERS AND CAREER AVERAGES IN ALL FIRST-CLASS MATCHES FOR YORKSHIRE (Continued)

Player	Date of Birth	Date of Death (if known)	First Played	Last Played	M	Inns	NO	Runs	HS	Av'ge	100s	Runs	Wkts	Av'ge	Ct/St
Jarvis, P W ....©	June 29, 1965		1981	1993	138	160	46	1,898	80	16.64	0	11,990	449	26.70	36
Johnson, C	Sept 5, 1947		1969	1979	100	152	14	2,960	107	21.44	2	265	4	66.25	50
Johnson, J	May 16, 1916		1936	1939	3	3	2	5	4*	5.00	0	27	5	5.40	1
Johnson, M	Apr 23, 1958		1981	1981	4	4	2	2	1	1.00	0	301	7	43.00	—
Joy, J	Sept 29, 1826	Sept 27, 1889	1849	1867	3	5	0	107	74	21.40	0	5	0	—	3
Judson, A	July 10, 1885	Apr 8, 1975	1920	1920	1	1					—	5	0	—	—
§ Katich, S M	Aug 21, 1975		2002	2002	1	2	0	37	21	18.50	0	25	0	—	1
Kaye, Harold S *	May 9, 1882	Nov 6, 1953	1907	1908	18	25	1	243	37	10.12	0				9
Kaye, Haven	June 11, 1846	Jan 24, 1892	1872	1873	8	14	0	117	33	8.35	0				3
Keedy, G	Nov 27, 1974		1994	1994	1	1	0	1	1	1.00	0				—
§ Keighley, W G * ....©	Jan 10, 1925		1947	1951	35	51	5	1,227	110	26.67	1	18	0	—	12
Kellett, S A	Oct 16, 1967		1989	1995	86	147	10	4,204	125*	30.68	7	7	0	—	74
Kennie, G	May 17, 1904		1927	1927	1	2	0	6	6	3.00	0				1
Kettleborough, R A	Mar 15, 1973		1994	1997	13	19	2	446	108	26.23	1	153	3	51.00	9
Kilburn, S	Oct 16, 1868	Sept 25, 1940	1896	1896	1	1	0	8	8	8.00	0				—
Kilner, N	July 21, 1895	Apr 28, 1979	1919	1923	69	73	7	1,253	112	18.98	2				34
Kilner, R ....©	Oct 17, 1890	Apr 5, 1928	1911	1927	365	478	46	13,018	206*	30.13	15	14,855	857	17.33	231
King, A M	Oct 8, 1932		1955	1955	1	1	0	12	12	12.00	0				—
Kippax, P J	Oct 15, 1940		1961	1962	4	7	2	37	9	7.40	0	279	8	34.87	1
§ Kirby, S P ....©	Oct 4, 1977		2001	2004	47	61	14	342	57	7.27	0	5,143	182	28.25	11
§ Kruis, G J	May 9, 1974		2005	2009	54	64	31	617	50*	18.69	0	5,431	154	35.26	11
§ Lambert, G A	Jan 4, 1980		2000	2000	2	3	2	6	3*	6.00	0	133	4	33.25	1
Lancaster, W W	Feb 4, 1873	Dec 30, 1938	1895	1895	7	10	0	163	51	16.30	0	29	0	—	1
§ Landon, C W *	May 30, 1850	Mar 5, 1903	1878	1882	9	13	0	51	18	3.92	0	74	1	—	7
§ Law, W *	Apr 9, 1851	Dec 20, 1892	1871	1873	4	7	0	51	22	7.28	0				3
Lawson, M A K	Oct 24, 1985		2004	2007	15	21	5	197	44	12.31	0	1,699	42	40.45	2
Leadbeater, B ....©	Aug 14, 1943		1966	1979	144	236	27	5,247	140*	25.10	1	5	1	5.00	80
Leadbeater, E	Aug 15, 1927		1949	1956	81	94	29	898	91	13.81	0	5,657	201	28.14	49
Leadbeater, H *	Dec 31, 1863	Oct 9, 1928	1884	1890	6	10	2	141	65	17.62	0	11	0	—	4
Leatham, G A B *	Apr 30, 1851	June 19, 1932	1874	1886	12	18	5	61	14	4.69	0				21/7

362

LIST OF PLAYERS AND CAREER AVERAGES IN ALL FIRST-CLASS MATCHES FOR YORKSHIRE (Continued)

Player	Date of Birth	Date of Death (if known)	First Played	Last Played	M	Inns	NO	Runs	HS	Av'ge	100s	Runs	Wkts	Av'ge	Ct/St
Leather, R S *	Aug 17, 1880	Jan 31, 1913	1906	1906	1	2	0	19	14	9.50	0	—	—	—	1
Lee, C	Mar 17, 1924	Sept 4, 1999	1952	1952	2	4	0	98	74	24.50	0	—	—	—	—
Lee, F	© Nov 18, 1856	Sept 13, 1896	1882	1890	105	182	10	3,622	165	21.05	3	—	—	—	53/1
Lee, G H	Aug 24, 1854	Oct 4, 1919	1879	1879	5	2	0	13	13	6.50	0	—	—	—	—
Lee, Herbert	July 2, 1856	Feb 4, 1908	1885	1885	2	6	0	20	9	3.33	0	—	—	—	2
Lee, J E *	Mar 23, 1838	Apr 2, 1880	1867	1867	2	3	0	9	6	3.00	0	—	—	—	—
Lee, J E	Dec 23, 1988		2006	2009	2	3	1	24	21*	12.00	0	149	2	74.50	—
Lees A Z	**Apr 14, 1993**		**2010**	**2011**	**4**	**2**	**0**	**38**	**38**	**19.00**	**0**	—	—	—	**1**
Legard, A D *	June 19, 1878	Aug 15, 1939	1910	1910	1	2	0	26	15	13.00	0	—	—	—	—
§ Lehmann, D S	© Feb 5, 1970		1997	2006	88	137	8	8,871	339	68.76	26	1,952	61	32.00	35
Lester, E I	© Feb 18, 1923		1945	1956	228	339	27	10,616	186	34.02	24	160	3	53.33	106
Leyland, M	© July 20, 1900	Jan 1, 1967	1920	1946	548	720	82	26,180	263	41.03	62	11,079	409	27.08	204
Lilley A E	**Apr 17, 1992**		**2011**	**2011**	**1**	**1**	**0**	**0**	**0**	**0.00**	**0**	**34**	**1**	**34.00**	—
Linaker, L	Apr 8, 1885	Nov 17, 1961	1909	1909	1	2	1	0	0	0.00	0	28	1	28.00	—
Lister, B	Dec 9, 1850	Dec 3, 1919	1874	1878	7	11	1	36	10	3.60	0	64	1	64.00	2
§ Lister-Kaye, K A *	Mar 27, 1892	Feb 28, 1955	1928	1928	2	2	1	13	7*	13.00	0	—	—	—	—
Lister, J *	May 14, 1930	Jan 28, 1991	1954	1954	2	4	0	35	16	8.75	0	—	—	—	8
Lockwood, E	Apr 4, 1845	Dec 19, 1921	1868	1884	214	364	29	7,789	208	23.25	6	2,265	141	16.06	164/2
Lockwood, H	Oct 20, 1855	Feb 18, 1930	1877	1882	16	27	2	408	90	16.32	0	37	0	—	8
Lodge, J T	Apr 16, 1921		1948	1948	2	3	0	48	30	16.00	0	17	0	—	—
Love, J D	Apr 22, 1955		1975	1989	247	388	58	10,263	170*	31.10	13	835	12	69.58	123
Lowe, G E	Jan 12, 1878	Aug 15, 1932	1902	1902	1	1	1	5	5*	—	0	—	—	—	—
Lowe J R	Oct 19, 1991		2010	2010	1	1	0	5	5	5.00	0	—	—	—	—
Lowson, F A	© July 1, 1925	Sept 8, 1984	1949	1958	252	404	31	13,897	259*	37.25	30	15	0	—	180
§ Loxley-Firth, E *	Mar 7, 1886	Jan 8, 1949	1912	1912	2	4	0	43	37	10.75	0	—	—	—	—
§ Lucas, D S	© Aug 19, 1978		2005	2005	1	—	—	—	—	—	—	84	8	10.50	—
Lumb, E *	© Sept 12, 1852	Apr 5, 1891	1872	1886	14	23	4	311	70*	16.36	0	199	5	39.80	5
§ Lumb, M J	© Feb 12, 1980		2000	2006	78	135	12	4,194	144	34.09	8	—	—	—	43
§ Lumb, R G	© Feb 27, 1950		1970	1984	239	395	30	11,525	165*	31.57	22	5	0	—	129
Lupton, A W *	© Feb 23, 1879	Apr 14, 1944	1908	1927	104	79	15	668	43*	10.43	0	88	0	—	25

LIST OF PLAYERS AND CAREER AVERAGES IN ALL FIRST-CLASS MATCHES FOR YORKSHIRE (Continued)

Player	Date of Birth	Date of Death (if known)	First Played	Last Played	M	Inns	NO	Runs	HS	Av'ge	100s	Runs	Wkts	Av'ge	Ct/St
Lynas, G G	Sept 7, 1832	Dec 8, 1896	1867	1867	2	3	1	4	4*	2.00	0	181	3	60.33	2
Lyth A ©	**© Sept 25, 1987**		**2007**	**2011**	**47**	**81**	**1**	**2,978**	**142**	**37.22**	**4**	—	—	—	**41**
Macaulay, G G ©	Dec 7, 1897	Dec 13, 1940	1920	1935	445	430	112	5,717	125*	17.97	0	30,554	1,774	17.22	361
McGrath A ©	**Oct 6, 1975**		**1995**	**2011**	**228**	**388**	**26**	**13,443**	**211**	**37.13**	**32**	**4,163**	**109**	**38.19**	**163**
McHugh F P	Nov 15, 1925		1949	1949	3	1	0	2	2	2.00	0	147	4	36.75	—
Marshall, A	July 10, 1849	Aug 3, 1891	1874	1874	1	2	0	2	2	1.00	0	11	0	—	1
§ Martyn, D R	Oct 21, 1971		2003	2003	1	2	0	342	238	171.00	1	—	—	—	2
Mason, A	May 2, 1921		1947	1950	18	19	3	105	22	6.56	0	1,473	51	28.88	6
Maude, E *	Dec 31, 1839	July 2, 1876	1866	1866	2	2	0	17	16	8.50	0	—	—	—	—
Metcalfe, A A ©	© Dec 25, 1963		1983	1995	184	317	19	10,465	216*	35.11	25	344	3	114.66	72
Micklethwait, W H *	Dec 13, 1885	Oct 7, 1947	1911	1911	1	1	0	44	44	44.00	0	—	—	—	—
Middlebrook, J D	May 13, 1977		1998	2001	23	31	3	485	84	17.32	0	1,458	49	29.75	14
Middlebrook, W	May 23, 1858	Apr 26, 1919	1888	1889	17	27	7	88	19*	4.40	0	895	50	17.90	17
Midgley, C A *	Nov 11, 1877	Nov 29, 1933	1906	1906	4	6	2	115	59*	28.75	0	149	8	18.62	3
Milburn, S M	Sept 29, 1972		1992	1995	6	8	2	22	7	3.66	0	431	14	30.78	1
§ Milligan, F W * ©	© Mar 19, 1870	Mar 31, 1900	1894	1898	81	113	10	1,879	74	18.24	0	2,736	112	24.42	40
Mitchell, A ©	© Sept 13, 1902	Dec 25, 1976	1922	1945	401	550	69	18,189	189	37.81	39	291	5	58.20	406
Mitchell, F * ©	© Aug 13, 1872	Oct 11, 1935	1894	1904	83	125	5	4,104	194	34.20	10	16	1	16.00	52
Monks, G D	Sept 3, 1929		1952	1952	1	1	0	3	3	3.00	0	—	—	—	1
Moorhouse, R ©	© Sept 7, 1866	Jan 7, 1921	1888	1899	206	315	45	5,217	113	19.32	3	1,232	43	28.65	92
§ Morkel, M	Oct 6, 1984		2008	2008	1	2	0	8	8	4.00	0	33	1	33.00	—
Morris, A C	Oct 4, 1976		1995	1997	16	23	2	362	60	17.23	0	508	9	56.44	12
Mosley, H	Mar 8, 1852	Nov 29, 1933	1881	1881	1	2	1	0	0	0.00	0	34	3	11.33	—
Motley A *	Feb 5, 1858	Sept 28, 1897	1879	1879	2	4	0	10	8*	2.50	0	135	7	19.28	—
Mounsey, J T	Aug 30, 1871	Apr 6, 1949	1891	1897	92	145	21	1,939	64	15.63	0	444	10	44.40	45
Moxon, M D ©	© May 4, 1960		1981	1997	277	476	42	18,973	274*	43.71	41	1,213	22	55.13	190
Myers, H	Jan 2, 1875	June 12, 1944	1901	1910	201	289	46	4,450	91	18.31	0	7,095	282	25.15	106
Myers, M	Apr 12, 1847	Dec 8, 1919	1876	1878	22	40	4	537	49	14.91	0	20	0	—	11
§ Naved-ul-Hasan, Rana	Feb 28, 1978		2008	2009	11	16	3	207	32	15.92	0	1,018	26	39.15	3
Naylor, J E	Dec 11, 1930	June 26, 1996	1953	1953	1	1	—	—	—	—	—	88	0	—	1

LIST OF PLAYERS AND CAREER AVERAGES IN ALL FIRST-CLASS MATCHES FOR YORKSHIRE (Continued)

Player	Date of Birth	Date of Death (if known)	First Played	Last Played	M	Inns	NO	Runs	HS	Av'ge	100s	Runs	Wkts	Av'ge	Ct/St
Newstead, J T	Sept 8, 1877 ©	Mar 25, 1952	1903	1913	96	128	17	1,791	100*	16.13	1	5,555	297	18.70	75
Nicholson, A G	June 25, 1938	Nov 5, 1985	1962	1975	282	267	125	1,667	50	11.73	0	17,296	876	19.74	85
Nicholson, N G	Oct 17, 1963		1988	1989	5	8	3	134	56*	26.80	0	25	0	—	5
Oates, William	Jan 1, 1852	Dec 9, 1940	1874	1875	7	13	7	34	14*	5.66	0	—	—	—	5/1
Oates, W F	June 11, 1929	May 15, 2001	1956	1956	3	3	0	20	9	6.66	0	—	—	—	1
Old, C M	Dec 22, 1948 ©		1966	1982	222	262	56	4,785	116	23.22	5	13,409	647	20.72	131
Oldham, S	July 26, 1948		1974	1985	59	39	18	212	50	10.09	0	3,849	130	29.60	18
Oldroyd, E	Oct 1, 1888 ©	Dec 29, 1964	1910	1931	383	509	58	15,891	194	35.23	37	1,658	42	39.47	203
Oyston, J	May 12, 1869	July 15, 1942	1900	1909	15	21	8	96	22	7.38	0	872	31	28.12	3
Padgett, D E V	July 20, 1934 ©		1951	1971	487	774	63	20,306	161*	28.55	29	208	6	34.66	250
Padgett, G H	Oct 9, 1931		1952	1952	6	7	4	56	32*	18.66	0	336	4	84.00	5
Padgett, J	Nov 21, 1860	Aug 2, 1943	1882	1889	6	9	0	92	22	10.22	0	—	0	—	2
Parker, B	June 23, 1970		1992	1998	44	71	10	1,839	138*	30.14	2	3	0	—	19
§ Parkin, C H	Feb 18, 1886	June 15, 1943	1906	1906	1	1	0	0	0	0.00	0	25	2	12.50	—
Parratt, J	Mar 24, 1859	May 6, 1905	1888	1890	2	2	0	11	11	5.50	0	75	1	75.00	—
§ Parton, J W	Jan 31, 1863	Jan 30, 1906	1889	1889	1	2	0	16	14	8.00	0	4	1	4.00	4
Patterson S A	**Oct 3, 1983**		**2005**	**2011**	**40**	**49**	**15**	**480**	**53**	**14.11**	**0**	**3,157**	**88**	**35.87**	**10**
Pearson, H E	Aug 7, 1851	July 8, 1903	1878	1880	4	7	5	31	10*	15.50	0	90	5	18.00	1
Pearson, J H	May 14, 1915	May 13, 2007	1934	1936	3	3	0	54	44	18.00	0	—	—	—	—
Peate, E	Mar 2, 1855	Mar 11, 1900	1879	1887	154	226	61	1,793	95	10.86	0	9,986	794	12.57	97
Peel, R	Feb 12, 1857	Aug 12, 1941	1882	1897	318	510	42	9,322	210*	19.91	6	20,638	1,311	15.74	141
Penny, J H	Sept 29, 1856	July 29, 1902	1891	1891	1	1	0	8	8*	8.00	0	—	—	—	—
Pickles, C S	Jan 30, 1966		1985	1992	58	76	21	1,336	66	24.29	0	3,638	83	43.83	24
Pickles, D	Nov 16, 1935		1957	1960	41	40	20	212	12	3.70	0	2,062	96	21.47	10
Pinder, G	July 15, 1841	Jan 15, 1903	1867	1880	125	199	44	1,639	57	10.57	0	325	19	17.10	145/102
Platt, R K	Dec 26, 1932		1955	1963	96	103	47	405	57*	7.23	0	6,389	282	22.65	35
Pollard, D	Aug 7, 1835	Mar 26, 1909	1865	1865	3	3	1	3	3	1.50	0	19	0	—	1
Pollitt, G	June 3, 1874	Not known	1899	1899	1	1	0	51	51	51.00	0	—	—	—	1
Prest, C H *	Dec 9, 1841	Mar 4, 1875	1864	1864	2	4	0	57	31	14.25	0	—	—	—	3
Preston, J M	Aug 23, 1864	Nov 26, 1890	1885	1889	79	134	11	1,935	93	15.73	0	3,232	178	18.15	36

LIST OF PLAYERS AND CAREER AVERAGES IN ALL FIRST-CLASS MATCHES FOR YORKSHIRE (Continued)

Player	Date of Birth	Date of Death (if known)	First Played	Last Played	M	Inns	NO	Runs	HS	Av'ge	100s	Runs	Wkts	Av'ge	Ct/St
Pride, T	July 23, 1864	Feb 16, 1919	1887	1887	1	1	0	1	1	1.00	0				4/3
Priestley, I M	Sept 25, 1967		1989	1989	2	4	2	25	23	12.50	0	119	4	29.75	
Pullan, P	Mar 29, 1857	Mar 3, 1901	1884	1884	1	1	1	14	14	14.00	0	5	0		
Pyrah R M	**© Nov 1, 1982**		**2004**	**2011**	**33**	**44**	**5**	**1,177**	**134***	**30.17**	**3**	**1773**	**45**	**39.40**	**15**
§ Radcliffe, E J R H ©	Jan 27, 1884	Nov 23, 1969	1909	1911	64	89	13	826	54	10.86	0	134	2	67.00	21
Ramage, A	Nov 29, 1957		1979	1983	23	22	9	219	52	16.84	0	1,649	44	37.47	21
Ramsden, G	Mar 2, 1983		2000	2000	1	1	1	0	0*		0	68	1	68.00	0
Randhawa G S	Jan 25, 1992		2011	2011	1	1	0	5	5	**5.00**	0	62	2	31.00	
Raper, J R S ©	Aug 9, 1909	Mar 9, 1997	1936	1947	3	4	0	24	15	6.00	0				1
Rashid A U	**© Feb 17, 1988**		**2006**	**2011**	**75**	**110**	**21**	**3,096**	**157***	**34.78**	**4**	**8,387**	**249**	**33.68**	**43**
Rawlin, E R	Oct 4, 1897	Jan 11, 1943	1927	1936	8	10	1	72	31	8.00	0	498	21	23.71	2
Rawlin, J T	Nov 10, 1856	Jan 19, 1924	1880	1885	27	36	2	274	55	8.05	0	258	11	23.45	13
Rawlinson, E B	Apr 10, 1837	Feb 17, 1892	1867	1875	37	68	1	991	55	15.73	0	62	5	12.40	16
Redfearn, J	May 13, 1862	Jan 14, 1931	1890	1890	1	1	0	5	5	5.00	0				
Render, G W A	Jan 5, 1887	Sept 17, 1922	1919	1919	1	1	0	5	5*	5.00	0				
Rhodes, A C	Oct 14, 1906	May 21, 1957	1932	1934	61	70	19	917	64*	17.98	0	3,026	107	28.28	45
Rhodes, H E *	Jan 11, 1852	Sept 10, 1889	1878	1883	10	16	1	269	64	17.93	0				1
Rhodes, S J	June 17, 1964		1981	1984	3	2	0	41	35	41.00	0				3
Rhodes, Wilfred ©	Oct 29, 1877	July 8, 1973	1898	1930	883	1,195	162	31,075	267*	30.08	46	57,634	3,598	16.01	586
Rhodes, William	Mar 4, 1883	Aug 5, 1941	1911	1911	7	12	1	1	1*	1.00	0	40	0		3
Richardson, J A *	Aug 4, 1908	Apr 2, 1985	1936	1947	23	39	2	308	61	30.80	1	90	2	45.00	18
§ Richardson, R B ©	Jan 12, 1962		1993	1994	13	23	2	1,310	112	34.47	1	23	1	23.00	11
§ Richardson, S A	Sept 5, 1977		2000	2003	4	5	1	377	69	17.95	0				
Riley, H	Aug 17, 1875	Nov 6, 1922	1895	1900	17	28	0	36	25*	9.00	0	54	1	54.00	
Riley, M *	Apr 5, 1851	June 1, 1899	1878	1882	57	66	1	361	92	13.37	0	10	0		3
Ringrose, W	Sept 2, 1871	Sept 14, 1943	1901	1906	84	66	9	353	23	6.19	0	3,224	155	20.80	25
Robinson, A L ©	Aug 17, 1946		1971	1977	104	69	31	365	30*	9.60	0	4,927	196	25.13	48
Robinson, Edward *	Dec 27, 1862	Sept 3, 1942	1887	1887	1	2	0	23	23*	23.00	0				
Robinson, Emmott ©	Nov 16, 1883	Nov 17, 1969	1919	1931	413	455	77	9,651	135*	25.53	7	19,645	893	21.99	318
Robinson, E P ©	Nov 10, 1911	Nov 10, 1998	1934	1949	208	253	46	2,596	75*	12.54	0	15,141	735	20.60	189
Robinson, H	May 12, 1858	Dec 14, 1909	1879	1879	1	2	0	5	4	2.50	0	20	1	20.00	

LIST OF PLAYERS AND CAREER AVERAGES IN ALL FIRST-CLASS MATCHES FOR YORKSHIRE *(Continued)*

Player	Date of Birth	Date of Death (if known)	First Played	Last Played	M	Inns	NO	Runs	HS	Av'ge	100s	Runs	Wkts	Av'ge	Ct/St
Robinson, M A ©	Nov 23, 1966		1991	1995	90	93	36	240	23	4.21	0	6,866	218	31.49	17
Robinson, P E ©	Aug 3, 1963		1984	1991	132	217	31	6,668	189	35.84	7	238	1	238.00	96
Robinson, W	Nov 29, 1851	Aug 14, 1919	1876	1877	7	14	1	151	68	11.61	0	—	—	—	3
Roebuck C G ©	Aug 14, 1991		2010	2010	1	1	0	23	23	23.00	0	—	—	—	—
Root J E	**Dec 30, 1990**		**2010**	**2011**	**17**	**33**	**5**	**975**	**160**	**34.82**	**1**	**346**	**7**	**49.42**	**6**
Roper, E *	Apr 8, 1851	Apr 27, 1921	1878	1880	5	7	1	85	68	14.16	0	—	—	—	2
Rothery, J W ©	Sept 5, 1877	June 2, 1919	1903	1910	150	236	18	4,614	161	21.16	3	44	2	22.00	45
Rowbotham, J ©	July 8, 1831	Dec 22, 1899	1861	1876	68	162	9	2,624	113	17.15	3	37	2	12.33	52
§ Rudolph J A ©	May 4, 1981		2007	2011	68	112	8	5429	228*	52.20	18	311	1	311.00	79
Rudston, H	Nov 22, 1879	April 14, 1962	1902	1907	21	30	0	609	164	20.30	1	—	—	—	3
Ryan, M	June 23, 1933		1954	1965	150	149	58	682	26*	7.49	0	9,466	413	22.92	59
Ryder, L	Aug 28, 1899	Jan 24, 1955	1924	1924	2	2	0	2	1	1.00	0	151	4	37.75	2
Sanderson B W	Jan 3, 1989		2008	2010	3	3	1	6	6*	6.00	0	190	6	31.66	—
Savile, G *	Apr 26, 1847	Sept 4, 1904	1867	1874	5	7	0	140	65	20.00	0	—	—	—	2
Sayers J J ©	**Nov 5, 1983**		**2004**	**2011**	**85**	**143**	**11**	**4,531**	**187**	**34.32**	**9**	**166**	**6**	**27.66**	**53**
Schofield, C J	Mar 21, 1976		1996	1996	1	1	0	25	25	25.00	0	112	5	22.40	—
Schofield, D	Oct 9, 1947		1970	1974	3	4	0	13	6*	—	0	27	2	13.50	1
Scott, E	July 6, 1834	Dec 3, 1898	1864	1864	3	1	0	8	8	8.00	0	—	—	—	2
Sedgwick, H A	Apr 8, 1883	Dec 28, 1957	1906	1906	3	5	2	53	34	17.66	0	327	16	20.43	1
Sellers, Arthur *	May 31, 1870	Sept 25, 1941	1890	1899	49	88	1	1,643	105	18.88	2	84	2	42.00	40
Sellers, A B * ©	Mar 5, 1907	Feb 20, 1981	1932	1948	334	437	51	8,949	204	23.18	4	653	8	81.62	264
Shackleton, A	Mar 9, 1908	Nov 16, 1971	1928	1934	9	11	5	49	25	8.16	0	130	6	21.66	3
Shahzad, Ajmal ©	**July 27, 1985**		**2006**	**2011**	**42**	**55**	**14**	**1111**	**88**	**27.09**	**0**	**3,986**	**117**	**34.06**	**5**
Sharp, K ©	Apr. 6, 1959		1976	1990	195	320	35	8,426	181	29.56	11	836	12	69.66	95
§ Sharpe, C M *	Sept 6, 1851	June 25, 1935	1875	1875	1	1	0	15	15	15.00	0	17	—	—	—
Sharpe, P J ©	Dec 27, 1936		1958	1974	411	666	71	17,685	203*	29.72	23	140	2	70.00	525
Shaw, J	Feb 17, 1964		1984	1988	61	58	27	340	15	10.96	0	4,101	123	33.34	9
Shaw, J	Mar 12, 1865	Jan 22, 1921	1896	1897	3	3	0	8	7	2.66	0	181	7	25.85	2
Sheepshanks, E R *	Mar 22, 1910	Dec 31, 1937	1929	1929	1	1	0	26	26	26.00	0	—	—	—	—
Shepherd, D A *	Mar 10, 1916	May 29, 1998	1938	1938	1	1	0	0	0	0.00	0	—	—	—	—

LIST OF PLAYERS AND CAREER AVERAGES IN ALL FIRST-CLASS MATCHES FOR YORKSHIRE (Continued)

Player	Date of Birth	Date of Death (if known)	First Played	Last Played	M	Inns	NO	Runs	HS	Av'ge	100s	Runs	Wkts	Av'ge	Ct/St
Shotton, W	Dec 1, 1840	May 26, 1909	1865	1874	2	4	0	13	7	3.25	0	13,852	558	24.82	60
Sidebottom, A ...C	Apr 1, 1954		1973	1991	216	249	50	4,243	124	22.33	1	5,460	225	24.26	24
Sidebottom R J	**Jan 15, 1978**		**1997**	**2011**	**70**	**97**	**29**	**971**	**61**	**14.27**	**0**				**7**
Sidgwick, R *	Aug 7, 1851		1882	1882	9	13	0	64	17	4.92	0				7
Silverwood, C E W ..C	Mar 5, 1975		1993	2005	131	179	33	2,369	80	16.22	0	11,413	427	27.62	30
Silvester, S	Mar 12, 1951		1976	1977	6	7	4	30	14	10.00	0	313	12	26.08	2
Simpson, E T B *	Mar 5, 1867		1889	1889	1	2	0	1	1	0.50	0				—
§ Sims, Rev H H M *	Mar 15, 1853	Oct 5, 1885	1875	1877	5	10	1	109	35*	12.11	0				2
Slinn, W	Dec 13, 1826	June 19, 1888	1861	1864	5	9	4	22	11	2.00	0	742	48	15.45	5
Smailes, T F ...C	Mar 27, 1910	Dec 1, 1970	1932	1948	262	339	42	5,686	117	19.14	3	16,593	802	20.68	153
Smales, K	Sept 15, 1927		1948	1950	13	19	3	165	45	10.31	0	766	22	34.81	4
Smith, A F	Mar 7, 1847	Jan 6, 1915	1868	1874	28	49	4	692	89	15.37	0				11
Smith, E (Barnsley)	July 11, 1888	Jan 2, 1972	1914	1926	16	21	5	169	49	10.56	0	1,090	46	23.69	6
Smith, Ernest (Morley)*C	Oct 19, 1869	Feb 9, 1945	1888	1907	154	234	18	4,453	129	20.61	2	6,278	248	25.31	112
Smith, Fred (Idle) *	Dec 26, 1885	Not known	1911	1911	1	1	0	11	11	11.00	0	45	2	22.50	—
Smith, Fred (Yeadon)	Dec 18, 1879	Oct 20, 1905	1903	1903	13	19	1	292	55	16.22	0				3
Smith, G	Jan 13, 1876	Jan 16, 1929	1901	1906	2	2	1	7	7	7.00	0	62	0		3
Smith, J	Mar 23, 1833	Feb 12, 1909	1865	1865	2	3	0	28	16	9.33	0	72	6	12.00	3
Smith, N	Apr 1, 1949		1970	1971	8	11	3	82	20	13.66	0				14/3
Smith, R	Apr 6, 1944		1969	1970	5	8	3	99	37*	19.80	0				—
Smith, Walker	Aug 14, 1847	July 7, 1900	1874	1874	5	9	0	152	59	16.88	0				3
§ Smith, William	Nov 1, 1839	Apr 19, 1897	1865	1874	11	19	3	260	90	16.25	0				8
Smithson, G A ...C	Nov 1, 1926	Sept 6, 1970	1946	1950	39	60	5	1,449	169	26.34	2	84	1	84.00	21
Smurthwaite, J	Oct 17, 1916	Oct 20, 1989	1938	1939	7	9	5	29	20*	7.25	0	237	12	19.75	4
Sowden, A	Dec 1, 1853	July 5, 1921	1878	1887	8	11	0	137	37	12.45	0	22	0		1
Squire, D	Dec 31, 1864	Apr 28, 1922	1893	1893	1	2	0			0.00	0	25	0		—
Squires, P J	Aug 4, 1951		1972	1976	49	84	8	1,271	70	16.72	0	32	0		14
Stanley, H C *	Feb 16, 1888	May 18, 1934	1911	1913	8	13	0	155	42	11.92	0				6
§ Stanyforth, R T *	May 30, 1892	Feb 20, 1964	1928	1928	3	3	0	26	10	8.66	0				2
Stead, D	June 22, 1939	Apr 15, 1980	1959	1959	2	3	0	8	8	2.66	0				—
§ Stemp, R D ...C	Dec 11, 1967		1993	1998	104	135	36	1,267	65	12.79	0	8,557	241	35.50	49

LIST OF PLAYERS AND CAREER AVERAGES IN ALL FIRST-CLASS MATCHES FOR YORKSHIRE (Continued)

Player	Date of Birth	Date of Death (if known)	First Played	Last Played	M	Inns	NO	Runs	HS	Av'ge	100s	Runs	Wkts	Av'ge	Ct/St
Stephenson, E	June 5, 1832	July 5, 1898	1861	1873	36	61	5	803	67	14.33	0	—	—	—	30/27
Stephenson, J S *	Nov 10, 1903	Oct 7, 1975	1923	1926	16	19	2	182	60	10.70	0	65	0	—	6
Stevenson, G B *	Dec 16, 1955	©	1973	1986	177	217	32	3,856	115*	20.84	2	13,254	464	28.56	73
Stott, W B	© July 18, 1934		1952	1963	187	309	19	9,168	186	31.61	17	112	7	16.00	91
Stringer, P M	Feb 23, 1943		1967	1969	13	17	8	101	15*	11.22	0	696	32	21.75	7
Stuchbury, S	June 22, 1954		1978	1981	3	3	2	7	4*	7.00	0	236	8	29.50	—
§ Sugg, F H	Jan 11, 1862	May 29, 1933	1883	1883	8	12	1	80	13*	10.00	0	—	—	—	4/1
§ Sugg, W	May 21, 1860	May 21, 1933	1881	1881	1	1	0	9	9	9.00	0	—	—	—	—
Sullivan, J H B *	Sept 21, 1890		1912	1912	1	2	0	41	26	20.50	0	43	0	—	—
Sutcliffe, H	Nov 24, 1894	Jan 22, 1978	1919	1945	602	864	96	38,558	313	50.20	112	381	8	47.62	402
Sutcliffe, W H H *	© Oct 10, 1926	Sept 16, 1998	1948	1957	177	273	34	6,247	181	26.13	6	152	6	25.33	80
Swallow, I G	Dec 18, 1962		1983	1989	61	82	18	1,296	114	20.25	1	3,270	64	51.09	28
§ Swanepoel, P J	Mar 30, 1977		2003	2003	2	3	0	20	17	6.66	0	129	3	43.00	1
§ Tait, J	Oct 7, 1872	Sept 6, 1954	1898	1899	2	2	1	7	3*	3.50	0	—	—	—	1
Tasker, J *	© Feb 4, 1887	Aug 24, 1975	1912	1913	31	43	4	586	67	15.02	0	—	—	—	14
Tattersall, G *	Apr 21, 1882	June 29, 1972	1905	1905	1	2	0	26	26	13.00	0	—	—	—	—
Taylor, C R	Feb 21, 1981		2001	2005	16	27	3	416	52*	17.33	0	26	0	—	8
Taylor, H	Dec 18, 1900	Oct 28, 1988	1924	1925	9	13	0	153	36	11.76	0	—	—	—	8
Taylor, H S	Dec 11, 1856	Nov 16, 1896	1879	1879	3	5	0	36	22	7.20	0	—	—	—	1
Taylor, J	Apr 2, 1850	May 27, 1924	1880	1881	9	13	1	107	44	8.91	0	—	—	—	4
Taylor, K	Aug 21, 1935		1953	1968	303	505	35	12,864	203*	27.37	16	3,680	129	28.52	146
Taylor, N S	June 2, 1963		1982	1983	8	6	1	10	4*	2.00	0	720	22	32.72	2
Taylor, T L *	© May 25, 1878	Mar. 16, 1960	1899	1906	82	122	5	3,933	156	35.11	8	—	—	—	47/2
§ Tendulkar, S R	Apr 24, 1973		1992	1992	16	25	2	1,070	100	46.52	1	195	4	48.75	10
Thewlis, H	Aug 31, 1865	Nov 30, 1920	1888	1888	2	4	1	4	2*	1.33	0	—	—	—	2
Thewlis, John Jun.	Sept 21, 1850	Aug 9, 1901	1879	1879	3	4	0	21	10	5.25	0	—	—	—	—
Thewlis, John Sen.	June 30, 1828	Dec 29, 1899	1861	1875	44	80	3	1,280	108	16.62	1	545	16	34.06	21/1
Thornicroft, N D.	Jan 23, 1985		2002	2007	7	10	4	50	30	8.33	0	—	—	—	2
Thornton, G *	July 20, 1854	Apr 18, 1915	1881	1881	3	4	0	21	7	5.25	0	—	—	—	2
Thornton, G *	Dec 24, 1867	Jan 31, 1939	1891	1891	3	4	0	21	16	5.25	0	74	2	37.00	—

LIST OF PLAYERS AND CAREER AVERAGES IN ALL FIRST-CLASS MATCHES FOR YORKSHIRE (Continued)

Player	Date of Birth	Date of Death (if known)	First Played	Last Played	M	Inns	NO	Runs	HS	Av'ge	100s	Runs	Wkts	Av'ge	Ct/St
Thorpe, G	Feb 20, 1834	Mar 2, 1899	1864	1864	1	2	1	14	9*	14.00	0	—	—	—	2
Threapleton, J W	July 20, 1857	July 30, 1918	1881	1881	1	1	1	8	8*	—	0	—	—	—	2/1
Tinsley, H J	Feb 20, 1865	Dec 10, 1938	1890	1891	9	13	0	56	15	4.30	0	57	4	14.25	1
Townsley, R A J	June 24, 1952		1974	1975	2	1	0	22	12	5.50	0	0	0	—	1
Towse, A D	Apr 22, 1968		1988	1988	1	1	0	1	1	1.00	0	50	3	16.66	—
Trueman, F S ©	Feb 6, 1931	July 1, 2006	1949	1968	459	533	81	6,852	104	15.15	2	29,890	1,745	17.12	325
Tunnicliffe, J	Aug 26, 1866	July 11, 1948	1891	1907	472	768	57	19,435	243	27.33	22	388	7	55.42	665
Turner, A	Sept 2, 1885	Aug 29, 1951	1910	1911	9	16	1	163	37	10.86	0	—	—	—	7
Turner, B	July 25, 1938		1960	1961	2	4	2	7	3*	3.50	0	47	2	11.75	2
Turner, C ©	Jan 11, 1902	Nov 19, 1968	1925	1946	200	266	32	6,132	130	26.20	2	5,320	173	30.75	181
Turner, F I	Sept 3, 1894	Oct 18, 1954	1924	1924	5	7	0	33	12	4.71	0	—	—	—	1
Tyson, C T	Jan 24, 1889	Apr 3, 1940	1921	1921	3	5	2	232	100*	77.33	2	—	—	—	—
Ullathorne, C E	Apr 11, 1845	May 2, 1904	1868	1875	27	46	8	283	28	7.44	0	—	—	—	19
Ulyett, G ©	Oct 21, 1851	June 18, 1898	1873	1893	355	618	31	14,157	199*	24.11	15	8,181	457	17.90	235
§ Usher, J	Feb 26, 1859	Aug 10, 1905	1888	1888	1	2	0	7	5	3.50	0	31	2	15.50	1
van Geloven, J	Jan 4, 1934	Aug 21, 2003	1955	1955	1	2	1	17	16	17.00	0	224	6	37.33	2
§ Vaughan, M P ©	Oct 29, 1974		1993	2009	151	267	14	9,160	183	36.20	20	4,268	92	46.39	55
§ Verelst, H W *	July 2, 1846	Apr 5, 1918	1868	1869	3	4	1	66	33*	22.00	0	—	—	—	1
Verity, H	May 18, 1905	July 31, 1943	1930	1939	278	294	77	3,898	101	17.96	1	21,353	1,558	13.70	191
Waddington, A ©	Feb 4, 1893	Oct 28, 1959	1919	1927	255	250	65	2,396	114	12.95	1	16,203	835	19.40	222
Wade, S ©	Feb 8, 1858	Nov 5, 1931	1886	1890	65	111	20	1,438	104*	15.80	0	2,498	133	18.78	31
Wainwright, D J ©	Mar 21, 1985		2004	2011	29	36	11	914	104*	36.56	0	2,480	69	35.94	6
Wainwright, E	Apr 8, 1865	Oct 28, 1919	1888	1902	352	545	36	11,092	228	21.53	18	17,744	998	17.77	327
Wainwright, W	Jan 21, 1882	Dec 31, 1961	1903	1905	24	36	3	648	62	19.63	0	582	19	30.63	21
Wake, W R *	May 21, 1852	Mar 14, 1896	1881	1881	3	3	0	13	11	4.33	0	—	—	—	2
Walker, A *	June 22, 1844	Dec 31, 1870	1863	1870	9	16	1	138	26	9.20	0	74	1	74.00	1
Walker, C	June 26, 1919	Dec 3, 1992	1947	1948	5	9	2	268	91	38.28	0	71	2	35.50	3
Walker, T	Apr 3, 1854	Aug 28, 1925	1879	1880	14	22	2	179	30	8.95	0	7	0	—	1
Waller, G	Dec 3, 1864	Dec 11, 1937	1893	1894	3	4	0	17	13	4.25	0	70	4	17.50	1

LIST OF PLAYERS AND CAREER AVERAGES IN ALL FIRST-CLASS MATCHES FOR YORKSHIRE (Continued)

Player	Date of Birth	Date of Death (if known)	First Played	Last Played	M	Inns	NO	Runs	HS	Av'ge	100s	Runs	Wkts	Av'ge	Ct/St
Wallgate, L *	Nov 12, 1849	May 9, 1887	1875	1878	3	3	0	9	6	3.00	0	17	1	17.00	3
Ward, A	Nov 21, 1865	Jan 6, 1939	1886	1886	4	7	1	41	22	6.83	0	1	0	—	1
Ward, F	Aug 31, 1881	Feb 28, 1948	1903	1903	1	1	1			0.00	0	16	0	—	—
Ward, H P *	Jan 20, 1899	Dec 16, 1946	1920	1920	1	1	0	10	10*	—	0	—	—	—	—
Wardall, T A ◎	Apr 19, 1862	Dec 20, 1932	1884	1894	43	73	1	1,003	106	14.12	2	489	23	21.26	25
Wardlaw I ◎	**Jun 29, 1985**		**2011**	**2011**	**1**	**0**	**0**	**0**		—	**0**	**68**	**1**	**68.00**	**1**
Wardle, J H ◎	Jan 8, 1923	July 23, 1985	1946	1958	330	418	57	5,765	79	15.96	0	27,917	1,539	18.13	210
Waring, J S	Oct 1, 1942		1963	1966	28	27	15	137	26	11.41	0	1,122	53	21.16	17
Washington, S	Nov 4, 1838	Apr 17, 1919	1870	1870	1	1	0	9	9	9.00	0	—	—	—	—
Washington, W A ◎	Dec 11, 1879	Oct 20, 1927	1900	1902	44	62	6	1,290	100*	23.03	1	—	—	—	18
Watson, H	Sept 26, 1880	Nov 24, 1951	1908	1914	29	35	11	141	41		0	75	0	—	46/10
Watson, W ◎	Mar 7, 1920	Apr 24, 2004	1939	1957	283	430	65	13,953	214*	38.22	26	—	—	—	170
Waud, B W * ◎	June 4, 1837	May 30, 1889	1862	1864	6	10	1	165	42	18.33	0	—	—	—	2
Webster, C	June 9, 1838	Jan 6, 1881	1861	1868	5	5	1	30	10	7.50	0	—	—	—	—
Webster, H H	May 8, 1844	Mar 5, 1915	1868	1868	2	3	0	10	10	3.33	0	—	—	—	—
§ Weekes, L C	July 19, 1971		1994	2000	2	2	0	10	10	10.00	0	191	10	19.10	1
West, J	Oct 16, 1844	Jan 27, 1890	1868	1876	38	64	13	461	41	9.03	0	853	53	16.09	14
Wharf, A G	June 4, 1975		1994	1997	7	9	1	186	62	23.25	0	111	5	22.20	2
Whatmough, F J	Dec 4, 1856	June 3, 1904	1878	1882	7	11	1	51	20	5.10	0	—	—	—	4
Wheater, C H *	Mar 4, 1860	May 11, 1885	1880	1880	2	4	1	45	27	15.00	0	7	0	—	—
White, Sir A W * ◎	Oct 14, 1877	Dec 16, 1945	1908	1920	97	128	28	1,457	55	14.57	0	—	—	—	50
White, C ◎	Dec 16, 1969		1990	2007	221	350	45	10,376	186	34.01	19	7,649	276	27.71	140
Whitehead, J P	Sept 3, 1925	Aug 15, 2000	1946	1951	37	38	17	387	58*	18.42	0	2,610	96	27.47	68
Whitehead, Lees	Mar 14, 1864	Nov 22, 1913	1889	1904	119	172	38	2,073	67*	15.47	0	2,408	99	24.32	—
Whitehead, Luther	June 25, 1869	Jan 16, 1931	1893	1893	2	4	0	21	13	5.25	0	—	—	—	21
Whiteley, J P	Feb 28, 1955		1978	1982	45	38	17	231	26	11.00	0	2,410	70	34.42	2
Whiting, C P	Apr 18, 1888	Jan 14, 1959	1914	1920	6	10	0	92	26	11.50	0	416	15	27.73	—
Whitwell, J F *	Feb 22, 1869	Nov 6, 1932	1890	1890	10	14	2	8	4	4.00	0	11		4.00	2
§ Whitwell, W F *	Dec 12, 1867	Apr 12, 1942	1890	1890	10	14	2	67	26	5.58	0	518	25	20.72	5
Widdup, S	Nov 10, 1977		2000	2001	11	18	1	245	44	14.41	0	22	1	22.00	

Player	Date of Birth	Date of Death (if known)	First Played	Last Played	M	Inns	NO	Runs	HS	Av'ge	100s	Runs	Wkts	Av'ge	Ct/St
Wigley, D H	Oct 26, 1981		2002	2002	1	2	1	19	15	19.00	0	116	1	116.00	—
§ Wilkinson, A J A *	May 28, 1835	Dec 11, 1905	1865	1868	5	6	0	129	53	21.50	0	57	0	—	1
Wilkinson, F	May 23, 1914	Mar 26, 1984	1937	1939	14	14	1	73	18*	5.61	0	590	26	22.69	12
Wilkinson, H *	© Dec 11, 1877	Apr 15, 1967	1903	1905	48	75	3	1,382	113	19.19	1	121	3	40.33	19
Wilkinson, R	Nov 11, 1977		1998	1998	1	1	0	9	9	9.00	0	35	1	35.00	4
Wilkinson, W H	Mar 12, 1881	June 4, 1961	1903	1910	126	192	14	3,812	103	21.41	1	971	31	31.32	93
Williams, A C	Mar 1, 1887	June 1, 1966	1911	1919	12	14	10	95	48*	23.75	0	678	30	22.60	6
Wilson, B B	© Dec 11, 1879	Sept 14, 1957	1906	1914	185	308	12	8,053	208	27.50	15	278	12	139.00	53
Wilson, C E M *	© May 15, 1875	Feb 8, 1944	1896	1899	8	13	3	256	91*	25.60	0	257	12	21.41	3
Wilson, D	Aug 7, 1937		1957	1974	392	502	85	5,788	83	13.88	0	22,626	1,104	20.49	235
Wilson, E R *	© Mar 25, 1879	July 21, 1957	1899	1923	66	72	14	902	104*	16.70	1	3,106	197	15.76	30
Wilson, Geoffrey *	© Aug 21, 1895	Nov 29, 1960	1919	1924	92	94	14	983	70	12.28	0	11	0	—	33
Wilson, G A *	Feb 2, 1916	Sept 24, 2002	1936	1939	15	25	5	352	55*	17.60	0	138	1	138.00	7
Wilson, John *	June 30, 1857	Nov 11, 1931	1887	1888	4	5	1	17	13*	4.25	0	165	12	13.75	3
Wilson, J P *	Apr 3, 1889	Oct 3, 1959	1911	1912	9	14	1	81	36	6.23	0	24	1	24.00	2
Wilson, J V	Jan 17, 1921	June 5, 2008	1946	1962	477	724	75	20,548	230	31.66	29	313	3	104.33	520
Wood, A	© Aug 25, 1898	Apr 1, 1973	1927	1946	408	481	80	8,579	123*	21.39	1	33	1	33.00	612/243
Wood, B	Dec 26, 1942		1964	1964	5	7	2	63	35	12.60	0				4
Wood, C H	July 26, 1934	June 28, 2006	1959	1959	4	4	1	22	10	7.33	0	319	11	29.00	1
Wood, G W	Nov 18, 1862	Dec 4, 1948	1895	1895	2	2	0	2	1	1.00	0				0/1
Wood, H *	Mar 22, 1855	July 31, 1941	1879	1880	10	16	1	156	36	10.40	0	212	10	21.20	8
Wood, J H *			1881	1881	2	1	0	14	14	14.00	0				—
Wood, M J	© Apr 6, 1977		1997	2007	128	222	20	6,742	207	33.37	16	27	2	13.50	113
Wood, R	June 3, 1929	May 22, 1990	1952	1956	22	18	4	60	17	4.28	0	1,346	51	26.39	5
Woodford, J D	Sept 9, 1943		1968	1972	38	61	2	1,204	101	20.40	1	185	4	46.25	12
Woodhead, F E *	May 29, 1868	Aug 25, 1943	1893	1894	4	8	0	57	18	7.12	0				3
Woodhouse, W H *	Apr 16, 1856	Mar 4, 1938	1884	1885	9	13	0	218	63	16.76	0				6
Wormald, A	May 10, 1855	Feb 6, 1940	1885	1891	7	11	3	161	80	20.12	0				10/2

LIST OF PLAYERS AND CAREER AVERAGES IN ALL FIRST-CLASS MATCHES FOR YORKSHIRE (Continued)

Player	Date of Birth	Date of Death (if known)	First Played	Last Played	M	Inns	NO	Runs	HS	Av'ge	100s	Runs	Wkts	Av'ge	Ct/St
Worsley, W A * ©	Apr 5, 1890	Dec 4, 1973	1928	1929	60	50	4	722	60	15.69	0	—	—	—	32
Wrathmell, L F	Jan 22, 1855	Sept 16, 1928	1886	1886	2	2	0	18	17	9.00	0	—	—	—	—
Wright, R	July 19, 1852	May 25, 1891	1877	1877	2	4	1	28	22	9.33	0	—	—	—	—
Wright, T J *	Mar 5, 1900	Nov 7, 1962	1919	1919	1	1	0	12	12	12.00	0	—	—	—	—
Yardley, N W D * ©	Mar 19, 1915	Oct 4, 1989	1936	1955	302	420	56	11,632	183*	31.95	17	5,818	195	29.83	220
Yeadon, J	Dec 10, 1861	May 30, 1914	1888	1888	3	6	2	41	22	10.25	0	—	—	—	5/3
§ Younus Khan	Nov 29, 1977		2007	2007	13	19	2	824	217*	48.47	3	342	8	42.75	11
§ Yuvraj Singh	Dec 12, 1981		2003	2003	7	12	2	145	56	14.50	0	130	3	43.33	12

In the career averages it should be noted that the bowling analysis for the second Cambridgeshire innings at Ashton-under-Lyne in 1865 has not been found. G R Atkinson took 3 wickets, W Cuttell 2, G Freeman 4 and R Iddison 1. The respective bowling averages have been calculated excluding these wickets.

MOST FIRST-CLASS APPEARANCES FOR YORKSHIRE

Matches	Player	Matches	Player	Matches	Player
883	W Rhodes (1898-1930)	496	R Illingworth (1951-1983)	429	D L Bairstow (1970-1990)
717	G H Hirst (1891-1929)	491	† J G Binks (1955-1969)	427	A Dolphin (1905-1927)
676	D Denton (1894-1920)	487	D E V Padgett (1951-1971)	425	P Carrick (1970-1993)
602	H Sutcliffe (1919-1945)	485	P Holmes (1913-1933)	414	G Boycott (1962-1986)
548	M Leyland (1920-1947)	477	J V Wilson (1946-1962)	413	E. Robinson (1919-1931)
536	D B Close (1949-1970)	472	J Tunnicliffe (1891-1907)	411	P J Sharpe (1958-1974)
517	D Hunter (1888-1909)	459	F S Trueman (1949-1968)	408	A Wood (1927-1946)
513	S Haigh (1895-1913)	456	J H Hampshire (1961-1981)	401	A Mitchell (1922-1945)
510	Lord Hawke (1881-1911)	445	G G Macaulay (1920-1935)		

† Kept wicket in 412 consecutive Championship matches 1955-1969

MOST TOTAL APPEARANCES FOR YORKSHIRE
(First-Class, Domestic List A and t20)

Matches	Player	Matches	Player
883	W Rhodes (1898-1930)	512	M D Moxon (1980-1997)
827	D L Bairstow (1970-1990)	510	Lord Hawke (1881-1911)
727	P Carrick (1970-1993)	500	P J Sharpe (1958-1974)
717	R J Blakey (1985-2004)	485	P Holmes (1913-1933)
717	G H Hirst (1891-1929)	477	J V Wilson (1946-1962)
687	J H Hampshire (1961-1981)	472	J Tunicliffe (1891-1907)
676	D Denton (1894-1920)	470	F S Trueman (1949-1968)
674	G Boycott (1962-1986)	467	J D Love (1975-1989)
602	H Sutcliffe (1919-1945)	451	D Wilson (1957-1974)
577	D Byas (1986-2001)	449	A Sidebottom (1973-1991)
568	D B Close (1949-1970)	445	G G Macauley (1920-1935)
563	A McGrath (1995-2011)	440	C M Old (1966-1982)
548	M Leyland (1920-1947)	427	A Dolphin (1905-1927)
545	C White (1990-2007)	413	E Robinson (1919-1931)
544	D E V Padgett (1951-1971)	411	P J Hartley (1985-1997)
536	R Illingworth (1951-1983)	408	A Wood (1927-1946)
521	J G Binks (1955-1969)	401	A Mitchell (1922-1945)
517	D Hunter (1888-1909)	401	A G Nicholson (1962-1975)
513	S Haigh (1895-1913)		

374

FRIENDS PROVIDENT TROPHY, CHELTENHAM & GLOUCESTER TROPHY, GILLETTE CUP AND NATWEST TROPHY 1963-2009

WINNERS 1965, 1969 AND 2002
SEMI-FINALISTS 1980, 1982, 1995, 1996, 1999, 2004, 2005 AND 2008

Played 137, Won 77 (in Yorkshire 36, Away 41). Lost 54 (in Yorkshire 21, Away 33).
No Result 4 (in Yorkshire 3, Away 1). Abandoned 2 (in Yorkshire 1, Away 1)

Highest Score:	By Yorkshire:	411:6 v. Devon at Exmouth, 2004
	Against Yorkshire:	339:7 by Northamptonshire at Northampton, 2006
†Lowest Score:	By Yorkshire:	76 v. Surrey at Harrogate, 1970
	Against Yorkshire:	53 by Ireland at Leeds, 1997
Highest Individual Score:	For Yorkshire:	160 M J Wood v. Devon at Exmouth, 2004
	Against Yorkshire:	177 S A Newman for Surrey at The Oval, 2009

Highest Partnerships: For Yorkshire:

1st wkt	242*	M D Moxon (107*) and A A Metcalfe (127*) v. Warwickshire at Leeds, 1990
2nd wkt	202	G Boycott (87) and C W J Athey (115) v. Kent at Leeds, 1980
3rd wkt	164	A McGrath (105*) and J A Rudolph (82) v. Scotland at Leeds, 2008
4th wkt	207	S A Kellett (107) and C White (113) v. Ireland at Leeds, 1995
5th wkt	160*	G M Fellows (80*) and C White (73*) v Surrey at Leeds, 2001
6th wkt	128*	A McGrath (72*) and G M Fellows (68*) v. Essex at Chelmsford, 2002
7th wkt	102	D L Bairstow (92) and C M Old (55*) v. Worcestershire at Leeds, 1982
8th wkt	79	P J Hartley (83) and D Gough (46) v. Ireland at Leeds, 1997
9th wkt	66	T T Bresnan (55) and A Shahzad (33) v. Durham at Chester-le-Street, 2008
10th wkt	29*	R Illingworth (32*) and A G Nicholson (15*) v. Warwickshire at Birmingham, 1968

Best Bowling:	For Yorkshire:	7 for 27 D Gough v. Ireland at Leeds, 1997
	Against Yorkshire:	7 for 33 R D Jackman for Surrey at Harrogate, 1970
Most Economical Bowling:	For Yorkshire:	12-9-4-1 D Wilson v. Norfolk at Lakenham, 1969
	Against Yorkshire:	12-6-10-0 D L Underwood for Kent at Canterbury, 1981
Most Expensive Bowling:	For Yorkshire:	10-0-82-3 T T Bresnan v. Northamptonshire at Northampton, 2006
	Against Yorkshire:	12-1-96-0 M E. Waugh for Essex at Chelmsford, 1995

†Lowest score is either the lowest all-out score or the lowest score at completion of 60 overs (65 overs in 1963. 50 overs from 1999)

Centuries (23)

C W J Athey	115	v. Kent at Leeds, 1980
G Boycott	146	v. Surrey at Lord's, 1965
M T G Elliott	128*	v. Somerset at Lord's, 2002
J H Hampshire	110	v. Durham at Middlesbrough, 1978
S A Kellett	107	v. Ireland at Leeds, 1995
D S Lehmann (2)	105	v. Glamorgan at Cardiff, 1997
	118*	v. Northamptonshire at Northampton, 2006
A McGrath (3)	135*	v. Lancashire at Manchester, 2007
	100	v. Durham at Leeds, 2007
	105*	v. Scotland at Leeds, 2008
A A Metcalfe	127*	v. Warwickshire at Leeds, 1990
M D Moxon (2)	107*	v. Warwickshire at Leeds, 1990
	137	v. Nottinghamshire at Leeds, 1996
J A Rudolph (2)	100	v. Leicestershire at Leeds, 2007
	118	v Gloucestershire at Leeds, 2009
M P Vaughan	116*	v Lancashire at Manchester, 2004
C White (4)	113	v. Ireland at Leeds, 1995
	100*	v. Surrey at Leeds, 2002
	112	v. Northamptonshire at Northampton, 2006
	101*	v. Durham at Chester-le-Street, 2006
M J Wood (2)	118*	v. Cambridgeshire at March, 2003
	160	v. Devon at Exmouth, 2004
Younus Khan	100	v. Nottinghamshire at Nottingham, 2007

5 Wickets in an Innings (8)

D Gough (2)	7 for 27 v. Ireland at Leeds, 1997
	5 for 30 v. Yorkshire CB at Harrogate, 2000
P J Hartley	5 for 46 v. Hampshire at Southampton, 1990
M J Hoggard	5 for 65 v. Somerset at Lord's, 2002
R Illingworth	5 for 29 v. Surrey at Lord's, 1965
A Sidebottom	5 for 27 v. Glamorgan at Leeds, 1987
G B Stevenson	5 for 27 v. Berkshire at Reading, 1983
F S Trueman	6 for 15 v. Somerset at Taunton, 1965

Man of the Match Awards

M D Moxon	5
J H Hampshire	4
C White	4
M P Vaughan	3
C W J Athey	2
M G Bevan	2
G Boycott	2
G L Brophy	2
D Gough	2
A McGrath	2
A A Metcalfe	2
P J Sharpe	2
C E W Silverwood	2
M J Wood	2

D L Bairstow, T T Bresnan, P Carrick, D B Close, M T G Elliott, G M Fellows, S D Fletcher, P J Hartley, P M Hutchison, R Illingworth, S A Kellett, B Leadbeater, D S Lehmann, M J Lumb, R M Pyrah, A Sidebottom, G B Stevenson, F S Trueman (1 each). (54 Awards: 32 Players).

versus Derbyshire: Played 5, Won 3 (in Yorkshire 1, Away 2), Lost 1 (in Yorkshire), No Result 1 (Away)

Highest Score:	By Yorkshire	253:4 at Derby, 2007
	By Derbyshire	251:6 at Leeds, 2006
Lowest Score:	By Yorkshire	219:8 at Lord's, 1969
	By Derbyshire	94 at Leeds, 2008
Highest Individual Score:	For Yorkshire	81 J A Rudolph at Derby, 2007
	For Derbyshire	100 C R Taylor at Leeds, 2006
Best Bowling:	For Yorkshire	3-16 A McGrath at Leeds, 2008
	For Derbyshire	3-31 A Ward at Lord's, 1969

versus Durham: Played 9, Won 5 (in Yorkshire 3, Away 2), Lost 4 (in Yorkshire 2, Away 2)

Highest Score:	By Yorkshire	268:7 at Chester-le-Street, 2009
	By Durham	266:8 at Leeds, 2007
Lowest Score:	By Yorkshire	135 at Harrogate, 1973
	By Durham	166 at Leeds, 2009
Highest Individual Score:	For Yorkshire	110 J H Hampshire at Middlesbrough, 1978
	For Durham	124* J P Maher at Chester-le-Street, 2006
Best Bowling:	For Yorkshire	4-9 C M Old at Middlesbrough, 1978
	For Durham	5-15 B R Lander at Harrogate, 1973

versus Essex: Played 4, Won 3 (in Yorkshire 1, Away 2), Lost 1 (Away)

Highest Score:	By Yorkshire	307:3 at Chelmsford, 1995
	By Essex	285:8 at Chelmsford, 2008
Lowest Score:	By Yorkshire	198 at Chelmsford, 2008
	By Essex	132 at Leeds, 1982
Highest Individual Score:	For Yorkshire	92 S A Kellett at Chelmsford, 1995
	For Essex	95 A N Cook at Chelmsford, 2008
Best Bowling:	For Yorkshire	3-21 A Sidebottom at Leeds, 1982
	For Essex:	3-30 R N ten Doeschate at Chelmsford, 2008

versus Glamorgan: Played 2, Won 1 (in Yorkshire), Lost 1 (Away)

Highest Score:	By Yorkshire	236:8	at Cardiff, 1997
	By Glamorgan	237:9	at Cardiff, 1997
Lowest Score:	By Yorkshire	—	
	By Glamorgan	83	at Leeds, 1987

Highest Individual

Score:	For Yorkshire	105	D S Lehmann at Cardiff, 1997
	For Glamorgan	62	M P Maynard at Cardiff, 1997
Best Bowling:	For Yorkshire	5-27	A Sidebottom at Leeds, 1987
	For Glamorgan	3-26	D A Cosker at Cardiff, 1997

versus Gloucestershire: Played 7, Won 2 (Away 2), Lost 5 (in Yorkshire 2, Away 3)

Highest Score:	By Yorkshire	243:6	at Bristol, 2004
		243:8	at Bristol, 1993
	By Gloucestershire	269	at Leeds, 2009
Lowest Score:	By Yorkshire	217:9	at Bristol, 2009
	By Gloucestershire	201	at Bristol, 2008

Highest Individual

Score:	For Yorkshire	118	J A Rudolph at Leeds, 2009
	For Gloucestershire	143*	C M Spearman at Bristol, 2004
Best Bowling:	For Yorkshire	4-31	T T Bresnan at Bristol, 2008
	For Gloucestershire	4-21	M J Procter at Leeds, 1976

versus Hampshire: Played 5, Won 2 (in Yorkshire 1, Away 1), Lost 3 (in Yorkshire 0, Away 3)

Highest Score:	By Yorkshire	233:6	at Bradford, 1974
	By Hampshire	261	at Bournemouth, 1977
Lowest Score:	By Yorkshire	118	at Southampton, 1990
	By Hampshire	192	at Bradford, 1974

Highest Individual

Score:	For Yorkshire	93*	C W J Athey at Southampton, 1980
	For Hampshire	100	S M Ervine at Southampton, 2005
Best Bowling:	For Yorkshire	5-46	P J Hartley at Southampton, 1990
	For Hampshire	5-35	J M Rice at Bournemouth, 1977

versus Kent: Played 3, Won 1 (in Yorkshire 1, Away 0), Lost 2 (in Yorkshire 0, Away 2)

Highest Score:	By Yorkshire	279:6	at Leeds, 1980
	By Kent	233	at Leeds, 1980
Lowest Score:	By Yorkshire	148	at Canterbury, 1971
	By Kent	233	at Leeds, 1980

Highest Individual

Score:	For Yorkshire	115	C W J Athey at Leeds, 1980
	For Kent	118*	C J Tavaré at Canterbury, 1981
Best Bowling:	For Yorkshire	4-35	A Sidebottom at Leeds, 1980
	For Kent	5-25	B D Julien at Canterbury, 1971

versus Lancashire: Played 12, Won 5 (in Yorkshire 2, Away 3), Lost 6 (in Yorkshire 1, Away 5), No result 1 (in Yorkshire)

Highest Score:	By Yorkshire	292:4	at Leeds, 2006
	By Lancashire	293:9	at Manchester, 1996
Lowest Score:	By Yorkshire	173	at Leeds, 1974
	By Lancashire	169	at Leeds, 1995

Highest Individual

Score:	For Yorkshire	135*	A McGrath at Manchester, 2007
	For Lancashire	141*	B J Hodge at Manchester, 2007
Best Bowling:	For Yorkshire	4-18	G S Blewett at Manchester, 1999
	For Lancashire	4-17	P Lever at Leeds, 1974

versus Leicestershire: Played 7, Won 3 (in Yorkshire 1, Away 2), Lost 4 (in Yorkshire 3, Away 1)

Highest Score:	By Yorkshire	310:5	at Leicester, 1997
	By Leicestershire	284:4	at Leeds, 2007
Lowest Score:	By Yorkshire	109	at Leeds, 1975
	By Leicestershire	168	at Leicester, 1965
Highest Individual			
Score:	For Yorkshire	100	J A Rudolph at Leeds, 2007
	For Leicestershire	90	I J Sutcliffe at Leicester, 1997
Best Bowling:	For Yorkshire	4-18	H P Cooper at Leeds, 1975
	For Leicestershire	5-34	P A J DeFreitas at Leeds, 1987

versus Middlesex: Played 5, Won 2 (in Yorkshire 2, Away 0), Lost 3 (in Yorkshire 1, Away 2)

Highest Score:	By Yorkshire	205:9	at Leeds, 1986
	By Middlesex	225:7	at Leeds, 1988
Lowest Score:	By Yorkshire	90	at Lord's, 1964
	By Middlesex	151	at Lord's, 1964
Highest Individual			
Score:	For Yorkshire	73*	D Byas at Leeds, 1996
	For Middlesex	104	P N Weekes at Leeds, 1996
Best Bowling:	For Yorkshire	4-29	H P Cooper at Lord's, 1979 and C Shaw at Leeds, 1988
	For Middlesex	4-24	N G Cowans at Leeds, 1986

versus Northamptonshire: Played 8, Won 4 (in Yorkshire 2, Away 2), Lost 4 (in Yorkshire 2, Away 2)

Highest Score:	By Yorkshire	341:3	at Northampton, 2006
	By Northamptonshire	339:7	at Northampton, 2006
Lowest Score:	By Yorkshire	165	at Leeds, 1983
	By Northamptonshire	211:7	at Leeds, 1983
Highest Individual			
Score:	For Yorkshire	118*	D S Lehmann at Northampton, 2006
	For Northamptonshire	161	D J G Sales at Northampton, 2006
Best Bowling:	For Yorkshire	4-36	D Gough at Northampton, 2000
	For Northamptonshire	5-33	B J Griffiths at Leeds, 1983

versus Nottinghamshire: Played 6, Won 5 (in Yorkshire 4, Away 1), Lost 0, Abandoned 1 (in Yorkshire)

Highest Score:	By Yorkshire	345:5	at Leeds, 1996
	By Nottinghamshire	243	at Nottingham, 2007
Lowest Score:	By Yorkshire	191	at Scarborough, 1969
	By Nottinghamshire	123	at Scarborough, 1969
Highest Individual			
Score:	For Yorkshire	137	M D Moxon at Leeds, 1996
	For Nottinghamshire	100*	J B Bolus at Middlesbrough, 1963
Best Bowling:	For Yorkshire	4-30	F S Trueman at Middlesbrough, 1963
	For Nottinghamshire	4-33	K Gilhouley at Middlesbrough, 1963

versus Somerset: Played 5, Won 2 (in Yorkshire 0, Away 2), Lost 3 (in Yorkshire 2, Away 1)

Highest Score:	By Yorkshire	260:4	at Lord's, 2002
	By Somerset	256:8	at Lord's, 2002
Lowest Score:	By Yorkshire	150	at Taunton, 1966
	By Somerset	63	at Taunton, 1965
Highest Individual			
Score:	For Yorkshire	128*	M T G Elliott at Lord's, 2002
	For Somerset	87*	I V A Richards at Leeds, 1985
Best Bowling:	For Yorkshire	6-15	F S Trueman at Taunton, 1965
	For Somerset	4-33	R Palmer at Taunton, 1966

versus Surrey: Played 9, Won 5 (in Yorkshire 2, Away 3), Lost 4 (in Yorkshire 2, Away 2)

Highest Score:	By Yorkshire	330:6	at The Oval, 2009
	By Surrey	329:8	at The Oval, 2009
Lowest Score:	By Yorkshire	76	at Harrogate, 1970
	By Surrey	134	at The Oval, 1969 and 134:8 at Harrogate, 1970

Highest Individual

Score:	For Yorkshire	146	G Boycott at Lord's, 1965
	For Surrey	177	S A Newman at The Oval, 2009
Best Bowling:	For Yorkshire	5-29	R Illingworth at Lord's, 1965
	For Surrey	7-33	R D Jackman at Harrogate, 1970

versus Sussex: Played 6, Won 2, (in Yorkshire 1, Away 1), Lost 4 (in Yorkshire 2, Away 2)

Highest Score:	By Yorkshire	270	at Hove, 1963
	By Sussex	292	at Hove, 1963
Lowest Score:	By Yorkshire	125	at Leeds, 1986
	By Sussex	212:9	at Hove, 1996

Highest Individual

Score:	For Yorkshire	82	M P Vaughan at Leeds, 2009
	For Sussex	90	J M Parks at Hove, 1963
Best Bowling:	For Yorkshire	4-35	T T Bresnan at Leeds, 2009
	For Sussex	4-17	G S Le Roux at Leeds, 1986

versus Warwickshire: Played 10, Won 2 (in Yorkshire 1, Away 1), Lost 6 (in Yorkshire 3, Away 3), No Result 1 (in Yorkshire), Abandoned 1 (Away)

Highest Score:	By Yorkshire	242:0	at Leeds, 1990
	By Warwickshire	245	at Leeds, 1993
Lowest Score:	By Yorkshire	123	at Birmingham, 1991
	By Warwickshire	157	at Birmingham, 1965

Highest Individual

Score:	For Yorkshire	127*	A A Metcalfe at Leeds, 1990
	For Warwickshire	113	K D Smith at Birmingham, 1982
Best Bowling:	For Yorkshire	3-26	P Carrick at Leeds, 1990
	For Warwickshire	4-16	A A Donald at Birmingham, 1991

versus Worcestershire: Played 5, Won 2 (in Yorkshire), Lost 2 (Away), No Result 1 (in Yorkshire)

Highest Score:	By Yorkshire	290:7	at Leeds, 1982
	By Worcestershire	286:5	at Leeds, 1982
Lowest Score:	By Yorkshire	177	at Worcester, 2003
	By Worcestershire	215:7	at Leeds, 2007

Highest Individual

Score:	For Yorkshire	92	D L Bairstow at Leeds, 1982
	For Worcestershire	105	G M Turner at Leeds, 1982
Best Bowling:	For Yorkshire	3-41	I J Harvey at Leeds, 2005
	For Worcestershire	5-49	M Hayward at Worcester, 2003

versus Ireland: Played 4, Won 4 (in Yorkshire 3, Away 1), Lost 0

Highest Score:	By Yorkshire	299:6	at Leeds, 1995
	By Ireland	228:7	at Leeds, 1995
Lowest Score:	By Yorkshire	249	at Leeds, 1997
	By Ireland	53	at Leeds, 1997

Highest Individual

Score:	For Yorkshire	113	C White at Leeds, 1995
	For Ireland	82	S J S Warke at Leeds, 1995
Best Bowling:	For Yorkshire	7-27	D Gough at Leeds, 1997
	For Ireland	3-26	P McCrum at Leeds, 1997

versus Scotland: Played 5, Won 5 (in Yorkshire 3, Away 2)

Highest Score:	By Yorkshire	259:8	at Edinburgh, 2007
	By Scotland	244	at Leeds, 2008
Lowest Score:	By Yorkshire	—	
	By Scotland	193:8	at Edinburgh, 2008
Highest Individual			
Score:	For Yorkshire	105*	A McGrath at Leeds, 2008
	For Scotland	73	I L Philip at Leeds, 1989
Best Bowling:	For Yorkshire	3-22	T T Bresnan at Edinburgh, 2007
	For Scotland	3-62	J A R Blain at Edinburgh, 2007

versus Bedfordshire: Played 1, Won 1 (Away)

Highest Score:	By Yorkshire	212:6	at Luton, 2001
	By Bedfordshire	211:9	at Luton, 2001
Highest Individual			
Score:	For Yorkshire	88	D S Lehmann at Luton, 2001
	For Bedfordshire	34	O J Clayton at Luton, 2001
Best Bowling:	For Yorkshire	4-39	R J Sidebottom at Luton, 2001
	For Bedfordshire	4-54	S Rashid at Luton, 2001

versus Berkshire: Played 2, Won 2 (Away 2)

Highest Score:	By Yorkshire	131:3	at Reading, 1983
	By Berkshire	128:9	at Reading, 1983
Lowest Score:	By Yorkshire	Have not been dismissed,	
		nor batted through entire overs	
	By Berkshire	105	at Finchampstead, 1988
Highest Individual			
Score:	For Yorkshire	74*	A A Metcalfe at Finchampstead, 1988
	For Berkshire	29	G R J Roope at Reading, 1983
Best Bowling:	For Yorkshire	5-27	G B Stevenson at Reading, 1983
	For Berkshire	1-15	M Lickley at Reading, 1983

versus Cambridgeshire: Played 3, Won 3 (in Yorkshire 2, Away 1)

Highest Score:	By Yorkshire	299:5	at March, 2003
	By Cambridgeshire	214:8	at March, 2003
Lowest Score:	By Cambridgeshire	176:8	at Leeds, 1986
Highest Individual			
Score:	For Yorkshire	118*	M J Wood March, 2003
	For Cambridgeshire	85	J D R Benson at Leeds, 1986
Best Bowling:	For Yorkshire	3-11	A G Nicholson at Castleford, 1967
	For Cambridgeshire	3-53	Ajaz Akhtar at March, 2003

versus Cheshire: Played 1, Won 1 (Away)

Highest Score:	By Yorkshire	160:0	at Oxton, 1985
	By Cheshire	159:7	at Oxton, 1985
Highest Individual			
Score:	For Yorkshire	82*	M D Moxon at Oxton, 1985
	For Cheshire	46	K Teesdale at Oxton, 1985
Best Bowling:	For Yorkshire	2-17	G B Stevenson at Oxton, 1985
	For Cheshire	No wicket taken	

versus Devon: Played 4, Won 4, (Away 4)

Highest Score:	By Yorkshire	411:6	at Exmouth, 2004
	By Devon	279:8	at Exmouth, 2004
Lowest Score:	By Devon	80	at Exmouth, 1998
Highest Individual			
Score:	For Yorkshire	160	M J Wood at Exmouth, 2004
	For Devon	83	P M Roebuck at Exmouth, 1994
Best Bowling:	For Yorkshire	4-26	D S Lehmann at Exmouth, 2002
	For Devon	2-42	A O F Le Fleming at Exmouth, 1994

versus Dorset: Played 1, Won 1, (Away)

Scores:	By Yorkshire	101:2	at Bournemouth, 2004
	By Dorset	97	at Bournemouth, 2004

Highest Individual

Score:	For Yorkshire	71*	M J Wood at Bournemouth, 2004
	For Dorset	23	C L Park at Bournemouth, 2004
Best Bowling:	For Yorkshire	4-18	C E W Silverwood at Bournemouth, 2004
	For Devon	2-31	D J L Worrad at Bournemouth, 2004

versus Herefordshire: Played 1, Won 1 (Away)

Highest Score:	By Yorkshire	275:8	at Kington, 1999
	By Herefordshire	124:5	at Kington, 1999

Highest Individual

Score:	For Yorkshire	77	G S Blewett at Kington, 1999
	For Herefordshire	39	R D Hughes at Kington, 1999
Best Bowling:	For Yorkshire	2-22	G M Hamilton at Kington, 1999
	For Herefordshire	2-41	C W Boroughs at Kington, 1999

versus Norfolk: Played 2, Won 2 (in Yorkshire 1, Away 1)

Highest Score:	By Yorkshire	167	at Lakenham, 1969
	By Norfolk	104	at Leeds, 1990
Lowest Score:	By Yorkshire	167	at Lakenham, 1969
	By Norfolk	78	at Lakenham, 1969

Highest Individual

Score:	For Yorkshire	56*	M D Moxon at Leeds, 1990
	For Norfolk	25	R J Finney at Leeds, 1990
Best Bowling:	For Yorkshire	3-8	P Carrick at Leeds, 1990
	For Norfolk	6-48	T I Moore at Lakenham, 1969

versus Northumberland: Played 1, Won 1 (Away)

Highest Score:	By Yorkshire	138:2	(51.3 overs) at Leeds, 1992
	By Northumberland	137	at Leeds, 1992

Highest Individual

Score:	For Yorkshire	38	S A Kellett at Leeds, 1992
	For Northumberland	47	G R Morris at Leeds, 1992
Best Bowling:	For Yorkshire	3-18	M A Robinson at Leeds, 1992
	For Northumberland	2-22	S Greensword at Leeds, 1992

versus Shropshire: Played 2, Won 1 (Away 1), Lost 1 (Away 1)

Highest Score:	By Yorkshire	192	at Telford, 1984
	By Shropshire	229:5	at Telford, 1984
Lowest Score:	By Yorkshire	192	at Telford, 1984
	By Shropshire	185	at Wellington, 1976

Highest Individual

Score:	For Yorkshire	59	J H Hampshire at Wellington, 1976
	For Shropshire	80	Mushtaq Mohammed at Telford, 1984
Best Bowling:	For Yorkshire	3-17	A L Robinson at Wellington, 1976
	For Shropshire	3-26	Mushtaq Mohammed at Telford, 1984

versus Wiltshire: Played 1, Won 1 (Away)

Highest Score:	By Yorkshire	304:7	at Trowbridge, 1987
	By Wiltshire	175	at Trowbridge, 1987

Highest Individual

Score:	For Yorkshire	85	A A Metcalfe at Trowbridge, 1987
	For Wiltshire	62	J J Newman at Trowbridge, 1987
Best Bowling:	For Yorkshire	4-40	K Sharp at Trowbridge, 1987
	For Wiltshire	2-38	R C Cooper at Trowbridge, 1987

versus Yorkshire Cricket Board: Played 1, Won 1 (Away)

Scores:	By Yorkshire	240:5	at Harrogate, 2000
	By Yorkshire CB	130	at Harrogate, 2000

Highest Individual

Score:	For Yorkshire	70	M P Vaughan at Harrogate, 2000
	For Yorkshire CB	31	R A Kettleborough at Harrogate, 2000
Best Bowling:	For Yorkshire	5-30	D Gough at Harrogate, 2000
	For Yorkshire CB	1-25	A E McKenna at Harrogate, 2000

CAREER AVERAGES FOR YORKSHIRE

FRIENDS PROVIDENT TROPHY, CHELTENHAM & GLOUCESTER TROPHY, GILLETTE CUP AND NATWEST TROPHY 1963-2009

Player	M	Inns	NO	Runs	HS	Av'ge	100s	50s	Runs	Wkts	Av'ge	Ct/St
Athey, C W J ...	15	15	2	485	115	37.30	1	2	41	1	41.00	2
Bairstow, D L ..	34	27	5	492	92	22.36	—	2	—	—	—	38/3
Balderstone, J C	5	3	0	65	34	21.66	—	—	10	1	10.00	1
Batty, J D	3	2	0	7	4	3.50	—	—	97	1	97.00	1
Bevan, M G	8	8	2	388	91*	64.66	—	4	89	3	29.66	—
Binks, J G	16	10	1	107	22	11.88	—	—	—	—	—	15/6
Blain, J A R ...	3	2	0	13	7	6.50	—	—	63	3	21.00	—
Blakey, R J ...	48	35	13	516	75	23.45	—	2	—	—	—	54/5
Blewett, G S ...	3	3	0	83	77	27.66	—	1	57	7	8.14	1
Booth, P A	1	1	1	6	6*	—	—	—	33	0	—	—
Bore, M K	3	2	1	0	0*	0.00	—	—	98	5	19.60	—
Boycott, G	40	39	4	1378	146	39.37	1	9	238	8	29.75	9
Bresnan, T T ..	**36**	**20**	**4**	**309**	**55**	**19.31**	**—**	**1**	**1360**	**47**	**28.93**	**8**
Brophy, G L ...	**23**	**19**	**7**	**437**	**68**	**36.41**	**—**	**4**	**—**	**—**	**—**	**29/3**
Byas, D	34	32	3	912	73*	31.45	—	5	23	1	23.00	23
Carrick, P	32	23	3	320	54	16.00	—	1	741	24	30.87	6
Chapman, C ...	1	—	—	—	—	—	—	—	—	—	—	1
Claydon, M E ..	7	2	0	15	9	7.50	—	—	293	8	36.62	—
Close, D B	15	15	2	407	96	31.30	—	2	357	22	16.22	6
Cooper, H P ...	11	9	4	49	17	9.80	—	—	347	15	23.13	2
Cope, G A	4	2	2	1	1*	—	—	—	130	5	26.00	1
Craven, V J	4	3	1	38	26	19.00	—	—	41	2	20.50	2
Dawson, R K J .	22	7	0	77	24	11.00	—	—	762	15	50.80	9
Dawood, I	4	3	0	26	23	8.66	—	—	—	—	—	1/1
Dennis, S J	5	2	0	14	14	7.00	—	—	202	6	33.66	—
Elliott, M T G ..	1	1	1	128	128*	—	1	—	—	—	—	—
Fellows, G M ..	12	8	3	230	68*	46.00	—	2	55	0	—	3
Fisher, I D	3	1	0	5	5	5.00	—	—	87	3	29.00	2
Fletcher, S D ..	15	7	4	36	16*	12.00	—	—	576	15	38.40	2
Gale, A W	**26**	**22**	**4**	**567**	**69***	**35.43**	**—**	**4**	**—**	**—**	**—**	**2**
Gilbert, C R ...	3	2	0	9	6	4.50	—	—	134	6	22.33	—
Gillespie, J N ..	11	2	1	15	15*	15.00	—	—	363	9	40.33	3
Gough, D	44	20	8	251	46	14.76	—	—	1596	86	18.55	9
Gray, A K D ...	3	1	0	0	0	0.00	—	—	152	5	30.40	3
Grayson, A P ...	7	6	0	91	29	15.16	—	—	241	4	60.25	3
Guy, S M	12	7	1	45	22	7.50	—	—	—	—	—	17/3
Hamilton, G M .	9	8	3	146	39	29.20	—	—	254	15	16.93	2
Hampshire, A W	1	1	0	0	0	0.00	—	—	—	—	—	1
Hampshire, J H .	32	31	5	877	110	33.73	1	6	4	0	—	10
Harden R J	4	4	0	54	37	13.50	—	—	—	—	—	—
Hartley, P J ...	28	17	8	250	83	27.77	—	2	1108	45	24.62	2
Hartley, S N ...	15	12	0	263	69	21.91	—	2	114	1	114.00	5
Harvey, I J	4	4	0	151	74	37.75	—	2	184	6	30.66	1
Hoggard, M J ..	16	4	4	8	7*	—	—	—	555	23	24.13	1
Hutchison, P M .	3	1	1	4	4*	—	—	—	62	5	12.40	—
Hutton, R A	13	10	2	136	61	17.00	—	1	341	13	26.23	3
Illingworth, R ..	15	10	7	150	45	50.00	—	—	260	8	32.50	7
Jaques, P A ...	**6**	**6**	**1**	**211**	**55***	**42.20**	**—**	**2**	**—**	**—**	**—**	**2**
Jarvis, P W	16	9	2	86	16	12.28	—	—	655	19	34.47	3
Johnson, C	4	4	0	62	44	15.50	—	—	—	—	—	—
Katich, S M ...	1	1	1	40	40*	—	—	—	—	—	—	—
Kellett, S A	9	7	0	246	107	35.14	1	1	—	—	—	6
Kirby, S P	2	1	0	0	0	0.00	—	—	74	2	37.00	—
Kruis, G J	25	9	5	42	11	10.50	—	—	774	26	29.76	3
Leadbeater, B ..	9	9	0	155	76	17.22	—	1	47	3	15.66	2

Player	M	Inns	NO	Runs	HS	Av'ge	100s	50s	Runs	Wkts	Av'ge	Ct/St
Lehmann, D S ..	23	19	5	853	118*	60.92	2	6	462	20	23.10	4
Lester, E I	1	1	0	0	0	0.00	—	—	—	—	—	—
Love, J D	21	18	3	266	67	17.73	—	3	39	2	19.50	5
Lumb, M J	20	18	3	628	89	41.86	—	4	—	—	—	6
Lumb, R G	12	12	0	222	56	18.50	—	1	—	—	—	—
Lyth, A	**11**	**9**	**1**	**218**	**83**	**27.25**	—	**1**	—	—	—	**4**
McGrath, A ...	**60**	**54**	**8**	**1879**	**135***	**40.84**	**3**	**15**	**732**	**22**	**33.27**	**19**
Metcalfe, A A ..	20	20	3	714	127*	42.00	1	5	44	2	22.00	4
Middlebrook, J D	2	1	1	6	6*	—	—	—	38	0	—	3
Morris, A C ...	1	1	1	1	1*	—	—	—	43	1	43.00	—
Moxon, M D ...	34	34	6	1316	137	47.00	2	10	68	4	17.00	12
Nicholson, A G .	17	12	4	42	15*	5.25	—	—	467	21	22.23	6
Old, C M	28	23	3	268	55*	13.40	—	1	799	43	18.58	7
Oldham, S	8	5	3	35	19	17.50	—	—	309	15	20.60	—
Padgett, D E V .	17	15	1	309	46	22.07	—	—	—	—	—	4
Parker, B	6	4	0	87	69	21.75	—	1	—	—	—	—
Patterson, S A .	**9**	**3**	**3**	**17**	**14***	—	—	—	**320**	**7**	**45.71**	—
Pickles, C S	3	2	0	15	12	7.50	—	—	111	4	27.75	1
Pyrah, R M ...	**28**	**18**	**5**	**273**	**67**	**21.00**	—	**1**	**1015**	**40**	**25.37**	**12**
Ramage, A	4	1	0	14	14	14.00	—	—	167	4	41.75	1
Rana Naved -ul-Hasan	7	7	1	134	53*	22.33	—	1	324	10	32.40	4
Rashid, A U ...	**18**	**11**	**2**	**105**	**41***	**11.66**	—	—	**466**	**13**	**35.84**	**5**
Richardson, R B	5	5	0	194	90	38.80	—	2	—	—	—	—
Robinson, A L .	5	2	1	18	18*	18.00	—	—	179	9	19.88	1
Robinson, M A .	11	4	3	1	1*	1.00	—	—	390	12	32.50	—
Robinson, P E .	8	5	0	113	66	22.60	—	1	—	—	—	3
Rudolph, J A ...	26	25	3	873	118	39.68	2	5	8	0	—	16
Ryan, M	3	2	1	7	6*	7.00	—	—	149	5	29.80	3
Sayers, J J	**6**	**6**	**0**	**111**	**51**	**18.50**	—	**1**	—	—	—	**1**
Shahzad, A	**8**	**6**	**2**	**110**	**43***	**27.25**	—	—	**292**	**7**	**41.71**	**2**
Sharp, K	17	13	2	228	50	20.72	—	1	47	4	11.75	6
Sharpe, P J	22	20	1	331	68	17.42	—	2	—	—	—	18
Shaw, C	6	5	2	10	6*	3.33	—	—	194	11	17.63	—
Sidebottom, A .	25	16	5	192	45	17.45	—	—	700	37	18.91	9
Sidebottom, R J .	14	2	1	13	7*	13.00	—	—	432	20	21.60	4
Silverwood,CEW	26	12	3	161	61	17.88	—	1	841	27	31.15	7
Smith, N	1	1	0	5	5	5.00	—	—	—	—	—	—
Squires, P J ...	2	2	0	46	42	23.00	—	—	—	—	—	1
Stemp, R D	11	3	2	1	1*	1.00	—	—	406	14	29.00	1
Stevenson, G B .	19	13	1	190	34	15.83	—	—	612	30	20.40	5
Stott, W B	2	2	0	30	30	15.00	—	—	—	—	—	—
Stringer, P M ...	2	2	2	7	5*	—	—	—	21	4	5.25	—
Swallow, I G ...	2	1	1	17	17*	—	—	—	16	0	—	—
Taylor, C R	1											
Taylor, K	10	10	0	135	30	13.50	—	—	168	11	15.27	3
Tendulkar, S R .	2	2	1	53	32*	53.00	—	—	—	—	—	1
Thornicroft, N D	2	1	1	10	10*	—	—	—	97	1	97.00	1
Trueman, F S ...	11	9	1	127	28	15.87	—	—	348	21	16.57	5
Vaughan, M P .	41	40	3	1356	116*	36.64	1	10	333	6	55.50	10
Wainwright, D J	**7**	**4**	**3**	**50**	**15***	**50.00**	—	—	**237**	**7**	**33.85**	**4**
Waring, J	1	1	1	1	1*	—	—	—	11	0	—	—
White, C	60	55	14	1809	113	44.12	4	10	1130	40	28.25	19
Whiteley, J P ...	1								48	0	—	—
Wilson, D	15	13	1	72	16	6.00	—	—	391	21	18.62	10
Wood, M J	28	28	6	908	160	41.27	2	3	45	3	15.00	11
Woodford, J D .	1	1	0	15	15	15.00	—	—	—	—	—	—
Younus Khan ...	7	6	0	234	100	39.00	1	0	124	2	62.00	3
Yuvraj Singh ...	1	1	0	27	27	27.00	—	—	27	0	—	—

WINNERS OF THE GILLETTE CUP, NATWEST TROPHY, CHELTENHAM & GLOUCESTER TROPHY AND FRIENDS PROVIDENT TROPHY 1963-2009

GILLETTE CUP

1963 **Sussex**, who beat Worcestershire by 14 runs
1964 **Sussex**, who beat Warwickshire by 8 wickets
1965 **Yorkshire**, who beat Surrey by 175 runs
1966 **Warwickshire**, who beat Worcestershire by 5 wickets
1967 **Kent**, who beat Somerset by 32 runs
1968 **Warwickshire**, who beat Sussex by 4 wickets
1969 **Yorkshire**, who beat Derbyshire by 69 runs
1970 **Lancashire**, who beat Sussex by 6 wickets
1971 **Lancashire**, who beat Kent by 24 runs
1972 **Lancashire**, who beat Warwickshire by 4 wickets
1973 **Gloucestershire**, who beat Sussex by 40 runs
1974 **Kent**, who beat Lancashire by 4 wickets
1975 **Lancashire**, who beat Middlesex by 7 wickets
1976 **Northamptonshire**, who beat Lancashire by 4 wickets
1977 **Middlesex**, who beat Glamorgan by 5 wickets
1978 **Sussex**, who beat Somerset by 5 wickets
1979 **Somerset**, who beat Northamptonshire by 45 runs
1980 **Middlesex**, who beat Surrey by 7 wickets

NATWEST TROPHY

1981 **Derbyshire**, who beat Northamptonshire by losing fewer wickets with the scores level.
1982 **Surrey**, who beat Warwickshire by 9 wickets
1983 **Somerset**, who beat Kent by 24 runs
1984 **Middlesex**, who beat Kent by 4 wickets
1985 **Essex**, who beat Nottinghamshire by 1 run
1986 **Sussex**, who beat Lancashire by 7 wickets
1987 **Nottinghamshire**, who beat Northamptonshire by 3 wickets
1988 **Middlesex**, who beat Worcestershire by 3 wickets
1989 **Warwickshire**, who beat Middlesex by 4 wickets
1990 **Lancashire**, who beat Northamptonshire by 7 wickets
1991 **Hampshire**, who beat Surrey by 4 wickets
1992 **Northamptonshire**, who beat Leicestershire by 8 wickets
1993 **Warwickshire**, who beat Sussex by 5 wickets
1994 **Worcestershire**, who beat Warwickshire by 8 wickets
1995 **Warwickshire**, who beat Northamptonshire by 4 wickets
1996 **Lancashire**, who beat Essex by 129 runs
1997 **Essex**, who beat Warwickshire by 9 wickets
1998 **Lancashire**, who beat Derbyshire by 9 wickets
1999 **Gloucestershire**, who beat Somerset by 50 runs
2000 **Gloucestershire,** who beat Warwickshire by 22 runs

CHELTENHAM & GLOUCESTER TROPHY

2001 **Somerset**, who beat Leicestershire by 41 runs
2002 **Yorkshire**, who beat Somerset by 6 wickets
2003 **Gloucestershire**, who beat Worcestershire by 7 wickets
2004 **Gloucestershire**, who beat Worcestershire by 8 wickets
2005 **Hampshire**, who beat Warwickshire by 18 runs
2006 **Sussex**, who beat Lancashire by 15 runs

FRIENDS PROVIDENT TROPHY

2007 **Durham**, who beat Hampshire by 125 runs
2008 **Essex,** who beat Kent by 5 wickets
2009 **Hampshire,** who beat Sussex by 6 wickets

BENSON AND HEDGES CUP 1972-2002

WINNERS 1987
LOSING FINALISTS 1972, 1999 SEMI-FINALISTS 1979, 1984, 1991, 1996, 1998, 2001

Played 146, Won 80 (in Yorkshire 40, Away 40), Lost 58 (in Yorkshire 28, Away 30),
No Result 8

Highest Score:	By Yorkshire	317:5 v. Scotland at Leeds, 1986
	Against Yorkshire	291:9 by Gloucestershire at Lord's, 1999
†Lowest Score:	By Yorkshire	81 v. Lancashire at Leeds 2002
	Against Yorkshire	50 by Hampshire at Leeds, 1991
Highest Individual Score:	For Yorkshire	142 G Boycott v. Worcestershire at Worcester, 1980
	Against Yorkshire	136* N Hussain for Essex at Chelmsford, 2002

Highest Partnerships: For Yorkshire

1st wkt	213	M D Moxon (141*) and A A Metcalfe (84) v. Glamorgan at Cardiff, 1991
2nd wkt	148*	G Boycott (69*) and C W J Athey (74*) v. Combined Universities at Oxford, 1980
3rd wkt	184	M P Vaughan (70) and D S Lehmann (119) v. Durham at Leeds, 1998
4th wkt	118	D S Lehmann (103) and G M Fellows (38) v. Derbyshire at Leeds, 2001
5th wkt	114	B Leadbeater (42*) and C M Old (72) v. Sussex at Hove, 1976
6th wkt	167*	M G Bevan (95*) and R J Blakey (80*) v. Lancashire at Manchester, 1996.
7th wkt	149	J D Love (118*) and C M Old (78*) v. Scotland at Bradford, 1981
8th wkt	48*	J D Love (40*) and P J Hartley (7*) v. Surrey at Leeds, 1987
9th wkt	41	K Sharp (64*) and P W Jarvis (11) v. Worcestershire at Leeds, 1987
10th wkt	80*	D L Bairstow (103*) and M Johnson (4*) v. Derbyshire at Derby, 1981

Best Bowling:	For Yorkshire	6 for 27 A G Nicholson v. Minor Counties at Middlesbrough, 1972
	Against Yorkshire	7 for 32 R G D Willis for Warwickshire at Birmingham, 1981

Most Economical Bowling:

	For Yorkshire	11-9-3-1 C M Old v. Middlesex at Lord's, 1979
	Against Yorkshire	11-5-7-2 A R Butcher for Surrey at Bradford, 1976

Most Expensive Bowling:

	For Yorkshire	11-2-72-2 PJ Hartley v. Worcestershire at Worcester, 1988
	Against Yorkshire	10-0-80-0 R N Dalton for Minor Counties, Leeds, 1997

†Lowest score is either the lowest all out score or the lowest score at completion of 55 overs.

Centuries (17)

D L Bairstow	103* v. Derbyshire at Derby, 1981
G Boycott (3)	102 v. Northamptonshire at Middlesbrough, 1977
	142 v. Worcestershire at Worcester, 1980
	106 v. Northamptonshire at Bradford, 1984
D Byas (2)	116* v. Surrey at The Oval, 1996
	104* v. Hampshire at Leeds, 1999
D S Lehmann (3)	102* v. Derbyshire at Derby, 1998
	119 v. Durham at Leeds, 1998
	103 v. Derbyshire at Leeds, 2001
J D Love	118* v. Scotland at Bradford, 1981
A McGrath	109* v. Minor Counties at Leeds, 1997
A A Metcalfe	114 v. Lancashire at Manchester, 1991
M D Moxon (2)	106* v. Lancashire at Leeds, 1986
	141* v. Glamorgan at Cardiff, 1991
K Sharp	105* v. Scotland at Leeds, 1986
M P Vaughan	125* v. Somerset at Taunton, 2001
M J Wood	115* v. Derbyshire at Derby, 2002

5 Wickets in an Innings (11)

P J Hartley	5 for 43 v. Scotland at Leeds, 1986
M D Moxon	5 for 31 v. Warwickshire at Leeds, 1991
A G Nicholson (2)	6 for 27 v. Minor Counties at Middlesbrough, 1972
	5 for 24 v. Derbyshire at Bradford, 1975
S Oldham	5 for 32 v. Minor Counties at Scunthorpe, 1975
A Sidebottom	5 for 27 v. Worcestershire at Bradford, 1985
C E W Silverwood	5 for 28 v. Scotland, at Leeds, 1996
G B Stevenson (2)	5 for 28 v. Kent at Canterbury, 1978
	5 for 50 v. Worcestershire at Leeds, 1982
C White	5 for 25 v. Lancashire at Leeds, 2000
D Wilson	5 for 26 v. Lancashire at Bradford, 1972

Gold Awards

G Boycott	9
D L Bairstow	7
M D Moxon	7
D S Lehmann	5
A A Metcalfe	5
C White	4
C W J Athey	3
M G Bevan	3
D Byas	3
J D Love	3
C M Old	3
A Sidebottom	3
R J Blakey	2
J H Hampshire	2
P J Hartley	2
R A Hutton	2
C E W Silverwood	2
M P Vaughan	2

P Carrick, D Gough, G M Hamilton, S N Hartley, C Johnson, A McGrath, A G Nicholson, S Oldham, P E Robinson, R D Stemp, G B Stevenson, D Wilson, M J Wood (1 each). (78 Awards: 31 Players).

ANALYSIS OF RESULTS

Opponents	Played	Won	Tied	Lost	No Result	Abandoned
Derbyshire	14	10	0	1	1	2
Durham	5	4	0	1	0	0
Essex	5	2	0	3	0	0
Glamorgan	1	1	0	0	0	0
Gloucestershire	3	1	0	2	0	0
Hampshire	5	4	0	1	0	0
Kent	4	2	0	2	0	0
Lancashire	16	6	0	9	0	1
Leicestershire	7	3	0	4	0	0
Middlesex	4	1	0	2	1	0
Northamptonshire	9	3	0	5	1	0
Nottinghamshire	16	6	0	8	2	0
Somerset	4	1	0	3	0	0
Surrey	7	3	0	4	0	0
Sussex	3	3	0	0	0	0
Warwickshire	11	7	0	4	0	0
Worcestershire	11	4	0	7	0	0
Combined Universities	3	1	0	2	0	0
Minor Counties	11	11	0	0	0	0
Scotland	7	7	0	0	0	0
Totals	146	80	0	58	5	3

BENSON & HEDGES CUP 1972-2002

Player	M	Inns	NO	Runs	HS	Av'ge	100s	50s	Runs	Wkts	Av'ge	Ct/St
Athey, C W J ...	29	26	4	608	94*	27.63	—	5	75	4	18.75	13
Bairstow, D L ..	85	59	14	945	103*	21.00	1	1	17	0	—	— 117/5
Baker, T M	3	1	0	3	3	3.00	—	—	67	3	22.33	2
Batty, J D	4	1	1	2	2*	—	—	—	109	1	109.00	1
Berry, P J	1								28	0	—	
Bevan, M G	10	9	4	544	95*	108.80	—	7	25	1	25.00	1
Blakey, R J	74	64	18	1308	80*	28.43	—	6	—	—	—	71/6
Blewett, G S ..	3	3	0	84	71	28.00	—	1	23	0	—	
Booth, P A	2	1	0	1	1	1.00	—	—	47	2	23.50	—
Bore, M K	6	3	2	13	7*	13.00	—	—	193	8	24.12	1
Boycott, G	57	55	9	2052	142	44.60	3	16	227	2	113.50	14
Bresnan, T T ...	6	4	3	23	16	23.00	—	—	119	3	39.66	1
Byas, D	58	55	5	1427	116*	28.54	2	7	155	5	31.00	17
Carrick, P	60	38	7	340	53	10.96	—	1	1590	42	37.85	9
Cooper, H P ..	28	15	6	76	20*	8.44	—	—	799	42	19.02	4
Cope, G A	4	4	4	34	18*	—	—	—	131	1	131.00	—
Craven, V J	1	1	0	1	1	1.00	—	—				1
Dawson, R K J .	3	3	2	16	8	16.00	—	—	35	5	7.00	1
Dennis, S J	9	2	0	10	10	5.00	—	—	327	7	46.71	1
Fellows, G M ..	20	18	4	219	38	15.64	—	—	192	9	21.33	3
Fisher, I D	1								26	1	26.00	1
Fletcher, S D ...	27	6	3	20	15*	6.66	—	—	974	35	27.82	6
Gough, D	39	19	6	177	48*	13.62	—	—	1245	45	27.66	11
Gray, A K D ...	3	3	1	17	10*	8.50	—	—	50	1	50.00	—
Grayson, A P ...	9	7	1	117	22*	19.50	—	—	118	3	39.33	2
Hamilton, G M .	17	10	3	170	31	24.29	—	—	474	22	21.55	1
Hampshire, J H .	44	37	4	866	85*	26.24	—	4	—	—	—	12
Harden R J	3	2	0	43	35	21.50	—	—	—	—	—	—
Hartley, P J	43	26	10	195	29*	12.18	—	—	1539	61	25.22	12
Hartley, S N ...	25	22	6	460	65*	28.75	—	2	421	18	23.38	7
Hoggard, M J ..	11	3	3	10	7*	—	—	—	350	13	26.92	1
Hutchison, P M .	6	2	2	6	4*	—	—	—	112	10	11.20	—
Hutton, R A ...	15	8	3	118	33*	23.60	—	—	434	21	20.66	5
Illingworth, R ..	2	1	1	9	9*	—	—	—	51	5	10.20	
Jarvis, P W	32	14	4	110	42	11.00	—	—	1006	52	19.34	4
Johnson, C	23	16	5	366	73*	33.27	—	1	23	0	—	9
Johnson, M	4	2	2	4	4*	—	—	—	138	7	19.71	—
Kellett, S A	14	12	1	239	45	21.72	—	—	—	—	—	6
Kirby, S P	1	1	0	0	0	0.00	—	—	43	0	—	
Leadbeater, B ..	21	21	5	601	90	37.56	—	4	10	0	—	5
Lehmann, D S ..	30	30	4	1285	119	49.92	3	8	306	12	25.50	13
Love, J D	42	39	12	1113	118*	41.22	1	5	7	0	—	7
Lumb, M J	11	9	1	126	43	15.75	—	—	—	—	—	3
Lumb, R G	36	34	3	937	90	30.22	—	6	—	—	—	6
McGrath, A	33	31	1	740	109*	24.66	1	1	10	2	5.00	11
Metcalfe, A A ..	31	31	4	1277	114	47.29	1	8	—	—	—	8
Middlebrook, JD	2	1	0	3	3	3.00	—	—	75	0	—	1
Morris, A C	1								4	0	—	1
Moxon, M D ...	50	50	7	1863	141*	43.32	2	14	242	9	26.88	19
Nicholson, A G .	19	5	4	15	8	15.00	—	—	478	35	13.65	2

BENSON & HEDGES CUP 1972-2002

Player	M	Inns	NO	Runs	HS	Av'ge	100s	50s	Runs	Wkts	Av'ge	Ct/St
Old, C M	47	31	7	571	78*	23.79	—	3	1171	71	16.49	11
Oldham, S	26	9	3	13	4*	2.16	—	—	763	44	17.34	7
Parker, B	10	7	2	154	58	30.80	—	1	—	—	—	3
Pickles, C S	10	7	2	96	37*	19.20	—	—	348	5	69.60	1
Ramage, A	10	4	3	30	17*	30.00	—	—	353	12	29.41	2
Richardson, R B	2	2	0	59	52	29.50	—	1	—	—	—	—
Robinson, A L ..	18	6	4	15	6*	7.50	—	—	505	15	33.66	2
Robinson, M A .	10	5	2	5	3*	1.66	—	—	305	14	21.78	—
Robinson, P E .	22	18	3	431	73*	28.73	—	2	—	—	—	7
Sharp, K	45	40	3	1073	105*	29.00	1	6	—	—	—	15
Sharpe, P J	15	14	3	297	89*	27.00	—	2	—	—	—	12
Shaw, C	4	1	1	4	4*	—	—	—	60	2	30.00	—
Sidebottom, A ..	52	27	9	247	32	13.72	—	—	1580	72	21.94	13
Sidebottom, R J .	20	7	2	20	8	4.00	—	—	622	12	51.83	8
Silverwood, CEW	32	17	2	150·	56	10.00	—	1	1136	50	22.72	7
Squires, P J	7	7	1	60	27	10.00	—	—	—	—	—	1
Stemp, R D	17	4	1	3	2	1.00	—	—	612	19	32.21	—
Stevenson, G B .	44	28	6	234	36	10.63	—	—	1567	74	21.17	8
Stutchbury, S ...	2	1	1	6	6*	—	—	—	89	3	29.66	—
Swallow, I G ...	4	3	2	18	10*	18.00	—	—	151	2	75.50	5
Tendulkar, S R .	2	2	0	23	16	11.50	—	—	65	3	21.66	1
Vaughan, M P ..	40	38	3	1190	125*	34.00	1	7	515	19	27.11	12
Wharf, A G	2	—	—	—	—	—	—	—	89	5	17.80	—
White, C	46	42	7	924	93	26.40	—	5	1479	47	31.46	15
Wilson, D	5	—	—	—	—	—	—	—	153	11	13.90	1
Wood, M J	12	10	2	248	115*	31.00	1	1	—	—	—	4
Woodford, J D ..	11	6	2	41	17*	10.25	—	—	226	17	13.29	5

CLYDESDALE BANK 40, PRO40, NATIONAL AND SUNDAY LEAGUES 1969-2011

JOHN PLAYER SPECIAL LEAGUE WINNERS 1983

Played 660, Won 297 (in Yorkshire 163, Away 134), Lost 303 (in Yorkshire 136, Away 167)
Ties 4   No Result 24   Abandoned 32

Highest Score:	By Yorkshire	352:6 v. Nottinghamshire at Scarborough, 2001
	Against Yorkshire	375:4 by Surrey at Scarborough, 1994
†Lowest Score:	By Yorkshire	54 v. Essex at Leeds, 2003
	Against Yorkshire	23 by Middlesex at Leeds, 1974

Highest Individual
| **Score:** | For Yorkshire | 191 D S Lehmann v. Nottinghamshire at Scarborough, 2001 |
| | Against Yorkshire | 155* B A Richards for Hampshire at Hull, 1970 |

Most Runs in a Season: 851 J A Rudolph in 2010

†Lowest score is the lowest all-out score or the lowest score at completion of allotted overs

Highest
Partnerships: For Yorkshire

1st wkt	233*	A W Gale (125*) and J A Rudolph (101*) v. Essex at Chelmsford, 2010
2nd wkt	172	D Byas (86) and D S Lehmann (99) v. Kent at Maidstone, 1998
3rd wkt	176	R J Blakey (86) and S R Tendulkar (107) v. Lancashire at Leeds, 1992
4th wkt	198*	M T G Elliott (115*) and A McGrath (85*) v. Kent at Leeds, 2002
5th wkt	190	R J Blakey (96) and M J Foster (118) v. Leicestershire at Leicester, 1993
6th wkt	110	B Leadbeater (69) and C Johnson (51*) v. Nottinghamshire at Hull, 1972
7th wkt	129*	D Byas (74*) and D Gough (72*) v. Leicestershire at Leicester, 1991
8th wkt	89	R J Blakey (60) and R K J Dawson (41) v. Leicestershire at Scarborough, 2002
9th wkt	88	S N Hartley (67) and A Ramage (32*) v. Middlesex at Lord's, 1982
10th wkt	64	R J Blakey (47) and R J Sidebottom (30*) v. Glamorgan at Leeds, 2002

| **Best Bowling:** | For Yorkshire | 7 for 15 R A Hutton v. Worcestershire at Leeds, 1969 |
| | Against Yorkshire | 6 for 15 A A Donald for Warwickshire at Birmingham, 1995 |

Most Economical Bowling:
	For Yorkshire	8-5-3-3 A L Robinson v. Derbyshire at Scarborough, 1973
	Against Yorkshire	8-4-6-2 P J Sainsbury for Hampshire at Hull, 1970
		8-5-6-3 M J Procter for Gloucestershire at Cheltenham, 1979

Most Expensive Bowling:
| | For Yorkshire | 9-0-87-1 T T Bresnan v. Somerset at Taunton, 2005 |
| | Against Yorkshire | 9-0-78-1 Mohammed Akram for Surrey at The Oval, 2005 |

Most Wickets In A Season: 37 M J Hoggard in 2000

Centuries (56)

C W J Athey	118	v. Leicestershire at Leicester, 1978
J M Bairstow	114	v. Middlesex at Lord's 2011
M G Bevan (2)	103*	v. Gloucestershire at Middlesbrough, 1995
	101	v. Worcestershire at Scarborough, 1995
G Boycott (2)	104*	v. Glamorgan at Colwyn Bay, 1973
	108*	v. Northamptonshire at Huddersfield, 1974
R J Blakey (3)	100*	v. Gloucestershire at Cheltenham, 1990
	130*	v. Kent at Scarborough, 1991
	105*	v. Warwickshire at Scarborough, 1992
D Byas (3)	106*	v. Derbyshire at Chesterfield, 1993
	101*	v. Nottinghamshire at Leeds, 1994
	111*	v. Lancashire at Leeds, 1996
M T G Elliott (2)	109	v. Leicestershire at Leicester, 2002
	115*	v. Kent at Leeds, 2002
S P Fleming	139*	v. Warwickshire at Leeds, 2003
M J Foster	118	v. Leicestershire at Leicester, 1993
A W Gale (2)	125*	v Essex at Chelmsford, 2010
	112	v. Kent at Canterbury, 2011
J H Hampshire (6)	108	v. Nottinghamshire at Sheffield, 1970
	119	v. Leicestershire at Hull, 1971
	106*	v. Lancashire at Manchester, 1972
	111*	v. Sussex at Hastings, 1973
	100*	v. Warwickshire at Birmingham, 1975
	114*	v. Northamptonshire at Scarborough, 1978
P A Jaques	105	v Sussex at Leeds, 2004
S A Kellett	118*	v. Derbyshire at Leeds, 1992
D S Lehmann (3)	103	v. Leicestershire at Scarborough, 2001
	191	v. Nottinghamshire at Scarborough, 2001
	104	v. Somerset at Taunton, 2002
J D Love (3)	100*	v. Gloucestershire at Gloucester, 1985
	104*	v. Nottinghamshire at Hull, 1986
	118*	v. Surrey at Leeds, 1987
R G Lumb	101	v. Nottinghamshire at Scarborough, 1976
A Lyth	109*	v Sussex at Scarborough, 2009
A McGrath (2)	102	v. Kent at Canterbury, 2001
	148	v. Somerset at Taunton, 2006
A A Metcalfe (2)	115*	v. Gloucestershire at Scarborough, 1984
	116	v. Middlesex at Lord's, 1991
M D Moxon (3)	105	v. Somerset at Scarborough, 1990
	129*	v. Surrey at The Oval, 1991
	112	v. Sussex at Middlesbrough, 1991
R B Richardson	103	v. Nottinghamshire at Nottingham, 1993
J A Rudolph (7)	127	v. Somerset at Scarborough, 2007
	120	v. Leicestershire at Leeds, 2008
	101*	v Essex at Chelmsford, 2010
	105	v. Derbyshire at Chesterfield, 2010
	124*	v. Middlesex at Scarborough, 2010
	106	v. Warwickshire at Scarborough, 2010
	132*	v. Sussex at Scarborough 2011
K Sharp (2)	112*	v. Worcestershire at Worcester, 1985
	114	v. Essex at Chelmsford, 1985
S R Tendulkar	107	v. Lancashire at Leeds, 1992
M P Vaughan	116*	v. Kent at Leeds, 2005
C White	148	v. Leicestershire at Leicester, 1997
M J Wood (2)	105*	v. Somerset at Taunton, 2002
	111	v. Surrey at The Oval, 2005

CLYDESDALE BANK 40, PRO40, NATIONAL AND SUNDAY LEAGUES 1969-2011 *(Continued)*

5 Wickets in an Innings (31)

C W J Athey	5 for 35 v. Derbyshire at Chesterfield, 1981	
M G Bevan	5 for 29 v. Sussex at Eastbourne, 1996	
P Carrick (2)	5 for 22 v. Glamorgan at Leeds, 1991	
	5 for 40 v. Sussex at Middlesbrough, 1991	
H P Cooper (2)	6 for 14 v. Worcestershire at Worcester, 1975	
	5 for 30 v. Worcestershire at Middlesbrough, 1978	
D Gough (2)	5 for 13 v. Sussex at Hove, 1994	
	5 for 25 v. Surrey at Leeds, 1998	
G M Hamilton (2)	5 for 16 v. Hampshire at Leeds, 1998	
	5 for 34 v. Sussex at Scarborough, 2000	
P .J. Hartley (2)	5 for 38 v. Worcestershire at Worcester, 1990	
	5 for 36 v. Sussex at Scarborough, 1993	
M J Hoggard (2)	5 for 28 v. Leicestershire at Leicester, 2000	
	5 for 30 v. Northamptonshire at Northampton, 2000 (consecutive matches)	
R A Hutton	7 for 15 v. Worcestershire at Leeds, 1969	
P W Jarvis (3)	6 for 27 v. Somerset at Taunton, 1989	
	5 for 18 v. Derbyshire at Leeds, 1990	
	5 for 29 v. Northamptonshire at Northampton, 1992	
A G Nicholson (2)	6 for 36 v. Somerset at Sheffield, 1972	
	5 for 17 v. Nottinghamshire at Hull, 1972 (Consecutive matches).	
C M Old (2)	5 for 33 v. Sussex at Hove, 1971	
	5 for 38 v. Northamptonshire at Sheffield, 1972	
S A Patterson	6 for 32 v. Derbyshire at Leeds, 2010	
C Shaw	5 for 41 v. Hampshire at Bournemouth, 1984	
R J Sidebottom (2)	6 for 40 v. Glamorgan at Cardiff, 1998	
	5 for 42 v. Leicestershire at Leicester, 2003	
G B Stevenson	5 for 41 v. Leicestershire at Leicester, 1976	
S Stuchbury	5 for 16 v. Leicestershire at Leicester, 1982	
N D Thornicroft	5 for 42 v. Gloucestershire at Leeds, 2003	
C White	5 for 19 v. Somerset at Scarborough, 2002	
D Wilson	6 for 18 v. Kent at Canterbury, 1969	

versus Derbyshire: Played 41, Won 22 (in Yorkshire 12, Away 10), Lost 15 (in Yorkshire 8, Away 7), Tied 1 (Away), No Result 1, Abandoned 2

Highest Score:	By Yorkshire	276:6 at Chesterfield, 2010
	By Derbyshire	268:6 at Chesterfield, 2010
Lowest Score:	By Yorkshire	117 at Huddersfield, 1978
	By Derbyshire	87 at Scarborough, 1973
Highest Individual Score:	For Yorkshire	118* S A Kellett at Leeds, 1992
	For Derbyshire	109* C J Adams at Derby, 1997
Best Bowling:	For Yorkshire	6-32 S A Patterson at Leeds, 2010
	For Derbyshire	4-14 A E Warner at Chesterfield, 1995

versus Durham:

	Played 15, Won 7 (in Yorkshire 4, Away 3)	
	Lost 6 (in Yorkshire 3, Away 3), No Result 1, Abandoned 1	
Highest Score:	By Yorkshire	269:5 at Chester-le-Street, 2002
	By Durham	256:4 at Chester-le-Street, 2005
Lowest Score:	By Yorkshire	122 at Chester-le-Street, 2007
	By Durham	121 at Scarborough, 1997
Highest Individual Score:	For Yorkshire	83 A W Gale at Scarborough, 2009
	For Durham	114 W Larkins at Leeds, 1993
Best Bowling:	For Yorkshire	4-18 C White at Scarborough, 1997
	For Durham	4-20 S J E Brown at Leeds, 1995

versus Essex:

	Played 38, Won 16 (in Yorkshire 9, Away 7)	
	Lost 19 (in Yorkshire 10, Away 9), Abandoned 3	
Highest Score:	By Yorkshire	264:6 at Ilford, 1997
	By Essex	262:9 at Ilford, 1997
Lowest Score:	By Yorkshire	54 at Leeds, 2003
	By Essex	108 at Leeds, 1996
Highest Individual Score:	For Yorkshire	125* A W Gale at Chelmsford, 2010
	For Essex	114 N Hussain at Leeds, 1999
Best Bowling:	For Yorkshire	4-21 C White at Leeds, 1996
	For Essex	6-18 R E East at Hull, 1969

versus Glamorgan:

	Played 36, Won 16 (in Yorkshire 8, Away 8),	
	Lost 18 (in Yorkshire 7, Away 11), Abandoned 2	
Highest Score:	By Yorkshire	253:4 at Leeds, 1991
	By Glamorgan	238:8 at Colwyn Bay, 2003
Lowest Score:	By Yorkshire	139 at Hull, 1981
	By Glamorgan	90 at Neath, 1969
Highest Individual Score:	For Yorkshire	104* G Boycott at Colwyn Bay, 1973
	For Glamorgan	97* G P Ellis at Leeds, 1976
Best Bowling:	For Yorkshire	6-40 R J Sidebottom at Cardiff, 1998
	For Glamorgan	5-16 G C Holmes at Swansea, 1985

versus Gloucestershire:

	Played 42, Won 17 (in Yorkshire 11, Away 6),	
	Lost 20 (in Yorkshire 6, Away 14), No Result 3, Abandoned 2	
Highest Score:	By Yorkshire	262:7 at Bristol, 1996
	By Gloucestershire	294:6 at Cheltenham, 2010
Lowest Score:	By Yorkshire	115 at Leeds, 1973
	By Gloucestershire	90 at Tewkesbury, 1972
Highest Individual Score:	For Yorkshire	115* A A Metcalfe at Scarborough, 1984
	For Gloucestershire	146* S Young at Leeds, 1997
Best Bowling:	For Yorkshire	5-42 N D Thornicroft at Leeds, 2003
	For Gloucestershire	5-33 M C J Ball at Leeds, 2003

versus Hampshire: Played 34, Won 13 (in Yorkshire 7, Away 6), Lost 19 (in Yorkshire 9, Away 10), No Result 1, Abandoned 1

Highest Score:	By Yorkshire	264:2 at Southampton, 1995
	By Hampshire	257:6 at Middlesbrough, 1985
Lowest Score:	By Yorkshire	74:9 at Hull, 1970
	By Hampshire	122 at Leeds, 1994
Highest Individual Score:	For Yorkshire	98* M G Bevan at Leeds, 1996
	For Hampshire	155* B A Richards at Hull, 1970
Best Bowling:	For Yorkshire	5-16 G M Hamilton at Leeds, 1998
	For Hampshire	5-31 D W White at Southampton, 1969

versus Kent: Played 47, Won 19 (in Yorkshire 11, Away 8), Lost 25 (in Yorkshire 9, Away 16) No Result 1, Abandoned 2

Highest Score:	By Yorkshire	299:3 at Leeds, 2002
	By Kent	266:5 at Maidstone, 1998
Lowest Score:	By Yorkshire	75 at Leeds, 1995
	By Kent	105 at Canterbury, 1969
Highest Individual Score:	For Yorkshire	130* R J Blakey at Scarborough, 1991
	For Kent	118* M H Denness at Scarborough, 1976
Best Bowling:	For Yorkshire	6-18 D Wilson at Canterbury, 1969
	For Kent	4-13 M V Fleming at Canterbury, 1996

versus Lancashire: Played 34, Won 10 (in Yorkshire 4, Away 6), Lost 19 (in Yorkshire 11, Away 8), No Result 3, Abandoned 2

Highest Score:	By Yorkshire	260:6 at Leeds, 1992
	By Lancashire	264:3 at Leeds, 1992
Lowest Score:	By Yorkshire	81 at Leeds, 1998
	By Lancashire	68 at Leeds, 2000
Highest Individual Score:	For Yorkshire	111* D Byas at Leeds, 1996
	For Lancashire	102* N J Speak at Leeds, 1992
Best Bowling:	For Yorkshire	4-14 C White at Leeds, 2000
	For Lancashire	6-25 G Chapple at Leeds, 1998

versus Leicestershire: Played 47, Won 21 (in Yorkshire 14, Away 7), Lost 22 (in Yorkshire 11, Away 11), Tie 1, No Result 2, Abandoned 1

Highest Score:	By Yorkshire	318:7 at Leicester, 1993
	By Leicestershire	302:7 at Leeds, 2008
Lowest Score:	By Yorkshire	89:9 at Leicester, 1989
	By Leicestershire	53 at Leicester, 2000
Highest Individual Score:	For Yorkshire	148 C White at Leicester, 1997
	For Leicestershire	108 N E Briers at Bradford, 1984
Best Bowling:	For Yorkshire	5-16 S Stuchbury at Leicester, 1982
	For Leicestershire	5-24 C W Henderson at Leeds, 2004

versus Middlesex: Played 37, Won 19 (in Yorkshire 11, Away 8), Lost 14 (in Yorkshire 3, Away 11), No Results 4

Highest Score:	By Yorkshire	275-4 at Lord's 2011
	By Middlesex	273:6 at Southgate, 2004
Lowest Score:	By Yorkshire	94 at Lord's, 1969
	By Middlesex	23 at Leeds, 1974
Highest Individual Score:	For Yorkshire	124* J A Rudolph at Scarborough, 2010
	For Middlesex	125* O A Shah at Southgate, 2004
Best Bowling:	For Yorkshire	4-6 R Illingworth at Hull, 1983
	For Middlesex	4-22 K P Dutch at Lord's, 1998

versus Northamptonshire: Played 37, Won 25 (in Yorkshire 12, Away 13), Lost 9 (in Yorkshire 5, Away 4), No Result 2, Abandoned 1

Highest Score:	By Yorkshire	251:4 at Tring, 1990
	By Northamptonshire	282:4 at Middlesbrough, 1982
Lowest Score:	By Yorkshire	112 at Northampton, 1975
	By Northamptonshire	109 at Northampton, 2000
Highest Individual Score:	For Yorkshire	114* J H Hampshire, Scarborough, 1978
	For Northamptonshire	104* P Willey at Bradford, 1976
Best Bowling:	For Yorkshire	5-29 P W Jarvis at Northampton, 1992
	For Northamptonshire	5-15 Sarfraz Nawaz, Northampton, 1975

versus Nottinghamshire: Played 37, Won 16 (in Yorkshire 11, Away 5), Lost 16 (in Yorkshire 6, Away 10), Tie 1, No Result 3, Abandoned 1

Highest Score:	By Yorkshire	352:6 at Scarborough, 2001
	By Nottinghamshire	291:6 at Nottingham, 2004
Lowest Score:	By Yorkshire	147 at Nottingham, 1975
	By Nottinghamshire	66 at Bradford, 1969
Highest Individual Score:	For Yorkshire	191 D S Lehmann at Scarborough, 2001
	For Nottinghamshire	123 D W Randall at Nottingham, 1987
Best Bowling:	For Yorkshire	5-17 A G Nicholson at Hull, 1972
	For Nottinghamshire	5-41 C L Cairns at Scarborough, 1996

versus Somerset: Played 43, Won 21 (in Yorkshire 13, Away 8), Lost 20 (in Yorkshire 8, Away 12), No Result 1, Abandoned 1

Highest Score:	By Yorkshire	343:9 at Taunton, 2005
	By Somerset	345:4 at Taunton, 2005
Lowest Score:	By Yorkshire	110 at Scarborough, 1977
	By Somerset	139 at Taunton, 2004
Highest Individual Score:	For Yorkshire	148 A McGrath at Taunton, 2006
	For Somerset	131 D B Close at Bath, 1974
Best Bowling:	For Yorkshire	6-27 P W Jarvis at Taunton, 1989
	For Somerset	5-27 J Garner at Bath, 1985

versus Surrey: Played 39, Won 15 (in Yorkshire 9, Away 6), Lost 22 (in Yorkshire 8, Away 14), Abandoned 2

Highest Score:	By Yorkshire	334:5 at The Oval, 2005
	By Surrey	375:4 at Scarborough, 1994
Lowest Score:	By Yorkshire	91 at Scarborough, 1970
	By Surrey	90 at Leeds, 1996
Highest Individual Score:	For Yorkshire	129* M D Moxon at The Oval, 1991
	For Surrey	136 M A Lynch at Bradford, 1985
Best Bowling:	For Yorkshire	5-25 D Gough at Leeds, 1998
	For Surrey	5-22 R D Jackman at The Oval, 1978

versus Sussex: Played 39, Won 17 (in Yorkshire 9, Away 8),
Lost 17 (in Yorkshire 8, Away 9), Abandoned 5

Highest Score:	By Yorkshire	302:4 at Scarborough, 2011
	By Sussex	272:6 at Arundel, 2000
Lowest Score:	By Yorkshire	89 at Hove, 1998
	By Sussex	108 at Hove, 1971
Highest Individual		
	For Yorkshire	132* J A Rudolph at Scarborough, 2011
	For Sussex	129 A W Greig at Scarborough, 1976
Best Bowling:	For Yorkshire	5-13 D Gough at Hove, 1994
	For Sussex	4-10 M H Yardy at Hove, 2011

versus Warwickshire: Played 42, Won 15 (in Yorkshire 8, Away 7),
Lost 20 (in Yorkshire 10, Away 10), Tied 1, No Result 1,
Abandoned 5

Highest Score:	By Yorkshire	274:3 at Leeds, 2003
	By Warwickshire	309:3 at Birmingham, 2005
Lowest Score:	By Yorkshire	56 at Birmingham, 1995
	By Warwickshire	59 at Leeds, 2001
Highest Individual Score:	For Yorkshire	139* S P Fleming at Leeds, 2003
	For Warwickshire	137 I R Bell at Birmingham, 2005
Best Bowling:	For Yorkshire	4-21 C E W Silverwood at Leeds, 2001
	For Warwickshire	6-15 A A Donald at Birmingham, 1995

versus Worcestershire: Played 44, Won 22 (in Yorkshire 7, Away 15),
Lost 20 (in Yorkshire 13, Away 7), No Result 1, Abandoned 1

Highest Score:	By Yorkshire	231:4 at Leeds, 2011
	By Worcestershire	251:4 at Scarborough, 1995
Lowest Score:	By Yorkshire	90 at Worcester, 1987
	By Worcestershire	86 at Leeds, 1969
Highest Individual Score:	For Yorkshire	112* K Sharp at Worcester, 1985
	For Worcestershire	113* G A Hick at Scarborough, 1995
Best Bowling:	For Yorkshire	7-15 R A Hutton at Leeds, 1969
	For Worcestershire	5-30 R J Chapman at Worcester, 1998

versus Netherlands: Played 4, Won 2 (in Yorkshire 1, Away 1),
Lost 2 (in Yorkshire 1, Away 1)

Highest Score:	By Yorkshire	204:6 at Leeds, 2010
	By Netherlands	200:8 at Leeds, 2010
Lowest Score:	By Yorkshire	123 at Amsterdam, 2011
	By Netherlands	154:9 at Rotterdam, 2010
Highest Individual Score:	For Yorkshire	83* J A Rudolph at Leeds, 2010
	For Netherlands	62 M G Dighton at Leeds, 2010
Best Bowling:	For Yorkshire	4-24 R M Pyrah at Rotterdam, 2010
	For Netherlands	3-26 Mudassar Bukhari at Leeds, 2011

versus Scotland: Played 4, Won 4 (in Yorkshire 2, Away 2),

Highest Score:	By Yorkshire	240:5 at Leeds, 2004
	By Scotland	203:9 at Edinburgh, 2005
Lowest Score:	By Yorkshire	199:8 at Edinburgh, 2004
	By Scotland	140 at Edinburgh, 2004
Highest Individual Score:	For Yorkshire	88* D S Lehmann at Leeds, 2004
	For Scotland	78 J A Beukes at Edinburgh, 2005
Best Bowling:	For Yorkshire	4-20 R K J Dawson at Edinburgh, 2004
	For Scotland	3-47 Asim Butt at Edinburgh, 2004

CAREER AVERAGES FOR YORKSHIRE

CLYDESDALE BANK 40, PRO40, NATIONAL AND SUNDAY LEAGUE RECORDS
1969-2011

Player	M	Inns	NO	Runs	HS	Av'ge	100s	50s	Runs	Wkts	Av'ge	Ct/St
M A Ashraf ...	3	0	0	0	0	—	—	—	129	2	64.50	1
Athey, C W J ...	94	86	8	2560	118	32.82	1	18	315	14	22.50	30
Azeem Rafiq ..	2	0	0	0	—	—	—	—	36	1	36.00	1
Bairstow, D L ..	279	227	51	3677	83*	20.89	—	16	—	—	—	234/23
Bairstow J M ..	27	23	3	564	114	28.20	1	2	—	—	—	17/1
Baker, T M ...	1	0	0	0	0	—	—	—	22	1	22.00	1
Balderstone, J C	8	8	2	108	46	18.00	—	—	28	1	28.00	2
Ballance G S ..	10	10	3	364	81*	52.00	—	2	—	—	—	4
Batty, J D ..	31	13	6	41	13*	5.86	—	—	1091	40	27.27	16
Best, T L	5	1	1	8	8*	—	—	—	166	10	16.60	1
Bevan, M G	29	27	5	1108	103*	50.36	2	7	399	23	17.34	9
Binks, J G	14	11	2	140	34	15.55	—	—	—	—	—	11/2
Blain, J A R	11	6	3	21	11*	7.00	—	—	364	11	33.08	3
Blakey, R J ...	249	218	52	5531	130*	33.31	3	27	—	—	—	244/48
Blewett, G S ..	11	11	0	178	48	16.18	—	—	116	4	29.00	6
Booth, P A	2								67	1	67.00	1
Bore, M K	44	18	7	67	15	6.09	—	—	1300	37	35.13	14
Boycott, G ...	163	157	24	5051	108*	37.97	2	37	611	14	43.64	69
Bresnan T T ...	88	65	18	800	61	17.02	—	2	3019	89	33.92	26
Broadhurst, M ..	1	—	—	—	—	—	—	—	27	0	—	—
Brophy G L ...	40	35	5	779	93*	25.96	—	5	—	—	—	35/10
Byas, D	217	211	27	5352	111*	29.08	3	28	463	19	24.36	88
Carrick, P	210	143	42	1481	48*	14.66	—	—	5030	170	29.58	53
Chapman, C A..	7	6	3	89	36*	29.66	—	—	—	—	—	2
Cleary, M F	4	3	1	50	23*	25.00	—	—	159	2	79.50	—
Close, D B	17	16	0	224	50	14.00	—	1	118	1	118.00	8
Cooper, H P ...	103	50	24	358	29*	13.76	—	—	3038	120	25.31	20
Cope, G A	28	14	7	61	16*	8.71	—	—	750	18	41.66	6
Coverdale, S P .	3	3	2	18	17*	18.00	—	—	—	—	—	3
Craven, V J	36	34	4	540	59	18.00	—	2	297	18	16.50	11
Dalton, A J	17	16	1	280	55	18.66	—	1	—	—	—	7
Dawood, I	20	16	4	212	57	17.66	—	1	—	—	—	17/7
Dawson, R K J .	65	46	9	303	44	8.18	—	—	1914	70	27.34	20
Dennis, S J	41	19	11	87	16*	10.87	—	—	1188	27	44.00	6
Elliott, M T G ..	5	5	2	266	115*	88.66	2	—	—	—	—	—
Elstub, C J	9	3	3	4	4*	—	—	—	259	11	23.55	—
Fellows, M G ..	62	52	8	893	67	20.29	—	4	589	13	45.30	21
Fisher, I D	24	11	3	63	20	7.87	—	—	595	25	23.80	3
Fleming, S P ...	7	7	1	285	139*	47.50	1	1	—	—	—	3
Fletcher, S D ..	86	19	11	53	11*	6.62	—	—	3136	114	27.50	26
Foster, M J	20	14	1	199	118	15.30	1	—	370	6	61.66	6
Gale A W	63	59	5	1739	125*	32.20	2	8	—	—	—	15
Gilbert, C R	1	1	0	9	9	9.00	—	—	40	2	20.00	—
Gillespie, J N ..	7	2	0	14	11	7.00	—	—	238	9	26.44	3
Gough, D	129	80	24	845	72*	15.08	—	1	3929	159	24.71	23
Gray, A K D ...	24	14	6	111	30*	13.87	—	—	612	17	36.00	5
Grayson, A P ..	49	35	6	367	55	12.65	—	1	1051	31	33.90	14
Guy S M	18	14	3	188	40	17.09	—	—	—	—	—	18/8
Hamilton, G M .	74	52	12	743	57*	18.57	—	2	2033	81	25.09	12
Hampshire, A W .	3	2	0	3	3	1.50	—	—	—	—	—	—

Player	M	Inns	NO	Runs	HS	Av'ge	100s	50s	Runs	Wkts	Av'ge	Ct/St
Hampshire, J H .	155	152	15	4505	119	32.88	6	26	22	1	22.00	47
Hannon-Dalby, O J									144	5	28.80	3
	4	0	0	0	0	—	—	—				1
Harden, R J	12	10	2	133	42	16.62	—	—				
Hartley, P J	145	102	31	1164	52	16.39	—	2	4778	174	27.45	26
Hartley, S N .	130	119	25	2087	83*	22.20	—	9	1587	48	33.06	40
Harvey, I J	24	23	2	486	69	23.14	—	1	766	24	31.91	7
Hodgson L J ...	6	2	0	9	9	4.50	—	—	161	4	40.25	1
Hoggard, M J ..	56	21	12	23	5*	2.55	—	—	1777	82	21.67	5
Hutchinson, P M .	23	8	5	8	2*	2.66	—	—	670	28	23.92	3
Hutton, R A	77	60	19	761	65	18.56	—	3	2215	94	23.56	19
Illingworth, R ..	23	4	3	12	8*	12.00	—	—	453	26	17.42	7
Ingham, P G ...	12	10	4	312	87*	52.00	—	2	—	—	—	2
Inzamam-ul-Haq	3	3	0	69	53	23.00	—	1				
Jaques, P A	20	19	1	788	105	43.77	1	7	—	—	—	11
Jarvis, P W	94	49	21	316	38*	11.28	—	—	2914	138	21.11	25
Johnson, C.....	100	81	17	1186	67*	18.53	—	3	5	2	2.50	24
Johnson, M	10	4	1	30	15*	10.00	—	—	317	5	63.40	2
Katich, S M ...	2	2	1	39	39*	39.00	—	—	—	—	—	2
Kellett, S A	30	30	2	697	118*	24.89	1	3	16	0	—	6
Kettleborough, RA	10	6	3	71	28	23.66	—	—	72	3	24.00	4
Kirby, S P	25	10	3	38	15	5.42	—	—	919	22	41.77	6
Kruis, G J	30	13	6	96	31*	13.71	—	—	1019	36	28.30	6
Lawson, M A K .	4	4	0	30	20	7.50	—	—	141	3	47.00	1
Leadbeater, B ..	73	68	14	1423	86*	26.35	—	6	38	2	19.00	18
Lee, J E	4	0	0	0	0	—	—	—	116	7	16.57	—
Lees A Z	1	1	1	12	12*	—	—	—				—
Lehmann, D S ..	77	77	11	3091	191	46.83	3	24	1222	47	26.00	24
Love, J D	157	146	18	2919	118*	22.80	3	10	83	3	27.66	32
Lucas, D S	5	2	0	40	32	20.00	—	—	187	3	62.33	1
Lumb, M J	71	69	4	1838	92	28.27	—	14	28	0	—	22
Lumb, R G	87	75	10	1588	101	24.43	1	9				15
Lyth A	41	37	2	969	109*	27.68	1	4	14	0	—	13
McGrath A	176	164	29	4422	148	32.75	2	28	1707	52	32.82	60
Metcalfe, A A ..	140	135	7	3529	116	27.57	2	23	—	—	—	32
Middlebrook, JD	14	9	2	52	15*	7.42	—	—	417	13	32.07	1
Milburn, S M ..	4	2	1	14	13*	14.00	—	—	118	2	59.00	1
Morris, A C.	23	15	3	208	48*	17.33	—	—	362	15	24.13	4
Moxon, M D ...	151	143	8	4128	129*	30.57	3	24	868	21	41.33	46
Nicholson, A G .	83	28	14	97	13*	6.92	—	—	1998	117	17.07	8
Nicholson, N G .	2	2	1	1	1*	1.00	—	—	—	—	—	2
Old, C M	143	112	27	1711	82*	20.12	—	6	3847	192	20.03	38
Oldham, S	71	26	15	144	38*	13.09	—	—	2064	83	24.86	10
Padgett, D E V .	40	39	2	760	68	20.54	—	2	25	1	25.00	9
Parker, B	56	49	6	723	42	16.81	—	—	18	0	—	8
Patterson S A ..	33	11	9	65	25*	32.50	—	—	1196	45	26.57	5
Pickles, C S	56	38	17	259	30*	12.33	—	—	1896	53	35.77	20
Pyrah R M	56	36	10	484	69	18.61	—	1	1521	59	25.77	15
Ramage, A	20	12	5	90	32*	12.85	—	—	658	14	47.00	—
Ramsden, G	1	—	—	—	—	—	—	—	26	2	13.00	—
Rana Neved -ul-Hasan	10	9	0	241	74	26.77	—	2	357	16	22.31	1
Rashid A U	38	23	10	272	42*	20.92	—	—	1260	46	27.39	14

Player	M	Inns	NO	Runs	HS	Av'ge	100s	50s	Runs	Wkts	Av'ge	Ct/St
Rhodes, S J	2	1	0	6	6	6.00	—	—	—	—	—	3
Richardson, R B	21	21	6	740	103	49.33	1	5	—	—	—	5
Robinson, A L ..	69	28	14	94	14	6.71	—	—	1904	81	23.50	11
Robinson, M A .	65	21	11	35	7	3.50	—	—	2030	63	32.22	7
Robinson, P E ..	104	100	12	2194	78*	24.93	—	11	—	—	—	37
Root J E	7	7	1	235	63	39.16	—	2	103	2	51.50	3
Rudolph J A ...	39	37	7	2217	132*	73.90	7	14	29	0	—	16
Sanderson B W .	10	2	1	14	12*	—	—	—	247	8	30.87	5
Sayers J J	20	20	2	387	62	21.50	—	3	79	1	79.00	1
Scofield, D	3	1	0	0	0	0.00	—	—	111	2	55.50	1
Shahzad A	21	15	4	125	59*	11.36	—	1	839	22	38.13	5
Sharp, K	141	135	13	3392	114	27.80	2	20	1	0	—	45
Sharpe, P J ...	52	50	0	871	81	17.42	—	4	11	0	—	22
Shaw, C	38	14	7	113	26	16.14	—	—	1142	45	25.37	4
Sidebottom, A ..	156	86	33	835	52*	15.75	—	1	4561	149	30.61	29
Sidebottom R J	73	39	19	258	30*	12.90	—	—	2289	83	27.57	12
Silverwood, CEW	106	64	27	555	58	15.00	—	2	3168	146	21.69	11
Smith, N	6	1	1	0	0*	—	—	—	—	—	—	2
Smith, R	3	2	0	17	17	8.50	—	—	—	—	—	1
Squires, P J	47	39	4	602	79*	17.20	—	3	4	0	—	8
Stemp, R D	60	21	7	114	23*	8.14	—	—	1978	67	29.52	13
Stevenson, G B .	153	116	16	1275	81*	12.75	—	2	4641	186	24.95	25
Stringer, P M ..	9	6	4	22	13*	11.00	—	—	235	11	21.36	—
Stuchbury, S ...	20	7	3	15	9*	3.75	—	—	588	26	22.61	2
Swallow, I G ...	2	1	0	2	2	2.00	—	—	31	0	—	—
Swanepoel, P J .	3	2	2	9	8*	—	—	—	100	3	33.33	—
Taylor, C R	5	5	0	102	28	20.40	—	—	—	—	—	—
Tendulkar, S R .	13	13	1	464	107	38.66	1	1	102	3	34.00	1
Thornicroft, N D	11	6	3	42	20	14.00	—	—	447	15	29.80	1
Townsley, R A J	5	4	1	81	34	27.00	—	—	62	0	—	1
Vaughan, M P ..	101	99	7	2344	116*	25.47	1	11	988	34	29.05	34
Wainwright D J .	40	16	10	100	26	16.66	—	—	1145	29	39.48	12
I Wardlaw	1	1	0	1	1	1.00	—	—	15	0	—	—
Warren, A C ...	1	1	0	3	3	3.00	—	—	35	1	35.00	—
Wharf, A G	4	1	1	2	2*	—	—	—	87	3	29.00	1
White, C	185	168	18	3643	148	24.28	1	13	3479	159	21.88	50
Whiteley, J P ..	5	4	0	19	14	4.75	—	—	147	2	73.50	1
Widdup, S	4	4	0	49	38	12.25	—	—	—	—	—	2
Wilson, D	39	32	7	352	46	14.08	—	—	958	42	22.80	11
Wood, M J	103	94	6	2053	111	23.32	2	10	26	0	—	41
Woodford, J D ..	60	50	12	834	69*	21.94	—	2	1401	60	23.35	20
Younus Khan ...	4	2	0	14	14	7.00	—	—	20	0	—	2
Yuvraj Singh ...	8	8	0	169	50	21.12	—	1	170	3	56.66	1

ALL LIMITED-OVERS COMPETITIONS (LIST A) OF 40 TO 65 OVERS 1963-2011

Player	M	Inns	NO	Runs	HS	Av'ge	100s	50s	Runs	Wkts	Av'ge	Ct/St
Ashraf, M A	3	0	0	0	—	—	—	—	129	2	64.50	1
Athey, C W J ...	138	127	14	3653	118	32.32	2	25	431	19	22.68	45
Azeem Rafiq	2	0	0	0	—	—	—	—	36	1	36.00	1
Bairstow, D L ...	398	313	70	5114	103*	21.04	1	19	17	0	—	389/31
Bairstow, J M ...	27	23	3	564	114	28.20	1	2	—	—	—	17/1
Baker, T M	4	1	0	3	3	3.00	—	—	89	4	22.25	3
Balderstone, J C ...	13	11	2	173	46	19.22	—	—	38	2	19.00	3
Ballance, G S	10	10	3	364	33	52.00	—	2	—	—	—	4
Batty, J D	38	16	7	50	13*	5.55	—	—	1297	42	30.88	18
Berry, P J	1	0	0	0	—	—	—	—	28	0	—	
Best, T L	5	1	1	8	8*	—	—	—	166	10	16.60	1
Bevan, M G	47	44	11	2040	103*	61.82	2	18	513	27	19.00	10
Binks, J G	30	21	3	247	34	13.72	—	—	—	—	—	26/8
Blain, J A R	14	8	3	34	11*	6.80	—	—	427	14	30.50	3
Blakey, R J	371	317	83	7355	130*	31.43	3	35	—	—	—	369/59
Blewett, G S	17	17	0	345	77	20.29	—	2	196	11	17.81	7
Booth, P A	5	2	1	7	6*	7.00	—	—	147	3	49.00	1
Bore, M K	53	23	10	80	15	6.15	—	—	1591	50	31.82	15
Boycott, G	260	251	37	8481	146	39.63	6	62	1076	24	44.83	92
Bresnan, T T	130	89	25	1132	61	17.68	—	3	4498	139	32.35	35
Broadhurst, M	1	—	—	—	—	—	—	—	27	0	—	
Brophy, G L	63	54	12	1216	93*	28.95	—	9	—	—	—	64/13
Byas, D	309	298	35	7691	116*	29.24	5	43	641	25	25.64	128
Carrick, P	302	204	52	2141	54	14.08	—	2	7361	236	31.19	68
Chapman, C A ...	8	6	3	89	36*	29.66	—	—	—	—	—	3
Claydon, M E ...	7	2	0	15	9	7.50	—	—	293	8	36.62	—
Cleary, M F	4	3	1	50	23*	25.00	—	—	159	2	79.50	—
Close, D B	32	31	2	631	96	21.75	—	3	475	23	20.65	14
Cooper, H P	142	74	34	483	29*	12.07	—	—	4184	177	23.63	26
Cope, G A	36	20	13	96	18*	13.71	—	—	1011	24	42.12	9
Coverdale, S P	3	3	2	18	17*	18.00	—	—	—	—	—	3
Craven, V J	41	38	5	579	59	17.54	—	2	338	20	16.90	14
Dalton, A J	17	16	1	280	55	18.66	—	1	—	—	—	7
Dawood, I	24	19	4	238	57	15.86	—	1	—	—	—	18/8
Dawson, R K J ...	90	56	11	396	41	8.80	—	—	2711	90	30.12	30
Dennis, S J	55	23	11	111	16*	9.25	—	—	1717	40	42.92	7
Elliott, M T G ...	6	6	3	394	128*	131.33	3	—	—	—	—	—
Elstub, C J	9	9	3	4	4*	—	—	—	259	11	23.54	—
Fellows, G M	94	78	15	1342	80*	21.30	—	6	836	22	38.00	27
Fisher, I D	28	12	3	68	20	7.55	—	—	708	29	24.41	6
Fleming, S P	7	7	1	285	139*	47.50	1	1	—	—	—	3
Fletcher, S D	128	32	18	109	16*	7.78	—	—	4686	164	28.57	34
Foster, M J	20	14	1	199	118	15.30	1	—	370	6	61.66	6
Gale, A W	89	81	9	2306	125*	32.02	2	12	—	—	—	17
Gilbert, C R	4	3	0	18	9	6.00	—	—	174	8	21.75	—
Gillespie, J N ...	18	4	1	29	15*	9.66	—	—	601	18	33.38	6
Gough, D	212	119	33	1273	72*	14.80	—	1	6770	290	23.34	43
Gray, A K D	30	18	7	128	30*	11.63	—	—	814	23	35.39	8
Grayson, A P	65	48	7	575	55	14.02	—	1	1410	38	37.10	19
Guy, S M	30	21	4	233	40	13.70	—	—	—	—	—	35/11

Player	M	Inns	NO	Runs	HS	Av'ge	100s	50s	Runs	Wkts	Av'ge	Ct/St
Hamilton, G M 100	70	18	1059	57*	20.36	—	2	2761	118	23.39	15	
Hampshire, A W ...	4	3	0	3	3	1.00	—	—	—	—	—	1
Hampshire, J H ...231	220	24	6248	119	31.87	7	36	26	1	26.00	69
Hannon-Dalby, O J	**4**	**0**	**0**	**0**			—	—	**144**	**5**	**28.80**	**3**
Harden, R J	19	16	2	230	42	16.42	—	—	—	—	—	1
Hartley, P J 216	145	49	1609	83	16.76	—	4	7425	280	26.51	40
Hartley, S N 170	153	31	2810	83*	23.03	—	13	2122	67	31.67	52
Harvey, I J	28	27	2	637	74	25.48	—	3	950	30	31.66	8
Hodgson, L J	6	2	0	9	9	4.50	—	—	161	4	40.25	1
Hoggard, M J	83	28	19	41	7*	4.55	—	—	2682	118	22.72	7
Hutchison, P M ...	32	11	8	18	4*	6.00	—	—	844	43	19.62	3
Hutton, R A 105	78	24	1015	65	18.79	—	4	2990	128	23.35	27
Illingworth, R ...	40	15	11	171	45	42.75	—	—	764	39	19.58	14
Ingham, P G	12	10	4	312	87*	52.00	—	2	—	—	—	2
Inzamam-ul-Haq ...	3	3	0	69	53	23.00	—	1	—	—	—	—
Jaques, P A	**26**	**24**	**2**	**999**	**105**	**43.43**	**1**	**9**	—	—	—	**13**
Jarvis, P W 142	72	27	512	42	11.37	—	—	4575	209	21.88	32
Johnson, C 127	101	22	1614	73*	20.43	—	4	28	2	14.00	33
Johnson, M	14	6	3	34	15*	11.33	—	—	455	12	37.91	2
Katich, S M	3	3	2	79	46*	79.00	—	—	—	—	—	2
Kellett, S A	53	49	3	1182	118*	25.69	2	4	16	0	—	12
Kettleborough, R A .	10	6	3	71	28	23.66	—	—	72	3	24.00	4
Kirby, S P	28	12	3	38	15	4.22	—	—	1036	24	43.16	6
Kruis, G J	55	22	11	138	31*	12.54	—	—	1793	62	28.91	9
Lawson, M A K ...	4	4	0	30	20	7.50	—	—	141	3	47.00	1
Leadbeater, B 103	98	19	2179	90	27.58	—	11	95	5	19.00	25
Lee, J E	4	0	0	0	0	—	—	—	116	7	16.57	—
Lees, A Z	**1**	**1**	**1**	**12**	**12***	—	—	—	—	—	—	**-**
Lehmann, D S 130	126	20	5229	191	49.33	8	38	1990	79	25.18	41
Lester, E I	1	1	0	0	0	0.00	—	—	—	—	—	—
Love, J D 220	203	33	4298	118*	25.28	4	18	129	5	25.80	44
Lucas, D S	5	2	0	40	32	20.00	—	—	187	3	62.33	1
Lumb, M J 102	96	6	2592	92	29.45	—	18	28	0	—	31
Lumb, R G 135	121	13	2747	101	25.43	1	16	—	—	—	21
Lyth, A	**52**	**46**	**3**	**1187**	**109***	**27.60**	**1**	**5**	**14**	**0**	—	**17**
McGrath, A 269	249	39	7041	148	33.52	6	44	2449	76	31.22	90
Metcalfe, A A 191	186	14	5520	127*	32.09	4	36	44	2	22.00	44
Middlebrook, J D ...	18	11	3	61	15*	7.62	—	—	530	13	40.76	5
Milburn, S M	4	2	1	14	13*	14.00	—	—	118	2	59.00	1
Morris, A C	25	16	4	209	48*	17.41	—	—	409	16	25.56	5
Moxon, M D 235	227	21	7307	141*	35.47	7	48	1178	34	34.64	77
Nicholson, A G ...119	45	22	154	15*	6.69	—	—	2943	173	17.01	16
Nicholson, N G ...	2	2	1	1	1*	1.00	—	—	—	—	—	2
Old, C M 218	166	37	2550	82*	19.76	—	10	5817	306	19.00	56
Oldham, S 105	40	21	192	38*	10.10	—	—	3136	142	22.08	17
Padgett, D E V	57	54	3	1069	68	20.96	—	2	25	1	25.00	13
Parker, B	72	60	8	964	69	18.53	—	1	18	0	—	11
Patterson, S A	**42**	**14**	**12**	**82**	**25***	**41.00**	—	—	**1516**	**52**	**29.15**	**5**
Pickles, C S	69	47	19	370	37*	13.21	—	—	2355	62	37.98	22
Pyrah, R M	**84**	**54**	**15**	**757**	**69**	**19.41**	—	**2**	**2536**	**99**	**25.61**	**27**
Ramage, A	34	17	8	134	32*	14.88	—	—	1178	30	39.26	3
Ramsden, G	1	—	—	—	—	—	—	—	26	2	13.00	—

Player	M	Inns	NO	Runs	HS	Av'ge	100s	50s	Runs	Wkts	Av'ge	Ct/St
Rana Naved												
-ul-Hasan	17	16	1	375	74	25.00	—	3	681	26	26.19	5
Rashid, A U	56	34	12	377	42*	17.13	—	—	1726	59	29.25	19
Rhodes, S J	2	1	0	6	6	6.00	—	—	—	—	—	3
Richardson, R B ...	28	28	6	993	103	45.13	1	8	—	—	—	5
Robinson, A L	92	36	19	127	18*	7.47	—	—	2588	105	24.64	14
Robinson, M A	86	30	16	41	7	2.92	—	—	2725	89	30.61	7
Robinson, P E 134	123	15	2738	78*	25.35	—	14		—	—	—	47
Root, J E	7	7	1	235	63	39.16	—	2	103	2	51.50	3
Rudolph, J A	65	62	10	3090	132*	59.42	9	19	37	0	—	32
Ryan, M	3	2	1	7	6*	7.00	—	—	149	5	29.80	3
Sanderson, B W	10	2	1	14	12*	14.00	—	—	247	8	30.87	5
Sayers, J J	26	26	2	498	62	20.75	—	4	79	1	79.00	2
Scofield, D	3	1	0	0	0	0.00	—	—	111	2	55.50	1
Shahzad, A	29	21	6	235	59*	15.66	—	1	1131	29	39.00	7
Sharp, K	203	188	18	4693	114	27.60	3	27	48	4	12.00	66
Sharpe, P J	89	84	4	1499	89*	18.73	—	8	11	0	16.50	52
Shaw, C	48	20	10	127	26	12.70	—	—	1396	58	24.06	8
Sidebottom, A 233	129	47	1273	52*	15.52	—	1		6841	258	26.51	51
Sidebottom, R J ...107	48	22	291	30*	11.19	—	—		3343	115	29.06	24
Silverwood,C E W ..164	93	32	866	61	14.19	—	4		5145	223	23.07	25
Smith, N	7	2	1	5	5	5.00	—	—	—	—	—	2
Smith, R	3	2	0	17	17	8.50	—	—	—	—	—	1
Squires, P J	56	48	5	708	79*	16.46	—	3	4	0	—	10
Stemp, R D	88	28	10	118	23*	6.55	—	—	2996	100	29.96	14
Stevenson, G B 216	157	23	1699	81*	12.67	—	2		6820	290	23.51	38
Stott, W B	2	2	0	30	30	15.00	—	—	—	—	—	—
Stringer, P M	11	8	6	29	13*	14.50	—	—	256	15	17.06	—
Stuchbury, S	22	8	4	21	9*	5.25	—	—	677	29	23.34	2
Swallow, I G	8	5	3	37	17*	18.50	—	—	198	2	99.00	5
Swanepoel, P G	3	2	2	9	8*	—	—	—	100	3	33,33	—
Taylor, C R	6	5	0	102	28	20.40	—	—	—	—	—	—
Taylor, K	10	10	0	135	30	13.50	—	—	168	11	15.27	3
Tendulkar, S R	17	17	2	540	107	36.00	1	1	167	6	27.83	3
Thornicroft, N D ...	13	7	4	52	20	17.33	—	—	544	16	34.00	2
Townsley, R A J	5	4	1	81	34	27.00	—	—	62	0	—	1
Trueman, F S	11	9	1	127	28	15.87	—	—	348	21	16.57	5
Vaughan, M P 182	177	13	4890	125*	29.81	3	28		1836	59	31.11	56
Wainwright, D J ...47	20	13	150	26	21.42	—	—		1382	36	38.38	16
Wardlaw, I	1	1	0	1	1	1.00	—	—	15	0	—	—
Waring, J	1	1	1	1	1*	—	—	—	11	0	—	—
Warren, A C	1	1	0	3	3	3.00	—	—	35	1	35.00	—
Wharf, A G	6	1	1	2	2*	—	—	—	176	8	22.00	1
White, C	291	265	39	6376	148	28.21	5	28	6088	246	24.74	84
Whiteley, J P	6	4	0	19	14	4.75	—	—	195	2	97.50	1
Widdup, S	4	4	0	49	38	12.25	—	—	—	—	—	1
Wilson, D	59	45	8	424	46	11.45	—	—	1502	74	20.29	22
Wood, M J 143	132	14	3209	160	27.19	5	14		71	3	23.66	56
Woodford, J D	72	57	14	890	69*	20.69	—	2	1627	77	21.12	25
Younus Khan	11	8	0	248	100	31.00	1	—	144	2	72.00	5
Yuvraj Singh	9	9	0	196	50	21.77	—	1	197	3	65.66	1

YORKSHIRE T20i CRICKETERS 2003-2010 (Correct to January 14, 2011)

For England

Player	M	I	NO	Runs	HS	Av'ge	100s	50s	Balls	Runs	W	Av'ge	Best	4wI	Ct/St
BRESNAN, T T 2006-11	16	10	5	76	23*	15.20	—	—	310	389	11	35.36	3-10	—	5
RASHID, A U 2009	5	2	1	10	9*	10.00	—	—	84	120	3	40.00	1-11	—	1
SHAHZAD, A 2010-11	3	1	1	0	0*	—	—	—	66	97	3	32.33	2-38	—	1
VAUGHAN, M P ...2005-7	2	2	0	27	27	13.50	—	—	—	—	—	—	—	—	—

For Scotland

BLAIN, J A R 2007-8	6	3	1	4	3*	2.00	—	—	120	108	6	18.00	2-23	—	1
HAMILTON, G M .2007-10	12	8	0	90	32	11.25	—	—	—	—	—	—	—	—	3

YORKSHIRE PLAYERS WHO PLAYED ALL THEIR T20i CRICKET AFTER LEAVING YORKSHIRE

For England

BATTY, G J 2009	1	1	0	4	4	4.00	—	—	18	17	0	—	—	—	—
GOUGH, D 2005-06	2	0	0	0	—	—	—	—	41	49	3	16.33	3-16	—	3
LUMB, M J 2010	7	7	0	137	33	19.57	—	—	—	—	—	—	—	—	5
SIDEBOTTOM, R J .2007-10	18	1	1	5	5*	—	—	—	367	437	23	19.00	3-16	—	—

Overseas Players

(Qualification: 24 t20 matches for Yorkshire)

For South Africa

RUDOLPH, J A 2006	1	1	1	6	6*	—	—	—	—	—	—	—	—	—	—

TWENTY20 CUP 2003-2011

BEST SEASONS — QUARTER-FINALISTS 2006 & 2007

Played 88, Won 37 (in Yorkshire 21, Away 16), Lost 43 (in Yorkshire 18 Away 25)
Tied 2 (in Yorkshire 1, Away 1), No Result 3 (Away), Abandoned 3 (in Yorkshire)

Highest Score:	By Yorkshire	213:7 v. Worcestershire at Leeds, 2010
	Against Yorkshire	222:5 by Derbyshire at Leeds, 2010
†Lowest Score:	By Yorkshire	90:9 v. Durham at Chester-le-Street, 2009
	Against Yorkshire	98 by Durham at Chester-le-Street, 2006

Highest Individual
| **Score:** | For Yorkshire | 109 I J Harvey v. Derbyshire at Leeds, 2005 |
| | Against Yorkshire | 111 D L Maddy for Leicestershire at Leeds, 2004 |

†Lowest score is the lowest all-out score or the lowest score at completion of allotted overs

Highest
Partnerships: For Yorkshire

1st wkt	104	A W Gale (43) and J A R Rudolph (61) v. Leicestershire at Leicester, 2009
2nd wkt	137*	A W Gale (60*) and H H Gibbs (76*) v. Durham at Leeds, 2010
3rd wkt	121	J A Rudolph (56) and A McGrath (59) v. Leicestershire at Leicester, 2008
4th wkt	93	P A Jaques (92) and T T Bresnan (42) v. Leicestershire at Leeds, 2004
5th wkt	82	J E Root (46*) and G S Ballance (46) v. Derbyshire at Leeds, 2011
6th wkt	65	A McGrath (39) and A U Rashid (34) v. Worcestershire at Worcester, 2010
7th wkt	56	V J Craven (44) and R J Blakey (18) v. Durham at Chester-le-Street, 2004
8th wkt	43*	R M Pyrah (22*) and C J McKay (21*) v. Worcestershire at Worcester, 2010
9th wkt	33*	A U Rashid (5*) and D Gough (20*) v. Lancashire at Leeds, 2008
10th wkt	28*	A U Rashid (28*) and G J Kruis (12*) v. Durham at Chester-le-Street, 2009

| **Best Bowling:** | For Yorkshire: | 5 for 16 R M Pyrah v. Durham at Scarborough, 2011 |
| | Against Yorkshire | 4 for 9 C K Langerveldt for Derbyshire at Leeds, 2008 |

Most Economical Bowling (4 overs):
| | For Yorkshire | 4-0-12-2 T T Bresnan v. Lancashire at Manchester, 2008 |
| | Against Yorkshire | 4-0-9-4 C K Langeveldt for Derbyshire at Leeds, 2008 |

Most Expensive Bowling:
| | For Yorkshire | 4-0-65-2 M J Hoggard v. Lancashire at Leeds, 2005 |
| | Against Yorkshire | 4-0-58-0 G Welch for Derbyshire at Leeds, 2003 |

| **versus Derbyshire:** | Played 13, Won 8 (in Yorkshire 3, Away 5), Lost 4 (in Yorkshire), No Result 1 (Away) |

Highest Score:	By Yorkshire	210:3 at Derby, 2006
	By Derbyshire	222:5 at Leeds, 2010
Lowest Score:	By Yorkshire	108:9 at Derby, 2004
	By Derbyshire	119:7 at Leeds, 2007
Highest Individual Score:		
	For Yorkshire	109 I J Harvey at Leeds, 2005
	For Derbyshire	100* G M Smith at Leeds, 2008
Best Bowling:	For Yorkshire	4 for 21 B W Sanderson at Derby, 2011
	For Derbyshire	4 for 9 C K Langeveldt at Leeds, 2008

versus Durham: Played 16, Won 9 (in Yorkshire 6, Away 3), Lost 5 (in Yorkshire 1, Away 4), Tied 1 (in Yorkshire), No Result 1 (Away)

Highest Score:	By Yorkshire	198:4 at Leeds, 2003
	By Durham	159:7 at Leeds, 2008
Lowest Score:	By Yorkshire	90:9 at Chester-le-Street, 2009
	By Durham	98 at Chester-le-Street, 2006
Highest Individual Score:		
	For Yorkshire	76* H H Gibbs at Leeds, 2010
	For Durham	57* D M Benkenstein at Chester-le-street, 2010
Best Bowling:	For Yorkshire	5 for 16 R M Pyrah at Scarborough, 2011
	For Durham	4 for 38 S J Harmison at Leeds, 2008

versus Essex: Played 1, Lost 1 (Away)

Scores:	By Yorkshire	143:7 at Chelmsford, 2006
	By Essex	149:5 at Chelmsford, 2006
Highest Individual Score:		
	For Yorkshire	43 G L Brophy at Chelmsford, 2006
	For Essex	48* J S Foster at Chelmsford, 2006
Best Bowling:	For Yorkshire	2 for 22 A Shahzad at Chelmsford, 2006
	For Essex	2 for 11 T J Phillips at Chelmsford, 2006

versus Lancashire: Played 16, Won 8 (in Yorkshire 5, Away 3), Lost 7 (in Yorkshire 2, Away 5), Abandoned 1 (in Yorkshire)

Highest Score:	By Yorkshire	170:2 at Leeds, 2004
	By Lancashire	207 at Manchester, 2005
Lowest Score:	By Yorkshire	97 at Manchester, 2005
	By Lancashire	104:3 at Manchester, 2003
Highest Individual Score:		
	For Yorkshire	108* I J Harvey at Leeds, 2004
	For Lancashire	101 S G Law at Manchester, 2005
Best Bowling	For Yorkshire	4 for 26 A U Rashid at Leeds, 2011
	For Lancashire	3 for 10 D G Cork at Manchester, 2005

versus Leicestershire: Played 13, Won 3 (in Yorkshire 1, Away 2), Lost 9 (in Yorkshire 4, Away 5), Abandoned 1 (in Yorkshire)

Highest Score:	By Yorkshire	211:6 at Leeds, 2004
	By Leicestershire	221:3 at Leeds, 2004
Lowest Score:	By Yorkshire	134 at Leeds, 2006
	By Leicestershire	148:3 at Leeds, 2009 and 148:8 at Leicester, 2010
Highest Individual Score:		
	For Yorkshire	92 P A Jaques at Leeds, 2004
	For Leicestershire	111 D L Maddy at Leeds, 2004
Best Bowling:	For Yorkshire	4 for 20 A U Rashid at Leeds, 2010
	For Leicestershire	3 for 3 J K H Naik at Leeds, 2011

versus Northamptonshire: Played 4, Won 1 (Away), Lost 1 (in Yorkshire), Tied 1 (Away), Abandoned 1 (in Yorkshire)

Highest Score:	By Yorkshire	180:3 at Northampton, 2010
	By Northamptonshire	180:5 at Northampton, 2010
Lowest Score:	By Yorkshire	144 at Northampton, 2011
	By Northamptonshire	132-7 at Northampton, 2011
Highest Individual Score:		
	For Yorkshire	101* H H Gibbs at Northampton, 2010
	For Northamptonshire	53 W P U J C Vaas at Northampton, 2010
Best Bowling:	For Yorkshire	3 for 23 A U Rashid at Leeds, 2010
	For Northamptonshire	4 for 23 A J Hall at Northampton 2011

versus Nottinghamshire: Played 16, Won 6 (in Yorkshire 4, Away 2), Lost 10 (in Yorkshire 4, Away 6)

Highest Score:
By Yorkshire 207:7 at Nottingham, 2004
By Nottinghamshire 215:6 at Nottingham, 2011

Lowest Score:
By Yorkshire 112:7 at Nottingham, 2010
By Nottinghamshire 136:8 at Nottingham, 2008

Highest Individual Score:
For Yorkshire 96* M J Wood at Nottingham, 2004
For Nottinghamshire 91 M A Ealham at Nottingham, 2004

Best Bowling:
For Yorkshire 4 for 23 Rana Naved-ul-Hasan at Leeds, 2009
For Nottinghamshire 3 for 42 S C G MacGill at Leeds, 2003

versus Sussex: Played 1, Lost 1 (Away)

Scores:
By Yorkshire 155 at Hove, 2007
By Sussex 193:5 at Hove, 2007

Highest Individual Score:
For Yorkshire 47 C White at Hove, 2007
For Sussex 57 M W Goodwin at Hove, 2007

Best Bowling:
For Yorkshire 2 for 32 Younus Khan at Hove, 2007
For Sussex 3 for 26 Rana Naved-ul-Hasan at Hove, 2007

versus Warwickshire: Played 4, Lost 3 (in Yorkshire 2, Away 1), No Result 1 (Away)

Highest Score:
By Yorkshire 161:8 at Leeds, 2011
By Warwickshire 164:5 at Leeds, 2011

Lowest Score:
By Yorkshire 121:9 at Leeds, 2010
By Warwickshire 145:8 at Birmingham, 2010

Highest Individual Score:
For Yorkshire 54 A W Gale at Leeds, 2011
For Warwickshire 64 W T S Porterfield at Leeds, 2011

Best Bowling:
For Yorkshire 3 for 22 R M Pyrah at Leeds, 2010
For Warwickshire 4 for 19 K H D Barker at Birmingham, 2010

versus Worcestershire: Played 4, Won 2 (in Yorkshire), Lost 2 (Away)

Highest Score:
By Yorkshire 213:7 at Leeds, 2010
By Worcestershire 208:7 at Worcester, 2010

Lowest Score:
By Yorkshire 142 at Worcester 2011
By Worcestershire 109 at Leeds, 2010

Highest Individual Score:
For Yorkshire 59 A Lyth at Leeds, 2010
For Worcestershire 69* G M Andrew at Leeds, 2011

Best Bowling:
For Yorkshire 4 for 21 R M Pyrah at Leeds, 2011
For Worcestershire 4 for 31 Shakib al Hasan at Worcester, 2011

CAREER AVERAGES FOR YORKSHIRE

TWENTY20 CUP 2003-2011

Player	M	Inns	NO	Runs	HS	Av'ge	100s	50s	Runs	Wkts	Av'ge	Ct/St
Azeem Rafiq ..	23	10	6	42	11*	10.50	—	—	615	19	32.36	10
Bairstow, J M .	30	25	4	422	49*	20.09	—	—	—	—	—	6/2
Ballance, G S ..	16	13	2	225	48*	20.45	—	—	—	—	—	4
Best, T L	8	3	2	10	10*	10.00	—	—	243	7	34.71	4
Blakey, R J	7	5	1	119	32	29.75	—	—	—	—	—	5/1
Bresnan T T ...	48	33	12	368	42	17.52	—	—	1188	49	24.24	15
Brophy, G L ...	49	42	7	664	57*	18.97	—	2	—	—	—	21/6
Claydon, M E ..	7	2	2	14	12*	—	—	—	188	5	37.60	2
Craven, V J	6	6	4	76	44*	38.00	—	—	67	0	—	3
Dawood, I	11	8	3	44	15	8.80	—	—	—	—	—	5/2
Dawson, R K J .	22	8	3	71	22	14.20	—	—	558	24	23.25	7
Fleming, S P ..	4	4	0	62	58	15.50	—	1	—	—	—	1
Gale, A W	67	61	7	1548	91	28.66	-	13	—	—	—	25
Gibbs, H H	15	15	3	443	101*	36.91	1	2	—	—	—	8
Gilbert, C R	13	9	2	107	36*	15.28	—	—	—	—	—	7
Gillespie, J N ..	17	4	2	14	8*	7.00	—	—	422	17	24.82	5
Gough, D	17	7	3	42	20*	10.50	—	—	416	16	26.00	2
Gray, A K D ..	8	3	0	17	13	5.66	—	—	211	9	23.44	4
Guy, S M	10	6	1	44	13	8.80	—	—	—	—	—	2
Hamilton, G M .	3	3	1	41	41*	20.50	—	—	—	—	—	1
Harvey, I J	10	10	1	438	109	48.66	2	2	258	10	25.80	4
Hodgson, L J...	2	1	1	39	39*	—	—	—	59	2	29.50	1
Hoggard, M J ..	15	2	1	19	18	19.00	—	—	472	13	36.30	4
Jaques, P A	13	13	1	455	92	37.91	—	3	15	0	—	2
Kirby, S P	3	—	—	—	—	—	—	—	119	4	29.75	1
Kruis, G J	20	5	3	41	22	20.50	—	—	486	19	25.57	6
Lawson, M A K .	2	1	1	4	4*	—	—	—	87	3	29.00	1
Lehmann, D S ..	9	9	3	252	48	42.00	—	—	180	8	22.50	4
Lumb, M J.....	26	26	3	442	84*	19.21	—	4	65	3	21.66	8
Lyth A	34	30	1	550	59	18.96	—	1	—	—	—	12
McGrath, A ...	66	61	12	1403	73*	28.63	—	8	698	23	30.34	26
McKay, C J	8	6	3	54	21*	18.00	—	—	258	10	25.80	1
Patterson, S A .	20	4	3	3	3*	3.00	—	—	653	17	38.41	3
Pyrah, R M ...	62	41	12	312	33*	10.75	—	—	1261	64	19.70	24
Rana Naved-ul-Hasan	8	8	2	63	20*	10.50	—	—	159	11	14.45	2
Rashid, A U ...	41	28	6	238	34	10.81	—	—	1088	50	21.76	14
Root, J E	9	7	2	106	46*	21.20	—	—	34	1	34.00	2
Rudolph, J A ...	39	35	5	710	61	23.66	—	3	145	6	24.16	7
Sanderson, B W .	4	—	—	—	—	—	—	—	74	6	12.33	—
Sayers, J J	12	9	0	172	44	19.11	—	—	—	—	—	2
Shahzad, A	22	16	4	129	20	10.75	—	—	576	17	33.88	5
Sidebottom, R J	13	8	4	63	16*	15.75	—	—	354	12	29.50	7
Silverwood, C E W	9	5	2	32	13*	10.66	—	—	264	7	37.71	4
Swanepoel, P....	2	1	1	2	2*	—	—	—	60	3	20.00	1
Taylor, C R	2	2	1	10	10*	10.00	—	—	—	—	—	—
Vaughan, M P ..	16	16	1	292	41*	19.46	—	—	81	1	81.00	2
Wainwright, D J .	26	9	6	23	6*	7.66	—	—	551	21	26.23	9
Wardlaw, I	4	0	0	0	0	—	—	—	65	2	32.50	—
Warren, A C ...	2	—	—	—	—	—	—	—	70	4	17.50	—
White, C	33	31	0	570	55	18.38	—	2	132	2	66.00	8
Wood, M J.....	15	15	3	328	96*	27.33	—	2	32	2	16.00	11
Younus Khan ...	2	2	0	55	40	27.50	—	—	32	2	16.00	0
Yuvraj Singh ...	5	5	0	154	71	30.80	—	1	51	5	10.20	0

SECOND ELEVEN RECORDS
in the
SECOND ELEVEN CHAMPIONSHIP 1959-1961 AND 1975-2011

SUMMARY OF RESULTS BY SEASON

Season	Played	Won	Lost	Drawn	Tied	Abandoned	Position in Championship
1959	10	4	1	5	0	0	7
1960	10	1	3	6	0	0	14
1961	9	2	2	5	0	1	11
1975	14	4	0	10	0	0	4
1976	14	5	5	4	0	0	5
1977	16	9	0	7	0	1	1
1978	15	5	2	8	0	0	4
1979	16	5	0	11	0	0	3
1980	14	5	2	7	0	1	5
1981	16	2	3	11	0	0	11
1982	16	2	3	11	0	0	14 =
1983	11	5	1	5	0	3	2
1984	15	9	3	3	0	0	1
1985	14	3	3	8	0	1	12
1986	16	5	1	10	0	0	5
1987	15	5	2	8	0	1	1 =
1988	16	4	1	11	0	0	9
1989	17	2	3	12	0	0	9 =
1990	16	1	6	9	0	0	17
1991	16	8	1	7	0	0	1
1992	17	5	2	10	0	0	5
1993	17	6	1	10	0	0	3
1994	17	6	2	9	0	0	2
1995	17	7	1	9	0	0	5
1996	17	6	3	8	0	0	4
1997	16	8	5	3	0	1	2
1998	15	4	2	9	0	0	9
1999	16	3	8	5	0	1	14
2000	14	5	2	7	0	1	5
2001	12	8	2	2	0	1	2
2002	12	5	1	6	0	0	3
2003	10	7	1	2	0	0	1
2004	7	2	0	5	0	1	8
2005	12	2	4	6	0	0	10
2006	14	6	4	4	0	0	3
2007	12	4	5	3	0	0	10
2008	12	4	4	4	0	2	5
2009	9	5	0	4	0	0	(Group A) 2
2010	9	2	4	3	0	0	(Group A) 8
2011	9	0	4	4	1	0	(Group A) 10
Totals	550	181	97	271	1	15	

Matches abandoned without a ball being bowled are not counted as a match played.
The Championship was divided into two groups from 2009, each team playng each other
once. The two group winners played for the Championship.

ANALYSIS OF RESULTS AGAINST EACH OPPONENT

County	Played	Won	Lost	Drawn	Tied	Abandoned	First Played
Derbyshire	52	12	8	32	0	2	1959
Durham	26	9	4	13	0	2	1992
Essex	13	9	2	2	0	0	1990
Glamorgan	38	10	3	25	0	2	1975
Gloucestershire	10	3	3	4	0	0	1990
Hampshire	12	4	1	7	0	0	1990
Kent	26	5	4	17	0	1	1981
Lancashire	63	14	17	32	0	3	1959
Leicestershire	26	10	5	10	1	0	1975
MCC Young Cricketers	3	3	0	0	0	0	2005
MCC Universities	1	0	0	1	0	0	2011
Middlesex	18	7	2	9	0	0	1977
Northamptonshire	45	13	5	27	0	1	1959
Nottinghamshire	54	17	10	27	0	2	1959
Scotland	2	1	0	1	0	0	2007
Somerset	18	9	3	6	0	0	1988
Surrey	36	9	9	18	0	2	1976
Sussex	16	6	5	5	0	0	1990
Warwickshire	56	21	12	23	0	0	1959
Worcestershire	35	19	4	12	0	0	1961
Totals	550	181	97	271	1	15	

Note: Matches abandoned are not included in the total played.

Highest Total

By Yorkshire: 538 for 9 wkts dec v. Worcestershire at Stamford Bridge, 2007
Against Yorkshire: 567 for 7 wkts dec by Middlesex at RAF Vine Lane, Uxbridge, 2000

Lowest Total

By Yorkshire: 69 v. Lancashire at Heywood, 1983
Against Yorkshire: 36 by Lancashire at Elland, 1979

Highest Individual Score

For Yorkshire: 273* by R J Blakey v. Northamptonshire at Northampton, 1986
Against Yorkshire: 235 by O A Shah for Middlesex at Leeds, 1999

Century in Each Innings

For Yorkshire:	C White	209* and 115*	v. Worcestershire at Worcester, 1990
	K Sharp	150* and 127	v. Essex at Elland, 1991
	A A Metcalfe	109 and 136*	v. Somerset at North Perrott, 1994
	R A Kettleborough	123 and 192*	v. Nottinghamshire at Todmorden, 1996
	C R Taylor	201* and 129	v. Sussex at Hove, 2005
	A W Gale	131 and 123	v. Somerset at Taunton, 2006
	J J Sayers	157 and 105	v. Lancashire at Leeds, 2007
Against Yorkshire:	N Nannan	100 and 102*	for Nottinghamshire at Harrogate, 1979
	G D Lloyd	134 and 103	for Lancashire at Scarborough, 1989
	A J Swann	131 and 100	for Northamptonshire at York, 1998
	G J Kennis	114 and 114	for Somerset at Taunton, 1999

Best Bowling in an Innings

For Yorkshire: 9 for 27 by G A Cope v. Northamptonshire at Northampton, 1979
Against Yorkshire: 8 for 15 by I Folley for Lancashire at Heywood, 1983

Best Bowling in a Match

For Yorkshire: 13 for 92 (6 for 48 and 7 for 44) by M K Bore v. Lancashire at Harrogate, 1976
Against Yorkshire: 13 for 100 (7 for 45 and 6 for 55) by N J Perry for Glamorgan at Cardiff, 1978

Totals of 450 and over

By Yorkshire (25)

Score	Versus	Ground	Season
538 for 9 wkts dec	Worcestershire	Stamford Bridge	2007
534 for 5 wkts dec	Lancashire	Stamford Bridge	2003
530 for 8 wkts dec	Nottinghamshire	Middlesbrough	2000
514 for 3 wkts dec	Somerset	Taunton	1988
509 for 4 wkts dec	Northamptonshire	Northampton	1986
502	Derbyshire	Chesterfield	2003
501 for 5 wkts dec	MCC Young Cricketers	Stamford Bridge	2009
497	Derbyshire	Chesterfield	2005
495 for 5 wkts dec	Somerset	Taunton	2006
488 for 8 wkts dec	Warwickshire	Harrogate	1984
486 for 6 wkts dec	Glamorgan	Leeds	1986
476 for 3 wkts dec	Glamorgan	Gorseinon	1984
475 for 9 wkts dec	Nottinghamshire	Nottingham	1995
474 for 3 wkts dec	Glamorgan	Todmorden	2003
470	Lancashire	Leeds	2006
474	Durham	Stamford Bridge	2003
469	Warwickshire	Castleford	1999
462	Scotland	Stamford Bridge	2007
461 for 8 wkts dec	Essex	Stamford Bridge	2006
459 for 3 wkts dec	Leicestershire	Oakham	1997
459 for 6 wkts dec	Glamorgan	Bradford	1992
457 for 9 wkts dec	Kent	Canterbury	1983
456 for 6 wkts dec	Nottinghamshire	York	1986
456 for 5 wkts dec	Gloucestershire	Todmorden	1990
454 for 9 wkts dec	Derbyshire	Chesterfield	1959
452 for 9 wkts dec	Glamorgan	Cardiff	2005

Against Yorkshire (12)

Score	For	Ground	Season
567 for 7 wkts dec	Middlesex	RAF Vine Lane, Uxbridge	2000
555 for 7 wkts dec	Derbyshire	Stamford Bridge	2002
525 for 7 wkts dec	Sussex	Hove	2005
493 for 8 wkts dec	Nottinghamshire	Lady Bay, Nottingham	2002
488 for 8 wkts dec	Warwickshire	Castleford	1999
486	Essex	Chelmsford	2000
485	Gloucestershire	North Park, Cheltenham	2001
477	Lancashire	Headingley	2006
471	Warwickshire	Clifton Park, York	2010
458	Lancashire	Bradford	1997
454 for 7 wkts dec	Lancashire	Todmorden	1993
450 for 7 wkts (inns closed)	Derbyshire	Bradford	1980

Completed Innings under 75

By Yorkshire (3)

Score	Versus	Ground	Season
69	Lancashire	Heywood	1983
74	Derbyshire	Chesterfield	1960
74	Nottinghamshire	Bradford	1998

Against Yorkshire (10)

Score	By	Ground	Season
36	Lancashire	Elland	1979
49	Leicestershire	Leicester	2008
50	Lancashire	Liverpool	1984
60	Derbyshire	Bradford	1977
60	Surrey	Sunbury-on-Thames	1977
62	MCC	High Wycombe	2005
64	Nottinghamshire	Brodsworth	1959
66	Leicestershire	Lutterworth	1977
72	Sussex	Horsham	2003
74	Worcestershire	Barnsley	1978

Individual Scores of 150 and over (60)

Score	Player	Versus	Ground	Season
273*	R J Blakey	Northamptonshire	Northampton	1986
238*	K Sharp	Somerset	Taunton	1988
233	P E Robinson	Kent	Canterbury	1983
221*	K Sharp	Gloucestershire	Todmorden	1990
219	G M Hamilton	Derbyshire	Chesterfield	2003
218*	A McGrath	Surrey	Elland	1994
212	G S Ballance	MCC Young Cricketers	Stamford Bridge	2009
209*	C White	Worcestershire	Worcester	1990
205	C R Taylor	Glamorgan	Todmorden	2003
204	B Parker	Gloucestershire	Bristol	1993
203	A McGrath	Durham	Headingley	2005
202*	J M Bairstow	Leicestershire	Oakham	2009
202	M J Wood	Essex	Stamford Bridge	2006
201*	C R Taylor	Sussex	Hove	2005
200*	D Byas	Worcestershire	Worcester	1992
192*	R A Kettleborough	Nottinghamshire	Todmorden	1996
191	P E Robinson	Warwickshire	Harrogate	1984
191	M J Wood	Derbyshire	Rotherham	2000
191	M J Lumb	Nottinghamshire	Middlesbrough	2000
189*	C S Pickles	Gloucestershire	Bristol	1991
186	A McGrath	MCC Universities	York	2011
184	J D Love	Worcestershire	Headingley	1976
183	A W Gale	Durham	Stamford Bridge	2006
174	G L Brophy	Worcestershire	Stamford Bridge	2007
173	S N Hartley	Warwickshire	Edgbaston	1980
173	A A Metcalfe	Glamorgan	Gorseinon	1984
173	B Parker	Sussex	Hove	1996
173	R A Kettleborough	Leicestershire	Oakham School	1997

Individual Scores of 150 and over *(Continued)*

Score	Player	Versus	Ground	Season
172	A C Morris	Lancashire	York	1995
170*	R A J Townsley	Glamorgan	Harrogate	1975
169	J E Root	Warwickshire	York	2010
168	M J Wood	Leicestershire	Oakham School	1997
166	A A Metcalfe	Lancashire	York	1984
166	C A Chapman	Northamptonshire	York	1998
165*	A Lyth	Durham	Stamford Bridge	2006
165	J J Sayers	Sussex	Hove	2006
164*	A W Gale	Leicestershire	Harrogate	2002
164	J C Balderstone	Nottinghamshire	Harrogate	1960
163*	J E Root	Leicestershire	Oakham	2009
163	A A Metcalfe	Derbyshire	Chesterfield	1992
162*	D Byas	Surrey	Scarborough	1987
160	A A Metcalfe	Somerset	Bradford	1993
157	J J Sayers	Lancashire	Headingley	2007
155	S M Guy	Derbyshire	Chesterfield	2005
154*	C R Taylor	Surrey	Whitgift School	2005
153*	A A Metcalfe	Warwickshire	Bingley	1995
153	C White	Worcestershire	Marske-by-the-Sea	1991
153	R A Stead	Surrey	Todmorden	2002
152	A A Metcalfe	Gloucestershire	Bristol	1993
151*	P E Robinson	Nottinghamshire	York	1986
151*	S J Foster	Kent	Elland	1992
151*	J J Sayers	Durham	Stamford Bridge	2004
151	P J Hartley	Somerset	Clevedon	1989
151	A McGrath	Somerset	Elland	1995
151	V J Craven	Glamorgan	Todmorden	2003
150*	K Sharp	Essex	Elland	1991
150*	G M Fellows	Hampshire	Todmorden	1998
150*	S M Guy	Nottinghamshire	Headingley	2005
150*	J A Leaning	Worcestershire	Worcester	2011
150	K Sharp	Glamorgan	Ebbw Vale	1983
150	S N Hartley	Nottinghamshire	Worksop	1988
150	C R Taylor	Derbyshire	Chesterfield	2003

7 Wickets in an Innings (30)

Analysis	Player	Versus	Ground	Season
9 for 27	G A Cope	Northamptonshire	Northampton	1977
9 for 62	M K Bore	Warwicshire	Scarborough	1976
8 for 53	S J Dennis	Nottinghamshire	Nottingham	1983
8 for 57	M K Bore	Lancashire	Manchester	1977
8 for 79	P J Berry	Derbyshire	Harrogate	1991
7 for 13	P Carrick	Northamptonshire	Marske-by-the-Sea	1977
7 for 21	S Silvester	Surrey	Sunbury-on-Thames	1977
7 for 22	J A R Blain	Surrey	Purley	2004
7 for 32	P W Jarvis	Surrey	The Oval	1984
7 for 34	P Carrick	Glamorgan	Leeds	1986
7 for 37	P M Hutchison	Warwickshire	Coventry	2001

7 Wickets in an Innings *(Continued)*

Analysis	Player	Versus	Ground	Season
7 for 39	G M Hamilton	Sussex	Leeds	1995
7 for 40	M K Bore	Worcestershire	Old Hill	1976
7 for 44	M K Bore	Lancashire	Harrogate	1976
7 for 44	J P Whiteley	Worcestershire	Leeds	1979
7 for 51	J D Middlebrook	Derbyshire	Rotherham	2000
7 for 53	J P Whiteley	Warwickshire	Birmingham	1980
7 for 55	C White	Leicestershire	Bradford	1990
7 for 58	K Gillhouley	Derbyshire	Chesterfield	1960
7 for 58	P J Hartley	Lancashire	Leeds	1985
7 for 63	M J Hoggard	Worcestershire	Harrogate	1998
7 for 65	M K Bore	Nottinghamshire	Steetley	1976
7 for 70	J D Batty	Leicestershire	Bradford	1992
7 for 71	J D Batty	Hampshire	Harrogate	1994
7 for 81	K Gillhouley	Lancashire	Scarborough	1960
7 for 84	I J Houseman	Kent	Canterbury	1989
7 for 88	I G Swallow	Nottinghamshire	Nottingham	1983
7 for 90	A P Grayson	Kent	Folkestone	1991
7 for 93	D Pickles	Nottinghamshire	Nottingham	1960
7 for 94	K Gillhouley	Northamptonshire	Redcar	1960

12 Wickets in a Match (6)

Analysis		Player	Versus	Ground	Season
13 for 92	(6-48 and 7-44)	M K Bore	Lancashire	Harrogate	1976
13 for 110	(7-70 and 6-40)	J D Batty	Leicestershire	Bradford	1992
13 for 111	(4-49 and 9-62)	M K Bore	Warwickshire	Scarborough	1976
12 for 69	(5-32 and 7-37)	P M Hutchison	Warwickshire	Coventry	2001
	(5-39 and 7-81)	K Gillhouley	Lancashire	Scarborough	1960
12 for 163	(5-78 and 7-84)	I J Houseman	Kent	Canterbury	1989

Hat-tricks (4)

Player	Versus	Ground	Season
I G Swallow	Warwickshire	Harrogate	1984
S D Fletcher	Nottinghamshire	Marske-by-the-Sea	1987
I G Swallow	Derbyshire	Chesterfield	1988
M Broadhurst	Essex	Southend-on-Sea	1992

ANNUAL REPORT
and
Statement of Account
for the year ended
December 31, 2011

CHAIRMAN'S REPORT

*Looking back on 2011 I would summarise
the year in three simple words:*
DISAPPOINTING YET OPTIMISTIC

On the playing side of our business I think we
all entered the season feeling fairly confident that
we would do reasonably well after finishing third
in 2010. We certainly felt that we had a platform
to build upon and that our players would develop
and prosper with the experiences they had
already established.

COLIN GRAVES

Unfortunately the dreams turned to nightmares as despite winning the
last match of the season at home to Somerset we plummeted headlong
into Division 2 for 2012.

Yes, I was disappointed, frustrated and annoyed that all our high
expectations were evaporated into a sense of reality, that in 2012 we
would not be playing Championship cricket at the highest level of competition. My frustrations were also well documented in the Press, as I
knew many of our members, supporters and sponsors were feeling the
same, and even though the truth may hurt some players it had to be said
that we under-performed badly and some players did not step up to the
mark when the opportunity was there to take.

On the positive side of our performances we saw a new generation of
future stars emerging, and Messrs Bairstow, Root, Ballance and Rafiq
are fantastic prospects for, hopefully, many years to come in the
Yorkshire colours. Ryan Sidebottom was welcomed back to the county
by everybody, and he performed fantastically, both with ball and bat. I
hope that the rest of the team take a lead from Ryan's efforts and prove
that they, too, have the capability to perform at the highest level.

Andrew Gale, our captain, was as disappointed as myself, and was even more frustrated when he had to miss the last six weeks with a broken arm. The Board has every confidence in our captain, and I ask all the players to totally support him in 2012, as he deserves some success with his total dedication to the Club, members and players.

On the management/coaching side I also felt for Martyn Moxon as Director of Professional Cricket, who is totally passionate for the Club to do well and to achieve success in winning trophies and competitions. At the end of the year, and with a great deal of consideration, we totally revamped the coaching structure, as we all believed that we had become stale and stereotyped in our support for the players and strategy. In 2012 we welcome Jason Gillespie, Paul Farbrace and Richard Damms as a new coaching-management team supporting Martyn and Ian Dews, and we all look forward to a new positive era for the Club.

Financially, as you will read in Charles Hartwell's report, our performance was as per our budgeted expectations — another substantial loss on the back of no Test Match at Headingley Carnegie in 2011. This just proves that developing stadia such as ours requires regular income to support the infrastructure and maintenance of such venues. On the positive side of this, under our Staging Agreement with the ECB we will have International Test Match cricket at Headingley Carnegie each year until at least 2019.

As a Board we have invested heavily in players, coaching, the ground facilities and supporting the community, so let us all look forward to some success in the future to reward our expectations and ambitions.

I must also take this opportunity to thank our partners, investors and sponsors in helping us through a very difficult year, and I cannot praise too highly HSBC, Leeds City Council and Leeds Metropolitan University for their fantastic support for the Board and the Club.

To our sponsors I acknowledge that you may be disappointed like many of us. However, now is the time we require your continued support, so please stick with us as I feel optimistic that you will be associated with a winning Yorkshire team in the future.

I must also pay tribute to the Members' Committee, the Archives Committee, the Museum of Cricket under David Hall, the Yorkshire County Cricket Club Charitable Youth Trust, the Yorkshire Cricket Foundation the Yorkshire Supporters' Association, the Players' Association, Geoff Holmes and Vivien Stone who operate the bookstall so successfully, Yorkshire Cricket Board and all our many volunteers who help the Club in various ways.

At this point I must also thank our retiring President, Ray Illingworth, who has carried out his duties admirably and has represented the Club in a most distinguished and professional manner. It has been a privilege and pleasure to work with such a great cricketing legend.

One other important thank-you is to all our staff at The Yorkshire County Cricket Club, who this year had to endure difficult times under tight budget controls and staff reductions. To you all, I cannot thank you enough, and your efforts are greatly appreciated by me, the Board and the members. The Board would like to congratulate Andy Fogarty, our Head Groundsman, who won the ECB 2011 Groundsman of the Year Award, Four-Day Category, and was runner up in the One-Day category. These awards are a credit to the hard work of all the ground staff. Well done.

To my fellow Board members, I also pay tribute to you for your encouragement, advice and support in helping to steer The Yorkshire County Cricket Club in a direction that we all wish to go — financially viable and professionally successful. Here, I must mention one Mr Geoffrey Boycott, who retires from the Board this year after seven years' service and is being proposed by your Board as our next President.

Geoffrey has been immense as a Board member, ambassador, supporter, fundraiser and broadcaster, and is famed for his cricketing knowledge throughout the world. It has been a privilege to work with such a great person and enthusiast for The Yorkshire County Cricket Club, and I cannot recommend too highly that you support the Board's nomination of "GB" as the next President of The Yorkshire County Cricket Club. He thoroughly deserves the highest honour the Club can bestow upon him.

Finally, to you our members, I owe you a sincere debt of gratitude for your continued support. I know at times you may think, "why do I continue my membership?" when you look at performances, match scheduling, financial results and other areas of disappointment or complaint.

I would therefore ask you personally to take away those negative thoughts, and let's all be positive and look forward with optimism to a new, successful season. I know that our players, coaches and staff are all desperate to do well in 2012 — however, we need your continued support for the good of The Yorkshire County Cricket Club.

May I wish you all a very enjoyable 2012 season, and I look forward to meeting you during the season.

COLIN GRAVES
Chairman
The Yorkshire
County Cricket Club

FINANCE DIRECTOR'S REPORT

Although it is disappointing to report a second consecutive loss, I am encouraged that despite some one-off expenditure the Club is able to report a deficit before tax that is consistent with budget. We can look forward to a return to sustained surpluses from 2012 when a full schedule of international cricket returns to our Club.

CHARLES HARTWELL

I have changed the format of the Income and Expenditure Account this year, and I believe that the revised format gives more insight into how the Club is performing. Total year-on-year revenue has fallen by £379k (6.5 per cent) to £5.4m.

However, like-for-like revenue has actually increased by six per cent. Three-quarters of this increase is attributable to the ODI, which fell on a Friday in 2011 as opposed to a Sunday in 2010, with the balance of growth attributable to improved revenues at the Yorkshire v. Lancashire Friends Life t20, and commission receivable from Scarborough CC, which was helped by the staging of their first Friends Life t20 match.

Total trading expenditure (excluding interest and depreciation) has fallen by £1.1m (18 per cent). If International cricket expenses are stripped out the Club managed to achieve a 10 per cent reduction in expenditure. This was driven through forward-price agreements of utility prices, tight control over general facility overhead and savings driven from headcount reduction, including not replacing the Chief Executive. The cost of staging the One-Day International was higher in 2011 than 2010 due to the fixture falling on a Friday rather than a Sunday, which resulted in a higher staging fee and higher overall hospitality costs due to increased demand.

The Balance Sheet is consistent with expectation. Reductions in the value of fixed assets are a function of depreciation, and there has been minimal capital investment during 2011, mainly comprising final costs of the Carnegie Pavilion. Short-term creditors have increased from £3.6m to £6.0m. £1m of this increase relates to deferred income (advance ticket sales) for the forthcoming Test Match, the balance representing the reclassification of term-loan commitments from long-term to short-term liabilities as capital repayment holidays come to an end. In addition, as expected and agreed with HSBC, the Club ended the year overdrawn and the cash asset in 2010 became a liability in 2011.

The Sales and Marketing Director left the Club in December 2011, which presented an opportunity to reassess the commercial offering and focus on the opportunities that lie ahead in both cricket and non-cricket activities. Headcount savings recorded in 2011 will not, however, be repeated in 2012. Hopefully, this investment should improve the customer experience for members and visitors to the ground and drive sustained increases to both the top and bottom lines.

To summarise, 2011 performed in line with budget in respect of both income and expenditure. I fully expect to report marked and sustained improvement to the Club's trading position from 2012, driven by the return of Test cricket. From a debt position the Club's objective is to repay term debt as soon as possible, while ensuring that there is sufficient operating cash to cover any unforeseen incremental cost or downside to revenue. To this end I am looking at rephasing long-term capital -debt repayments to balance the desire to repay debt with cash-flow risk. I would like to take this opportunity to thank our Chairman, HSBC and Leeds City Council for their continued support.

I am happy to record that both Domestic and International attendances exceeded expectation. 1st XI match attendances were 93,584 (72,439 at Headingley and 21,145 at Scarborough) and a sellout crowd of 16,573 attended the One-Day International. In terms of spectator volume by match category 39,193 watched LV County Championship Cricket, 38,980 watched Friends Life t20 and 15,411 watched CB40 .

There are always a considerable number of empty seats at domestic-cricket matches, and I would encourage every member to bring friends and family to a game whenever possible. With the exception of Graham's excellent catering provision in the Cricket Centre, the Club does not directly benefit from the sale of food and beverages within the ground (the Club receives a fixed annual payment) and it is always challenging to strike a balance between setting ticket prices that attract more spectators and ensuring that overall revenue is sufficient to, firstly, cover the costs of the match and, secondly, to generate a contribution towards the considerable costs that a ground of this size incurs.

There will be investment in new staff during 2012. In addition, there will be investment in member and guest facilities. The Long Room will benefit from a new carpet, and within the Cricket Centre the kitchen and serving area will have a complete refurbishment.

Graham and Linda will therefore be able to enhance their offering on match days, and also cater for the increasing demands for parties and corporate events. There will also be enhancements to the Club's retail facilities in response to recommendations from Barbara Noble. The Club will celebrate its 150th anniversary in 2013, and there will be a number of special events throughout 2013 to mark this milestone. The sesqui-centennial anniversary of the Club should provide a great excuse to promote and be proud of our great Club.

Finally, I would like to take this opportunity to state my appreciation of the Yorkshire Cricket Taverners. From within their number the Taverners play an active role in the Club, and their generous annual donation is both welcome and appreciated, as is the work of all our volunteers and committees.

I look forward to a prosperous and exciting 2012 season, and wish you all the very best.

CHARLES HARTWELL ACA
Director of Finance
Yorkshire County Cricket Club

DIRECTOR OF PROFESSIONAL CRICKET'S REPORT

Last season was easily the most challenging and frustrating of my coaching career. It started full of optimism and anticipation after a positive 2010 season, but finished with huge disappointment.

We knew 2011 would be a challenge when we decided to "go it on our own" and not employ an overseas player or replace Jacques Rudolph. To be relegated from Division 1 of the LV Championship was not part of the plan.

Although in hindsight some may argue that this was a mistake, I still believe the players had earned the right in 2010 to be given the opportunity to play 1st XI cricket last season. The most frustrating thing for me was the fact that we had a number of opportunities to win games but were unable to capitalise on strong positions as a result of a period of poor play, and the advantage was lost.

MARTYN MOXON

We played some very good cricket at times, but didn't play well enough for long enough to win enough games. We were competitive, and fought hard on a number of occasions not to be beaten, but the current points system doesn't reward draws. Our inexperience showed at times with some careless batting and an inability to maintain pressure when we were bowling. A lot of good work was wasted.

Our one-day cricket was very inconsistent. We got off to a bad start in the CB40 and never really recovered, although along the way there were some good performances. In the Friends Life t20 having a team so inexperienced at this form of the game was always going to make it difficult, but again we took some notable scalps. Towards the end of this competition the players were starting to grow into their roles, and I don't believe there is any shortcut in t20 cricket — players need to play it to learn. It is a very difficult game to succeed in immediately. Players need to learn and trust their method.

Although there was negativity about last season, there were also a number of positives that came out of a disappointing summer. There was certainly no lack of effort, and the players showed fighting spirit on numerous occasions. I have great belief in this group of players. They

419

work hard and want to be successful. However, we need to be smarter and more mature as a group. We are trying to put together a squad of largely homegrown players who will be successful for Yorkshire for a sustained period, and I believe this group are capable of achieving that (England selections permitting — but that's another topic!)

There were some excellent individual performances during the season, and the emergence of Joe Root and Gary Ballance and the continuing development of Jonathan Bairstow were the stand-out highlights.

We have signed Phil Jaques to add quality and experience to our batting resources, and at the time of writing we are exploring the possibility of making another signing to make the squad a strong unit with lots of competition for places.

Although the priority for 2012 is promotion back into Division 1 of the LVCC, I want us to be competitive on all fronts and see more consistency in our one-day cricket. Make no mistake, promotion is no forgone conclusion; we will have to play at our best for the whole season. Look at Northampton shire last year: they were at the top of the table all season, only to miss out in the final game. I can assure you that we are all working very hard to give ourselves the best chance of success, and there is a determination to come back strongly in 2012.

There has also been a reorganisation of the coaching structure since the end of last season. This has been on the agenda for a couple of years, and it was felt that we needed a more efficient, streamlined structure that would give coaches specific responsibility. The positions within the new structure were advertised worldwide, and I am delighted with the outcome. We have assembled a group of coaches in Jason Gillespie, Paul Farbrace, Ian Dews and Richard Damms who have great expertise and a wide range of experience. This will be a team who will work together to give the players the support they need to perform and develop.

I would like to take this opportunity of thanking Craig White, Kevin Sharp, Steve Oldham and John Blain for the work they have done at the Club, and wish them well for the future.

Although 2011 was disappointing, I believe there is plenty to be optimistic about for the future.

Thank you for your continued support.

MARTYN MOXON
Director of Professional Cricket
Yorkshire County Cricket Club

MEMBERS' COMMITTEE
CHAIRMAN'S REPORT

The following served on the Members' Committee during the year.

Chairman:	**Mr S J Mann**
Elected Members:	**Mrs C Evers**
	Mr R Levin
	Mr S J Mann
	Mr E Stephens
Appointed Members:	**Mr G Clark**
	Mr A Kilburn
	Mr R W Stott
In Attendance:	**Mr R Kaye,** Sales and Marketing Director
	Mr R Smith, Board Drector

There were seven full Committee meetings during the year. A full minute of each meeting was presented to the Board of the Club, and a summary appears on the Club website. Four Members Forums were held during the season in the Long Room prior to the start of play.

There was one change to the list of attendees at Committee meetings. Mr Richard Kaye, who held executive responsibility for sales and marketing attended each meeting. Mr Richard Levin was re-elected at the March AGM to continue for a further four years as an elected member.

The Member Forums continue to play a key role as a method of communication. The attendance of Club executives enables members to hear background explanations to policy decisions and provides a platform for objective feedback and comment to the Club. If these gatherings are to continue to be productive there is a need for attendees to ensure that comment is constructive and questions are of substance. Each meeting in 2011 attracted over 70 members. Possibly the highlight was the final forum of the season in early September when the Club captain attended and answered a range of questions on playing issues. Given the disappointments in the season it says much of the calibre of the captain that he was prepared to talk to the membership in such a frank and honest manner. His attendance was greatly appreciated by all.

Fixtures and venues continue to be a subject of debate each year. In 2011, as in previous years, there was a detailed dialogue with the Club on the following season's programme. The committee have supported the Club's view that a more balanced schedule is required so that there is first-class cricket at Headingley Carnegie in each month of the season.

The fixtures for 2012 show that yet again it has been impossible for the ECB to respond to what appears a simple and not unreasonable request. The committee will continue to pursue a balanced approach to scheduling.

While first-class fixtures are firmly committed to Headingley Carnegie and Scarborough, there is an annual request to take second-team games around the county as much as possible. It was very much appreciated that the Club agreed to a play a fixture at

STEPHEN MANN

Harrogate in 2011 to coincide with the opening of the new pavilion.

Lengthy discussions took place on membership numbers and the costs of attending both Yorkshire matches and Tests. While there has been a small decline in membership the general level has remained steady for the last few years. Efforts should be made to entice former members back and to make membership a more worthwhile commodity. A basic principle is to ensure that the cost of attending is not a barrier. County cricket, and Yorkshire in particular, should not price people out of going.

A number of marketing topics were raised, particularly the shop. The Club were asked to review its activities, opening hours, layout and merchandise. It was not felt unreasonable to ask for the shop to be open on all match days and throughout the time spectators are on the ground.

My sincere thanks to the membership for making the role of chairman of the Members' Committee so enjoyable. Yorkshire may not have the largest membership, but they do have a membership that supports the various teams at home and away in far greater numbers than any other county. Long may that be the case.

Finally, best wishes and sincere a thank you for his inclusive style to Richard Kaye, who left at the end of the year to take up a role with the ECB. I would also like to thank all my committee colleagues for their support and work throughout the year.

STEPHEN MANN,
Chairman,
Members' Committee
Yorkshire County Cricket Club

INDEPENDENT AUDITORS' REPORT

TO THE MEMBERS OF THE YORKSHIRE
COUNTY CRICKET CLUB

We have audited the financial statements of The Yorkshire County Cricket Club for the year ended December 31, 2011. The financial reporting framework that has been applied in their preparation is applicable in law and UK Accounting Standards (UK Generally Accepted Accounting Practice).

This report is made solely to the Club's members, as a body, in accordance with Section 9 of the Friendly and Industrial and Provident Societies Act 1968. Our audit work has been undertaken so that we might state to the Club's members those matters we are required to state to them in an auditor's report and for no other purpose. To the fullest extent permitted by law, we do not accept or assume responsibility to anyone other than the Club and the Club's members, as a body, for our audit work, for this report, or for the opinions we have formed.

Respective responsibilities of directors and auditor

As more fully explained in the Statement of Directors' Responsibilities the Club's directors are responsible for the preparation of financial statements which give a true and fair view. Our responsibility is to audit, and express an opinion on, the financial statements in accordance with applicable law and International Standards on Auditing (UK and Ireland). Those standards require us to comply with the Auditing Practices Board's (APB's) Ethical Standards for Auditors.

Scope of the audit of the financial statements

A description of the scope of an audit of financial statements is provided on the APB's website at www.frc.org.uk/apb/scope/private.cfm.

Opinion on financial statements

In our opinion the financial statements:

- give a true and fair view, in accordance with UK Generally Accepted Accounting Practice, of the state of the Club's affairs as at 31 December 2011 and of its deficit for the year then ended; and

- have been properly prepared in accordance with the Industrial and Provident Societies Acts 1965 to 2003.

Matters on which we are required to report by exception

We have nothing to report in respect of the following.

Under the Industrial and Provident Societies Acts 1965 to 2003 we are required to report to you if, in our opinion:

• a satisfactory system of control over transactions has not been maintained; or

• the association has not kept proper accounting records; or

• the financial statements are not in agreement with the books of account; or

• we have not received all the information and explanations we need for our audit.

A J SILLS (Senior Statutory Auditor) for and on behalf of KPMG LLP, Statutory Auditor

Chartered Accountants,

Leeds   FEBRUARY 7, 2012

CORPORATE GOVERNANCE

The Board is accountable to the Club's members for good corporate governance, and this statement describes how the principles of governance are applied.

THE BOARD

The Board is responsible for approving Club policy and strategy. It meets monthly, or more frequently if business needs require, and has a schedule of matters specifically reserved to it for decision, including all significant commercial issues and all capital expenditure.

The Executive Management Team supply the Board with appropriate and timely information, and the Board Members are free to seek any further information they consider necessary.

NOMINATIONS COMMITTEE

The Nominations Committee is formally constituted with written terms of reference, which are defined in the Club Rules and reviewed regularly. It consists of the President, Secretary and two other Board members, currently C J Graves and R A Smith.

RELATIONS WITH MEMBERS

The Club encourages effective communication with its members, and a specific Committee, as defined in the Club Rules, is appointed for that purpose.

INTERNAL CONTROL

The Board acknowledges its responsibility to maintain a sound system of internal control relating to operational, financial and compliance controls and risk management to safeguard the members' interests and the Club's assets, and will regularly review its effectiveness. Such a system, however, is designed to manage and meet the Club's particular needs and mitigate the risks to which it is exposed, rather than eliminate the risk of failure to achieve business objectives, and can provide only reasonable and not absolute assurance against material mis-statement or loss.

The Club considers its key components to provide effective internal control and improve business efficiency are:

- Regular meetings with senior management to review and assess progress made against objectives and deal with any problems which arise from such reviews.

- A financial reporting system of annual budgets, periodic forecasts and detailed monthly reporting which includes cash-flow forecasts. Budgets and forecasts are reviewed and approved by the Board.

- A defined management and organisation structure with defined responsibilities and appropriate authorisation limits and short lines of communication to the Executive Chairman.

ACCOUNTABILITY AND AUDIT

The Board's responsibilities

The following statement, which should be read in conjunction with the Report of the Independent Auditors, is made with a view to distinguishing for members the respective responsibilities of the Board and of the auditors in relation to the accounts:

The Board is required by UK law to prepare accounts which give a true and fair view of the state of affairs of the Club at the end of the financial year and of the surplus or deficiency of the Club for the financial year then ended.

The Board is also responsible for maintaining adequate accounting records and for taking reasonable steps to safeguard the assets of the Club and detect irregularities and fraud.

The Board confirms that in preparing the Club's accounts appropriate policies have been consistently applied and applicable accounting standards complied with. Further, in all material respects the accounts are supported by prudent judgments and estimates made by reference to information available at the time of their preparation.

All Board members bring independent judgment to bear on their deliberations concerning strategy and performance. The Board is satisfied that it has had access to sufficient information to enable it to make proper decisions in a timely manner, and the Chairman has ensured that Board Members were kept properly briefed.

INCOME AND EXPENDITURE ACCOUNT
for the year ended 31st December, 2011

	Note	2011 £	2010 £
Income			
International ticket and hospitality revenue		936,582	1,590,236
Domestic ticket and hospitality revenue		508,559	453,930
Subscriptions		583,405	564,763
England and Wales Cricket Board		1,971,717	1,728,006
Commercial income		1,389,695	1,447,399
Other income		41,923	26,922
		5,431,881	5,811,256
Cost of sales			
International match and hospitality expenditure		429,997	1,007,472
Domestic match and hospitality costs (home fixtures)		279,979	334,932
Retail		92,027	67,600
Catering		30,560	39,828
		(832,563)	(1,449,832)
Cricket expenses			
Staff remuneration and employment expenses		2,038,804	1,978,757
Match expenses (away fixtures)		245,618	275,278
Development expenses		254,505	291,237
Other cricket expenses		30,932	34,548
		(2,569,859)	(2,579,820)
Overhead			
Infrastructure and ground operations		585,681	714,692
Commercial		530,581	709,815
Administration		394,720	548,429
Ticket and membership office		125,063	140,312
		(1,636,045)	(2,113,248)
Earnings /(loss) before interest, tax, depreciation and amortisation		393,414	(331,644)
Below the line expenditure:			
Loan Interest		(1,026,764)	(945,424)
Depreciation		(732,208)	(895,771)
Release of Capital Grants		181,960	165,672
		(1,577,012)	(1,675,523)
(Deficit) for the year before taxation		(1,183,598)	(2,007,167)
Taxation	4	723,495	148,158
(Deficit) for the year after taxation		(460,103)	(1,859,009)

BALANCE SHEET

as at 31st December, 2011

	Note	2011 £	2011 £	2010 £	2010 £
Assets employed:					
Fixed Assets	5		28,957,564		29,478,215
Current assets:					
Stocks		40,044		42,350	
Debtors	6	982,623		264,730	
Cash at bank and in hand		—		415,494	
		1,022,667		722,574	
Creditors: amounts falling due within one year	7	(5,967,888)		(3,612,557)	
Net current liabilities			(4,945,221)		(2,889,983)
Total assets less current liabilities			24,012,343		26,588,232
Funded by:					
Creditors: amounts falling due after more than one year	8		21,221,274		23,160,524
Deferred income — capital grants	9		5,003,623		5,180,160
			26,224,897		28,340,684
Capital and Reserves					
Called up share capital	11		275		286
Capital redemption reserve	12		564		552
Income and expenditure account	12		(2,213,393)		(1,753,290)
			(2,212,554)		(1,752,452)
			24,012,343		26,588,232

These accounts were approved by the Board on 7th February 2012

C J GRAVES, Chairman

R A SMITH, Director

There were no other gains and losses in the current or preceding year other than those stated above. The accompanying notes form an integral part of these accounts.

CASH FLOW STATEMENT

for the year ended 31st December, 2011

	Note	2011 £	2010 £
Cash inflow from operating activities	13	**14,857**	3,849,113
Returns on investments and servicing of finance	14	**(1,026,764)**	(945,424)
Capital expenditure and financial investment	14	**(232,427)**	(1,819,769)
Cash (outflow) / inflow before financing		**(1,244,334)**	1,083,920
Financing	14	**(481,735)**	(327,228)
(Decrease) / increase in cash in the period		**(1,725,850)**	756,692

Reconciliation of net cash flow to movement in net debt

(Decrease) / increase in cash in period		**(1,725,850)**	756,692
HSBC loan		—	(20,750)
C J Graves loan		—	(200,000)
Debentures		**(32,633)**	(207,915)
Other loans - ECB net repayment		**305,000**	631,500
New finance leases		—	(2,151,880)
Capital element of finance-lease repayments		**209,150**	124,311
		(1,244,333)	(1,068,042)

ANALYSIS OF NET DEBT

	At 1 Jan 2011 £	Cash flow 2011 £	Other changes 2011 £	At 31 Dec 2011 £
Cash at bank and in hand	415,494	(415,494)	—	—
Overdraft - current	—	(1,310,356)	—	(1,310,356)
	415,494	**(1,725,850)**	**—**	**(1,310,356)**
Debt due within one year:				
HSBC loan	—	—	(568,502)	(568,502)
Leeds City Council loan	—	—	(743,000)	(743,000)
Other loans ECB	(455,000)	305,000	—	(150,000)
Finance leases less than one year	(209,563)	209,150	(209,120)	(209,533)
Debt due after one year:				
HSBC loan	(4,169,014)	—	568,502	(3,600,512)
Leeds City Council loan	(8,507,000)	—	743,000	(7,764,000)
Pride Appeal loan	(1,005,000)	—	—	(1,005,000)
Graves Family Trusts loans	(3,600,000)	—	—	(3,600,000)
C J Graves loan	(400,000)	—	—	(400,000)
Debentures	(291,263)	(32,633)	—	(323,896)
Finance leases more than one year	(1,819,696)	—	209,120	(1,610,576)
	(20,456,536)	**481,517**	**—**	**(19,975,019)**
Total	**(20,041,042)**	**(1,244,333)**	**—**	**(21,285,375)**

NOTES TO THE ACCOUNTS

for the year ended 31st December, 2011

1. Accounting policies

The accounts have been prepared in accordance with applicable accounting standards and under the historical cost convention. The principal accounting policies of the Club have remained unchanged from the previous year.

The format of the Income and Expenditure Account has been changed in the year to provide more meaningful analysis of the Club's financial performance. Comparatives have been adjusted accordingly.

(a) Income

All income is accounted for on an accruals basis, except for donations which are accounted for in the year of receipt.

Income represents amounts receivable from the Club's principal activities. Income is analysed between international-ticket and hospitality revenue, domestic-ticket and hospitality revenue, subscriptions, England and Wales Cricket Board, commercial and other income.

Subscriptions

Subscription income comprises amounts receivable from members in respect of the current season. Subscriptions received in respect of future seasons are treated as deferred income.

Domestic-ticket and hospitality revenue

Relate to amounts received from gate charges, ticket sales, hospitality and guarantees directly attributable to staging domestic-cricket matches in Yorkshire.

International-ticket and hospitality revenue

Relate to amounts received from gate charges, ticket sales, hospitality and guarantees directly attributable to staging international cricket matches in Yorkshire.

England and Wales Cricket Board (ECB)

ECB income relates to fees receivable, including performance-related elements, in the current season distributed from central funds in accordance with the First Class Memorandum of Understanding. ECB fees received in respect of future seasons are treated as deferred income. ECB distributions receivable to fund capital projects are treated as deferred income and are released to the Income and Expenditure Account by equal instalments over the expected useful lives of the relevant assets in accordance with accounting policy (b) Fixed assets and depreciation, as set out below.

Commercial and other income

Commercial income relates to amounts received, net of related expenditure, from ground advertising, catering guarantees, box lettings, facility hire, dinners and other events.

Advertising income received in respect of future seasons is treated as deferred income.

Other income relates to amounts received, net of related expenditure, from retail, Cricket Centre bar, Taverners' Club, fund-raising activities and other sundry items.

(b) Fixed assets and depreciation

All expenditure in connection with the development of Headingley Carnegie Cricket Ground and the related facilities has been capitalised. Finance costs relating to and incurred during the period of construction were also capitalised. Depreciation is only charged once a discrete phase of the development is completed.

Depreciation is calculated to write down the cost of fixed assets by equal annual instalments over their expected useful lives.

The periods generally applicable are:

Headingley Carnegie Cricket Ground and Cricket Centre

Buildings	Carnegie Pavilion	125 years
	Other buildings	50 years
Fixtures		4 years
Plant & Equipment	Between 4 and 10 years	
Office equipment		
Telephone system		4 years
Computer equipment		2 years

Freehold land is not depreciated.

All other expenditure on repairs to Headingley Carnegie Cricket Ground and other grounds is written off as and when incurred.

(c) Carnegie Pavilion

The Club's contribution towards the design and build cost of the Carnegie Pavilion is £3m, of which £1.5m is payable over 20 years under a 125-year lease agreement. The £3m, together with the associated legal, professional and capital fit-out costs of the areas within the Pavilion that the Club occupies, have been capitalised and depreciated over the 125-year lease term. The £1.5m payable under the lease agreement has been treated as a finance lease within the financial statements with the capital element reported within Creditors (Finance leases), and the interest element charged to the Income and Expenditure Account on a straight-line basis over the 20-year term.

(d) Stocks

Stocks represent goods for resale, and are stated at the lower of cost and net realisable value.

(e) Grants

Capital grants relating to the development of Headingley Carnegie Cricket Ground (including the Yorkshire Cricket Museum) and Cricket Centre are included within the Balance Sheet as deferred income, and are released to the Income and Expenditure Account by equal instalments over the expected useful lives of the relevant assets in accordance with accounting policy (b) Fixed assets and depreciation, as set out above.

Grants of a revenue nature are credited to the Income and Expenditure Account in the same period as their related expenditure.

(f) Cricket Centre

The Cricket Centre was operated by the Club as a joint venture with Leeds City Council until April 2011. Under this arrangement the Club had a 60 per cent interest in the profits earned by the Centre. For the period January to April 2011 inclusive (and throughout 2010) profit was recognised when received by the Club with full provision being made for anticipated losses. Losses attributable to Leeds City Council were deducted from the related revenue grant. Post April 2011 all income and expenditure generated by the Centre was attributable to the Club. The assets of the Cricket Centre are all owned and controlled by the Club.

The Cricket Centre bar operation did not form part of the joint venture, and all income and expenditure relating to the bar is solely attributable to the Club.

(g) Contribution to pension funds

The pension costs charged to the Income and Expenditure account represent the amount of contributions payable in respect of the accounting period.

(h) Leased assets

Assets acquired under finance leases are capitalised and the outstanding future lease obligations are shown in Creditors. Operating lease rentals are charged to the Income and Expenditure account on a straight-line basis over the period of the lease.

(i) Deferred taxation

Deferred tax is recognised on all timing differences where the transactions or the events that give the Club an obligation to pay more tax in the future have occurred by the balance-sheet date. Deferred tax assets are recognised when it is more likely than not that they will be recovered. Deferred tax is measured by using rates of tax that have been enacted or substantively enacted by the balance-sheet date.

(j) Disclosure of information to Auditor

The members of the Board who held office at the date of approval of the Annual Report and Accounts confirm that, so far as they are aware, there is no relevant information of which the Club's auditor is unaware; or each member has taken all the steps that he ought to have taken as a member to make himself aware of any relevant audit information or to establish that the Club's auditor is aware of that information.

2. Financial Position

The Club is in a net current liability position of £5.0m (2010: £2.9m). This includes deferred income of £2.0m (2010: £1.0m). Details of the loan and overdraft maturity analysis which impact on the financial position can be found in Note 8.

The Board fully expect the Club to return to consistent annual profitability from 2012. However they are aware that 2012 will be challenging due to starting 2012 with an overdraft — a concequence of not having a Test Match in 2011. However, Mr C J Graves has agreed to provide such cash-flow support as the Club requires during 2012, and the Club is in discussion with HSBC and Leeds City Council with the objective of restructuring term-debt repayments in order to balance operating cash flow with the repayment of debt.

The Board therefore considers it appropriate to prepare the financial statements on a going-concern basis.

3. Directors' remuneration

	2011 £	2010 £
Wages and salaries	—	72,779
Social security costs	—	8,950
Pension costs	—	9,863
	—	91,592

4. Taxation

	2011	2010
UK corporation tax	—	—
Total current tax	—	—
Deferred tax (see Note 10)	(723,495)	(148,158)
Tax on (deficit) on ordinary activities	(723,495)	(148,158)
(Deficit) on ordinary activities before taxation	(1,183,598)	(2,007,167)
Current tax at 26.5% (2010: 27.0%)	(313,654)	(541,935)
Effects of:		
Non-taxable income	(96,324)	(77,079)
Depreciation for the period in excess of capital allowances	148,063	156,762
Losses not utilised	261,915	462,252
Total current tax (see above)	£ —	£ —

5. Fixed assets (See next page)

Headingley Carnegie Cricket Ground

	Cricket Centre		Freehold Land and Buildings £	Plant and Equipment £	Assets in the Course of Construction £	Leasehold Improvements (Carnegie Pavilion) £	Office Equipment £	Total £
	Freehold Land and Buildings £	Plant & Equipment £						
Cost								
January 1, 2011	535,837	758,603	24,991,887	4,551,960	298,846	4,297,037	363,487	35,797,657
Additions	—	—	—	15,565	2,346	210,616	3,900	232,427
Transfers	—	—	301,192	—	(301,192)	—	—	—
December 31, 2011	535,837	758,603	25,293,079	4,567,525	—	4,507,653	367,387	36,030,084
Depreciation								
January 1, 2011	82,156	664,158	1,649,737	3,586,006	—	17,188	320,197	6,319,442
Provided in the year	9,885	70,306	235,435	359,595	—	55,614	22,243	753,078
December 31, 2011	92,041	734,464	1,885,172	3,945,601	—	72,802	342,440	7,072,520
Net book value								
December 31, 2011	**443,796**	**24,139**	**23,407,907**	**621,924**	**—**	**4,434,851**	**24,947**	**28,957,564**
December 31, 2010	453,681	94,445	23,342,150	965,954	298,846	4,279,849	43,290	29,478,215

Improvements to Leasehold Property consist of the Club's share of the costs associated with the design and build of the Carnegie Pavilion. This cost includes a £3m base-capital contribution (£1.5m of which has been treated as a finance lease, with the outstanding capital balance shown within creditors). The remaining £1.5m represents costs associated with fit-out, structural amendments, legal and consultancy fees. The total cost is depreciated over 125 years, which represents the useful economic life of the building.

433

	2011	2010
	£	£

6. Debtors

Trade debtors	126,382	139,197
Deferred tax asset (see Note 10)	723,495	—
Other debtors	132,746	125,533
	982,623	264,730

7. Creditors: amounts falling due within one year

Leeds City Council loan	743,000	—
Bank Loan	568,502	—
Bank overdraft (secured)	1,310,356	—
ECB loans	150,000	455,000
Trade creditors	291,319	599,454
Finance leases	209,533	209,563
Social security and other taxes	239,441	888,876
Other creditors	329,563	308,129
Accruals	172,925	167,956
Deferred income	1,953,249	983,579
	5,967,888	3,612,557

8. Creditors: amounts falling due after more than one year

Leeds City Council Loan	7,764,000	8,507,000
Bank Loan	3,600,512	4,169,014
Pride Appeal Loans	1,005,000	1,005,000
CJ and J Graves Accumulation and Maintenance Trusts Loans	3,600,000	3,600,000
C J Graves Loan	400,000	400,000
Debentures	323,896	291,263
Finance Leases	1,610,576	1,819,696
Deferred income	2,917,290	3,368,551
	21,221,274	23,160,524

Loan and overdraft maturity analysis:

In one year or less or on demand	2,981,391	664,563
In more than one year but not more than two years	1,575,034	2,886,566
In more than two years but not more than five years	8,888,000	7,243,000
In more than five years	7,840,950	9,662,407
	21,285,375	20,456,535

The Leeds City Council loan is repayable by April 30, 2020, at an interest rate of 4.5 per cent per annum. The Club has given a First Legal Charge over the freehold property known as Headingley Carnegie Cricket Ground, St Michael's Lane, Leeds, to Leeds City Council in respect of this loan. Mr C J Graves has provided a shortfall guarantee in respect of this loan. The Club has also given a First Legal Charge to HSBC Bank plc over the Cricket Centre known as 41/43 St Michael's Lane, Headingley, Leeds, and a Second Legal Charge over the property known as Headingley Carnegie Cricket Ground, St Michael's Lane, Leeds, in respect of the bank loan and overdrafts. HSBC Bank plc also has a fixed and floating charge over all the assets of the Club, subject to the Legal Charges referred to above. This loan is repayable by April 30, 2019, and bears an interest rate of 4.0 per cent over the Bank's base rate, increasing to 4.00 per cent over the Bank's base rate from January 2011. Mr C J Graves has also provided a £6m guarantee in respect of the indebtedness to HSBC Bank plc. The Pride Appeal loans primarily consist of a £1m loan received from Mr C J Graves, which is interest free and repayable on demand with 12 months' notice. The C J Graves Accumulation and Maintenance Trust and J Graves Accumulation and Maintenance Trust each bear interest at the rate of 5.5 per cent per annum and are repayable in April 2014.

	2011 £	2010 £
9. Deferred income -capital grants		
At January 1, 2011	**5,180,160**	5,036,256
Received in year	**5,423**	309,576
Released to Income and Expenditure Account	**(181,960)**	(165,672)
At December 31, 2011	**5,003,623**	5,180,160

Grants received during the year relate to the final balance of a grant to design and build the Yorkshire Cricket Museum. This grant was made by The Yorkshire Cricket Foundation. The total grant is £300,000. The associated design and build cost of the Museum has been released from Assets in the Course of Construction during the year.

10. Provision for Liabilities		
— Deferred Taxation Asset / (Liability)		
At January 1, 2011	—	148,158
(Credit) to Income and Expenditure Account for the year	**(723,495)**	(148,158)
At December 31, 2011	**(723,495)**	—

The elements of deferred taxation are as follows :		
Difference between accumulated depreciation and capital allowances	**(240,111)**	(363,827)
Tax losses	**963,606**	363,827
	(723,495)	—

11. Share capital		
Allotted, called up and fully paid Ordinary shares of 5p each	**275**	286

During the year the Club allotted one Ordinary share to each of 19 new qualifying members and redeemed 237 Ordinary shares in respect of retiring members. Each member of the Club owns one Ordinary share, and the rights attached thereto are contained within the Club's rules.

12. Reserves.

	Income and Expenditure Account	Capital Redemption Reserve
At January 1, 2011	**(1,753,290)**	552
Deficit for the year	**(460,103)**	—
Shares in respect of retiring members	—	12
At December 31, 2011	**(2,213,393)**	564

13. Reconciliation of operating profit to cash flow		
(Deficit) for the year before taxation	**(1,183,598)**	(2,007,167)
Loan interest and similar amounts payable	**1,026,764**	945,424
Operating (Deficit)	**(156,834)**	(1,061,743)
Depreciation of tangible assets	**753,078**	895,771
Capital grants received	**5,423**	309,576
Release of capital grants	**(181,960)**	(165,672)
(Decrease) / increase in stock	**2,307**	16,811
(Decrease) / increase in debtors	**5,602**	88,484
(Decrease) / increase in creditors	**(931,167)**	59,871
Increase in deferred income	**518,409**	3,706,015
Cash inflow from operating activities	**14,857**	3,849,113

435

	2011	2010
	£	£

14. Analysis of cash flows

Returns on investment and servicing of finance

Loan interest and facility fees	(1,026,764)	(945,424)
	(1,026,764)	(945,424)

Capital expenditure and financial investment

Purchase of tangible fixed assets	(232,427)	(1,819,769)

Financing

Other loans received in year:

ECB	182,500	425,000
Debentures	32,633	207,915
HSBC	—	20,750
C J Graves	—	200,000
ECB loan repayment	(487,500)	(1,056,500)
Capital element of finance-lease rental payments	(209,150)	(124,312)
Issue of ordinary share capital	1	1 3
Repurchase of ordinary share capital	—	(95)
	(481,516)	(327,229)

15. Leasing commitments

Operating lease payments amounting to £41,569 (2010: £46,221) are due within one year. The leases to which these amounts relate expire as follows:

	2011 Land and buildings £	2011 Other £	2010 Land and buildings £	2010 Other £
In one year or less	—	861	—	8,233
Between two and five years	—	10,708	—	7,988
In five years or more	30,000	—	30,000	—
	£30,000	**£11,569**	£30,000	£16,221

16. Related party transactions

Mr C J Graves is the Chairman of Costcutter Supermarkets Group Limited. The Club has purchased printing and software maintenance from Costcutter Supermarkets Group Limited. The turnover for the year is £1,200 (2010: £1,792) of which £600 remains outstanding at December 31, 2011 (2010: £588). Costcutter are also sponsors of the Club and boxholders at Headingley Carnegie Cricket Ground under the Club's normal commercial terms. During the year Mr R A Smith was a Board Member and Trustee of the Yorkshire Cricket Foundation (YCF). During 2011 the YCF awarded capital grants of £5,424 (2010: £294,576), and non-capital grants of £8,850 (2010 : £44,622).

17. Pensions

The Club operates defined contribution pension schemes for the benefit of certain employees. The amounts paid during the year were £191,781 (2010: £198,425). The assets of these schemes are administered in funds independent from those of the Club.

18. Audit Fee

The Club paid its auditors £16,000 (2010: £16,000) in respect of the audit of its Financial Statements.

436